The Political Writings of Alexander Hamilton

Few of America's founders influenced its political system more than Alexander Hamilton. He played a leading role in writing and ratifying the Constitution, was de facto leader of one of America's first two political parties, and was influential in interpreting the scope of the national government's constitutional powers. This comprehensive collection provides Hamilton's most enduringly important political writings, covering his entire public career, from 1775 to his death in 1804. Readers are introduced to Hamilton – in his own words – as defender of the American cause, as an early proponent of a stronger national government, as a founder and protector of the American Constitution, as the nation's first secretary of the treasury, as President George Washington's trusted foreign policy advisor, and as a leader of the Federalist Party. Presented in a convenient two-volume set, this book provides a unique insight into the political ideas of one of America's leading founders; a must-have reference source.

CARSON HOLLOWAY is Professor of Political Science at the University of Nebraska at Omaha. His articles have appeared in *The Review of Politics*, *Interpretation: A Journal of Political Philosophy*, *Perspectives on Political Science*, *First Things*, and *Public Discourse*. He is the author of *Hamilton versus Jefferson in the Washington Administration: Completing the Founding or Betraying the Founding?* (Cambridge University Press, 2015).

BRADFORD P. WILSON is Executive Director of the James Madison Program in American Ideals and Institutions, Lecturer in Politics, and Faculty Fellow of Butler College at Princeton University. He is the author/editor of five books on American political and constitutional thought. His writings have appeared in the *Review of Metaphysics*, *American Political Science Review*, and *Academic Questions*, and as chapters in edited volumes.

Alexander Hamilton

The Political Writings
of Alexander Hamilton

Volume II: 1789–1884

Edited by

Carson Holloway
University of Nebraska Omaha

Bradford P. Wilson
Princeton University

CAMBRIDGE
UNIVERSITY PRESS

CAMBRIDGE
UNIVERSITY PRESS

University Printing House, Cambridge CB2 8BS, United Kingdom

One Liberty Plaza, 20th Floor, New York, NY 10006, USA

477 Williamstown Road, Port Melbourne, VIC 3207, Australia

314–321, 3rd Floor, Plot 3, Splendor Forum, Jasola District Centre, New Delhi – 110025, India

79 Anson Road, #06-04/06, Singapore 079906

Cambridge University Press is part of the University of Cambridge.

It furthers the University's mission by disseminating knowledge in the pursuit of
education, learning, and research at the highest international levels of excellence.

www.cambridge.org
Information on this title: www.cambridge.org/9781107088474
DOI: 10.1017/9781316104897

First published 2017

Printed in the United States of America by Sheridan Books, Inc.

A catalogue record for this publication is available from the British Library.

ISBN – 2-Volume Set 978-1-107-08847-4 Hardback
ISBN – Volume I 978-1-108-42222-2 Hardback
ISBN – Volume II 978-1-108-42223-9 Hardback

Cambridge University Press has no responsibility for the persistence or accuracy of URLs
for external or third-party internet websites referred to in this publication and does not
guarantee that any content on such websites is, or will remain, accurate or appropriate.

This book is dedicated to the memory of Alexander Hamilton, American Patriot and Statesman.

Contents

Part 4: Elder Statesman: 1801–1804

Appendix: Hamilton's Death and Legacy

Acknowledgments

We wish to express our gratitude to Cambridge University Press for publishing this work. We must particularly thank our editor, Robert Dreesen, his assistant, Brianda Reyes, and content manager, Claire Sissen, for guiding us through the process of preparing these volumes for publication. Our thanks are also due to those scholars who acted as reviewers for the project and who offered us their support and helpful suggestions for improvement. In addition, we wish to thank Hamilton scholars Ron Chernow and Joanne Freeman for encouraging us to undertake this project when we were first considering it, and our friends Darren Staloff and Matthew Franck for being an ongoing source of insight into Hamilton, his time, and the issues he confronted. Finally, we gratefully acknowledge the efforts of earlier editors and compilers of Hamilton's writings, whose work has inspired and helped to guide our own.

Carson Holloway would like to thank the Heritage Foundation for its support for his work. During the 2014–2015 academic year he held a fellowship in American political thought at Heritage's B. Kenneth Simon Center for Principles and Politics. This fellowship provided him with much needed time to work on this project. He also thanks the Center's director, David Azerrad, and its associate director, Arthur Milikh, for their intellectual companionship and friendship. He also wishes to express his gratitude to his colleagues at the University of Nebraska at Omaha for their friendship and encouragement, and to graduate student Bryan Brooks, who provided valuable assistance in compiling the materials for this work. Finally, he is grateful to his wife, Shari, and his daughters – Maria, Anna, Elizabeth, Catherine, Jane, and Emily – for their love and support.

Bradford Wilson wishes to thank Robert P. George for his friendship and learned advice as this project matured, and the James Madison Program in American Ideals and Institutions at Princeton University for providing such an hospitable home for scholarly work on the political thought of American statesmen. He thanks Duanyi Wang for her assistance with our preparation of the manuscript. He also wishes to express his love and gratitude for his understanding and ever supportive family – Elle, Lauren, Darren, Julia, Nathan, and his beloved grandchildren.

Introduction

Alexander Hamilton continues to hold an unassailable place in the first rank of the American founders. To most minds, Hamilton belongs with that handful of men – such as George Washington, Thomas Jefferson, John Adams, James Madison, and Benjamin Franklin – whose contributions to establishing the American republic are most worthy of our remembrance and our study. Thanks to many fine biographies – and, more recently, a very popular Broadway musical – the general contours of Hamilton's meteoric career are well known: orphan immigrant to the North American colonies, aide de camp to General Washington during the revolutionary war, framer of the Constitution, organizer and lead author of *The Federalist*, the nation's first secretary of the treasury, leader of the Federalist Party, victim of Aaron Burr's bullet in their infamous duel of 1804.

Hamilton's contribution as a political thinker, however, is less appreciated than it should be. To be sure, there have been numerous scholarly studies – both books and articles – of his political thought. The output here, however, has not been as great as it might be, given the massive amount that Hamilton wrote about politics, and his almost invariable recurrence to fundamental principles whenever he examined a political question. Hamilton rarely addressed an issue that came to his attention without relating it to some enduring aspect of human nature, some fundamental political principle, some axiom or maxim of conduct – even as he also reminded his readers of the role of prudence in statesmanship by emphasizing that such principles and maxims often admitted of exceptions in particular circumstances.

It is with a view to fostering greater interest in and study of Hamilton's political thought and statesmanship that we offer this two-volume collection of his political writings. Of course, we recognize with respect and gratitude earlier Hamilton collections. We believe this work, however, makes a unique contribution insofar as it is both more comprehensive than some of the earlier collections and more focused than others. On the one hand, there have been volumes that have offered either a relatively small number of Hamilton's most famous works from across his lifetime or a handful from some specific period of his career. On the other hand, there are Joanne B. Freeman's Library of America collection of Hamilton's writings and Harold C. Syrett's *Papers of Alexander Hamilton*. The former will remain useful for historians and a popular audience interested in Hamilton's life, but for that very reason it includes a good deal of

Hamilton's personal correspondence and therefore necessarily has to exclude many writings of enduring political interest. The latter, a masterful achievement, will remain essential to Hamilton specialists, but it is so comprehensive – twenty-seven volumes – that it cannot offer the convenience of this work. And by including everything that Hamilton wrote, and much that was written to him, Syrett's Hamilton *Papers* present a large body of material that is not of direct interest to the student of politics. In contrast to these earlier works, then, we have striven to include *all* that is of enduring political interest but *only* what is of enduring political interest. By bringing these political writings together in a single two-volume work, and thus making them easier and more convenient of access, we hope to encourage more students of political theory and statesmanship to turn their attention to Hamilton's political thought.

We say we have *striven* to include all that is of enduring political interest because we admittedly have only imperfectly succeeded in doing so. Hamilton wrote so much about politics that it is impossible to include everything of interest while keeping the compilation to a reasonable and manageable size. Our primary principle of selection has been to include whatever touches on matters of principle – political, philosophic, legal, and constitutional – and its application to practice. We have therefore excluded the vast archive of Hamilton's writings in the daily conduct of administrative duties and in commenting to political allies on the horserace aspects of politics.

The Political Writings of Alexander Hamilton is divided into two volumes, and each volume is further divided into parts that correspond to the main periods of Hamilton's political career. Volume II, the present volume, is broken into four parts that follow Hamilton's political thought from his service as the nation's first secretary of the treasury up through his political retirement and to the time of his death. Part 1: Financial Founding Father: 1789–1792 presents the most important works that Hamilton produced in order to construct and defend his financial program for the infant republic. Here the reader will encounter Hamilton's great state papers – his *Report on the Public Credit*, *Report on a National Bank*, *Report on Manufactures*, as well as his *Opinion on the Constitutionality of a National Bank*. We have also included his written defenses of his program in response to the criticisms of Thomas Jefferson and James Madison, notably Hamilton's 1792 letter to Edward Carrington and his "Objections and Answers Respecting the Administration," prepared for George Washington.

The later part of Hamilton's tenure as secretary of the treasury was consumed with problems of foreign policy. Materials relevant to this period of his public life are contained in Part 2: The Challenges of Foreign Policy: 1793–1795. Here we have included letters and other documents Hamilton wrote regarding the leading diplomatic difficulty the country faced: the proper American response to the wars arising out of the French Revolution. The second section of the volume also presents a considerable portion of the newspaper articles Hamilton produced defending the administration's foreign policy and criticizing the French Revolution, including the entirety of his famous *Pacificus* series.

In 1795 Hamilton left the Washington administration and returned to his private law practice. He remained, however, deeply involved in national politics, acting as the de facto leader of the emerging Federalist Party, in opposition to the Republican Party led by Thomas Jefferson. During this time Hamilton wrote copious amounts of newspaper commentary and advised President Washington almost continually. After Washington was succeeded by John Adams, Hamilton continued to advise and influence Adams's cabinet. Part 3: Federalist Party Leader: 1795–1800 traces this stage of Hamilton's public career. In the realm of foreign policy, Hamilton wrote the majority of essays entitled *The Defense*, a series of articles in support of the Jay Treaty, some of which are presented here. He also continued and sharpened his public critique of the French Revolution, and returned to the army in the context of the quasi-war with France. In domestic politics, Hamilton acted a seemingly strange and memorable part. He wrote a letter arguing that his fellow Federalist, John Adams, was unfit to continue as president of the United States. Then, when the Electoral College failed to produce a winner and the election was thrown into the House of Representatives, Hamilton argued strenuously that Federalists should support the election of Hamilton's bitter rival, Thomas Jefferson. Although he disagreed with Jefferson politically, Hamilton thought he was a far better and safer choice than the alternative, Aaron Burr, who Hamilton viewed as an unprincipled adventurer. Writings pertaining to these and other matters of interest are offered in Part 3.

Part 4: Elder Statesman: 1801–1804 presents writings from the final years of Hamilton's life, when he was politically marginalized in the wake of the Republican triumph of 1800 but still following national politics closely and commenting on it frequently. Here, perhaps not surprisingly, Hamilton re-emerged as a sharp critic of Thomas Jefferson, the man he had helped elect to the presidency. Hamilton penned another newspaper series, *The Examination*, in which he criticized Jefferson's policies as president, laying particular emphasis on the constitutional questions raised by the repeal of the Judiciary Act. Later he also wrote in criticism of Jefferson's handling of the Louisiana Purchase. These and other materials are presented in this final part of the collection, the last few entries of which concern Hamilton's final public act: his fatal duel with vice president Aaron Burr.

We have also included an appendix to the work, "Hamilton's Death and Legacy." This section includes some firsthand accounts of Hamilton's last hours, as well as some appreciations of his life, character, and career offered by other American statesmen who knew him well.

We have made some light modifications to Hamilton's original texts in order to ease the task of the contemporary reader. Our most extensive intervention has been to modernize Hamilton's punctuation. He generally used far more commas and semicolons than we do today, although he also sometimes omitted them where we would find them necessary. Our aim here has always been to preserve his meaning while also making it more immediately evident to the modern reader. Put another way, we wanted to save the reader the mental effort involved in "translating" Hamilton's punctuation, so that the reader's mind could instead be occupied wholly with following the train of Hamilton's thought and appreciating the eloquence of his expression. We have also modernized Hamilton's spelling and capitalization, although we have left the latter undisturbed when Hamilton capitalized a whole word with the intention of emphasizing it. Likewise, italics are retained for words that Hamilton himself chose to emphasize.

We have generally followed the editors of *The Papers of Alexander Hamilton* in supplying the missing letters from obviously incomplete words and in supplying missing words. In order to make the text more readable, however, we have omitted the various brackets that they used. Where Hamilton supplied a later list of errata to a published work we have simply made the corrections in our text itself without noting them. We have filled out Hamilton's abbreviations in cases in which they would have been confusing. Occasional blank spaces left in the text are Hamilton's own.

Our preference has been to include whole works, but in some cases it has been necessary to omit passages that were not of sufficient interest but were taking up valuable space. We have generally indicated in the entry title when we have excerpted a work, although we have simply dropped irrelevant postscripts from some letters.

Footnotes are always Hamilton's own. Any editorial remarks we thought necessary to add have been placed in numbered endnotes.

We are grateful to Columbia University Press for allowing us to use *The Papers of Alexander Hamilton* as the source for most of the documents included in our volumes. Readers interested in the contexts of and references in Hamilton's writings would do well to consult the editorial notes in *The Papers of Alexander Hamilton*.

PART 1

Financial Founding Father: 1789–1792

Letter to Henry Lee, December 1, 1789

My Dear Friend,

I have just received your letter of the 16th instant.

I am sure you are sincere when you say you would not subject me to an impropriety. Nor do I know that there would be any in my answering your queries. But you remember the saying with regard to Caesar's wife. I think the spirit of it applicable to every man concerned in the administration of the finances of a country. With respect to the conduct of such men—*Suspicion* is ever eagle eyed, and the most innocent things are apt to be misinterpreted.

Be assured of the affection & friendship of Yr.

A. Hamilton

Excerpts from a Report Relative to a Provision for the Support of Public Credit, January 9, 1790

The secretary of the treasury, in obedience to the resolution of the House of Representatives, of the twenty-first day of September last, has, during the recess of Congress, applied himself to the consideration of a proper plan for the support of the public credit, with all the attention which was due to the authority of the House, and to the magnitude of the object.

In the discharge of this duty, he has felt, in no small degree, the anxieties which naturally flow from a just estimate of the difficulty of the task, from a well-founded diffidence of his own qualifications for executing it with success, and from a deep and solemn conviction of the momentous nature of the truth contained in the resolution under which his investigations have been conducted, "That an *adequate* provision for the support of the Public Credit, is a matter of high importance to the honor and prosperity of the United States."

With an ardent desire that his well-meant endeavors may be conducive to the real advantage of the nation, and with the utmost deference to the superior judgment of the House, he now respectfully submits the result of his enquiries and reflections to their indulgent construction.

In the opinion of the secretary, the wisdom of the House, in giving their explicit sanction to the proposition which has been stated, cannot but be applauded by all who will seriously consider, and trace through their obvious consequences, these plain and undeniable truths.

That exigencies are to be expected to occur, in the affairs of nations, in which there will be a necessity for borrowing.

That loans in times of public danger, especially from foreign war, are found an indispensable resource, even to the wealthiest of them.

And that in a country, which, like this, is possessed of little active wealth, or in other words, little monied capital, the necessity for that resource, must, in such emergencies, be proportionably urgent.

And as on the one hand, the necessity for borrowing in particular emergencies cannot be doubted, so on the other, it is equally evident, that to be able to borrow upon *good terms*, it is essential that the credit of a nation should be well established.

For when the credit of a country is in any degree questionable, it never fails to give an extravagant premium, in one shape or another, upon all the loans it has occasion to make. Nor does the evil end here; the same disadvantage must be sustained upon whatever is to be bought on terms of future payment.

From this constant necessity of *borrowing* and *buying dear*, it is easy to conceive how immensely the expenses of a nation, in a course of time, will be augmented by an unsound state of the public credit.

To attempt to enumerate the complicated variety of mischiefs in the whole system of the social economy, which proceed from a neglect of the maxims that uphold public credit, and justify the solicitude manifested by the House on this point, would be an improper intrusion on their time and patience.

In so strong a light nevertheless do they appear to the secretary, that on their due observance at the present critical juncture, materially depends, in his judgment, the individual and aggregate prosperity of the citizens of the United States; their relief from the embarrassments they now experience; their character as a People; the cause of good government.

If the maintenance of public credit, then, be truly so important, the next enquiry which suggests itself is, by what means it is to be effected? The ready answer to which question is, by good faith, by a punctual performance of contracts. States, like individuals, who observe their engagements are respected and trusted: while the reverse is the fate of those who pursue an opposite conduct.

Every breach of the public engagements, whether from choice or necessity, is in different degrees hurtful to public credit. When such a necessity does truly exist, the evils of it are only to be palliated by a scrupulous attention, on the part of the government, to carry the violation no farther than the necessity absolutely requires, and to manifest, if the nature of the case admits of it, a sincere disposition to make reparation, whenever circumstances shall permit. But with every possible mitigation, credit must suffer, and numerous mischiefs ensue. It is therefore highly important, when an appearance of necessity seems to press upon the public councils, that they should examine well its reality, and be perfectly assured that there is no method of escaping from it, before they yield to its suggestions. For though it cannot safely be affirmed that occasions have never existed, or may not exist, in which violations of the public faith, in this respect, are inevitable; yet there is great reason to believe that they exist far less frequently than precedents indicate; and are oftenest either pretended through levity or want of firmness, or supposed through want of knowledge. Expedients might often have been devised to effect, consistently with good faith, what has been done in contravention of it. Those who are most commonly creditors of a nation, are, generally speaking, enlightened men; and there are signal examples to warrant a conclusion that when a candid and fair appeal is made to them, they will understand their true interest too well to refuse their concurrence in such modifications of their claims as any real necessity may demand.

While the observance of that good faith which is the basis of public credit is recommended by the strongest inducements of political expediency, it is enforced by considerations of still greater authority. There are arguments for it which rest on the immutable principles of moral obligation. And in proportion as the mind is disposed to contemplate, in the order of Providence, an intimate connection between public virtue and public happiness, will be its repugnancy to a violation of those principles.

This reflection derives additional strength from the nature of the debt of the United States. It was the price of liberty. The faith of America has been repeatedly pledged for it, and with solemnities that give peculiar force to the obligation. There is indeed reason to regret that it has not hitherto been kept; that the necessities of the war, conspiring with inexperience in the subjects of finance, produced direct infractions; and that the subsequent period has been a continued scene of negative violation, or noncompliance. But a diminution of this regret arises from the reflection that the last seven years have exhibited an earnest and uniform effort, on the part of the government of the union, to retrieve the national credit by doing justice to the creditors of the nation, and that the embarrassments of a defective constitution, which defeated this laudable effort, have ceased.

From this evidence of a favorable disposition, given by the former government, the institution of a new one, clothed with powers competent to calling forth the resources of the community, has excited correspondent expectations. A general belief, accordingly, prevails that the credit of the United States will quickly be established on the firm foundation of an effectual provision for the existing debt. The influence which this has had at home is witnessed by the rapid increase that has taken place in the market value of the public securities. From January to November, they rose thirty-three and a third percent, and from that period to this time they have risen fifty percent more. And the intelligence from abroad announces effects proportionably favorable to our national credit and consequence.

It cannot but merit particular attention that among ourselves the most enlightened friends of good government are those whose expectations are the highest.

To justify and preserve their confidence; to promote the increasing respectability of the American name; to answer the calls of justice; to restore landed property to its due value; to furnish new resources both to agriculture and commerce; to cement more closely the union of the states; to add to their security against foreign attack; to establish public order on the basis of an upright and liberal policy. These are the great and invaluable ends to be secured by a proper and adequate provision, at the present period, for the support of public credit.

To this provision we are invited not only by the general considerations which have been noticed, but by others of a more particular nature. It will procure to every class of the community some important advantages, and remove some no less important disadvantages.

The advantage to the public creditors from the increased value of that part of their property which constitutes the public debt needs no explanation.

But there is a consequence of this, less obvious, though not less true, in which every other citizen is interested. It is a well-known fact that in countries in which the national debt is properly funded, and an object of established confidence, it answers most of the purposes of money. Transfers of stock or public debt are there equivalent to payments in specie; or in other words, stock, in the principal transactions of business, passes current as specie. The same thing would in all probability happen here under the like circumstances.

The benefits of this are various and obvious.

First. Trade is extended by it, because there is a larger capital to carry it on, and the merchant can at the same time afford to trade for smaller profits, as his stock, which, when unemployed, brings him in an interest from the government, serves him also as money when he has a call for it in his commercial operations.

Secondly. Agriculture and manufactures are also promoted by it: For the like reason, that more capital can be commanded to be employed in both, and because the merchant, whose enterprise in foreign trade gives to them activity and extension, has greater means for enterprise.

Thirdly. The interest of money will be lowered by it, for this is always in a ratio to the quantity of money and to the quickness of circulation. This circumstance will enable both the public and individuals to borrow on easier and cheaper terms.

And from the combination of these effects, additional aids will be furnished to labor, to industry, and to arts of every kind.

But these good effects of a public debt are only to be looked for when, by being well funded, it has acquired an *adequate* and *stable* value. Till then, it has rather a contrary tendency. The fluctuation and insecurity incident to it in an unfunded state render it a mere commodity, and a precarious one. As such, being only an object of occasional and particular speculation, all the money applied to it is so much diverted from the more useful channels of circulation, for which the thing itself affords no substitute: So that, in fact, one serious inconvenience of an unfunded debt is that it contributes to the scarcity of money.

This distinction, which has been little if at all attended to, is of the greatest moment. It involves a question immediately interesting to every part of the community, which is no other than this—Whether the public debt, by a provision for it on true principles, shall be rendered a *substitute* for money; or whether, by being left as it is, or by being provided for in such a manner as will wound those principles and destroy confidence, it shall be suffered to continue as it is, a pernicious drain of our cash from the channels of productive industry.

The effect which the funding of the public debt, on right principles, would have upon landed property is one of the circumstances attending such an arrangement which has been least adverted to, though it deserves the most particular attention. The present depreciated state of that species of property is a serious calamity. The value of cultivated lands, in most of the states, has fallen since the revolution from 25 to 50 percent. In those farthest south the decrease is still more considerable. Indeed, if the representations continually received from that quarter may be credited, lands there will command no price which may not be deemed an almost total sacrifice.

This decrease in the value of lands ought, in a great measure, to be attributed to the scarcity of money. Consequently, whatever produces an augmentation of the monied capital of the country must have a proportional effect in raising that value. The beneficial tendency of a funded debt, in this respect, has been manifested by the most decisive experience in Great Britain.

The proprietors of lands would not only feel the benefit of this increase in the value of their property, and of a more prompt and better sale, when they had occasion to sell, but the necessity of selling would be, itself, greatly diminished. As the same cause would contribute to the facility of loans, there is reason to believe that such of them as are indebted would be able through that resource to satisfy their more urgent creditors.

It ought not, however, to be expected that the advantages, described as likely to result from funding the public debt, would be instantaneous. It might require some time to bring the value of stock to its natural level and to attach to it that fixed confidence which is necessary to its quality as money. Yet the late rapid rise of the public securities encourages an expectation that the progress of stock to the desirable point will be much more expeditious than could have been foreseen. And as in the meantime it will be increasing in value, there is room to conclude that it will, from the outset, answer many of the purposes in contemplation. Particularly it seems to be probable that from creditors, who are not themselves necessitous, it will early meet with a ready reception in payment of debts at its current price.

Having now taken a concise view of the inducements to a proper provision for the public debt, the next enquiry which presents itself is, what ought to be the nature of such a provision? This requires some preliminary discussions.

It is agreed on all hands that that part of the debt which has been contracted abroad, and is denominated the foreign debt, ought to be provided for according to the precise terms of the contracts relating to it. The discussions which can arise, therefore, will have reference essentially to the domestic part of it, or to that which has been contracted at home. It is to be regretted that there is not the same unanimity of sentiment on this part as on the other.

The secretary has too much deference for the opinions of every part of the community not to have observed one which has, more than once, made its appearance in the public prints, and which is occasionally to be met with in conversation. It involves this question, whether a discrimination ought not to be made between original holders of the public securities and present possessors by purchase. Those who advocate a discrimination are for making a full provision for the securities of the former, at their nominal value, but contend that the latter ought to receive no more than the cost to them, and the interest: And the idea is sometimes suggested of making good the difference to the primitive possessor.

In favor of this scheme it is alleged that it would be unreasonable to pay twenty shillings in the pound to one who had not given more for it than three or four. And it is added that it would be hard to aggravate the misfortune of the first owner, who, probably through necessity, parted with his property at so great a loss, by obliging him to contribute to the profit of the person who had speculated on his distresses.

The secretary, after the most mature reflection on the force of this argument, is induced to reject the doctrine it contains as equally unjust and impolitic, as highly injurious, even to the original holders of public securities, as ruinous to public credit.

It is inconsistent with justice, because in the first place, it is a breach of contract, in violation of the rights of a fair purchaser.

The nature of the contract in its origin is that the public will pay the sum expressed in the security to the first holder or his *assignee*. The *intent*, in making the security assignable, is that the proprietor may be able to make use of his property by selling it for as much as it *may be worth in the market*, and that the buyer may be *safe* in the purchase.

Every buyer therefore stands exactly in the place of the seller, has the same right with him to the identical sum expressed in the security, and having acquired that right by fair purchase, and in conformity to the original *agreement* and *intention* of the government, his claim cannot be disputed without manifest injustice.

That he is to be considered as a fair purchaser results from this: Whatever necessity the seller may have been under was occasioned by the government in not making a proper provision for its debts. The buyer had no agency in it and therefore ought not to suffer. He is not even chargeable with having taken an undue advantage. He paid what the commodity was worth in the market, and took the risks of reimbursement upon himself. He of course gave a fair equivalent and ought to reap the benefit of his hazard, a hazard which was far from inconsiderable, and which, perhaps, turned on little less than a revolution in government.

That the case of those who parted with their securities from necessity is a hard one cannot be denied. But whatever complaint of injury or claim of redress they may have respects the government solely. They have not only nothing to object to the persons who relieved their necessities, by giving them the current price of their property, but they are even under an implied condition to contribute to the reimbursement of those persons. They knew that by the terms of the contract with themselves the public were bound to pay to those to whom they should convey their title the sums stipulated to be paid to them and that as citizens of the United States they were to bear their proportion of the contribution for that purpose. This, by the act of assignment, they tacitly engage to do; and if they had an option, they could not, with integrity or good faith, refuse to do it without the consent of those to whom they sold.

But though many of the original holders sold from necessity, it does not follow that this was the case with all of them. It may well be supposed that some of them did it either through want of confidence in an eventual provision, or from the allurements of some profitable speculation. How shall these different classes be discriminated from each other? How shall it be ascertained in any case that the money which the original holder obtained for his security was not more beneficial to him than if he had held it to the present time, to avail himself of the provision which shall be made? How shall it be known whether if the purchaser had employed his money in some other way he would not be in a better situation than by having applied it in the purchase of securities, though he should now receive their full amount? And if neither of these things can be known, how shall it be determined whether a discrimination, independent of the breach of contract, would not do a real injury to purchasers, and if it included a compensation to the primitive proprietors would not give them an advantage to which they had no equitable pretension?

It may well be imagined, also, that there are not wanting instances in which individuals, urged by a present necessity, parted with the securities received by them from the public, and shortly after replaced them with others, as an indemnity for their first loss. Shall they be deprived of the indemnity which they have endeavored to secure by so provident an arrangement?

Questions of this sort, on a close inspection, multiply themselves without end, and demonstrate the injustice of a discrimination, even on the most subtle calculations of equity, abstracted from the obligation of contract.

The difficulties too of regulating the details of a plan for that purpose, which would have even the semblance of equity, would be found immense. It may well be doubted whether they would not be insurmountable, and replete with such absurd, as well as inequitable consequences, as to disgust even the proposers of the measure.

As a specimen of its capricious operation, it will be sufficient to notice the effect it would have upon two persons who may be supposed two years ago to have purchased, each, securities at three shillings in the pound, and one of them to retain those bought by him till the discrimination should take place, the other to have parted with those bought by him within a month past, at nine shillings. The former, who had had most confidence in the government, would in this case only receive at the rate of three shillings and the interest; while the latter, who had had less confidence, would receive *for what cost him the same money* at the rate of nine shillings, and his representative, *standing in his place*, would be entitled to a like rate.

The impolicy of a discrimination results from two considerations; one, that it proceeds upon a principle destructive of that *quality* of the public debt, or the stock of the nation, which is essential to its capacity for answering the purposes of money—that is the *security* of *transfer*; the other, that as well on this account, as because it includes a breach of faith, it renders property in the funds less valuable; consequently induces lenders to demand a higher premium for what they lend, and produces every other inconvenience of a bad state of public credit.

It will be perceived at first sight that the transferable quality of stock is essential to its operation as money, and that this depends on the idea of complete security to the transferree, and a firm persuasion that no distinction can in any circumstances be made between him and the original proprietor.

The precedent of an invasion of this fundamental principle would of course tend to deprive the community of an advantage with which no temporary saving could bear the least comparison.

And it will as readily be perceived that the same cause would operate a diminution of the value of stock in the hands of the first as well as of every other holder. The price which any man who should incline to purchase would be willing to give for it would be in a compound ratio to the immediate profit it afforded, and to the chance of the continuance of his profit. If there was supposed to be any hazard of the latter, the risk would be taken into the calculation, and either there would be no purchase at all, or it would be at a proportionably less price.

For this diminution of the value of stock every person who should be about to lend to the government would demand a compensation, and would add to the actual difference, between the nominal and the market value, and equivalent for the chance of greater decrease, which, in a precarious state of public credit, is always to be taken into the account.

Every compensation of this sort, it is evident, would be an absolute loss to the government.

In the preceding discussion of the impolicy of a discrimination, the injurious tendency of it to those who continue to be the holders of the securities they received from the government has been explained. Nothing need be added on this head except that this is an additional and interesting light in which the injustice of the measure may be seen. It would not only divest present proprietors by purchase of the rights they had acquired under the sanction of public faith, but it would depreciate the property of the remaining original holders.

It is equally unnecessary to add anything to what has been already said to demonstrate the fatal influence which the principle of discrimination would have on the public credit.

But there is still a point in view in which it will appear perhaps even more exceptionable than in either of the former. It would be repugnant to an express provision of the Constitution of the United States. This provision is that "all debts contracted and engagements entered into before the adoption of that Constitution shall be as valid against the United States under it, as under the confederation," which amounts to a constitutional ratification of the contracts respecting the debt in the state in which they existed under the confederation. And resorting to that standard, there can be no doubt that the rights of assignees and original holders must be considered as equal.

In exploding thus fully the principle of discrimination, the secretary is happy in reflecting that he is the only advocate of what has been already sanctioned by the formal and express authority of the government of the Union, in these emphatic terms—"The remaining class of creditors (say Congress in their circular address to the states, of the 26th of April 1783) is composed partly of such of our fellow citizens as originally lent to the public the use of their funds, or have since manifested *most confidence* in their country, by receiving transfers from the lenders, and partly of those whose property has been either advanced or assumed for the public service. To *discriminate* the merits of these several descriptions of creditors would be a task equally unnecessary and invidious. If the voice of humanity plead more loudly in favor of some than of others, the voice of policy, no less than of justice, pleads in favor of all. A wise nation will never permit those who relieve the wants of their country, or who *rely most* on its *faith*, its *firmness*, and its *resources*, when either of them is distrusted, to suffer by the event."

The secretary, concluding that a discrimination between the different classes of creditors of the United States cannot with propriety be *made*, proceeds to examine whether a difference ought to be permitted to *remain* between them and another description of public creditors—Those of the states individually.

The secretary, after mature reflection on this point, entertains a full conviction that an assumption of the debts of the particular states by the union, and a like provision for them as for those of the union, will be a measure of sound policy and substantial justice.

It would, in the opinion of the secretary, contribute, in an eminent degree, to an orderly, stable, and satisfactory arrangement of the national finances.

Admitting, as ought to be the case, that a provision must be made in some way or other, for the entire debt, it will follow that no greater revenues will be required, whether that provision be made wholly by the United States, or partly by them, and partly by the states separately.

The principal question then must be, whether such a provision cannot be more conveniently and effectually made by one general plan issuing from one authority than by different plans originating in different authorities.

In the first case there can be no competition for resources; in the last, there must be such a competition. The consequences of this, without the greatest caution on both sides, might be interfering regulations, and thence collision and confusion. Particular branches of industry might also be oppressed by it. The most productive objects of revenue are not numerous. Either these must be wholly engrossed by one side, which might lessen the efficacy of the provisions by the other, or both must have recourse to the same objects in different modes, which might occasion an accumulation upon them beyond what they could properly bear. If this should not happen, the caution requisite to avoiding it would prevent the revenue's deriving the full benefit of each object. The danger of interference and of excess would be apt to impose restraints very unfriendly to the complete command of those resources which are the most convenient, and to compel the having recourse to others, less eligible in themselves, and less agreeable to the community.

The difficulty of an effectual command of the public resources, in case of separate provisions for the debt, may be seen in another and perhaps more striking light. It would naturally happen that different states, from local considerations, would in some instances have recourse to different objects, in others to the same objects, in different degrees, for procuring the funds of which they stood in need. It is easy to conceive how this diversity would affect the aggregate revenue of the country. By the supposition, articles which yielded a full supply in some states would yield nothing, or an insufficient product, in others. And hence the public revenue would not derive the full benefit of those articles from state regulations. Neither could the deficiencies be made good by those of the union. It is a provision of the national Constitution that "all duties, imposts and excises, shall be uniform throughout the United States." And as the general government would be under a necessity from motives of policy of paying regard to the duty which may have been previously imposed upon any article, though but in a single state, it would be constrained either to refrain wholly from any further imposition upon such article where it had been already rated as high as was proper, or to confine itself to the difference between the existing rate and what the article would reasonably bear. Thus the preoccupancy of an article by a single state would tend to arrest or abridge the impositions of the union on that article. And as it is supposable that a great variety of articles might be placed in this situation by dissimilar arrangements of the particular states, it is evident that the aggregate revenue of the country would be likely to be very materially contracted by the plan of separate provisions.

If all the public creditors receive their dues from one source, distributed with an equal hand, their interest will be the same. And having the same interests, they will unite in the support of the fiscal arrangements of the government: As these, too, can be made with more convenience where there is no competition: These circumstances combined will insure to the revenue laws a more ready and more satisfactory execution.

If on the contrary there are distinct provisions, there will be distinct interests, drawing different ways. That union and concert of views among the creditors, which in every government is of great importance to their security and to that of public credit, will not only not exist, but will be likely to give place to mutual jealousy and opposition. And from this cause the operation of the systems which may be adopted, both by the particular states and by the union, with relation to their respective debts, will be in danger of being counteracted.

There are several reasons which render it probable that the situation of the state creditors would be worse than that of the creditors of the union, if there be not a national assumption of the state debts. Of these it will be sufficient to mention two; one, that a principal branch of revenue is exclusively vested in the union; the other, that a state must always be checked in the imposition of taxes on articles of consumption from the want of power to extend the same regulation to the other states, and from the tendency of partial duties to injure its industry and commerce. Should the state creditors stand upon a less eligible footing than the others it is unnatural to expect they would see with pleasure a provision for them. The influence which their dissatisfaction might have could not but operate injuriously, both for the creditors and the credit of the United States.

Hence it is even the interest of the creditors of the union that those of the individual states should be comprehended in a general provision. Any attempt to secure to the former either exclusive or peculiar advantages would materially hazard their interests.

Neither would it be just that one class of the public creditors should be more favored than the other. The objects for which both descriptions of the debt were contracted are in the main the same. Indeed a great part of the particular debts of the States has arisen from assumptions by them on account of the union. And it is most equitable that there should be the same measure of retribution for all.

There is an objection, however, to an assumption of the state debts which deserves particular notice. It may be supposed that it would increase the difficulty of an equitable settlement between them and the United States.

The principles of that settlement, whenever they shall be discussed, will require all the moderation and wisdom of the government. In the opinion of the secretary, that discussion, till further lights are obtained, would be premature.

All therefore which he would now think advisable on the point in question would be that the amount of the debts assumed and provided for should be charged to the respective states to abide an eventual arrangement. This the United States, as assignees to the creditors, would have an indisputable right to do.

But as it might be a satisfaction to the House to have before them some plan for the liquidation of accounts between the union and its members, which, including the assumption of the state debts, would consist with equity: The secretary will submit in this place such thoughts on the subject as have occurred to his own mind or been suggested to him, most compatible, in his judgment, with the end proposed.

Let each state be charged with all the money advanced to it out of the treasury of the United States, liquidated according to the specie value, at the time of each advance, with interest at six percent.

Let it also be charged with the amount, in specie value, of all its securities which shall be assumed, with the interest upon them to the time when interest shall become payable by the United States.

Let it be credited for all monies paid and articles furnished to the United States, and for all other expenditures during the war, either towards general or particular defense, whether authorized or unauthorized by the United States; the whole liquidated to specie value, and bearing an interest of six percent from the several times at which the several payments, advances, and expenditures accrued.

And let all sums of continental money now in the treasuries of the respective states, which shall be paid into the treasury of the United States, be credited at specie value.

Upon a statement of the accounts according to these principles, there can be little doubt that balances would appear in favor of all the states against the United States.

To equalize the contributions of the states, let each be then charged with its proportion of the aggregate of those balances, according to some equitable ratio, to be devised for that purpose.

If the contributions should be found disproportionate, the result of this adjustment would be that some states would be creditors, some debtors to the union.

Should this be the case, as it will be attended with less inconvenience for the United States to have to pay balances to than to receive them from the particular states, it may perhaps be practicable to effect the former by a second process, in the nature of a transfer of the amount of the debts of debtor states to the credit of creditor states, observing the ratio by which the first apportionment shall have been made. This, whilst it would destroy the balances due from the former, would increase those due to the latter. These to be provided for by the United States at a reasonable interest, but not to be transferable.

The expediency of this second process must depend on a knowledge of the result of the first. If the inequalities should be too great, the arrangement may be impracticable, without unduly increasing the debt of the United States. But it is not likely that this would be the case. It is also to be remarked that though this second process might not, upon the principle of apportionment, bring the thing to the point aimed at, yet it may approach so nearly to it, as to avoid essentially the embarrassment of having considerable balances to collect from any of the states.

The whole of this arrangement to be under the superintendence of commissioners, vested with equitable discretion and final authority.

The operation of the plan is exemplified in the schedule A.

The general principle of it seems to be equitable, for it appears difficult to conceive a good reason why the expenses for the particular defense of a part in a common war should not be a common charge, as well as those incurred professedly for the general defense. The defense of each part is that of the whole; and unless all the expenditures are brought into a common mass, the tendency must be to add to the calamities suffered, by being the most exposed to the ravages of war, an increase of burthens.

This plan seems to be susceptible of no objection which does not belong to every other that proceeds on the idea of a final adjustment of accounts. The difficulty of settling a ratio is common to all. This must, probably, either be sought for in the proportions of the requisitions, during the war, or in the decision of commissioners appointed with plenary power. The rule prescribed in the Constitution with regard to representation and direct taxes would evidently not be applicable to the situation of parties during the period in question.

The existing debt of the United States is excluded from the computation, as it ought to be, because it will be provided for out of a general fund.

The only discussion of a preliminary kind, which remains, relates to the distinctions of the debt into principal and interest. It is well known that the arrears of the latter bear a large proportion to the amount of the former. The immediate payment of these arrears is evidently impracticable, and a question arises, what ought to be done with them?

There is good reason to conclude that the impressions of many are more favorable to the claim of the principal than to that of the interest, at least so far as to produce an opinion that an inferior provision might suffice for the latter.

But to the secretary this opinion does not appear to be well-founded. His investigations of the subject have led him to a conclusion that the arrears of interest have pretensions at least equal to the principal.

The liquidated debt, traced to its origin, falls under two principal discriminations. One, relating to loans, the other to services performed and articles supplied.

The part arising from loans was at first made payable at fixed periods, which have long since elapsed, with an early option to lenders either to receive back their money at the expiration of those periods or to continue it at interest 'till the whole amount of continental bills circulating should not exceed the sum in circulation at the time of each loan. This contingency, in the sense of the contract, never happened; and the presumption is that the creditors preferred continuing their money indefinitely at interest to receiving it in a depreciated and depreciating state.

The other parts of it were chiefly for objects which ought to have been paid for at the time, that is, when the services were performed or the supplies furnished, and were not accompanied with any contract for interest.

But by different acts of government and administration, concurred in by the creditors, these parts of the debt have been converted into a capital, bearing an interest of six percent per annum, but without any definite period of redemption. A portion of the loan-office debt has been exchanged for new securities of that import. And the whole of it seems to have acquired that character after the expiration of the periods prefixed for re-payment.

If this view of the subject be a just one, the capital of the debt of the United States may be considered in the light of an annuity at the rate of six percent per annum, redeemable at the pleasure of the government by payment of the principal. For it seems to be a clear position that when a public contracts a debt payable with interest, without any precise time being stipulated or understood for payment of the capital, that time is a matter of pure discretion with the government, which is at liberty to consult its own convenience respecting it, taking care to pay the interest with punctuality.

Wherefore, as long as the United States should pay the interest of their debt as it accrued, their creditors would have no right to demand the principal.

But with regard to the arrears of interest, the case is different. These are now due, and those to whom they are due have a right to claim immediate payment. To say that it would be impracticable to comply would not vary the nature of the right. Nor can this idea of impracticability be honorably carried further than to justify the proposition of a new contract upon the basis of a commutation of that right for an equivalent. This equivalent too ought to be a real and fair one. And what other fair equivalent can be imagined for the detention of money but a reasonable interest? Or what can be the standard of that interest but the market rate, or the rate which the government pays in ordinary cases?

From this view of the matter, which appears to be the accurate and true one, it will follow that the arrears of interest are entitled to an equal provision with the principal of the debt.

The result of the foregoing discussions is this—That there ought to be no discrimination between the original holders of the debt and present possessors by purchase—That it is expedient there should be an assumption of the state debts by the Union, and that the arrears of interest should be provided for on an equal footing with the principal.

The interesting problem now occurs. Is it in the power of the United States, consistently with those prudential considerations which ought not to be overlooked, to make a provision equal to the purpose of funding the whole debt, at the rates of interest which it now bears, in addition to the sum which will be necessary for the current service of the government?

The secretary will not say that such provision would exceed the abilities of the country, but he is clearly of opinion that to make it would require the extension of taxation to a degree and to objects which the true interest of the public creditors forbids. It is therefore to be hoped, and even to be expected, that they will cheerfully concur in such modifications of their claims, on fair and equitable principles, as will facilitate to the government an arrangement substantial, durable, and satisfactory to the community. The importance of the last characteristic will strike every discerning mind. No plan, however flattering in appearance, to which it did not belong, could be truly entitled to confidence.

It will not be forgotten, that exigencies may, ere long, arise, which would call for resources greatly beyond what is now deemed sufficient for the current service; and that, should the faculties of the country be exhausted or even *strained* to provide for the public debt, there could be less reliance on the sacredness of the provision.

But while the secretary yields to the force of these considerations, he does not lose sight of those fundamental principles of good faith, which dictate that every practicable exertion ought to be made scrupulously to fulfill the engagements of the government; that no change in the rights of its creditors ought to be attempted without their voluntary consent; and that this consent ought to be voluntary in fact as well as in name. Consequently, that every proposal of a change ought to be in the shape of an appeal to their reason and to their interest, not to their necessities. To this end it is requisite that a fair equivalent should be offered for what may be asked to be given up, and unquestionable security for the remainder. Without this, an alteration, consistently with the credit and honor of the nation, would be impracticable.

It remains to see what can be proposed in conformity to these views.

It has been remarked that the capital of the debt of the union is to be viewed in the light of an annuity at the rate of six percent per annum, redeemable at the pleasure of the government by payment of the principal. And it will not be required that the arrears of interest should be considered in a more favorable light. The same character, in general, may be applied to the debts of the individual states.

This view of the subject admits that the United States would have it in their power to avail themselves of any fall in the market rate of interest for reducing that of the debt.

This property of the debt is favorable to the public, unfavorable to the creditor. And may facilitate an arrangement for the reduction of interest upon the basis of a fair equivalent.

Probabilities are always a rational ground of contract. The secretary conceives that there is good reason to believe, if effectual measures are taken to establish public credit, that the government rate of interest in the United States will, in a very short time, fall at least as low as five percent, and that in a period not exceeding twenty years it will sink still lower, probably to four.

There are two principal causes which will be likely to produce this effect; one, the low rate of interest in Europe; the other, the increase of the monied capital of the nation by the funding of the public debt.

From three to four percent is deemed good interest in several parts of Europe. Even less is deemed so in some places. And it is on the decline, the increasing plenty of money continually tending to lower it. It is presumable that no country will be able to borrow of foreigners upon better terms than the United States, because none can, perhaps, afford so good security. Our situation exposes us less than that of any other nation to those casualties which are the chief causes of expense; our encumbrances, in proportion to our real means, are less, though these cannot immediately be brought so readily into action, and our progress in resources from the early state of the country, and the immense tracts of unsettled territory, must necessarily exceed that of any other. The advantages of this situation have already engaged the attention of the European moneylenders, particularly among the Dutch. And as they become better understood, they will have the greater influence. Hence as large a proportion of the cash of Europe as may be wanted will be, in a certain sense, in our market, for the use of government. And this will naturally have the effect of a reduction of the rate of interest, not indeed to the level of the places which send their money to market, but to something much nearer to it than our present rate.

The influence which the funding of the debt is calculated to have in lowering interest has been already remarked and explained. It is hardly possible that it should not be materially affected by such an increase of the monied capital of the nation as would result from the proper funding of seventy millions of dollars. But the probability of a decrease in the rate of interest acquires confirmation from facts which existed prior to the revolution. It is well known that in some of the states money might with facility be borrowed, on good security, at five percent and, not unfrequently, even at less.

The most enlightened of the public creditors will be most sensible of the justness of this view of the subject and of the propriety of the use which will be made of it.

The secretary, in pursuance of it, will assume, as a probability sufficiently great to be a ground of calculation, both on the part of the government and of its creditors—That the interest of money in the United States will, in five years, fall to five percent and, in twenty, to four. The probability in the mind of the secretary is rather that the fall may be more rapid and more considerable; but he prefers a mean, as most likely to engage the assent of the creditors, and more equitable in itself; because it is predicated on probabilities, which may err on one side as well as on the other.

Premising these things, the secretary submits to the House the expediency of proposing a loan to the full amount of the debt, as well of the particular states as of the union, upon the following terms.

First—That for every hundred dollars subscribed, payable in the debt (as well interest as principal), the subscribed be entitled, at his option, either

To have two thirds funded at an annuity, or yearly interest of six percent, redeemable at the pleasure of the government by payment of the principal; and to receive the other third in lands in the western territory, at the rate of twenty cents per acre. Or,

To have the whole sum funded at an annuity or yearly interest of four percent, irredeemable by any payment exceeding five dollars per annum on account both of principal and interest; and to receive, as a compensation for the reduction of interest, fifteen dollars and eighty cents, payable in lands, as in the preceding case. Or

To have sixty-six dollars and two thirds of a dollar funded immediately at an annuity or yearly interest of six percent, irredeemable by any payment exceeding four dollars and two thirds of a dollar per annum, on account both of principal and interest; and to have, at the end of ten years, twenty-six dollars and eighty-eight cents, funded at the like interest and rate of redemption. Or

To have an annuity for the remainder of life, upon the contingency of living to a given age, not less distant than ten years, computing interest at four percent. Or

To have an annuity for the remainder of life, upon the contingency of the survivorship of the youngest of two persons, computing interest, in this case also, at four percent.

In addition to the foregoing loan, payable wholly in the debt, the secretary would propose that one should be opened for ten millions of dollars, on the following plan.

That for every hundred dollars subscribed, payable one half in specie and the other half in debt (as well principal as interest), the subscriber be entitled to an annuity or yearly interest of five percent, irredeemable by any payment exceeding six dollars per annum, on account both of principal and interest...

In order to keep up a due circulation of money, it will be expedient that the interest of the debt should be paid quarter-yearly. This regulation will, at the same time, conduce to the advantage of the public creditors, giving them, in fact, by the anticipation of payment, a higher rate of interest; which may, with propriety, be taken into the estimate of the compensation to be made to them. Six percent per annum, paid in this mode, will truly be worth six dollars and one hundred and thirty-five thousandth parts of a dollar, computing the market interest at the same rate.

The secretary thinks it advisable to hold out various propositions, all of them compatible with the public interest, because it is, in his opinion, of the greatest consequence, that the debt should, with the consent of the creditors, be remolded into such a shape as will bring the expenditure of the nation to a level with its income. 'Till this shall be accomplished, the finances of the United

States will never wear a proper countenance. Arrears of interest, continually accruing, will be as continual a monument either of inability or of ill faith, and will not cease to have an evil influence on public credit. In nothing are appearances of greater moment than in whatever regards credit. Opinion is the soul of it, and this is affected by appearances as well as realities. By offering an option to the creditors between a number of plans, the change meditated will be more likely to be accomplished. Different tempers will be governed by different views of the subject.

But while the secretary would endeavor to effect a change in the form of the debt by new loans, in order to render it more susceptible of an adequate provision, he would not think it proper to aim at procuring the concurrence of the creditors by operating upon their necessities.

Hence whatever surplus of revenue might remain, after satisfying the interest of the new loans and the demand for the current service, ought to be divided among those creditors, if any, who may not think fit to subscribe to them. But for this purpose, under the circumstance of depending propositions, a temporary appropriation will be most advisable, and the sum must be limited to four percent, as the revenues will only be calculated to produce, in that proportion, to the entire debt.

The secretary confides for the success of the propositions to be made on the goodness of the reasons upon which they rest, on the fairness of the equivalent to be offered in each case, on the discernment of the creditors of their true interest, and on their disposition to facilitate the arrangements of the government and to render them satisfactory to the community...

Persuaded as the secretary is, that the proper funding of the present debt will render it a national blessing: Yet he is so far from acceding to the position, in the latitude in which it is sometimes laid down, that "public debts are public benefits," a position inviting to prodigality, and liable to dangerous abuse, that he ardently wishes to see it incorporated as a fundamental maxim in the system of public credit of the United States that the creation of debt should always be accompanied with the means of extinguishment. This he regards as the true secret for rendering public credit immortal. And he presumes that it is difficult to conceive a situation in which there may not be an adherence to the maxim. At least he feels an unfeigned solicitude that this may be attempted by the United States, and that they may commence their measures for the establishment of credit with the observance of it...

The secretary has now completed the objects which he proposed to himself to comprise in the present report. He has, for the most part, omitted details, as well to avoid fatiguing the attention of the House, as because more time would have been desirable even to digest the general principles of the plan. If these should be found right, the particular modifications will readily suggest themselves in the progress of the work.

The secretary, in the views which have directed his pursuit of the subject, has been influenced, in the first place, by the consideration that his duty from the very terms of the resolution of the House obliged him to propose what appeared to him an adequate provision for the support of the public credit, adapted at the same time to the real circumstances of the United States; and in the next, by the reflection that measures which will not bear the test of future unbiased examination can neither be productive of individual reputation, nor (which is of much greater consequence) public honor or advantage.

Deeply impressed, as the secretary is, with a full and deliberate conviction that the establishment of public credit, upon the basis of a satisfactory provision for the public debt, is, under the present circumstances of this country, the true desideratum towards relief from individual and national embarrassments; that without it, these embarrassments will be likely to press still more severely upon the community—He cannot but indulge an anxious wish that an effectual plan for that purpose may, during the present session, be the result of the united wisdom of the legislature.

He is fully convinced that it is of the greatest importance that no further delay should attend the making of the requisite provision; not only because it will give a better impression of the good faith of the country, and will bring earlier relief to the creditors; both which circumstances are of great moment to public credit: but, because the advantages to the community from raising stock as speedily as possible to its natural value will be incomparably greater than any that can result from its continuance below that standard. No profit, which could be derived from purchases in the market on account of the government to any practicable extent, would be an equivalent for the loss which would be sustained by the purchases of foreigners at a low value. Not to repeat that governmental purchases to be honorable ought to be preceded by a provision. Delay, by disseminating doubt, would sink the price of stock; and as the temptation to foreign speculations, from the lowness of the price, would be too great to be neglected, millions would probably be lost to the United States.

All which is humbly submitted.

Alexander Hamilton, Secretary of the Treasury.

Memorandum to George Washington, May 28, 1790

The secretary of the treasury conceives it to be his duty most respectfully to represent to the president of the United States, that there are, in his judgment, objections of a very serious & weighty nature to the resolutions of the two houses of Congress of the twenty first instant, concerning certain arrears of pay due to the officers and soldiers of the lines of Virginia and North Carolina.

The third of those resolutions directs, that in cases where *payment* has not been made to the original claimant in person, or to his representative, *it* shall be made to the original claimant, or to such person or persons only, as shall produce a power of attorney, duly attested by *two justices* of the peace of the county, in which such person or persons reside, authorizing him or them to receive a certain specified sum.

By the law of most if not all the states, claims of this kind are in their nature assignable for valuable consideration; and the assignor may constitute the assignee, his attorney or agent, to receive the amount. The import of every such assignment is a contract, express, or implied, on the part of the assignor, that the assignee shall receive the sum assigned to his own use. In making it, no precise form is necessary, but any instrument, competent to conveying with clearness & precision the sense of the parties, suffices; There is no need of the cooperation of any justice of the peace, or other magistrate whatever.

The practice of the Treasury and of the public officers in other departments, in the adjustment and satisfaction of claims upon the United States, has uniformly corresponded with the rules of that law.

A regulation therefore having a retrospective operation, and prescribing, with regard to past transactions, new and unknown requisites, by which the admission of claims is to be guided, is an infraction of the rights of individuals, acquired under preexisting laws, and a contravention of the public faith, pledged by the course of public proceedings. It has consequently a tendency not less unfriendly to public credit, than to the security of property.

Such is the regulation contained in the resolution above referred to. It defeats all previous assignments not accompanied with a *Power of Attorney* attested by *two Justices* of the peace of *the County* where the assignor resides; a formality, which for obvious reasons cannot be presumed to have attended any of them, and which does not appear to have been observed, with respect to those upon which applications for payment have hitherto been made.

It is to be remarked that the assignee has no method of compelling the assignor to perfect the transfer by a new instrument, in conformity to the rule prescribed; if even the existence of such a power, the execution of which would involve a legal controversy, could be a satisfactory cause for altering by a new law that state of things, which antecedent law and usage had established between the parties.

It is perhaps, too, questionable, whether an assignee, however equitable his pretensions were, could, under the operation of the provision, which has been recited, have any remedy whatever for the recovery of the money or value which he may have paid to the assignor. It is not certain, that a legislative act, decreeing payment to a different person, would not be a legal bar; but if the existence of such a remedy were certain, it would be but a very inconclusive consideration. The assignment may have been a security for a precarious or desperate debt, which security will be wrested from the assignee; or it may have been a composition between an insolvent debtor and his creditor, & the only resource of the latter; or the assignor may be absent and incapable either of benefiting by the provision, or of being called to an account: and in every case the assignee would be left to the casualty of the ability of the assignor to repay; to the perplexity, trouble and expense of a suit at law. In respect to the soldiers the presumption would be, in the greater number of cases, that the pursuit of redress would be worse than acquiescence in the loss. To vary the risks of parties; to supersede the contracts between them; to turn over a creditor, without his consent, from one *debtor* to *another*; to take away a right to a *specific thing* leaving only the chance of a remedy for retribution are not less positive violations of property, than a direct confiscation.

It appears from the debates in the House of Representatives, and it may be inferred from the nature of the proceeding, that a suggestion of fraud has been the occasion of it. Fraud is certainly a good objection to any contract, and where it is properly ascertained, invalidates it. But the power of ascertaining it is the peculiar province of the Judiciary Department. The principles of good government conspire with those of justice to place it there. 'Tis there only that such an investigation of the fact can be had as ought to precede a decision. 'Tis there only the parties can be heard and evidence on both sides produced; without which *surmise* must be substituted to *Proof*, and *Conjecture* to *fact*.

This, then, is the dilemma incident to legislative interference. Either the legislature must erect itself into a court of justice and determine each case upon its own merits, after a full hearing of the allegations and proofs of the parties; or it must proceed upon vague suggestions, loose reports, or at best upon partial & problematical testimony, to condemn in the gross and in the dark, the fairest and most unexceptionable claims, as well as those which may happen to be fraudulent and exceptionable. The first would be an usurpation of the judiciary authority; the last is at variance with the rules of property, the dictates of Equity and the maxims of good government.

All admit the truth of these positions as general rules. But when a departure from it is advocated for any particular purpose, it is usually alleged that there are exceptions to it; that there are certain extraordinary cases, in which the public good demands & justifies an extraordinary interposition of the Legislature.

This doctrine in relation to extraordinary cases is not to be denied; but it is highly important, that the nature of those cases should be carefully distinguished.

It is evident that every such interposition, deviating from the usual course of law and justice, and infringing the established rules of property, which ought as far as possible to be held sacred and inviolable, is an overleaping of the ordinary and regular bounds of legislative discretion; and is in the nature of a resort to first principles. Nothing therefore but some urgent public necessity, some impending national Calamity, something that threatens direct and general mischief to the society, for which there is no adequate redress in the established course of things, can, it is presumed, be a sufficient cause for the employment of so extraordinary a remedy. An accommodation to the interests of a small part of the community, in a case of inconsiderable magnitude on a national scale, cannot, in the judgment of the secretary, be entitled to that character.

If partial inconveniencies and hardships occasion legislative interferences in private contracts, the intercourses of business become uncertain, the security of property is lessened, the confidence in government destroyed or weakened.

The Constitution of the United States interdicts the states individually from passing any law impairing the obligation of contracts. This, to the more enlightened part of the community, was not one of the least recommendations of that Constitution. The too frequent intermeddlings of the state legislatures, in relation to private contracts, were extensively felt and seriously lamented; and a constitution which promised a preventative, was, by those who felt and thought in that manner, eagerly embraced. Precedents of similar interferences by the Legislature of the United States cannot fail to alarm the same class of persons, and at the same time to diminish the respect of the state legislatures for the interdiction alluded to. The *example* of the national government in a matter of this kind may be expected to have a far more powerful influence than the *precepts* of its Constitution.

The present case is that of a particular class of men, highly meritorious indeed, but inconsiderable in point of numbers, and the whole of the property in question less than fifty thousand dollars, which, when distributed among those who are principally to be benefited by the regulation, does not exceed twenty five dollars per man. The relief of the individuals, who may have been subjects of imposition, in so limited a case, seems a very inadequate cause for a measure which breaks in upon those great principles that constitute the foundations of property.

The eligibility of the measure is the more doubtful, as the Courts of Justice are competent to the relief, which it is the object of the resolutions to give, as far as the fact of fraud, or imposition, or undue advantage can be substantiated. It is true that many of the individuals would probably not be in a condition to seek that relief, from their own resources; but the aid of government may in this respect be afforded in a way which will be consistent with the established order of things. The secretary, from the information communicated to him, believing it to be probable that undue advantages had been taken, had conceived a plan for the purpose of the following kind; that measures should be adopted for procuring the appointment of an agent, or attorney by the original claimants, or if deceased, by their legal representatives; that payment of the money should be deferred until this had been effected; that the amount of the sums due should then be placed in the hands of the proper officer for the purpose of payment; that a demand should be made upon him on behalf of the original claimants by their agent; and as a like demand would of course be made by the assignees, that the parties should be informed that a legal adjudication was necessary to ascertain the validity of their respective pretentions; and that in this state of things, the attorney general should be directed either to prosecute or defend for the original claimants, as should appear to him most likely to ensure justice. A step of this kind appeared to the secretary to be warranted and dictated as well by a due regard to the defenseless situation of the parties, who may have been prejudiced, as by considerations resulting from the propriety of discouraging similar practices.

It is with reluctance and pain that the secretary is induced to make this representation to the president. The respect which he entertains for the decisions of the two houses of Congress; the respect which is due to those movements of humanity, towards the supposed sufferers, and of indignation against those who are presumed to have taken an undue advantage; an unwillingness to present before the mind of the president, especially at the present juncture, considerations which may occasion perplexity or anxiety, concur in rendering the task peculiarly unwelcome: Yet the principles which appear to the secretary to have been invaded in this instance are, in his estimation, of such fundamental consequence to the stability, character, & success of the government, and at the same time so immediately interesting to the department entrusted to his care, that he feels himself irresistibly impelled by a sense of duty, as well to the chief magistrate as to the community, to made a full communication of his impressions & reflections.

He is sensible, that an inflexible adherence to the principles contended for must often have an air of rigor, and will sometimes be productive of particular inconveniencies. The general rules of property, & all those general rules which form the links of society, frequently involve in their ordinary operation particular hardships and injuries; yet the public order and the general happiness require a steady conformity to them. It is perhaps always better, that partial evils should be submitted to, than that principles should be violated. In the infancy of our present government, peculiar strictness and circumspection are called for by the too numerous instances of relaxations, which in other quarters & on other occasions, have discredited our public measures.

The secretary is not unaware of the delicacy of an opposition to the resolutions in question, by the president, should his view of the subject coincide with that of the secretary: Yet he begs leave on this point to remark, that such an opposition in a Case, in which a small part of the community only is directly concerned, would be less likely to have disagreeable consequences, than in one which should affect a very considerable portion of it: and the prevention of an ill precedent, if it be truly one, may prove a decisive obstacle to other cases of greater extent and magnitude and of a more critical tendency. If the objections are as solid as they appear to the secretary to be, he trusts they cannot fail, with the sanction of the president, to engage the approbation, not only of the generality of considerate men, but of the community at large. And if momentary dissatisfaction should happen to exist in particular parts of the union, it is to be hoped that it will be speedily removed by the measures which, under the direction of the president, may be pursued for obtaining the same end in an unexceptionable mode, for the success of which the secretary will not fail to exert his most zealous endeavors.

It is proper that the president should be informed that, if objections should be made by him, they will, in all probability, be effectual, as the resolutions passed in the Senate with no greater majority than twelve to ten.

The secretary feels an unreserved confidence in the justice and magnanimity of the president, that whatever may be his view of the subject, he will at least impute the present representation to an earnest and anxious conviction, in the mind of the secretary, of the truth and importance of the principles which he supports, & of the inauspicious tendency of the measure to which he objects, cooperating with a pure and ardent zeal for the public good, and for the honor & prosperity of the administration of the chief magistrate.

All which is humbly submitted

Alexr. Hamilton
Secretary of the Treasury

Address to the Public Creditors, September 1, 1790

It is probable that many of you are not sufficiently apprised of the advantages of your own situation, and that for want of judging rightly of it and of your future prospects, you may be tempted to part with your securities much below their true value and considerably below what it is probable they will sell for in eight or nine months from this time.

To guard you against an unnecessary sacrifice of your interests by a precipitate sale, I will now state to you, in a plain and concise way, what has been done for you in the course of the last session of Congress, and what you may reasonably expect.

Effectual provision has been made for *actually* paying you six percent yearly on two thirds of the principal of your debt, that is, 4 percent on the whole amount of your principal. And at the end of ten years you are to receive six percent yearly on the remaining third of your principal, that is, two percent more on the whole of your principal. And like *effectual* provision has been made for *actually* paying you three percent yearly on whatever arrears of interest may be due to you on your principal. For this interest you are not even to wait to the end of a year, but you are to receive it, in quarter-yearly payments, that is to say, one fourth part at the end of every three months; and it is to be paid to you not in new certificates, or paper money, but in actual gold and silver. To secure this to you, the duties which have been laid on goods imported and on the tonnage of ships or vessels (and which there is every reason from the experience we have had to believe will be sufficient) are absolutely *mortgaged* to you till the whole of your debt is discharged. You will not have to depend, as under most of the state governments, upon a provision from year to year, with an entire uncertainty whether it would be continued, and with many examples of fickleness and change; but you will have to depend on a permanent provision made once for all, for the sacredness of which, the faith, not of a single state, but of all the states is solemnly bound to you, and which cannot be undone or altered without the concurrence of three different branches of the government—the House of Representatives, the Senate, and the president of the United States. It cannot be supposed that if one of the two branches of Congress should hereafter be disposed to do so disgraceful and ruinous a thing as to repeal a law on which the credit of the government was at stake, that the other branch would be willing to concur in so pernicious a measure; or if both should be so unwise and dishonest, that the President of the United States would give his assent to it, or if he dissented, that two thirds of both houses of Congress would be inclined to persist in spite of his disapprobation. Whoever considers the nature of our government with discernment will see that though obstacles and delays will frequently stand in the way of the adoption of good measures, yet when once adopted they are likely to be stable and permanent: It will be far more difficult to *undo* than to *do*.

To destroy your confidence in future, there are too many publications which represent to you that Congress have by their late proceedings violated their past engagements, and that you can place no greater reliance upon those they now make than those they have heretofore made. Whether representations like these proceed from a sincere opinion in persons who have not accurately considered the matter, or from those who wish to depreciate the government, or from those who wish to buy securities cheap, or from all these descriptions of persons, I cannot say; but from whatever source they proceed they are certainly not candid nor just.

Congress it is true submit to your consideration some alterations in the nature of your claims upon the government for certain equivalents, which they hold out to you, and of which you are to judge. A principal object they have in doing this is to obtain a suspension of the payment of one third of the interest to which you are entitled for ten years, in order to avoid the necessity of burthening the community, or carrying taxation to objects which might be displeasing to them. And you cannot wonder that a government, so lately formed, and not without considerable opposition, should be cautious in this respect.

But whether you will accept the terms offered to you is certainly left to your own choice. There is not a syllable in the law that obliges you to do it. On the contrary, there is in it an express ratification of your former contracts; and to remove all possibility of future cavil about the true import or obligation, all questions of discrimination and the like, new titles are offered to you, of the like import in substance with your old ones. And your rights are thus established, and their meaning defined, so as to render their future operation under the sanction of the Constitution unequivocal. They are only not violated, but if possible they have received additional strength, and have become still more inviolable.

So far is there from being anything compulsory in the acts of the government in the case that those of you who do not choose to subscribe to the new terms are to receive during the time allotted for determining upon them exactly as much as those who do subscribe. And the faith of the government remains pledged to you to fulfill its engagements, which must be performed as fast as its resources can be brought into action for the purpose. Your only security before the late arrangement was the faith of government: There were no funds pledged to you which have been taken away: You have still the faith of government upon a renewed assurance as your pledge, and while you are deliberating on the new proposals you are to receive a payment on account.

You are therefore to decide according to your own judgment whether an acceptance of the new terms, under all their circumstances, are preferable or not to a dependence on the future resources of the country for more. This is a question of prudent calculation, which you are at liberty to determine as you please.

Whence it is evident that whatever other objections may be against the propriety of the provision which has been made for the public debt, the charge of a breach of contract is not well-founded.

The better to form a comparison between the terms proposed and those of your former contract, it may be well to recollect that the latter will be satisfied by a provision, *annually* made, for paying you six percent. Whatever the policy of the government may hereafter dictate, there is nothing in the existing contract that calls for a *permanent appropriation* of funds. Such a *permanent appropriation*, however, forms a part of the new loans, and will be of the essence of the new contract.

These remarks are intended to satisfy you that there is no cause from anything that has happened for a diminution, but on the contrary much reason for an increase of your confidence in the property you possess, as holders of the public debt.

I return to the subject of the value of your securities: Their present price, if compared with that at which they were current before the establishment of the new constitution, will be deemed to be *high*, and is as great as at this time could reasonably have been expected; but compared with their true value, and the solidity of the footing on which they stand, is still far too low. The rise which has already taken place is an earnest to you of their probable future rise: Such of you who do not incline to be permanent holders will at least do well to postpone a sale till after March, when the first payment of interest is to be made. The effect of this on the price of securities must undoubtedly be very favorable, and you may then calculate on a better market.

The holders of state securities have still stronger reasons for keeping those they have, the price of which, in most of the states, is out of all proportion lower than that of the present securities of the United States, and must in all probability undergo a considerable change for the better, as soon as funds are actually appropriated for them, which is not now the case, but which must of course be so at the ensuing session in December. The present debt of the United States, having been provided for out of the duties on imposts and tonnage only, seems to leave no doubt of the facility of devising the means of providing for the amount which has been assumed of the state debts.

Letter to John Jay, November 13, 1790

My Dear Sir

I enclose you copies of two resolutions[1] which have passed the house of representatives of Virginia. Others had been proposed and disagreed to. But the war was still going on. A spirited remonstrance to Congress is talked of.

This is the first symptom of a spirit which must either be killed or will kill the Constitution of the United States. I send the resolutions to you that it may be considered what ought to be done.

Ought not the collective weight of the different parts of the government to be employed in exploding the principles they contain? This question arises out a sudden & indigested thought.

I remain Dr Sir   Your Affectionate & Obedient   hum servant
A. Hamilton

Excerpt from the Report on a National Bank, December 13, 1790

In obedience to the order of the House of Representatives of the ninth day of August last, requiring the secretary of the treasury to prepare and report on this day such further provision as may, in his opinion, be necessary for establishing the public credit

The said secretary further respectfully reports

That from a conviction (as suggested in his report No. 1 herewith presented) that a national bank is an institution of primary importance to the prosperous administration of the finances, and would be of the greatest utility in the operations connected with the support of the public credit, his attention has been drawn to devising the plan of such an institution, upon a scale which will entitle it to the confidence and be likely to render it equal to the exigencies of the public.

Previously to entering upon the detail of this plan, he entreats the indulgence of the House towards some preliminary reflections naturally arising out of the subject, which he hopes will be deemed neither useless nor out of place. Public opinion being the ultimate arbiter of every measure of government, it can scarcely appear improper, in deference to that, to accompany the origination of any new proposition with explanations, which the superior information of those to whom it is immediately addressed would render superfluous.

It is a fact well understood that public banks have found admission and patronage among the principal and most enlightened commercial nations. They have successively obtained in Italy, Germany, Holland, England, and France, as well as in the United States. And it is a circumstance which cannot but have considerable weight in a candid estimate of their tendency that after an experience of centuries there exists not a question about their utility in the countries in which they have been so long established. Theorists and men of business unite in the acknowledgment of it.

Trade and industry, wherever they have been tried, have been indebted to them for important aid. And government has been repeatedly under the greatest obligations to them in dangerous and distressing emergencies. That of the United States, as well in some of the most critical conjunctures of the late war as since the peace, has received assistance from those established among us, with which it could not have dispensed.

With this two fold evidence before us, it might be expected that there would be a perfect union of opinions in their favor. Yet doubts have been entertained, jealousies and prejudices have circulated; and though the experiment is every day dissipating them within the spheres in which effects are best known, yet there are still persons by whom they have not been entirely renounced. To give a full and accurate view of the subject would be to make a treatise of a report; but there are certain aspects in which it may be cursorily exhibited, which may perhaps conduce to a just impression of its merits. These will involve a comparison of the advantages with the disadvantages, real or supposed, of such institutions.

The following are among the principal advantages of a bank.

First. The augmentation of the active or productive capital of a country. Gold and silver, when they are employed merely as the instruments of exchange and alienation, have been not improperly denominated dead stock; but when deposited in banks, to become the basis of a paper circulation, which takes their character and place as the signs or representatives of value, they then acquire life, or, in other words, an active and productive quality. This idea, which appears rather subtle and abstract in a general form, may be made obvious and palpable by entering into a few particulars. It is evident, for instance, that the money which a merchant keeps in his chest, waiting for a favorable opportunity to employ it, produces nothing 'till that opportunity arrives. But if instead of locking it up in this manner he either deposits it in a bank, or invests it in the stock of a bank, it yields a profit during the interval, in which he partakes or not according to the choice he may have made of being a depositor or a proprietor; and when any advantageous speculation offers, in order to be able to embrace it, he has only to withdraw his money if a depositor, or if a proprietor to obtain a loan from the bank, or to dispose of his stock; an alternative seldom or never attended with difficulty, when the affairs of the institution are in a prosperous train. His money thus deposited or invested is a fund upon which himself and others can borrow to a much larger amount. It is a well-established fact that banks in good credit can circulate a far greater sum than the actual quantum of their capital in gold & silver. The extent of the possible excess seems indeterminate, though it has been conjecturally stated at the proportions of two and three to one. This faculty is produced in various ways. First, a great proportion of the notes, which are issued and pass current as cash, are indefinitely suspended in circulation from the confidence which each holder has that he can at any moment turn them into gold and silver. Secondly, every loan which a bank makes is, in its first shape, a credit given to the borrower on its books, the amount of which it stands ready to pay, either in its own notes, or in gold or silver, at his option. But in a great number of cases no actual payment is made in either. The borrower frequently, by a check or order, transfers his credit to some other person to whom he has a payment to make; who, in his turn is as often content with a similar credit, because he is satisfied that he can, whenever he pleases, either convert it into cash or pass it to some other hand as an equivalent for it. And in this manner the credit keeps circulating, performing in every stage the office of money, till it is extinguished by a discount with some person who has a payment to make to the bank, to an equal or greater amount. Thus large sums are lent and paid, frequently through a variety of hands, without the intervention of a single piece of coin. Thirdly, there is always a large quantity of gold and silver in the repositories of the bank, besides its own stock, which is placed there with a view partly to its safekeeping and partly to the accommodation of an institution which is itself a source of general accommodation. These deposits are of immense consequence in the operations of a bank. Though liable to be redrawn at any moment, experience proves that the money so much oftener changes proprietors than place, and that what is drawn out is generally so speedily replaced as to authorize the counting upon the sums deposited as an *effective fund*; which, concurring with the stock of the bank, enables it to extend its loans, and to answer all the demands for coin, whether in consequence of those loans or arising from the occasional return of its notes.

These different circumstances explain the manner in which the ability of a bank to circulate a greater sum than its actual capital in coin is acquired. This, however, must be gradual; and must be preceded by a firm establishment of confidence; a confidence which may be bestowed on the most rational grounds; since the excess in question will always be bottomed on good security of one kind or another. This every well conducted bank carefully requires before it will consent to advance either its money or its credit; and where there is an auxiliary capital (as will be the case in the plan hereafter submitted) which, together with the capital in coin, define the boundary that shall not be exceeded by the engagements of the bank, the security may, consistently with all the maxims of a reasonable circumspection, be regarded as complete.

The same circumstances illustrate the truth of the position that it is one of the properties of banks to increase the active capital of a country. This, in other words, is the sum of them. The money of one individual, while he is waiting for an opportunity to employ it, by being either deposited in the bank for safekeeping or invested in its Stock, is in a condition to administer to the wants of others, without being put out of his own reach when occasion presents. This yields an extra profit, arising from what is paid for the use of his money by others, when he could not himself make use of it; and keeps the money itself in a state of incessant activity. In the almost infinite vicissitudes and competitions of mercantile enterprise, there never can be danger of an intermission of demand, or that the money will remain for a moment idle in the vaults of the bank. This additional employment given to money, and the faculty of a bank to lend and circulate a greater sum than the amount of its stock in coin, are to all the purposes of trade and industry an absolute increase of capital. Purchases and undertakings, in general, can be carried on by any given sum of bank paper or credit, as effectually as by an equal sum of gold and silver. And thus by contributing to enlarge the mass of industrious and commercial enterprise, banks become nurseries of national wealth: a consequence as satisfactorily verified by experience as it is clearly deducible in theory.

Secondly. Greater facility to the government in obtaining pecuniary aids, especially in sudden emergencies. This is another and an undisputed advantage of public banks, one which, as already remarked, has been realized in signal instances among ourselves. The reason is obvious: The capitals of a great number of individuals are, by this operation, collected to a point and placed under one direction. The mass, formed by this union, is in a certain sense magnified by the credit attached to it: And while this mass is always ready, and can at once be put in motion in aid of the government, the interest of the bank to afford that aid, independent of regard to the public safety and welfare, is a sure pledge for its disposition to go as far in its compliances as can in prudence be desired. There is in the nature of things, as will be more particularly noticed in another place, an intimate connection of interest between the government and the bank of a nation.

Thirdly. The facilitating of the payment of taxes. This advantage is produced in two ways. Those who are in a situation to have access to the bank can have the assistance of loans to answer with punctuality the public calls upon them. This accommodation has been sensibly felt in the payment of the duties heretofore laid by those who reside where establishments of this nature exist. This, however, though an extensive, is not an universal benefit. The other way in which the effect here contemplated is produced, and in which the benefit is general, is the increasing of the quantity of circulating medium and the quickening of circulation. The manner in which the first happens has already been traced. The last may require some illustration. When payments are to be made between different places, having an intercourse of business with each other, if there happen to be no private bills at market, and there are no bank notes which have a currency in both, the consequence is that coin must be remitted. This is attended with trouble, delay, expense, and risk. If on the contrary there are bank notes current in both places, the transmission of these by the post, or any other speedy or convenient conveyance, answers the purpose; and these again, in the alternations of demand, are frequently returned very soon after to the place from whence they were first sent: Whence the transportation and retransportation of the metals are obviated; and a more convenient and more expeditious medium of payment is substituted. Nor is this all. The metals, instead of being suspended from their usual functions during this process of vibration from place to place, continue in activity and administer still to the ordinary circulation, which of course is prevented from suffering either diminution or stagnation. These circumstances are additional causes of what, in a practical sense, or to the purposes of business, may be called greater plenty of money. And it is evident that whatever enhances the quantity of circulating money adds to the ease with which every industrious member of the community may acquire that portion of it of which he stands in need, and enables him the better to pay his taxes, as well as to supply his other wants. Even where the circulation of the bank paper is not general it must still have the same effect, though in a less degree. For whatever furnishes additional supplies to the channels of circulation in one quarter naturally contributes to keep the streams fuller elsewhere. This last view of the subject serves both to illustrate the position that banks tend to facilitate the payment of taxes, and to exemplify their utility to business of every kind in which money is an agent.

It would be to intrude too much on the patience of the house to prolong the details of the advantages of banks, especially as all those which might still be particularized are readily to be inferred as consequences from those which have been enumerated. Their disadvantages, real or supposed, are now to be reviewed. The most serious of the charges which have been brought against them are—

That they serve to increase usury:

That they tend to prevent other kinds of lending:

That they furnish temptations to overtrading:

That they afford aid to ignorant adventurers who disturb the natural and beneficial course of trade:

That they give to bankrupt and fraudulent traders a fictitious credit, which enables them to maintain false appearances and to extend their impositions: And lastly

That they have a tendency to banish gold and silver from the country.

There is great reason to believe that on a close and candid survey it will be discovered that these charges are either destitute of foundation or that, as far as the evils they suggest have been found to exist, they have proceeded from other, or partial, or temporary causes, are not inherent in the nature and permanent tendency of such institutions; or are more than counterbalanced by opposite advantages. This survey shall be had in the order in which the charges have been stated.

The first of them is that banks serve to increase usury.

It is a truth, which ought not to be denied, that the method of conducting business, which is essential to bank operations, has among us, in particular instances, given occasion to usurious transactions. The punctuality in payments which they necessarily exact has sometimes obliged those who have adventured beyond both their capital and their *credit* to procure money, at any price, and consequently to resort to usurers for aid.

But experience and practice gradually bring a cure to this evil. A general habit of punctuality among traders is the natural consequence of the necessity of observing it with the bank, a circumstance which itself more than compensates for any occasional ill which may have sprung from that necessity in the particular under consideration. As far therefore as traders depend on each other for pecuniary supplies, they can calculate their expectations with greater certainty; and are in proportionably less danger of disappointments which might compel them to have recourse to so pernicious an expedient as that of borrowing at usury; the mischiefs of which, after a few examples, naturally inspire great care, in all but men of desperate circumstances, to avoid the possibility of being subjected to them. One, and not the least of the evils incident to the use of that expedient, if the fact be known or even strongly suspected, is loss of credit with the bank itself.

The directors of a bank too, though in order to extend its business and its popularity in the infancy of an institution they may be tempted to go further in accommodations, than the strict rules of prudence will warrant, grow more circumspect of course as its affairs become better established, and as the evils of too great facility are experimentally demonstrated. They become more attentive to the situation and conduct of those with whom they deal; they observe more narrowly their operations and pursuits; they economize the credit, they give to those of suspicious solidity, they refuse it to those whose career is more manifestly hazardous. In a word, in the course of practice, from the very nature of things, the *interest* will make it the *policy* of a bank to succor the wary and industrious, to discredit the rash and unthrifty, to discountenance both usurious lenders and usurious borrowers.

There is a leading view in which the tendency of banks will be seen to be to abridge rather than to promote usury. This relates to their property of increasing the quantity and quickening the circulation of money. If it be evident that usury will prevail or diminish according to the proportion which the demand for borrowing bears to the quantity of money at market to be lent, whatever has the property just mentioned, whether it be in the shape of paper or of coin, by contributing to render the supply more equal to the demand must tend to counteract the progress of usury.

But bank-lending, it is pretended, is an impediment to other kinds of lending; which, by confining the resource of borrowing to a particular class, leaves the rest of the community more destitute and therefore more exposed to the extortions of usurers. As the profits of bank stock exceed the legal rate of interest, the possessors of money, it is argued, prefer investing it in that article to lending it at this rate; to which there are the additional motives of a more prompt command of the capital, and of more frequent and exact returns, without trouble or perplexity in the collection. This constitutes the second charge which has been enumerated.

The fact on which this charge rests is not to be admitted without several qualifications, particularly in reference to the state of things in this country. First. The great bulk of the stock of a bank will consist of the funds of men in trade among ourselves, and monied foreigners; the former of whom could not spare their capitals out of their reach to be invested in loans for long periods on mortgages or personal security; and the latter of whom would not be willing to be subjected to the casualties, delays, and embarrassments of such a disposition of their money in a distant country. Secondly. There will always be a considerable proportion of those who are properly the money lenders of a country who, from that spirit of caution which usually characterizes this description of men, will incline rather to vest their funds in mortgages on real estate than in the stock of a bank, which they are apt to consider as a more precarious security.

These considerations serve in a material degree to narrow the foundation of the objection as to the point of fact. But there is a more satisfactory answer to it. The effect supposed, as far as it has existence, is temporary. The reverse of it takes place in the general and permanent operation of the thing.

The capital of every public bank will of course be restricted within a certain defined limit. It is the province of legislative prudence so to adjust this limit that while it will not be too contracted for the demand which the course of business may create, and for the security which the public ought to have for the solidity of the paper which may be issued by the bank, it will still be within the compass of the pecuniary resources of the community; so that there may be an easy practicability of completing the subscriptions to it. When this is once done, the supposed effect of necessity ceases. There is then no longer room for the investment of any additional capital. Stock may indeed change hands by one person selling and another buying; but the money, which the buyer takes out of the common mass to purchase the stock, the seller receives and restores to it. Hence the future surpluses which may accumulate must take their natural course, and lending at interest must go on as if there were no such institution.

It must indeed flow in a more copious stream. The bank furnishes an extraordinary supply for borrowers within its immediate sphere. A larger supply consequently remains for borrowers elsewhere. In proportion as the circulation of the bank is extended there is an augmentation of the aggregate mass of money for answering the aggregate mass of demand. Hence a greater facility in obtaining it for every purpose.

It ought not to escape without a remark that as far as the citizens of other countries become adventurers in the bank there is a positive increase of the gold and silver of the country. It is true that from this a half yearly rent is drawn back, accruing from the dividends upon the stock. But as this rent arises from the employment of the capital by our own citizens, it is probable that it is more than replaced by the profits of that employment. It is also likely that a part of it is, in the course of trade, converted into the products of our country: And it may even prove an incentive, in some cases, to emigration to a country in which the character of citizen is as easy to be acquired as it is estimable and important. This view of the subject furnishes an answer to an objection which has been deduced from the circumstance here taken notice of, namely the income resulting to foreigners from the part of the stock, owned by them, which has been represented as tending to drain the country of its specie. In this objection, the original investment of the capital, and the constant use of it afterwards, seem both to have been overlooked.

That banks furnish temptations to overtrading is the third of the enumerated objections. This must mean that by affording additional aids to mercantile enterprise, they induce the merchant sometimes to adventure beyond the prudent or salutary point. But the very statement of the thing shows that the subject of the charge is an occasional ill incident to a general good. Credit of every kind (as a species of which only can bank lending have the effect supposed) must be in different degrees chargeable with the same inconvenience. It is even applicable to gold and silver when they abound in circulation. But would it be wise on this account to decry the precious metals, to root out credit, or to proscribe the means of that enterprise which is the main spring of trade and a principal source of national wealth because it now and then runs into excesses, of which overtrading is one?

If the abuses of a beneficial thing are to determine its condemnation, there is scarcely a source of public prosperity which will not speedily be closed. In every case the evil is to be compared with the good; and in the present case such a comparison will issue in this, that the new and increased energies derived to commercial enterprise from the aid of banks are a source of general profit and advantage which greatly outweigh the partial ills of the overtrading of a few individuals at particular times, or of numbers in particular conjunctures.

The fourth and fifth charges may be considered together. These relate to the aid which is sometimes afforded by banks to unskillful adventurers and fraudulent traders. These charges also have some degree of foundation, though far less than has been pretended, and they add to the instances of partial ills connected with more extensive and overbalancing benefits.

The practice of giving fictitious credit to improper persons is one of those evils which experience guided by interest speedily corrects. The bank itself is in so much jeopardy of being a sufferer by it that it has the strongest of all inducements to be on its guard. It may not only be injured immediately by the delinquencies of the persons to whom such credit is given, but eventually by the incapacities of others whom their impositions or failures may have ruined.

Nor is there much danger of a bank's being betrayed into this error from want of information. The directors themselves, being for the most part selected from the class of traders, are to be expected to possess individually an accurate knowledge of the characters and situations of those who come within that description. And they have, in addition to this, the course of dealing of the persons themselves with the bank to assist their judgment, which is in most cases a good index of the state in which those persons are. The artifices and shifts, which those in desperate or declining circumstances are obliged to employ to keep up the countenance which the rules of the bank require, and the train of their connections, are so many prognostics not difficult to be interpreted of the fate which awaits them. Hence it not unfrequently happens that banks are the first to discover the unsoundness of such characters, and, by withholding credit, to announce to the public that they are not entitled to it.

If banks in spite of every precaution are sometimes betrayed into giving a false credit to the persons described, they more frequently enable honest and industrious men of small or perhaps of no capital to undertake and prosecute business with advantage to themselves and to the community, and assist merchants of both capital and credit who meet with fortuitous and unforeseen shocks, which might without such helps prove fatal to them and to others, to make head against their misfortunes, and finally to retrieve their affairs: Circumstances which form no inconsiderable encomium on the utility of banks.

But the last and heaviest charge is still to be examined. This is that banks tend to banish the gold and silver of the country.

The force of this objection rests upon their being an engine of paper credit, which by furnishing a substitute for the metals is supposed to promote their exportation. It is an objection which if it has any foundation lies not against banks peculiarly, but against every species of paper credit.

The most common answer given to it is that the thing supposed is of little or no consequence, that it is immaterial what serves the purpose of money, whether paper or gold and silver, that the effect of both upon industry is the same, and that the intrinsic wealth of a nation is to be measured, not by the abundance of the precious metals contained in it, but by the quantity of the productions of its labor and industry.

This answer is not destitute of solidity, though not entirely satisfactory. It is certain that the vivification of industry, by a full circulation, with the aid of a proper and well regulated paper credit, may more than compensate for the loss of a part of the gold and silver of a nation, if the consequence of avoiding that loss should be a scanty or defective circulation.

But the positive and permanent increase or decrease of the precious metals in a country can hardly ever be a matter of indifference. As the commodity taken in lieu of every other, it is a species of the most effective wealth; and as the money of the world, it is of great concern to the state that it possess a sufficiency of it to face any demands which the protection of its external interests may create.

The objection seems to admit of another and a more conclusive answer which controverts the fact itself. A nation that has no mines of its own must derive the precious metals from others, generally speaking, in exchange for the products of its labor and industry. The quantity it will possess will therefore, in the ordinary course of things, be regulated by the favorable or unfavorable balance of its trade; that is, by the proportion between its abilities to supply foreigners and its wants of them; between the amount of its exportations and that of its importations. Hence the state of its agriculture and manufactures, the quantity and *quality* of its labor and industry, must, in the main, influence and determine the increase or decrease of its gold and silver.

If this be true, the inference seems to be that well constituted banks favor the increase of the precious metals. It has been shown that they augment in different ways the active capital of the country. This it is which generates employment, which animates and expands labor and industry. Every addition which is made to it by contributing to put in motion a greater quantity of both tends to create a greater quantity of the products of both: And, by furnishing more materials for exportation, conduces to a favorable balance of trade and consequently to the introduction and increase of gold and silver.

This conclusion appears to be drawn from solid premises. There are, however, objections to be made to it.

It may be said that as bank paper affords a substitute for specie it serves to counteract that rigorous necessity for the metals as a medium of circulation which, in the case of a wrong balance, might restrain in some degree their exportation; and it may be added that from the same cause, in the same case, it would retard those economical and parsimonious reforms in the manner of living which the scarcity of money is calculated to produce, and which might be necessary to rectify such wrong balance.

There is perhaps some truth in both these observations, but they appear to be of a nature rather to form exceptions to the generality of the conclusion than to overthrow it. The state of things in which the *absolute exigencies* of circulation can be supposed to resist with any effect the urgent demands for specie which a wrong balance of trade may occasion presents an *extreme case*. And a situation in which a too expensive manner of living of a community compared with its means can stand in need of a corrective from distress or necessity is one which perhaps rarely results but from extraordinary and adventitious causes: such, for example, as a national revolution which unsettles all the established habits of a people and inflames the appetite for extravagance by the illusions of an ideal wealth, engendered by the continual multiplication of a depreciating currency or some similar cause. There is good reason to believe that where the laws are wise and well executed, and the inviolability of property and contracts maintained, the economy of a people will in the general course of things correspond with its means.

The support of industry is probably in every case of more consequence towards correcting a wrong balance of trade than any practicable retrenchments in the expenses of families or individuals: And the stagnation of it would be likely to have more effect in prolonging than any such savings in shortening its continuance. That stagnation is a natural consequence of an inadequate medium, which, without the aid of bank circulation, would in the cases supposed be severely felt.

It also deserves notice that as the circulation is always in a compound ratio to the fund upon which it depends and to the demand for it, and as that fund is itself affected by the exportation of the metals, there is no danger of its being overstocked, as in the case of paper issued at the pleasure of the government; or of its preventing the consequences of any unfavorable balance from being sufficiently felt to produce the reforms alluded to, as far as circumstances may require and admit.

Nothing can be more fallible than the comparisons which have been made between different countries to illustrate the truth of the position under consideration. The comparative quantity of gold and silver in different countries depends upon an infinite variety of facts and combinations, all of which ought to be known, in order to judge whether the existence or nonexistence of paper currencies has any share in the relative proportions they contain. The *mass* and *value* of the productions of the labor and industry of each, compared with its wants; the nature of its establishments abroad; the kind of wars in which it is usually engaged; the relations it bears to the countries which are the original possessors of those metals; the privileges it enjoys in their trade; these and a number of other circumstances are all to be taken into the account and render the investigation too complex to justify any reliance on the vague and general surmises which have been hitherto hazarded on the point.

In the foregoing discussion the objection has been considered as applying to the permanent expulsion and diminution of the metals. Their temporary exportation for particular purposes has not been contemplated. This, it must be confessed, is facilitated by banks from the faculty they possess of supplying their place. But their utility is in nothing more conspicuous than in these very cases. They enable the government to pay its foreign debts and to answer any exigencies which the external concerns of the community may have produced. They enable the merchant to support his credit (on which the prosperity of trade depends) when special circumstances prevent remittances in other modes. They enable him also to prosecute enterprises which ultimately tend to an augmentation of the species of wealth in question. It is evident that gold and silver may often be employed in procuring commodities abroad which, in a circuitous commerce, replace the original fund with considerable addition. But it is not to be inferred from this facility given to temporary exportation that banks, which are so friendly to trade and industry, are in their general tendency inimical to the increase of the precious metals.

These several views of the subject appear sufficient to impress a full conviction of the utility of banks and to demonstrate that they are of great importance, not only in relation to the administration of the finances, but in the general system of the political economy.

The judgment of many concerning them has no doubt been perplexed by the misinterpretation of appearances which were to be ascribed to other causes. The general devastation of personal property occasioned by the late war naturally produced, on the one hand, a great demand for money, and on the other a great deficiency of it to answer the demand. Some injudicious laws, which grew out of the public distresses, by impairing confidence and causing a part of the inadequate sum in the country to be locked up, aggravated the evil: The dissipated habits, contracted by many individuals during the war, which after the peace plunged them into expenses beyond their incomes: The number of adventurers without capital and in many instances without information, who at that epoch rushed into trade, and were obliged to make any sacrifices to support a transient credit; the employment of considerable sums in speculations upon the public debt, which from its unsettled state was incapable of becoming itself a substitute: All these circumstances concurring necessarily led to usurious borrowing, produced most of the inconveniencies, and were the true causes of most of the appearances; which, where the banks were established, have been by some erroneously placed to their account: a mistake which they might easily have avoided by turning their eyes towards places where there were none and where, nevertheless, the same evils would have been perceived to exist, even in a greater degree than where those institutions had obtained.

These evils have either ceased or been greatly mitigated. Their more complete extinction may be looked for from that additional security to property which the Constitution of the United States happily gives (a circumstance of prodigious moment in the scale both of public and private prosperity), from the attraction of foreign capital under the auspices of that security to be employed upon objects & in enterprises for which the state of this country opens a wide and inviting field, from the consistency and stability which the public debt is fast acquiring, as well in the public opinion, at home and abroad, as in fact; from the augmentation of capital which that circumstance and the quarter yearly payment of interest will afford; and from the more copious circulation, which will be likely to be created by a well constituted national bank.

The establishment of banks in this country seems to be recommended by reasons of a peculiar nature. Previously to the revolution circulation was in a great measure carried on by paper emitted by the several local governments. In Pennsylvania alone the quantity of it was near a million and a half of dollars. This auxiliary may be said to be now at an end. And it is generally supposed that there has been for some time past a deficiency of circulating medium. How far that deficiency is to be considered as real or imaginary is not susceptible of demonstration, but there are circumstances and appearances which, in relation to the country at large, countenance the supposition of its reality.

The circumstances are, besides the fact just mentioned respecting paper emissions, the vast tracts of waste land and the little advanced state of manufactures. The progressive settlement of the former, while it promises ample retribution in the generation of future resources, diminishes or obstructs in the meantime the *active* wealth of the country. It not only draws off a part of the circulating money and places it in a more passive state, but it diverts into its own channels a portion of that species of labor and industry which would otherwise be employed in furnishing materials for foreign trade, and which by contributing to a favorable balance would assist the introduction of specie. In the early periods of new settlements, the settlers not only furnish no surplus for exportation but they consume a part of that which is produced by the labor of others. The same thing is a cause that manufactures do not advance or advance slowly. And notwithstanding some hypotheses to the contrary, there are many things to induce a suspicion that the precious metals will not abound in any country which has not mines or variety of manufactures. They have been sometimes acquired by the sword, but the modern system of war has expelled this resource, and it is one upon which it is to be hoped the United States will never be inclined to rely.

The appearances alluded to are greater prevalency of direct barter in the more interior districts of the country, which, however, has been for some time past gradually lessening; and greater difficulty, generally, in the advantageous alienation of improved real estate; which, also, has, of late, diminished, but is still seriously felt in different parts of the Union. The difficulty of getting money, which has been a general complaint, is not added to the number, because it is the complaint of all times, and one in which imagination must ever have too great scope to permit an appeal to it.

If the supposition of such a deficiency be in any degree founded, and some aid to circulation be desirable, it remains to inquire what ought to be the nature of that aid.

The emitting of paper money by the authority of government is wisely prohibited to the individual states by the national Constitution. And the spirit of that prohibition ought not to be disregarded by the government of the United States. Though paper emissions under a general authority might have some advantages not applicable, and be free from some disadvantages which are applicable, to the like emissions by the states separately, yet they are of a nature so liable to abuse, and it may even be affirmed so certain of being abused, that the wisdom of the government will be shown in never trusting itself with the use of so seducing and dangerous an expedient. In times of tranquility it might have no ill consequence, it might even perhaps be managed in a way to be productive of good; but in great and trying emergencies there is almost a moral certainty of its becoming mischievous. The stamping of paper is an operation so much easier than the laying of taxes that a government in the practice of paper emissions would rarely fail in any such emergency to indulge itself too far in the employment of that resource to avoid as much as possible one less auspicious to present popularity. If it should not even be carried so far as to be rendered an absolute bubble, it would at least be likely to be extended to a degree which would occasion an inflated and artificial state of things incompatible with the regular and prosperous course of the political economy.

Among other material differences between a paper currency issued by the mere authority of government and one issued by a bank payable in coin is this—That in the first case there is no standard to which an appeal can be made, as to the quantity which will only satisfy or which will surcharge the circulation; in the last, that standard results from the demand. If more should be issued than is necessary, it will return upon the bank. Its emissions, as elsewhere intimated, must always be in a compound ratio to the fund and to the demand: Whence it is evident that there is a limitation in the nature of the thing: While the discretion of the government is the only measure of the extent of the emissions by its own authority.

This consideration further illustrates the danger of emissions of that sort, and the preference which is due to bank paper.

The payment of the interest of the public debt, at thirteen different places, is a weighty reason, peculiar to our immediate situation, for desiring a bank circulation. Without a paper in general currency, equivalent to gold and silver, a considerable proportion of the specie of the country must always be suspended from circulation and left to accumulate, preparatorily to each day of payment; and as often as one approaches, there must in several cases be an actual transportation of the metals at both expense and risk from their natural and proper reservoirs to distant places. This necessity will be felt very injuriously to the trade of some of the states, and will embarrass not a little the operations of the treasury in those states. It will also obstruct those negotiations between different parts of the Union by the instrumentality of treasury bills which have already afforded valuable accommodations to trade in general.

Assuming it then as a consequence from what has been said that a national bank is a desirable institution, two inquiries emerge. Is there no such institution already in being which has a claim to that character, and which supersedes the propriety or necessity of another? If there be none, what are the principles upon which one ought to be established?

There are at present three banks in the United States. That of North America, established in the city of Philadelphia; that of New York, established in the city of New York; that of Massachusetts, established in the city of Boston. Of these three the first is the only one which has at any time had a direct relation to the government of the United States.

The Bank of North America originated in a resolution of Congress of the 26th of May 1781, founded upon a proposition of the superintendent of finance, which was afterwards carried into execution by an ordinance of the 31st of December following, entitled, "An Ordinance to incorporate the Subscribers to the Bank of North America."

The aid afforded to the United States by this institution during the remaining period of the war was of essential consequence, and its conduct towards them since the peace has not weakened its title to their patronage and favor. So far its pretensions to the character in question are respectable, but there are circumstances which militate against them, and considerations which indicate the propriety of an establishment on different principles.

The directors of this bank, on behalf of their constituents, have since *accepted* and *acted* under a new charter from the state of Pennsylvania, materially variant from their original one, and which so narrows the foundation of the institution as to render it an incompetent basis for the extensive purposes of a national bank.

The limit assigned by the ordinance of Congress to the stock of the bank is ten millions of dollars. The last charter of Pennsylvania confines it to two millions. Questions naturally arise whether there be not a direct repugnancy between two charters so differently circumstanced, and whether the acceptance of the one is not to be deemed a virtual surrender of the other. But perhaps it is neither advisable nor necessary to attempt a solution of them.

There is nothing in the Acts of Congress which imply an exclusive right in the institution to which they relate, except during the term of the war. There is therefore nothing, if the public good require it, which prevents the establishment of another. It may, however, be incidentally remarked that in the general opinion of the citizens of the United States, the Bank of North America has taken the station of a bank of Pennsylvania only. This is a strong argument for a new institution, or for a renovation of the old, to restore it to the situation in which it originally stood in the view of the United States.

But though the ordinance of Congress contains no grant of exclusive privileges, there may be room to allege that the government of the United States ought not, in point of candor and equity, to establish any rival or interfering institution in prejudice of the one already established, especially as this has, from services rendered, well founded claims to protection and regard.

The justice of such an observation ought within proper bounds to be admitted. A new establishment of the sort ought not to be made without cogent and sincere reasons of public good. And in the manner of doing it every facility should be given to a consolidation of the old with the new, upon terms not injurious to the parties concerned. But there is no ground to maintain that, in a case in which the government has made no condition restricting its authority, it ought voluntarily to restrict it through regard to the interests of a particular institution, when those of the state dictate a different course; especially too after such circumstances have intervened, as characterize the actual situation of the Bank of North America.

The inducements to a new disposition of the thing are now to be considered. The first of them which occurs is the at least ambiguous situation in which the

Bank of North America has placed itself by the acceptance of its last charter. If this has rendered it the mere bank of a particular state, liable to dissolution at the expiration of fourteen years, to which term the act of that state has restricted its duration, it would be neither fit nor expedient to accept it as an equivalent for a bank of the United States.

The restriction of its capital also, which according to the same supposition cannot be extended beyond two millions of dollars, is a conclusive reason for a different establishment. So small a capital promises neither the requisite aid to government nor the requisite security to the community. It may answer very well the purposes of local accommodation, but is an inadequate foundation for a circulation coextensive with the United States, embracing the whole of their revenues, and affecting every individual into whose hands the paper may come.

And inadequate as such a capital would be to the essential ends of a national bank, it is liable to being rendered still more so by that principle of the constitution of the Bank of North America, contained equally in its old and in its new charter, which leaves the increase of the *actual* capital at any time (now far short of the allowed extent) to the discretion of the directors or stockholders. It is naturally to be expected that the allurements of an advanced price of stock and of large dividends may disincline those who are interested to an extension of capital, from which they will be apt to fear a diminution of profits. And from this circumstance the interest and accommodation of the public (as well individually as collectively) are made more subordinate to the interest, real or imagined, of the stockholders than they ought to be. It is true that unless the latter be consulted there can be no bank (in the sense at least in which institutions of this kind, worthy of confidence, can be established in this country), but it does not follow that this is alone to be consulted, or that it even ought to be paramount. Public utility is more truly the object of public banks than private profit. And it is the business of government to constitute them on such principles that, while the latter will result in a sufficient degree to afford competent motives to engage in them, the former be not made subservient to it. To effect this, a principal object of attention ought to be to give free scope to the creation of an ample capital; and with this view fixing the bounds which are deemed safe and convenient, to leave no discretion either to stop short of them or to overpass them. The want of this precaution in the establishment of the Bank of North America is a further and an important reason for desiring one differently constituted.

There may be room, at first sight, for a supposition that as the profits of a bank will bear a proportion to the extent of its operations, and as, for this reason, the interest of the stockholders will not be disadvantageously affected by any necessary augmentations of capital, there is no cause to apprehend that they will be indisposed to such augmentations. But most men in matters of this nature prefer the certainties they enjoy to probabilities depending on untried experiments, especially when these promise rather that they will not be injured than that they will be benefited.

From the influence of this principle, and a desire of enhancing its profits, the directors of a bank will be more apt to overstrain its faculties in the attempt to face the additional demands which the course of business may create than to set on foot new subscriptions which may hazard a diminution of the profits and even a temporary reduction of the price of stock.

Banks are among the best expedients for lowering the rate of interest in a country; but to have this effect their capitals must be completely equal to all the demands of business, and such as will tend to remove the idea that the accommodations they afford are in any degree favors, an idea very apt to accompany the parsimonious dispensation of contracted funds. In this, as in every other case, the plenty of the commodity ought to beget a moderation of the price.

The want of a principle of rotation in the constitution of the Bank of North America is another argument for a variation of the establishment. Scarcely one of the reasons which militate against this principle in the constitution of a country is applicable to that of a bank, while there are strong reasons in favor of it in relation to the one which do not apply to the other. The knowledge to be derived from experience is the only circumstance common to both which pleads against rotation in the directing officers of a bank.

But the objects of the government of a nation and those of the government of a bank are so widely different as greatly to weaken the force of that consideration in reference to the latter. Almost every important case of legislation requires, towards a right decision, a general and an accurate acquaintance with the affairs of the state, and habits of thinking seldom acquired but from a familiarity with public concerns. The administration of a bank, on the contrary, is regulated by a few simple fixed maxims, the application of which is not difficult to any man of judgment, especially if instructed in the principles of trade. It is in general a constant succession of the same details.

But though this be the case, the idea of the advantages of experience is not to be slighted. Room ought to be left for the regular transmission of official information: And for this purpose the head of the direction ought to be excepted from the principle of rotation. With this exception, and with the aid of the information of the subordinate officers, there can be no danger of any ill effects from want of experience or knowledge; especially as the periodical exclusion ought not to reach the whole of the directors at one time.

The argument in favor of the principle of rotation is this, that by lessening the danger of combinations among the directors to make the institution subservient to party views, or to the accommodation, preferably, of any particular set of men, it will render the public confidence more firm, stable, and unqualified.

When it is considered that the directors of a bank are not elected by the great body of the community, in which a diversity of views will naturally prevail at different conjunctures, but by a small and select class of men, among whom it is far more easy to cultivate a steady adherence to the same persons and objects; and that those directors have it in their power so immediately to conciliate, by obliging the most influential of this class, it is easy to perceive that without the principle of rotation, changes in that body can rarely happen but as a concession which they may themselves think it expedient to make to public opinion.

The continual administration of an institution of this kind by the same persons will never fail, with or without cause, from their conduct to excite distrust and discontent. The necessary secrecy of their transactions gives unlimited scope to imagination to infer that something is or may be wrong. And this *inevitable* mystery is a solid reason for inserting in the constitution of a bank the necessity of a change of men. As neither the mass of the parties interested nor the public in general can be permitted to be witnesses of the interior management of the directors, it is reasonable that both should have that check upon their conduct, and that security against the prevalency of a partial or pernicious system, which will be produced by the certainty of periodical changes. Such too is the delicacy of the credit of a bank that everything which can fortify confidence and repel suspicion, without injuring its operations, ought carefully to be sought after in its formation.

A further consideration in favor of a change is the improper rule by which the right of voting for directors is regulated in the plan upon which the Bank of North America was originally constituted, namely a vote for each share, and the want of a rule in the last charter; unless the silence of it, on that point, may signify that every stockholder is to have an equal and a single vote, which would be a rule in a different extreme not less erroneous. It is of importance that a rule should be established on this head, as it is one of those things which ought not to be left to discretion; and it is consequently of equal importance that the rule should be a proper one.

A vote for each share renders a combination between a few principal stockholders to monopolize the power and benefits of the bank too easy. An equal vote to each stockholder, however great or small his interest in the institution, allows not that degree of weight to large stockholders which it is reasonable they should have, and which perhaps their security and that of the bank require. A prudent mean is to be preferred. A conviction of this has produced a byelaw of the corporation of the bank of North America, which evidently aims at such a mean. But a reflection arises here that a like majority with that which enacted this law may at any moment repeal it.

The last inducement which shall be mentioned is the want of precautions to guard against a foreign influence insinuating itself into the direction of the bank. It seems scarcely reconcilable with a due caution to permit that any but citizens should be eligible as directors of a national bank, or that nonresident foreigners should be able to influence the appointment of directors by the votes of their proxies. In the event, however, of an incorporation of the Bank of North America in the plan, it may be necessary to qualify this principle so as to leave the right of foreigners who now hold shares of its stock unimpaired, but without the power of transmitting the privilege in question to foreign alienees.

It is to be considered that such a bank is not a mere matter of private property, but a political machine of the greatest importance to the state.

There are other variations from the constitution of the Bank of North America, not of inconsiderable moment, which appear desirable, but which are not of magnitude enough to claim a preliminary discussion. These will be seen in the plan which will be submitted in the sequel.

If the objections which have been stated to the constitution of the Bank of North America are admitted to be well founded, they will nevertheless not derogate from the merit of the main design, or of the services which that bank has rendered, or of the benefits which it has produced. The creation of such an institution at the time it took place was a measure dictated by wisdom. Its utility has been amply evinced by its fruits. American Independence owes much to it. And it is very conceivable that reasons of the moment may have rendered those features in it inexpedient which a revision, with a permanent view, suggests as desirable.

The order of the subject leads next to an inquiry into the principles upon which a national bank ought to be organized.

The situation of the United States naturally inspires a wish that the form of the institution could admit of a plurality of branches. But various considerations discourage from pursuing this idea. The complexity of such a plan would be apt to inspire doubts which might deter from adventuring in it. And the practicability of a safe and orderly administration, though not to be abandoned as desperate, cannot be made so manifest in perspective as to promise the removal of those doubts or to justify the government in adopting the idea as an original experiment. The most that would seem advisable on this point is to insert a provision which may lead to it hereafter if experience shall more clearly demonstrate its utility, and satisfy those who may have the direction that it may be adopted with safety. It is certain that it would have some advantages both peculiar and important. Besides more general accommodation, it would lessen the danger of a run upon the bank.

The argument against it is that each branch must be under a distinct though subordinate direction, to which a considerable latitude of discretion must of necessity be entrusted. And as the property of the whole institution would be liable for the engagements of each part, that and its credit would be at stake, upon the prudence of the directors of every part. The mismanagement of either branch might hazard serious disorder in the whole.

Another wish dictated by the particular situation of the country is that the bank could be so constituted as to be made an immediate instrument of loans to the proprietors of land, but this wish also yields to the difficulty of accomplishing it. Land is alone an unfit fund for a bank circulation. If the notes issued upon it were not to be payable in coin, on demand or at a short date, this would amount to nothing more than a repetition of the paper emissions which are now exploded by the general voice. If the notes are to be payable in coin, the land must first be converted into it by sale or mortgage. The difficulty of effecting the latter is the very thing which begets the desire of finding another resource, and the former would not be practicable on a sudden emergency but with sacrifices which would make the cure worse than the disease. Neither is the idea of constituting the fund partly of coin and partly of land free from impediments. These two species of property do not for the most part unite in the same hands.

Will the monied man consent to enter into a partnership with the landholder by which *the latter* will share in the profits *which will be* made *by the money of the former?* The money, it is evident, will be the agent or efficient cause of the profits. The land can only be regarded as an additional security. It is not difficult to foresee that a union on such terms will not readily be formed. If the landholders are to procure the money by sale or mortgage of a part of their lands, this they can as well do when the stock consists wholly of money as if it were to be compounded of money and land.

To procure for the landholders the assistance of loans is the great desideratum. Supposing other difficulties surmounted and a fund created, composed partly of coin and partly of land, yet the benefit contemplated could only then be obtained by the banks advancing them its notes for the whole or part of the value of the lands they had subscribed to the stock. If this advance was small, the relief aimed at would not be given; if it was large, the quantity of notes issued would be a cause of *distrust*, and if received at all they would be likely to return speedily upon the bank for payment; which, after exhausting its coin, might be under a necessity of turning its lands into money at any price that could be obtained for them, to the irreparable prejudice of the proprietors.

Considerations of public advantage suggest a further wish, which is that the bank could be established upon principles that would cause the profits of it to redound to the immediate benefit of the state. This is contemplated by many who speak of a national bank, but the idea seems liable to insuperable objections. To attach full confidence to an institution of this nature, it appears to be an essential ingredient in its structure that it shall be under a *private* not a *public* direction, under the guidance of *individual interest* not of *public policy*; which would be supposed to be, and in certain emergencies, under a feeble or too sanguine administration would really be, liable to being too much influenced by *public necessity*. The suspicion of this would most probably be a canker that would continually corrode the vitals of the credit of the bank, and would be most likely to prove fatal in those situations in which the public good would require that they should be most sound and vigorous. It would indeed be little less than a miracle, should the credit of the bank be at the disposal of the government, if in a long series of time there was not experienced a calamitous abuse of it. It is true that it would be the real interest of the government not to abuse it; its genuine policy to husband and cherish it with the most guarded circumspection as an inestimable treasure. But what government ever uniformly consulted its true interest in opposition to the temptations of momentary exigencies? What nation was ever blessed with a constant succession of upright and wise administrators?

The keen, steady, and, as it were, magnetic sense of their own interest as proprietors in the directors of a bank, pointing invariably to its true pole, the prosperity of the institution, is the only security that can always be relied upon for a careful and prudent administration. It is therefore the only basis on which an enlightened, unqualified, and permanent confidence can be expected to be erected and maintained.

The precedents of the banks established in several cities of Europe, Amsterdam, Hamburg, and others, may seem to militate against this position. Without a precise knowledge of all the peculiarities of their respective constitutions, it is difficult to pronounce how far this may be the case. That of Amsterdam, however, which we best know, is rather under a municipal than a governmental direction. Particular magistrates of the city, not officers of the republic, have the management of it. It is also a bank of deposit, not of loan or circulation, consequently less liable to abuse, as well as less useful. Its general business consists in receiving money for safekeeping, which if not called for within a certain time becomes a part of its stock and irreclaimable: But a credit is given for it on the books of the bank, which, being transferable, answers all the purposes of money.

The directors being magistrates of the city, and the stockholders in general its most influential citizens, it is evident that the principle of private interest must be prevalent in the management of the bank. And it is equally evident that, from the nature of its operations, that principle is less essential to it than to an institution constituted with a view to the accommodation of the public and individuals by direct loans and a paper circulation.

As far as may concern the aid of the bank, within the proper limits a good government has nothing more to wish for than it will always possess, though the management be in the hands of private individuals. As the institution, if rightly constituted, must depend for its renovation from time to time on the pleasure of the government, it will not be likely to feel a disposition to render itself, by its conduct, unworthy of public patronage. The government too in the administration of its finances has it in its power to reciprocate benefits to the bank, of not less importance than those which the bank affords to the government, and which besides are never unattended with an immediate and adequate compensation. Independent of these more particular considerations, the natural weight and influence of a good government will always go far towards procuring a compliance with its desires; and as the directors will usually be composed of some of the most discreet, respectable, and well informed citizens, it can hardly ever be difficult to make them sensible of the force of the inducements which ought to stimulate their exertions.

It will not follow from what has been said that the state may not be the holder of a part of the stock of a bank and consequently a sharer in the profits of it. It will only follow that it ought not to desire any participation in the direction of it, and therefore ought not to own the whole or a principal part of the stock; for if the mass of the property should belong to the public, and if the direction of it should be in private hands, this would be to commit the interests of the state to persons not interested, or not enough interested, in their proper management.

There is one thing, however, which the government owes to itself and to the community, at least to all that part of it who are not stockholders, which is to reserve to itself a right of ascertaining, as often as may be necessary, the state of the bank, excluding, however, all pretension to control. This right forms an article in the primitive constitution of the Bank of North America. And its propriety stands upon the clearest reasons. If the paper of a bank is to be permitted to insinuate itself into all the revenues and receipts of a country, if it is even to be tolerated as the substitute for gold and silver in all the transactions of business, it becomes in either view a national concern of the first magnitude. As such the ordinary rules of prudence require that the government should possess the means of ascertaining, whenever it thinks fit, that so delicate a trust is executed with fidelity and care. A right of this nature is not only desirable, as it respects the government, but it ought to be equally so to all those concerned in the institution as an additional title to public and private confidence, and as a thing which can only be formidable to practices that imply mismanagement. The presumption must always be that the characters who would be entrusted with the exercise of this right on behalf of the government will not be deficient in the discretion which it may require; at least the admitting of this presumption cannot be deemed too great a return of confidence for that very large portion of it which the government is required to place in the bank.

Abandoning, therefore, ideas, which however agreeable or desirable are neither practicable nor safe, the following plan for the constitution of a national bank is respectfully submitted to the consideration of the House.

Opinion on the Constitutionality of a National Bank, February 23, 1791

The secretary of the treasury, having perused with attention the papers containing the opinions of the secretary of state and attorney general concerning the constitutionality of the bill for establishing a national bank, proceeds according to the order of the president to submit the reasons which have induced him to entertain a different opinion.

It will naturally have been anticipated that in performing this task he would feel uncommon solicitude. Personal considerations alone arising from the reflection that the measure originated with him would be sufficient to produce it: The sense which he has manifested of the great importance of such an institution to the successful administration of the department under his particular care, and an expectation of serious ill consequences to result from a failure of the measure, do not permit him to be without anxiety on public accounts. But the chief solicitude arises from a firm persuasion that principles of construction like those espoused by the secretary of state and the attorney general would be fatal to the just & indispensable authority of the United States.

In entering upon the argument it ought to be premised that the objections of the secretary of state and attorney general are founded on a general denial of the authority of the United States to erect corporations. The latter indeed expressly admits that if there be anything in the bill which is not warranted by the Constitution, it is the clause of incorporation.

Now it appears to the secretary of the treasury that this *general principle* is *inherent* in the very *definition* of *Government* and *essential* to every step of the progress to be made by that of the United States, namely—that every power vested in a government is in its nature *sovereign* and includes by *force* of the *term* a right to employ all the *means* requisite and fairly *applicable* to the attainment of the *ends* of such power; and which are not precluded by restrictions & exceptions specified in the Constitution; or not immoral, or not contrary to the essential ends of political society.

This principle in its application to government in general would be admitted as an axiom. And it will be incumbent upon those who may incline to deny it to *prove* a distinction, and to show that a rule which in the general system of things is essential to the preservation of the social order is inapplicable to the United States.

The circumstances that the powers of sovereignty are in this country divided between the national and state governments does not afford the distinction required. It does not follow from this that each of the *portions* of powers delegated to the one or to the other is not sovereign *with regard to its proper objects*. It will only *follow* from it that each has sovereign power as to *certain things* and not as to *other things*. To deny that the government of the United States has sovereign power as to its declared purposes & trusts, because its power does not extend to all cases, would be equally to deny that the state governments have sovereign power in any case, because their power does not extend to every case. The tenth section of the first article of the Constitution exhibits a long list of very important things which they may not do. And thus the United States would furnish the singular spectacle of a *political society* without *sovereignty*, or of a people *governed* without *government*.

If it would be necessary to bring proof to a proposition so clear as that which affirms that the powers of the federal government, *as to its objects*, are sovereign, there is a clause of its Constitution which would be decisive. It is that which declares that the Constitution and the laws of the United States made in pursuance of it, and all treaties made or which shall be made under their authority, shall be the supreme law of the land. The power which can create the *Supreme law* of the land, in any case, is doubtless sovereign *as to such case*.

This general & indisputable principle puts at once an end to the *abstract* question—Whether the United States have power to *erect a corporation?* that is to say, to give a *legal* or *artificial capacity* to one or more persons, distinct from the natural. For it is unquestionably incident to *sovereign power* to erect corporations, and consequently to *that* of the United States, in *relation to the objects* entrusted to the management of the government. The difference is this—where the authority of the government is general, it can create corporations in *all cases*; where it is confined to certain branches of legislation, it can create corporations only in those cases.

Here then, as far as concerns the reasonings of the secretary of state & the attorney general, the affirmative of the constitutionality of the bill might be permitted to rest. It will occur to the president that the principle here advanced has been untouched by either of them.

For a more complete elucidation of the point nevertheless, the arguments which they have used against the power of the government to erect corporations, however foreign they are to the great & fundamental rule which has been stated, shall be particularly examined. And after showing that they do not tend to impair its force, it shall also be shown, that the power of incorporation incident to the government in certain cases does fairly extend to the particular case which is the object of the bill.

The first of these arguments is that the foundation of the Constitution is laid on this ground "that all powers not delegated to the United States by the Constitution nor prohibited to it by the States are reserved to the States or to the people," whence it is meant to be inferred that Congress can in no case exercise any power not included in those enumerated in the Constitution. And it is affirmed that the power of erecting a corporation is not included in any of the enumerated powers.

The main proposition here laid down in its true signification is not to be questioned. It is nothing more than a consequence of this republican maxim that all government is a delegation of power. But how much is delegated in each case is a question of fact to be made out by fair reasoning & construction upon the particular provisions of the Constitution—taking as guides the general principles & general ends of government.

It is not denied that there are *implied* as well as *express* powers, and that the former are as effectually delegated as the latter. And for the sake of accuracy it shall be mentioned that there is another class of powers, which may be properly denominated *resulting* powers. It will not be doubted that if the United States should make a conquest of any of the territories of its neighbors, they would possess sovereign jurisdiction over the conquered territory. This would rather be a result from the whole mass of the powers of the government & from the nature of political society than a consequence of either of the powers specially enumerated.

But be this as it may, it furnishes a striking illustration of the general doctrine contended for. It shows an extensive case in which a power of erecting corporations is either implied in, or would result from, some or all of the powers vested in the national government. The jurisdiction acquired over such conquered territory would certainly be competent to every species of legislation.

To return—It is conceded that implied powers are to be considered as delegated equally with express ones.

Then it follows that as a power of erecting a corporation may as well be *implied* as any other thing, it may as well be employed as an *instrument* or *mean* of carrying into execution any of the specified powers as any other instrument or mean whatever. The only question must be, in this as in every other case, whether the mean to be employed, or in this instance the corporation to be erected, has a natural relation to any of the acknowledged objects or lawful ends of the government. Thus a corporation may not be erected by Congress for superintending the police of the city of Philadelphia, because they are not authorized to *regulate* the *police* of that city; but one may be erected in relation to the collection of the taxes, or to the trade with foreign countries, or to the trade between the states, or with the Indian tribes, because it is the province of the federal government to regulate those objects & because it is incident to a general *sovereign* or *legislative power* to *regulate* a thing to employ all the means which relate to its regulation to the *best & greatest advantage*.

A strange fallacy seems to have crept into the manner of thinking & reasoning upon the subject. Imagination appears to have been unusually busy concerning it. An incorporation seems to have been regarded as some great, independent, substantive thing—as a political end of peculiar magnitude & moment; whereas it is truly to be considered as a *quality*, *capacity*, or *mean* to an end. Thus a mercantile company is formed with a certain capital for the purpose of carrying on a particular branch of business. Here the business to be prosecuted is the *end*; the association in order to form the requisite capital is the primary mean. Suppose that an incorporation were added to this; it would only be to add a new *quality* to that association, to give it an artificial capacity by which it would be enabled to prosecute the business with more safety & convenience.

That the importance of the power of incorporation has been exaggerated, leading to erroneous conclusions, will further appear from tracing it to its origin. The Roman law is the source of it, according to which a *voluntary* association of individuals at *any time* or *for any purpose* was capable of producing it. In England, whence our notions of it are immediately borrowed, it forms a part of the executive authority, & the exercise of it has been often *delegated* by that authority. Whence therefore the ground of the supposition that it lies beyond the reach of all those very important portions of sovereign power, legislative as well as executive, which belong to the government of the United States?

To this mode of reasoning respecting the right of employing all the means requisite to the execution of the specified powers of the government, it is objected that none but *necessary* & proper means are to be employed, & the secretary of state maintains that no means are to be considered as *necessary* but those without which the grant of the power would be *nugatory*. Nay so far does he go in his restrictive interpretation of the word as even to make the case of *necessity* which shall warrant the constitutional exercise of the power to depend on *casual* & *temporary* circumstances, an idea which alone refutes the construction. The *expediency* of exercising a particular power at a particular time must indeed depend on *circumstances*, but the constitutional right of exercising it must be uniform & invariable—the same to day, as tomorrow.

All the arguments therefore against the constitutionality of the bill derived from the accidental existence of certain state banks—institutions which *happen* to exist today, & for aught that concerns the government of the United States may disappear tomorrow— must not only be rejected as fallacious, but must be viewed as demonstrative that there is a *radical* source of error in the reasoning.

It is essential to the being of the national government that so erroneous a conception of the meaning of the word *necessary* should be exploded.

It is certain that neither the grammatical nor popular sense of the term requires that construction. According to both, *necessary* often means no more than *needful, requisite, incidental, useful,* or *conducive to*. It is a common mode of expression to say that it is *necessary* for a government or a person to do this or that thing, when nothing more is intended or understood than that the interests of the government or person require, or will be promoted, by the doing of this or that thing. The imagination can be at no loss for exemplifications of the use of the word in this sense.

And it is the true one in which it is to be understood as used in the Constitution. The whole turn of the clause containing it indicates that it was the intent of the Convention by that clause to give a liberal latitude to the exercise of the specified powers. The expressions have peculiar comprehensiveness. They are—"to make *all laws*, necessary & proper for *carrying into execution* the foregoing powers & all *other powers* vested by the constitution in the *government* of the United States, or in any *department* or *officer* thereof." To understand the word as the secretary of state does would be to depart from its obvious & popular sense and to give it a *restrictive* operation, an idea never before entertained. It would be to give it the same force as if the word *absolutely* or *indispensibly* had been prefixed to it.

Such a construction would beget endless uncertainty & embarrassment. The cases must be palpable & extreme in which it could be pronounced with certainty that a measure was absolutely necessary, or one without which the exercise of a given power would be nugatory. There are few measures of any government which would stand so severe a test. To insist upon it would be to make the criterion of the exercise of any implied power a *case of extreme necessity*, which is rather a rule to justify the overleaping of the bounds of constitutional authority than to govern the ordinary exercise of it.

It may be truly said of every government, as well as of that of the United States, that it has only a right to pass such laws as are necessary & proper to accomplish the objects entrusted to it. For no government has a right to do *merely what it pleases*. Hence by a process of reasoning similar to that of the secretary of state it might be proved that neither of the state governments has a right to incorporate a bank. It might be shown that all the public business of the state could be performed without a bank, and inferring thence that it was unnecessary it might be argued that it could not be done, because it is against the rule which has been just mentioned. A like mode of reasoning would prove that there was no power to incorporate the inhabitants of a town, with a view to a more perfect police: For it is certain that an incorporation may be dispensed with, though it is better to have one. It is to be remembered that there is no *express* power in any state constitution to erect corporations.

The *degree* in which a measure is necessary can never be a test of the *legal* right to adopt it. That must ever be a matter of opinion, and can only be a test of expediency. The *relation* between the *measure* and the *end*, between the *nature* of *the mean* employed towards the execution of a power and the object of that power, must be the criterion of constitutionality, not the more or less of *necessity* or *utility*.

The practice of the government is against the rule of construction advocated by the secretary of state. Of this the act concerning lighthouses, beacons, buoys, & public piers is a decisive example. This doubtless must be referred to the power of regulating trade, and is fairly relative to it. But it cannot be affirmed that the exercise of that power in this instance was strictly necessary, or that the power itself would be *nugatory* without that of regulating establishments of this nature.

This restrictive interpretation of the word *necessary* is also contrary to this sound maxim of construction, namely, that the powers contained in a constitution of government, especially those which concern the general administration of the affairs of a country, its finances, trade, defense, &c, ought to be construed liberally, in advancement of the public good. This rule does not depend on the particular form of a government or on the particular demarcation of the boundaries of its powers, but on the nature and objects of government itself. The means by which national exigencies are to be provided for, national inconveniencies obviated, national prosperity promoted, are of such infinite variety, extent, and complexity, that there must, of necessity, be great latitude of discretion in the selection & application of those means. Hence, consequently, the necessity & propriety of exercising the authorities entrusted to a government on principles of liberal construction.

The attorney general admits the *rule* but takes a distinction between a state and the federal constitution. The latter, he thinks, ought to be construed with greater strictness, because there is more danger of error in defining partial than general powers.

But the reason of the *rule* forbids such a distinction. This reason is—the variety & extent of public exigencies, a far greater proportion of which and of a far more critical kind, are objects of national than of state administration. The greater danger of error, as far as it is supposable, may be a prudential reason for caution in practice, but it cannot be a rule of restrictive interpretation.

In regard to the clause of the Constitution immediately under consideration, it is admitted by the attorney general that no *restrictive* effect can be ascribed to it. He defines the word necessary thus. "To be necessary is to be *incidental*, and may be denominated the natural means of executing a power."

But while, on the one hand, the construction of the secretary of state is deemed inadmissible, it will not be contended on the other, that the clause in question gives any *new* or *independent* power. But it gives an explicit sanction to the doctrine of *implied* powers and is equivalent to an admission of the proposition that the government, *as to its specified powers* and *objects*, has plenary & sovereign authority, in some cases paramount to that of the states, in others coordinate with it. For such is the plain import of the declaration that it may pass *all laws* necessary & proper to carry into execution those powers.

It is no valid objection to the doctrine to say that it is calculated to extend the powers of the general government throughout the entire sphere of state legislation. The same thing has been said and may be said with regard to every exercise of power by *implication* or *construction*. The moment the literal meaning is departed from there is a chance of error and abuse. And yet an adherence to the letter of its powers would at once arrest the motions of the government. It is not only agreed on all hands that the exercise of constructive powers is indispensable, but every act which has been passed is more or less an exemplification of it. One has been already mentioned, that relating to lighthouses &c. That which declares the power of the president to remove officers at pleasure acknowledges the same truth in another and a signal instance.

The truth is that difficulties on this point are inherent in the nature of the federal Constitution. They result inevitably from a division of the legislative power. The consequence of this division is that there will be cases clearly within the power of the national government, others clearly without its power, and a third class which will leave room for controversy & difference of opinion, & concerning which a reasonable latitude of judgment must be allowed.

But the doctrine which is contended for is not chargeable with the consequence imputed to it. It does not affirm that the national government is sovereign in all respects, but that it is sovereign to a certain extent: that is, to the extent of the objects of its specified powers.

It leaves therefore a criterion of what is constitutional and of what is not so. This criterion is the *end* to which the measure relates as a *mean*. If the end be clearly comprehended within any of the specified powers, & if the measure have an obvious relation to that end, and is not forbidden by any particular provision of the Constitution—it may safely be deemed to come within the compass of the national authority. There is also this further criterion which may materially assist the decision. Does the proposed measure abridge a preexisting right of any state or of any individual? If it does not, there is a strong presumption in favor of its constitutionality, & slighter relations to any declared object of the Constitution may be permitted to turn the scale.

The general objections which are to be inferred from the reasonings of the secretary of state and of the attorney general to the doctrine which has been advanced have been stated and it is hoped satisfactorily answered. Those of a more particular nature shall now be examined.

The secretary of state introduces his opinion with an observation that the proposed incorporation undertakes to create certain capacities, properties, or attributes which are *against* the laws of *alienage*, *descents*, *escheat* and *forfeiture*, *distribution* and *monopoly,* and to confer a power to make laws paramount to those of the states. And nothing says he, in another place, but a *necessity invincible by other means* can justify such a *prostration* of *laws* which constitute the pillars of our whole system of jurisprudence and are the foundation laws of the state governments.

If these are truly the foundation laws of the several states, then have most of them subverted their own foundations. For there is scarcely one of them which has not, since the establishment of its particular constitution, made material alterations in some of those branches of its jurisprudence, especially the law of descents. But it is not conceived how anything can be called the fundamental law of a state government which is not established in its constitution unalterable by the ordinary legislature. And with regard to the question of necessity it has been shown that this can only constitute a question of expediency, not of right.

To erect a corporation is to substitute a *legal* or *artificial* to a *natural* person, and where a number are concerned, to give them *individuality*. To that legal or artificial person once created, the common law of every state of itself *annexes* all those incidents and attributes which are represented as a prostration of the main pillars of their jurisprudence. It is certainly not accurate to say that the erection of a corporation is *against* those different *heads* of the state laws, because it is rather to create a kind of person or entity to which *they* are inapplicable, and to which the general rule of those laws assigns a different regimen. The laws of alienage cannot apply to an artificial person because it can have no country. Those of descent cannot apply to it because it can have no heirs. Those of escheat are foreign from it for the same reason. Those of forfeiture because it cannot commit a crime. Those of distribution because, though it may be dissolved, it cannot die. As truly might it be said that the exercise of the power of prescribing the rule by which foreigners shall be naturalized is *against* the law of alienage, while it is in fact only to put them in a situation to cease to be the subject of that law. To do a thing which is *against* a law is to do something which it forbids or which is a violation of it.

But if it were even to be admitted that the erection of a corporation is a direct alteration of the state laws in the enumerated particulars, it would do nothing towards proving that the measure was unconstitutional. If the government of the United States can do no act which amounts to an alteration of a state law, all its powers are nugatory. For almost every new law is an alteration, in some way or other of an old *law*, either *common* or *statute*.

There are laws concerning bankruptcy in some states—some states have laws regulating the values of foreign coins. Congress are empowered to establish uniform laws concerning bankruptcy throughout the United States and to regulate the values of foreign coins. The exercise of either of these powers by Congress necessarily involves an alteration of the laws of those states.

Again: Every person by the common law of each state may export his property to foreign countries at pleasure. But Congress, in pursuance of the power of regulating trade, may prohibit the exportation of commodities: in doing which, they would alter the common law of each state in abridgement of individual rights.

It can therefore never be good reasoning to say—this or that act is unconstitutional because it alters this or that law of a state. It must be shown that the act which makes the alteration is unconstitutional on other accounts, not *because* it makes the alteration.

There are two points in the suggestions of the secretary of state which have been noted that are peculiarly incorrect. One is that the proposed incorporation is against the laws of monopoly, because it stipulates an exclusive right of banking under the national authority. The other that it gives power to the institution to make laws paramount to those of the states.

But with regard to the first point, the bill neither prohibits any state from erecting as many banks as they please, nor any number of individuals from associating to carry on the business, & consequently is free from the charge of establishing a monopoly: for monopoly implies a *legal impediment* to the carrying on of the trade by others than those to whom it is granted.

And with regard to the second point there is still less foundation. The byelaws of such an institution as a bank can operate only upon its own members, can only concern the disposition of its own property, and must essentially resemble the rules of a private mercantile partnership. They are expressly not to be contrary to law, and law must here mean the law of a state as well as of the United States. There never can be a doubt that a law of the corporation, if contrary to a law of a state, must be overruled as void, unless the law of the state is contrary to that of the United States, and then the question will not be between the law of the state and that of the corporation but between the law of the state and that of the United States.

Another argument made use of by the secretary of state is the rejection of a proposition by the convention to empower Congress to make corporations, either generally or for some special purpose.

What was the precise nature or extent of this proposition, or what the reasons for refusing it, is not ascertained by any authentic document, or even by accurate recollection. As far as any such document exists it specifies only canals. If this was the amount of it, it would at most only prove that it was thought inexpedient to give a power to incorporate for the purpose of opening canals, for which purpose a special power would have been necessary, except with regard to the western territory, there being nothing in any part of the Constitution respecting the regulation of canals. It must be confessed, however, that very different accounts are given of the import of the proposition and of the motives for rejecting it. Some affirm that it was confined to the opening of canals and obstructions in rivers, others that it embraced banks, and others that it extended to the power of incorporating generally. Some again allege that it was disagreed to because it was thought improper to vest in Congress a power of erecting corporations—others because it was thought unnecessary to *specify* the power, and inexpedient to furnish an additional topic of objection to the Constitution. In this state of the matter no inference whatever can be drawn from it.

But whatever may have been the nature of the proposition or the reasons for rejecting it concludes nothing in respect to the real merits of the question. The secretary of state will not deny that whatever may have been the intention of the framers of a constitution or of a law, that intention is to be sought for in the instrument itself, according to the usual & established rules of construction. Nothing is more common than for laws to *express* and *effect* more or less than was intended. If then a power to erect a corporation, in any case, be deducible by fair inference from the whole or any part of the numerous provisions of the Constitution of the United States, arguments drawn from extrinsic circumstances regarding the intention of the Convention must be rejected.

Most of the arguments of the secretary of state which have not been considered in the foregoing remarks are of a nature rather to apply to the expediency than to the constitutionality of the bill. They will, however, be noticed in the discussions which will be necessary in reference to the particular heads of the powers of the government which are involved in the question.

Those of the attorney general will now properly come under review.

His first observation is that the power of incorporation is not *expressly* given to Congress. This shall be conceded, but in *this sense* only, that it is not declared in *express terms* that Congress may erect a *corporation*. But this cannot mean that there are not certain *express* powers, which *necessarily* include it.

For instance, Congress have express power "to exercise exclusive legislation in all cases whatsoever over such *district* (not exceeding ten miles square) as may by cession of particular states & the acceptance of Congress become the seat of the government of the United States; and to exercise *like authority* over all places purchased by consent of the legislature of the state in which the same shall be for the erection of forts, arsenals, dock yards, & other needful buildings."

Here then is express power to exercise *exclusive legislation in all cases whatsoever over certain places*, that is to do in respect to those places all that any government whatever may do: For language does not afford a more complete designation of sovereign power than in those comprehensive terms. It is in other words a power to pass all laws whatsoever, & consequently to pass laws for erecting corporations, as well as for any other purpose which is the proper object of law in a free government. Surely it can never be believed that Congress with *exclusive power of legislation in all cases whatsoever* cannot erect a corporation within the district which shall become the seat of government, for the better regulation of its police. And yet there is an unqualified denial of the power to erect corporations in every case on the part both of the secretary of state and of the attorney general. The former indeed speaks of that power in these emphatical terms, that it is *a right remaining exclusively with the states*.

As far then as there is an express power to do any *particular act of legislation*, there is an express one to erect corporations in the cases above described. But accurately speaking, no *particular power* is more than *implied* in a *general one*. Thus the power to lay a duty on a *gallon of rum* is only a particular *implied* in the general power to lay and collect taxes, duties, imposts, and excises. This serves to explain in what sense it may be said that Congress have not an express power to make corporations.

This may not be an improper place to take notice of an argument which was used in debate in the House of Representatives. It was there urged that if the Constitution intended to confer so important a power as that of erecting corporations, it would have been expressly mentioned. But the case which has been noticed is clearly one in which such a power exists, and yet without any specification or express grant of it further than as every *particular implied* in a general power can be said to be so granted.

But the argument itself is founded upon an exaggerated and erroneous conception of the nature of the power. It has been shown that it is not of so transcendent a kind as the reasoning supposes, and that viewed in a just light it is a mean which ought to have been left to *implication*, rather than an *end* which ought to have been *expressly* granted.

Having observed that the power of erecting corporations is not expressly granted to Congress, the attorney general proceeds thus:

"If it can be exercised by them, it must be

1. because the nature of the federal government implies it,
2. because it is involved in some of the specified powers of legislation, or
3. because it is necessary & proper to carry into execution some of the specified powers."

To be implied in the *nature of the federal government*, says he, would beget a doctrine so indefinite as to grasp every power.

This proposition, it ought to be remarked, is not precisely or even substantially that which has been relied upon. The proposition relied upon is that the *specified powers* of Congress are in their nature sovereign—that it is incident to sovereign power to erect corporations, & that therefore Congress have a right, within the *sphere & in relation to the objects of their power, to erect corporations.*

It shall, however, be supposed that the attorney general would consider the two propositions in the same light, & that the objection made to the one would be made to the other.

To this objection an answer has been already given. It is this: that the doctrine is stated with this express *qualification*, that the right to erect corporations does *only* extend to *cases & objects* within the *sphere* of the *specified powers* of the government. A general legislative authority implies a power to erect corporations *in all cases*—a particular legislative power implies authority to erect corporations in relation to cases arising under that power only. Hence the affirming that as an *incident* to sovereign power Congress may erect a corporation in relation to the *collection* of their taxes is no more than to affirm that they may do whatever else they please than the saying that they have a power to regulate trade would be to affirm that they have a power to regulate religion, or than the maintaining that they have sovereign power as to taxation would be to maintain that they have sovereign power as to everything else.

The attorney general undertakes in the next place to show that the power of erecting corporations is not involved in any of the specified powers of legislation confided to the national government.

In order to this he has attempted an enumeration of the particulars which he supposes to be comprehended under the several heads of the *powers* to lay & collect taxes &c—to borrow money on the credit of the United States—to regulate commerce with foreign nations, between the states, and with the Indian Tribes—to dispose of and make all needful rules & regulations respecting the territory or other property belonging to the United States; the design of which enumeration is to show *what is* included under those different heads of power, & *negatively* that the power of erecting corporations is not included.

The truth of this inference or conclusion must depend on the accuracy of the enumeration. If it can be shown that the enumeration is *defective*, the inference is destroyed. To do this will be attended with no difficulty.

The heads of the power to lay & collect taxes he states to be

1. To ascertain the subject of taxation &c.
2. to declare the quantum of taxation &c.
3. to prescribe the *mode* of *collection.*
4. to ordain the manner of accounting for the taxes &c.

The defectiveness of this enumeration consists in the generality of the third division "*to prescribe the mode* of collection," which is in itself an immense chapter. It will be shown hereafter that, among a vast variety of particulars, it comprises the very power in question, namely to *erect corporations.*

The heads of the power to borrow money are stated to be

1. to stipulate the sum to be lent.
2. an interest or no interest to be paid.
3. the time & manner of repaying, unless the loan be placed on an irredeemable fund.

This enumeration is liable to a variety of objections. It omits, in the first place, the *pledging* or *mortgaging* of a fund for the security of the money lent, an usual and in most cases an essential ingredient.

The idea of a stipulation of *an interest or no interest* is too confined. It should rather have been said to stipulate *the consideration* of the loan. Individuals often borrow upon considerations other than the payment of interest. So may government, and so they often find it necessary to do. Every one recollects the lottery tickets & other douceurs often given in Great Britain as collateral inducements to the lending of money to the government.

There are also frequently collateral conditions which the enumeration does not contemplate. Every contract which has been made for monies borrowed in Holland includes stipulations that the sum due shall be *free from taxes*, and from sequestration in time of war, and mortgages all the land & property of the United States for the reimbursement.

It is also known that a lottery is a common expedient for borrowing money which certainly does not fall under either of the enumerated heads.

The heads of the power to regulate commerce with foreign nations are stated to be

1. to prohibit them or their commodities from our ports.
2. to impose duties on *them* where none existed before, or to increase existing duties on them.
3. to subject *them* to any species of custom house regulation.
4. to grant *them* any exemptions or privileges which policy may suggest.

This enumeration is far more exceptionable than either of the former. It omits *everything* that relates to the *citizens, vessels,* or *commodities* of the United States. The following palpable omissions occur at once.

1. Of the power to prohibit the exportation of commodities which not only exists at all times, but which in time of war it would be necessary to exercise, particularly with relation to naval and warlike stores.
2. Of the power to prescribe rules concerning the *characteristics & privileges* of an American bottom—how she shall be navigated, as whether by citizens or foreigners, or by a proportion of each.
3. Of the power of regulating the manner of contracting with seamen, the police of ships on their voyages &c of which the act for the government & regulation of seamen in the merchants service is a specimen.

That the three preceding articles are omissions will not be doubted. There is a long list of items in addition which admit of little, if any, question, of which a few samples shall be given.

1. The granting of bounties to certain kinds of vessels & certain species of merchandise. Of this nature is the allowance on dried & pickled fish & salted provisions.
2. The prescribing of rules concerning the *inspection* of commodities to be exported. Though the states individually are competent to this regulation, yet there is no reason, in point of authority at least, why a general system might not be adopted by the United States.

3. The regulation of policies of insurance; of salvage upon goods found at sea, and the disposition of such goods.
4. The regulation of pilots.
5. The regulation of bills of exchange drawn by a merchant of *one state* upon a merchant of *another state*. This last rather belongs to the regulation of trade between the states, but is equally omitted in the specification under that head.

The last enumeration relates to the power "to dispose of & make *all needful rules and regulations* respecting the territory *or other property* belonging to the United States."
The heads of this power are said to be

1. to exert an ownership over the territory of the United States, which may be properly called the property of the United States, as in the western territory, and to *institute a government therein:* or
2. to exert an ownership over the other property of the United States.

This idea of exerting an ownership over the Territory or other property of the United States is particularly indefinite and vague. It does not at all satisfy the conception of what must have been intended by a power to make all needful *rules* and *regulations*; nor would there have been any use for a special clause which authorized nothing more. For the right of exerting an ownership is implied in the very definition of property.

It is admitted that in regard to the western territory something more is intended—even the institution of a government; that is, the creation of a body politic, or corporation of the highest nature; one, which in its maturity, will be able itself to create other corporations. Why then does not the same clause authorize the erection of a corporation in respect to the regulation or disposal of any other of the property of the United States? This idea will be enlarged upon in another place.

Hence it appears, that the enumerations which have been attempted by the attorney general are so imperfect as to authorize no conclusion whatever. They therefore have no tendency to disprove that each and every of the powers to which they relate includes that of erecting corporations, which they certainly do, as the subsequent illustrations will more & more evince.

It is presumed to have been satisfactorily shown in the course of the preceding observations

1. That the power of the government, *as to* the objects entrusted to its management, is in its nature sovereign.
2. That the right of erecting corporations is one, inherent in & inseparable from the idea of sovereign power.
3. That the position that the government of the United States can exercise no power but such as is delegated to it by its Constitution does not militate against this principle.

4. That the word *necessary* in the general clause can have no *restrictive* operation derogating from the force of this principle, indeed, that the degree in which a measure is or is not necessary cannot be a *test* of *constitutional* right, but of expediency only.
5. That the power to erect corporations is not to be considered as an *independent & substantive* power but as an *incidental & auxiliary* one, and was therefore more properly left to implication than expressly granted.
6. That the principle in question does not extend the power of the government beyond the prescribed limits, because it only affirms a power to *incorporate* for *purposes within the sphere of the specified powers.*

And lastly that the right to exercise such a power, in certain cases, is unequivocally granted in the most *positive & comprehensive* terms.

To all which it only remains to be added that such a power has actually been exercised in two very eminent instances: namely in the erection of two governments, one northwest of the river Ohio, and the other south west—*the last, independent of any antecedent compact.*

And there results a full & complete demonstration that the secretary of state & attorney general are mistaken when they deny generally the power of the national government to erect corporations.

It shall now be endeavored to be shown that there is a power to erect one of the kind proposed by the bill. This will be done by tracing a natural & obvious relation between the institution of a bank and the objects of several of the enumerated powers of the government, and by showing that, *politically* speaking, it is necessary to the effectual execution of one or more of those powers. In the course of this investigation, various instances will be stated, by way of illustration, of a right to erect corporations under those powers.

Some preliminary observations maybe proper.

The proposed bank is to consist of an association of persons for the purpose of creating a joint capital to be employed, chiefly and essentially, in loans. So far the object is not only lawful, but it is the mere exercise of a right which the law allows to every individual. The bank of New York, which is not incorporated, is an example of such an association. The bill proposes in addition that the government shall become a joint proprietor in this undertaking, and that it shall permit the bills of the company payable on demand to be receivable in its revenues & stipulates that it shall not grant privileges similar to those which are to be allowed to this company to any others. All this is incontrovertibly within the compass of the discretion of the government. The only question is whether it has a right to incorporate this company in order to enable it the more effectually to accomplish *ends*, which are in themselves lawful.

To establish such a right it remains to show the relation of such an institution to one or more of the specified powers of the government.

Accordingly it is affirmed that it has a relation more or less direct to the power of collecting taxes, to that of borrowing money, to that of regulating trade between the states, and to those of raising, supporting, & maintaining fleets & armies. To the two former the relation may be said to be *immediate*.

And, in the last place, it will be argued that it is *clearly* within the provision which authorizes the making of all *needful* rules & *regulations* concerning the *property* of the United States, as the same has been practiced upon by the government.

A bank relates to the collection of taxes in two ways: *indirectly*, by increasing the quantity of circulating medium & quickening circulation, which facilitates the means of paying—*directly*, by creating a *convenient species* of *medium* in which they are to be paid.

To designate or appoint the money or *thing* in which taxes are to be paid is not only a proper but a necessary *exercise* of the power of collecting them. Accordingly Congress, in the law concerning the collection of the duties on imports & tonnage, have provided that they shall be payable in gold & silver. But while it was an indispensable part of the work to say in what they should be paid, the choice of the specific thing was mere matter of discretion. The payment might have been required in the commodities themselves. Taxes in kind, however ill judged, are not without precedents, even in the United States. Or it might have been in the paper money of the several states, or in the bills of the bank of North America, New York, and Massachusetts, all or either of them; or it might have been in bills issued under the authority of the United States.

No part of this can, it is presumed, be disputed. The appointment, then, of the *money* or *thing* in which the taxes are to be paid is an incident to the power of collection. And among the expedients which may be adopted is that of bills issued under the authority of the United States.

Now the manner of issuing these bills is again matter of discretion. The government might, doubtless, proceed in the following manner. It might provide that they should be issued under the direction of certain officers, payable on demand; and in order to support their credit & give them a ready circulation, it might, besides giving them a currency in its taxes, set apart out of any monies in its treasury a given sum and appropriate it under the direction of those officers as a fund for answering the bills as presented for payment.

The constitutionality of all this would not admit of a question. And yet it would amount to the institution of a bank, with a view to the more convenient collection of taxes. For the simplest and most precise idea of a bank is a deposit of coin or other property as a fund for *circulating* a *credit* upon it, which is to answer the purpose of money. That such an arrangement would be equivalent to the establishment of a bank would become obvious if the place where the fund to be set apart was kept should be made a receptacle of the monies of all other persons who should incline to deposit them there for safekeeping; and would become still more so if the officers charged with the direction of the fund were authorized to make discounts at the usual rate of interest, upon good security. To deny the power of the government to add these ingredients to the plan would be to refine away all government.

This process serves to exemplify the natural & direct relation which may subsist between the institution of a bank and the collection of taxes. It is true that the species of bank which has been designated does not include the idea of incorporation. But the argument intended to be founded upon it is this: that the institution comprehended in the idea of a bank being one immediately relative to the collection of taxes, *in regard to the appointment* of *the money or thing* in which they are to be paid, the sovereign power of providing for the collection of taxes necessarily includes the right of granting a corporate capacity to such an institution, as a requisite to its greater security, utility, and more convenient management.

A further process will still more clearly illustrate the point. Suppose, when the species of bank which has been described was about to be instituted, it were to be urged that in order to secure to it a due degree of confidence the fund ought not only to be set apart & appropriated generally, but ought to be specifically vested in the officers who were to have the direction of it, and in their *successors* in office, to the end that it might acquire the character of *private property* incapable of being resumed without a violation of the sanctions by which the rights of property are protected & occasioning more serious & general alarm, the apprehension of which might operate as a check upon the government— such a proposition might be opposed by arguments against the expediency of it or the solidity of the reason assigned for it, but it is not conceivable what could be urged against its constitutionality.

And yet such a disposition of the thing would amount to the erection of a corporation. For the true definition of a corporation seems to be this. It is a *legal* person, or a person created by act of law, consisting of one or more natural persons authorized to hold property or a franchise in succession in a legal as contradistinguished from a natural capacity.

Let the illustration proceed a step further. Suppose a bank of the nature which has been described with or without incorporation had been instituted, & that experience had evinced, as it probably would, that being wholly under public direction it possessed not the confidence requisite to the credit of its bills— Suppose also that, by some of those adverse conjunctures which occasionally attend nations, there had been a very great drain of the specie of the country, so as not only to cause general distress for want of an adequate medium of circulation, but to produce, in consequence of that circumstance, considerable defalcations in the public revenues—suppose also, that there was no bank instituted in any state—in such a posture of things, would it not be most manifest that the incorporation of a bank, like that proposed by the bill, would be a measure immediately relative to the *effectual collection* of the taxes and completely within the province of the sovereign power of providing by all laws necessary & proper for that collection?

If it be said that such a state of things would render that necessary & therefore constitutional which is not so now—the answer to this, and a solid one it doubtless is, must still be that which has been already stated—Circumstances may affect the expediency of the measure, but they can neither add to nor diminish its constitutionality.

A bank has a direct relation to the power of borrowing money because it is an usual and in sudden emergencies an essential instrument in the obtaining of loans to government.

A nation is threatened with a war. Large sums are wanted, on a sudden, to make the requisite preparations. Taxes are laid for the purpose, but it requires time to obtain the benefit of them. Anticipation is indispensable. If there be a bank the supply can at once be had; if there be none loans from individuals must be sought. The progress of these is often too slow for the exigency: in some situations they are not practicable at all. Frequently when they are, it is of great consequence to be able to anticipate the product of them by advances from a bank.

The essentiality of such an institution as an instrument of loans is exemplified at this very moment. An Indian expedition is to be prosecuted. The only fund out of which the money can arise consistently with the public engagements is a tax which will only begin to be collected in July next. The preparations, however, are instantly to be made. The money must therefore be borrowed. And of whom could it be borrowed, if there were no public banks?

It happens that there are institutions of this kind, but if there were none it would be indispensable to create one.

Let it then be supposed that the necessity existed (as but for a casualty would be the case), that proposals were made for obtaining a loan, that a number of individuals came forward and said, we are willing to accommodate the government with this money; with what we have in hand and the credit we can raise upon it we doubt not of being able to furnish the sum required: but in order to this it is indispensable that we should be incorporated as a bank. This is essential towards putting it in our power to do what is desired and we are obliged on that account to make it the *consideration* or condition of the loan.

Can it be believed that a compliance with this proposition would be unconstitutional? Does not this alone evince the contrary? It is a necessary part of a power to borrow to be able to stipulate the consideration or conditions of a loan. It is evident, as has been remarked elsewhere, that this is not confined to the mere stipulation of a sum of money by way of interest—why may it not be deemed to extend, where a government is the contracting party, to the stipulation of a *franchise?* If it may, & it is not perceived why it may not, then the grant of a corporate capacity may be stipulated as a consideration of the loan. There seems to be nothing unfit or foreign from the nature of the thing in giving individuality or a corporate capacity to a number of persons who are willing to lend a sum of money to the government, the better to enable them to do it, and make them an ordinary instrument of loans in future emergencies of the state.

But the more general view of the subject is still more satisfactory. The legislative power of borrowing money, & of making all laws necessary & proper for carrying into execution that power, seems obviously competent to the appointment of the *organ* through which the abilities and wills of individuals may be most efficaciously exerted for the accommodation of the government by loans.

The attorney general opposes to this reasoning the following observation. "To borrow money presupposes the accumulation of a fund to be lent, and is secondary to the creation of an ability to lend." This is plausible in theory, but it is not true in fact. In a great number of cases a previous accumulation of a fund equal to the whole sum required does not exist. And nothing more can be actually presupposed than that there exist resources which, put into activity to the greatest advantage by the nature of the operation with the government, will be equal to the effect desired to be produced. All the provisions and operations of government must be presumed to contemplate things as they *really* are.

The institution of a bank has also a natural relation to the regulation of trade between the states, in so far as it is conducive to the creation of a convenient medium of *exchange* between them and to the keeping up a full circulation by preventing the frequent displacement of the metals in reciprocal remittances. Money is the very hinge on which commerce turns. And this does not mean merely gold & silver; many other things have served the purpose with different degrees of utility. Paper has been extensively employed.

It cannot therefore be admitted with the attorney general that the regulation of trade between the states, as it concerns the medium of circulation & exchange, ought to be considered as confined to coin. It is even supposable in argument that the whole, or the greatest part of the coin of the country, might be carried out of it.

The secretary of state objects to the relation here insisted upon by the following mode of reasoning—"To erect a bank, says he, & to regulate commerce, are very different acts. He who erects a bank creates a subject of commerce; so does he who makes a bushel of wheat or digs a dollar out of the mines. Yet neither of these persons regulates commerce thereby." To make a thing which may be bought & sold is not to *prescribe* regulations for *buying & selling*: thus making the regulation of commerce to consist in prescribing rules for *buying & selling*.

This indeed is a species of regulation of trade; but is one which falls more aptly within the province of the local jurisdictions than within that of the general government, whose care must be presumed to have been intended to be directed to those general political arrangements concerning trade on which its aggregate interests depend, rather than to the details of buying and selling.

Accordingly, such only are the regulations to be found in the laws of the United States, whose objects are to give encouragement to the enterprise of our own merchants and to advance our navigation and manufactures.

And it is in reference to these general relations of commerce that an establishment which furnishes facilities to circulation and a convenient medium of exchange & alienation is to be regarded as a regulation of trade.

The secretary of state further argues that if this was a regulation of commerce, it would be void *as extending as much to the internal commerce of every state as to its external*. But what regulation of commerce does not extend to the internal commerce of every state? What are all the duties upon imported articles amounting to prohibitions but so many bounties upon domestic manufactures affecting the interests of different classes of citizens in different ways? What are all the provisions in the coasting act which relate to the trade between district and district of the same State? In short, what regulation of trade between the states but must affect the internal trade of each state? What can operate upon the whole but must extend to every part!

The relation of a bank to the execution of the powers that concern the common defense has been anticipated. It has been noted that at this very moment the aid of such an institution is essential to the measures to be pursued for the protection of our frontier.

It now remains to show that the incorporation of a bank is within the operation of the provision which authorizes Congress to make all needful rules & regulations concerning the property of the United States. But it is previously necessary to advert to a distinction which has been taken by the attorney general.

He admits that the word *property* may signify personal property however acquired. And yet asserts that it cannot signify money arising from the sources of revenue pointed out in the Constitution, because, says he, "the disposal & regulation of money is the final cause for raising it by taxes."

But it would be more accurate to say that the *object* to which money is intended to be applied is the *final cause* for raising it, than that the disposal and regulation of it is *such*. The support of government, the support of troops for the common defense, the payment of the public debt, are the true *final causes* for raising money. The disposition & regulation of it when raised are the steps by which it is applied to the *ends* for which it was raised, not the ends themselves. Hence therefore the money to be raised by taxes as well as any other personal property must be supposed to come within the meaning, as they certainly do within the letter, of the authority to make all needful rules & regulations concerning the property of the United States.

A case will make this plainer: suppose the public debt discharged and the funds now pledged for it liberated. In some instances it would be found expedient to repeal the taxes; in others the repeal might injure our own industry, our agriculture, and manufactures. In these cases they would of course be retained. Here then would be monies arising from the authorized sources of revenue which would not fall within the rule by which the attorney general endeavors to except them from other personal property & from the operation of the clause in question.

The monies being in the coffers of the government, what is to hinder such a disposition to be made of them as is contemplated in the bill or what an incorporation of the parties concerned under the clause which has been cited?

It is admitted that with regard to the western territory they give a power to erect a corporation—that is, to institute a government. And by what rule of construction can it be maintained that the same words in a constitution of government will not have the same effect when applied to one species of property as to another, as far as the subject is capable of it?—or that a legislative power to make all needful rules & regulations or to pass all laws necessary & proper concerning the public property which is admitted to authorize an incorporation in one case will not authorize it in another?—will justify the institution of a government over the western territory, & will not justify the incorporation of a bank for the more useful management of the money of the nation? If it will do the last as well as the first, then under this provision alone the bill is constitutional, because it contemplates that the United States shall be joint proprietors of the stock of the bank.

There is an observation of the secretary of state to this effect, which may require notice in this place. Congress, says he, are not to lay taxes *ad libitum for any purpose they please*, but only to pay the debts or provide for the *welfare* of the Union. Certainly no inference can be drawn from this against the power of applying their money for the institution of a bank. It is true that they cannot without breach of trust lay taxes for any other purpose than the general welfare, but so neither can any other government. The welfare of the community is the only legitimate end for which money can be raised on the community. Congress can be considered as under only one restriction which does not apply to other governments—They cannot rightfully apply the money they raise to any purpose *merely* or purely local. But with this exception they have as large a discretion in relation to the *application* of money as any legislature whatever. The constitutional *test* of a right application must always be whether it be for a purpose of *general* or *local* nature. If the former, there can be no want of constitutional power. The quality of the object, as how far it will really promote or not the welfare of the union, must be matter of conscientious discretion. And the arguments for or against a measure in this light must be arguments concerning expediency or inexpediency, not constitutional right. Whatever relates to the general order of the finances, to the general interests of trade &c, being general objects are constitutional ones for *the application* of *money*.

A bank then whose bills are to circulate in all the revenues of the country is *evidently* a general object, and for that very reason a constitutional one as far as regards the appropriation of money to it. Whether it will really be a beneficial one or not is worthy of careful examination, but is no more a constitutional point in the particular referred to than the question whether the western lands shall be sold for twenty or thirty cents per acre.

A hope is entertained that it has by this time been made to appear to the satisfaction of the president that a bank has a natural relation to the power of collecting taxes; to that of borrowing money; to that of regulating trade; to that of providing for the common defense: and that as the bill under consideration contemplates the government in the light of a joint proprietor of the stock of the bank, it brings the case within the provision of the clause of the Constitution which immediately respects the property of the United States.

Under a conviction that such a relation subsists, the secretary of the treasury with all deference conceives that it will result as a necessary consequence from the position, that all the specified powers of the government are sovereign as to the proper objects, that the incorporation of a bank is a constitutional measure, and that the objections taken to the bill in this respect are ill founded.

But from an earnest desire to give the utmost possible satisfaction to the mind of the president on so delicate and important a subject, the secretary of the treasury will ask his indulgence while he gives some additional illustrations of cases in which a power of erecting corporations may be exercised, under some of those heads of the specified powers of the government which are alleged to include the right of incorporating a bank.

1. It does not appear susceptible of a doubt that if Congress had thought proper to provide in the collection law that the bonds to be given for the duties should be given to the collector of each district in the name of the collector of the district A. or B. as the case might require, to enure to him & his successors in office, in trust for the United States, that it would have been consistent with the Constitution to make such an arrangement. And yet this, it is conceived, would amount to an incorporation.

2. It is not an unusual expedient of taxation to farm particular branches of revenue, that is to mortgage or sell the product of them for certain definite sums, leaving the collection to the parties to whom they are mortgaged or sold. There are even examples of this in the United States. Suppose that there was any particular branch of revenue which it was manifestly expedient to place on this footing, & there were a number of persons willing to engage with the government, upon condition that they should be incorporated & the funds vested in them, as well for their greater safety as for the more convenient recovery & management of the taxes. Is it supposable that there could be any constitutional obstacle to the measure? It is presumed that there could be none. It is certainly a mode of collection which it would be in the discretion of the government to adopt, though the circumstances must be very extraordinary that would induce the secretary to think it expedient.

3. Suppose a new & unexplored branch of trade should present itself with some foreign country. Suppose it was manifest that to undertake it with advantage required an union of the capitals of a number of individuals, & that those individuals would not be disposed to embark without an incorporation, as well to obviate that consequence of a private partnership, which makes every individual liable in his whole estate for the debts of the company to their utmost extent, as for the more convenient management of the business— what reason can there be to doubt that the national government would have a constitutional right to institute and incorporate such a company? None.

They possess a general authority to regulate trade with foreign countries. This is a mean which has been practiced to that end by all the principal commercial nations, who have trading companies to this day which have subsisted for centuries. Why may not the United States *constitutionally* employ the means *usual* in other countries for attaining the ends entrusted to them?

A power to make all needful rules & regulations concerning territory has been construed to mean a power to erect a government. A power to *regulate* trade is a power to make all needful rules & regulations concerning trade. Why may it not then include that of erecting a trading company as well as in the other case to erect a government?

It is remarkable, that the state conventions who have proposed amendments in relation to this point have most, if not all, of them expressed themselves nearly thus—"Congress shall not grant monopolies, nor *erect any company* with exclusive advantages of commerce," thus at the same time expressing their sense that the power to erect trading companies or corporations was inherent in Congress, & objecting to it no further than as to the grant of *exclusive* privileges.

The secretary entertains all the doubts which prevail concerning the utility of such companies, but he cannot fashion to his own mind a reason to induce a doubt that there is a constitutional authority in the United States to establish them. If such a reason were demanded, none could be given unless it were this— that Congress cannot erect a corporation, which would be no better than to say they cannot do it because they cannot do it: first presuming an inability without reason, & then assigning that *inability* as the cause of itself.

Illustrations of this kind might be multiplied without end. They shall, however, be pursued no further.

There is a sort of evidence on this point, arising from an aggregate view of the Constitution, which is of no inconsiderable weight. The very general power of laying & collecting taxes & appropriating their proceeds—that of borrowing money indefinitely—that of coining money & regulating foreign coins—that of making all needful rules and regulations respecting the property of the United States—these powers combined, as well as the reason & nature of the thing, speak strongly this language: That it is the manifest design and scope of the Constitution to vest in Congress all the powers requisite to the effectual administration of the finances of the United States. As far as concerns this object there appears to be no parsimony of power.

To suppose then that the government is precluded from the employment of so usual as well as so important an instrument for the administration of its finances as that of a bank is to suppose what does not coincide with the general tenor & complexion of the Constitution, and what is not agreeable to impressions that any mere spectator would entertain concerning it. Little less than a prohibitory clause can destroy the strong presumptions which result from the general aspect of the government. Nothing but demonstration should exclude the idea that the power exists.

In all questions of this nature the practice of mankind ought to have great weight against the theories of individuals.

The fact, for instance, that all the principal commercial nations have made use of trading corporations or companies for the purposes of *external commerce* is a satisfactory proof that the establishment of them is an incident to the regulation of that commerce.

This other fact, that banks are an usual engine in the administration of national finances, & an ordinary & the most effectual instrument of loans &

one which in this country has been found essential, pleads strongly against the supposition that a government clothed with most of the most important prerogatives of sovereignty in relation to the revenues, its debts, its credit, its defense, its trade, its intercourse with foreign nations—is forbidden to make use of that instrument as an appendage to its own authority.

It has been stated as an auxiliary test of constitutional authority to try whether it abridges any preexisting right of any state or any individual. The proposed incorporation will stand the most severe examination on this point. Each state may still erect as many banks as it pleases; every individual may still carry on the banking business to any extent he pleases.

Another criterion may be this, whether the institution or thing has a more direct relation as to its uses to the objects of the reserved powers of the state governments than to those of the powers delegated by the United States. This rule indeed is less precise than the former, but it may still serve as some guide. Surely a bank has more reference to the objects entrusted to the national government than to those, left to the care of the state governments. The common defense is decisive in this comparison.

It is presumed that nothing of consequence in the observations of the secretary of state and attorney general has been left unnoticed.

There are indeed a variety of observations of the secretary of state designed to show that the utilities ascribed to a bank in relation to the collection of taxes and to trade could be obtained without it, to analyze which would prolong the discussion beyond all bounds. It shall be forborne for two reasons—first because the report concerning the bank may speak for itself in this respect; and secondly because all those observations are grounded on the erroneous idea that the *quantum* of necessity or utility is the test of a constitutional exercise of power.

One or two remarks only shall be made: one is that he has taken no notice of a very essential advantage to trade in general which is mentioned in the report as peculiar to the existence of a bank circulation equal in the public estimation to gold & silver. It is this, that it renders it unnecessary to *lock* up the money of the country to accumulate for months successively in order to the periodical payment of interest. The other is this; that his arguments to show that treasury orders & bills of exchange from the course of trade will prevent any considerable displacement of the metals are founded on a partial view of the subject. A case will prove this: The sums collected in a state may be small in comparison with the debt due to it. The balance of its trade, direct & circuitous, with the seat of government may be even or nearly so. Here then without bank bills, which in that state answer the purpose of coin, there must be a displacement of the coin in proportion to the difference between the sum collected in the state and that to be paid in it. With bank bills no such displacement would take place, or, as far as it did, it would be gradual & insensible. In many other ways also would there be at least a temporary & inconvenient displacement of the coin, even where the course of trade would eventually return it to its proper channels.

The difference of the two situations in point of convenience to the treasury can only be appreciated by one who experiences the embarrassments of making provision for the payment of the interest on a stock continually changing place in thirteen different places.

One thing which has been omitted just occurs, although it is not very material to the main argument. The secretary of state affirms that the bill only contemplates a re-payment, not a loan to the government. But here he is certainly mistaken. It is true the government invests in the stock of the bank a sum equal to that which it receives on loan. But let it be remembered that it does not therefore cease to be a proprietor of the stock, which would be the case if the money received back were in the nature of a repayment. It remains a proprietor still, & will share in the profit or loss of the institution, according as the dividend is more or less than the interest it is to pay on the sum borrowed. Hence that sum is manifestly and in the strictest sense a loan.

Excerpts from the Report on Manufactures, December 5, 1791

The secretary of the treasury, in obedience to the order of the House of Representatives of the 15th day of January 1790, has applied his attention, at as early a period as his other duties would permit, to the subject of manufactures, and particularly to the means of promoting such as will tend to render the United States independent on foreign nations for military and other essential supplies. And he thereupon respectfully submits the following report.

The expediency of encouraging manufactures in the United States, which was not long since deemed very questionable, appears at this time to be pretty generally admitted. The embarrassments which have obstructed the progress of our external trade have led to serious reflections on the necessity of enlarging the sphere of our domestic commerce: the restrictive regulations, which in foreign markets abridge the vent of the increasing surplus of our agricultural produce, serve to beget an earnest desire that a more extensive demand for that surplus may be created at home: And the complete success which has rewarded manufacturing enterprise in some valuable branches, conspiring with the promising symptoms which attend some less mature essays in others, justify a hope that the obstacles to the growth of this species of industry are less formidable than they were apprehended to be; and that it is not difficult to find, in its further extension, a full indemnification for any external disadvantages which are or may be experienced, as well as an accession of resources, favorable to national independence and safety.

There still are, nevertheless, respectable patrons of opinions unfriendly to the encouragement of manufactures. The following are, substantially, the arguments by which these opinions are defended.

"In every country (say those who entertain them) agriculture is the most beneficial and *productive* object of human industry. This position, generally if not universally true, applies with peculiar emphasis to the United States on account of their immense tracts of fertile territory, uninhabited and unimproved. Nothing can afford so advantageous an employment for capital and labor as the conversion of this extensive wilderness into cultivated farms. Nothing equally with this can contribute to the population, strength, and real riches of the country."

"To endeavor by the extraordinary patronage of government to accelerate the growth of manufactures is in fact to endeavor, by force and art, to transfer the natural current of industry from a more to a less beneficial channel. Whatever has such a tendency must necessarily be unwise. Indeed it can hardly ever be wise in a government to attempt to give a direction to the industry of its citizens. This under the quicksighted guidance of private interest will, if left to itself, infallibly find its own way to the most profitable employment: and 'tis by such employment that the public prosperity will be most effectually promoted. To leave industry to itself, therefore, is, in almost every case, the soundest as well as the simplest policy."

"This policy is not only recommended to the United States by considerations which affect all nations, it is, in a manner, dictated to them by the imperious force of a very peculiar situation. The smallness of their population compared with their territory—the constant allurements to emigration from the settled to the unsettled parts of the country—the facility with which the less independent condition of an artisan can be exchanged for the more independent condition of a farmer, these and similar causes conspire to produce, and for a length of time must continue to occasion, a scarcity of hands for manufacturing occupation, and dearness of labor generally. To these disadvantages for the prosecution of manufactures a deficiency of pecuniary capital being added, the prospect of a successful competition with the manufactures of Europe must be regarded as little less than desperate. Extensive manufactures can only be the offspring of a redundant, at least of a full population. Till the latter shall characterize the situation of this country, 'tis vain to hope for the former."

"If, contrary to the natural course of things, an unseasonable and premature spring can be given to certain fabrics by heavy duties, prohibitions, bounties, or by other forced expedients, this will only be to sacrifice the interests of the community to those of particular classes. Besides the misdirection of labor, a virtual monopoly will be given to the persons employed on such fabrics; and an enhancement of price, the inevitable consequence of every monopoly, must be defrayed at the expense of the other parts of the society. It is far preferable that those persons should be engaged in the cultivation of the earth, and that we should procure in exchange for its productions the commodities with which foreigners are able to supply us in greater perfection, and upon better terms."

This mode of reasoning is founded upon facts and principles which have certainly respectable pretensions. If it had governed the conduct of nations more generally than it has done there is room to suppose that it might have carried them faster to prosperity and greatness than they have attained by the pursuit of maxims too widely opposite. Most general theories, however, admit of numerous exceptions, and there are few, if any, of the political kind, which do not blend a considerable portion of error with the truths they inculcate.

In order to an accurate judgment how far that which has been just stated ought to be deemed liable to a similar imputation, it is necessary to advert carefully to the considerations which plead in favor of manufactures and which appear to recommend the special and positive encouragement of them in certain cases, and under certain reasonable limitations.

It ought readily to be conceded, that the cultivation of the earth—as the primary and most certain source of national supply—as the immediate and chief source of subsistence to man—as the principal source of those materials which constitute the nutriment of other kinds of labor—as including a state most favorable to the freedom and independence of the human mind—one, perhaps, most conducive to the multiplication of the human species—has *intrinsically a strong claim to preeminence over every other kind of industry*.

But, that it has a title to anything like an exclusive predilection, in any country, ought to be admitted with great caution. That it is even more productive than every other branch of industry requires more evidence than has yet been given in support of the position. That its real interests, precious and important as without the help of exaggeration they truly are, will be advanced rather than injured by the due encouragement of manufactures may, it is believed, be satisfactorily demonstrated. And it is also believed that the expediency of such encouragement in a general view may be shown to be recommended by the most cogent and persuasive motives of national policy.

It has been maintained that agriculture is not only the most productive but the only productive species of industry. The reality of this suggestion in either aspect has, however, not been verified by any accurate detail of facts and calculations; and the general arguments which are adduced to prove it are rather subtle and paradoxical than solid or convincing.

Those which maintain its exclusive productiveness are to this effect.

Labor bestowed upon the cultivation of land produces enough not only to replace all the necessary expenses incurred in the business, and to maintain the persons who are employed in it, but to afford together with the *ordinary profit* on the stock or capital of the farmer a net surplus or *rent* for the landlord or proprietor of the soil. But the labor of artificers does nothing more than replace the stock which employs them (or which furnishes materials, tools, and wages) and yield the *ordinary profit* upon that stock. It yields nothing equivalent to the *rent* of land. Neither does it add anything to the *total value* of the *whole annual produce* of the land and labor of the country. The additional value given to those parts of the produce of land which are wrought into manufactures is counterbalanced by the value of those other parts of that produce, which are consumed by the manufacturers. It can therefore only be by saving or *parsimony*, not by the positive *productiveness* of their labor, that the classes of artificers can in any degree augment the revenue of the society.

To this it has been answered—

I. "That inasmuch as it is acknowledged that manufacturing labor reproduces a value equal to that which is expended or consumed in carrying it on, and continues in existence the original stock or capital employed—it ought on that account alone to escape being considered as wholly unproductive: That though it should be admitted, as alleged, that the consumption of the produce of the soil by the classes of artificers or manufacturers is exactly equal to the value added by their labor to the materials upon which it is exerted, yet it would not thence follow that it added nothing to the revenue of the society, or to the aggregate value of the annual produce of its land and labor. If the consumption for any given period amounted to a *given sum* and the *increased* value of the produce manufactured in the same period to a *like sum*, the total amount of the consumption and production during that period would be equal to the *two sums*, and consequently double the value of the agricultural produce consumed. And though the increment of value produced by the classes of artificers should at no time exceed the value of the produce of the land consumed by them, yet there would be at every moment, in consequence of their labor, a greater value of goods in the market than would exist independent of it."

II. "That the position that artificers can augment the revenue of a society only by parsimony is true in no other sense than in one which is equally applicable to husbandmen or cultivators. It may be alike affirmed of all these classes that the fund acquired by their labor and destined for their support is not, in an ordinary way, more than equal to it. And hence it will follow that augmentations of the wealth or capital of the community (except in the instances of some extraordinary dexterity or skill) can only proceed, with respect to any of them, from the savings of the more thrifty and parsimonious."

III. "That the annual produce of the land and labor of a country can only be increased in two ways—by some improvement in the *productive powers* of the useful labor which actually exists within it, or by some increase in the quantity of such labor: That with regard to the first, the labor of artificers being capable of greater subdivision and simplicity of operation than that of cultivators, it is susceptible in a proportionably greater degree of improvement in its *productive powers*, whether to be derived from an accession of skill or from the application of ingenious machinery, in which particular, therefore, the labor employed in the culture of land can pretend to no advantage over that engaged in manufactures: That with regard to an augmentation of the quantity of useful labor, this, excluding adventitious circumstances, must depend essentially upon an increase of *capital*, which again must depend upon the savings made out of the revenues of those who furnish or manage *that* which is at any time employed, whether in agriculture, or in manufactures, or in any other way."

But while the *exclusive* productiveness of agricultural labor has been thus denied and refuted, the superiority of its productiveness has been conceded without hesitation. As this concession involves a point of considerable magnitude in relation to maxims of public administration, the grounds on which it rests are worthy of a distinct and particular examination.

One of the arguments made use of in support of the idea may be pronounced both quaint and superficial. It amounts to this—That in the productions of the soil, nature cooperates with man, and that the effect of their joint labor must be greater than that of the labor of man alone.

This, however, is far from being a necessary inference. It is very conceivable that the labor of man alone laid out upon a work requiring great skill and art to bring it to perfection may be more productive, *in value*, than the labor of nature and man combined, when directed towards more simple operations and objects: And when it is recollected to what an extent the agency of nature in the application of the mechanical powers is made auxiliary to the prosecution of manufactures, the suggestion which has been noticed loses even the appearance of plausibility.

It might also be observed, with a contrary view, that the labor employed in agriculture is in a great measure periodical and occasional, depending on seasons, liable to various and long intermissions, while that occupied in many manufactures is constant and regular, extending through the year, embracing in some instances night as well as day. It is also probable that there are among the cultivators of land more examples of remissness than among artificers. The farmer, from the peculiar fertility of his land, or some other favorable circumstance, may frequently obtain a livelihood even with a considerable degree of carelessness in the mode of cultivation; but the artisan can with difficulty effect the same object without exerting himself pretty equally with all those who are engaged in the same pursuit. And if it may likewise be assumed as a fact that manufactures open a wider field to exertions of ingenuity than agriculture, it would not be a strained conjecture that the labor employed in the former, being at once more *constant*, more uniform, and more ingenious than that which is employed in the latter, will be found at the same time more productive.

But it is not meant to lay stress on observations of this nature—they ought only to serve as a counterbalance to those of a similar complexion. Circumstances so vague and general, as well as so abstract, can afford little instruction in a matter of this kind.

Another, and that which seems to be the principal argument offered for the superior productiveness of agricultural labor, turns upon the allegation that labor employed in manufactures yields nothing equivalent to the rent of land, or to that net surplus, as it is called, which accrues to the proprietor of the soil.

But this distinction, important as it has been deemed, appears rather *verbal* than *substantial*.

It is easily discernible that what in the first instance is divided into two parts under the denominations of the *ordinary profit* of the stock of the farmer and *rent* to the landlord is in the second instance united under the general appellation of the *ordinary profit* on the stock of the undertaker, and that this formal or verbal distribution constitutes the whole difference in the two cases. It seems to have been overlooked that the land is itself a stock or capital, advanced or lent by its owner to the occupier or tenant, and that the rent he receives is only the ordinary profit of a certain stock in land, not managed by the proprietor himself but by another to whom he lends or lets it, and who on his part advances a second capital to stock & improve the land, upon which he also receives the usual profit. The rent of the landlord and the profit of the farmer are therefore nothing more than the *ordinary profits* of *two* capitals belonging to *two* different persons and united in the cultivation of a farm: As in the other case, the surplus which arises upon any manufactory, after replacing the expenses of carrying it on, answers to the ordinary profits of *one* or *more* capitals engaged in the prosecution of such manufactory. It is said *one* or *more* capitals because in fact the same thing which is contemplated in the case of the farm sometimes happens in that of a manufactory. There is one who furnishes a part of the capital or lends a part of the money by which it is carried on, and another who carries it on with the addition of his own capital. Out of the surplus which remains after defraying expenses an interest is paid to the money lender for the portion of the capital furnished by him, which exactly agrees with the rent paid to the landlord; and the residue of that surplus constitutes the profit of the undertaker or manufacturer and agrees with what is denominated the ordinary profits on the stock of the farmer. Both together make the ordinary profits of two capitals employed in a manufactory; as in the other case the rent of the landlord and the revenue of the farmer compose the ordinary profits of two capitals employed in the cultivation of a farm.

The rent therefore accruing to the proprietor of the land, far from being a criterion of *exclusive* productiveness, as has been argued, is no criterion even of superior productiveness. The question must still be whether the surplus, after defraying expenses of a *given capital* employed in the *purchase* and *improvement* of a piece of land, is greater or less than that of a like capital employed in the prosecution of a manufactory: or whether the *whole value produced* from a *given capital* and a *given quantity of labor* employed in one way be greater or less than the *whole value produced* from an *equal capital* and an *equal quantity of labor* employed in the other way: or rather, perhaps whether the business of agriculture or that of manufactures will yield the greatest product, according to a *compound ratio* of the quantity of the capital and the quantity of labor, which are employed in the one or in the other.

The solution of either of these questions is not easy; it involves numerous and complicated details, depending on an accurate knowledge of the objects to be compared. It is not known that the comparison has ever yet been made upon sufficient data properly ascertained and analyzed. To be able to make it on the present occasion with satisfactory precision would demand more previous enquiry and investigation than there has been hitherto either leisure or opportunity to accomplish.

Some essays, however, have been made towards acquiring the requisite information, which have rather served to throw doubt upon than to confirm the hypothesis under examination: But it ought to be acknowledged that they have been too little diversified and are too imperfect to authorize a definitive conclusion either way, leading rather to probable conjecture than to certain deduction. They render it probable that there are various branches of manufactures in which a given capital will yield a greater *total* product, and a considerably greater *net* product, than an equal capital invested in the purchase and improvement of lands; and that there are also *some* branches in which both the *gross* and the *net* produce will exceed that of agricultural industry, according to a compound ratio of capital and labor: But it is on this last point that there appears to be the greatest room for doubt. It is far less difficult to infer generally that the *net produce* of capital engaged in manufacturing enterprises is greater than that of capital engaged in agriculture.

In stating these results, the purchase and improvement of lands under previous cultivation are alone contemplated. The comparison is more in favor of agriculture when it is made with reference to the settlement of new and waste lands, but an argument drawn from so temporary a circumstance could have no weight in determining the general question concerning the permanent relative productiveness of the two species of industry. How far it ought to influence the policy of the United States on the score of particular situation will be adverted to in another place.

The foregoing suggestions are *not designed to inculcate an opinion that manufacturing industry is more productive than that of agriculture*. They are intended rather to show that the reverse of this proposition is not ascertained; that the general arguments which are brought to establish it are not satisfactory; and consequently that a supposition of the superior productiveness of tillage ought to be no obstacle to listening to any substantial inducements to the encouragement of manufactures, which may be otherwise perceived to exist, through an apprehension that they may have a tendency to divert labor from a more to a less profitable employment.

It is extremely probable that on a full and accurate development of the matter, on the ground of fact and calculation, it would be discovered that there is no material difference between the aggregate productiveness of the one and of the other kind of industry, and that the propriety of the encouragements which may in any case be proposed to be given to either ought to be determined upon considerations irrelative to any comparison of that nature.

II. But without contending for the superior productiveness of manufacturing industry, it may conduce to a better judgment of the policy, which ought to be pursued respecting its encouragement, to contemplate the subject under some additional aspects, tending not only to confirm the idea that this kind of industry has been improperly represented as unproductive in itself, but to evince in addition that the establishment and diffusion of manufactures have the effect of rendering the total mass of useful and productive labor in a community *greater than it would otherwise be*. In prosecuting this discussion, it may be necessary briefly to resume and review some of the topics which have been already touched.

To affirm that the labor of the manufacturer is unproductive, because he consumes as much of the produce of land as he adds value to the raw materials which he manufactures, is not better founded than it would be to affirm that the labor of the farmer, which furnishes materials to the manufacturer, is unproductive *because he consumes an equal value of manufactured articles*. Each furnishes a certain portion of the produce of his labor to the other, and each destroys a correspondent portion of the produce of the labor of the other. In the meantime, the maintenance of two citizens instead of one is going on, the state has two members instead of one, and they together consume twice the value of what is produced from the land.

If instead of a farmer and artificer there were a farmer only, he would be under the necessity of devoting a part of his labor to the fabrication of clothing and other articles, which he would procure of the artificer in the case of there being such a person; and of course he would be able to devote less labor to the cultivation of his farm, and would draw from it a proportionably less product. The whole quantity of production in this state of things, in provisions, raw materials, and manufactures, would certainly not exceed in value the amount of what would be produced in provisions and raw materials only, if there were an artificer as well as a farmer.

Again—if there were both an artificer and a farmer, the latter would be left at liberty to pursue exclusively the cultivation of his farm. A greater quantity of provisions and raw materials would of course be produced—equal at least, as has been already observed, to the whole amount of the provisions, raw materials, and manufactures which would exist on a contrary supposition. The artificer at the same time would be going on in the production of manufactured commodities, to an amount sufficient not only to repay the farmer in those commodities for the provisions and materials which were procured from him, but to furnish the artificer himself with a supply of similar commodities for his own use. Thus, then, there would be two quantities or values in existence instead of one; and the revenue and consumption would be double in one case what it would be in the other.

If in place of both these suppositions, there were supposed to be two farmers and no artificer, each of whom applied a part of his labor to the culture of land and another part to the fabrication of manufactures—in this case the portion of the labor of both bestowed upon land would produce the same quantity of provisions and raw materials only as would be produced by the entire sum of the labor of one applied in the same manner, and the portion of the labor of both bestowed upon manufactures would produce the same quantity of manufactures only as would be produced by the entire sum of the labor of one applied in the same manner. Hence the produce of the labor of the two farmers would not be greater than the produce of the labor of the farmer and artificer; and hence it results that the labor of the artificer is as positively productive as that of the farmer, and as positively augments the revenue of the society.

The labor of the artificer replaces to the farmer that portion of his labor with which he provides the materials of exchange with the artificer, and which he would otherwise have been compelled to apply to manufactures: and while the artificer thus enables the farmer to enlarge his stock of agricultural industry, a portion of which he purchases for his own use, *he also supplies himself with the manufactured articles of which he stands in need.*

He does still more—Besides this equivalent which he gives for the portion of agricultural labor consumed by him and this supply of manufactured commodities for his own consumption—he furnishes still a surplus which compensates for the use of the capital advanced either by himself or some other person, for carrying on the business. This is the ordinary profit of the stock employed in the manufactory, and is, in every sense, as effective an addition to the income of the society as the rent of land.

The produce of the labor of the artificer consequently may be regarded as composed of three parts: one by which the provisions for his subsistence and the materials for his work are purchased of the farmer, one by which he supplies himself with manufactured necessaries, and a third which constitutes the profit on the stock employed. The two last portions seem to have been overlooked in the system which represents manufacturing industry as barren and unproductive.

In the course of the preceding illustrations, the products of equal quantities of the labor of the farmer and artificer have been treated as if equal to each other. But this is not to be understood as intending to assert any such precise equality. It is merely a manner of expression adopted for the sake of simplicity and perspicuity. Whether the value of the produce of the labor of the farmer be somewhat more or less than that of the artificer is not material to the main scope of the argument, which hitherto has only aimed at showing that the one as well as the other occasions a positive augmentation of the total produce and revenue of the society.

It is now proper to proceed a step further and to enumerate the principal circumstances from which it may be inferred—That manufacturing establishments not only occasion a positive augmentation of the produce and revenue of the society, but that they contribute essentially to rendering them greater than they could possibly be without such establishments. These circumstances are—

1. The division of labor.
2. An extension of the use of machinery.
3. Additional employment to the classes of the community not ordinarily engaged in business.
4. The promoting of emigration from foreign countries.
5. The furnishing greater scope for the diversity of talents and dispositions which discriminate men from each other.
6. The affording a more ample and various field for enterprise.
7. The creating in some instances a new, and securing in all, a more certain and steady demand for the surplus produce of the soil.

Each of these circumstances has a considerable influence upon the total mass of industrious effort in a community. Together they add to it a degree of energy and effect which are not easily conceived. Some comments upon each of them, in the order in which they have been stated, may serve to explain their importance.

I. As to the division of labor.

It has justly been observed that there is scarcely anything of greater moment in the economy of a nation than the proper division of labor. The separation of occupations causes each to be carried to a much greater perfection than it could possible acquire if they were blended. This arises principally from three circumstances.

1st. The greater skill and dexterity naturally resulting from a constant and undivided application to a single object. It is evident that these properties must increase in proportion to the separation and simplification of objects and the steadiness of the attention devoted to each, and must be less in proportion to the complication of objects and the number among which the attention is distracted.

2nd. The economy of time—by avoiding the loss of it, incident to a frequent transition from one operation to another of a different nature. This depends on various circumstances—the transition itself—the orderly disposition of the implements, machines, and materials employed in the operation to be relinquished—the preparatory steps to the commencement of a new one—the interruption of the impulse, which the mind of the workman acquires, from being engaged in a particular operation—the distractions, hesitations, and reluctances which attend the passage from one kind of business to another.

3rd. An extension of the use of machinery. A man occupied on a single object will have it more in his power and will be more naturally led to exert his imagination in devising methods to facilitate and abridge labor than if he were perplexed by a variety of independent and dissimilar operations. Besides this, the fabrication of machines, in numerous instances, becoming itself a distinct trade, the artist who follows it has all the advantages which have been enumerated for improvement in his particular art; and in both ways the invention and application of machinery are extended.

And from these causes united, the mere separation of the occupation of the cultivator from that of the artificer has the effect of augmenting the *productive powers* of labor, and with them the total mass of the produce or revenue of a country. In this single view of the subject, therefore, the utility of artificers or manufacturers towards promoting an increase of productive industry is apparent.

II. As to an extension of the use of machinery a point which though partly anticipated requires to be placed in one or two additional lights.

The employment of machinery forms an item of great importance in the general mass of national industry. 'Tis an artificial force brought in aid of the natural force of man, and, to all the purposes of labor, is an increase of hands, an accession of strength, *unencumbered too by the expense of maintaining the laborer.* May it not therefore be fairly inferred that those occupations which give greatest scope to the use of this auxiliary contribute most to the general stock of industrious effort, and, in consequence, to the general product of industry?

It shall be taken for granted, and the truth of the position referred to observation, that manufacturing pursuits are susceptible in a greater degree of the application of machinery than those of agriculture. If so, all the difference is lost to a community, which, instead of manufacturing for itself, procures the fabrics requisite to its supply from other countries. The substitution of foreign for domestic manufactures is a transfer to foreign nations of the advantages accruing from the employment of machinery, in the modes in which it is capable of being employed with most utility and to the greatest extent.

The cotton mill invented in England within the last twenty years is a signal illustration of the general proposition which has been just advanced. In consequence of it all, the different processes for spinning cotton are performed by means of machines, which are put in motion by water, and attended chiefly by women and children, and by a smaller number of persons in the whole than are requisite in the ordinary mode of spinning. And it is an advantage of great moment that the operations of this mill continue with convenience during the night as well as through the day. The prodigious effect of such a machine is easily conceived. To this invention is to be attributed essentially the immense progress which has been so suddenly made in Great Britain in the various fabrics of cotton.

III. As to the additional employment of classes of the community not ordinarily engaged in the particular business.

This is not among the least valuable of the means by which manufacturing institutions contribute to augment the general stock of industry and production. In places where those institutions prevail, besides the persons regularly engaged in them, they afford occasional and extra employment to industrious individuals and families, who are willing to devote the leisure resulting from the intermissions of their ordinary pursuits to collateral labors, as a resource of multiplying their acquisitions or their enjoyments. The husbandman himself experiences a new source of profit and support from the increased industry of his wife and daughters, invited and stimulated by the demands of the neighboring manufactories.

Besides this advantage of occasional employment to classes having different occupations, there is another of a nature allied to it and of a similar tendency. This is—the employment of persons who would otherwise be idle (and in many cases a burden on the community), either from the bias of temper, habit, infirmity of body, or some other cause, indisposing or disqualifying them for the toils of the country. It is worthy of particular remark that in general, women and children are rendered more useful and the latter more early useful by manufacturing establishments than they would otherwise be. Of the number of persons employed in the cotton manufactories of Great Britain, it is computed that 4/7 nearly are women and children, of whom the greatest proportion are children and many of them of a very tender age.

And thus it appears to be one of the attributes of manufactures, and one of no small consequence, to give occasion to the exertion of a greater quantity of industry, even by the *same number* of persons, where they happen to prevail, than would exist if there were no such establishments.

IV. As to the promoting of emigration from foreign countries. Men reluctantly quit one course of occupation and livelihood for another, unless invited to it by very apparent and proximate advantages. Many, who would go from one country to another if they had a prospect of continuing with more benefit the callings to which they have been educated, will often not be tempted to change their situation by the hope of doing better in some other way. Manufacturers, who listening to the powerful invitations of a better price for their fabrics, or their labor, of greater cheapness of provisions and raw materials, of an exemption from the chief part of the taxes, burdens, and restraints which they endure in the old world, of greater personal independence and consequence under the operation of a more equal government, and of what is far more precious than mere religious toleration—a perfect equality of religious privileges; would probably flock from Europe to the United States to pursue their own trades or professions, if they were once made sensible of the advantages they would enjoy and were inspired with an assurance of encouragement and employment, will, with difficulty, be induced to transplant themselves, with a view to becoming cultivators of land.

If it be true then, that it is the interest of the United States to open every possible avenue to emigration from abroad, it affords a weighty argument for the encouragement of manufactures, which for the reasons just assigned, will have the strongest tendency to multiply the inducements to it.

Here is perceived an important resource, not only for extending the population, and with it the useful and productive labor of the country, but likewise for the prosecution of manufactures without deducting from the number of hands which might otherwise be drawn to tillage, and even for the indemnification of agriculture for such as might happen to be diverted from it. Many whom manufacturing views would induce to emigrate would afterwards yield to the temptations which the particular situation of this country holds out to agricultural pursuits. And while agriculture would in other respects derive many signal and unmingled advantages from the growth of manufactures, it is a problem whether it would gain or lose as to the article of the number of persons employed in carrying it on.

V. As to the furnishing greater scope for the diversity of talents and dispositions which discriminate men from each other.

This is a much more powerful mean of augmenting the fund of national industry than may at first sight appear. It is a just observation that minds of the strongest and most active powers for their proper objects fall below mediocrity and labor without effect if confined to uncongenial pursuits. And it is thence to be inferred that the results of human exertion may be immensely increased by diversifying its objects. When all the different kinds of industry obtain in a community, each individual can find his proper element and can call into activity the whole vigor of his nature. And the community is benefitted by the services of its respective members in the manner in which each can serve it with most effect.

If there be anything in a remark often to be met with—namely that there is, in the genius of the people of this country, a peculiar aptitude for mechanic improvements, it would operate as a forcible reason for giving opportunities to the exercise of that species of talent by the propagation of manufactures.

VI. As to the affording a more ample and various field for enterprise.

This also is of greater consequence in the general scale of national exertion than might perhaps on a superficial view be supposed, and has effects not altogether dissimilar from those of the circumstance last noticed. To cherish and stimulate the activity of the human mind by multiplying the objects of enterprise is not among the least considerable of the expedients by which the wealth of a nation may be promoted. Even things in themselves not positively advantageous sometimes become so by their tendency to provoke exertion. Every new scene which is opened to the busy nature of man to rouse and exert itself is the addition of a new energy to the general stock of effort.

The spirit of enterprise, useful and prolific as it is, must necessarily be contracted or expanded in proportion to the simplicity or variety of the occupations and productions which are to be found in a society. It must be less in a nation of mere cultivators than in a nation of cultivators and merchants, less in a nation of cultivators and merchants than in a nation of cultivators, artificers, and merchants.

VII. As to the creating in some instances a new, and securing in all, a more certain and steady demand for the surplus produce of the soil.

This is among the most important of the circumstances which have been indicated. It is a principal mean by which the establishment of manufactures contributes to an augmentation of the produce or revenue of a country and has an immediate and direct relation to the prosperity of agriculture.

It is evident that the exertions of the husbandman will be steady or fluctuating, vigorous or feeble, in proportion to the steadiness or fluctuation, adequateness, or inadequateness of the markets on which he must depend for the vent of the surplus which may be produced by his labor, and that such surplus in the ordinary course of things will be greater or less in the same proportion.

For the purpose of this vent, a domestic market is greatly to be preferred to a foreign one, because it is in the nature of things far more to be relied upon.

It is a primary object of the policy of nations to be able to supply themselves with subsistence from their own soils; and manufacturing nations, as far as circumstances permit, endeavor to procure from the same source the raw materials necessary for their own fabrics. This disposition, urged by the spirit of monopoly, is sometimes even carried to an injudicious extreme. It seems not always to be recollected that nations who have neither mines nor manufactures can only obtain the manufactured articles of which they stand in need by an exchange of the products of their soils, and that, if those who can best furnish them with such articles are unwilling to give a due course to this exchange, they must of necessity make every possible effort to manufacture for themselves, the effect of which is that the manufacturing nations abridge the natural advantages of their situation, through an unwillingness to permit the agricultural countries to enjoy the advantages of theirs, and sacrifice the interests of a mutually beneficial intercourse to the vain project of *selling everything* and *buying nothing*.

But it is also a consequence of the policy which has been noted that the foreign demand for the products of agricultural countries is, in a great degree, rather casual and occasional than certain or constant. To what extent injurious interruptions of the demand for some of the staple commodities of the United States may have been experienced from that cause must be referred to the judgment of those who are engaged in carrying on the commerce of the country; but it may be safely assumed that such interruptions are at times very inconveniently felt, and that cases not unfrequently occur in which markets are so confined and restricted as to render the demand very unequal to the supply.

Independently likewise of the artificial impediments which are created by the policy in question, there are natural causes tending to render the external demand for the surplus of agricultural nations a precarious reliance. The differences of seasons in the countries which are the consumers make immense differences in the produce of their own soils in different years, and consequently in the degrees of their necessity for foreign supply. Plentiful harvests with them, especially if similar ones occur at the same time in the countries which are the furnishers, occasion of course a glut in the markets of the latter.

Considering how fast and how much the progress of new settlements in the United States must increase the surplus produce of the soil, and weighing seriously the tendency of the system which prevails among most of the commercial nations of Europe, whatever dependence may be placed on the force of natural circumstances to counteract the effects of an artificial policy there appear strong reasons to regard the foreign demand for that surplus as too uncertain a reliance, and to desire a substitute for it in an extensive domestic market.

To secure such a market there is no other expedient than to promote manufacturing establishments. Manufacturers, who constitute the most numerous class after the cultivators of land, are for that reason the principal consumers of the surplus of their labor.

This idea of an extensive domestic market for the surplus produce of the soil is of the first consequence. It is of all things that which most effectually conduces to a flourishing state of agriculture. If the effect of manufactories should be to detach a portion of the hands which would otherwise be engaged in tillage, it might possibly cause a smaller quantity of lands to be under cultivation; but by their tendency to procure a more certain demand for the surplus produce of the soil, they would, at the same time, cause the lands which were in cultivation to be better improved and more productive. And while by their influence the condition of each individual farmer would be meliorated, the total mass of agricultural production would probably be increased. For this must evidently depend as much, if not more, upon the degree of improvement than upon the number of acres under culture.

It merits particular observation that the multiplication of manufactories not only furnishes a market for those articles which have been accustomed to be produced in abundance in a country, but it likewise creates a demand for such as were either unknown or produced in inconsiderable quantities. The bowels as well as the surface of the earth are ransacked for articles which were before neglected. Animals, plants, and minerals acquire an utility and value which were before unexplored.

The foregoing considerations seem sufficient to establish, as general propositions, that it is the interest of nations to diversify the industrious pursuits of the individuals who compose them—that the establishment of manufactures is calculated not only to increase the general stock of useful and productive labor, but even to improve the state of agriculture in particular, certainly to advance the interests of those who are engaged in it. There are other views that will be hereafter taken of the subject, which, it is conceived, will serve to confirm these inferences.

III. Previously to a further discussion of the objections to the encouragement of manufactures which have been stated, it will be of use to see what can be said in reference to the particular situation of the United States against the conclusions appearing to result from what has been already offered.

It may be observed, and the idea is of no inconsiderable weight, that however true it might be that a state which possessing large tracts of vacant and fertile territory was at the same time secluded from foreign commerce would find its interest and the interest of agriculture in diverting a part of its population from tillage to manufactures; yet it will not follow that the same is true of a state which having such vacant and fertile territory has at the same time ample opportunity of procuring from abroad, on good terms, all the fabrics of which it stands in need for the supply of its inhabitants. The power of doing this at least secures the great advantage of a division of labor, leaving the farmer free to pursue exclusively the culture of his land, and enabling him to procure with its products the manufactured supplies requisite either to his wants or to his enjoyments. And though it should be true that in settled countries the diversification of industry is conducive to an increase in the productive powers of labor and to an augmentation of revenue and capital, yet it is scarcely conceivable that there can be anything of so solid and permanent advantage to an uncultivated and unpeopled country as to convert its wastes into cultivated and inhabited districts. If the revenue in the meantime should be less, the capital in the event must be greater.

To these observations, the following appears to be a satisfactory answer—

1. If the system of perfect liberty to industry and commerce were the prevailing system of nations—the arguments which dissuade a country in the predicament of the United States from the zealous pursuits of manufactures would doubtless have great force. It will not be affirmed that they might not be permitted, with few exceptions, to serve as a rule of national conduct. In such a state of things, each country would have the full benefit of its peculiar advantages to compensate for its deficiencies or disadvantages. If one nation were in condition to supply manufactured articles on better terms than another, that other might find an abundant indemnification in a superior capacity to furnish the produce of the soil. And a free exchange, mutually beneficial, of the commodities which each was able to supply, on the best terms, might be carried on between them, supporting in full vigor the industry of each. And though the circumstances which have been mentioned, and others which will be unfolded hereafter, render it probable that nations merely agricultural would not enjoy the same degree of opulence in proportion to their numbers as those which united manufactures with agriculture; yet the progressive improvement of the lands of the former might, in the end, atone for an inferior degree of opulence in the meantime: and in a case in which opposite considerations are pretty equally balanced, the option ought perhaps always to be in favor of leaving industry to its own direction.

But the system which has been mentioned is far from characterizing the general policy of nations. The prevalent one has been regulated by an opposite spirit.

The consequence of it is that the United States are to a certain extent in the situation of a country precluded from foreign commerce. They can indeed without difficulty obtain from abroad the manufactured supplies of which they are in want, but they experience numerous and very injurious impediments to the emission and vent of their own commodities. Nor is this the case in reference to a single foreign nation only. The regulations of several countries with which we have the most extensive intercourse throw serious obstructions in the way of the principal staples of the United States.

In such a position of things the United States cannot exchange with Europe on equal terms, and the want of reciprocity would render them the victim of a system which should induce them to confine their views to agriculture and refrain from manufactures. A constant and increasing necessity on their part for the commodities of Europe, and only a partial and occasional demand for their own in return, could not but expose them to a state of impoverishment compared with the opulence to which their political and natural advantages authorize them to aspire.

Remarks of this kind are not made in the spirit of complaint. 'Tis for the nations whose regulations are alluded to to judge for themselves whether, by aiming at too much they do not lose more than they gain. 'Tis for the United States to consider by what means they can render themselves least dependent on the combinations, right or wrong, of foreign policy.

It is no small consolation that already the measures which have embarrassed our trade have accelerated internal improvements, which upon the whole have bettered our affairs. To diversify and extend these improvements is the surest and safest method of indemnifying ourselves for any inconveniences which those or similar measures have a tendency to beget. If Europe will not take from us the products of our soil upon terms consistent with our interest, the natural remedy is to contract as fast as possible our wants of her.

2. The conversion of their waste into cultivated lands is certainly a point of great moment in the political calculations of the United States. But the degree in which this may possibly be retarded by the encouragement of manufactories does not appear to countervail the powerful inducements to affording that encouragement.

An observation made in another place is of a nature to have great influence upon this question. If it cannot be denied that the interests even of agriculture may be advanced more by having such of the lands of a state as are occupied under good cultivation than by having a greater quantity occupied under a much inferior cultivation, and if manufactories, for the reasons assigned, must be admitted to have a tendency to promote a more steady and vigorous cultivation of the lands occupied than would happen without them—it will follow that they are capable of indemnifying a country for a diminution of the progress of new settlements, and may serve to increase both the capital value and the income of its lands, even though they should abridge the number of acres under tillage.

But it does by no means follow that the progress of new settlements would be retarded by the extension of manufactures. The desire of being an independent proprietor of land is founded on such strong principles in the human breast that where the opportunity of becoming so is as great as it is in the United States, the proportion will be small of those, whose situations would otherwise lead to it, who would be diverted from it towards manufactures. And it is highly probable, as already intimated, that the accessions of foreigners, who originally drawn over by manufacturing views would afterwards abandon them for agricultural, would be more than equivalent for those of our own citizens who might happen to be detached from them.

The remaining objections to a particular encouragement of manufactures in the United States now require to be examined.

One of these turns on the proposition that industry, if left to itself, will naturally find its way to the most useful and profitable employment: whence it is inferred, that manufactures without the aid of government will grow up as soon and as fast as the natural state of things and the interest of the community may require.

Against the solidity of this hypothesis, in the full latitude of the terms, very cogent reasons may be offered. These have relation to—the strong influence of habit and the spirit of imitation—the fear of want of success in untried enterprises—the intrinsic difficulties incident to first essays towards a competition with those who have previously attained to perfection in the business to be attempted—the bounties, premiums, and other artificial encouragements with which foreign nations second the exertions of their own citizens in the branches in which they are to be rivaled.

Experience teaches that men are often so much governed by what they are accustomed to see and practice that the simplest and most obvious improvements in the most ordinary occupations are adopted with hesitation, reluctance, and by slow gradations. The spontaneous transition to new pursuits, in a community long habituated to different ones, may be expected to be attended with proportionably greater difficulty. When former occupations ceased to yield a profit adequate to the subsistence of their followers, or when there was an absolute deficiency of employment in them owing to the superabundance of hands, changes would ensue; but these changes would be likely to be more tardy than might consist with the interest either of individuals or of the society. In many cases they would not happen while a bare support could be ensured by an adherence to ancient courses, though a resort to a more profitable employment might be practicable. To produce the desirable changes as early as may be expedient may therefore require the incitement and patronage of government.

The apprehension of failing in new attempts is perhaps a more serious impediment. There are dispositions apt to be attracted by the mere novelty of an undertaking—but these are not always those best calculated to give it success. To this it is of importance that the confidence of cautious sagacious capitalists, both citizens and foreigners, should be excited. And to inspire this description of persons with confidence, it is essential that they should be made to see in any project which is new, and for that reason alone if for no other precarious, the prospect of such a degree of countenance and support from government as may be capable of overcoming the obstacles inseparable from first experiments.

The superiority antecedently enjoyed by nations who have preoccupied and perfected a branch of industry constitutes a more formidable obstacle than either of those which have been mentioned to the introduction of the same branch into a country in which it did not before exist. To maintain between the recent establishments of one country and the long matured establishments of another country a competition upon equal terms, both as to quality and price, is in most cases impracticable. The disparity in the one or in the other, or in both, must necessarily be so considerable as to forbid a successful rivalship, without the extraordinary aid and protection of government.

But the greatest obstacle of all to the successful prosecution of a new branch of industry in a country in which it was before unknown consists, as far as the instances apply, in the bounties, premiums, and other aids which are granted in a variety of cases by the nations in which the establishments to be imitated are previously introduced. It is well known (and particular examples in the course of this report will be cited) that certain nations grant bounties on the exportation of particular commodities to enable their own workmen to undersell and supplant all competitors in the countries to which those commodities are sent. Hence the undertakers of a new manufacture have to contend not only with the natural disadvantages of a new undertaking, but with the gratuities and remunerations which other governments bestow. To be enabled to contend with success it is evident that the interference and aid of their own government are indispensable.

Combinations by those engaged in a particular branch of business in one country to frustrate the first efforts to introduce it into another by temporary sacrifices, recompensed perhaps by extraordinary indemnifications of the government of such country, are believed to have existed and are not to be regarded as destitute of probability. The existence or assurance of aid from the government of the country in which the business is to be introduced may be essential to fortify adventurers against the dread of such combinations to defeat their efforts[2] if formed, and to prevent their being formed, by demonstrating that they must in the end prove fruitless.

Whatever room there may be for an expectation that the industry of a people, under the direction of private interest, will upon equal terms find out the most beneficial employment for itself, there is none for a reliance that it will struggle against the force of unequal terms, or will of itself surmount all the adventitious barriers to a successful competition, which may have been erected either by the advantages naturally acquired from practice and previous possession of the ground or by those which may have sprung from positive regulations and an artificial policy. This general reflection might alone suffice as an answer to the objection under examination, exclusively of the weighty considerations which have been particularly urged.

The objections to the pursuit of manufactures in the United States which next present themselves to discussion represent an impracticability of success, arising from three causes—scarcity of hands—dearness of labor—want of capital.

The two first circumstances are to a certain extent real, and, within due limits, ought to be admitted as obstacles to the success of manufacturing enterprise in the United States. But there are various considerations which lessen their force and tend to afford an assurance that they are not sufficient to prevent the advantageous prosecution of many very useful and extensive manufactories.

With regard to scarcity of hands, the fact itself must be applied with no small qualification to certain parts of the United States. There are large districts which may be considered as pretty fully peopled, and which notwithstanding a continual drain for distant settlement are thickly interspersed with flourishing and increasing towns. If these districts have not already reached the point at which the complaint of scarcity of hands ceases, they are not remote from it and are approaching fast towards it: And having perhaps fewer attractions to agriculture, than some other parts of the Union, they exhibit a proportionably stronger tendency towards other kinds of industry. In these districts may be discerned no inconsiderable maturity for manufacturing establishments.

But there are circumstances which have been already noticed with another view that materially diminish everywhere the effect of a scarcity of hands. These circumstances are—the great use which can be made of women and children, on which point a very pregnant and instructive fact has been mentioned—the vast extension given by late improvements to the employment of machines, which substituting the agency of fire and water, has prodigiously lessened the necessity for manual labor—the employment of persons ordinarily engaged in other occupations during the seasons or hours of leisure, which, besides giving occasion to the exertion of a greater quantity of labor by the same number of persons, and thereby increasing the general stock of labor, as has been elsewhere remarked, may also be taken into the calculation as a resource for obviating the scarcity of hands—lastly the attraction of foreign emigrants. Whoever inspects, with a careful eye, the composition of our towns will be made sensible to what an extent this resource may be relied upon. This exhibits a large proportion of ingenious and valuable workmen, in different arts and trades, who, by expatriating from Europe, have improved their own condition and added to the industry and wealth of the United States. It is a natural inference from the experience we have already had that as soon as the United States shall present the countenance of a serious prosecution of manufactures—as soon as foreign artists shall be made sensible that the state of things here affords a moral certainty of employment and encouragement—competent numbers of European workmen will transplant themselves effectually to ensure the success of the design. How indeed can it otherwise happen considering the various and powerful inducements which the situation of this country offers, addressing themselves to so many strong passions and feelings, to so many general and particular interests?

It may be affirmed therefore, in respect to hands for carrying on manufactures, that we shall in a great measure trade upon a foreign stock, reserving our own for the cultivation of our lands and the manning of our ships, as far as character and circumstances shall incline. It is not unworthy of remark that the objection to the success of manufactures deduced from the scarcity of hands is alike applicable to trade and navigation, and yet these are perceived to flourish without any sensible impediment from that cause.

As to the dearness of labor (another of the obstacles alleged) this has relation principally to two circumstances, one that which has been just discussed, or the scarcity of hands, the other the greatness of profits.

As far as it is a consequence of the scarcity of hands, it is mitigated by all the considerations which have been adduced as lessening that deficiency.

It is certain too that the disparity in this respect between some of the most manufacturing parts of Europe and a large proportion of the United States is not nearly so great as is commonly imagined. It is also much less in regard to artificers and manufacturers than in regard to country laborers; and while a careful comparison shows that there is, in this particular, much exaggeration, it is also evident that the effect of the degree of disparity which does truly exist is diminished in proportion to the use which can be made of machinery.

To illustrate this last idea—Let it be supposed that the difference of price in two countries of a given quantity of manual labor requisite to the fabrication of a given article is as 10, and that some *mechanic power* is introduced into both countries, which performing half the necessary labor leaves only half to be done by hand, it is evident that the difference in the cost of the fabrication of the article in question in the two countries, as far as it is connected with the price of labor, will be reduced from 10 to 5 in consequence of the introduction of that *power*.

This circumstance is worthy of the most particular attention. It diminishes immensely one of the objections most strenuously urged against the success of manufactures in the United States.

To procure all such machines as are known in any part of Europe can only require a proper provision and due pains. The knowledge of several of the most important of them is already possessed. The preparation of them here is in most cases practicable on nearly equal terms. As far as they depend on water, some superiority of advantages may be claimed from the uncommon variety and greater cheapness of situations adapted to mill seats, with which different parts of the United States abound.

So far as the dearness of labor may be a consequence of the greatness of profits in any branch of business, it is no obstacle to its success. The undertaker can afford to pay the price.

There are grounds to conclude that undertakers of manufactures in this country can at this time afford to pay higher wages to the workmen they may employ than are paid to similar workmen in Europe. The prices of foreign fabrics in the markets of the United States, which will for a long time regulate the prices of the domestic ones, may be considered as compounded of the following ingredients—The first cost of materials, including the taxes, if any, which are paid upon them where they are made; the expense of grounds, buildings, machinery, and tools; the wages of the persons employed in the manufactory; the profits on the capital or stock employed; the commissions of agents to purchase them where they are made; the expense of transportation to the United

States, including insurance and other incidental charges; the taxes or duties, if any, and fees of office, which are paid on their exportation; the taxes or duties, and fees of office, which are paid on their importation.

As to the first of these items, the cost of materials, the advantage upon the whole is at present on the side of the United States, and the difference in their favor must increase in proportion as a certain and extensive domestic demand shall induce the proprietors of land to devote more of their attention to the production of those materials. It ought not to escape observation, in a comparison on this point, that some of the principal manufacturing countries of Europe are much more dependent on foreign supply for the materials of their manufactures than would be the United States, who are capable of supplying themselves with a greater abundance as well as a greater variety of the requisite materials.

As to the second item, the expense of grounds, buildings, machinery, and tools, an equality at least may be assumed, since advantages in some particulars will counterbalance temporary disadvantages in others.

As to the third item, or the article of wages, the comparison certainly turns against the United States, though as before observed not in so great a degree as is commonly supposed.

The fourth item is alike applicable to the foreign and to the domestic manufacture. It is indeed more properly a *result* than a particular to be compared.

But with respect to all the remaining items, they are alone applicable to the foreign manufacture, and in the strictest sense extraordinaries, constituting a sum of extra charge on the foreign fabric, which cannot be estimated at less than from 15 to 30 percent on the cost of it at the manufactory.

This sum of extra charge may confidently be regarded as more than a counterpoise for the real difference in the price of labor, and is a satisfactory proof that manufactures may prosper in defiance of it in the United States. To the general allegation, connected with the circumstances of scarcity of hands and dearness of labor, that extensive manufactures can only grow out of a redundant or full population, it will be sufficient to answer generally that the fact has been otherwise—That the situation alleged to be an essential condition of success has not been that of several nations at periods when they had already attained to maturity in a variety of manufactures.

The supposed want of capital for the prosecution of manufactures in the United States is the most indefinite of the objections which are usually opposed to it.

It is very difficult to pronounce anything precise concerning the real extent of the monied capital of a country, and still more concerning the proportion which it bears to the objects that invite the employment of capital. It is not less difficult to pronounce how far the *effect* of any given quantity of money, as capital, or in other words as a medium for circulating the industry and property of a nation, may be increased by the very circumstance of the additional motion which is given to it by new objects of employment. That effect, like the momentum of descending bodies, may not improperly be represented as in a compound ratio to *mass* and *velocity*. It seems pretty certain that a given sum of money, in a situation in which the quick impulses of commercial activity were little felt, would appear inadequate to the circulation of as great a quantity of industry and property as in one in which their full influence was experienced.

It is not obvious why the same objection might not as well be made to external commerce as to manufactures, since it is manifest that our immense tracts of land occupied and unoccupied are capable of giving employment to more capital than is actually bestowed upon them. It is certain that the United States offer a vast field for the advantageous employment of capital, but it does not follow that there will not be found, in one way or another, a sufficient fund for the successful prosecution of any species of industry which is likely to prove truly beneficial.

The following considerations are of a nature to remove all inquietude on the score of want of capital.

The introduction of banks, as has been shown on another occasion, has a powerful tendency to extend the active capital of a country. Experience of the utility of these institutions is multiplying them in the United States. It is probable that they will be established wherever they can exist with advantage; and wherever they can be supported, if administered with prudence, they will add new energies to all pecuniary operations.

The aid of foreign capital may safely and with considerable latitude be taken into calculation. Its instrumentality has been long experienced in our external commerce, and it has begun to be felt in various other modes. Not only our funds but our agriculture and other internal improvements have been animated by it. It has already in a few instances extended even to our manufactures.

It is a well known fact that there are parts of Europe which have more capital than profitable domestic objects of employment. Hence, among other proofs, the large loans continually furnished to foreign states. And it is equally certain that the capital of other parts may find more profitable employment in the United States than at home. And notwithstanding there are weighty inducements to prefer the employment of capital at home even at less profit to an investment of it abroad though with greater gain, yet these inducements are overruled either by a deficiency of employment or by a very material difference in profit. Both these causes operate to produce a transfer of foreign capital to the United States. 'Tis certain that various objects in this country hold out advantages which are with difficulty to be equaled elsewhere; and under the increasingly favorable impressions which are entertained of our government, the attractions will become more and more strong. These impressions will prove a rich mine of prosperity to the country, if they are confirmed and strengthened by the progress of our affairs. And to secure this advantage, little more is now necessary than to foster industry and cultivate order and tranquility at home and abroad.

It is not impossible that there may be persons disposed to look with a jealous eye on the introduction of foreign capital, as if it were an instrument to deprive our own citizens of the profits of our own industry: But perhaps there never could be a more unreasonable jealousy. Instead of being viewed as a rival, it ought to be considered as a most valuable auxiliary, conducing to put in motion a greater quantity of productive labor and a greater portion of useful enterprise than could exist without it. It is at least evident that in a country situated like the United States, with an infinite fund of resources yet to be unfolded, every farthing of foreign capital which is laid out in internal ameliorations and in industrious establishments of a permanent nature is a precious acquisition.

And whatever be the objects which originally attract foreign capital, when once introduced it may be directed towards any purpose of beneficial exertion which is desired. And to detain it among us there can be no expedient so effectual as to enlarge the sphere within which it may be usefully employed: Though induced merely with views to speculations in the funds, it may afterwards be rendered subservient to the interests of agriculture, commerce, & manufactures.

But the attraction of foreign capital for the direct purpose of manufactures ought not to be deemed a chimerical expectation. There are already examples of it, as remarked in another place. And the examples, if the disposition be cultivated, can hardly fail to multiply. There are also instances of another kind which serve to strengthen the expectation. Enterprises for improving the public communications by cutting canals, opening the obstructions in rivers, and erecting bridges have received very material aid from the same source.

When the manufacturing capitalist of Europe shall advert to the many important advantages which have been intimated in the course of this report, he cannot but perceive very powerful inducements to a transfer of himself and his capital to the United States. Among the reflections which a most interesting peculiarity of situation is calculated to suggest, it cannot escape his observation, as a circumstance of moment in the calculation, that the progressive population and improvement of the United States ensure a continually increasing domestic demand for the fabrics which he shall produce, not to be affected by any external casualties or vicissitudes.

But while there are circumstances sufficiently strong to authorize a considerable degree of reliance on the aid of foreign capital towards the attainment of the object in view, it is satisfactory to have good grounds of assurance that there are domestic resources of themselves adequate to it. It happens that there is a species of capital actually existing within the United States which relieves from all inquietude on the score of want of capital—This is the funded debt.

The effect of a funded debt as a species of capital has been noticed upon a former occasion, but a more particular elucidation of the point seems to be required by the stress which is here laid upon it. This shall accordingly be attempted.

Public funds answer the purpose of capital from the estimation in which they are usually held by monied men, and consequently from the ease and dispatch with which they can be turned into money. This capacity of prompt convertibility into money causes a transfer of stock to be in a great number of cases equivalent to a payment in coin. And where it does not happen to suit the party who is to receive to accept a transfer of stock, the party who is to pay is never at a loss to find elsewhere a purchaser of his stock, who will furnish him in lieu of it with the coin of which he stands in need. Hence in a sound and settled state of the public funds a man possessed of a sum in them can embrace any scheme of business which offers with as much confidence as if he were possessed of an equal sum in coin.

This operation of public funds as capital is too obvious to be denied, but it is objected to the idea of their operating as an *augmentation* of the capital of the community that they serve to occasion the *destruction* of some other capital to an equal amount.

The capital which alone they can be supposed to destroy must consist of— The annual revenue, which is applied to the payment of interest on the debt and to the gradual redemption of the principal—The amount of the coin, which is employed in circulating the funds, or, in other words, in effecting the different alienations which they undergo.

But the following appears to be the true and accurate view of this matter.

1st. As to the point of the annual revenue requisite for payment of interest and redemption of principal.

As a determinate proportion will tend to perspicuity in the reasoning, let it be supposed that the annual revenue to be applied, corresponding with the modification of the 6 percent stock of the United States, is in the ratio of eight upon the hundred, that is in the first instance six on account of interest and two on account of principal.

Thus far it is evident that the capital destroyed to the capital created would bear no greater proportion than 8 to 100. There would be withdrawn from the total mass of other capitals a sum of eight dollars to be paid to the public creditor, while he would be possessed of a sum of one hundred dollars, ready to be applied to any purpose, to be embarked in any enterprise which might appear to him eligible. Here then the *augmentation* of capital, or the excess of that which is produced beyond that which is destroyed, is equal to ninety two dollars. To this conclusion it may be objected that the sum of eight dollars is to be withdrawn annually until the whole hundred is extinguished, and it may be inferred that in process of time a capital will be destroyed equal to that which is at first created.

But it is nevertheless true that during the whole of the interval between the creation of the capital of 100 dollars and its reduction to a sum not greater than that of the annual revenue appropriated to its redemption—there will be a greater active capital in existence than if no debt had been contracted. The sum drawn from other capitals *in any one year* will not exceed eight dollars, but there will be *at every instant of time* during the whole period in question a sum corresponding *with so much of the principal* as remains *unredeemed* in the hands of some person or other employed, or ready to be employed, in some profitable undertaking. There will therefore constantly be more capital in capacity to be employed than capital taken from employment. The excess for the first year has been stated to be ninety two dollars; it will diminish yearly, but there always will be an excess, until the principal of the debt is brought to a level with the *redeeming annuity*, that is, in the case which has been assumed by way of example, to *eight dollars*. The reality of this excess becomes palpable if it be supposed, as often happens, that the citizen of a foreign country imports into the United States 100 dollars for the purchase of an equal sum of public debt. Here is an absolute augmentation of the mass of circulating coin to the extent of 100 dollars. At the end of a year the foreigner is presumed to draw back eight dollars on account of his principal and interest, but he still leaves ninety two of his original deposit in circulation, as he in like manner leaves eighty four at the end of the second year, drawing back then also the annuity of eight dollars: And thus the matter proceeds, the capital left in circulation diminishing each year, and coming nearer to the level of the annuity drawn back. There are, however, some differences in the ultimate operation of the part of the debt which is purchased by foreigners and that which remains in the hands of citizens. But the general effect in each case, though in different degrees, is to add to the active capital of the country.

Hitherto the reasoning has proceeded on a concession of the position that there is a destruction of some other capital to the extent of the annuity appropriated to the payment of the interest and the redemption of the principal of the debt, but in this, too much has been conceded. There is at most a temporary transfer of some other capital to the amount of the annuity, from those who pay to the creditor who receives, which he again restores to the circulation to resume the offices of a capital. This he does either immediately by employing the money in some branch of Industry, or mediately by lending it to some other person who does so employ it or by spending it on his own maintenance. In either supposition there is no destruction of capital, there is nothing more than a suspension of its motion for a time; that is, while it is passing from the hands of those who pay into the public coffers, & thence through the public creditor into some other channel of circulation. When the payments of interest are periodical and quick and made by instrumentality of banks, the diversion or suspension of capital may almost be denominated momentary. Hence the deduction on this account is far less than it at first sight appears to be.

There is evidently, as far as regards the annuity, no destruction nor transfer of any other capital than that portion of the income of each individual, which goes to make up the annuity. The land which furnishes the farmer with the sum which he is to contribute remains the same; and the like may be observed of other capitals. Indeed as far as the tax, which is the object of contribution (as frequently happens, when it does not oppress by its weight) may have been a motive to *greater exertion* in any occupation; it may even serve to increase the contributory capital: This idea is not without importance in the general view of the subject.

It remains to see what further deduction ought to be made from the capital which is created by the existence of the debt on account of the coin which is employed in its circulation. This is susceptible of much less precise calculation than the article which has been just discussed. It is impossible to say what proportion of coin is necessary to carry on the alienations which any species of property usually undergoes. The quantity indeed varies according to circumstances. But it may still without hesitation be pronounced, from the quickness of the rotation, or rather of the transitions, that the *medium* of circulation always bears but a small proportion to the amount of the *property* circulated. And it is thence satisfactorily deducible that the coin employed in the negotiations of the funds and which serves to give them activity as capital is incomparably less than the sum of the debt negotiated for the purposes of business.

It ought not, however, to be omitted that the negotiation of the funds becomes itself a distinct business, which employs and by employing diverts a portion of the circulating coin from other pursuits. But making due allowance for this circumstance there is no reason to conclude that the effect of the diversion of coin in the whole operation bears any considerable proportion to the amount of the capital to which it gives activity. The sum of the debt in circulation is continually at the command of any useful enterprise—the coin itself which circulates it is never more than momentarily suspended from its ordinary functions. It experiences an incessant and rapid flux and reflux to and from the channels of industry to those of speculations in the funds.

There are strong circumstances in confirmation of this theory. The force of monied capital which has been displayed in Great Britain, and the height to which every species of industry has grown up under it, defy a solution from the quantity of coin which that kingdom has ever possessed. Accordingly it has been coeval with its funding system, the prevailing opinion of the men of business, and of the generality of the most sagacious theorists of that country, that the operation of the public funds as capital has contributed to the effect in question. Among ourselves appearances thus far favor the same conclusion. Industry in general seems to have been reanimated. There are symptoms indicating an extension of our commerce. Our navigation has certainly of late had a considerable spring, and there appears to be in many parts of the Union a command of capital which till lately, since the revolution at least, was unknown. But it is at the same time to be acknowledged that other circumstances have concurred (and in a great degree) in producing the present state of things, and that the appearances are not yet sufficiently decisive to be entirely relied upon.

In the question under discussion it is important to distinguish between an *absolute increase of capital, or an accession of real wealth*, and *an artificial increase of capital*, as an engine of business, or as an instrument of industry and commerce. In the first sense, a funded debt has no pretensions to being deemed an increase of capital; in the last it has pretensions which are not easy to be controverted. Of a similar nature is bank credit and in an inferior degree every species of private credit.

But though a funded debt is not in the first instance an absolute increase of capital, or an augmentation of real wealth, yet by serving as a new power in the operation of industry it has within certain bounds a tendency to increase the real wealth of a community in like manner as money borrowed by a thrifty farmer to be laid out in the improvement of his farm may, in the end, add to his stock of real riches.

There are respectable individuals who from a just aversion to an accumulation of public debt are unwilling to concede to it any kind of utility, who can discern no good to alleviate the ill with which they suppose it pregnant, who cannot be persuaded that it ought in any sense to be viewed as an increase of capital lest it should be inferred that the more debt the more capital, the greater the burdens the greater the blessings of the community.

But it interests the public councils to estimate every object as it truly is, to appreciate how far the good in any measure is compensated by the ill, or the ill by the good. Either of them is seldom unmixed.

Neither will it follow that an accumulation of debt is desirable because a certain degree of it operates as capital. There may be a plethora in the political as in the natural body; there may be a state of things in which any such artificial capital is unnecessary. The debt too may be swelled to such a size as that the greatest part of it may cease to be useful as a capital, serving only to pamper the dissipation of idle and dissolute individuals: as that the sums required to pay the interest upon it may become oppressive and beyond the means which a government can employ, consistently with its tranquility, to raise them; as that the resources of taxation, to face the debt, may have been strained too far to admit of extensions adequate to exigencies which regard the public safety.

Where this critical point is cannot be pronounced, but it is impossible to believe that there is not such a point.

And as the vicissitudes of nations beget a perpetual tendency to the accumulation of debt, there ought to be in every government a perpetual, anxious, and unceasing effort to reduce that which at any time exists, as fast as shall be practicable consistently with integrity and good faith.

Reasonings on a subject comprehending ideas so abstract and complex, so little reducible to precise calculation, as those which enter into the question just discussed are always attended with a danger of running into fallacies. Due allowance ought therefore to be made for this possibility. But as far as the nature of the subject admits of it, there appears to be satisfactory ground for a belief that the public funds operate as a resource of capital to the citizens of the United States, and, if they are a resource at all, it is an extensive one...

There remains to be noticed an objection to the encouragement of manufactures of a nature different from those which question the probability of success. This is derived from its supposed tendency to give a monopoly of advantages to particular classes at the expense of the rest of the community, who, it is affirmed, would be able to procure the requisite supplies of manufactured articles on better terms from foreigners than from our own citizens, and who, it is alleged, are reduced to a necessity of paying an enhanced price for whatever they want by every measure which obstructs the free competition of foreign commodities.

It is not an unreasonable supposition that measures which serve to abridge the free competition of foreign articles have a tendency to occasion an enhancement of prices, and it is not to be denied that such is the effect in a number of cases; but the fact does not uniformly correspond with the theory. A reduction of prices has in several instances immediately succeeded the establishment of a domestic manufacture. Whether it be that foreign manufacturers endeavor to supplant by underselling our own, or whatever else be the cause, the effect has been such as is stated, and the reverse of what might have been expected.

But though it were true that the immediate and certain effect of regulations controlling the competition of foreign with domestic fabrics was an increase of price, it is universally true that the contrary is the ultimate effect with every successful manufacture. When a domestic manufacture has attained to perfection, and has engaged in the prosecution of it a competent number of persons, it invariably becomes cheaper. Being free from the heavy charges which attend the importation of foreign commodities, it can be afforded, and accordingly seldom or never fails to be sold cheaper, in process of time, than was the foreign article for which it is a substitute. The internal competition which takes place soon does away everything like monopoly, and by degrees reduces the price of the article to the *minimum* of a reasonable profit on the capital employed. This accords with the reason of the thing and with experience.

Whence it follows that it is the interest of a community, with a view to eventual and permanent economy, to encourage the growth of manufactures. In a national view, a temporary enhancement of price must always be well compensated by a permanent reduction of it.

It is a reflection which may with propriety be indulged here that this eventual diminution of the prices of manufactured articles, which is the result of internal manufacturing establishments, has a direct and very important tendency to benefit agriculture. It enables the farmer to procure with a smaller quantity of his labor the manufactured produce of which he stands in need, and consequently increases the value of his income and property.

The objections which are commonly made to the expediency of encouraging, and to the probability of succeeding, in manufacturing pursuits in the United States having now been discussed, the considerations which have appeared in the course of the discussion recommending that species of industry to the patronage of the government will be materially strengthened by a few general and some particular topics which have been naturally reserved for subsequent notice.

I. There seems to be a moral certainty that the trade of a country which is both manufacturing and agricultural will be more lucrative and prosperous than that of a country which is merely agricultural.

One reason for this is found in that general effort of nations (which has been already mentioned) to procure from their own soils the articles of prime necessity requisite to their own consumption and use, and which serves to render their demand for a foreign supply of such articles in a great degree occasional and contingent. Hence, while the necessities of nations exclusively devoted to agriculture for the fabrics of manufacturing states are constant and regular, the wants of the latter for the products of the former are liable to very considerable fluctuations and interruptions. The great inequalities resulting from difference of seasons have been elsewhere remarked: This uniformity of demand on one side, and unsteadiness of it on the other, must necessarily have a tendency to cause the general course of the exchange of commodities between the parties to turn to the disadvantage of the merely agricultural states. Peculiarity of situation, a climate and soil adapted to the production of peculiar commodities, may sometimes contradict the rule; but there is every reason to believe that it will be found in the main a just one.

Another circumstance which gives a superiority of commercial advantages to states that manufacture as well as cultivate consists in the more numerous attractions which a more diversified market offers to foreign customers, and greater scope which it affords to mercantile enterprise. It is a position of indisputable truth in commerce, depending too on very obvious reasons, that the greatest resort will ever be to those marts where commodities, while equally abundant, are most various. Each difference of kind holds out an additional inducement. And it is a position not less clear that the field of enterprise must be enlarged to the merchants of a country in proportion to the variety as well as the abundance of commodities which they find at home for exportation to foreign markets.

A third circumstance, perhaps not inferior to either of the other two, conferring the superiority which has been stated has relation to the stagnations of demand for certain commodities which at some time or other interfere more or less with the sale of all. The nation which can bring to market but few articles is likely to be more quickly and sensibly affected by such stagnations than one which is always possessed of a great variety of commodities. The former frequently finds too great a proportion of its stock of materials for sale or exchange lying on hand—or is obliged to make injurious sacrifices to supply its wants of foreign articles which are *numerous* and *urgent* in proportion to the smallness of the number of its own. The latter commonly finds itself indemnified by the high prices of some articles for the low prices of others—and the prompt and advantageous sale of those articles which are in demand enables its merchant the better to wait for a favorable change in respect to those which are not. There is ground to believe that a difference of situation in this particular has immensely different effects upon the wealth and prosperity of nations.

From these circumstances collectively two important inferences are to be drawn: one, that there is always a higher probability of a favorable balance of trade in regard to countries in which manufactures founded on the basis of a thriving agriculture flourish than in regard to those which are confined wholly or almost wholly to agriculture; the other (which is also a consequence of the first), that countries of the former description are likely to possess more pecuniary wealth, or money, than those of the latter.

Facts appear to correspond with this conclusion. The importations of manufactured supplies seem invariably to drain the merely agricultural people of their wealth. Let the situation of the manufacturing countries of Europe be compared in this particular with that of countries which only cultivate, and the disparity will be striking. Other causes, it is true, help to account for this disparity between some of them, and among these causes the relative state of agriculture; but between others of them the most prominent circumstance of dissimilitude arises from the comparative state of manufactures. In corroboration of the same idea, it ought not to escape remark that the West India Islands, the soils of which are the most fertile, and the nation which in the greatest degree supplies the rest of the world with the precious metals, exchange to a loss with almost every other country.

As far as experience at home may guide, it will lead to the same conclusion. Previous to the revolution, the quantity of coin possessed by the colonies which now compose the United States appeared to be inadequate to their circulation; and their debt to Great Britain was progressive. Since the Revolution, the states in which manufactures have most increased have recovered fastest from the injuries of the late war and abound most in pecuniary resources.

It ought to be admitted, however, in this as in the preceding case, that causes irrelative to the state of manufactures account, in a degree, for the phenomena remarked. The continual progress of new settlements has a natural tendency to occasion an unfavorable balance of trade, though it indemnifies for the inconvenience by that increase of the national capital which flows from the conversion of waste into improved lands: And the different degrees of external commerce which are carried on by the different states may make material differences in the comparative state of their wealth. The first circumstance has reference to the deficiency of coin and the increase of debt previous to the revolution, the last to the advantages which the most manufacturing states appear to have enjoyed, over the others, since the termination of the late war.

But the uniform appearance of an abundance of specie, as the concomitant of a flourishing state of manufactures, and of the reverse, where they do not prevail, afford a strong presumption of their favorable operation upon the wealth of a country.

Not only the wealth but the independence and security of a country appear to be materially connected with the prosperity of manufactures. Every nation with a view to those great objects ought to endeavor to possess within itself all the essentials of national supply. These comprise the means of *subsistence*, *habitation*, *clothing*, and *defense*.

The possession of these is necessary to the perfection of the body politic, to the safety as well as to the welfare of the society; the want of either is the want of an important organ of political life and motion; and in the various crises which await a state, it must severely feel the effects of any such deficiency. The extreme embarrassments of the United States during the late war, from an incapacity of supplying themselves, are still matter of keen recollection: A future war might be expected again to exemplify the mischiefs and dangers of a situation to which that incapacity is still in too great a degree applicable, unless changed by timely and vigorous exertion. To effect this change as fast as shall be prudent merits all the attention and all the zeal of our public councils; 'tis the next great work to be accomplished.

The want of a navy to protect our external commerce, as long as it shall continue, must render it a peculiarly precarious reliance for the supply of essential articles, and must serve to strengthen prodigiously the arguments in favor of manufactures.

To these general considerations are added some of a more particular nature.

Our distance from Europe, the great fountain of manufactured supply, subjects us in the existing state of things to inconvenience and loss in two ways.

The bulkiness of those commodities which are the chief productions of the soil necessarily imposes very heavy charges on their transportation to distant markets. These charges, in the cases in which the nations to whom our products are sent maintain a competition in the supply of their own markets, principally fall upon us and form material deductions from the primitive value of the articles furnished. The charges on manufactured supplies brought from Europe are greatly enhanced by the same circumstance of distance. These charges, again, in the cases in which our own industry maintains no competition in our own markets, also principally fall upon us, and are an additional cause of extraordinary deduction from the primitive value of our own products, these being the materials of exchange for the foreign fabrics which we consume.

The equality and moderation of individual property and the growing settlements of new districts occasion in this country an unusual demand for coarse manufactures, the charges of which being greater in proportion to their greater bulk augment the disadvantage which has been just described.

As in most countries domestic supplies maintain a very considerable competition with such foreign productions of the soil as are imported for sale; if the extensive establishment of manufactories in the United States does not create a similar competition in respect to manufactured articles, it appears to be clearly deducible from the considerations which have been mentioned that they must sustain a double loss in their exchanges with foreign nations, strongly conducive to an unfavorable balance of trade, and very prejudicial to their interests.

These disadvantages press with no small weight on the landed interest of the country. In seasons of peace they cause a serious deduction from the intrinsic value of the products of the soil. In the time of a war, which should either involve ourselves or another nation possessing a considerable share of our carrying trade, the charges on the transportation of our commodities, bulky as most of them are, could hardly fail to prove a grievous burthen to the farmer, while obliged to depend in so great degree as he now does upon foreign markets for the vent of the surplus of his labor.

As far as the prosperity of the fisheries of the United States is impeded by the want of an adequate market there arises another special reason for desiring the extension of manufactures. Besides the fish, which in many places would be likely to make a part of the subsistence of the persons employed, it is known that the oils, bones, and skins of marine animals are of extensive use in various manufactures. Hence the prospect of an additional demand for the produce of the fisheries.

One more point of view only remains in which to consider the expediency of encouraging manufactures in the United States.

It is not uncommon to meet with an opinion that though the promoting of manufactures may be the interest of a part of the Union, it is contrary to that of another part. The northern & southern regions are sometimes represented as having adverse interests in this respect. Those are called manufacturing, these agricultural states; and a species of opposition is imagined to subsist between the manufacturing and agricultural interests.

This idea of an opposition between those two interests is the common error of the early periods of every country, but experience gradually dissipates it. Indeed they are perceived so often to succor and to befriend each other that they come at length to be considered as one: a supposition which has been frequently abused and is not universally true. Particular encouragements of particular manufactures may be of a nature to sacrifice the interests of landholders to those of manufacturers; but it is nevertheless a maxim well established by experience, and generally acknowledged where there has been sufficient experience, that the *aggregate* prosperity of manufactures and the *aggregate* prosperity of agriculture are intimately connected. In the course of the discussion which has had place, various weighty considerations have been adduced operating in support of that maxim. Perhaps the superior steadiness of the demand of a domestic market for the surplus produce of the soil is alone a convincing argument of its truth.

Ideas of a contrariety of interests between the northern and southern regions of the Union are in the main as unfounded as they are mischievous. The diversity of circumstances on which such contrariety is usually predicated authorizes a directly contrary conclusion. Mutual wants constitute one of the strongest links of political connection, and the extent of these bears a natural proportion to the diversity in the means of mutual supply.

Suggestions of an opposite complexion are ever to be deplored as unfriendly to the steady pursuit of one great common cause and to the perfect harmony of all the parts.

In proportion as the mind is accustomed to trace the intimate connection of interest which subsists between all the parts of a society united under the *same* government—the infinite variety of channels which serve to circulate the prosperity of each to and through the rest—in that proportion will it be little apt to be disturbed by solicitudes and apprehensions which originate in local discriminations. It is a truth as important as it is agreeable, and one to which it is not easy to imagine exceptions, that everything tending to establish *substantial* and *permanent order* in the affairs of a country, to increase the total mass of industry and opulence, is ultimately beneficial to every part of it. On the credit of this great truth an acquiescence may safely be accorded from every quarter to all institutions & arrangements which promise a confirmation of public order and an augmentation of national resource.

But there are more particular considerations which serve to fortify the idea that the encouragement of manufactures is the interest of all parts of the Union. If the northern and middle states should be the principal scenes of such establishments, they would immediately benefit the more southern by creating a demand for productions, some of which they have in common with the other states, and others of which are either peculiar to them, or more abundant, or of better quality than elsewhere. These productions principally are timber, flax, hemp, cotton, wool, raw silk, indigo, iron, lead, furs, hides, skins and coals. Of these articles cotton & indigo are peculiar to the southern states, as are hitherto *lead & coal.* Flax and hemp are or may be raised in greater abundance there than in the more northern states; and the wool of Virginia is said to be of better quality than that of any other state, a circumstance rendered the more probable by the reflection that Virginia embraces the same latitudes with the finest wool countries of Europe. The climate of the south is also better adapted to the production of silk.

The extensive cultivation of cotton can perhaps hardly be expected but from the previous establishment of domestic manufactories of the article, and the surest encouragement and vent for the others would result from similar establishments in respect to them.

If then it satisfactorily appears that it is the interest of the United States generally to encourage manufactures, it merits particular attention that there are circumstances which render the present a critical moment for entering with zeal upon the important business. The effort cannot fail to be materially seconded by a considerable and increasing influx of money in consequence of foreign speculations in the funds—and by the disorders which exist in different parts of Europe.

The first circumstance not only facilitates the execution of manufacturing enterprises, but it indicates them as a necessary mean to turn the thing itself to advantage and to prevent its being eventually an evil. If useful employment be not found for the money of foreigners brought to the country to be invested in purchases of the public debt, it will quickly be re-exported to defray the expense of an extraordinary consumption of foreign luxuries; and distressing drains of our specie may hereafter be experienced to pay the interest and redeem the principal of the purchased debt.

This useful employment too ought to be of a nature to produce solid and permanent improvements. If the money merely serves to give a temporary spring to foreign commerce, as it cannot procure new and lasting outlets for the products of the country, there will be no real or durable advantage gained. As far as it shall find its way in agricultural ameliorations, in opening canals, and in similar improvements, it will be productive of substantial utility. But there is reason to doubt whether in such channels it is likely to find sufficient employment, and still more whether many of those who possess it would be as readily attracted to objects of this nature as to manufacturing pursuits, which bear greater analogy to those to which they are accustomed and to the spirit generated by them.

To open the one field as well as the other will at least secure a better prospect of useful employment for whatever accession of money there has been or may be.

There is at the present juncture a certain fermentation of mind, a certain activity of speculation and enterprise, which if properly directed may be made subservient to useful purposes; but which if left entirely to itself, may be attended with pernicious effects.

The disturbed state of Europe inclining its citizens to emigration, the requisite workmen will be more easily acquired than at another time; and the effect of multiplying the opportunities of employment to those who emigrate may be an increase of the number and extent of valuable acquisitions to the population arts and industry of the country. To find pleasure in the calamities of other nations would be criminal; but to benefit ourselves, by opening an asylum to those who suffer in consequence of them, is as justifiable as it is politic.

A full view having now been taken of the inducements to the promotion of manufactures in the United States, accompanied with an examination of the principal objections which are commonly urged *in opposition*, it is proper in the next place to consider the means by which it may be effected, as introductory to a specification of the objects which in the present state of things appear the most fit to be encouraged, and of the particular measures which it may be advisable to adopt, in respect to each.

In order to a better judgment of the means proper to be resorted to by the United States, it will be of use to advert to those which have been employed with success in other countries. The principal of these are.

I. Protecting duties—or duties on those foreign articles which are the rivals of the domestic ones intended to be encouraged.

Duties of this nature evidently amount to a virtual bounty on the domestic fabrics, since by enhancing the charges on foreign articles they enable the national manufacturers to undersell all their foreign competitors. The propriety of this species of encouragement need not be dwelt upon, as it is not only a clear result from the numerous topics which have been suggested, but is sanctioned by the laws of the United States in a variety of instances; it has the additional recommendation of being a resource of revenue. Indeed all the duties imposed on imported articles, though with an exclusive view to revenue, have the effect in contemplation, and except where they fall on raw materials wear a beneficent aspect towards the manufactures of the country.

II. Prohibitions of rival articles or duties equivalent to prohibitions.

This is another and an efficacious mean of encouraging national manufactures, but in general it is only fit to be employed when a manufacture has made such a progress and is in so many hands as to insure a due competition and an adequate supply on reasonable terms. Of duties equivalent to prohibitions, there are examples in the laws of the United States, and there are other cases to which the principle may be advantageously extended, but they are not numerous.

Considering a monopoly of the domestic market to its own manufacturers as the reigning policy of manufacturing nations, a similar policy on the part of the United States in every proper instance is dictated, it might almost be said, by the principles of distributive justice; certainly by the duty of endeavoring to secure to their own citizens a reciprocity of advantages.

III. Prohibitions of the exportation of the materials of manufactures.

The desire of securing a cheap and plentiful supply for the national workmen, and, where the article is either peculiar to the country, or of peculiar quality there, the jealousy of enabling foreign workmen to rival those of the nation with its own materials, are the leading motives to this species of regulation. It ought not to be affirmed that it is in no instance proper, but it is certainly one which ought to be adopted with great circumspection and only in very plain cases. It is seen at once that its immediate operation is to abridge the demand and keep down the price of the produce of some other branch of industry, generally speaking of agriculture, to the prejudice of those who carry it on; and though if it be really essential to the prosperity of any very important national manufacture, it may happen that those who are injured in the first instance may be eventually indemnified by the superior steadiness of an extensive domestic market, depending on that prosperity: yet in a matter in which there is so much room for nice and difficult combinations, in which such opposite considerations combat each other, prudence seems to dictate that the expedient in question ought to be indulged with a sparing hand.

IV. Pecuniary bounties.

This has been found one of the most efficacious means of encouraging manufactures, and it is in some views the best. Though it has not yet been practiced upon by the government of the United States (unless the allowance on the exportation of dried and pickled fish and salted meat could be considered as a bounty), and though it is less favored by public opinion than some other modes.

Its advantages, are these—

1. It is a species of encouragement more positive and direct than any other, and for that very reason has a more immediate tendency to stimulate and uphold new enterprises, increasing the chances of profit and diminishing the risks of loss in the first attempts.

2. It avoids the inconvenience of a temporary augmentation of price, which is incident to some other modes, or it produces it to a less degree, either by making no addition to the charges on the rival foreign article, as in the case of protecting duties, or by making a smaller addition. The first happens when the fund for the bounty is derived from a different object (which may or may not increase the price of some other article, according to the nature of that object), the second when the fund is derived from the same or a similar object of foreign manufacture. One percent duty on the foreign article converted into a bounty on the domestic will have an equal effect with a duty of two percent, exclusive of such bounty; and the price of the foreign commodity is liable to be raised in the one case in the proportion of 1 percent, in the other, in that of two percent. Indeed the bounty when drawn from another source is calculated to promote a reduction of price, because, without laying any new charge on the foreign article, it serves to introduce a competition with it, and to increase the total quantity of the article in the market.

3. Bounties have not, like high protecting duties, a tendency to produce scarcity. An increase of price is not always the immediate, though where the progress

of a domestic manufacture does not counteract a rise, it is commonly the ultimate effect of an additional duty. In the interval between the laying of the duty and a proportional increase of price, it may discourage importation by interfering with the profits to be expected from the sale of the article.

4. Bounties are sometimes not only the best but the only proper expedient for uniting the encouragement of a new object of agriculture with that of a new object of manufacture. It is the interest of the farmer to have the production of the raw material promoted by counteracting the interference of the foreign material of the same kind. It is the interest of the manufacturer to have the material abundant and cheap. If, prior to the domestic production of the material in sufficient quantity to supply the manufacturer on good terms, a duty be laid upon the importation of it from abroad, with a view to promote the raising of it at home, the interests both of the farmer and manufacturer will be disserved. By either destroying the requisite supply, or raising the price of the article beyond what can be afforded to be given for it by the conductor of an infant manufacture, it is abandoned or fails; and there being no domestic manufactories to create a demand for the raw material which is raised by the farmer, it is in vain that the competition of the like foreign article may have been destroyed.

It cannot escape notice that a duty upon the importation of an article can no otherwise aid the domestic production of it than giving the latter greater advantages in the home market. It can have no influence upon the advantageous sale of the article produced in foreign markets, no tendency, therefore, to promote its exportation.

The true way to conciliate these two interests is to lay a duty on foreign *manufactures* of the material the growth of which is desired to be encouraged, and to apply the produce of that duty by way of bounty, either upon the production of the material itself, or upon its manufacture at home, or upon both. In this disposition of the thing the manufacturer commences his enterprise under every advantage which is attainable as to quantity or price of the raw material: And the farmer, if the bounty be immediately to him, is enabled by it to enter into a successful competition with the foreign material; if the bounty be to the manufacturer on so much of the domestic material as he consumes, the operation is nearly the same; he has a motive of interest to prefer the domestic commodity, if of equal quality, even at a higher price than the foreign, so long as the difference of price is anything short of the bounty which is allowed upon the article.

Except the simple and ordinary kinds of household manufactures, or those for which there are very commanding local advantages, pecuniary bounties are in most cases indispensable to the introduction of a new branch. A stimulus and a support not less powerful and direct is, generally speaking, essential to the overcoming of the obstacles which arise from the competitions of superior skill and maturity elsewhere. Bounties are especially essential in regard to articles upon which those foreigners who have been accustomed to supply a country are in the practice of granting them.

The continuance of bounties on manufactures long established must almost always be of questionable policy: Because a presumption would arise in every such case that there were natural and inherent impediments to success. But in new undertakings they are as justifiable as they are oftentimes necessary.

There is a degree of prejudice against bounties from an appearance of giving away the public money without an immediate consideration, and from a supposition that they serve to enrich particular classes at the expense of the community.

But neither of these sources of dislike will bear a serious examination. There is no purpose to which public money can be more beneficially applied than to the acquisition of a new and useful branch of industry, no consideration more valuable than a permanent addition to the general stock of productive labor.

As to the second source of objection, it equally lies against other modes of encouragement which are admitted to be eligible. As often as a duty upon a foreign article makes an addition to its price, it causes an extra expense to the community for the benefit of the domestic manufacturer. A bounty does no more: But it is the interest of the society in each case to submit to a temporary expense, which is more than compensated by an increase of industry and wealth, by an augmentation of resources and independence, & by the circumstance of eventual cheapness, which has been noticed in another place.

It would deserve attention, however, in the employment of this species of encouragement in the United States, as a reason for moderating the degree of it in the instances in which it might be deemed eligible, that the great distance of this country from Europe imposes very heavy charges on all the fabrics which are brought from thence, amounting from 15 to 30 percent on their value, according to their bulk.

A question has been made concerning the constitutional right of the government of the United States to apply this species of encouragement, but there is certainly no good foundation for such a question. The National legislature has express authority "To lay and Collect taxes, duties, imposts and excises, to pay the debts and provide for the *Common defence* and *general welfare*," with no other qualifications than that "all duties, imposts and excises, shall be *uniform* throughout the United States," that no capitation or other direct tax shall be laid unless in proportion to numbers ascertained by a census or enumeration taken on the principles prescribed in the Constitution, and that "no tax or duty shall be laid on articles exported from any state." These three qualifications excepted, the power to *raise money* is *plenary* and *indefinite;* and the objects to which it may be *appropriated* are no less comprehensive than the payment of the public debts and the providing for the common defense and "*general Welfare.*" The terms "*general Welfare*" were doubtless intended to signify more than was expressed or imported in those which preceded; otherwise numerous exigencies incident to the affairs of a nation would have been left without a provision. The phrase is as comprehensive as any that could have been used; because it was not fit that the constitutional authority of the Union to appropriate its revenues should have been restricted within narrower limits than the "General Welfare" and because this necessarily embraces a vast variety of particulars, which are susceptible neither of specification nor of definition.

It is therefore of necessity left to the discretion of the national legislature to pronounce upon the objects which concern the general welfare, and for which under that description an appropriation of money is requisite and proper. And there seems to be no room for a doubt that whatever concerns the general interests of *learning*, of *agriculture*, of *manufactures*, and of *commerce* are within the sphere of the national councils *as far as regards an application of money*.

The only qualification of the generality of the phrase in question which seems to be admissible, is this—That the object to which an appropriation of money is to be made be *general* and not *local*, its operation extending in fact, or by possibility, throughout the Union, and not being confined to a particular spot.

No objection ought to arise to this construction from a supposition that it would imply a power to do whatever else should appear to Congress conducive to the general welfare. A power to appropriate money with this latitude which is granted too in *express terms* would not carry a power to do any other thing not authorized in the Constitution, either expressly or by fair implication.

V. Premiums

These are of a nature allied to bounties, though distinguishable from them in some important features.

Bounties are applicable to the whole quantity of an article produced, or manufactured, or exported, and involve a correspondent expense. Premiums serve to reward some particular excellence or superiority, some extraordinary exertion or skill, and are dispensed only in a small number of cases. But their effect is to stimulate general effort. Contrived so as to be both honorary and lucrative, they address themselves to different passions, touching the chords as well of emulation as of interest. They are accordingly a very economical mean of exciting the enterprise of a whole community.

There are various societies in different countries whose object is the dispensation of premiums for the encouragement of *agriculture*, *arts*, *manufactures*, and *commerce*; and though they are for the most part voluntary associations, with comparatively slender funds, their utility has been immense. Much has been done by this mean in Great Britain: Scotland in particular owes materially to it a prodigious amelioration of condition. From a similar establishment in the United States, supplied and supported by the government of the Union, vast benefits might reasonably be expected. Some further ideas on this head shall accordingly be submitted in the conclusion of this report.

VI. The Exemption of the materials of manufactures from duty.

The policy of that exemption as a general rule, particularly in reference to new establishments, is obvious. It can hardly ever be advisable to add the obstructions of fiscal burdens to the difficulties which naturally embarrass a new manufacture; and where it is matured and in condition to become an object of revenue, it is generally speaking better that the fabric than the material should be the subject of taxation. Ideas of proportion between the quantum of the tax and the value of the article can be more easily adjusted in the former than in the latter case. An argument for exemptions of this kind in the United States is to be derived from the practice, as far as their necessities have permitted, of those nations whom we are to meet as competitors in our own and in foreign markets.

There are, however, exceptions to it, of which some examples will be given under the next head.

The laws of the Union afford instances of the observance of the policy here recommended, but it will probably be found advisable to extend it to some other cases. Of a nature bearing some affinity to that policy is the regulation which exempts from duty the tools and implements, as well as the books, cloths, and household furniture of foreign artists who come to reside in the United States, an advantage already secured to them by the laws of the Union, and which it is in every view proper to continue.

VII. Drawbacks of the duties which are imposed on the materials of manufactures.

It has already been observed as a general rule that duties on those materials ought with certain exceptions to be forborne. Of these exceptions, three cases occur which may serve as examples—one—where the material is itself an object of general or extensive consumption and a fit and productive source of revenue: Another, where a manufacture of a simpler kind, the competition of which with a like domestic article is desired to be restrained, partakes of the nature of a raw material from being capable by a further process to be converted into a manufacture of a different kind, the introduction or growth of which is desired to be encouraged; a third where the material itself is a production of the country and in sufficient abundance to furnish cheap and plentiful supply to the national manufacturer.

Under the first description comes the article of molasses. It is not only a fair object of revenue, but being a sweet it is just that the consumers of it should pay a duty as well as the consumers of sugar.

Cottons and linens in their white state fall under the second description. A duty upon such as are imported is proper to promote the domestic manufacture of similar articles in the same state. A drawback of that duty is proper to encourage the printing and staining at home of those which are brought from abroad: When the first of these manufactures has attained sufficient maturity in a country, to furnish a full supply for the second the utility of the drawback ceases.

The article of hemp either now does or may be expected soon to exemplify the third case in the United States.

Where duties on the materials of manufactures are not laid for the purpose of preventing a competition with some domestic production, the same reasons which recommend, as a general rule, the exemption of those materials from duties would recommend as a like general rule the allowance of drawbacks in favor of the manufacturer. Accordingly such drawbacks are familiar in countries which systematically pursue the business of manufactures, which furnishes an argument for the observance of a similar policy in the United States; and the idea has been adopted by the laws of the Union in the instances of salt and molasses. It is believed that it will be found advantageous to extend it to some other articles.

VIII. The encouragement of new inventions and discoveries at home, and of the introduction into the United States of such as may have been made in other countries, particularly those which relate to machinery.

This is among the most useful and unexceptionable of the aids which can be given to manufactures. The usual means of that encouragement are pecuniary rewards and, for a time, exclusive privileges. The first must be employed according to the occasion and the utility of the invention or discovery: For the last, so far as respects "authors and inventors," provision has been made by law. But it is desirable in regard to improvements and secrets of extraordinary value to be able to extend the same benefit to introducers as well as authors and inventors, a policy which has been practiced with advantage in other countries. Here, however, as in some other cases, there is cause to regret that the competency of the authority of the national government to the *good* which might be done is not without a question. Many aids might be given to industry, many internal improvements of primary magnitude might be promoted, by an authority operating throughout the Union, which cannot be effected as well, if at all, by an authority confined within the limits of a single state.

But if the legislature of the Union cannot do all the good that might be wished, it is at least desirable that all may be done which is practicable. Means for promoting the introduction of foreign improvements, though less efficaciously than might be accomplished with more adequate authority, will form a part of the plan intended to be submitted in the close of this report.

It is customary with manufacturing nations to prohibit, under severe penalties, the exportation of implements and machines which they have either invented or improved. There are already objects for a similar regulation in the United States; and others may be expected to occur from time to time. The adoption of it seems to be dictated by the principle of reciprocity. Greater liberality, in such respects, might better comport with the general spirit of the country; but a selfish and exclusive policy in other quarters will not always permit the free indulgence of a spirit which would place us upon an unequal footing. As far as prohibitions tend to prevent foreign competitors from deriving the benefit of the improvements made at home, they tend to increase the advantages of those by whom they may have been introduced and operate as an encouragement to exertion.

IX. Judicious regulations for the inspection of manufactured commodities.

This is not among the least important of the means by which the prosperity of manufactures may be promoted. It is indeed in many cases one of the most essential. Contributing to prevent frauds upon consumers at home and exporters to foreign countries—to improve the quality & preserve the character of the national manufactures, it cannot fail to aid the expeditious and advantageous sale of them, and to serve as a guard against successful competition from other quarters. The reputation of the flour and lumber of some states and of the potash of others has been established by an attention to this point. And the like good name might be procured for those articles, wheresoever produced, by a judicious and uniform system of inspection throughout the ports of the

United States. A like system might also be extended with advantage to other commodities.

X. The facilitating of pecuniary remittances from place to place is a point of considerable moment to trade in general, and to manufactures in particular, by rendering more easy the purchase of raw materials and provisions and the payment for manufactured supplies. A general circulation of bank paper, which is to be expected from the institution lately established, will be a most valuable mean to this end. But much good would also accrue from some additional provisions respecting inland bills of exchange. If those drawn in one state payable in another were made negotiable everywhere, and interest and damages allowed in case of protest, it would greatly promote negotiations between the citizens of different states by rendering them more secure, and with it the convenience and advantage of the merchants and manufacturers of each.

XI. The facilitating of the transportation of commodities.

Improvements favoring this object intimately concern all the domestic interests of a community, but they may without impropriety be mentioned as having an important relation to manufactures. There is perhaps scarcely anything which has been better calculated to assist the manufactures of Great Britain than the ameliorations of the public roads of that kingdom, and the great progress which has been of late made in opening canals. Of the former, the United States stand much in need, and for the latter they present uncommon facilities.

The symptoms of attention to the improvement of inland navigation, which have lately appeared in some quarters, must fill with pleasure every breast warmed with a true zeal for the prosperity of the country. These examples, it is to be hoped, will stimulate the exertions of the government and the citizens of every state. There can certainly be no object more worthy of the cares of the local administrations, and it were to be wished that there was no doubt of the power of the national government to lend its direct aid on a comprehensive plan. This is one of those improvements which could be prosecuted with more efficacy by the whole than by any part or parts of the Union. There are cases in which the general interest will be in danger to be sacrificed to the collision of some supposed local interests. Jealousies in matters of this kind are as apt to exist as they are apt to be erroneous.

The following remarks are sufficiently judicious and pertinent to deserve a literal quotation. "Good roads, canals, and navigable rivers, by diminishing the expense of carriage, put the *remote parts of a country* more nearly upon a level with those in the neighborhood of the town. They are *upon that account* the greatest of all improvements. They encourage the cultivation of the remote, which must always be the most extensive circle of the country. They are advantageous to the town by breaking down the monopoly of the country in its neighborhood. They are advantageous *even to that part of the country*. Though they introduce some rival commodities into the old market, they open many new markets to its produce. Monopoly besides is a great enemy to good management, which can never be universally established but in consequence of that free and universal competition which forces everybody to have recourse to it for the sake of self defense. It is not more than fifty years ago that *some of the countries in the neighborhood of London petitioned the Parliament against the extension of the turnpike roads into the remoter counties. Those remoter counties, they pretended, from the cheapness of labor, would be able to sell their grass and corn cheaper in the London market than themselves, and they would thereby reduce their rents and ruin their cultivation.* Their rents however have risen and their cultivation has been improved, since that time."[3]

Specimens of a spirit similar to that which governed the counties here spoken of present themselves too frequently to the eye of an impartial observer and render it a wish of patriotism that the body in this country in whose councils a local or partial spirit is least likely to predominate were at liberty to pursue and promote the general interest in those instances in which there might be danger of the interference of such a spirit.

The foregoing are the principal of the means by which the growth of manufactures is ordinarily promoted. It is, however, not merely necessary that the measures of government which have a direct view to manufactures should be calculated to assist and protect them, but that those which only collaterally affect them in the general course of the administration should be guarded from any peculiar tendency to injure them.

There are certain species of taxes which are apt to be oppressive to different parts of the community, and among other ill effects have a very unfriendly aspect towards manufactures. All poll or capitation taxes are of this nature. They either proceed according to a fixed rate, which operates unequally and injuriously to the industrious poor, or they vest a discretion in certain officers to make estimates and assessments which are necessarily vague, conjectural, and liable to abuse. They ought therefore to be abstained from in all but cases of distressing emergency.

All such taxes (including all taxes on occupations) which proceed according to the amount of capital *supposed* to be employed in a business, or of profits *supposed* to be made in it, are unavoidably hurtful to industry. It is in vain that the evil may be endeavored to be mitigated by leaving it, in the first instance, in the option of the party to be taxed to declare the amount of his capital or profits.

Men engaged in any trade of business have commonly weighty reasons to avoid disclosures which would expose with anything like accuracy the real state of their affairs. They most frequently find it better to risk oppression than to avail themselves of so inconvenient a refuge. And the consequence is that they often suffer oppression.

When the disclosure too if made is not definitive but controllable by the discretion, or in other words by the passions & prejudices of the revenue officers, it is not only an ineffectual protection, but the possibility of its being so is an additional reason for not resorting to it.

Allowing to the public officers the most equitable dispositions, yet where they are to exercise a discretion without certain data they cannot fail to be often misled by appearances. The quantity of business which seems to be going on is, in a vast number of cases, a very deceitful criterion of the profits which are made; yet it is perhaps the best they can have, and it is the one on which they will most naturally rely. A business therefore which may rather require aid from the government than be in a capacity to be contributory to it may find itself crushed by the mistaken conjectures of the assessors of taxes.

Arbitrary taxes, under which denomination are comprised all those that leave the *quantum* of the tax to be raised on each person to the *discretion* of certain officers, are as contrary to the genius of liberty as to the maxims of industry. In this light they have been viewed by the most judicious observers on government, who have bestowed upon them the severest epithets of reprobation, as constituting one of the worst features usually to be met with in the practice of despotic governments.

It is certain at least that such taxes are particularly inimical to the success of manufacturing industry, and ought carefully to be avoided by a government which desires to promote it.

Letter to Edward Carrington, May 26, 1792

My Dear Sir,

Believing that I possess a share of your personal friendship and confidence and yielding to that which I feel towards you—persuaded also that our political creed is the same on *two essential points*, 1st the necessity of *union* to the respectability and happiness of this country, and 2nd the necessity of an *efficient* general government to maintain that union—I have concluded to unbosom myself to you on the present state of political parties and views. I ask no reply to what I shall say. I only ask that you will be persuaded the representations I shall make are agreeable to the real and sincere impressions of my mind. You will make the due allowances for the influence of circumstances upon it—you will consult your own observations and you will draw such a conclusion as shall appear to you proper.

When I accepted the office I now hold, it was under a full persuasion that from similarity of thinking, conspiring with personal goodwill, I should have the firm support of Mr. Madison in the *general course* of my administration. Aware of the intrinsic difficulties of the situation and of the powers of Mr. Madison, I do not believe I should have accepted under a different supposition.

I have mentioned the similarity of thinking between that gentleman and myself. This was relative not merely to the general principles of national policy and government but to the leading points which were likely to constitute questions in the administration of the finances. I mean, 1. the expediency of *funding* the debt, 2. the inexpediency of *discrimination* between original and present holders, 3. the expediency of *assuming* the state debts.

As to the first point, the evidence of Mr. Madison's sentiments at one period is to be found in the address of Congress of April 26th, 1783, which was planned by him in conformity to his own ideas and without any previous suggestions from the Committee and with his hearty cooperation in every part of the business. His conversations upon various occasions since have been expressive of a continuance in the same sentiment, nor indeed has he yet contradicted it by any part of his official conduct. How far there is reason to apprehend a change in this particular will be stated hereafter.

As to the second part, the same address is an evidence of Mr. Madison's sentiments at the same period. And I had been informed that at a later period he had been in the Legislature of Virginia a strenuous and successful opponent of the principle of discrimination. Add to this that a variety of conversations had taken place between him and myself respecting the public debt down to the commencement of the new government, in none of which had he glanced at the idea of a change of opinion. I wrote him a letter after my appointment in the recess of Congress to obtain his sentiments on the subject of the finances. In his answer there is not a lisp of his new system.

As to the third point, the question of an assumption of the state debts by the U. States was in discussion when the Convention that framed the present government was sitting at Philadelphia; and in a long conversation which I had with Mr. Madison in an afternoon's walk I well remember that we were perfectly agreed in the expediency and propriety of such a measure, though we were both of opinion that it would be more advisable to make it a measure of administration than an article of constitution, from the impolicy of multiplying obstacles to its reception on collateral details.

Under these circumstances, you will naturally imagine that it must have been matter of surprise to me when I was apprised that it was Mr. Madison's intention to oppose my plan on both the last mentioned points.

Before the debate commenced I had a conversation with him on my report, in the course of which I alluded to the calculation I had made of his sentiments and the grounds of that calculation. He did not deny them but alleged in his justification that the very considerable alienation of the debt, subsequent to the periods at which he had opposed a discrimination, had essentially changed the state of the question—and that, as to the assumption, he had contemplated it to take place *as matters stood at the peace.*

While the change of opinion avowed on the point of discrimination diminished my respect for the force of Mr. Madison's mind and the soundness of his judgment—and while the idea of reserving and setting afloat a vast mass of already extinguished debt as the condition of a measure the leading objects of which were an accession of strength to the national government and an assurance of order and vigor in the national finances by doing away the necessity of thirteen complicated and conflicting systems of finance— appeared to me somewhat extraordinary: Yet my previous impressions of the fairness of Mr. Madison's character and my reliance on his good will towards me disposed me to believe that his suggestions were sincere, and even, on the point of an assumption of the debts of the states as they stood at the peace, to lean towards a cooperation in his view, 'till on feeling the ground I found the thing impracticable, and on further reflection I thought it liable to immense difficulties. It was tried and failed with little countenance.

At this time and afterwards repeated intimations were given to me that Mr. Madison, from a spirit of rivalship or some other cause, had become personally unfriendly to me; and one gentleman in particular, whose honor I have no reason to doubt, assured me that Mr. Madison in a conversation with him had made a pretty direct attempt to insinuate unfavorable impressions of me.

Still I suspended my opinion on the subject. I knew the malevolent officiousness of mankind too well to yield a very ready acquiescence to the suggestions which were made, and resolved to wait 'till time and more experience should afford a solution.

It was not 'till the last session that I became unequivocally convinced of the following truth—"*That Mr. Madison cooperating with Mr. Jefferson is at the head of a faction decidedly hostile to me and my administration, and actuated by views in my judgment subversive of the principles of good government and dangerous to the union, peace, and happiness of the Country.*"

These are strong expressions; they may pain your friendship for one or both of the gentlemen whom I have named. I have not lightly resolved to hazard them. They are the result of a *serious alarm* in my mind for the public welfare, and of a full conviction that what I have alleged is a truth, and a truth which ought to be told and well attended to by all the friends of union and efficient national government. The suggestion will, I hope, at least awaken attention, free from the bias of former prepossessions.

This conviction in my mind is the result of a long train of circumstances, many of them minute. To attempt to detail them all would fill a volume. I shall therefore confine myself to the mention of a few.

First—As to the point of opposition to me and my administration.

Mr. Jefferson with very little reserve manifests his dislike of the funding system generally, calling in question the expediency of funding a debt at all. Some expressions which he has dropped in my own presence (sometimes without sufficient attention to delicacy) will not permit me to doubt on this point representations which I have had from various respectable quarters. I do not mean that he advocates directly the undoing of what has been done, but he censures the whole on principles which, if they should become general, could not but end in the subversion of the system.

In various conversations with *foreigners* as well as citizens he has thrown censure on my *principles* of government and on my measures of administration. He has predicted that the people would not long tolerate my proceedings & that I should not long maintain my ground. Some of those whom he *immediately* and *notoriously* moves have *even* whispered suspicions of the rectitude of my motives and conduct. In the question concerning the bank he not only delivered an opinion in writing against its constitutionality & expediency, but he did it *in a style and manner* which I felt as partaking of asperity and ill humor towards me. As one of the trustees of the sinking fund, I have experienced in almost every leading question opposition from him. When any turn of things in the community has threatened either odium or embarrassment to me, he has not been able to suppress the satisfaction which it gave him.

A part of this is of course information and might be misrepresentation. But it comes through so many channels and so well accords with what falls under my own observation that I can entertain no doubt.

I find a strong confirmation in the following circumstances. *Freneau*, the present printer of the *National Gazette*, who was a journeyman with Childs & Swain at New York, was a known Anti-Federalist. It is reduced to a certainty that he was brought to Philadelphia by Mr. Jefferson to be the conductor of a newspaper. It is notorious that contemporarily with the commencement of his paper he was a clerk in the Department of State for foreign languages. Hence a clear inference that his paper has been set on foot and is conducted under the patronage & not against the views of Mr. Jefferson. What then is the complexion of this paper? Let any impartial man peruse all the numbers down to the present day; and I never was more mistaken if he does not pronounce that it is a paper devoted to the subversion of me & the measures in which I have had an agency; and I am little less mistaken if he do not pronounce that it is a paper of a tendency *generally unfriendly* to the government of the U. States.

It may be said that a newspaper, being open to all the publications which are offered to it, its complexion may be influenced by other views than those of the editor. But the fact here is that wherever the editor appears it is in a correspondent dress. The paragraphs which appear as his own, the publications not original which are selected for his press, are of the same malignant and unfriendly aspect, so as not to leave a doubt of the temper which directs the publication.

Again *Brown*, who publishes an evening paper called *The Federal Gazette*, was originally a zealous Federalist and personally friendly to me. He has been employed by Mr. Jefferson as a printer to the government for the publication of the laws, and for some time past 'till lately the complexion of his press was equally bitter and unfriendly to me & to the government.

Lately, Col. Pickering, in consequence of certain attacks upon him, got hold of some instances of malconduct of his which have served to hold him in check and seemed to have varied his tone a little. I don't lay so much stress on this last case as on the former. There I find an internal evidence which is as conclusive as can be expected in any similar case. Thus far as to Mr. Jefferson.

With regard to Mr. Madison—the matter stands thus. I have not heard, but in the one instance to which I have alluded, of his having held language unfriendly to me in private conversation. But in his public conduct there has been a more uniform & persevering opposition than I have been able to resolve into a sincere difference of opinion. I cannot persuade myself that Mr. Madison and I, whose politics had formerly so much the *same point of departure*, should now diverge so widely in our opinions of the measures which are proper to be pursued. The opinion I once entertained of the candor and simplicity and fairness of Mr. Madison's character has, I acknowledge, given way to a decided opinion that *it is one of a peculiarly artificial and complicated kind.*

For a considerable part of the last session Mr. Madison lay in a great measure *perdu*. But it was evident from his votes & a variety of little movements and appearances that he was the prompter of Mr. Giles & others who were the open instruments of opposition. Two facts occurred in the course of the session which I view as unequivocal demonstrations of his disposition towards me. In one, a direct and decisive blow was aimed. When the Department of the Treasury was established, Mr. Madison was an unequivocal advocate of the principles which prevailed in it and of the powers and duties which were assigned by it to the head of the department. This appeared both from his private and public discourses, and I will add that I have personal evidence that Mr. Madison is as well convinced as any man in the U. States of the necessity of the arrangement which characterizes that establishment to the orderly conducting of the business of the finances.

Mr. Madison nevertheless opposed directly a reference to me to report *ways & means* for the western expedition, & combated *on principle* the propriety of such references.

He well knew that if he had prevailed, a certain consequence was my *resignation*—that I would not be fool enough to make pecuniary sacrifices and endure a life of extreme drudgery without opportunity either to do material good or to acquire reputation; and frequently with a responsibility in reputation for measures in which I had no hand and in respect to which the part I had acted, if any, could not be known.

To accomplish this point, an effectual train, as was supposed, was laid. Besides those who ordinarily acted under Mr. Madison's banners, several, who had generally acted with me, from various motives, vanity, self importance, &c. &c. were enlisted.

My overthrow was anticipated as certain and Mr. Madison, *laying aside his wonted caution*, boldly led his troops as he imagined to a certain victory. He was disappointed. Though *late* I became apprised of the danger, measures of counteraction were adopted, & when the question was called, Mr. Madison was confounded to find characters voting against him whom he had counted upon as certain.

Towards the close of the session another, though a more covert, attack was made. It was in the shape of a proposition to insert in the supplementary act respecting the public debt something by way of instruction to the trustees "to make their purchases of the debt at the *lowest* market price." In the course of the discussion of this point, Mr. Madison dealt much in *insidious insinuations* calculated to give an impression that the public money under my particular direction had been unfaithfully applied to put undue advantages in the pockets of speculators, & to support the debt at an *artificial* price for their benefit. The whole manner of this transaction left no doubt in anyone's mind that Mr. Madison was actuated by *personal* & political animosity.

As to this last instance, it is but candid to acknowledge that Mr. Madison had a better right to act the enemy than on any former occasion. I had some short time before, subsequent to his conduct respecting the reference, declared openly my opinion of the views by which he was actuated towards me & my determination to consider & treat him as a political enemy.

An intervening proof of Mr. Madison's unfriendly intrigues to my disadvantage is to be found in the following incident which I relate to you upon my honor, but from the nature of it you will perceive in the *strictest confidence*. The president, having prepared his speech at the commencement of the ensuing session, communicated it to Mr. Madison for his remarks. It contained among other things a *clause* concerning weights & measures, hinting the advantage of an invariable standard, which *preceded*, in the original state of the speech, a clause concerning the mint. Mr. Madison suggested a transposition of these clauses & the addition of certain words which I now forget, importing an *immediate connection* between the two subjects. You may recollect that Mr. Jefferson proposes that the *unit of weight* & the *unit in the coins* shall be the same, & that my propositions are to preserve the dollar as the unit, adhering to its present quantity of silver, & establishing the same proportion of alloy in the silver as in the gold coins. The evident design of this maneuver was to connect the president's opinion in favor of Mr. Jefferson's idea in contradiction to mine, & the worst of it is, *without his being aware of the tendency of the thing*. It happened that the president showed me the speech, altered in conformity to Mr. Madison's suggestion, just before it was copied for the purpose of being delivered. I remarked to him the tendency of the alteration. *He declared that he had not been aware of it & had no such intention, & without hesitation agreed to expunge the words which were designed to connect the two subjects.*

This transaction, in my opinion, not only furnishes a proof of Mr. Madison's *intrigues* in opposition to my measures, but charges him with an *abuse* of the president's confidence in him by endeavoring to make him, without his knowledge, take part with one officer against another in a case in which they had given different opinions to the legislature of the country. *I forbore to awaken the president's mind to this last inference*, but it is among the circumstances which have convinced me that Mr. Madison's true character is the reverse of that *simple, fair, candid one* which he has assumed.

I have informed you that Mr. Freneau was brought to Philadelphia by Mr. Jefferson to be the conductor of a newspaper. My information announced Mr. Madison as the mean of negotiation while he was at New York last summer. This and the general coincidence & close intimacy between the two gentlemen leave no doubt that their views are substantially the same.

Secondly, as to the tendency of the views of the two gentlemen who have been named.

Mr. Jefferson is an avowed enemy to a funded debt. Mr. Madison disavows in public any intention to *undo* what has been done, but in a private conversation with Mr. Charles Carroll (Senator), this gentleman's name I mention confidentially though he mentioned the matter to Mr. King & several other gentlemen as well as myself, & if any chance should bring you together you would easily bring him to repeat it to you, he favored the sentiment in Mr. Mercer's speech that a legislature had no right to *fund* the debt by mortgaging permanently the public revenues because they had no right to bind posterity. The inference is that what has been unlawfully done may be undone.

The discourse of partisans in the legislature & the publications in the party newspapers direct their main battery against the *principle* of a funded debt, & represent it in the most odious light as a perfect *Pandora's box*.

If Mr. Barnwell of St. Carolina, who appears to be a man of nice honor, may be credited, Mr. Giles declared in a conversation with him that if there was a question for reversing the funding system on the abstract point of the right of pledging & the futility of preserving public faith, he should be for reversal, merely to demonstrate his sense of the defect of right & the inutility of the thing. If positions equally extravagant were not publicly advanced by some of the party & secretly countenanced by the most guarded & *discreet* of them, one would be led, from the absurdity of the declaration, to suspect misapprehension. But from what is *known* anything may be *believed*.

Whatever were the original merits of the funding system, after having been so solemnly adopted, & after so great a transfer of property under it, what would become of the government should it be reversed? What of the national reputation? Upon what system of morality can so atrocious a doctrine be maintained? In me I confess it excites *indignation & horror!*

What are we to think of those maxims of government by which the power of a legislature is denied to bind the nation by a *contract* in an affair of *property* for twenty-four years? For this is precisely the case of the debt. What are to become of all the legal rights of property, of all charters to corporations, nay, of all grants to a man, his heirs, & assigns forever, if this doctrine be true? What is the term for which a government is in capacity to *contract?* Questions might be multiplied without end to demonstrate the perniciousness & absurdity of such a doctrine.

In almost all the questions great & small which have arisen since the first session of Congress, Mr. Jefferson & Mr. Madison have been found among those who were disposed to narrow the federal authority. The question of a national bank is one example. The question of bounties to the fisheries is another. Mr. Madison resisted it on the ground of constitutionality, 'till it was evident by the intermediate questions taken that the bill would pass & he then, under the wretched subterfuge of a change of a single word "bounty" for "allowance," went over to the majority & voted for the bill. In the militia bill & in a variety of minor cases he has leaned to abridging the exercise of federal authority, & leaving as much as possible to the states & he has lost no opportunity of *sounding the alarm* with great affected solemnity at encroachments meditated on the rights of the states, & of holding up the bugbear of a faction in the government having designs unfriendly to liberty.

This kind of conduct has appeared to me the more extraordinary on the part of Mr. Madison as I know for a certainty it was a primary article in his creed that the real danger in our system was the subversion of the national authority by the preponderancy of the state governments. All his measures have proceeded on an opposite supposition.

I recur again to the instance of Freneau's paper. In matters of this kind one cannot have direct proof of men's latent views; they must be inferred from circumstances. As the coadjutor of Mr. Jefferson in the establishment of this paper, I include Mr. Madison in the consequences imputable to it.

In respect to our foreign politics, the views of these gentlemen are in my judgment equally unsound & dangerous. *They have a womanish attachment to France and a womanish resentment against Great Britain.* They would draw us into the closest embrace of the former & involve us in all the consequences of her politics, & they would risk the peace of the country in their endeavors to keep us at the greatest possible distance from the latter. This disposition goes to a length particularly in Mr. Jefferson of which, till lately, I had no adequate idea. Various circumstances prove to me that if these gentlemen were left to pursue their own course there would be in less than six months *an open war between the U. States & Great Britain.*

I trust I have a due sense of the conduct of France towards this country in the late Revolution, & that I shall always be among the foremost in making her every suitable return; but there is a wide difference between this & implicating ourselves in all her politics; between bearing good will to her & hating and wrangling with all those whom she hates. The neutral & the pacific policy appears to me to mark the true path to the U. States.

Having now delineated to you what I conceive to be the true complexion of the politics of these gentlemen, I will now attempt a solution of these strange appearances.

Mr. Jefferson, it is known, did not in the first instance cordially acquiesce in the new Constitution for the U. States; he had many doubts & reserves. He left this country before we had experienced the imbecilities of the former.

In France he saw government only on the side of its abuses. He drank deeply of the French philosophy, in religion, in science, in politics. He came from France in the moment of a fermentation which he had had a share in exciting, & in the passions and feelings of which he shared both from temperament and situation.

He came here probably with a too partial idea of his own powers, and with the expectation of a greater share in the direction of our councils than he has in reality enjoyed. I am not sure that he had not peculiarly marked out for himself the department of the finances.

He came electrified *plus* with attachment to France and with the project of knitting together the two countries in the closest political bands.

Mr. Madison had always entertained an exalted opinion of the talents, knowledge, and virtues of Mr. Jefferson. The sentiment was probably reciprocal. A close correspondence subsisted between them during the time of Mr. Jefferson's absence from this country. A close intimacy arose upon his return.

Whether any peculiar opinions of Mr. Jefferson concerning the public debt wrought a change in the sentiments of Mr. Madison (for it is certain that the former is more radically wrong than the latter) or whether Mr. Madison, seduced by the expectation of popularity and possibly by the calculation of advantage to the state of Virginia, was led to change his own opinion—certain it is that a very material *change* took place, & that the two gentlemen were united in the new ideas. Mr. Jefferson was indiscreetly open in his approbation of Mr. Madison's principles upon his first coming to the seat of government. I say indiscreetly because a gentleman in the administration in one department ought not to have taken sides against another in another department.

The course of this business & a variety of circumstances which took place left Mr. Madison a very discontented & chagrined man and begot some degree of ill humor in Mr. Jefferson.

Attempts were made by these gentlemen in different ways to produce a commercial warfare with Great Britain. In this too they were disappointed. And as they had the liveliest wishes on the subject their dissatisfaction has been proportionally great, and as I had not favored the project, I was comprehended in their displeasure.

These causes and perhaps some others created, much sooner than I was aware of it, a systematic opposition to me on the part of those gentlemen. My subversion, I am now satisfied, has been long an object with them.

Subsequent events have increased the spirit of opposition and the feelings of personal mortification on the part of these gentlemen.

A mighty stand was made on the affair of the bank. There was much *commitment* in that case. I prevailed.

On the mint business I was opposed from the same quarter, & with still less success. In the affair of ways & means for the western expedition—on the supplementary arrangements concerning the debt except as to the additional assumption, my views have been equally prevalent in opposition to theirs. This current of success on one side & defeat on the other has rendered the opposition furious, & has produced a disposition to subvert their competitors even at the expense of the government.

Another circumstance has contributed to widening the breach. 'Tis evident beyond a question from every movement that Mr. Jefferson aims with ardent desire at the presidential chair. This too is an important object of the party politics. It is supposed, from the nature of my former personal & political connections, that I may favor some other candidate more than Mr. Jefferson when the question shall occur by the retreat of the present gentleman. My influence therefore with the community becomes a thing, on ambitious & personal grounds, to be resisted & destroyed.

You know how much it was a point to establish the secretary of state as the officer who was to administer the government in defect of the president & vice president. Here I acknowledge, though I took far less part than was supposed, I run counter to Mr. Jefferson's wishes; but if I had had no other reason for it, I had already *experienced opposition* from him which rendered it a measure of *self-defense*.

It is possible too (for men easily heat their imaginations when their passions are heated) that they have by degrees persuaded themselves of what they may have at first only sported to influence others—namely that there is some dreadful combination against state government & republicanism, which according to them are convertible terms. But there is so much absurdity in this supposition that the admission of it tends to apologize for their hearts at the expense of their heads.

Under the influence of all these circumstances, the attachment to the government of the U. States, originally weak in Mr. Jefferson's mind, has given way to something very like dislike; in Mr. Madison's, it is so counteracted by personal feelings as to be more an affair of the head than of the heart—more the result of a conviction of the necessity of Union than of cordiality to the thing itself. I hope it does not stand worse than this with him.

In such a state of mind both these gentlemen are prepared to hazard a great deal to effect a change. Most of the important measures of every government are connected with the treasury. To subvert the present head of it they deem it expedient to risk rendering the government itself odious, perhaps foolishly thinking that they can easily recover the lost affections & confidence of the people, and not appreciating as they ought to do the natural resistance to government which in every community results from the human passions, the degree to which this is strengthened by the *organized rivality* of state governments, & the infinite danger that the national government once rendered odious will be kept so by these powerful & indefatigable enemies.

They forget an old but a very just, though a coarse, saying—That it is much easier to raise the Devil than to lay him.

Poor *Knox* has come in for a share of their persecution as a man who generally thinks with me & who has a portion of the president's good will & confidence.

In giving you this picture of political parties my design is, I confess, to awaken your attention, if it has not yet been awakened, to the conduct of the gentlemen in question. If my opinion of them is founded it is certainly of great moment to the public weal that they should be understood. I rely on the strength of your mind to appreciate men as they merit—when you have a clue to their real views.

A word on another point. I am told that serious apprehensions are disseminated in your state as to the existence of a monarchical party meditating the destruction of state & republican government. If it is possible that so absurd an idea can gain ground it is necessary that it should be combated. I assure you on my *private faith* and *honor* as a man that there is not in my judgment a shadow of foundation of it. A very small number of men indeed may entertain theories less republican than Mr. Jefferson & Mr. Madison; but I am persuaded there is not a man among them who would not regard as both *criminal* & *visionary* any attempt to subvert the republican system of the country. Most of these men rather *fear* that it may not justify itself by its fruits than feel a predilection for a different form; and their fears are not diminished by the factions & fanatical politics which they find prevailing among a certain set of gentlemen and threatening to disturb the tranquility and order of the government.

As to the destruction of state governments, the *great* and *real* anxiety is to be able to preserve the national from the too potent and counteracting influence of those governments. As to my own political creed, I give it to you with the utmost sincerity. I am *affectionately* attached to the republican theory. I desire *above all things* to see the *equality* of political rights exclusive of all *hereditary* distinction firmly established by a practical demonstration of its being consistent with the order and happiness of society.

As to state governments, the prevailing bias of my judgment is that if they can be circumscribed within bounds consistent with the preservation of the national government, they will prove useful and salutary. If the states were all of the size of Connecticut, Maryland, or New Jersey, I should decidedly regard the local governments as both safe & useful. As the thing now is, however, I acknowledge the most serious apprehensions that the government of the U. States will not be able to maintain itself against their influence. I see that influence already penetrating into the national councils & perverting their direction.

Hence a disposition on my part towards a liberal construction of the powers of the national government and to erect every fence to guard it from depredations which is, in my opinion, consistent with constitutional propriety.

As to any combination to prostrate the state governments, I disavow and deny it. From an apprehension lest the judiciary should not work efficiently or harmoniously I have been desirous of seeing some rational scheme of connection adopted as an amendment to the Constitution; otherwise I am for maintaining things as they are, though I doubt much the possibility of it, from a tendency in the nature of things towards the preponderancy of the state governments.

I said that I was *affectionately* attached to the republican theory. This is the real language of my heart which I open to you in the sincerity of friendship; & I add that I have strong hopes of the success of that theory; but in candor I ought also to add that I am far from being without doubts. I consider its success as yet a problem.

It is yet to be determined by experience whether it be consistent with that *stability* and *order* in government which are essential to public strength & private security and happiness. On the whole, the only enemy which republicanism has to fear in this country is in the spirit of faction and anarchy. If this will not permit the ends of government to be attained under it—if it engenders disorders in the community, all regular & orderly minds will wish for a change—and the demagogues who have produced the disorder will make it for their own aggrandizement. This is the old story.

If I were disposed to promote monarchy & overthrow state governments, I would mount the hobby horse of popularity—I would cry out usurpation—danger to liberty &c. &c—I would endeavor to prostrate the national government—raise a ferment—and then "ride in the whirlwind and direct the storm." That there are men acting with Jefferson & Madison who have this in view I verily believe. I could lay my finger on some of them. That Madison does *not* mean it I also verily believe, and I rather believe the same of Jefferson, but I read him upon the whole thus—"A man of profound ambition & violent passions."

You must be by this time tired of my epistle. Perhaps I have treated certain characters with too much severity. I have, however, not meant to do them injustice—and from the bottom of my soul believe I have drawn them truly and that it is of the utmost consequence to the public weal they should be viewed in their true colors. I yield to this impression. I will only add that I make no clandestine attacks on the gentlemen concerned. They are both apprised indirectly from myself of the opinion I entertain of their views. With the truest regard and esteem.

Letter to George Washington, August 18, 1792

Sir,

I am happy to be able at length to send you answers to the objections which were communicated in your letter of the 29th of July.

They have unavoidably been drawn in haste, too much so to do perfect justice to the subject, and have been copied just as they flowed from my heart and pen, without revision or correction. You will observe that here and there some severity appears. I have not fortitude enough always to hear with calmness calumnies which necessarily include me as a principal agent in the measures censured, of the falsehood of which I have the most unqualified consciousness. I trust that I shall always be able to bear, as I ought, imputations of error of judgment; but I acknowledge that I cannot be entirely patient under charges which impeach the integrity of my public motives or conduct. I feel that I merit them *in no degree*, and expressions of indignation sometimes escape me in spite of every effort to suppress them. I rely on your goodness for the proper allowances.

> With high respect and the most affectionate
> attachment, I have the honor to be,
> Sir   Your most Obedient   & humble servant
> Alexander Hamilton

Objections and Answers Respecting the Administration, August 18, 1792

1. Object. The public debt is greater than we can possibly pay before other causes of adding to it will occur, and this has been artificially created by adding together the *whole amount* of the debtor and creditor sides of the account.

Answer. The public debt was produced by the late war. It is not the fault of the present government that it exists, unless it can be proved that public morality and policy do not require of a government an honest provision for its debts. Whether it is greater than can be paid before new causes of adding to it will occur is a problem incapable of being solved but by experience, and this would be the case if it were not one fourth as much as it is. If the policy of the country be prudent, cautious, and *neutral* towards foreign nations there is a rational probability that war may be avoided long enough to wipe off the debt. The Dutch in a situation not near so favorable for it as that of the U. States have enjoyed intervals of peace longer than with proper exertions would suffice for the purpose. The debt of the U. States compared with its present and growing abilities is really a very light one. It is little more than 15,000,000 of pounds Sterling, about the annual expenditure of Great Britain.

But whether the public debt shall be extinguished or not within a moderate period depends on the temper of the people. If they are rendered dissatisfied by misrepresentations of the measures of the government, the government will be deprived of an efficient command of the resources of the community towards extinguishing the debt. And thus those who clamor are likely to be the principal causes of protracting the existence of the debt.

As to having been artificially increased, this is denied; perhaps indeed the true reproach of the system which has been adopted is that it has artificially diminished the debt, as will be explained by and by.

The assertion that the debt has been increased by adding together the whole amount of the debtor and creditor sides of the account, not being very easy to be understood, is not easy to be answered.

But an answer shall be attempted.

The thirteen states in their *joint* capacity owed a *certain* sum. The same states in their separate capacities owed *another sum*. These two sums constituted the *aggregate* of the *public debt*. The public in a political sense, compounded of the governments of the Union and of the several states, was the debtor. The individuals who held the various evidences of debt were the creditors. It would be nonsense to say that the combining of *the two parts* of the public debt is adding together the debtor and creditor sides of the account. So great an absurdity cannot be supposed to be intended by the objection. Another meaning must therefore be sought for.

It may possibly exist in the following misconception. The states individually, when they liquidated the accounts of individuals for services and supplies towards the common defense during the late war and gave certificates for the sums due, would naturally charge them to the U. States as contributions to the common cause. The U. States in assuming to pay those certificates charge themselves with them. And it may be supposed that here is a double charge for the same thing.

But as the amount of the sum assumed for each state is by the system adopted to be charged to such state, it of course goes in extinguishment of so much of the first charge as is equal to the sum assumed, and leaves the U. States chargeable only once, as ought to be the case.

Or perhaps the meaning of the objection may be found in the following mode of reasoning. Some states, from having disproportionately contributed during the war, would probably on a settlement of accounts be found debtors, independently of the assumption. The assuming of the debts of such states increases the balances against them, and as these balances will ultimately be remitted from the impracticability of enforcing their payment, the sums assumed will be an extra charge upon the U. States increasing the mass of the debt.

This objection takes it for granted that the balances of the debtor states will not be exacted, which by the way is no part of the system, and if it should eventually not prove true the foundation of the reasoning would fail. For it is evident if the balances are to be collected (unless there be some undiscovered error in the principle by which the accounts are to be adjusted) that one side of the account will counterpoise the other. And everything as to the quantum of debt will remain *in statu quo*.

But it shall be taken for granted that the balances will be remitted; and still the consequence alleged does not result. The reverse of it may even take place. In reasoning upon this point it must be remembered that impracticability would be alike an obstacle to the collection of balances without, as with, the assumption.

This being the case, whether the balances to be remitted will be increased or diminished must depend on the relative proportions of outstanding debts. If a former *debtor* state owes to individuals a smaller sum in proportion to its contributive faculty than a former *creditor* state, the assumption of the debts of both to be provided for out of a *common fund* raised upon them proportionally must necessarily, on the idea of a remission of balances, tend to restore equality between them and lessen the balance of the debtor state to be remitted.

How the thing may work upon the whole cannot be pronounced without a knowledge of the situation of the account of each state, but all circumstances that are known render it probable that the ultimate effect will be favorable to justice between the states and that there will be inconsiderable balances either on one side or on the other.

It was observed that perhaps the true reproach of the system which has been adopted is that it has artificially decreased the debt. This is explained thus—

In the case of the debt of the U. States, interest upon two thirds of the principal only at 6 percent is immediately paid—interest upon the remaining third was deferred for ten years—and only 3 percent has been allowed upon the arrears of interest, making one third of the whole debt.

In the case of the separate debts of the states interest upon 4/9 only of the entire sum is immediately paid, interest upon 2/9 was deferred for 10 years, and only 3 percent allowed on 3/9.

The market rate of interest at the time of adopting the funding system was 6 percent. Computing according to this rate of interest—the then present value of 100 dollars of debt upon an average, principal and interest, was about 73 dollars.

And the present *actual* value in the market of 100 dollars, as the several kinds of stock are sold, is no more than 83 dollars & 61 cents. This computation is not made on equal sums of the several kinds of stock according to which the average value of 100 dollars would be only 78.75, but it is made on the proportions which constitute the mass of the debt.

At 73 to 100 the diminution on 60,000,000 is 16,200,000 dollars; at 83.61 to 100 it is 9,834,000 dollars.

But as the U. States having a right to redeem in certain proportions need never give more than par for the 6 percent, the diminution to them as purchasers at the present market prices is 12,168,000 dollars.

If it be said that the U. States are engaged to pay the whole sum at the nominal value, the answer is that they are always at liberty if they have the means to purchase at the market prices, and in all those purchases they gain the difference between the nominal sums and the lesser market rates.

If the whole debt had been provided for at 6 percent, the market rate of interest when the funding system passed, the market value throughout would undoubtedly have been 100 for 100. The debt may then rather be said to have been artificially decreased by the nature of the provision.

The conclusion from the whole is that assuming it as a principle that the public debts of the different descriptions were honestly to be provided for and paid—it is the reverse of true that there has been an artificial increase of them. To argue on a different principle is to presuppose dishonesty, and make it an objection to doing right.

Objection II. This accumulation of debt has taken forever out of our power those easy sources of revenue which applied &c.

Answer. There having been no accumulation of debt, if what is here pretended to have been the consequence were true, it would only be to be regretted as the unavoidable consequence of an unfortunate state of things. But the supposed consequence does by *no means* exist. The only sources of taxation which have been touched are imported articles and the single internal object of distilled spirits. Lands, houses, the great mass of personal as well as the whole of real property remain essentially free. In short, the chief sources of taxation are free for extraordinary conjunctures; and it is one of the distinguishing merits of the system which has been adopted that it has rendered this far more the case than it was before. It is only to look into the different states to be convinced of it. In most of them real estate is wholly exempted. In some, very small burdens rest upon it for the purpose of the internal governments. In all, the burdens of the people have been lightened. It is a mockery of truth to represent the U. States as a community burdened and exhausted by taxes.

Objection 3.

Answer. This is a mere painting and exaggeration. With the exception of a very few articles, the duties on imports are still moderate, lower than in any country of whose regulations we have knowledge, except perhaps Holland, where, having few productions or commodities of their own, their export trade depends on the reexportation of foreign articles.

It is true the merchants have complained, but so they did of the first impost law for a time, and so men always will do at an augmentation of taxes which touch the business they carry on, especially in a country where no or scarcely any *such* taxes before existed. The collection, it is not doubted, will be essentially secure. Evasions have existed in a degree and will continue to exist. Perhaps they may be somewhat increased; to what extent can only be determined by experience, but there are no symptoms to induce an opinion that they will materially increase. As to the idea of a war upon the citizens to collect the impost duties, it can only be regarded as a figure of rhetoric.

The excise law no doubt is a good topic of declamation. But can it be doubted that it is an excellent and a very fit mean of revenue?

As to the partiality of its operation, it is no more so than any other tax on a consumable commodity, adjusting itself upon exactly the same principles. The consumer in the main pays the tax—and if some parts of the U. States consume more domestic spirits, others consume more foreign—and both are taxed. There is perhaps, upon the whole, no article of more *general* and *equal consumption* than distilled spirits.

As to its *unproductiveness*, unless enforced by *arbitrary* and *vexatious* means, facts testify the contrary. Already, under all the obstacles arising from its novelty and the prejudices against it in some states, it has been considerably productive. And it is not enforced by any arbitrary or vexatious means; at least the precautions in the existing laws for the collection of the tax will not appear in that light but to men who regard all taxes and all the means of enforcing them as arbitrary and vexatious. Here, however, there is abundant room for fancy to operate. The standard is in the mind, and different minds will have different standards.

The observation relating to the commitment of the authority of the government in parts where resistance is most probable and coercion least practicable has more weight than any other part of this objection. It must be confessed that a hazard of this nature has been run, but if there were motives sufficiently cogent for it, it was wisely run. It does not follow that a measure is bad because it is attended with a degree of danger.

The general inducements to a provision for the public debt are—I. To preserve the public faith and integrity by fulfilling as far as was practicable the public engagements. II. To manifest a due respect for property by satisfying the public obligations in the hands of the public creditors and which were as much their property as their houses or their lands, their hats or their coats. III. To revive and establish public credit, the palladium of public safety. IV. To preserve the government itself by showing it worthy of the confidence which was placed in it, to procure to the community the blessings which in innumerable ways attend confidence in the government, and to avoid the evils which in as many ways attend the want of confidence in it.

The particular inducements to an assumption of the state debts were—I. To consolidate the finances of the country and give an assurance of permanent order in them, avoiding the collisions of thirteen different and independent systems of finance under concurrent and coequal authorities and the scramblings for revenue which would have been incident to so many different systems. II. To secure to the government of the Union, by avoiding those entanglements, an effectual command of the resources of the Union for present and future exigencies. III. To *equalize the condition* of the *citizens* of the several states in the important article of taxation, rescuing a part of them from being oppressed with burdens beyond their strength on account of extraordinary exertions in the war and through the want of certain adventitious resources which it was the good fortune of others to possess.

A mind naturally attached to order and system and capable of appreciating their immense value, unless misled by particular feelings, is struck at once with the prodigious advantages which in the course of time must attend such a simplification of the financial affairs of the country as results from placing all the parts of the public debt upon one footing—under one direction—regulated by one provision. The want of this sound policy has been a continual source of disorder and embarrassment in the affairs of the United Netherlands.

The true justice of the case of the public debt consists in that equalization of the condition of the citizens of all the states which must arise from a consolidation of the debt and common contributions towards its extinguishment. Little inequalities as to the past can bear no comparison with the more lasting inequalities which, without the assumption, would have characterized the future condition of the people of the U. States, leaving upon those who had done most or suffered most a great additional weight of burden.

If the foregoing inducements to a provision for the public debt (including an assumption of the state debts) were sufficiently cogent—then the justification of the excise law lies within a narrow compass. Some further source of revenue, besides the duties on imports, was indispensable, and none equally productive would have been so little exceptionable to the mass of the people.

Other reasons cooperated in the minds of some able men to render an excise at an early period desirable. They thought it well to lay hold of so valuable a resource of revenue before it was generally preoccupied by the state governments. They supposed it not amiss that the authority of the national government should be visible in some branch of internal revenue, lest a total non-exercise of it should beget an impression that it was never to be exercised & next that it ought not to be exercised. It was supposed too that a thing of the kind could not be introduced with a greater prospect of easy success than at a period when the government enjoyed the advantage of first impressions—when state factions to resist its authority were not yet matured—when so much aid was to be derived from the popularity and firmness of the actual chief magistrate.

Facts hitherto do not indicate the measure to have been rash or ill-advised. The law is in operation with perfect acquiescence in all the states north of New York, though they contribute most largely. In New York and New Jersey it is in full operation with some very partial complainings fast wearing away. In the greatest part of Pennsylvania it is in operation and with increasing good humor towards it. The four western counties continue exceptions. In Delaware it has had some struggle, which by the last accounts was surmounted. In Maryland and Virginia it is in operation and without material conflict. In South Carolina it is now in pretty full operation, though in the interior parts it has had some serious opposition to overcome. In Georgia no material difficulty has been experienced. North Carolina, Kentucky, & the four western counties of Pennsylvania present the only remaining impediments of any consequence to the full execution of the law. The latest advices from N.C. & Kentucky were more favorable than the former.

It may be added as a well-established fact that the effect of the law has been to encourage new enterprises in most of the states in the business of domestic distillation. A proof that it is perceived to operate favorably to the manufacture and that the measure cannot long remain unpopular anywhere.

Objection IV. Propositions have been made in Congress & projects are on foot still to increase the mass of the debt.

Ans. Propositions have been made and no doubt will be renewed by the states interested to complete the assumption of the state debts. This would add in the first instance to the mass of the *debt of the U. States* between three and four millions of dollars, but it would not increase the mass of the *public debt* at all. It would only transfer from particular states to the Union debts which already exist and which, if the states indebted are honest, must be provided for. It happens that Massachusetts and South Carolina would be chiefly benefited. And there is a moral certainty that Massachusetts will have a balance in her favor more than equal to her remaining debt and a probability that South Carolina will have a balance sufficient to cover hers—so that there is not likely to be an eventual increase even of the *debt of the United States* by the further assumption. The immense exertions of Massachusetts during the late war and particularly in the latter periods of it when too many of the states failed in their federal duty are known to every well informed man. It would not be too strong to say that they were in a great degree the pivot of the revolution. The exertions, sufferings, sacrifices, and losses of South Carolina need not be insisted upon. The other states have comparatively none or inconsiderable debts. Can that policy be condemned which aims at putting the burdened states upon an equal footing with the rest? Can that policy be very liberal which resists so equitable an arrangement? It has been said that if they had exerted themselves since the peace their situation would have been different. But Massachusetts threw her citizens into rebellion by heavier taxes than were paid in any other state, and South Carolina has done as much since the peace as could have been expected considering the exhausted state in which the war left her.

The only proposition during the last session or at any antecedent one which would truly have swelled the debt artificially was one which Mr. Madison made in the first session & which was renewed in the last and generally voted for by those who oppose the system that has prevailed. The object of this proposition was *that all the parts* of the state debts which have been *paid* or other*wise absorbed by them* should be assumed for the benefit of the states and funded by the U. States. This measure if it had succeeded would truly have produced an immense artificial increase of the debt, but it has twice failed & there is no probability that it will ever succeed.

Objection 5. By borrowing at 2/3 &c.

Answer. First—All the foreign loans which were made by the U. States prior to the present government, taking into the calculation charges & premiums, cost them more than 6 percent. Since the establishment of the present government they borrowed first at about 5 ¼ including charges & since at about 4 ¼ including charges. And it is questionable in the present state of Europe whether they can obtain any further loans at so low a rate.

The system which is reprobated is the very cause that we have been able to borrow monies on so good terms. If one that would have inspired less confidence, certainly if the substitutes which have been proposed from a certain quarter had obtained, we could not have procured loans even at six percent. The Dutch were largely adventurers in our domestic debt before the present government. They did not embark far till they had made inquiries of influential public characters as to the light in which the debt was & would be considered in the hands of alienees—and had received assurances that assignees would be regarded in the same light as original holders. What would have been the state of our credit with them if they had been disappointed, or indeed if our conduct had been in any respect inconsistent with the notions entertained in Europe concerning the maxims of public credit?

The inference is that our being able to borrow on low terms is a consequence of the system which is the object of censure and that the thing itself, which is made the basis of another system, would not have existed under it.

Secondly. It will not be pretended that we could have borrowed at the proposed low rate of interest in the U. States; and all our exertions to borrow in Europe which have been unremitted, as occasions presented, have not hitherto produced above ___ of dollars in space of ___; not even a sufficient sum to change the form of our foreign debt.

Thirdly. If it were possible to borrow the whole sum abroad within a short period to pay off our debt, it is not easy to imagine a more pernicious operation than this would have been. It would first have transferred to foreigners by a violent expedient the whole amount of our debt; and creating a money plethora in the country, a momentary scene of extravagance would have followed & the excess would quickly have flowed back: The evils of which situation need not be enlarged upon. If it be said that the operation might have been gradual, then the end proposed would not have been attained.

Lastly. The plan which has been adopted secures in the first instance the *identical advantage* which in the other plan would have been *eventual* and *contingent*. It puts one third of the whole debt at an interest of 3 percent only—and by deferring the payment of interest on a third of the remainder effectually reduces the interest on that part. It is evident that a *suspension* of interest is in fact a *reduction* of interest. The money which would go towards paying interest in the interval of suspension is an accumulating fund to be applied towards payment of it when it becomes due, proportionably reducing the provision then to be made.

In reality, on the principles of the funding system, the United States reduced the interest on their whole debt upon *an average* to about 4 ½ percent, nearly the lowest rate they have any chance to borrow at, and lower than they could possibly have borrowed at, in an attempt to reduce the interest on the whole capital by borrowing and paying; probably by one percent. A demand for large loans by forcing the market would unavoidably have raised their price upon the borrower. The above average of 4 ½ percent is found by calculation, computing the then present value of the deferred stock at the time of passing the funding act and of course 3 percent on the 3 percent stock.

The funding system, then, secured in the very outset the *precise advantage* which it is alleged would have accrued from leaving the whole debt redeemable at pleasure. But this is not all. It did more. It left the government still in a condition to enjoy upon 5/9 of the entire debt the advantage of extinguishing it by loans at a low rate of interest, if they are obtainable. The 3 percents which are one third of the whole may always be purchased in the market below par, till the market rate of interest falls to 3 percent. The deferred will be purchasable below par till near the period of the actual payment of interest. And this further advantage will result: in all these purchases the public will enjoy not only the advantage of a reduction of interest on the sums borrowed but the additional advantage of purchasing the debt under par, that is for less than 20/ in the pound.

If it be said that the like advantage might have been enjoyed under another system, the assertion would be without foundation. Unless some equivalent had been given for the reduction of interest in the irredeemable quality annexed to the debt, nothing was left consistently with the principles of public credit but to provide for the whole debt at 6 percent. This evidently would have kept the whole at par, and no advantage could have been derived by purchases under the nominal value. The reduction of interest by borrowing at a lower rate is all that would have been practicable and this advantage has been secured by the funding system in the very outset and without any second process.

If no provision for the interest had been made, not only public credit would have been sacrificed, but by means of it the borrowing at a low rate of interest or at any rate would have been impracticable.

There is no reproach which has been thrown upon the funding system so unmerited as that which charges it with being a bad bargain for the public or with a tendency to prolong the extinguishment of the debt. The bargain has if anything been too good on the side of the public, and it is impossible for the debt to be in a more convenient form than it is for a rapid extinguishment.

Some gentlemen seem to forget that the faculties of every country are limited. They talk as if the government could extend its revenue *ad libitum* to pay off the debt. Whereas every rational calculation of the abilities of the country will prove that the power of redemption which has been reserved over the debt is quite equal to those abilities, and that a greater power would be useless. If happily the abilities of the country should exceed this estimate, there is nothing to hinder the surplus being employed in purchases. As long as the three percents & deferred exist, those purchases will be under par. If for the stock bearing an immediate interest of six percent more than par is given—the government can afford it from the saving made in the first instance.

Upon the whole then it is the merit of the funding system to have conciliated these three important points—the restoration of public credit—a reduction of the rate of interest—and an organization of the debt convenient for speedy extinguishment.

Object 6. The irredeemable quality was given to the debt for the *avowed* purpose of inviting its transfer to foreign countries.

This assertion is a palpable misrepresentation. The *avowed purpose* of that quality of the debt, as explained in the report of the secretary of the treasury, and in the arguments in Congress, was to give an *equivalent* for the reduction of interest, that is for deferring the payment of interest on ⅓ of the principal for three years and for allowing only 3 percent on the arrears of interest.

It was indeed argued, in confirmation of the reality of the equivalent, that foreigners would be willing to give more where a high rate of interest was *fixed* than where it was liable to fluctuate with the market. And this has been verified by the fact—for the 6 percents could not have risen for a moment above par if the rate could have been lowered by redeeming the debt at pleasure. But the inviting of the transfer to foreigners was never assigned as a motive to the arrangement.

And what is more, that transfer will be probably slower with the portion of irredeemability which is attached to the debt than without it, because a larger capital would be requisite to purchase 100 dollars in the former than in the latter case. And the capital of foreigners is limited as well as our own.

It appears to be taken for granted that if the debt had not been funded in its present shape foreigners would not have purchased it as they now do, than which nothing can be more ill-founded or more contrary to experience. Under the old confederation, when there was no provision at all, foreigners had purchased five or six millions of the debt. If any provision had been made capable of producing confidence, their purchases would have gone on just as they now do; and the only material difference would have been that what they got from us then would have cost them less than what they now get from us does cost them. Whether it is to the disadvantage of the country that they pay more is submitted.

Even a provision which should not have inspired full confidence would not have prevented foreign purchases. The commodity would have been cheap in proportion to the risks to be run. And full-handed Dutchmen would not have scrupled to amass large sums, for trifling considerations, in the hope that time & experience would introduce juster notions into the public councils.

Our debt would still have gone from us & with it our reputation & credit.

Objection 7.

Answer. The same glooming forebodings were heard in England in the early periods of its funding system. But they have never been realized. The money invested by foreigners in the purchase of its debt being employed in its commerce, agriculture, and manufactures increased the wealth and capital of the nation, more than in proportion to the annual drain for the payment of interest, and created the ability to bear it.

The objection seems to forget that the debt is not transferred for nothing—that the capital paid for the debt is always an equivalent for the interest to be paid to the purchasers. If that capital is well employed in a young country like this, it must be considerably increased so as to yield a greater revenue than the interest of the money. The country therefore will be a gainer by it and will be able to pay the interest without inconvenience.

But the objectors suppose that all the money which comes in goes out again in an increased consumption of foreign luxuries. This, however, is taking for granted what never happened in any industrious country & what appearances among us do not warrant. The expense of living generally speaking is not sensibly increased. Large investments are every day making in ship building, house building, manufactures, & other improvements public & private.

The transfer too of the whole debt is a very improbable supposition. A large part of it will continue to be holden by our own citizens. And the interest of that part which is owned by foreigners will not be annually exported as is supposed. A considerable part will be invested in new speculations, in lands, canals, roads, manufactures, commerce. Facts warrant this supposition. The agents of the Dutch have actually made large investments in a variety of such speculations. A young country like this is peculiarly attractive. New objects will be continually opening and the money of foreigners will be made instrumental to their advancement.

8th Object.

Ans. This is a mere hypothesis in which theorists differ. There are no decisive facts on which to rest the question.

The supposed tendency of bank paper to banish specie is from its capacity of serving as a substitute for it in circulation. But as the quantity circulated is proportioned to the demand for it in circulation, the presumption is that a greater quantity of industry is put in motion by it, so as to call for a proportionably greater quantity of *circulating medium* and prevent the banishment of the specie.

But however this may be it is agreed among sound theorists that banks more than compensate for the loss of the specie in other ways. Smith, who was witness to their effects in Scotland, where too a very adverse fortune attended some of them, bears his testimony to their beneficial effects in these strong terms (*Wealth of Nations* Vol. I Book II. Ch. II. Page 441 to 444).

9 Objection. The 10 or 12 percent &c.

Answer. 1. The profits of the bank have not hitherto exceeded the rate of 8 percent per annum & perhaps never may. It is questionable whether they can legally make more than 10 percent.

2. These profits can in no just sense be said to be taken out of the pockets of the people. They are compounded of two things—1. the interest paid by the government on that part of the public debt which is incorporated in the stock of the bank—2. the interest paid by those *individuals who borrow* money of the bank on the *sums they borrow*.

As to the first, it is no *new grant* to the bank. It is the old interest on a part of the old debt of the country, subscribed by the proprietors of that debt towards constituting the stock of the bank. It would have been equally payable if the bank had never existed. It is therefore nothing new taken out of the pockets of the people.

As to the second, it may with equal propriety be said, when one individual borrows money of another, that the interest which the borrower pays to the lender is taken out of the *pockets of the people*. The case here is not only parallel but the same. It is a case of one or more individuals borrowing money of a company of individuals associated to lend. None but the actual borrowers pay in either case. The rest of the community have nothing to do with it.

If a man receives a bank bill for the ox or the bushel of wheat which he sells, he pays no more interest upon it than upon the same sum in gold or silver; that is he pays none at all.

So that whether the paper banishes specie or not it is the same thing to every individual through whose hands it circulates, as to the point of interest. Specie no more than bank paper can be borrowed without paying interest for it, and when either is not borrowed no interest is paid. As far as the government is a sharer in the profits of the bank, which is in the proportion of 1/5, the contrary of what is supposed happens. *Money is put into the pockets of the People.*

All this is so plain and so palpable that the assertion which is made betrays extreme ignorance or extreme disingenuousness. It is destitute even of color.

10 Objection.

This is a copious subject which has been fully discussed in the report of the secretary of the treasury on the subject of manufactures from page ___ to ___. It is true that the capital, that is the *specie*, which is employed in paper speculation, while so employed, is barren and useless, but the paper itself constitutes a *new capital*, which, being saleable and transferable at any moment, enables the proprietor to undertake any piece of business as well as an equal sum in coin.

And as the amount of the debt circulated is much greater than the amount of the *specie* which circulates it, the new capital put in motion by it considerably exceeds the old one which is *suspended*. And there is more capital to carry on the productive labor of the society. Everything that has value is capital—an acre of ground, a horse or a cow or a public or a private obligation, which may with different degrees of convenience be applied to industrious enterprise. That which, like public stock, can at any instant be turned into money is of equal utility with money as capital.

Let it be examined whether at those places where there is most debt afloat and most money employed in its circulation, there is not at the same time a greater plenty of money for every other purpose. It will be found that there is.

But it is in fact quite immaterial to the government, as far as regards the propriety of its measures.

The debt existed. It was to be provided for. In whatever shape the provision was made the object of speculation and the speculation would have existed. Nothing but abolishing the debt could have obviated it. It is therefore the fault of the Revolution, not of the government, that paper speculation exists.

An unsound or precarious provision would have increased this species of speculation in its most odious forms. The defects & casualties of the system would have been as much subjects of speculation as the debt itself.

The difference is that under a bad system the public stock would have been too uncertain an article to be a substitute for money & all the money employed in it would have been diverted from useful employment without anything to compensate for it. Under a good system the stock becomes more than a substitute for the money employed in negotiating it.

Objection 11. Paper speculation nourishes in our citizens &c.

Answer. This proposition within certain limits is true. Jobbing in the funds has some bad effects among those engaged in it. It fosters a spirit of gambling and diverts a certain number of individuals from other pursuits. But if the proposition be true that stock operates as capital, the effect upon the citizens at large is different. It promotes among them industry by furnishing a larger field of employment. Though this effect of a funded debt has been called in question in England by some theorists, yet most theorists & all practical men allow its existence. And there is no doubt, as already intimated, that if we look into those scenes among ourselves where the largest portions of the debt are accumulated we shall perceive that a new spring has been given to industry in various branches.

But be all this as it may, the observation made under the last head applies here. The debt was the creature of the Revolution. It was to be provided for. Being so, in whatever form it must have become an object of speculation and jobbing.

Objection 12. The funding of the debt has furnished effectual means of corrupting &c.

Answer. This is one of those assertions which can only be denied and pronounced to be malignant and false. No facts exist to support it, and being a mere matter of fact, no *argument* can be brought to repel it.

The assertors beg the question. They assume to themselves and to those who think with them infallibility. Take their words for it, they are the only honest men in the community. But compare the tenor of men's lives and *at least* as large a proportion of virtuous and independent characters will be found among those whom they malign as among themselves.

A member of a majority of the legislature would say to these defamers—

"In your vocabulary, gentlemen, *creditor* and *enemy* appear to be synonymous terms—the *support of public credit* and *corruption* of similar import—an *enlarged* and *liberal* construction of the Constitution for the public good and for the maintenance of the due energy of the national authority of the same meaning with usurpation and a conspiracy to overturn the republican government of the country—every man of a different opinion from your own an ambitious despot or a corrupt knave. You bring everything to the standard of your narrow and depraved ideas, and you condemn without mercy or even decency whatever does not accord with it. Every man who is either too long or too short for your political couch must be stretched or lopped to suit it. But your pretensions must be rejected, your insinuations despised. Your politics originate in immorality, in a disregard of the maxims of good faith and the rights of property, and if they could prevail must end in national disgrace and confusion. Your rules of construction for the authorities vested in the government of the Union would arrest all its essential movements and bring it back in practice to the same state of imbecility which rendered the old confederation contemptible. Your principles of liberty are principles of licentiousness incompatible with all government. You sacrifice everything that is venerable and substantial in society to the vain reveries of a false and newfangled philosophy. As to the motives by which I have been influenced, I leave my general conduct in private and public life to speak for them. Go and learn among my *fellow citizens* whether I have not uniformly maintained the character of an honest man. As to the love of liberty and country you have given no stronger proofs of being actuated by it than I have done. Cease then to arrogate to yourself and to your party all the patriotism and virtue of the country. Renounce if you can the intolerant spirit by which you are governed—and begin to reform yourself instead of reprobating others, by beginning to doubt of your own infallibility."

Such is the answer which would naturally be given by a member of the majority in the legislature to such an objector. And it is the only one that could be given, until some evidence of the supposed corruption should be produced.

As far as I know, there is not a member of the legislature who can properly be called a stockjobber or a paper dealer. There are several of them who were proprietors of public debt in various ways. Some for money lent & property furnished for the use of the public during the war, others for sums received in payment of debts—and it is supposable enough that some of them had been purchasers of the public debt, with intention to hold it as a valuable & convenient property, considering an honorable provision for it as matter of course.

It is a strange perversion of ideas, and as novel as it is extraordinary, that men should be deemed corrupt & criminal for becoming proprietors in the funds of their country. Yet I believe the number of members of Congress is very small who have ever been considerably proprietors in the funds.

And as to improper speculations on measures depending before Congress, I believe never was any *body* of men freer from them.

There are indeed several members of Congress who have become proprietors in the Bank of the United States, and a *few* of them to a pretty large amount, say 50 or 60 shares; but all operations of this kind were necessarily subsequent to the determination upon the measure. The subscriptions were of course subsequent & purchases still more so. Can there be anything really blamable in this? Can it be culpable to invest property in an institution which has been established for the most important national purposes? Can that property be supposed to corrupt the holder? It would indeed tend to render him friendly to the preservation of the bank; but in this there would be no collision between duty & interest, and it could give him no improper bias in other questions.

To uphold public credit and to be friendly to the bank must be presupposed to be *corrupt things* before the being a proprietor in the funds or of bank stock can be supposed to have a *corrupting influence*. The being a proprietor in either case is a very different thing from being, in a proper sense of the term, a stockjobber. On this point of the corruption of the legislature one more observation of great weight remains. Those who oppose a *funded* debt and mean any provision for it contemplate an *annual* one. Now, it is impossible to conceive a more fruitful source of legislative corruption than this. All the members of it who should incline to speculate would have an annual opportunity of speculating upon their influence in the legislature to promote or retard or put off a provision. Every session the question whether the annual provision should be continued would be an occasion of pernicious caballing and corrupt bargaining. In this very view when the subject was in deliberation, it was impossible not to wish it declared upon once for all & out of the way.

Objection the 13. The Corrupt Squadron &c.

Here again the objectors beg the question. They take it for granted that their constructions of the Constitution are right and that the opposite ones are wrong, and with great good nature and candor ascribe the effect of a difference of opinion to a disposition to get rid of the limitations on the government.

Those who have advocated the constructions which have obtained have met their opponents on the ground of fair argument and they think have refuted them. How shall it be determined which side is right?

There are some things which the general government has clearly a right to do—there are others which it has clearly no right to meddle with, and there is a good deal of middle ground about which honest & well disposed men may differ. The most that can be said is that some of this middle ground may have been occupied by the national legislature; and this surely is no evidence of a disposition to get rid of the limitations in the Constitution, nor can it be viewed in that light by men of candor.

The truth is, one description of men is disposed to do the essential business of the nation by a liberal construction of the powers of the government, another from disaffection would fritter away those powers—a third from an overweening jealousy would do the same thing—a fourth from party & personal opposition are torturing the Constitution into objections to everything they do not like.

The bank is one of the measures which is deemed by some the greatest stretch of power, and yet its constitutionality has been established in the most satisfactory manner.

And the most incorrigible theorist among its opponents would in one month's experience as head of the Department of the Treasury be compelled to acknowledge that it is an absolutely indispensable engine in the management of the finances and would quickly become a convert to its perfect constitutionality.

Objection XIV. The ultimate object of all

To this there is no other answer than a flat denial—except this, that the project from its absurdity refutes itself.

The idea of introducing a monarchy or aristocracy into this country, by employing the influence and force of a government continually changing hands towards it, is one of those visionary things that none but madmen could meditate and that no wise men will believe.

If it could be done at all, which is utterly incredible, it would require a long series of time, certainly beyond the life of any individual to effect it. Who then would enter into such plot? For what purpose of interest or ambition?

To hope that the people may be cajoled into giving their sanctions to such institutions is still more chimerical. A people so enlightened and so diversified as the people of this country can surely never be brought to it but from convulsions and disorders in consequence of the acts of popular demagogues.

The truth unquestionably is that the only path to a subversion of the republican system of the country is by flattering the prejudices of the people and exciting their jealousies and apprehensions to throw affairs into confusion and bring on civil commotion. Tired at length of anarchy, or want of government, they may take shelter in the arms of monarchy for repose and security.

Those, then, who resist a confirmation of public order are the true artificers of monarchy—not that this is the intention of the generality of them. Yet it would not be difficult to lay the finger upon some of their party who may justly be suspected. When a man unprincipled in private life, desperate in his fortune, bold in his temper, possessed of considerable talents, having the advantage of military habits—despotic in his ordinary demeanour—known to have scoffed in private at the principles of liberty—when such a man is seen to mount the hobby horse of popularity—to join in the cry of danger to liberty—to take every opportunity of embarrassing the general government & bringing it under suspicion—to flatter and fall in with all the nonsense of the zealots of the day—it may justly be suspected that his object is to throw things into confusion that he may "ride the storm and direct the whirlwind."

It has aptly been observed that *Cato* was the Tory, *Caesar* the whig, of his day. The former frequently resisted—the latter always flattered the follies of the people. Yet the former perished with the republic, the latter destroyed it.

No popular government was ever without its Catalines & its Caesars. These are its true enemies.

As far as I am informed the anxiety of those who are calumniated is to keep the government in the state in which it is, which they fear will be no easy task, from a natural tendency in the state of things to exalt the local on the ruins of the national government. Some of them appear to wish, in a constitutional way, a change in the judiciary department of the government, from an apprehension that an orderly and effectual administration of justice cannot be obtained without a more intimate connection between the state and national tribunals. But even this is not an object of any set of men as a party. There is a difference of opinion about it on various grounds among those who have generally acted together. As to any other change of consequence, I believe nobody dreams of it.

'Tis curious to observe the anticipations of the different parties. One side appears to believe that there is a serious plot to overturn the state governments and substitute monarchy to the present republican system. The other side firmly believes that there is a serious plot to overturn the general government & elevate the separate power of the states upon its ruins. Both sides may be equally wrong & their mutual jealousies may be materially causes of the appearances which mutually disturb them, and sharpen them against each other.

Objection the 15. This change was contemplated &c.

This is a palpable misrepresentation. No man that I know of contemplated the introducing into this country of a monarchy. A very small number (not more than three or four) manifested theoretical opinions favorable in the abstract to a constitution like that of Great Britain, but everyone agreed that such a constitution except as to the general distribution of departments and powers was out of the question in reference to this country. The member who was most explicit on this point (a member from New York) declared in strong terms that the republican theory ought to be adhered to in this country as long as there was any chance of its success—that the idea of a perfect equality of political rights among the citizens, exclusive of all permanent or hereditary distinctions, was of a nature to engage the good wishes of every good man, whatever might be his theoretic doubts—that it merited his best efforts to give success to it in practice—that hitherto from an incompetent structure of the government it had not had a fair trial, and that the endeavor ought then to be to secure to it a better chance of success by a government more capable of energy and order.

There is not a man at present in either branch of the legislature who, that I recollect, had held language in the convention favorable to monarchy.

The basis therefore of this suggestion fails.

16. So many of them &c.

This has been answered above. Neither description of character is to be found in the legislature. In the Senate there are 9 or ten who were members of the Convention; in the House of Representatives not more than six or seven. Of those who are in the last-mentioned house—none can be considered as influential but Mr. Madison and Mr. Gerry. Are they monarchy men?

As to the 17th, 18th, and 19th heads—They are rather inferences from and comments upon what is before suggested than specific objections. The answer to them must therefore be derived from what is said under other heads.

It is certainly much to be regretted that party discriminations are so far geographical as they have been, and that ideas of a severance of the Union are creeping in both north and south. In the south it is supposed that more government than is expedient is desired by the north. In the north it is believed that the prejudices of the south are incompatible with the necessary degree of government and with the attainment of the essential ends of national union. In both quarters there are respectable men who talk of separation as a thing dictated by the different geniuses and different prejudices of the parts. But happily their number is not considerable—& the prevailing sentiment of the people is in favor of their true interest, union. And it is to be hoped that the efforts of wise men will be able to prevent a schism, which would be injurious in different degrees to different portions of the Union, but would seriously wound the prosperity of all.

As to the sacrifice of southern to northern prejudices—if the conflict has been between *prejudices* and *prejudices*, it is certainly to be wished for mutual gratification that there had been mutual concession; but if the conflict has been between *great* and *substantial* national objects on the one hand, and theoretical prejudices on the other, it is difficult to desire that the former should in any instance have yielded.

Objection 20. The owers of the debt are in the southern and the holders of it in the northern division.

Answer. If this were literally true it would be no argument for or against anything. It would be still politically and morally right for the debtors to pay their creditors.

But it is in *no sense* true. The owers of the debt are the people of *every* state, south, middle, north. The holders are the individual creditors—citizens of the United Netherlands, Great Britain, France, & of these states, north, middle, south. Though some men who constantly substitute hypothesis to fact, imagination to evidence, assert and reassert that the inhabitants of the south contribute *more* than those of the north, yet there is no pretence that they contribute *all*; and even the assertion of greater contribution is unsupported by documents facts, or, it may be added, probabilities. Though the inhabitants of the south manufacture less than those of the north, which is the great argument, yet it does not follow that they consume more of taxable articles. It is a solid answer to this that *whites* live better, wear more and better cloths, and consume more luxuries, than blacks who constitute so considerable a part of the population of the south—that the inhabitants of cities and towns, which abound so much more in the north than in the south, consume more of foreign articles than the inhabitants of the country—that it is a general rule that communities consume & contribute in proportion to their active or circulating wealth and that the northern regions have more active or circulating wealth than the southern.

If official documents are consulted, though for obvious reasons they are not decisive, they contradict rather than confirm the hypothesis of greater proportional contribution in the southern division.

But to make the allegation in the objection true, it is necessary not merely that the inhabitants of the south should contribute more, but that they should contribute *all*.

It must be confessed that a much larger proportion of the debt is *owned* by inhabitants of the states from Pennsylvania to New Hampshire inclusively than in the states south of Pennsylvania.

But as to the primitive debt of the United States, that was the case in its original concoction. This arose from two causes. I. From the war having more constantly been carried on in the northern quarter, which led to obtaining more men and greater supplies in that quarter; and credit having been, for a considerable time, the main instrument of the government, a consequent accumulation of debt in that quarter took place. II. From the greater ability of the northern and middle states to furnish men money and other supplies, and from the greater quantity of men, money, and other supplies which they did furnish. The loan office debt, the army debt, the debt of the five great departments was *contracted* in a much larger proportion in the northern and middle than in the southern states.

It must be confessed too that by the attractions of a superior monied capital the disparity has increased, but it was great in the beginning.

As to the assumed debt, the proportion in the south was at the first somewhat larger than in the north; and it must be acknowledged that this has since, from the same superiority of monied capital in the north, ceased to be the case.

But if the northern people who were originally greater creditors than the southern have become still more so as purchasers, is it any reason that an honorable provision should not be made for their debt? Or is the government to blame for having made it? Did the northern people take their property by violence from the southern, or did they purchase and pay for it?

It may be answered that they obtained a considerable part of it by speculation, taking advantage of superior opportunities of information.

But admitting this to be true in all the latitude in which it is commonly stated—Is a government to bend the general maxims of policy and to mold its measures according to the accidental course of private speculations? Is it to do this or omit that in cases of great national importance because one set of individuals may gain, another lose, from unequal opportunities of information, from unequal degrees of resource, craft, confidence, or enterprise?

Moreover—There is much exaggeration in stating the manner of the alienation of the debt. The principal speculations in state debt, whatever may be pretended, certainly began after the promulgation of the plan for assuming by the report of the secretary of the treasury to the House of Representatives. The resources of individuals in this country are too limited to have admitted of much progress in purchases before the knowledge of that plan was diffused throughout the country. After that, purchasers and sellers were upon equal ground. If the purchasers speculated upon the sellers, in many instances the sellers speculated upon the purchasers. Each made his calculation of chances and founded upon it an exchange of money for certificates. It has turned out generally that the buyer had the best of the bargain; but the seller got the value of his commodity according to his estimate of it, and probably in a great number of instances more. This shall be explained:

It happened that Mr. Madison and some other distinguished characters of the south started in opposition to the assumption. The high opinion entertained of them made it be taken for granted in that quarter that the opposition would be successful. The securities quickly rose by means of purchases beyond their former prices. It was imagined that they would soon return to their old station by a rejection of the proposition for assuming. And the certificate holders were eager to part with them at their current prices, calculating on a loss to the purchasers from their future fall. The representation is not conjectural; it is founded in information from respectable and intelligent southern characters—and may be ascertained by inquiry.

Hence it happened that the inhabitants of the southern states sustained a considerable loss by the opposition to the assumption from southern gentlemen and their too great confidence in the efficacy of that opposition.

Further—A great part of the debt which has been purchased by northern of southern citizens has been at high prices, in numerous instances beyond the true value. In the late delirium of speculation large sums were purchased at 25 percent above par and upwards.

The southern people upon the whole have not parted with their property for nothing. They parted with it voluntarily—in most cases upon fair terms, without surprise or deception, in many cases for more than its value. Tis their own fault if the purchase money has not been beneficial to them—and the presumption is that it has been so in a material degree.

Let then any candid and upright mind, weighing all the circumstances, pronounce whether there be any real hardship in the inhabitants of the south being required to contribute their proportion to a provision for the debt as it now exists—whether, if at liberty, they could honestly dispute the doing of it, or whether they can even in candor and good faith complain of being obliged to do it.

If they can, it is time to unlearn all the ancient notions of justice and morality, and to adopt a new system of ethics.

Observation 21. The Antifederal champions &c.

Answer. All that can be said in answer to this has been already said.

It is much to be wished that the true state of the case may not have been that the Antifederal champions have been encouraged in their activity by the countenance which has been given to their principles by certain Federalists, who in an envious and ambitious struggle for power, influence, and preeminence have embraced as auxiliaries the numerous party originally disaffected to the government in the hope that these, united with the factious and feeble-minded Federalists whom they can detach, will give them the predominancy. This would be nothing more than the old story of personal and party emulation.

The Anti-Federal champions alluded to may be taught to abate their exultation by being told that the great body of the Federalists, or rather the great body of the people, are of opinion that none of their predictions have been fulfilled—That the beneficial effects of the government have exceeded expectation and are witnessed by the general prosperity of the nation.

Explanatory Notes

1 The resolutions held that the parts of the act for providing for the debt that assumed the state debts were unconstitutional, and that the parts that limited the ability of the government to redeem the debt were dangerous to the rights and subversive of the interests of the people. See *PAH*, 7: 150 n. 1.
2 The original reads "effects," but we think "efforts" far more likely.
3 Here Hamilton quotes Adam Smith's *Wealth of Nations*. See *PAH*, 10: 116 n. 100.

PART 2

The Challenges of Foreign Policy: 1793–1795

For the Gazette of the United States, March–April, 1793

The late war with Great Britain produced three parties in the U. States, an *English* party, a *French* party, and an *American* party, if the latter can with propriety be called a party. These parties continue to the present moment. There are persons among us who appear to be more alive to the interests of France, on the one hand, and to those of Great Britain, on the other, than to those of the U. States. Both these dispositions are to be condemned and will be rejected by every true American.

A dispassionate and virtuous citizen of the U. States will scorn to stand on any but purely *American* ground. It will be his study to render his feeling and affections neutral and impartial towards all foreign nations. His prayer will be for peace and that his country may be as much as possible kept out of the destructive vortex of foreign politics. To speak figuratively, he will regard his own country as a wife to whom he is bound to be exclusively faithful and affectionate, and he will watch with a jealous attention every propensity of his heart to wander towards a foreign country, which he will regard as a mistress that may pervert his fidelity and mar his happiness. 'Tis to be regretted that there are persons among us who appear to have a passion for a foreign mistress, as violent as it is irregular—and who, in the paroxysms of their love, seem, perhaps without being themselves sensible of it, too ready to sacrifice the real welfare of the political family to their partiality for the object of their tenderness.

These reflections are suggested by an attempt which appears to be making under different shapes to diffuse among the people an opinion that in certain events the United States are bound to take part with France in the expected war with G. Britain. This effort is not prudent, is not commendable. It tends unnecessarily to hazard the public peace by holding out to Great Britain an appearance that a disposition to take such a part exists in this country. It tends to embarrass the councils of the country by leading the public opinion to prejudge the question. Discussions on one side will produce discussions on the other, and in one way or the other impressions may be formed contrary to the true policy of the nation.

The treaty between France and the U. States is in possession of the public. But whether there be any secret article defining the extent and force of any of its stipulations—whether there have been any official explanations respecting their true import and application, which may give a complexion different from that which the words may seem to bear—these, and perhaps other circumstances necessary to a right judgment, are unknown.

But without knowing them it may justly be doubted whether there be anything in the treaty, as it appears, that under the *existing circumstances* of the parties can oblige the U. States to embark.

It is understood that *general guarantees*, where no precise stipulations point out special succors or special duties, have the least force of any species of national engagement, leaving much to reciprocal convenience. It is moreover a good excuse for not fulfilling a stipulation, especially if not very definite or precise, that it would *uselessly* expose the party who is to perform to a *great extremity* of danger.

If all or nearly all the maritime powers shall be combined against France, what could the U. States do towards preserving her American possessions against attacks of those powers, which is the object of the guarantee on their part—and who could say to what they would expose themselves by embarking in a war on the side of France in her present situation?

But a still more serious question arises. Are the U. States bound to fulfill to the *present ruling powers* of France, in the midst of a *pending* and *disputed* revolution, the stipulations made with the former government—with a prince who has been dethroned and decapitated?

It may be answered that treaties are made between *nations* not between *governments*, and that the obligations they create attach themselves to the contracting nations, whatever changes in the form of their government take place. This, as a general principle, is true. But it is true only in reference to a *change* which has been finally *established* and *secured*, not to one which is *depending* and *in contest*, and which may never be consummated. Such is the condition of France at this time. It is therefore in the discretion of the U. States to judge when the new government is so established as to be a proper organ of the national will, in claiming the performance of any stipulations which have been made with the late sovereign of France.

These considerations at least justify a suspension of the public opinion on the points in question, and afford a good ground of hope that if the powers at war with France will act with moderation & justice towards this country we shall be able to continue in our present happy condition and avoid the terrible calamities of war. Which that God may grant must be the fervent prayer of every good citizen!

Answer to Question the 3rd Proposed by the President of the U. States, April 18, 1793

"If received," meaning a minister from the Republic of France, "shall it be absolutely or with qualifications, and if with qualifications of what kind."

It is conceived to be advisable that the reception of the expected minister from the Republic of France should be qualified by a previous declaration substantially to this effect—"that the government of the United States uniformly entertaining cordial wishes for the happiness of the French nation, and disposed to maintain with it an amicable communication and intercourse, uninterrupted by political vicissitudes, does not hesitate to receive him in the character which his credentials import; yet considering the origin, course, and circumstances of the relations contracted between the two countries, and the existing position of the affairs of France, it is deemed advisable and proper on the part of the United States to reserve to future consideration and discussion the question—whether the operation of the treaties by which those relations were formed ought not to be deemed temporarily and provisionally suspended—and under this impression it is thought due to a spirit of candid and friendly procedure to apprise him before hand of the intention to reserve that question, lest silence on the point should occasion misconstruction."

The grounds of this opinion are as follow—

The treaties between the United States and France were made with His Most Christian Majesty, his heirs, and successors. The government of France which existed at the time those treaties were made gave way in the first instance to a new constitution, formed by the representatives of the nation and accepted by the king, which went into regular operation. Of a sudden, a tumultuous rising took place—the king was seized, imprisoned, and declared to be suspended by the authority of the National Assembly, a body delegated to exercise the legislative functions of the already established government—in no shape authorized to divest any other of the constituted authorities of its legal capacities or powers. So far, then, what was done was a manifest assumption of power.

To justify it, it is alleged to have been necessary for the safety of the nation, to prevent the success of a counter-revolution, meditated or patronized by the king.

On the other side it is affirmed that the whole transaction was merely the execution of a plan, which had been for some time projected and had been gradually ripening, to bring about an abolition of the royalty and the establishment of a republican government.

No satisfactory proof is known to have been produced to fix upon the king the charges which have been brought against him.

On the other hand, declarations have escaped from characters who took a lead in the measure of suppressing the royalty, which seem to amount to a tacit acknowledgement that the events of the tenth of August were the result of a premeditated plan of the republican party to get rid of the monarchical power—rather than a necessary counteraction of mischievous designs on the part of the king.

Mr. Deseze—one of the counsel for the king makes these striking observations on the point—

"I know it has been said that he excited the insurrection to gain the end of his plan. But who is now ignorant that this insurrection had been planned, ripened—that it had its agents, its Consul, its Directory? Who knows not that there had been signed acts and treaties on this subject?"

"*Within this hall* has been contested the *glories* of the 10th of August. I do not come to dispute the glory; but since it has been *proved* that *this day was meditated*, how can it be attributed as a crime to him?"

The events of the tenth of August were followed on the second and third of September with the massacre of a great number of persons in different parts of France, including several distinguished individuals who were known to be attached either to the ancient government or to the constitution which had succeeded it.

The suspension of the king was accompanied by a call upon the primary assemblies to depute persons to represent them in a convention in order to the taking of such measures as the exigency of the conjuncture might require.

Under circumstances not free from precipitation, violence, and awe, deputies to a National Convention were chosen. They assembled on the ___ of September at Paris, and on the very day of their meeting decreed the abolition of royalty.

They proceeded in the next place to organize a temporary provisional government, charged with managing the affairs of the nation till *a constitution should be established*.

As a circumstance that gives a complexion to the course of things, it is proper to mention that the Jacobin Club at Paris (a society which with its branches in different parts of France appears to have had a prevailing influence over the affairs of the country), previous to the meeting of the Convention entered into measures with the avowed object of *purging* the Convention of those persons, favorers of royalty, who might have escaped the *attention* of the *primary assemblies*.

In the last place, the late king of France has been tried and condemned by the Convention and has suffered death.

Whether he has suffered justly or unjustly, whether he has been a guilty tyrant or an unfortunate victim, is at least a problem. There certainly can be no hazard in affirming that no proof has yet come to light sufficient to establish a belief that the death of Louis is an act of national justice.

It appears to be regarded in a different light throughout Europe and by a numerous and respectable part, if not by a majority, of the people of the United States.

Almost all Europe is or seems likely to be armed in opposition to the present rulers of France—with the declared or implied intention of restoring if possible the royalty, in the successor of the deceased monarch.

The present war, then, turns essentially on the point—what shall be the future government of France? Shall the royal authority be restored in the person of the successor of Louis, or shall a republic be constituted in exclusion of it?

Thus stand the material facts which regard the origin of our connections with France and the obligations or dispensations that now exist. They have been stated not with a view to indicate a definitive opinion concerning the propriety of the conduct of the present rulers of France, but to show that the course of the revolution there has been attended with circumstances which militate against a full conviction of its having been brought to its present *stage* by such a *free*, *regular*, and *deliberate* act of the nation, and with such a spirit of justice and humanity, as ought to silence all scruples about the validity of what has been done, and the morality of aiding it, even if consistent with policy.

This great and important question arises out of the facts which have been stated.

Are the United States bound, by the principles of the laws of nations, to consider the treaties heretofore made with France as in present force and operation between them and the actual governing powers of the French nation? Or may they elect to consider their operation as suspended, reserving also a right to judge finally whether any such changes have happened in the political affairs of France as may justify a renunciation of those treaties?

It is believed that they have an option to consider the operation of the treaties as suspended, and will have eventually a right to renounce them, if such changes shall take place as can *bona fide* be pronounced *to render* a continuance of the connections which result from them disadvantageous or dangerous.

There are two general propositions which may be opposed to this opinion. I. That a nation has a right, in its own discretion, to change its form of government, to abolish one and substitute another. II. That *real* treaties (of which description those in question are) bind the nations whose governments contract and continue in force notwithstanding any changes which happen in the forms of their government.

The truth of the first proposition ought to be admitted in its fullest latitude. But it will by no means follow that because a nation has a right to manage its own concerns as it thinks fit, and to make such changes in its political institutions as itself judges best calculated to promote its interests—that it has *therefore* a right to involve other nations, with whom it may have had connections, *absolutely* and *unconditionally* in the consequences of the changes which it may think proper to make. This would be to give to a nation or society not only a power over its own happiness but a power over the happiness of other nations or societies. It would be to extend the operations of the maxim much beyond the *reason* of it—which is simply that every nation ought to have a right to provide for its *own happiness*.

If then a nation thinks fit to make changes in its government, which render treaties that before subsisted between it and another nation useless or dangerous or hurtful to that other nation, it is a plain dictate of reason that the *latter* will have a right to renounce those treaties; because *it* also has a right to take care of its own happiness, and cannot be obliged to suffer this to be impaired by the means which its neighbor or ally may have adopted for its own advantage, contrary to the ancient state of things.

But it may be said that an obligation to submit to the inconveniencies that may ensue arises from the other maxim which has been stated, namely, that real treaties bind nations notwithstanding the changes which happen in the forms of their governments.

All general rules are to be construed with certain reasonable limitations. That which has been just mentioned must be understood in this sense—that changes in forms of government do not of course abrogate *real* treaties, that they continue absolutely binding on the party which makes the change, and will bind the other party, unless in due time and for just cause he declares his election to renounce them—that in good faith he ought not to renounce them, unless the change which happened does really render them useless or materially less advantageous or more dangerous than before. But for good and sufficient cause he may renounce them.

Nothing can be more evident than that the existing forms of government of two nations may enter far into the motives of a real treaty. Two republics may contract an alliance—the principal inducement to which may be a similarity of constitutions, producing common interest to defend their mutual rights and liberties. A change of the government of one of them into a monarchy or despotism may destroy this inducement and the main link of common interest. Two monarchies may form an alliance on a like principle, their common defense against a powerful neighboring republic. The change of the government of one of the allies may destroy the source of common sympathy and common interest and render it prudent for the other ally to renounce the connection and seek to fortify itself in some other quarter.

Two nations may form an alliance because each has confidence in the energy and efficacy of the government of the other. A revolution may subject one of them to a different form of government—feeble, fluctuating, and turbulent, liable to provoke wars & very little fitted to repel them. Even the connections of a nation with other foreign powers may enter into the motives of an alliance with it. If a dissolution of ancient connections shall have been a consequence of a revolution of government, the external political relations of the parties may have become so varied as to occasion an incompatibility of the alliance with the power which had changed its constitution with the other connections of its ally, connections perhaps essential to its welfare.

In such cases, reason, which is the touchstone of all similar maxims, would dictate that the party whose government had remained stationary would have a right, under a *bona fide* conviction that the change in the situation of the other party would render a future connection detrimental or dangerous, to declare the connection dissolved.

Contracts between nations as between individuals must lose their force where the considerations fail.

A treaty *pernicious* to the state is of itself void where no change in the situation of either of the parties takes place. By a much stronger reason it must become *voidable*, at the option of the other party, when the voluntary act of one of the allies has made so material a change in the condition of things as is always implied in a radical revolution of government.

Moreover, the maxim in question must, it is presumed, be understood with this further limitation—that the revolution be *consummated*—that the new government be *established* and recognized among nations—that there be an *undisputed* organ of the national will to claim the performance of the stipulations made with the former government.

It is not natural to presume that an ally is obliged to throw his weight into either scale—where the war involves the very point, what shall be the government of the country, and that too against the very party with whom the formal obligations of the alliance have been contracted.

It is more natural to conclude that in such a case the ally ought either to aid the party with whom the contract was immediately made—or to consider the operation of the alliance as suspended. The latter is undoubtedly his duty rather than the former where the nation appears to have pronounced the change.

A doctrine contrary to that here supported may involve an opposition of moral duties, and dilemmas of a very singular and embarrassing kind.

A nation may owe its existence or preservation entirely, or in a great degree, to the voluntary succors which it derived from the monarch of a country—the then lawful organ of the national will—the director of its sword and its purse—the dispenser of its aids and its favors. In consideration of the good offices promised or afforded by him, an alliance may have been formed—between the monarch, his heirs, and successors and the country indebted to him for those good offices—stipulating future cooperation and mutual aid. This monarch, without any particular crime on his part, may be afterwards deposed and expelled by his nation, or by a triumphant faction, which may perhaps momentarily direct the national voice. He may find in the assistance of neighboring powers friendly to his cause the means of endeavoring to reinstate himself.

In the midst of his efforts to accomplish this purpose—the ruling powers of the nation over which he had reigned call upon the country which had been saved by his friendship and patronage to perform the stipulations expressed in the alliance made with him and embark in a war against their friend and benefactor, on the suggestion that the treaty being a *real* one, the actual rulers of the nation have a right to claim the benefit of it.

If there be no option in such case—would there not be a most perplexing conflict of opposite obligations?—of the faith supposed to be plighted by the treaty and of justice and gratitude towards a man, from whom essential benefits had been received, and who could oppose the *formal* and *express* terms of the contract to an abstract theoretic proposition? Would genuine honor, would true morality, permit the taking a hostile part against the friend and benefactor, being at the same time the original party to the contract?

Suppose the call of the actual rulers to be complied with and the war to have been entered into by the ally—suppose the expelled monarch to have reentered his former dominions, and to have been joined by one half of his former subjects—how would the obligation then stand? He will now have added to the title of being the formal party to the contract that of being the actual possessor of one half the country and of the wishes of one half the nation.

Is it supposable that in such a case the obligations of the alliance can continue in favor of those by whom he had been expelled? Or would they then revert again to the monarch? Or would they fluctuate with the alternations of good and ill fortune attending the one or the other party? Can a principle which would involve such a dilemma be true? Is it not evident that there must be an option to consider the operation of the alliance as suspended during the contest concerning the government—that on the one hand there may not be a necessity of taking part with the expelled monarch against the apparent will of the nation, or on the other a necessity of joining the ruling powers of the moment against the immediate party with whom the contract was made and from whom the consideration may have flowed?

If the opinions of writers be consulted, they will, as far as they go, confirm the sense of the maxim which is here contended for.

Grotius, while he asserts the general principle of the obligation of real treaties upon nations notwithstanding the changes in their governments, admits the qualification which has been insisted upon and expressly excepts the case where it appears that the motive to the treaty was "peculiar to the form of government, *as* when free states enter into an alliance for the defense of their liberties." Book II, Chap. 16. § XVI. No. 1.

And *Vattel*, who is the most systematic of the writers on the laws of nations, lays down the qualification in the greatest latitude. To give a correct idea of his meaning, it will be of use to transcribe the entire section with its marginal note. It is found—Book II, Chap. XII. § 197.

"The same question" (says he, to wit, that stated in the margin) "presents itself in *real* alliances, and in general in all alliances made with the state and not in particular with a king for the defense of his person. An ally ought doubtless to be defended against every invasion, against every foreign violence, and even against his rebellious subjects; in the same manner a republic ought to be defended against the enterprises of one who attempts to destroy the public liberty. But it ought to be remembered that an ally of the state or the nation is not its judge. If the nation has deposed its king in form, if the people of a republic have driven out their magistrates and set themselves at liberty, or acknowledged the authority of an usurper either expressly or tacitly, to oppose these domestic regulations by disputing their justice or validity would be to interfere with the government of the nation and to do it an injury. The ally *remains the ally of the state*, notwithstanding the change that has happened in it. *However* when this change renders the alliance *useless, dangerous*, or *disagreeable*, it may renounce it, for it may say upon a good foundation that it would not have entered into an alliance with that nation had it been under the present form of government."

It is not perceived that there is any ambiguity of expression or any other circumstance to throw the least obscurity upon the sense of the author. The precise question he raises is: what is the obligation of a *real* alliance when the king who is the ally is driven from the throne? He concludes, after several intermediate observations, that the *ally remains the ally of the state*, notwithstanding the change which has happened. Nevertheless, says he, when the change renders the alliance *useless, dangerous*, or *disagreeable*, it may be renounced.

It is observable that the question made by writers always is whether, in a real alliance, when the king who is the ally is deposed, the ally of the deposed king is bound to succor and support him. And though it is decided by the better opinions, as well as by the reason of the thing, that there is not an obligation to support him against the will of the nation, when his dethronement is to be ascribed to that source—yet there is never a single suggestion on the other hand of the ally of such dethroned king being obliged to assist his nation against him. The most that appears to be admitted in favor of the decision of the nation is that there is no support due to the dethroned prince.

Puffendorf puts this matter upon very proper ground. Referring to the opinion of Grotius, who with too much latitude lays it down "that a league made with a king is valid though that king or his successors be expelled from the kingdom *by his subjects*; for though he has lost his possession, the right to the crown still remains in him"—makes the following observation. "To me so much in this case seems to be certain, that if the terms of the league *expressly mention* and *intend* the defense of the prince's *person* and *family*, he ought to be assisted in the recovery of his kingdom. But if the league was formed for *public good* only, 'tis a *disputable* point whether the exiled prince can demand assistance in virtue of his league. *For the aids mentioned are presumed to have been promised against foreign enemies, without view of this particular case.* Not but that still such a league leaves *liberty* to assist a *lawful prince* against an *usurper*."

The presumption here stated is a natural and a proper one, and in its reason applies to both sides, to the exiled prince, who should demand succors against his nation, and to the nation, who having dethroned its prince should demand succors to support the act of dethronement and establish the revolution. The ally in such case is not bound to come in aid of either party—but may consider the operation of the alliance as suspended till the competition about the government is decided.

What a difference is there between asserting it to be a *disputable* point whether the ally of a dethroned prince in the case of a real treaty is not bound to assist him against the nation—and maintaining that the ally is bound at all events to assist the nation against him. For this is the consequence of asserting that such a treaty *ipso facto* attaches itself to the body of the nation, even in the course of a pending revolution, and without option either to suspend or renounce.

If the practice of nations be consulted—neither will that be found to confirm the proposition—that the obligation of real treaties extends unconditionally to the *actual governors* of nations, whatever changes take place. In the books which treat the subject, numerous examples of the contrary are quoted. The most prevailing practice has been to assist the *ancient* sovereign. In the very instance to which this discussion relates, this is the course which a great part of Europe directly or indirectly pursues.

It may be argued by way of objection to what has been said—that admitting the general principle of a right for sufficient cause to renounce, yet still, as the change in the present case is from a monarchy to a republic and no sufficient cause hitherto exists for a renunciation—the possibility of its arising hereafter in the progress of events does not appear a valid reason for resorting to the principle in question.

To this the answer is that no government has yet been instituted in France in lieu of that which has been pulled down—that the existing political powers are by the French themselves denominated provisional and are to give way to a constitution to be established.

It is therefore impossible to foresee what the future government of France will be—and in this state of uncertainty the right to *renounce* resolves itself of course into a right to *suspend*. The one is a consequence of the other, *applicable* to the *undetermined* state of things. If there be a right to renounce when the change of government proves to be of a nature to render an alliance useless or injurious—there must be a right, amidst a pending revolution, to wait to see what change will take place.

Should it be said that the treaty is binding now, no objectionable change having yet taken place, but may be renounced hereafter if any such change shall take place? The answer is that it is not possible to pronounce at present what is the *quality* of the change. Everything is in *transitu*. This state of suspense as to the object of option naturally suspends the option itself. The business may in its progress assume a variety of forms. If the issue may not be waited for, the obligations of the country may fluctuate indefinitely, be one thing today, another tomorrow, a consequence which is inadmissible.

Besides: the true reasoning would seem to be that to admit the *operation* of the treaties while the event is pending would be to take the chance of what that event shall be and would preclude a future renunciation.

Moreover: the right to consider the operation of the treaties as suspended results from this further consideration—that during a *pending revolution* an ally in a real treaty is not bound to pronounce between the competitors or contending parties.

The conclusion from the whole is that there is an option in the United States to hold the operation of the treaties suspended—and that in the event if the form of government established in France shall be such as to render a continuance of the treaties contrary to the interest of the United States, they may be renounced.

If there be such an option, there are strong reasons to show that the character and interest of the United States require that they should pursue the course of holding the operation of the treaties suspended.

Their character—because it was from Louis the XVI, the then sovereign of the country, that they received those succors which were so important in the establishment of their independence and liberty—It was with him, his heirs, and successors that they contracted the engagements by which they obtained those precious succors.

It is enough on their part to respect the right of the nation to change its government so far as not to side with the successors of the dethroned prince—as to receive their ambassador and keep up an amicable intercourse—as to be willing to render every good office not contrary to the duties of real neutrality.

To throw their weight into the scale of the new government would, it is to be feared, be considered by mankind as not consistent with a decent regard to the relations which subsisted between them and Louis the XVI—as not consistent with a due sense of the services they received from that unfortunate prince—as not consistent with national delicacy and decorum.

The character of the United States may be also concerned in keeping clear of any connection with the present government of France in other views.

A struggle for liberty is in itself respectable and glorious. When conducted with magnanimity, justice, and humanity it ought to command the admiration of every friend to human nature. But if sullied by crimes and extravagancies, it loses its respectability. Though success may rescue it from infamy, it cannot in the opinion of the sober part of mankind attach to it much positive merit or praise. But in the event of a want of success, a general execration must attend it.

It appears thus far but too probable that the pending revolution of France has sustained some serious blemishes. There is too much ground to anticipate that a sentence uncommonly severe will be passed upon it if it fails.

Will it be well for the United States to expose their reputation to the *issue* by implicating themselves as associates? Will their reputation be promoted by a successful issue? What will it suffer by the reverse? These questions suggest very serious considerations to a mind anxious for the reputation of the country— anxious that it may emulate a character of sobriety, moderation, justice, and love of order.

The *interest* of the United States seems to dictate the course recommended in many ways.

I. In reference to their character, from the considerations already stated.
II. In reference to their peace.

As the present treaties contain stipulations of military succors and military aids in certain cases which are likely to occur, there can be no doubt that *if* there be an option to consider them as not binding, as not in operation—the considering them as binding, as in operation, would be equivalent to making new treaties of similar import—and it is a well settled point that such stipulations entered into pending a war or with a view to a war is a departure from neutrality.

How far the parties opposed to France may think fit to treat us as enemies in consequence of this is a problem which experience only can solve—the solution of which will probably be regulated by their views of their own interest—by the circumstances which may occur—and it is far from impossible that these will restrain them so long as we in fact take no active part in favor of France.

But if there be an option to avoid it, it can hardly be wise to incur so great an additional risk and embarrassment—to implicate ourselves in the perplexities which may follow.

With regard to the good effect of the conduct which is advocated upon the powers at war with France, nothing need be said.

Considering our interest with reference even to France herself, some reasons may be urged in favor of considering the treaties as suspended.

It seems to be the general if not the universal sentiment that we ought not to embark in the war.

Suppose the French islands attacked and we called upon to perform the guarantee.

To avoid complying with it—we must either say—

That the war being *offensive* on the part of France, the *casus fœderis* does not exist.

Or, that as our cooperation would be *useless* to the object of the guarantee and attended with more than ordinary danger to ourselves, we cannot afford it.

Would the one or the other be satisfactory to France?

The first would probably *displease*—the last would *not please*. It is moreover the most questionable & the least reputable of all the objections which a nation is allowed to oppose to the performance of its engagements. We should not therefore be much more certain of avoiding the displeasure of the present ruling powers of France by considering the treaties as in operation than by considering their operation as suspended, taking it for granted that we are in either case to observe a neutral conduct *in fact*.

But suppose the contest unsuccessful on the part of the present governing powers of France. What would be our situation with the future government of that country?

Should we not be branded and detested by it as the worst of ingrates?

When it is added that the restoration of the monarchy would be very materially attributed to the interposition of Great Britain—the reflection just suggested acquires peculiar weight and importance.

But against this may be placed the consideration—that in the event of the success of the present governing powers we should stand on much worse ground by having considered the operation of the treaties as suspended than by having pursued a contrary conduct.

This is not clear, for the reasons just given, unless we are also willing, if called upon, to become parties in the war.

But admitting that the *course* of considering the treaties as in present operation would give us a claim of merit with France in the event of the establishment of the republic—our affairs with that country would not stand *so much the better* on this account as they would *stand worse* for giving operation to the treaties—should the monarchy be restored.

We should still have to offer a better claim to the friendship of France than any other power—the not taking side with her enemies—the early acknowledgement of the republic by the reception of its minister—and such good offices as have been and may be rendered, consistently with a sincere neutrality.

The reasons too which induced us not to go further will have their due weight in times that shall restore tranquility, moderation, and sober reflection! They will justify us even to France herself.

Is there not, however, danger that a refusal to admit the operation of the treaties might occasion an immediate rupture with France?

A danger of this sort cannot be supposed without supposing such a degree of intemperance on the part of France as will finally force us to *quarrel* with her or to *embark* with her.

And if such be her temper, a fair calculation of hazards will lead us to risk her displeasure in the first instance.

An inquiry naturally arises of this kind—Whether from the nature of the treaties they have any such intrinsic value as to render it inexpedient to put them in jeopardy by raising a question about their operation or validity?

Here it may freely be pronounced there is no difficulty. The military stipulations they contain are contrary to that neutrality in the quarrels of Europe which it is our true policy to cultivate and maintain. And the commercial stipulations to be found in them present no peculiar advantages. They secure to us nothing or scarcely anything which an inevitable course of circumstances would not produce. It would be our interest, in the abstract, to be disengaged from them and take the chance of future negotiation for a better treaty of commerce.

It might be observed by way of objection to what has been said—that an *admission* of the *operation* of the treaties has been considered as equivalent to taking part with France.

It is true that the two things have been considered as *equivalent* to each other—and in strict reasoning this ought to be the case. Because—

I. If there be an option, the effect of not using it would be to pass from a *state* of *neutrality* to that *of being an ally*—thereby *authorizing* the powers at war with France to treat us as an enemy.
II. If under the operation of the treaties we are not bound to embark in the war, it must be owing either to *casualty* or *inability*.

If the war is not *offensive* on the part of France, an attack on the West India Islands would leave us no escape but in the plea of inability.

The putting ourselves in a situation in which it might so happen that we could preserve our neutrality under no other plea than that of *inability* is in all the political legal relations of the subject to make ourselves a party. In other words, the placing ourselves in a position in which it would depend on casualty whether it would not become our duty to engage in the war—ought in a general question of *establishing* or *recognizing* a political relation with a foreign power embarked in war—to be regarded in the same light as taking part with that power in the war. To do a thing, or to contract or incur an obligation of doing it, are not in such a question materially different.

There remain some miscellaneous views of the subject which will serve to fortify the general reasoning.

I. The conduct of the present government of France gives a sanction to other nations to use some latitude of discretion in respect to their treaties with the former government. That government, it is understood, has formally declared null various stipulations of the ancient government with foreign powers—on the principle of their inapplicability to the new order of things. Were it to be urged that an erroneous conduct on the part of France will not justify a like conduct on our part, it might be solidly replied that a rule of practice formally adopted by any nation for regulating its political obligations towards other nations may justly be appealed to as a standard for regulating the obligations of other nations towards her. Suppose this general ground to have been explicitly taken by France, that all treaties made by the old government became void by the Revolution, unless recognized by the existing authority. Can it be doubted that every other nation would have had a right to adopt the same principle of conduct towards France? It cannot. By parity of reasoning, as far as France may in practice have pursued that principle, other nations may justifiably plead the example.

II. In addition to the embarrassment heretofore suggested as incident to the admission of the present operation of the treaties—this very particular one may attend our case. An *island* may be taken by Great Britain or Holland with the avowed intention of holding it for the future king of France, the successor of Louis the XVI. Can it be possible that a treaty made with Louis the XVI should *oblige* us to embark in the war to rescue a part of his dominions from his immediate successor? Under all the circumstances of the case, would the national integrity or delicacy permit it? Was it clear that Louis merited his death as a perfidious tyrant, the last question might receive a different answer from what can now be given to it. Ought the United States to involve themselves in a dilemma of this kind?

III. In national questions the general conduct of nations have great weight. When all Europe is or is likely to be armed in opposition to the authority of the present government of France, would it not be to carry theory to an extreme to pronounce that the United States are under an *absolute* indispensable obligation, not only to acknowledge respectfully the authority of that government, but to admit the immediate operation of treaties which would constitute them at once its ally?

IV. Prudence at least seems to dictate the course of *reserving* the question, in order that further reflection and a more complete development of circumstances may enable us to make a decision both *right* and *safe*. It does not appear necessary to precipitate the fixing of our relations to France beyond the possibility of retraction. It is putting too suddenly too much to hazard.

It may be asked—Does an unqualified reception of the minister determine the point?

Perhaps it does not. Yet there is no satisfactory guide by which to decide the precise import and extent of such a reception—by which to pronounce that it would not *conclude* us as to the treaties. There is great room to consider the epoch of receiving a minister from the Republic as that *when* we ought to explain ourselves on the point in question—and silence, at that time, as a waiver of our option.

It is probable that on the part of France it will be urged to have this effect, and if it should be truly so considered by her, to raise the question afterwards would lead to complaint, accusation, ill humor.

It seems most candid and most safe to anticipate—not to risk the imputation of inconsistency. It seems advisable to be able to say to foreign powers, if questioned—"In receiving the minister of France we have not acknowledged ourself its ally. We have reserved the point for future consideration."

It may be asked whether the reception at any rate is not inconsistent with the reservation recommended.

It does not appear to be so. The acknowledgement of a government by the reception of its ambassador, and the acknowledgement of it *as an ally*, are things different and *separable* from each other. However, the first, where a connection before existed between two nations, may imply the last, if nothing is said; this implication may clearly be repelled by a declaration that it is not the intention of the party. Such a declaration would be in the nature of a protest against the implication—and the declared intent would govern. It is a rule that "*Expressum facit cessare tacitum.*"

It may likewise be asked whether we are not too late for the ground proposed to be taken—whether the payments on account of the debt to France subsequent to the last change be not an acknowledgement that all engagements to the former government are to be fulfilled to the present.

The two objects of a debt in money and a treaty of alliance have no necessary connection. They are governed by considerations altogether different and irrelative.

The payment of a debt is a matter of perfect and strict obligation. It must be done at all events. It is to be regulated by circumstances of time and place—and ought to be done with precise punctuality.

In the case of a nation—whoever acquires *possession* of its political power, whoever becomes master of its *goods*, of the national property, must pay all the debts which the government of the nation has contracted.

In like manner, on the principle of reciprocity the sovereign in possession is to receive the debts due to the government of the nation. These debts are at all events to be paid—and *possession* alone can guide as to the party to whom they are to be paid.

Questions of property are very different from those of *political connection*.

Nobody can doubt that the debt due to France is at all events to be paid, whatever *form* of government may take place in that country.

Treaties between nations are capable of being affected by a great variety of considerations, casualties, and contingencies. Forms of government, it is evident, may be the considerations of them. Revolutions of government, by changing those forms, may consequently vary the obligations of parties.

Hence the payment of a debt to the sovereign in possession does not imply an admission of the present operation of political treaties. It may so happen that there is a strict obligation to pay the debt and a perfect right to withdraw from the treaties.

And while we are not bound to expose ourselves to the resentment of the governing power of France by refusing to pay a debt at the time and place stipulated, so neither are we bound, pending a contested revolution of government, to expose ourselves to the resentment of other nations by declaring ourselves the ally of that power, in virtue of treaties contracted with a former sovereign, who still pursues his claim to govern, supported by the general sense and arm of Europe.

On the Reception of Edmond Charles Genet in Philadelphia, May 14–16, 1793

It is observable that attempts are making to engage the good citizens of this place to give some public demonstrations of satisfaction on the arrival of M. Genet, the expected minister plenipotentiary from France.

The good sense and prudence of the citizens of Philadelphia, it is hoped, will guard them against being led into so unadvised a step.

Every discreet man must perceive at once that it is highly the interest of this country to remain at peace and as a mean to this to observe a strict neutrality in the present quarrel between the European powers.

Public manifestations even of strong wishes in our citizens in favor of any of the contending parties might interfere with this object, in tending to induce a belief that we may finally take a side.

If done at the seat of the general government it may be suspected to have been done with the countenance of the government. 'Tis easy to see that such a supposition might not be without inconvenience.

The step recommended would be the more delicate as nothing of the kind happened on the arrival of Mr. Ternant, the immediate predecessor of the expected gentleman. Mr. Ternant, having served with reputation & usefulness in our armies during the late war, had a personal claim to marks of esteem, as far as on considerations of public propriety it would have been right to bestow them. None were bestowed. To distinguish his successor would savor as little of kindness towards him as of prudence towards ourselves.

If we feel kind dispositions towards France for the assistance afforded us in our revolution, it will not do us honor to forget that Louis the XVI was then the sovereign of the country—that the succor afforded depended on his pleasure. *Of this we are sure*—there is no ambiguity. Whether he has suffered justly the melancholy fate which he has recently experienced is *at least a question*. No satisfactory evidence of the affirmative has yet appeared in this country. We have seen strong assertions but no proof. To the last awful moment he persevered in declaring his innocence.

In such a state of things any extraordinary honors to the representative of those who consigned him to so affecting a doom would be as little consonant with decorum and humanity as with true policy.

It will not be difficult, either, to perceive that in such a state of things[1]

Memorandum to George Washington, May 15, 1793

State of facts as supposed

Mr. Genet, minister plenipotentiary from the Republic of France, arrives at Charlestown. There he causes two privateers to be fitted out, to which he issues commissions to cruise against the enemies of France. There also the privateers are manned, and partly with citizens of the United States, who are enlisted or engaged for the purpose without the privity or permission of the government of this country, before even Mr. Genet has delivered his credentials and been recognized as a public minister. One or both these privateers make captures of British vessels in the neighborhood of our coasts and bring or send their prizes into our ports.

The British minister plenipotentiary among other things demands a restitution of these prizes. Ought the demands to be complied with?

I am of opinion that it ought to be complied with, and for the following reasons.

The proceedings in question are highly exceptionable both as they respect our rights and as they make us an instrument of hostilities against Great Britain.

The jurisdiction of every *independent* nation within its own territories naturally excludes all exercise of authority by any other government within those territories, unless by its own consent or in consequence of stipulations in treaties. Every such exercise of authority therefore not warranted by consent or treaty is an intrusion on the jurisdiction of the country within which it is exercised and amounts to an injury and affront, more or less great, according to the nature of the case.

The equipping, manning, and commissioning of vessels of war, the enlisting, levying, or raising of men for military service, whether by land or sea—all which are essentially of the same nature—are among the highest and most important exercises of sovereignty.

It is therefore an injury and affront of a very serious kind for one nation to do acts of the above description, within the territories of another, without its consent or permission. This is a principle so obvious—in itself—that it does not stand in need of confirmation from authorities.

Yet the following passage from Vattel, as to one of the points included in the case, is so pertinent and forcible that it cannot be improper to quote it. It is found—Book III, Chapt. II § 15—in these words.

"As the right of levying soldiers belongs solely to the nation, so no person is to enlist soldiers in a foreign country without the permission of the sovereign. They who undertake to enlist soldiers in a foreign country without the sovereign's permission and, in general, *whoever alienates the subjects of another*, violates one of *the most sacred rights*, both of the Prince and the state. Foreign *recruiters are hanged immediately* and very justly, as it is not to be presumed that their sovereign ordered them to commit the crime; and if they did receive such an order they ought not to obey it: their sovereign having no right to command what is contrary to the law of nature. It is not, I say, apprehended that these recruiters act by order of their sovereign, and usually they who have practiced seduction only are, if taken, severely punished. If they have used violence and made their escape, they are claimed and the men they carried off demanded. *But if it appears that they acted by order, such a proceeding in a foreign sovereign is justly considered as an injury, and as a sufficient cause for declaring war against him, unless he condescends to make suitable reparation.*"

The word soldiers here made use is to be understood to mean all persons engaged or enlisted for military service—seamen as well as landmen. The principle applies equally to the former as to the latter. This, it is imagined, will not be questioned.

In the case under consideration there was neither treaty nor consent to warrant what was done. And the case is much stronger than a mere levying of men.

The injury and insult to our government then, under the facts stated, cannot be doubted. The right to reparation follows of course.

It remains to inquire whether we are under an obligation to redress any injury which may have accrued to Great Britain from the irregularity committed towards us.

The existence of such an obligation is affirmed upon the following grounds.

It is manifestly contrary to the duty of a neutral nation to suffer itself to be made an *instrument* of hostility by one power at war against another. In doing it, such nation becomes an associate, a party.

The United States would become effectually an instrument of hostility to France against the other powers at war—if France could *ad libitum* build, equip, and commission, in their ports, vessels of war—man those vessels with their seamen—send them out of their ports to cruise against the enemies of France—bring or send the vessels and property taken from those enemies *into* their ports—dispose of them there, with a right to repeat these expeditions as often as she should find expedient.

By the same rule that France could do these things—she could issue commissions among us at pleasure for raising any number of troops—could march those troops towards our frontiers, attack from thence the territories of Spain or England—return with the plunder, which had been taken within our territories—go again on new expeditions, and repeat them as often as was found advantageous.

There can be no material differences between the two cases—between preparing the means in and carrying on from our ports naval expeditions—and preparing the means in and carrying on from our territories land expeditions against the enemies of France. The principle in each case would be the same.

And from both or either would result a state of war between us and those enemies of the worst kind for them, as long as it was tolerated. I say a state of war of the worst kind because while the resources of our country would be employed in annoying them, the instruments of this annoyance would be occasionally protected from pursuit by the privileges of our ostensible neutrality.

It is easy to see that such a state of things would not be tolerated longer than 'till it was perceived—and that we should quickly and with good reason be treated as an associate of the power whose instrument we had been made.

If it is inconsistent with the duties of neutrality to permit the practices described to an indefinite extent, it must be alike inconsistent with those duties to permit them to any extent. The quality of the fact, not the degree, must be the criterion.

It has indeed been agreed that we are bound to *prevent* the practices in question in future, and that an assurance shall be given to the British minister that *effective measures* will be taken for that purpose.

But it is denied that we are bound to interpose to remedy the effects which have hitherto ensued.

The obligation to prevent an injury usually, if not universally, includes that of repairing or redressing it when it has happened.

If it be contrary to the duty of the U. States as a neutral nation to suffer cruisers to be fitted out of their ports to annoy the British trade, it comports with their duty to remedy the injury which may have been sustained, when it is in their power so to do.

If it be said that what was done took place before the government could be prepared to prescribe a preventative, and that this creates a dispensation from the obligation to redress—

The answer is—

That a government is responsible for the conduct of all parts of the community over which it presides; that it is to be supposed to have at all times a competent police everywhere to prevent infractions of its duty towards foreign nations—that in the case in question the magistracy of the place ought not to have permitted what was done—and that the government is answerable for the consequences of its omissions.

It is true that in a number of cases a government may excuse itself for the nonperformance of its duty—on account of the want of time to take due precautions—from the consideration of the thing having been unexpected and unforeseen &c. &c. And justice often requires that excuses of this kind bona fide offered should be admitted as satisfactory.

But such things are only *excuses*, not *justifications*, and they are only then to be received when a remedy is not within the reach of the party.

If the privateers expedited from Charlestown had been sent to the French dominions, there to operate out of our reach, the excuse of want of time to take due precautions ought to have been satisfactory to Great Britain. But now that they have sent their prizes into our ports, that excuse cannot avail us. We have it in our power to administer a specific remedy by causing restitution of the property taken—and it is conceived to be our duty to do so.

It is objected to this that the commissions which were issued are valid between the parties at war, though irregular with respect to us—that the captures made under it are therefore valid captures, vesting the property in the captors, of which they cannot be deprived without a violation of their rights and an aggression on our part.

It is believed to be true that the commissions are in a legal sense valid as between the parties at war. But the inference drawn from this position does not seem to follow.

It has been seen that what has been done on the part of the French is a violation of our rights—for which we have a *claim to reparation* and a right to make war if it be refused.

We may reasonably demand then, as the reparation to which we are entitled, restitution of the property taken, with or without an apology for the infringement of our sovereignty. This we have a right to demand as a species of reparation consonant with the nature of the injury, and enabling us to do justice to the party in injuring whom we have been made instrumental.

It can therefore be no just cause of complaint on the part of the captors that they are required to surrender a property, *the means of acquiring which took their origin in a violation of our rights.*

On the other hand, there is a claim upon us to arrest the effects of the injury or annoyance to which we have been made accessory. To insist therefore upon the restitution of the property taken will be to enforce a *right* in order to the performance of a *duty*.

The effects of captures under the commissions, however valid between the parties at war, have no validity against us. Originating in a violation of our rights, we are no wise bound to respect them.

Why then (it may be asked) not send then to the animadversion and decision of the courts of justice?

Because, it is believed, they are not competent to the decision. The whole is an affair between the governments of the parties concerned—to be settled by reasons of state, not rules of law. 'Tis the case of an infringement of our sovereignty to the prejudice of a third party, in which the government is to demand a reparation, with the double view of vindicating its own rights and doing justice to the suffering party.

A comparison of this case with that of contraband articles can only mislead. A neutral nation has a general right to trade with a power at war. The exception of contraband articles is an exception of necessity; it is a qualification of the general right of the neutral nation in favor of the safety of the belligerent party. And from this cause and the difficulty of tracing it in the course of commercial dealings that for the peace of nations, the external penalty of confiscation is alone established. The neutral nation is only bound to abandon its subjects to that penalty, not to take internal measures to prevent and punish the practice.

The state of peace between two nations on the other hand makes it intrinsically criminal in either nation or in the subjects of either to engage in actual hostilities against the other. The sovereign of each nation is bound to prevent this by internal regulations and measures—and of course to give redress where the offence has been committed.

What has been agreed to be done in the present case acknowledges the distinction and establishes the consequences. While it was refused to interfere to prevent the shipment of arms, it has been agreed that measures should be taken towards punishing our citizens who engaged on board the privateers, and to assure the British minister that effectual measures would be taken to prevent a repetition of the thing complained. Hence a recognized distinction of principle and a virtual recognition of the consequences contended for.

As little to the purpose is the example of cases in which particular nations permit the levying of troops among them by the parties at war. The almost continually warlike posture of Europe can alone have produced the *toleration* of a practice so inconsistent with morality and humanity; but, allowing these examples their full force, they are at an *infinite distance from* the case of raising, equipping, and organizing within the neutral territory an armed force, sending it on expeditions against a party at war & bringing back their spoils into the neutral country.

If the view which has been taken of the subject is a just one, Great Britain will have a right to consider our refusal to cause restitution to be made as equivalent to our becoming an accomplice in the hostility—as a departure from neutrality—as an aggression upon her.

Hence we shall furnish a cause of war and endanger the existence of it.

I infer then that we equally owe it to ourselves and to Great Britain to cause restitution to be made of the property taken. In the case of so palpable and serious a violation of our rights, aggravated by several collateral circumstances, the mention of which is purposely waived, a decided conduct appears most consistent with our honor and with our future safety.

Alex Hamilton

Excerpt from a Letter to _____, May 18, 1793

You ask me if the newspapers of Philadelphia give a true picture of the conduct of its citizens on the occasion of the arrival of Mr. Genet, and whether the great body of them are really as indiscreet as those papers represent them. It gives me pleasure to be able to answer you in the negative. I can assure you upon the best evidence that, comparatively speaking, but a small proportion of them have had an agency in the business...

You ask who were its *promoters*.

I answer that with *very few exceptions* they were the same men who have been uniformly the enemies and the disturbers of the government of the U. States. It will not be surprising if we see ere long a curious *combination* growing up to control its measures with regard to foreign politics at the expense of the peace of the country—perhaps at a still greater expense. We too have our disorganizers. But I trust there is enough of virtue and good sense in the people of America to baffle every attempt against their prosperity—though masked under the specious garb of an extraordinary zeal for liberty. They practically, I doubt not, adopt this sacred maxim, that without government there is no true liberty.

I agree with you in the reflections you make on the tendency of public demonstrations of attachment to the cause of France. 'Tis certainly not wise to expose ourselves to the jealousy and resentment of the rest of the world by a fruitless display of zeal for that cause—it may do us much harm—it can do France no good (unless indeed we are to embark in the war with her, which nobody is so hardy as to avow, though some secretly *machinate* it). It cannot be without danger and inconvenience to our interests to impress on the nations of Europe an idea that we are actuated by the *same spirit* which has for some time past fatally misguided the measures of those who conduct the affairs of France and sullied a cause once glorious and that might have been triumphant.

The cause of France is compared with that of America during its late revolution. Would to Heaven that the comparison were just. Would to heaven that we could discern in the mirror of French affairs the same humanity, the same decorum, the same gravity, the same order, the same dignity, the same solemnity which distinguished the course of the American Revolution. Clouds & darkness would not then rest upon the issue as they now do.

I own I do not like the comparison. When I contemplate the horrid and systematic massacres of the 2nd & 3rd of September—When I observe that a Marat and a Robespierre, the notorious prompters of those bloody scenes—sit triumphantly in the Convention and take a conspicuous part in its measures—that an attempt to bring the assassins to justice has been obliged to be abandoned—When I see an unfortunate prince, whose reign was a continued demonstration of the goodness & benevolence of his heart, of his attachment to the people of whom he was the monarch—who, though educated in the lap of despotism, had given repeated proofs that he was not the enemy of liberty—brought precipitately and ignominiously to the block—without any substantial proof of guilt as yet disclosed—without even an authentic exhibition of motives, in decent regard to the opinions of mankind—When I find the doctrines of atheism openly advanced in the Convention and heard with loud applauses—When I see the sword of fanaticism extended to force a political creed upon citizens who were invited to submit to the arms of France as the harbingers of liberty—When I behold the hand of rapacity outstretched to prostrate and ravish the monuments of religious worship erected by those citizens and their ancestors. When I perceive passion, tumult, and violence usurping those seats where reason and cool deliberation ought to preside—

I acknowledge that I am glad to believe there is no real resemblance between what was the cause of America & what is the cause of France— that the difference is no less great than that between liberty & licentiousness. I regret whatever has a tendency to confound them, and I feel anxious, as an American, that the ebullitions of inconsiderate men among us may not tend to involve our reputation in the issue.

Defense of the President's Neutrality Proclamation, May 1793

1. It is a melancholy truth, which every new political occurrence more and more unfolds, that there is a description of men in this country irreconcilably adverse to the government of the United States, whose exertions, whatever be the springs of them, whether infatuation or depravity or both, tend to disturb the tranquility, order, and prosperity of this now peaceable, flourishing, and truly happy land. A real and enlightened friend to public felicity cannot observe new confirmations of this fact without feeling a deep and poignant regret that human nature should be so refractory and perverse; that amidst a profusion of the bounties and blessings of Providence, political as well as natural, inviting to contentment and gratitude, there should still be found men disposed to cherish and propagate disquietude and alarm; to render suspected and detested the instruments of the felicity in which they partake; to sacrifice the most substantial advantages that ever fell to the lot of a people at the shrine of personal envy, rivalship, and animosity, to the instigations of a turbulent and criminal ambition, or to the treacherous phantoms of an ever craving and never to be satisfied spirit of innovation; a spirit which seems to suggest to its votaries that the most natural and happy state of society is a state of continual revolution and change—that the welfare of a nation is in exact ratio to the rapidity of the political vicissitudes which it undergoes—to the frequency and violence of the tempests with which it is agitated.

2. Yet so the fact unfortunately is—such men there certainly are—and it is essential to our dearest interests, to the preservation of peace and good order, to the dignity and independence of our public councils—to the real and permanent security of liberty and property—that the citizens of the U. States should open their eyes to the true characters and designs of the men alluded to—should be upon their guard against their insidious and ruinous machinations.

3. At this moment a most dangerous combination exists. Those who for some time past have been busy in undermining the Constitution and government of the U. States by indirect attacks, by laboring to render its measures odious, by striving to destroy the confidence of the people in its administration—are now meditating a more direct and destructive war against it—and embodying and arranging their forces and systematizing their efforts. Secret clubs are formed and private consultations held. Emissaries are dispatched to

distant parts of the United States to effect a concert of views and measures among the members and partisans of the disorganizing corps in the several states. The language in the confidential circles is that the Constitution of the United States is too complex a system—that it savors too much of the pernicious doctrine of "balances and checks," that it requires to be simplified in its structure, to be purged of some monarchical and aristocratic ingredients which are said to have found their way into it, and to be stripped of some dangerous prerogatives with which it is pretended to be invested.

4. The noblest passion of the human soul, which nowhere burns with so pure and bright a flame as in the breasts of the people of the U. States, is if possible to be made subservient to this fatal project. That zeal for the liberty of mankind, which produced so universal a sympathy in the cause of France in the first stages of its revolution, and which, it is supposed, has not yet yielded to the just reprobation which a sober, temperate, and humane people, friends of religion, social order, and justice, enemies to tumult and massacre, to the wanton and lawless shedding of human blood, cannot but bestow upon those extravagancies, excesses, and outrages which have sullied and which endanger that cause—that laudable, it is not too much to say that holy, zeal is intended by every art of misrepresentation and deception to be made the instrument first of controlling, finally of overturning the government of the Union.

5. The ground which has been so wisely taken by the executive of the U. States, in regard to the present war of Europe against France, is to be the pretext of this mischievous attempt. The people are if possible to be made to believe that the proclamation of neutrality issued by the president of the U.S. was unauthorized, illegal, and officious—inconsistent with the treaties and plighted faith of the nation—inconsistent with a due sense of gratitude to France for the services rendered us in our late contest for independence and liberty—inconsistent with a due regard for the progress and success of republican principles. Already the presses begin to groan with invective against the chief magistrate of the Union for that prudent and necessary measure, a measure calculated to manifest to the world the pacific position of the government and to caution the citizens of the U. States against practices which would tend to involve us in a war the most unequal and calamitous in which it is possible for a country to be engaged—a war which would not be unlikely to prove pregnant with still greater dangers and disasters than that by which we established our existence as an independent nation.

6. What is the true solution of this extraordinary appearance? Are the professed the real motives of its authors? They are not. The true object is to disparage in the opinion and affections of his fellow citizens that man who at the head of our armies fought so successfully for the liberty and independence which are now our pride and our boast—who during the war supported the hopes, united the hearts, and nerved the arm of his countrymen—who at the close of it, unseduced by ambition & the love of power, soothed and appeased the discontents of his suffering companions in arms, and with them left the

proud scenes of a victorious field for the modest retreats of private life—
who could only have been drawn out of these favorite retreats to aid in the
glorious work of engrafting that liberty, which his sword had contributed
to win, upon a stock of which it stood in need and without which it could
not flourish—endure—a firm adequate national government—who at this
moment sacrifices his tranquility and every favorite pursuit to the peremptory call of his country to aid in giving solidity to a fabric which he has
assisted in rearing—whose whole conduct has been one continued proof of
his rectitude, moderation, disinterestedness, and patriotism, who, whether
the evidence of a uniform course of virtuous public actions be considered,
or the motives likely to actuate a man placed precisely in his situation be
estimated, it may safely be pronounced can have no other ambition than
that of doing good to his country & transmitting his fame unimpaired to
posterity. For what or for whom is he to hazard that rich harvest of glory,
which he has acquired that unexampled veneration and love of his fellow
citizens, which he so eminently possesses?

7. Yet the men alluded to, while they contend with affected zeal for gratitude
    towards a foreign nation, which in assisting us was and ought to have been
    influenced by considerations relative to its own interest—forgetting what is
    due to a fellow citizen who at every hazard rendered essential services to his
    country from the most patriotic motives—insidiously endeavor to despoil
    him of that precious reward of his services, the confidence and approbation
    of his fellow citizens.

8. The present attempt is but the renewal in another form of an attack some
    time since commenced, and which was only dropped because it was per-
    ceived to have excited a general indignation. Domestic arrangements of
    mere convenience, calculated to reconcile the economy of time with the
    attentions of decorum and civility, were then the topics of malevolent decla-
    mation. A more serious article of charge is now opened and seems intended
    to be urged with greater earnestness and vigor. The merits of it shall be
    examined in one or two succeeding papers, I trust in a manner that will
    evince to every candid mind to futility.

9. To be an able and firm supporter of the government of the Union is in the
    eyes of the men referred to a crime sufficient to justify the most malignant
    persecution. Hence the attacks which have been made and repeated with
    such persevering industry upon more than one public character in that gov-
    ernment. Hence the effort which is now going on to depreciate in the eyes
    and estimation of the people the man whom their unanimous suffrages have
    placed at the head of it.

10. Hence the pains which are taking to inculcate a discrimination between
    principles and *men* and to represent an attachment to the one as a species
    of war against the other; an endeavor, which has a tendency to stifle or
    weaken one of the best and most useful feelings of the human heart—a rev-
    erence for merit—and to take away one of the strongest incentives to public
    virtue—the expectation of public esteem.

11. A solicitude for the character who is attacked forms no part of the motives to this comment. He has deserved too much, and his countrymen are too sensible of it to render any advocation of him necessary. If his virtues and services do not secure his fame and ensure to him the unchangeable attachment of his fellow citizens, 'twere in vain to attempt to prop them by anonymous panegyric.

12. The design of the observations which have been made is merely to awaken the public attention to the views of a party engaged in a dangerous conspiracy against the tranquility and happiness of their country. Aware that their hostile aims against the government can never succeed til they have subverted the confidence of the people in its present chief magistrate, they have at length permitted the suggestions of their enmity to betray them into this hopeless and culpable attempt. If we can destroy his popularity (say they) our work is more than half completed.

13. In proportion as the citizens of the U. States value the Constitution on which their union and happiness depend, in proportion as they tender the blessings of peace and deprecate the calamities of war—ought to be their watchfulness against this success of the artifices which will be employed to endanger that Constitution and those blessings. A mortal blow is aimed at both.

14. It imports them infinitely not to be deceived by the protestations which are made—that no harm is meditated against the Constitution—that no design is entertained to involve the peace of the country. These appearances are necessary to the accomplishment of the plan which has been formed. It is known that the great body of the people are attached to the Constitution. It would therefore defeat the intention of destroying it to avow that it exists. It is also known that the people of the U. States are firmly attached to peace. It would consequently frustrate the design of engaging them in the war to tell them that such an object is in contemplation.

15. A more artful course has therefore been adopted. Professions of good will to the Constitution are made without reserve: But every possible art is employed to render the administration and the most zealous and useful friends of the government odious. The reasoning is obvious. If the people can be persuaded to dislike all the measures of the government and to dislike all or the greater part of those who have been most conspicuous in establishing or conducting it—the passage from this to the dislike and change of the Constitution will not be long nor difficult. The abstract idea of regard for a Constitution on paper will not long resist a thorough detestation of its practice.

16. In like manner, professions of a disposition to preserve the peace of the country are liberally made. But the means of effecting the end are condemned, and exertions are used to prejudice the community against them. A proclamation of neutrality in the most cautious form is represented as illegal—contrary to our engagements with and our duty towards one of the belligerent powers. The plain inference is that in the opinion of these

characters the U. States are under obligations which do not permit them to be neutral. Of course they are in a situation to become a party in the war from duty.

17. Pains are likewise taken to inflame the zeal of the people for the cause of France and to excite their resentments against the powers at war with her. To what end all this—but to beget if possible a temper in the community which may overrule the moderate or pacific views of the government.

Pacificus No. I, June 29, 1793

As attempts are making very dangerous to the peace and it is to be feared not very friendly to the Constitution of the U. States—it becomes the duty of those who wish well to both to endeavor to prevent their success.

The objections which have been raised against the proclamation of neutrality lately issued by the president have been urged in a spirit of acrimony and invective which demonstrates that more was in view than merely a free discussion of an important public measure; that the discussion covers a design of weakening the confidence of the people in the author of the measure, in order to remove or lessen a powerful obstacle to the success of an opposition to the government, which however it may change its form, according to circumstances, seems still to be adhered to and pursued with persevering industry.

This reflection adds to the motives connected with the measure itself to recommend endeavors by proper explanations to place it in a just light. Such explanations at least cannot but be satisfactory to those who may not have leisure or opportunity for pursuing themselves an investigation of the subject, and who may wish to perceive that the policy of the government is not inconsistent with its obligations or its honor.

The objections in question fall under four heads—

1. That the proclamation was without authority.
2. That it was contrary to our treaties with France.
3. That it was contrary to the gratitude which is due from this to that country for the succors rendered us in our own revolution.
4. That it was out of time & unnecessary.

In order to judge of the solidity of the first of these objections, it is necessary to examine what is the nature and design of a proclamation of neutrality.

The true nature & design of such an act is—to *make known* to the powers at war and to the citizens of the country whose government does the act that such country is in the condition of a nation at peace with the belligerent parties and under no obligations of treaty to become an *associate in the war* with either of them; that this being its situation its intention is to observe a conduct conformable with it and to perform towards each the duties of neutrality; and as a consequence of this state of things to give warning to all within its jurisdiction to abstain from acts that shall contravene those duties, under the penalties which the laws of the land (of which the law of nations is a part) annexes to acts of contravention.

This, and no more, is conceived to be the true import of a proclamation of neutrality.

It does not imply that the nation which makes the declaration will forbear to perform to any of the warring powers any stipulations in treaties which can be performed without rendering it an *associate* or *party* in the war. It therefore does not imply in our case that the U. States will not make those distinctions between the present belligerent powers which are stipulated in the 17th and 22nd articles of our treaty with France, because these distinctions are not incompatible with a state of neutrality; they will in no shape render the U. States an *associate* or *party* in the war. This must be evident when it is considered that even to furnish *determinate* succors of a certain number of ships or troops to a power at war, in consequence of *antecedent treaties having no particular reference to the existing war*, is not inconsistent with neutrality, a position well established by the doctrines of writers and the practice of nations.*

But no special aids, succors, or favors having relation to war, not positively and precisely stipulated by some treaty of the above description, can be afforded to either party without a breach of neutrality.

In stating that the proclamation of neutrality does not imply the nonperformance of any stipulations of treaties which are not of a nature to make the nation an associate or party in the war, it is conceded that an execution of the clause of guarantee contained in the 11th article of our treaty of alliance with France would be contrary to the sense and spirit of the proclamation, because it would engage us with our whole force as an *associate* or *auxiliary* in the war; it would be much more than the case of a definite limited succor, previously ascertained.

It follows that the proclamation is virtually a manifestation of the sense of the government that the U. States are, *under the circumstances of the case, not bound* to execute the clause of guarantee.

If this be a just view of the true force and import of the proclamation, it will remain to see whether the president in issuing it acted within his proper sphere, or stepped beyond the bounds of his constitutional authority and duty.

It will not be disputed that the management of the affairs of this country with foreign nations is confided to the government of the U. States.

It can as little be disputed that a proclamation of neutrality, where a nation is at liberty to keep out of a war in which other nations are engaged and means so to do, is a *usual* and a *proper* measure. *Its main object and effect are to prevent the nation being immediately responsible for acts done by its citizens, without the privity or connivance of the government, in contravention of the principles of neutrality.*[†]

An object this of the greatest importance to a country whose true interest lies in the preservation of peace.

---

* See Vatel Book III Chap. VI § 101.
† See Vatel Book III Chap. VII § 113.

The inquiry then is—what department of the government of the U. States is the proper one to make a declaration of neutrality in the cases in which the engagements of the nation permit and its interests require such a declaration.

A correct and well informed mind will discern at once that it can belong neither to the legislative nor judicial department and of course must belong to the executive.

The legislative department is not the *organ* of intercourse between the U. States and foreign nations. It is charged neither with *making* nor *interpreting* treaties. It is therefore not naturally that organ of the government which is to pronounce the existing condition of the nation with regard to foreign powers, or to admonish the citizens of their obligations and duties as founded upon that condition of things. Still less is it charged with enforcing the execution and observance of these obligations and those duties.

It is equally obvious that the act in question is foreign to the judiciary department of the government. The province of that department is to decide litigations in particular cases. It is indeed charged with the interpretation of treaties, but it exercises this function only in the litigated cases, that is where contending parties bring before it a specific controversy. It has no concern with pronouncing upon the external political relations of treaties between government and government. This position is too plain to need being insisted upon.

It must then of necessity belong to the executive department to exercise the function in question—when a proper case for the exercise of it occurs.

It appears to be connected with that department in various capacities, as the *organ* of intercourse between the nation and foreign nations—as the interpreter of the national treaties in those cases in which the judiciary is not competent, that is in the cases between government and government—as that power which is charged with the execution of the laws, of which treaties form a part—as that power which is charged with the command and application of the public force.

This view of the subject is so natural and obvious—so analogous to general theory and practice—that no doubt can be entertained of its justness, unless such doubt can be deduced from particular provisions of the Constitution of the U. States.

Let us see then if cause for such doubt is to be found in that Constitution.

The second article of the Constitution of the U. States, section 1st, establishes this general proposition, that "The Executive Power shall be vested in a President of the United States of America."

The same article in a succeeding section proceeds to designate particular cases of executive power. It declares among other things that the president shall be commander in chief of the army and navy of the U. States and of the militia of the several states when called into the actual service of the U. States, that he shall have power by and with the advice of the Senate to make treaties, that it shall be his duty to receive ambassadors and other public ministers and to take care that the laws be faithfully executed.

It would not consist with the rules of sound construction to consider this enumeration of particular authorities as derogating from the more comprehensive grant contained in the general clause, further than as it may be coupled with express restrictions or qualifications; as in regard to the cooperation of the Senate in the appointment of officers and the making of treaties, which are qualifications of the general executive powers of appointing officers and making treaties: Because the difficulty of a complete and perfect specification of all the cases of executive authority would naturally dictate the use of general terms—and would render it improbable that a specification of certain particulars was designed as a substitute for those terms when antecedently used. The different mode of expression employed in the Constitution in regard to the two powers, the legislative and the executive, serves to confirm this inference. In the article which grants the legislative powers of the government the expressions are—"*All Legislative powers herein granted shall be vested in a Congress of the* U. States"; in that which grants the executive power the expressions are, as already quoted, "The Executive Power shall be vested in a President of the U. States of America."

The enumeration ought rather therefore to be considered as intended by way of greater caution, to specify and regulate the principal articles implied in the definition of executive power, leaving the rest to flow from the general grant of that power, interpreted in conformity to other parts of the Constitution and to the principles of free government.

The general doctrine, then, of our Constitution is that the executive power of the nation is vested in the president, subject only to the *exceptions* and *qualifications* which are expressed in the instrument.

Two of these have been already noticed—the participation of the Senate in the appointment of officers and the making of treaties. A third remains to be mentioned, the right of the legislature "to declare war and grant letters of marque and reprisal."

With these exceptions the executive power of the Union is completely lodged in the president. This mode of construing the Constitution has indeed been recognized by Congress in formal acts, upon full consideration and debate. The power of removal from office is an important instance.

And since upon general principles, for reasons already given, the issuing of a proclamation of neutrality is merely an executive act; since also the general executive power of the Union is vested in the president, the conclusion is that the step which has been taken by him is liable to no just exception on the score of authority.

It may be observed that this inference would be just if the power of declaring war had not been vested in the legislature, but that this power naturally includes the right of judging whether the nation is under obligations to make war or not.

The answer to this is that, however true it may be that the right of the legislature to declare war includes the right of judging whether the nation be under obligations to make war or not—it will not follow that the executive is in any case excluded from a similar right of judgment in the execution of its own functions.

If the legislature have a right to make war on the one hand—it is on the other the duty of the executive to preserve peace till war is declared; and in fulfilling that duty it must necessarily possess a right of judging what is the nature of the obligations which the treaties of the country impose on the government; and when in pursuance of this right it has concluded that there is nothing in them inconsistent with a *state* of neutrality, it becomes both its province and its duty to enforce the laws incident to that state of the nation. The executive is charged with the execution of all laws, the laws of nations as well as the municipal law, which recognizes and adopts those laws. It is consequently bound, by faithfully executing the laws of neutrality, when that is the state of the nation, to avoid giving a cause of war to foreign powers.

This is the direct and proper end of the proclamation of neutrality. It declares to the U. States their situation with regard to the powers at war and makes known to the community that the laws incident to that situation will be enforced. In doing this, it conforms to an established usage of nations, the operation of which as before remarked is to obviate a responsibility on the part of the whole society for secret and unknown violations of the rights of any of the warring parties by its citizens.

Those who object to the proclamation will readily admit that it is the right and duty of the executive to judge of, or to interpret, those articles of our treaties which give to France particular privileges, in order to the enforcement of those privileges: But the necessary consequence of this is that the executive must judge what are the proper bounds of those privileges—what rights are given to other nations by our treaties with them—what rights the law of nature and nations gives and our treaties permit in respect to those nations with whom we have no treaties; in fine what are the reciprocal rights and obligations of the United States & of all & each of the powers at war.

The right of the executive to receive ambassadors and other public ministers may serve to illustrate the relative duties of the executive and legislative departments. This right includes that of judging, in the case of a revolution of government in a foreign country, whether the new rulers are competent organs of the national will and ought to be recognized or not: And where a treaty antecedently exists between the U. States and such nation, that right involves the power of giving operation or not to such treaty. For until the new government is *acknowledged*, the treaties between the nations, as far at least as regards *public* rights, are of course suspended.

This power of determining virtually in the case supposed upon the operation of national treaties as a consequence of the power to receive ambassadors and other public ministers is an important instance of the right of the executive to decide the obligations of the nation with regard to foreign nations. To apply it to the case of France, if there had been a treaty of alliance *offensive* and defensive between the U. States and that country, the unqualified acknowledgement of the new government would have put the U. States in a condition to become an associate in the war in which France was engaged—and would have laid the legislature under an obligation, if required, and there was otherwise no valid excuse, of exercising its power of declaring war.

This serves as an example of the right of the executive, in certain cases, to determine the condition of the nation, though it may consequentially affect the proper or improper exercise of the power of the legislature to declare war. The executive indeed cannot control the exercise of that power—further than by the exercise of its general right of objecting to all acts of the legislature, liable to being overruled by two thirds of both houses of Congress. The legislature is free to perform its own duties according to its own sense of them—though the executive in the exercise of its constitutional powers may establish an antecedent state of things which ought to weigh in the legislative decisions. From the division of the executive power there results, in reference to it, a *concurrent* authority in the distributed cases.

Hence in the case stated, though treaties can only be made by the president and Senate, their activity may be continued or suspended by the president alone.

No objection has been made to the president's having acknowledged the Republic of France by the reception of its minister without having consulted the Senate, though that body is connected with him in the making of treaties, and though the consequence of his act of reception is to give operation to the treaties heretofore made with that country: But he is censured for having declared the U. States to be in a state of peace & neutrality with regard to the powers at war, because the right of *changing* that state & *declaring war* belongs to the legislature.

It deserves to be remarked that as the participation of the Senate in the making of treaties and the power of the legislature to declare war are exceptions out of the general "Executive Power" vested in the president, they are to be construed strictly—and ought to be extended no further than is essential to their execution.

While therefore the legislature can alone declare war, can alone actually transfer the nation from a state of peace to a state of war—it belongs to the "Executive Power" to do whatever else the laws of nations cooperating with the treaties of the country enjoin in the intercourse of the U. States with foreign powers.

In this distribution of powers the wisdom of our Constitution is manifested. It is the province and duty of the executive to preserve to the nation the blessings of peace. The legislature alone can interrupt those blessings by placing the nation in a state of war.

But though it has been thought advisable to vindicate the authority of the executive on this broad and comprehensive ground—it was not absolutely necessary to do so. That clause of the Constitution which makes it his duty to "take care that the laws be faithfully executed" might alone have been relied upon and this simple process of argument pursued.

The president is the constitutional executor of the laws. Our treaties and the laws of nations form a part of the law of the land. He who is to execute the laws must first judge for himself of their meaning. In order to the observance of that conduct which the laws of nations, combined with our treaties, prescribed to this country in reference to the present war in Europe, it was necessary for the president to judge for himself whether there was anything in our treaties incompatible with an adherence to neutrality. Having judged that there was not, he had a right, and if in his opinion the interests of the nation required it, it was his duty, as executor of the laws, to proclaim the neutrality of the nation, to exhort all persons to observe it, and to warn them of the penalties which would attend its nonobservance.

The proclamation has been represented as enacting some new law. This is a view of it entirely erroneous. It only proclaims a *fact* with regard to the *existing state* of the nation, informs the citizens of what the laws previously established require of them in that state, & warns them that these laws will be put in execution against the infractors of them.

Pacificus No. II, July 3, 1793

The second & principal objection to the proclamation, namely that it is inconsistent with the treaties between the United States and France, will now be examined.

It has been already shown that it is not inconsistent with the performance of any of the stipulations in those treaties which would not make us an associate or party in the war, and particularly that it is compatible with the privileges secured to France by the 17th & 22nd articles of the Treaty of Commerce, which, except the clause of guarantee, constitute the most material discriminations to be found in our treaties in favor of that country.

Official documents have likewise appeared in the public papers, which are understood to be authentic, that serve as a comment upon the sense of the proclamation in this particular, proving that it was not deemed by the executive incompatible with the performance of the stipulations in those articles, and that in practice they are intended to be observed.

It has, however, been admitted that the declaration of neutrality excludes the idea of an execution of the clause of guarantee.

It becomes necessary therefore to examine whether the United States would have a valid justification for not complying with it, in case of their being called upon for that purpose by France.

Without knowing how far the reasons which have occurred to me may have influenced the president, there appear to me to exist very good and substantial grounds for a refusal.

The alliance between the United States and France is a *defensive alliance*. In the caption of it, it is denominated a "Treaty of Alliance eventual and *defensive*." In the body of it (Article the 2nd) it is again called a *defensive alliance*. The words of that article are as follow: "The essential and direct end of the present *Defensive Alliance* is to maintain effectually the liberty, sovereignty, and independence, absolute and unlimited, of the United States, as well in matters of government as of commerce."

The predominant quality or character then of our alliance with France is that it is *defensive* in its principle. Of course, the meaning, obligation, and force of every stipulation in the treaty must be tested and determined by that principle. It is not necessary (and would be absurd) that it should be repeated in every article. It is sufficient that it be once declared to be understood in every part of the treaty, unless coupled with express negative words excluding the implication.

The great question consequently is—What are the nature and effect of a defensive alliance? When does the *casus fœderis*, or *condition* of the contract, take place in such an alliance?

Reason, the concurring opinions of writers, and the practice of nations will answer—"When either of the allies is *attacked*, when war is made upon him, not when he makes war upon another." In other words, the stipulated assistance is to be given to the ally when engaged in a *defensive*, not when engaged in an *offensive*, war. This obligation to assist only in a defensive war constitutes the essential difference between a defensive alliance and one which is both offensive and defensive. In the latter case there is an obligation to cooperate as well when the war on the part of our ally is offensive as when it is defensive. To affirm therefore that the U. States are bound to assist France in the war in which she is at present engaged would be to convert our treaty with her into an alliance offensive and defensive, contrary to the express & reiterated declarations of the instrument itself.

This assertion implies that the war in question is an *offensive war* on the part of France.

And so it undoubtedly is with regard to all the powers with whom she was at war at the time of issuing the proclamation.

No position is better established than that the power which *first declares* or *actually begins* a war, whatever may have been the causes leading to it, is that which makes an *offensive war*. Nor is there any doubt that France first declared and began the war against Austria, Prussia, Savoy, Holland, England, and Spain.

Upon this point there is apt to be some incorrectness of ideas. Those who have not examined subjects of such a nature are led to imagine that the party which commits the first injury or gives the first provocation is on the offensive side in the war, though begun by the other party.

But the cause or occasion of the war and the war itself are things entirely distinct. 'Tis the commencement of the war itself that decides the question of being on the offensive or defensive. All writers on the laws of nations agree in this principle, but it is more accurately laid down in the following extract from Burlamaqui.*

"Neither are we to believe (says he) that he *who first injures* another begins by that an *offensive* war and that the other *who demands the satisfaction for the injury received* is *always* on the *defensive*. There are a great many *unjust acts which may kindle a war* and which, however, are not the war itself, as the ill treatment of a prince's ambassador, the plundering of his subjects, &c."

"If therefore we take up arms to revenge such an unjust act we commence an *offensive* but a just war; and the prince who has done the injury and will not give satisfaction makes a *defensive* but an unjust war."

"We must therefore affirm, in general, that the first who takes up arms whether *justly* or *unjustly* commences an *offensive* war, & he who opposes him, whether with or without reason, begins a defensive war."

* Vol. II Book IV Chap III Sections IV & V.

France then being on the *offensive* in the war in which she is engaged, and our alliance with her being *defensive* only, it follows that the *casus fœderis* or condition of our guarantee cannot take place, and that the U. States are free to refuse a performance of that guarantee if demanded.

Those who are disposed to justify indiscriminately everything in the conduct of France may reply that though the war in point of form may be offensive on her part, yet in point of principle it is defensive—was in each instance a mere anticipation of attacks meditated against her, and was justified by previous aggressions of the opposite parties.

It is believed that it would be a sufficient answer to this observation to say that in determining the *legal* and *positive* obligations of the U. States the only point of inquiry is—whether the war was *in fact* begun by France or by her enemies; that all beyond this would be too vague, too liable to dispute, too much matter of opinion to be a proper criterion of national conduct; that when a war breaks out between two nations, all other nations, in regard to the positive rights of the parties and their positive duties towards them, are bound to consider it as equally just on both sides—that consequently in a *defensive* alliance, when *war is made upon* one of the allies, the other is bound to fulfill the conditions stipulated on its part, without inquiry whether the war is rightfully begun or not—as on the other hand when war is begun by one of the allies the other is exempted from the obligation of assisting, however just the commencement of it may have been.

The foundation of this doctrine is the utility of clear and certain rules for determining the reciprocal duties of nations—that as little as possible may be left to opinion and the subterfuges of a refining or unfaithful casuistry.

Some writers indeed of great authority affirm that it is a tacit condition of every treaty of alliance that one ally is not bound to assist the other in a war manifestly unjust. But this is questioned on the ground which has been stated by other respectable authorities. And though the manifest injustice of the war has been affirmed by some to be a good cause for not executing the formal obligations of a treaty, I have nowhere found it maintained that the justice of a war is a consideration which can *oblige* a nation to do what its formal obligations do not require, as in the case of a *defensive* alliance, to furnish the succors stipulated, though the formal obligation did not exist, by reason of the ally having begun the war instead of being the party attacked.

But if this were not the true doctrine, an impartial examination would prove that with respect to some of the powers, France is not blameless in the circumstances which preceded and led to the war with those powers, that if she received she also gave cause of offense, and that the justice of the war on her side is, in those cases, not a little problematical.

There are prudential reasons which dissuade from going largely into this examination, unless it shall be rendered necessary by the future turn of the discussion.

It will be sufficient here to notice cursorily the following facts.

France committed an aggression upon Holland in declaring free the navigation of the Scheldt and acting upon that declaration, contrary to treaties in which she had explicitly acknowleged and even guaranteed the exclusive right of Holland to the navigation of that river, and contrary to the doctrines of the best writers and established usages of nations in such cases.

She gave a general and just cause of alarm to nations by that decree of the 19th of November 1792, whereby the Convention, in the name of the French nation, declare that they will grant *fraternity* and *assistance* to every people who *wish* to recover their liberty, and charge the executive power to send the necessary orders to *the generals* to give assistance to such people and to *defend those citizens who may have been or who may be vexed for the cause of liberty*, which decree was ordered to be printed *in all languages*.

When a nation has actually come to a resolution to throw off a yoke under which it may have groaned and to assert its liberties—it is justifiable and meritorious in another nation to afford assistance to the one which has been oppressed & is *in the act* of liberating itself; but it is not warrantable for any nation *beforehand* to hold out a general invitation to insurrection and revolution by promising to assist *every people* who may *wish* to recover their liberty and to defend *those citizens*, of every country, *who may have been or who may be vexed for the cause of liberty*; still less to commit to the GENERALS of its armies the discretionary power of judging when the citizens of a foreign country have been vexed for the cause of liberty by their own government.

The latter part of the decree amounted exactly to what France herself has most complained of—an interference by one nation in the internal government of another.

Vattel justly observes, as a consequence of the liberty & independence of nations—"That it does not belong to any foreign power to take cognizance of the administration of the *sovereign* of another country, to set himself up as a judge of his conduct or to oblige him to alter it."

Such a conduct as that indicated by this decree has a natural tendency to disturb the tranquility of nations, to excite fermentation and revolt everywhere, and therefore justified neutral powers who were in a situation to be affected by it in taking measures to repress the spirit by which it had been dictated.

But the principle of this decree received a more particular application to Great Britain by some subsequent circumstances.

Among the proofs of this are two answers which were given by the president of the National Convention at a public sitting on the 28th of November to two different addresses, one presented by a deputation from "the Society for constitutional information in London," the other by a deputation of English & Irish citizens at Paris.

The following are extracts from these answers.

"The shades of Penn, of *Hampden*, and of *Sydney* hover over your heads; and *the moment without doubt approaches in which the French will bring congratulations to the National Convention of Great Britain.*"

"Nature and *principles* draw *towards us* England, Scotland, and Ireland. Let the cries of friendship resound through the two republics." "Principles are waging war against tyranny, which will fall under the blows of philosophy. *Royalty in Europe is either destroyed or on the point of perishing*, on the ruins of feudality; and the *Declaration of Rights placed by the side of thrones is a devouring fire which will consume them.* WORTHY REPUBLICANS &c."

Declarations of this sort cannot but be considered as a direct application of the principle of the decree to Great Britain, as an open patronage of a revolution in that country, a conduct which, proceeding from the head of the body that governed France in the presence and on behalf of that body, was unquestionably an offense and injury to the nation to which it related.

The decree of the 15th of November is another cause of offense to all the governments of Europe. By That decree "*the French Nation declares* that it will *treat as enemies the people* who, *refusing* or *renouncing* liberty and equality, *are desirous* of preserving their *prince* and *privileged castes*—or of *entering into an accommodation* with them &c." This degree was little short of a declaration of war against all nations having *princes* and *privileged classes*.

The *incorporation* of the territories over which the arms of France had temporarily prevailed, *with* and *as a part* of herself, is another violation of the rights of nations into which the Convention was betrayed by an intemperate zeal, if not by a culpable ambition.

The laws of nations give to a power at war nothing more than a usufructuary or possessory right to the territories which it conquers, suspending the absolute dominion & property till a treaty of peace or something equivalent shall cede or relinquish the conquered territory to the conqueror. This principle is one of the greatest importance to the tranquility and security of nations, facilitating an adjustment of the quarrels and the preservation of ancient limits.

But France, by incorporating with herself in several instances the territories she had acquired, violated this important principle and multiplied indefinitely the obstacles to peace and accommodation. The doctrine *that a nation cannot consent to its own dismemberment but in a case of extreme necessity* immediately attached itself to all the incorporated territories. While the progressive augmentation of the dominions of the most powerful nation in Europe, on a principle not of temporary acquisition but of permanent union, threatened the independence of all other countries and give to neighboring neutral powers the justest cause of umbrage and alarm.

It is a principle well agreed & founded on the best reasons that whenever a particular nation adopts maxims of conduct contrary to those generally established among nations, calculated to disturb their tranquility & to expose their safety, they may justifiably make a common cause to oppose & control such nation.

Whatever partiality may be entertained for the general object of the French Revolution, it is impossible for any well-informed or sober-minded man not to condemn the proceedings which have been stated as repugnant to the general rights of nations, to the true principles of liberty, to the freedom of opinion of mankind, & not to acknowledge as a consequence of this that the justice of the war on the part of France, with regard to some of the powers with which she is engaged, is from those causes questionable enough to free the U. States from all embarrassment on that score, if it be at all incumbent upon them to go into the inquiry.

The policy of a defensive alliance is so essentially distinct from that of an offensive one that it is every way important not to confound their effects. The first kind has in view the prudent object of mutual defense when either of the allies is involuntarily forced into a war by the attack by some third power. The latter kind subjects the peace of each ally to the will of the other, and obliges each to partake in the wars of policy & interest, as well as in those of safety and defense, of the other. To preserve their boundaries distinct it is necessary that each kind should be governed by plain and obvious rules. This would not be the case if instead of taking the simple fact of who begun the war as a guide it was necessary to travel into metaphysical niceties about the justice or injustice of the cause which led to it. Since also the not furnishing a stipulated succor when it is due is itself a cause of war, it is very requisite that there should be some palpable criterion for ascertaining *when it is due*. This criterion as before observed in a defensive alliance is the *commencement* or not of the war by our ally, as a mere matter of fact.

Other topics calculated to illustrate the position that the U. States are not bound to execute the clause of guarantee are reserved for another paper.

Pacificus No. III, July 6, 1793

France at the time of issuing the proclamation was engaged & likely to be engaged in war with all or almost all Europe, without a single ally in that quarter of the globe.

In such a state of things it is evident that however she may be able to defend herself at home (a thing probably still practicable if her factions can be appeased, and system and order introduced) she cannot make any *external* efforts in any degree proportioned to those which can be made against her.

By this situation of things alone the U. States would be dispensed from an obligation to embark in her quarrel.

It is known that we are wholly destitute of naval force. France, with all the great maritime powers united against her, is unable to supply this deficiency. She cannot afford us that species of cooperation which is necessary to render our efforts useful to her and to prevent our experiencing the entire destruction of our trade and the most calamitous inconveniences in other respects.

Our guarantee does not respect France herself. It does not relate to her own immediate defense or preservation. It relates merely to the defense & preservation of her American colonies, objects of which (though of considerable importance) she might be deprived and yet remain a great and powerful and a happy nation.

In the actual situation of this country, and in relation to an object so secondary to France, it may fairly be maintained that an ability in her to supply in a competent degree our deficiency of naval force is a *condition* of our obligation to perform the guarantee on our part.

Had the United States a powerful marine or could they command one in time, this reasoning would not be solid; but circumstanced as they are it is presumed to be well founded.

There would be no proportion between the mischiefs and perils to which the U. States would expose themselves by embarking in the war and the benefit *which the nature of their stipulation aims at securing* to France, or that which it would be in their power actually to render her by becoming a party.

This disproportion would be a valid reason for not executing the guarantee. All contracts are to receive a reasonable construction. Self-preservation is the first duty of a nation, and though in the performance of stipulations relating to war good faith requires that the *ordinary hazards* of war should be fairly encountered, because they are directly contemplated by such stipulations, yet it does not require that *extraordinary* and *extreme* hazards should be run, especially where the object for which they are to be run is only a *partial* and *particular* interest of the ally for whom they are to be run.

As in the present instance good faith does not require that the U. States should put in jeopardy their essential interests, perhaps their very existence, in one of the most unequal contests in which a nation could be engaged—to secure to France what?—her West India Islands and other less important possessions in America. For it is to be remembered that the stipulations of the U. States do in no event reach beyond this point. If they were upon the strength of their guarantee to engage in the war, and could make any arrangement with the belligerent powers for securing to France those islands and those possessions, they would be at perfect liberty instantly to withdraw. They would not be bound to prosecute the war one moment longer.

They are under no obligation, in any event, as far as the faith of treaties is concerned, to assist France in the defense of her liberty, a topic on which so much has been said, so very little to the purpose as it regards the present question.

The contest in which the U. States would plunge themselves, were they to take part with France, would possibly be still more unequal than that in which France herself is engaged. With the possessions of Great Britain and Spain on both flanks, the numerous Indian tribes, under the influence and direction of those powers, along our whole interior frontier, with a long extended sea coast—with no maritime force of our own, and with the maritime force of all Europe against us, with no fortifications whatever and with a population not exceeding four millions—it is impossible to imagine a more unequal contest than that in which we should be involved in the case supposed, a contest from which we are dissuaded by the most cogent motives of self-preservation, as well as of interest.

We may learn from Vattel, one of the best writers on the laws of nations, that "if a state which has promised succors finds itself unable to furnish them, its very inability is its exemption; and if the furnishing the succors would expose it to an *evident* danger, this also is a lawful dispensation. The case would render the treaty *pernicious* to the state and *therefore not obligatory*. But this applies to an *imminent danger* threatening the *safety* of the State; *the case of such a danger is tacitly and necessarily reserved in every treaty*."*

If, too (as no sensible and candid man will deny), the extent of the present combination against France is in a degree to be ascribed to imprudences on her part—the *exemption* to the U. States is still more manifest and complete. No country is bound to partake in hazards of the most critical kind, which may have been produced or promoted by the indiscretion and intemperance of another. This is an obvious dictate of reason, with which the common sense and common practice of mankind coincide.

To the foregoing considerations it may perhaps be added, with no small degree of force, that military stipulations in national treaties contemplate only the *ordinary* case of *foreign war*, and are irrelative to the contests which grow

* See Book III Chap VI § 92.

out of REVOLUTIONS OF GOVERNMENT; unless where they have express reference to a revolution begun, or where there is a guarantee of the existing constitution of a nation, or where there is a *personal* alliance for the defense of a prince and his family.*

The revolution in France is the primitive source of the war in which she is engaged. The restoration of the monarchy is the avowed object of some of her enemies—and the implied one of all of them. That question then is essentially involved in the principle of the war, a question certainly never in the contemplation of that government with which our treaty was made, and it may thence be fairly inferred never intended to be embraced by it.

The inference would be that the U. States have fulfilled the utmost that could be claimed by the nation of France when they so far respected its decision as to recognize the newly constituted powers, giving operation to the Treaty of Alliance for *future occasions, but considering the present war as a tacit exception.* Perhaps, too, this exception is in other respects due to the circumstances under which the engagements between the two countries were contracted. It is impossible, prejudice apart, not to perceive a delicate embarrassment between the *theory* and *fact* of our political relations to France.

On these grounds, also, as well as on that of the present war being *offensive* on the side of France—The U. States have valid and honorable pleas to offer against the execution of the guarantee, if it should be claimed of them by France. And the president was in every view fully justified in pronouncing that the duty and interest of the U. States dictated a neutrality in the war.

* Puffendorf, Book VIII Chapt IX Section IX.

Pacificus No. IV, July 10, 1793

A third objection to the proclamation is that it is inconsistent with the gratitude due to France for the services rendered us in our own revolution.

Those who make this objection disavow at the same time all intention to advocate the position that the United States *ought to take part in the war*. They profess to be friends to our remaining at peace. What then do they mean by the objection?

If it be no breach of gratitude to refrain from joining France in the war—how can it be a breach of gratitude to declare that such is our disposition and intention?

The two positions are at variance with each other; and the true inference is either that those who make the objection really wish to engage this country in the war, or that they seek a pretext for censuring the conduct of the chief magistrate, for some purpose very different from the public good.

They endeavor in vain to elude this inference by saying that the proclamation places France upon an *equal* footing with her enemies, while our treaties require distinctions in her favor, and our relative situation would dictate kind offices to her, which ought not to be granted to her adversaries.

They are not ignorant that the proclamation is reconcilable with both those objects, as far as they have any foundation in truth or propriety.

It has been shown that the promise of "a *friendly* and *impartial* conduct" towards all the belligerent powers is not inconsistent with the performance of any stipulations in our treaties which would not include our becoming an associate in the wars; and it has been observed that the conduct of the executive, in regard to the 17th and 22nd articles of the Treaty of Commerce, is an unequivocal comment upon those terms. The expressions indeed were naturally to be understood with the exception of those matters of positive compact which would not amount to taking part in the war, for a nation then observes a friendly and impartial conduct towards two powers at war—when it only performs to one of them what it is obliged to do by the positive stipulations of antecedent treaties, those stipulations not amounting to a participation in the war.

Neither do those expressions imply that the U. States will not exercise their discretion in doing kind offices to some of the parties, without extending them to the others, *so long as those offices have no relation to war*: For kind offices of that description may, consistently with neutrality, be shown to one party and refused to another.

If the objectors mean that the U. States ought to favor France *in things relating to war and where they are not bound to do it by treaty*—they must in this case also abandon their pretension of being friends to peace. For such a conduct would be a violation of neutrality, which could not fail to produce war.

It follows then that the proclamation is reconcilable with all that those who censure it contend for, taking them upon their own ground—that nothing is to be done incompatible with the preservation of peace.

But though this would be a sufficient answer to the objection under consideration, yet it may not be without use to indulge some reflections on this very favorite topic of gratitude to France, since it is at this shrine we are continually invited to sacrifice the true interests of the country, as if *"All for love and the world well lost"*[2] were a fundamental maxim in politics.

Faith and justice between nations are virtues of a nature sacred and unequivocal. They cannot be too strongly inculcated nor too highly respected. Their obligations are definite and positive, their utility unquestionable: they relate to objects which with probity and sincerity generally admit of being brought within clear and intelligible rules.

But the same cannot be said of gratitude. It is not very often between nations that it can be pronounced with certainty that there exists a solid foundation for the sentiment—and how far it can justifiably be permitted to operate is always a question of still greater difficulty.

The basis of gratitude is a benefit received or intended, which there was no right to claim, originating in a regard to the interest or advantage of the party on whom the benefit is or is meant to be conferred. If a service is rendered from views *chiefly* relative to the immediate interest of the party who renders it, and is productive of reciprocal advantages, there seems scarcely in such a case to be an adequate basis for a sentiment like that of gratitude. The effect would be disproportioned to the cause, if it ought to beget more than a disposition to render in turn a correspondent good office, founded on *mutual* interest and *reciprocal* advantage. But gratitude would require more than this; it would require, to a certain extent, even a sacrifice of the interest of the party obliged to the service or benefit of the party by whom the obligation had been conferred.

Between individuals, occasion is not unfrequently given to the exercise of gratitude. Instances of conferring benefits from kind and benevolent dispositions or feelings towards the person benefitted, without any other interest on the part of the person who confers the benefit than the pleasure of doing a good action, occur every day among individuals. But among nations they perhaps never occur. It may be affirmed as a general principle that the predominant motive of good offices from one nation to another is the interest or advantage of the nations which performs them.

Indeed the rule of morality is in this respect not exactly the same between nations as between individuals. The duty of making its own welfare the guide of its actions is much stronger upon the former than upon the latter; in proportion to the greater magnitude and importance of national compared with individual happiness, to the greater permanency of the effects of national than of individual conduct. Existing millions and for the most part future generations are concerned in the present measures of a government: While the consequences of the private actions of an individual for the most part terminate with himself or are circumscribed within a narrow compass.

Whence it follows that an individual may on numerous occasions meritoriously indulge the emotions of generosity and benevolence, not only without an eye to, but even at the expense of his own interest. But a nation can rarely be justified in pursuing a similar course; and when it does so ought to confine itself within much stricter bounds.* Good offices, which are indifferent to the interest of a nation performing them, or which are compensated by the existence or expectation of some reasonable equivalent, or which produce an essential good to the nation to which they are rendered, without real detriment to the affairs of the nation rendering them, prescribe the limits of national generosity or benevolence.

It is not meant here to advocate a policy absolutely selfish or interested in nations, but to show that a policy regulated by their own interest, as far as justice and good faith permit, is and ought to be their prevailing policy: and that either to ascribe to them a different principle of action, or to deduce from the supposition of it arguments for a self-denying and self-sacrificing gratitude on the part of a nation which may have received from another good offices, is to misconceive or mistake what usually are and ought to be the springs of national conduct.

These general reflections will be auxiliary to a just estimate of our real situation with regard to France, of which a close view will be taken in a succeeding paper.

---

* This conclusion derives confirmation from the reflection that under every form of government, rulers are only trustees for the happiness and interest of their nation, and cannot, consistently with their trust, follow the suggestions of kindness or humanity towards others, to the prejudice of their constituent.

Pacificus No. V, July 13–17, 1793

France, the rival time immemorial of Great Britain, had in the course of the war which ended in 1763 suffered from the successful arms of the latter the severest losses and the most mortifying defeats. Britain from that moment had acquired an ascendant over France in the affairs of Europe and in the commerce of the world too decided to be endured without impatience or without an eager desire of finding a favorable opportunity to destroy it and repair the breach which had been made in the national glory. The animosity of wounded pride conspired with calculations of the interest of the state to give a keen edge to that impatience and to that desire.

The American Revolution offered the occasion. It attracted early the notice of France, though with extreme circumspection. As far as countenance and aid may be presumed to have been given prior to the epoch of the acknowledgement of our independence, it will be no unkind derogation to assert that they were marked neither with liberality nor with vigor, that they bore the appearance rather of a desire to keep alive disturbances which would embarrass a rival power than of a serious design to assist a revolution or a serious expectation that it would be effected.

The victories of Saratoga, the capture of an army, which went a great way towards deciding the issue of the contest, decided also the hesitations of France. They established in the government of that country a confidence in our ability to accomplish our purpose, and as a consequence of it produced the treaties of alliance and commerce.

It is impossible to see in all this anything more than the conduct of a rival nation, embracing a most promising opportunity to repress the pride and diminish the dangerous power of its rival by seconding a successful resistance to its authority and by lopping off a valuable portion of its dominions. The dismemberment of this country from Great Britain was an obvious and a very important interest of France. It cannot be doubted that it was the determining motive and an adequate compensation for the assistance afforded us.

Men of sense in this country deduced an encouragement to the part which their zeal for liberty prompted them to take in our revolution from the probability of the cooperation of France and Spain. It will be remembered that this argument was used in the publications of the day, but upon what was it bottomed? Upon the known competition between those powers and Great Britain, upon their evident interest to reduce her power and circumscribe her empire; not upon motives of regard to our interest or of attachment to our cause. Whoever should have alleged the latter as grounds of the expectation held out would have been justly considered as a visionary or a deceiver. And whoever shall now ascribe the aid we received to such motives would not deserve to be viewed in a better light.

The inference from these facts is not obscure. Aid and cooperation founded upon a great interest, *pursued* and *obtained* by the party affording them, is not a proper stock upon which to engraft that enthusiastic gratitude which is claimed from us by those *who love France more than the United States.*

This view of the subject, extorted by the extravagancy of such a claim, is not meant to disparage the just pretensions of France upon our *good will.* Though neither in the *motives* to the succors which she furnished us, nor in their *extent* (considering how powerfully *the point of honor in such a war* reinforced the considerations of interest, when she was once engaged) can be found a sufficient basis for that gratitude which is the theme of so much declamation. Yet we shall find in the manner of affording those succors just cause for our esteem and friendship.

France did not attempt, in the first instance, to take advantage of our situation to extort from us any humiliating or injurious concessions as the price of her assistance, nor afterwards in the progress of the war to impose hard terms as the condition of particular aids.

Though this course was certainly dictated by policy, yet it was an honorable and a magnanimous policy, such a one as always constitutes a title to the approbation and esteem of mankind and a claim to the friendship and acknowledgement of the party in whose favor it is practiced.

But these sentiments are satisfied on the part of a nation when they produce sincere wishes for the happiness of the party from whom it has experienced such conduct and a cordial disposition to *render all good and friendly offices which can be rendered without prejudice to its own solid and permanent interests.*

To ask of a nation so situated to make a sacrifice of substantial interest, to expose itself to the jealousy, ill will, or resentment of the rest of the world, to hazard in an eminent degree its own safety for the benefit of the party who may have observed towards it the conduct which has been described, would be to ask more than the nature of the case demands, more than the fundamental maxims of society authorize, more than the dictates of sound reason justify.

A question has arisen, with regard to the proper object of that gratitude which is so much insisted upon, whether the unfortunate prince by whom the assistance received was given, or the nation of whom he was the chief and the organ.

The arguments which support the latter idea are as follow—

"Louis the XVI was but the constitutional agent of the French nation. He acted for and on behalf of the nation; 'twas with their money and their blood he supported our cause. 'Tis to them, therefore, not to him that our obligations are due. Louis the XVI in taking our part was no doubt actuated by motives of state policy. An absolute prince could not love liberty. But the people of

France patronized our cause with zeal from sympathy in its object. The people therefore, not the monarch, were entitled to our sympathy."

This reasoning may be ingenious, but it is not founded in *nature* or *fact*.

Louis the XVI, though no more than the constitutional agent of the nation, had at the time the sole power of managing its affairs—the legal right of directing its will and its forces. It belonged to him to assist us or not, without consulting the nation; and he did assist us, without such consultation. His will alone was *active*, that of the nation *passive*. If there was any kindness in the decision demanding a return of kindness from us, it was the kindness of Louis the XVI—his heart was the depository of the sentiment. Let the genuine voice of nature then, unperverted by political subtleties, pronounce whether the acknowledgement which may be due for that kindness can be equitably transferred from him to others who had no share in the decision—whether the *principle of gratitude* ought to determine us to behold with indifference his misfortunes and with satisfaction the triumphs of his enemies.

The doctrine that the prince is only the organ of his nation is conclusive to enforce the obligations of good faith between nation and nation; in other words, the observance of duties stipulated in treaties for national purposes—and it will even suffice to continue to a nation a claim to the friendship and good will of another resulting from friendly offices done by its prince; but it would be to carry it too far and to render it too artificial to attribute to it the effect of transferring that claim from the prince to the nation, by way of opposition and contrast. Friendship, good will, gratitude for favors received have so inseparable a reference to the motives with which and to the persons by whom they were rendered as to be incapable of being transferred to *another* at *his expense*.

But Louis the XVI, it is said, acted from reasons of state without regard to our cause, while the people of France patronized it with zeal and attachment.

As far as the assertion with regard to the monarch is founded and is an objection to our gratitude to him, it destroys the whole fabric of gratitude to France; for our gratitude is and must be relative to the *services* rendered us. The nation can only claim it on the score of their having been rendered *by their agent with their means*. If the views with which he rendered them divested them of that merit which ought to inspire gratitude—none is due. The nation no more than their agent can claim it.

As to the individual good wishes of the citizens of France, as they did not produce the services rendered to us as a nation, they can be no foundation for national gratitude. They can only call for a reciprocation of individual good wishes. They cannot form the basis of public obligation.

But the assertion takes more for granted than there is reason to believe true.

Louis the XVI no doubt took part in our contest from reasons of state; but Louis the XVI was a humane, kind-hearted man. The acts of his youth had entitled him to this character. It is natural for a man of such a disposition to become interested in the cause of those whom he protects or aids; and if the concurrent testimony of the period may be credited, there was no man in France more personally friendly to the cause of this country than Louis the XVI. I am much misinformed if repeated declarations of the venerable Franklin did not attest this fact.

It is a just tribute to the people of France to admit that they manifested a lively interest in the cause of America; but, while motives are scanned, who can say how much of it is to be ascribed to the antipathy which they bore to their rival neighbors—how much to their sympathy in the object of our pursuit? It is certain that the love of liberty was not a *national* sentiment in France when a zeal for our cause first appeared among that people.

There is reason to believe, too, that the attachment to our cause, which ultimately became very extensive, if not general, did not originate with the mass of the French people. It began with the higher circles, more immediately connected with the government, and was thence transmitted through the nation.

This observation, besides its tendency to correct ideas which are calculated to give a false direction to the public feeling, may serve to check the spirit of illiberal invective which has been wantonly indulged against those distinguished friends of America, who, though the authors of the French Revolution, have fallen victims to it, because their principles would not permit them to go the length of an entire subversion of the monarchy.

The preachers of gratitude are not ashamed to brand *Louis* the XVI as a tyrant, and *La Fayette* as a traitor. But how can we wonder at this, when they insinuate a distrust even of a ____!

In urging the friendly disposition of our cause manifested by the people of France as a motive to our gratitude towards that people, it ought not to be forgotten that those dispositions were not confined to the inhabitants of that country. They were eminently shared by the people of the United Provinces, produced to us valuable pecuniary aids from their citizens, and finally involved them in the war on the same side with us. It may be added, too, that here the patronage of our cause emphatically began with the community, not originating as in France with the government, but finally implicating the government in the consequences.

Our cause had also numerous friends in other countries, even in that with which we were at war. Conducted with prudence, moderation, justice, and humanity, it may truly be said to have been a popular cause among mankind, conciliating the countenance of princes and the affection of nations.

The dispositions of the individual citizens of France can therefore in no sense be urged as constituting a peculiar claim to our gratitude. As far as there is foundation for it, it must be referred to the *services rendered*; and, in the first instance to the unfortunate monarch that rendered them. This is the conclusion of nature and reason.

Pacificus No. VI, July 17, 1793

The very men who not long since, with a holy zeal, would have been glad to make an *autos de fé* of any one who should have presumed to assign bounds to our obligations to Louis the XVI are now ready to consign to the flames those who venture even to think that he died a proper object of our sympathy or regret. The greatest pains are taken to excite against him our detestation. His supposed perjuries and crimes are sounded in the public ear, with all the exaggerations of intemperate declaiming. All the *unproved* and *contradicted allegations* which have been brought against him are taken for granted as the oracles of truth, on no better grounds than the mere general presumptions—that he could not have been a friend to a revolution which stripped him of so much power—that it is not likely the Convention would have pronounced him guilty and consigned him to so ignominious a fate if he had been really innocent.

It is very possible that time may disclose facts and proofs which will substantiate the guilt imputed to Louis; but these facts and proofs have not yet been authenticated to the world; and justice admonishes us to wait for their production and authentication.

Those who have most closely attended to the course of the transaction find least cause to be convinced of the criminality of the deceased monarch. While his counsel, whose characters give weight to their assertions with an air of conscious truth, boldly appeal to facts and proofs in the knowledge and possession of the Convention for the refutation of the charges brought against him—the members of that body, in all the debates upon the subject which have reached this country, either directly from France or circuitously through England, appear to have contented themselves with *assuming* the existence of the facts charged, and inferring from them a criminality which, after the abolition of the royalty, they were interested to establish.

The presumptions of guilt drawn from the suggestions which have been stated are more than counterbalanced by an opposite presumption which is too obvious not to have occurred to many, though I do not recollect yet to have met with it in print. It is this:

If the Convention had possessed *clear evidence* of the guilt of Louis, they would have promulgated it to the world in an *authentic* and *unquestionable* shape. Respect for the opinion of mankind, regard for their own character, the interest of their cause, made this an *indispensable* duty; nor can the omission be satisfactorily ascribed to any other reason than the want of *such evidence*.

The inference from this is that the melancholy catastrophe of Louis XVI was the result of a supposed political expediency rather than of real criminality.

In a case so circumstanced, does it, can it consist with our justice or our humanity to partake in the angry and vindictive passions which are endeavored to be excited against the unfortunate monarch? Was it a crime in him to have been born a prince? Could this circumstance forfeit his title to the commiseration due to his misfortunes as a man?

Would *gratitude* dictate to a people, situated as are the people of this country, to *lend their aid* to extend to the son the misfortunes of the father? Should we not be more certain of violating no obligation of that kind—of not implicating the delicacy of our national character—by taking no part in the contest—than by throwing our weight into either scale?

Would not a just estimate of the origin and progress of our relations to France, viewed with reference to the mere question of gratitude, lead us to this result—that we ought not to *take part* against the son and successor of a father, on whose *sole will* depended the assistance which we received—that we ought not to *take part* with him against the nation whose blood and whose treasure had been, in the hands of the father, the means of the assistance afforded us?

But we are sometimes told by way of answer that the cause of France is the cause of liberty: and that we are bound to assist the nation on the score of their being engaged in the defense of that cause. How far this idea ought to carry us will be the object of future examination.

It is only necessary here to observe that it presents a question essentially different from that which has been in discussion. If we are bound to assist the French nation, on the principle of their being embarked in the defense of liberty, this is a ground altogether foreign to that of gratitude. Gratitude has reference only *to kind offices received*. The obligation to assist the cause of liberty has reference to the merits of that cause and to the interest we have in its support. It is possible that the benefactor may be on one side—the defenders and supporters of liberty on the other, gratitude may point one way—the love of liberty another. It is therefore important to just conclusions not to confound the two things.

A sentiment of justice more than the importance of the question itself has led to so particular a discussion, respecting the proper object of whatever acknowledgment may be due from the United States for the aid which they received from France during their own revolution.

The extent of the obligation which it may impose is by far the most interesting inquiry. And though it is presumed that enough has been already said to evince that it does in no degree require us to embark in the war; yet there is another and very simple view of the subject, which is too convincing to be omitted.

The assistance lent us by France was afforded by a great and powerful nation, possessing numerous armies, a respectable fleet, and the means of rendering it a match for the force to be contended with. The position of Europe was favorable to the enterprise, a general disposition prevailing to see the power of Great Britain abridged. The cooperation of Spain was very much a matter of course, and the probability of other powers becoming engaged on the same side not remote. Great Britain was alone and likely to continue so—France had a great and persuasive interest in the separation of this country from Britain. In this situation, with *much to hope* and *not much to fear*, she took part in our quarrel.

France is at this time *singly* engaged with the greatest part of Europe, including all the first-rate powers except one, and in danger of being engaged with all the rest. To use the emphatic language of a member of the National Convention—she has but *one enemy*, and that is ALL EUROPE. Her internal affairs are *without doubt* in serious disorder. Her navy comparatively inconsiderable. The United States are a young nation; their population, though rapidly increasing, still small—their resources, though growing, not great; without armies, without fleets—capable from the nature of the country and the spirit of its inhabitants of immense exertions for self-defense, but little capable of those external efforts which could materially serve the cause of France. So far from having any direct interest in going to war, they have the strongest motives of interest to avoid it. By embarking with France in the war, they would have incomparably more to apprehend, than to hope.

This contrast of situations and inducements is alone a conclusive demonstration that the United States are not under an obligation from gratitude to join France in the war. The utter disparity between the circumstances of the service *to be rendered* and of the *service received* proves that the one cannot be an adequate basis of obligation for the other. There would be a want of equality, and consequently of reciprocity.

But complete justice would not be done to this question of gratitude, were no notice to be taken of the address which has appeared in the public papers (the authenticity of which has not been impeached) from the Convention of France to the United States, announcing the appointment of the present minister plenipotentiary. In that address the Convention informs us that "the support which the ancient French Court had afforded the United States to recover their independence was only the fruit of a base speculation, and that their glory offended its ambitious views, and the ambassadors of France bore the criminal orders of stopping the career of their prosperity."

If this information is to be admitted in the full force of the terms, it is very fatal to the claim of gratitude towards France. An observation similar to one made in a former paper occurs here. If the organ of the nation on whose will the aid given us depended acted not only from motives irrelative to our advantage but from unworthy motives or, as it is stated, from a *base* speculation; if afterwards he displayed a temper hostile to the confirmation of our security and prosperity, in a point so momentous as the establishment of a more adequate government; he acquired no title to our gratitude in the first instance, or he forfeited it in the second. And the nation of France, who can only claim it in virtue of the conduct of their agent, must together with him renounce the pretension. It is an obvious principle that if a nation can claim merit from the good deeds of its sovereign, it must answer for the demerit of his misdeeds. The rule to be a good one must apply both ways.

But some deductions are to be made from the suggestions contained in the address of the Convention in reference to the motives which evidently dictated the communication. Their zeal to alienate the good will of this country from the late monarch and to increase the odium of the French nation against the monarchy, which was so ardent as to make them overlook the tendency of their communication to disarm their votaries among us of the plea of gratitude, may justly be suspected of exaggeration.

The truth probably is that the *base speculation* charged amounts to nothing more than the government of France, in affording us assistance, was directed by the motives which have been attributed to it, namely, the desire of promoting the interest of France by lessening the power of Great Britain and opening a new channel of commerce to herself—that the orders said to have been given to the ambassadors of France to stop the career of our prosperity are resolvable into a speculative jealousy of the ministers of the day, lest the U. States by becoming as powerful and great as they are capable of becoming under an efficient government might prove formidable to the European possessions in America. With these qualifications and allowances the address offers no new discovery to the intelligent and unbiased friends of their country. They knew long ago that the interest of France had been the governing motive of the aid afforded us; and they saw clearly enough, in the conversation & conduct of her agents while the present Constitution of the United States was under consideration, that the government of which they were the instruments would have preferred our remaining under the old form, for the reason which has been stated. They perceived also that these views had their effect upon some of the devoted partisans of France among ourselves, as they now perceive that the same characters are embodying themselves with all the aid they can obtain, under the like influence, to resist the *operation* of that government of which they withstood the establishment.

All this was and is seen, and the body of the people of America are too discerning to be long in the dark about it. Too wise to have been misled by foreign or domestic machinations, they adopted a Constitution which was necessary to their safety and to their happiness. Too wise still to be ensnared by the same machinations, they will support the government they have established, and will take care of their own peace, in spite of the insidious efforts which are making to detach them from the one and to disturb the other.

The information which the address of the Convention contains ought to serve as an instructive lesson to the people of this country. It ought to teach us not to overrate *foreign friendships*—to be upon our guard against *foreign attachments*. The former will generally be found hollow and delusive; the latter will have a natural tendency to lead us aside from our own true interest and to make us the dupes of foreign influence. They introduce a principle of action which in its effects, if the expression may be allowed, is *anti-national*. Foreign influence is truly the Grecian Horse to a republic. We cannot be too careful to exclude its entrance. Nor ought we to imagine that it can only make its approaches in the gross form of direct bribery. It is then most dangerous when it comes under the patronage of our passions, under the auspices of national prejudice and partiality.

I trust the morals of this country are yet too good to leave much to apprehend on the score of bribery. Caresses, condescensions, flattery, in unison with our prepossessions, are infinitely more to be feared; and as far as there is opportunity for corruption, it is to be remembered that one foreign power can employ this resource as well as another, and that the effect must be much greater when it is combined with the other means of influence than where it stands alone.

Pacificus No. VII, July 27, 1793

The remaining objection to the proclamation of neutrality still to be discussed is that it was out of time and unnecessary.

To give color to this *objection* it is asked—why did not the proclamation appear when the war commenced with Austria & Prussia? Why was it forborne till Great Britain, Holland, and Spain became engaged? Why did not the government wait till the arrival at Philadelphia of the minister of the French Republic? Why did it volunteer a declaration not required of it by any of the belligerent parties?

To most of these questions solid answers have already appeared in the public prints. Little more can be done than to repeat and enforce them.

Austria and Prussia are not maritime powers. Contraventions of neutrality as against them were not likely to take place to any extent or in a shape that would attract their notice. It would therefore have been useless, if not ridiculous, to have made formal declaration on the subject while they were the only parties opposed to France.

But the reverse of this is the case with regard to Spain, Holland, & England. These are all commercial maritime nations. It was to be expected that their attention would be immediately drawn towards the U. States with sensibility, and even with jealousy. It was to be feared that some of our citizens might be tempted by the prospect of gain to go into measures which would injure them and commit the peace of the country. Attacks by some of these powers upon the possessions of France in America were to be looked for as a matter of course. While the views of the U. States as to that particular were problematical, they would naturally consider us as a power that might become their enemy. This they would have been the more apt to do on account of those public demonstrations of attachment to the cause of France, of which there has been so great a display. Jealousy, everybody knows, especially if sharpened by resentment, is apt to lead to ill treatment, ill treatment to hostility.

In proportion to the probability of our being regarded with a suspicious and consequently an unfriendly eye by the powers at war with France, in proportion to the danger of imprudencies being committed by any of our citizens, which might occasion a rupture with them—the policy on the part of the government of removing all doubt as to its own disposition, and of deciding the condition of the U. States in the view of the parties concerned, became obvious and urgent.

Were the U. States now what, if we do not rashly throw away the advantages we possess, they may expect to be in 15 or 20 years, there would have been more room for an insinuation which has been thrown out—namely that they ought to have secured to themselves some advantage as the consideration of their neutrality, an idea, however, of which the justice and magnanimity cannot be commended. But in their present situation, with their present strength and resources, an attempt of that kind could have only served to display pretensions at once excessive and unprincipled. The chance of obtaining any collateral advantage, if such a chance there was, by leaving a doubt upon our intentions as to peace or war, could not wisely have been put for a single instant in competition with the tendency of a contrary conduct to secure our peace.

The conduciveness of the declaration of neutrality to that end was not the only recommendation to an early adoption of the measure. It was of great importance that our own citizens should understand, as soon as possible, the opinion which the government entertained of the nature of our relations to the warring parties and of the propriety or expediency of our taking a side or remaining neuter. The arrangements of our merchants could not but be very differently affected by the one hypothesis or the other; and it would necessarily have been very detrimental and perplexing to them to have been left in uncertainty. It is not requisite to say how much our agriculture and other interests would have been likely to have suffered by embarrassments to our merchants.

The idea of its having been incumbent on the government to delay the measure for the coming of the minister of the French Republic is as absurd as it is humiliating. Did the executive stand in need of the logic of a foreign agent to enlighten it either as to the duties or the interests of the nation? Or was it bound to ask his consent to a step which appeared to itself consistent with the former and conducive to the latter?

The sense of our treaties was to be learnt from the treaties themselves. It was not difficult to pronounce beforehand that we had a greater interest in the preservation of peace than in any advantages with which France might tempt our participation in the war. Commercial privileges were all that she could offer of real value in our estimation, and a *carte blanche* on this head would have been an inadequate recompense for renouncing peace and committing ourselves voluntarily to the chances of so precarious and perilous a war. Besides, if the privileges which might have been conceded were not founded in a real permanent mutual interest—of what value would be the treaty that should concede them? Ought not the calculation in such case to be upon a speedy resumption of them, with perhaps a quarrel as the pretext? On the other hand, may we not trust that commercial privileges which are truly founded in mutual interest will grow out of that interest, without the necessity of giving a premium for them at the expense of our peace?

To what purpose then was the executive to have waited for the arrival of the minister? Was it to give opportunity to contentious discussions—to intriguing machinations—to the clamors of a faction won to a foreign interest?

Whether the declaration of neutrality issued upon or without the requisition of any of the belligerent powers can only be known to their respective ministers and to the proper officers of our government. But if it be true that it issued without any such requisition, it is an additional indication of the wisdom of the measure.

It is of much importance to the end of preserving peace that the belligerent powers should be thoroughly convinced of the sincerity of our intentions to observe the neutrality we profess; and it cannot fail to have weight in producing this conviction that the declaration of it was a spontaneous act—not stimulated by any requisition on the part of either of them—proceeding purely from our own view of our duty and interest.

It was not surely necessary for the government to wait for such a requisition, while there were advantages and no disadvantages in anticipating it. The benefit of an early notification to our merchants conspired with the consideration just mentioned to recommend the course which was pursued.

If, in addition to the rest, the early manifestation of the views of the government has had any effect in fixing the public opinion on the subject and in counteracting the success of the efforts which it was to be foreseen would be made to disunite it, this alone would be a great recommendation of the policy of having suffered no delay to intervene.

What has been already said in this and in preceding papers affords a full answer to the suggestion that the proclamation was unnecessary. It would be a waste of time to add anything more.

But there has been a criticism, several times repeated, which may deserve a moment's attention. It has been urged that the proclamation ought to have contained some reference to our treaties, and that the generality of the promise to observe a conduct *friendly* and *impartial* towards the belligerent powers ought to have been qualified with the expressions equivalent to these—*"as far as may consist with the treaties of the U. States."*

The insertion of such a clause would have entirely defeated the object of the proclamation by rendering the intention of the government equivocal. That object was to assure the powers at war and our own citizens that in the opinion of the executive it was consistent with the duty and interest of the nation to observe a neutrality in the war and that it was intended to pursue a conduct corresponding with that opinion. Words equivalent to those contended for would have rendered the other part of the declaration nugatory by *leaving it uncertain whether the executive did or did not believe a state of neutrality to be consistent with our treaties.* Neither foreign powers nor our own citizens would have been able to have drawn any conclusion from the proclamation, and both would have had a right to consider it as a mere equivocation.

By not inserting any such ambiguous expressions, the proclamation was susceptible of an intelligible and proper construction. While it denoted on the one hand that in the judgment of the executive there was nothing in our treaties obliging us *to become a party in the war*, it left it to be expected on the other— that all stipulations compatible with neutrality, according to the laws and usages of nations, would be enforced. It follows that the proclamation was in this particular exactly what it ought to have been.

The words "make known the disposition of the U. States" have also given a handle to cavil. It has been asked how could the president undertake to declare the disposition of the U. States. The people, for aught he knew, may have been in a very different sentiment. Thus a conformity with republican propriety and modesty is turned into a topic of accusation.

Had the president announced his own disposition, he would have been chargeable with egotism if not presumption. The constitutional organ of intercourse between the U. States & foreign nations—whenever he speaks to them, it is in that capacity; it is in the name and on behalf of the U. States. It must therefore be with greater propriety that he speaks of their disposition than of his own.

It is easy to imagine that occasions frequently occur in the communications to foreign governments and foreign agents—which render it necessary to speak of the friendship or *friendly disposition* of the U. States, of *their disposition* to cultivate harmony and good understanding, to reciprocate neighborly offices, &c. &c. It is usual for example when public ministers are received for some complimentary expressions to be interchanged. It is presumable that the late reception of the French minister did not pass without some assurance on the part of the president of the friendly disposition of the U. States towards France. Admitting it to have happened, would it be deemed an improper arrogation? If not, why it was more so to declare the disposition of the U. States to observe a neutrality in the existing war?

In all such cases nothing more is to be understood than an official expression of the *political* disposition of the nation *inferred* from its political relations, obligations, and interests. It is never to be supposed that the expression is meant to convey the precise state of the individual sentiments or opinions of the great mass of the people.

Kings and princes speak of their own dispositions. The magistrates of republics of the dispositions of their nations. The president therefore has evidently used the style adapted to his situation, & the criticism upon it is plainly a cavil.

Philo Pacificus, August 5, 1793

Mr. Dunlap,[3]

Your correspondent the OLD SOLDIER has given us a long string of quotations from Vattel & Burlamaqui—to prove what?

Why, *that the keeping of promises is of great importance to nations and to individuals.*

That real treaties are binding upon nations notwithstanding changes in the form of government.

And this parade of authorities is offered against something that Pacificus is pretended to have advanced, who indirectly is honored by this learned and good-natured writer with the epithets *highwayman, villain,* &c.

What are we to think of the understanding or candor of this Old Soldier, when the fact is that *Pacificus* has not uttered a syllable tending to draw into question either of the propositions which the authorities quoted tend to establish?

The reasoning of Pacificus throughout not only admits the sacredness of treaties, but proceeds upon the ground that the treaties both of ALLIANCE and of *amity* and *commerce* between the U. States and France are still *in full force between the two nations, notwithstanding the change which has happened in the government of France.*

All that he says turns upon an examination of *the true meaning of the engagements* contained in those treaties, not upon the obligatory force of the treaties themselves.

It follows that all the extracts quoted by your correspondent are entirely foreign from the purpose.

To contest the *meaning* of a promise is certainly a very different thing from disputing its validity or obligation.

But the *Old Soldier*, besides quoting authorities to prove what has not been denied, has been guilty of shamefully mutilating the strongest of those he has quoted, in a manner very material to its sense.

The entire passage is found in Vattel, Book II, Chapter XII, Section 197, in these words—

"If the nation has deposed its king in form, if the people of a republic have driven out their magistrates and set themselves at liberty, or acknowledged the authority of an usurper either expressly or tacitly; to oppose these domestic regulations, by disputing their justice or validity, would be to interfere in the government of a nation and to do it an injury. The ally remains the ally of the state notwithstanding the change that has happened. *However, when this change renders the alliance useless, dangerous, or disagreeable it may renounce it: for it may say upon a good foundation that it would not have entered into an alliance with that nation had it been under the present form of government."*

This last clause, which contains a very important qualification of the general principle, not being to the purpose of the *Old Soldier*, was bravely discarded.

It shows that the U. States, before they gave effect to their treaties with France under the new regimen, might have waited to see what government she would establish in place of the old (for as yet she has no constitution) in order that they might first judge whether a continuance of the alliance under the new form would or would not be *useless*, *dangerous*, or *disagreeable* to them.

But this course it is generally understood, & it appears from official communications, was not pursued. On the contrary, the executive has evidently proceeded upon the principle of giving immediate operation to the treaties with France; and its measures give rise to no question but about the true meaning of those treaties under the circumstances of the case.

The vindication of those measures on a different ground would therefore have been absurd, and has not been attempted by PACIFICUS.

Does the OLD SOLDIER, probably a *mercenary* as well as a veteran, think to deter by his vociferations PACIFICUS or any other independent man from defending against him and his accomplices the rights, the peace, the dignity, and the independence of the nation? If he does, he is grievously mistaken. The real patriots of the country will not be less ready to withstand the encroachments of the agents and myrmidons of France than they were to resist those of Great Britain. Their country is to them everything, and they disdain to bend their necks to the yoke of any foreign nation.

Memorandum to George Washington, August 5, 1793

I doubt the expediency of specially convening the Congress at this time, for the following reasons—

The Constitution requires that an extraordinary occasion should exist as the basis of the exercise of the power of the president to convene the legislature.

It is not perceived that any circumstance now exists which did not exist months ago of sufficient force to constitute an extraordinary occasion.

The war in Europe existed then, as it does now. Indian affairs are not understood to be at this time in a worse, if in so bad a posture, as they have been for a considerable time past.

Some additional incidents have indeed fallen out. The decision with regard to Mr. Genet's recall, the verdict of the jury in the case of Henfield, the supposed decree of the National Convention affecting our Treaty of Commerce with France.

But with regard to the first, it would be only a reason for the measure as far as the circumstance may be supposed likely to produce a war with France. According to ordinary calculation such a consequence ought not to be looked for—and the prudence is very questionable of manifesting by any public act that the executive did look for it.

The second is a matter which under the circumstances seems not of sufficient weight. The judges who tried the cause were united in their opinion of the law. The jury was universally believed in this city to have been selected for the purpose of acquittal, so as to take off much the force of the example and to afford no evidence that other juries would pursue the same course.

The supposed decree of the National Convention is an important consideration. But its authenticity is not yet out of question and it could hardly be acted upon till that was ascertained. And indeed it will deserve examination whether the executive would not itself be competent to whatever it would be prudent to do in the case.

The objections to the measure, at this time, are that unless there are reasons of sufficient force now for adopting it which did not exist before, the taking the step now would impeach the omitting of it hitherto and would expose the executive to much criticism and animadversion.

That the meeting of Congress could scarcely be accelerated for more than a month, allowing as ought to be done due time for the knowledge of the call to diffuse itself throughout the U. States, for the members to prepare for coming and for the distant ones to perform the journey. Sufficient time ought to be given for a full house. A month is so short a period as not to form a material object— and as consequently to bring into still greater question the propriety of acting upon grounds not much if anything stronger than existed when a call would have produced a considerable acceleration.

In proportion to the shortness of the period gained would be the public anxiety and alarm at the measure. It would be construed into an indication that something very extraordinary and urgent had occurred. And abroad as well as at home much speculation would be excited. This consideration, which was always a weighty objection to anticipating the meeting of Congress by a special call, has now great additional force for the reason just assigned.

No Jacobin No. V,
August 14, 1793

For the *American Daily Advertiser*

The observations hitherto made have been designed to vindicate the executive of the United States from the aspersions cast upon it by the JACOBIN. Let us now examine what has been the conduct of the agents of France.

Mr. Genet, charged with the commission of minister plenipotentiary from the French republic to the United States, arrived first at Charleston, in South Carolina. Instead of coming immediately on to the seat of government, as in propriety he ought to have done, he continued at that place, and on the road so long, as to excite no small degree of observation and surprise.

Here at once the system of *electrifying* the people (to use a favorite phrase of the agents of France) began to be put in execution. Discerning men saw from this first opening of the scene what was to be the progress of the drama. They perceived that negotiation with the constitutional organs of the nation was not the only mean to be relied upon for carrying the points with which the representative of France was charged, that popular intrigue was at least to second, if not to enforce, the efforts of negotiation.

During the stay of Mr. Genet at Charleston, without a possibility of sounding or knowing the disposition of our government on the point, he causes to be fitted out two privateers, under French colors and commissions, to cruise from our ports against the enemies of France. Citizens of the United States are engaged to serve on board these privateers, contrary to the natural duties of humanity between nations at peace, and contrary to the positive stipulations of our treaties with some of the powers at war with France. One of these privateers makes a prize of an English vessel, brings her into the port of Charleston, where a consul of France proceeds to try, condemn, and sell her, unwarranted by usage, by treaty, by precedent, by permission.

It is impossible for a conduct less friendly or less respectful than this to have been observed. To direct violations of our sovereignty, amounting to a serious aggression, was added a dangerous commitment of our peace, without even the ceremony of previously feeling the pulse of the government.

The incidents that attended Mr. Genet's arrival here previous to his reception, though justly subject to criticism, shall be passed over in silence. Breaches of decorum lose their importance when mingled with injuries and outrages.

This offensive commencement of his career was not made an objection to his reception, though it would probably have been so in any other country in the world. It has not been alleged either that there was any want of cordiality in that reception. We shall see what return has been made to this manifestation of moderation and friendship. Knowing, as we do, the opposition of the government to the pretension of fitting out privateers in our ports, it cannot be doubted that an early opportunity was taken to make known its disapprobation to the French minister. Nor is it possible that the executive of the United States can have neglected to remonstrate against so improper an exercise of consular jurisdiction as that which has been mentioned: yet we have seen that the practice of fitting out privateers has been openly persisted in. Their number has been so increased, and their depredations have been so multiplied, as to give just cause of alarm for the consequences to the peace of this country. It is also matter of notoriety that the consuls of France have gone on with the condemnation of prizes, that one of them has had the audacity, by a formal protest to the District Court of New York, not only to deny its jurisdiction, but to arrogate to himself a complete and exclusive jurisdiction over the case.

The aggravating circumstances which attended the fitting out the *Little Democrat* at this port under the very nose of the government; the means which were used to obtain a suspension of her progress until the return of the president to the seat of government; the refusal which those overtures met with; the intemperate and menacing declarations which they produced on the part of the French minister, have been the subject of general conversation.

How much more there is in the case—what further contempts of the government may have succeeded the return of the president, can only be matter of conjecture. We know, however, that the *Little Democrat* proceeded to sea; and we conclude from the known consistency of our chief magistrate that this could not have been with his consent.

Prosecutions have been instituted and carried on against some of our citizens for entering into the service of France. It is known that Mr. Genet has publicly espoused and patronized the practice; even, as is asserted, without contradiction to the seeing of counsel for carrying on the defense of the guilty; and we see but a few days since an advertisement from the consul of France at Philadelphia inviting to enter into her service not only her own citizens but all *friends in liberty*, including of course the citizens of the United States.

We read of cases in which one nation has raised men for military service in the dominions of another with the consent of the nation in whose territories they were raised; but the raising of men, not only without the consent, but against the will of the government of the country in which they are raised, is a novelty, reserved for the present day, to display the height of arrogance on one side, and the depth of humiliation on the other.

This is but a part of the picture.

No Jacobin No. VI,
August 16, 1793

For the *American Daily Advertiser*

Let it be supposed for argument-sake that the pretensions of the agents of France, as to fitting out privateers in our ports, enlisting our citizens to serve in them, and holding courts of admiralty within our jurisdiction, for the trial and condemnation of prizes, were well-founded, still the conclusion would be that their conduct is unwarrantable.

When the minister of one country residing in another differs from the government of the country in which he resides about the rights of the nation he represents, whether founded upon treaty or upon the laws of nations, his proper course is to state the subject of difference to his sovereign, who will judge whether his ideas are well or ill founded—whether the pretensions he may have advanced are to be supported or relinquished—if the former, whether further efforts of negotiation are or are not to be tried; or whether reprisals or war is to be resorted to for redressing any denial of right which may have taken place.

This is the only regular or justifiable mode in which he can proceed—the only one proper for the adjustment of differences of opinion between nation and nation.

Every ambassador or other diplomatic character enjoys by the laws of nations privileges and immunities of a high and peculiar nature. One of these is inviolability, or an exemption from punishment for crimes. This sacredness of condition imposes on him an obligation to act with the greatest circumspection and propriety, to abstain cautiously from all infractions of the laws—from all invasions of the authority of the government to which he has been delegated. His only justifiable weapons are negotiation, remonstrance, representation.

If instead of these he has recourse to others, if he undertakes to carry into practice, by *overt acts*, his own opinions of the rights of his country, within the jurisdiction of the nation with which he resides, and in defiance of the known sense and will of its government, he abuses the character with which he is invested, he insults and offends the government to which he has been sent, he makes himself a disturber of the public peace, dangerous in proportion as he is privileged, and richly merits to be dismissed for his temerity.

This is precisely what has been done. This it is that calls for the indignation of every true friend to his country—of every honest and independent citizen—of every man who respects himself and feels for the dignity and rights of the nation of which he is a member.

The man who loves France, equally with him who thinks that no foreign *love* ought to abate the fervor or to taint the purity of his attachment to his own country, ought to join in the reprobation of such conduct. It is directly calculated to endanger the good understanding which subsists between the two nations and to substitute to friendship mutual alienation and disgust.

No Jacobin No. VII,
August 23, 1793

For the *American Daily Advertiser*

One of the earliest exploits which distinguished the career of Mr. Genet after his arrival in this city was the placing himself at the head of a political club. The public papers have announced him member of the Society of the Friends to *Liberty* and *Equality*, and private report assigning to him the presidential chair, does full credit to his exertions to augment the numbers and to enlarge and animate the views of the Society.

The history of diplomatic enterprise affords no parallel to this: We should in vain look for a precedent of a foreign minister, in the country of his mission, becoming the declared head or even the acknowledged member of a *political association*. To what shall we ascribe so extraordinary a step? To a complete ignorance of the rules of propriety, or to a profound contempt for the people among whom he resides? Could he be insensible to the incompatibility between the new office he had accepted and the character with which he had been invested by his nation? Or did he imagine that the people of the United States were so uninformed or so infatuated as not to perceive the danger as well as the unfitness of such an example?

This proceeding of Mr. Genet, which has hitherto escaped without animadversion, though not without notice, is, in a high degree a subject of alarm. There is nothing which the policy of nations has been more careful to circumscribe within strict limits than the sphere of diplomatic agency. The rules of intercourse between foreign missionaries and the nations with which they reside are defined by exact metes and bounds: These rules forbid them to have any political intercourse but with the constitutional organs of the government to which they are sent. They prohibit in the most rigid manner all tampering with private individuals or classes of men—all attempts to acquire an influence in the community extrinsic to the government.

This is a point which particularly demands the exercise of republican jealousy. Foreign intrigues and machinations are among the most formidable enemies which republics have to encounter. These, however narrowed or watched, are always likely to have too much influence upon their affairs. If it should be permitted to the agents of foreign powers to insert themselves in popular societies—to mingle openly and directly in the parties, which will never fail, more or less, to divide a free country, the fruits cannot fail to be dissension, commotion, and, in the end, loss of liberty.

While foreign agents are confined within their proper bounds, a few individuals may be perverted from their duty, but the mass of the nation will remain sound—in condition to control and correct the treacheries, the delinquencies, and the vices of individuals. If, on the contrary, those agents are suffered to travel out of their sphere, and to disseminate their poisons among the people themselves, the whole social frame becomes distempered: The malady spreads itself throughout all the parts of the body politic, seizes upon the heart, and preys upon the vitals.

Of the pernicious tendency of foreign influence upon free communities, examples are numerous. But none can afford a more useful lesson than the case of Sweden, within our own memory. Owing to the distractions and calamities produced by the intermeddlings of foreign powers in the political party-ships of that country, Sweden, in a single day, without struggle or resistance, passed from a form of government essentially republican to that of an absolute monarchy. Let the example of this revolution, among the most extraordinary that are recorded in the annals of mankind, warn and instruct us: Let it teach us to dread and to shun the treacherous and destructive embraces of foreign influence more than war, pestilence, or famine.

Those of us who may feel less alarmed at its approaches, through a partiality for the quarter from which it comes, ought to remember that at some future day it may advance upon us under very different auspices: that a steady adherence to prudent and sound maxims of conduct is the only solid basis of security, and that to keep the Temple of Liberty always pure, it must never be permitted to be profaned by bad examples.

No Jacobin No. VIII,
August 26, 1793

For the *American Daily Advertiser*

It was intimated in the commencement of these papers that Mr. Genet had threatened to appeal from the president of the United States to the people. The fact, though understood from its source in this city, has of late acquired more formal authenticity.

A declaration of this nature demonstrates a total ignorance of the genius and character of the citizens of this country, as well as an entire want of delicacy and decorum in its author. The people of the United States are a people equally sober and enlightened; their notions of liberty are rational and orderly; they know that true liberty can only be supported on the basis of government and law—that the magistracy must be duly respected—that the officers whom they elect are the representatives of their power and dignity—that disrespect to these is offence to them—that an attempt by any foreign agent to sow discord between them and those to whom they have committed the guardianship of their interests is an enterprise against their tranquility and honor, as affrontive as it is dangerous. It supposes nothing less than that they are capable of arranging themselves under foreign banners to control and overturn the constitutional authorities they have themselves created.

When Mr. Genet conceived and expressed the idea of appealing from the president to the people, he must have considered the latter as light, vain, and precipitate; as likely to be governed by impulse more than reason; as susceptible of being flattered by a seeming deference to their authority into an approbation of a direct and contemptuous breach of it in the person of their executive representative; into measures inconsistent with their dignity, their interest, their peace, and their safety.

To endeavor by a lengthy comment to display the impropriety of this conduct would be to weaken the force of the fact. It speaks for itself. There is something in it which comes directly home to the feelings of every man whose feelings are truly American, who possesses and cherishes a becoming pride of national character, producing at once a spontaneous and unqualified indignation.

Yet there are men among us, who call themselves citizens of the United States, degenerate enough to become the apologists of Mr. Genet. He is (say they) a foreigner, not well acquainted with our language; his meaning may have been different from his expression; by the people, he may have intended their representatives in Congress. These are the best of the excuses offered for him.

But it happens that the only one of these suggestions which has the color of truth is that he is a foreigner, one of the grounds of his culpability.

He understands our language remarkably well, as he has proved by correct extemporaneous answers to popular addresses, and was not at all likely to have used expressions materially foreign to his meaning. He understands too well the distinction between the people and their representatives to have confounded the one with the other—to have intended Congress when he mentioned the people. Mr. Genet would blush to make such excuses for himself.

But there are not wanting persons who take a bolder flight and, rejecting the humble style of apology, assume the haughtier tone of justification. Why, say they, should not Mr. Genet talk of appealing from the president to the people? Is the president an absolute sovereign, or is he only the temporary agent of a free nation? If the latter, if the people are the sovereign, why should not an appeal be carried from him to them?

The answer to this rant is obvious and conclusive.

The general security of nations has established it as a sacred and inviolable maxim, forming an essential bulwark of their internal tranquility, that no agent of a foreign sovereign shall, on any pretext, attempt to create a schism between the citizens and the rulers of a state, whatever be its form of government, whether despotic or free, monarchical or republican. The interest of every nation is to every other always distinct, frequently rival. In the intercourses between nations, each can bring to the aid of its views all the influence of its power and wealth: If it were permitted to add to this potent agency, regularly exerted, the free employment of the means of cabal and sedition, every government would be in constant danger of being convulsed and subverted by every other. And as none would in practice tolerate a pretension so hostile to its safety, the admission of it in principle could only serve to multiply tenfold the occasions of war between nation and nation. The peace and safety of states therefore require that all pretense of right in the missionaries of one nation to influence the citizens of another to overrule the decisions of their own government should be rigorously excluded. This exclusion is the common interest of nations and of governments.

The right of appealing from the rulers of a nation to the nation itself, as far as it has foundation in truth, belongs exclusively to the members of that nation. By them alone can it be safely exercised. Their weapons must be those of reason and argument. They must rely wholly on convincing the judgment and conciliating the affections of the people. They must confine themselves within the limits of the laws, or the laws will punish them. They have no armies, no fleets, to second or enforce their logic.

But the case would be widely different with the representative of a foreign power. His appeal would be backed with all the strength, wealth, and weight of the nation to which he belonged. He would have in his hands powerful means of corrupting and intimidating; his harangues, *delivered under the muzzles of the cannons of his ships*, might have a force much greater than they could derive from their eloquence. Exempt by his character from the animadversion of the laws, he might boldly hazard what private persons could not attempt. After having in vain endeavored to convince a majority of the nation, and having only been able to seduce to his views a profligate and unthinking minority, he might then bring to the aid of his friends the purse and the sword of his own country. The calamities of a foreign might be added to the horrors of a civil war to accomplish what his appeal had fruitlessly essayed.

What an immense difference then between the appeal of the representative of a foreign nation and that of private citizens! What treason against the tranquility of nations to vindicate the propriety of such an appeal! What baseness, what prostitution in a citizen of this country, to become the advocate of a pretension so pernicious, so unheard of, so detestable! Language is too poor to give a name to so abandoned a renunciation of principle!

Views on the French Revolution, 1794

Facts, numerous and unequivocal, demonstrate that the present era is among the most extraordinary which have occurred in the history of human affairs. Opinions for a long time have been gradually gaining ground which threaten the foundations of religion, morality, and society. An attack was first made upon the Christian Revelation; for which natural religion was offered as the substitute. The Gospel was to be discarded as a gross imposture; but the being and attributes of a God, the obligations of piety, even the doctrine of a future state of rewards and punishments were to be retained and cherished.

In proportion as success has appeared to attend the plan, a bolder project has been unfolded. The very existence of a deity has been questioned, and in some instances denied. The duty of piety has been ridiculed, the perishable nature of man asserted, and his hopes bounded to the short span of his earthly state. DEATH has been proclaimed an ETERNAL SLEEP—"the dogma of the *immortality* of the soul a *cheat* invented to torment the living for the benefit of the dead." Irreligion, no longer confined to the closets of concealed sophists, nor to the haunts of wealthy riot, has more or less displayed its hideous front among all classes.

Wise and good men took a lead in delineating the odious character of despotism, in exhibiting the advantages of a moderate and well-balanced government, in inviting nations to contend for the enjoyment of rational liberty. Fanatics in political science have since exaggerated and perverted their doctrines. Theories of government unsuited to the nature of man, miscalculating the force of his passions, disregarding the lessons of experimental wisdom, have been projected and recommended. These have everywhere attracted sectaries, and everywhere the fabric of government has been in different degrees undermined.

A league has at length been cemented between the apostles and disciples of irreligion and of anarchy. Religion and government have both been stigmatized as abuses; as unwarrantable restraints upon the freedom of man; as causes of the corruption of his nature, intrinsically good; as sources of an artificial and false morality, which tyrannically robs him of the enjoyments for which his passions fit him; and as clogs upon his progress to the perfection for which he was destined.

As a corollary from these premises, it is a favorite tenet of the sect that religious opinion of any sort is unnecessary to society, that the maxims of a genuine morality and the authority of the magistracy and the laws are a sufficient and ought to be the only security for civil rights and private happiness.

As another corollary, it is occasionally maintained by the same sect that but a small portion of power is requisite to government; that even this portion is only temporarily necessary, in consequence of the bad habits which have been produced by the errors of ancient systems; and that as human nature shall refine and ameliorate by the operation of a more enlightened plan, government itself will become useless, and society will subsist and flourish free from its shackles.

If all the votaries of this new philosophy do not go the whole length of its frantic creed, they all go far enough to endanger the full extent of the mischiefs which are inherent in so wild and fatal a scheme, every modification of which aims a mortal blow at the vitals of human happiness.

The practical development of this pernicious system has been seen in France. It has served as an engine to subvert all her ancient institutions civil and religious, with all the checks that served to mitigate the rigor of authority; it has hurried her headlong through a rapid succession of dreadful revolutions, which have laid waste property, made havoc among the arts, overthrown cities, desolated provinces, unpeopled regions, crimsoned her soil with blood, and deluged it in crime, poverty, and wretchedness; and all this as yet for no better purpose than to erect on the ruins of former things a despotism unlimited and uncontrolled; leaving to a deluded, an abused, a plundered, a scourged, and an oppressed people not even the shadow of liberty to console them for a long train of substantial misfortunes, of bitter sufferings.

This horrid system seemed awhile to threaten the subversion of civilized society and the introduction of general disorder among mankind. And though the frightful evils which have been its first and only fruits have given a check to its progress, it is to be feared that the poison has spread too widely and penetrated too deeply to be as yet eradicated. Its activity has indeed been suspended, but the elements remain concocting for new eruptions as occasion shall permit. It is greatly to be apprehended that mankind is not near the end of the misfortunes which it is calculated to produce, and that it still portends a long train of convulsion, revolution, carnage, devastation, and misery.

Symptoms of the too great prevalence of this system in the United States are alarmingly visible. It was by its influence that efforts were made to embark this country in a common cause with France in the early period of the present war, to induce our government to sanction and promote her odious principles and views with the blood and treasure of our citizens. It is by its influence that every succeeding revolution has been approved or excused—all the horrors that have been committed justified or extenuated—that even the last usurpation, which contradicts all the ostensible principles of the Revolution, has been regarded with complacency; and the despotic constitution engendered by it slyly held up as a model not unworthy of our imitation.

In the progress of this system, impiety and infidelity have advanced with gigantic strides. Prodigious crimes heretofore unknown among us are seen. The chief and idol of[4]

Americanus No. I,
January 31, 1794

An examination into the question how far *regard to the cause of liberty* ought to induce the U. States to take part with France in the present war has been promised.[5] This promise shall now be performed, premising only that it is foreign to the immediate object of these papers—a vindication of the declaration of neutrality. That *executive* act must derive its defense from a just construction of existing treaties and laws. If shown to be consistent with these, the defense is complete.

Whether a mere regard to the cause of liberty, independent of treaty, ought to induce us to become *volunteers* in the war is a question, under our Constitution, not of executive but of legislative cognizance. It belongs to Congress to say—whether the nation shall of choice dismiss the olive branch and unfurl the banners of war.

In judging of the eligibility of the measure with a view to the question just stated, it would present itself under two aspects—

I. Whether the cause of France be truly the cause of liberty, pursued with justice and humanity, and in a manner likely to crown it with honorable success.
II. Whether the degree of service we could render by participating in the conflict was likely to compensate, by its utility to the cause, the evils which would probably flow from it to ourselves.

If either of these questions can be answered in the negative, it will result that the consideration which has been stated ought not to embark us in the war.

A discussion of the first point will not be entered upon. It would involve an examination too complicated for the compass of these papers; and after all, the subject gives so great scope to opinion, to imagination, to feeling that little could be expected from argument. The great leading facts are before the public, and by this time most men have drawn their conclusions so firmly that the issue alone can adjust their differences of opinion. There was a time when all men in this country entertained the same favorable view of the French Revolution. At the present time they all still unite in the wish that the troubles of France may terminate in the establishment of a free and good government, and all dispassionate well-informed men equally unite in the doubt whether this is likely to take place under the auspices of those who now govern the affairs of that country. But agreeing in these two points, there is a great and serious diversity of opinion as to the real merits and probable issue of the French Revolution.

None can deny that the cause of France has been stained by excesses and extravagances for which it is not easy, if possible, to find a parallel and at which reason and humanity recoil. Yet many find apologies & extenuations with which they satisfy themselves; they still see in the cause of France the cause of liberty; they are still sanguine in the hope that it will be crowned with success; that the French nation will establish for themselves not only a free but a republican government, capable of promoting solidly their happiness. Others on the contrary discern no adequate apology for the horrid and disgusting scenes which have been and continue to be acted. They conceive that the excesses which have been committed transcend greatly the measure of those which were reasonably to have been expected with every due allowance for circumstances. They perceive in them proofs of atrocious depravity in the most influential leaders of the Revolution. They observe that among these a Marat and a Robespierre, assassins still reeking with the blood of murdered fellow citizens, monsters who outdo the fabled enormities of a *Busiris* and a *Procrustes*, are predominant in influence as in iniquity. They find everywhere marks of an unexampled dissolution of all the social and moral ties. They see nowhere anything but principles and opinions so wild, so extreme, passions so turbulent, so tempestuous, as almost to forbid the hope of agreement in any rational or well organized system of government: They conclude that a state of things like this is calculated to extend disgust and disaffection throughout the nation, to nourish more and more a spirit of insurrection and mutiny, facilitating the progress of the invading armies and exciting in the bowels of France commotions of which it is impossible to compute the mischiefs, the duration, or the end: that if by the energy of the national character and the intrinsic difficulty of the enterprise the enemies of France shall be compelled to leave her to herself, this era may only prove the commencement of greater misfortunes: that after wading through seas of blood, in a furious and sanguinary civil war, France may find herself at length the slave of some victorious Scylla or Marius or Caesar: And they draw this afflicting inference from the whole view of the subject, that there is more reason to fear that the cause of true liberty has received a deep wound in the mismanagements of it by those who, unfortunately for the French nation, have for a considerable time past maintained an ascendant in its affairs—than to regard the Revolution of France, in the form it has latterly worn, as entitled to the honors due to that sacred and all important cause—or as a safe bark on which to freight the fortunes, the liberties, and the reputation of this now respectable and happy land.

Without undertaking to determine which of these opposite opinions rests most firmly on the evidence of facts, I shall content myself with observing that if the latter is conceived to have but a tolerable foundation, it is conclusive against the propriety of our engaging in the war, merely through regard for the cause of liberty: For when we resolve to put so vast a stake upon the chance of the die, we ought at least to be certain that the object for which we hazard is genuine, is substantial, is real.

Let us proceed to the discussion of the second question.

To judge of the degree of aid which we could afford to France in her present struggle, it may be of use to take a true view of the means with which we carried on the war that accomplished our own revolution.

Our supplies were derived from five sources—1. paper money— 2. domestic loans—3. foreign loans—4. pecuniary taxes—5. taxes in specific articles—6. military impress.

The first of these resources with a view to a future war may be put out of the question. Past experience would forbid its being again successfully employed, and no friend to the morals, property, or industry of the people, to public or private credit, would desire to see it revived.

The second would exist, but probably in a more limited extent. The circumstances of a depreciating paper, which the holders were glad, as they supposed, to realize, was a considerable motive to the loans obtained during the late war. The magnitude of them, however, even then, bore a small proportion to the aggregate expense.

The third resource would be equally out of the question with the first. The principal lending powers would be our enemies as they are now those of France.

The three remaining items—*pecuniary taxes*, taxes on specific articles, military impress, could be employed again in a future war and are the resources upon which we should have chiefly to rely: for the resources of domestic loans is by no means a very extensive one in a community where capitals are so moderate as in ours.

Though it is not to be doubted that the people of the U. States would hereafter as heretofore throw their whole property into common stock for their common defense against internal invasion or an unprovoked attack—who is there sanguine enough to believe that large contributions either in money or produce could be extracted from them to carry on an external war voluntarily undertaken for a foreign and speculative purpose?

The expectation were an illusion. Those who may entertain it ought to pause and reflect. Whatever enthusiasm might have been infused into a part of the community would quickly yield to more just and sober ideas inculcated by experience of the burdens & calamities of war. The circuitous logic by which it is attempted to be maintained that a participation in the war is necessary to the security of our own liberty would then appear, as it truly is, a mere delusion, propagated by bribed incendiaries or hair-brained enthusiasts. And the authors of the delusion would not fail to be execrated as the enemies of the public weal.

Viewing the matter dispassionately, we cannot but conclude that in a war of *choice*, not of *necessity*, like that in which we are invited to engage—it would be a bad calculation to look for great exertions of the community.

The business would move as heavily as it was in its origin impolitic. The faculty of the government to obtain pecuniary supplies would in such a situation be circumscribed within a narrow compass. Levies of men would not be likely to be more successful than those of money. No one would think of detaching the militia for distant expeditions abroad: And the experience we have had in our Indian enterprises does not authorize strong expectations of going far, by voluntary enlistments, where the question is not, as it was during the last war, the defense of the essential rights & interests of the country. The severe expedient of drafting from the militia a principal reliance in that war would put the authority of government in the case supposed to a very critical test.

This summary view of what would be our situation & prospects is alone sufficient to demonstrate the general position that our ability to promote the cause of France by external exertions could not be such as to be very material to the event.

Let us, however, for more complete elucidation inquire to what particular objects they could be directed.

Fleets we have not and could not have in time or to an extent to be of use in the contest.

Shall we raise an army and send it to France? She does not want soldiers. Her own population can amply furnish her armies. The number we could send, if we could get them there at all, would be of no weight in the scale.

The true wants of France are of system, order, money, provisions, arms, military stores.

System and order we could not give her by engaging in the war. The supply of money in that event would be out of our power. At present we can pay our debt to her in proportion as it becomes due. Then we could not even do this. Provisions and other supplies, as far as we are in condition to furnish them, could not then be furnished at all. The conveyance of them would become more difficult—& the forces we should be obliged ourselves to raise would consume our surplus.

Abandoning then, as of necessity we must, the idea of aiding France in Europe, shall we turn our attention to the succor of her islands? Alas, we should probably have here only to combat their own internal disorders to aid Frenchmen against Frenchmen—whites against blacks, or blacks against whites. If we may judge from the past conduct of the powers at war with France, their effort is immediately against herself—her islands are not in the first instance a serious object. But grant that they become so, is it evident, that we can cooperate efficaciously to their preservation? Or if we can what will this have to do with the preservation of French liberty? The dangers to this arise from the invasion of foreign armies carried into the bosom of France—from the still more formidable assaults of civil dissension and the spirit of anarchy.

Shall we attack the islands of the powers opposed to France?

How shall we without a competent fleet carry on the necessary expeditions for the purpose? Where is such a fleet? How shall we maintain our conquests after they are made? What influence could the capture of an island or two have upon the general issue of the contest? These questions answer themselves.

Or shall we endeavor to make a diversion in favor of France by attacking Canada on the one side & Florida on the other?

This certainly would be the most, indeed the only, eligible mode of aiding France in war. These enterprises may be considered as within the compass of our means.

But while this is admitted, it ought not to be regarded as a very easy task. The reduction of Canada ought not to be undertaken with less than ___ men; that of the Floridas with much fewer than ___, for reinforcement could be brought to both those countries from the West India possessions of their respective sovereigns. Relying on their naval superiority, they could spare from the islands all the troops which were not necessary to the preservation of their internal tranquility.

These armies are then to be raised and equipped and to be provided with all the requisite apparatus for operation. Proportionate magazines are to be formed for their accommodation and supply.

Some men, whose fate it is to think loosely, may imagine that a more summary substitute could be found in the militia. But the militia, an excellent auxiliary for internal defense, could not be advantageously employed in distant expeditions requiring time and perseverance. For these, men regularly engaged for a competent period are indispensable. The conquest of Canada at least may with decision be regarded as out of the reach of a militia operation.

If war was resolved upon, the very preparation of the means for the enterprises which have been mentioned would demand not less than a year. Before this period was elapsed, the fate of France, as far as foreign invasion is concerned, would probably be decided. It would be manifest either that she could or could not be subjugated by force of external coercion. Our interposition would therefore be too late to benefit her. It appears morally certain that the war against France cannot be of much duration. The exertions are too mighty to be long protracted.

The only way in which the enterprises in question could serve the cause of France would be by making a diversion of a part of those forces which would otherwise be directed against her. But this consequence could not be counted upon. It would be known that we could not be very early ready to attack with effect, and it would be an obvious policy to risk secondary objects rather than be diverted from the efficacious pursuit of the main one. It would be natural in such case to rely for indemnification on the successful result of the war in Europe. The governments concerned imagine that they have too much at stake upon that result not to hazard considerably elsewhere in order to secure the fairest chance of its being favorable to their wishes.

It would not probably render the matter better to precipitate our measures for the sake of a more speedy impulse. The parties ought in such case to count upon the abortion of our attempts from their immaturity and to rely the more confidently upon the means of resistance already on the spot.

We could not therefore flatter ourselves that the expedient last proposed—that of attacking the possessions of Great Britain and Spain in our neighborhood—would be materially serviceable to the cause of France.

But to give the argument its fairest course, I shall take notice of two particulars in respect to which our interference would be more sensibly felt. These are the depredations which our privateers might make upon the commerce of the maritime enemies of France, and the direct injury which would accrue to that of G. Britain from the interruption of intercourse between the two countries. Considering the shock lately sustained by mercantile credit in that country—the real importance to it of our imports from thence and of our exports thither, the large sums which are due and in a continual course of remittance from our merchants to her merchants—a war between the U. States and Great Britain could not fail to be seriously distressing to her.

Yet it would be weak to count upon very decisive influence of these circumstances. The public credit of G. Britain has still energy sufficient to enable her to struggle with much partial derangement. Her private credit, manifestly disordered by temporary causes, and propped as it has been by the public purse, seems to have recovered its impaired tone. Her commerce too suddenly interrupted by the breaking out of war, must have resumed its wonted channels in proportion as the progress of her naval preparations has tended to give it protection. And though the being at war with us would be very far from a matter of indifference either to her commerce or to her credit, yet it is not likely that it would arrest her career or overrule those paramount considerations which brought her into her present situation.

When we recollect how she maintained herself under a privation of our commerce, through a seven years war with us, united for certain periods of it with France, Spain, & Holland, though we perceive a material difference between her present and her then situation arising from that very effort, yet we cannot reasonably doubt that she would be able notwithstanding a similar privation to continue a war which in fact does not call for an equal exertion on her part, as long as the other powers with which she is associated shall be in condition to prosecute it with a hope of success. Nor is it probable, whatever may be the form or manner of the engagement, that Great Britain could, if disposed to peace, honorably make a separate retreat. It is the interest of all parties in such cases to assure to each other a cooperation: and it is presumable that this has taken place in some shape or other between the powers at present combined against France.

The conclusion from the several considerations which have been presented carefully & dispassionately weighed is this, that there is no probable prospect of this country rendering material service to the cause of France by engaging with her in the war.

It has been very truly observed in the course of the publications upon the subject—*that if France is not in some way or other wanting to herself, she will not stand in need of our assistance, and if she is, our assistance cannot save her.*

Pacificus

Americanus No. II,
February 7, 1794

Let us now turn to the other side of the medal. To be struck with it, it is not necessary to exaggerate.

All who are not willfully blind must see and acknowledge that this country at present enjoys an unexampled state of prosperity. That war would interrupt it need not be affirmed. We should then by war lose the advantage of that astonishing progress in strength, wealth, and improvement which we are now making, and which if continued for a few years will place our national rights and interests upon immovable foundations. This loss alone would be of infinite moment: it is such a one as no prudent or good man would encounter but for some clear necessity or some positive duty.

If while Europe is exhausting herself in a destructive war this country can maintain its peace, the issue will open to us a wide field of advantages which even imagination can with difficulty compass.

But a check to the *progress* of our prosperity is not the greatest evil to be anticipated. Considering the naval superiority of the enemies of France, we cannot doubt that our commerce would be in a great degree annihilated by a war. Our agriculture would of course with our commerce receive a deep wound. The exportations which now contribute to animate it could not fail to be essentially diminished. Our mechanics would experience their full share of the common calamity. That lively and profitable industry which now spreads a smile over all our cities and towns would feel an instantaneous and rapid decay.

Nine tenths of our present revenues are derived from commercial duties. Their declension must of course keep pace with that of trade. A substitute cannot be found in other sources of taxation without imposing heavy burthens on the people. To support public credit and carry on the war would suppose exactions really grievous. To abandon public credit would be to renounce an essential mean of carrying on the war, besides the sacrifice of the public creditors and the disgrace of a national bankruptcy.

We will not call in the aid of savage butcheries and depredations to heighten the picture. 'Tis enough to say that a general Indian war, incited by the united influence of Britain and Spain, would not fail to spread desolation throughout our frontier.

To a people who have so recently and so severely felt the evils of war, little more is necessary than to appeal to their own recollection for their magnitude and extent.

The war which now rages is, & for obvious reasons is likely to continue to be, carried on with unusual animosity and rancor. It is highly probable that the resentment of the combined powers against us if we should take part in the war would be if possible still more violent than it is against France. Our interference would be regarded as altogether officious and wanton. How far this idea might lead to an aggravation of the ordinary calamities of war would deserve serious reflection.

The certain evils of our joining France in the war are sufficient dissuasives from so intemperate a measure. The possible ones are of a nature to call for all our caution, all our prudence.

To defend its own rights, to vindicate its own honor, there are occasions when a nation ought to hazard even its existence. Should such an occasion occur, I trust those who are now most averse to commit the peace of the country will not be the last to face the danger, nor the first to turn their backs upon it.

But let us at least have the consolation of not having rashly courted misfortune. Let us have to act under the animating reflection of being engaged in repelling wrongs which we neither sought nor merited, in vindicating our rights, invaded without provocation, in defending our honor, violated without cause. Let us not have to reproach ourselves with having voluntarily bartered blessings for calamities.

But we are told that our own liberty is at stake upon the event of the war against France—that if she falls we shall be the next victim. The combined powers, it is said, will never forgive in us the origination of those principles which were the germs of the French Revolution. They will endeavor to eradicate them from the world.

If this suggestion were ever so well founded, it would perhaps be a sufficient answer to it to say that our interference is not likely to alter the case—that it could only serve prematurely to exhaust our strength.

But other answers more conclusive present themselves.

The war against France requires on the part of her enemies efforts unusually violent. They are obliged to strain every nerve, to exert every resource. However it may terminate, they must find themselves spent in an extreme degree, a situation not very favorable to the undertaking a new and, even to Europe combined, an immense enterprise.

To subvert by force republican liberty in this country, nothing short of entire conquest would suffice. This conquest, with our present increased population, greatly distant as we are from Europe, would either be impracticable or would demand such exertions as, following immediately upon those which will have been requisite to the subversion of the French Revolution, would be absolutely ruinous to the undertakers.

It is against all probability that an undertaking pernicious as this would be, even in the event of success, would be attempted against an unoffending nation by its geographical position so little connected with the political concerns of Europe.

But impediments would arise from more special causes. Suppose France subdued and a restoration of the monarchy in its ancient form or a partition effected. To uphold either state of things, after the general impulse in favor of liberty which has been given to the minds of 24 millions of people, would in one way or another find occupation for a considerable part of the forces which had brought it about. In the event of an unqualified restoration of the monarchy, if the future monarch did not stand in need of foreign legions for the support of his authority, still the powers who had been concerned in the restoration could not sufficiently rely upon the solidity of the order of things reestablished by them not to keep themselves in a posture to be prepared against the disturbance of it—'till there had been time to compose the discordant interests and passions produced by the Revolution and bring back the nation to ancient habits of subordination. In the event of a partition of France it would of course give occupation to the forces of the conquerors to secure the submission of the dismembered parts.

The new dismemberment of Poland will be another obstacle to the detaching of troops from Europe for a crusade against this country. The fruits of that transaction can only be secured to Russia and Prussia by the agency of large bodies of forces kept on foot for the purpose within the dismembered territories.

Of the powers combined against France there are only three whose interests have any material reference to this country—England, Spain, Holland.

As to Holland, it will be readily conceded that she can have no interest or feeling to induce her to embark in so mad & wicked a project. Let us see how the matter will stand with regard to Spain & England.

The object of the enterprise against us must either be the establishment in this country of a royal in place of our present republican government, the subjugation of the country to the dominion of one of the parties, or its division among them.

The establishment of an independent monarchy in this country would be so manifestly against the interests of both those nations, in the ordinary acceptation of this term in politics—that neither of them can be so absurd as to desire it.

It may be adopted as an axiom in our political calculation that no foreign power which has valuable colonies in America will be propitious to our remaining one people united under a vigorous government.

No man I believe but will think it probable, however disadvantageous the change in other respects, that a monarchical government, from its superior force, would ensure more effectually than our present form our permanent unity as a nation. This at least would be the indubitable conclusion of European calculators. From which may be confidently inferred a disinclination both in England and Spain to our undergoing a change of that kind.

The only thing that can be imagined capable of reconciling either of those powers to it would be the giving us for monarch a member of its own royal family and forming something like a family compact.

But here would arise a direct collision of interest between them. Which of them would agree that a prince of the family of the other should be reigning over this country, giving to that other a decided preponderancy in the scale of American affairs?

The subjugation of the U. States to the dominion of either of those powers would fall more strongly under a like consideration. 'Tis impossible that either of them should consent that the other should become master of this country— And neither of them without madness could desire a mastery which would cost more than 'twas worth to maintain it, and which from an irresistible course of things could be but of very short duration.

The third, namely the division of it between them, is the most colorable of the three suppositions—But even this would be the excess of folly in both.

Nothing could be more unwise in the first instance, in Great Britain, than to consent by that measure to divide with Spain the emoluments of our commerce which now in so great a degree center with her with a probability of continuing to do it as long as the natural relations of commerce are permitted to govern.

Spain too could not fail to be sensible that from obvious causes her dominion over the part which was allotted to her would be altogether transient.

The first collision between Britain and Spain would certainly have one of two effects—either a reunion of the whole country under Great Britain or a dismission of the yoke of both.

The latter by far the most probable would discover to both the extreme absurdity of the project.

The U. States, rooted as are now the ideas of independence, are happily too remote from Europe to be governed by her. Dominion over any part of them would be a real misfortune to any nation of that quarter of the globe.

To Great Britain the enterprise supposed would threaten serious consequences in more ways than one. It may safely be affirmed that she would run by it greater risk of bankruptcy and revolution than we of subjugation. A chief proportion of the burden would unavoidably fall upon her as the most monied & principal maritime power, & it may emphatically be said that she would make war upon her own commerce & credit. There is the strongest ground to believe that the nation would disrelish and oppose the project. The certainty of great evils attending it—the dread of much greater—experience of the disasters of the last war, would operate upon all. Many, not improbably a majority, would see in the enterprise a malicious and wanton hostility against liberty, of which they might themselves expect to be the next victim. Their judgments and their feelings would easily distinguish this case from that either of their former contest with us or their present contest with France. In the former they had pretensions to support which were plausible enough to mislead their pride and their interest. In the latter there were strong circumstances to rouse their passions, alarm their fears, and induce an acquiescence in the course which was pursued.

But a future attack upon us, as apprehended, would be so absolutely pretextless as not to be misunderstood. Our conduct will have been such as to entitle us to the reverse of unfriendly or hostile dispositions: While powerful motives of self-interest would advocate with them our cause.

But Britain, Spain, Austria, Prussia, and perhaps even Russia will have more need and a stronger desire of peace & repose to restore and recruit their wasted strength and exhausted treasuries—to reinvigorate the interior order and industry of their respective kingdoms relaxed and depressed by war—than either means or inclination to undertake so extravagant an enterprise against the liberty of this country.

If there can be any danger to us of that sort, it must arise from our voluntarily thrusting ourselves into the war. Once embarked, nations sometimes prosecute enterprises which they would not otherwise have dreamt of. The most violent resentment would no doubt in such case be kindled against us for what would be called a wanton and presumptuous intermeddling on our part. What this might produce it is not easy to calculate.

There are two great errors in our reasoning upon this subject. One is that the combined powers will certainly attribute to us the same principles which they deem so exceptionable in France, the other that our principles are in fact the same.

If left to themselves they will all, except one, naturally see in us a people who originally resorted to a revolution in government as a refuge from encroachment on rights and privileges *antecedently* enjoyed—not as a people who from choice have sought a radical and entire change in the established government in pursuit of new privileges and rights carried to an extreme not reconcilable perhaps with any form of regular government. They will see in us a people who have a due respect for property and personal security—who in the midst of our revolution abstained with exemplary moderation from everything violent or sanguinary, instituting governments adequate to the protection of persons and property; who since the completion of our revolution have in a very short period, from mere reasoning and reflection, without tumult or bloodshed, adopted a form of general government calculated as well as the nature of things would permit—to remedy antecedent defects—to give strength and security to the nation—to rest the foundations of liberty on the basis of justice, order, and law—who at all times have been content to govern ourselves; unmeddling in the governments or affairs of other nations: in fine, they will see in us sincere republicans but decided enemies to licentiousness and anarchy—sincere republicans but decided friends to the freedom of opinion, to the order and tranquility of all mankind. They will not see in us a people whose best passions have been misled and whose best qualities have been perverted from their true aim by headlong fanatical or designing leaders to the perpetration of acts from which humanity shrinks— to the commission of outrages, over which the eye of reason weeps—to the profession and practice of principles which tend to shake the foundations of morality—to dissolve the social bands—to disturb the peace of mankind—to substitute confusion to order, anarchy to government.

Such at least is the light in which the reason or the passions of the powers confederated against France lead them to view her principles and conduct. And it is to be lamented that so much cause has been given for their opinions. If on our part we give no incitement to their passions, facts too prominent and too decisive to be combated will forbid their reason to bestow the same character upon us.

It is therefore matter of real regret that there should be an effort on our part to level the distinctions which discriminate our case from that of France—to confound the two cases in the view of foreign powers—and to hazard our own principles by persuading ourselves of a similitude which does not exist.

Let us content ourselves with lamenting the errors into which a great, a gallant, an amiable, a respectable nation has been betrayed—with uniting our wishes and our prayers that the Supreme Ruler of the World will bring them back from those errors to a more sober and more just way of thinking and acting, and will overrule the complicated calamities which surround them to the establishment of a government under which they may be free secure and happy. But let us not corrupt ourselves by false comparisons or glosses—nor shut our eyes to the true nature of transactions which ought to grieve and warn us—not rashly mingle our destiny in the consequences of the errors and extravagances of another nation.

PACIFICUS

Letter to George Washington, April 14, 1794

Sir,

The present is beyond question a great, a difficult, & a perilous crisis in the affairs of this country. In such a crisis it is the duty of every man, according to situation, to contribute all in his power towards preventing evil and producing good. This consideration will I trust be a sufficient apology for the liberty I am about to take of submitting without an official call the ideas which occupy my mind concerning the actual posture of our public affairs. It cannot but be of great importance that the chief magistrate should be informed of the real state of things, and it is not easy for him to have this information but through those principal officers who have most frequent access to him. Hence an obligation on their part to communicate information on occasions like the present.

A course of accurate observation has impressed on my mind a full conviction that there exist in our councils three considerable parties—one decided for preserving peace by every effort which shall any way consist with the ultimate maintenance of the national honor and rights and disposed to cultivate with all nations a friendly understanding—another decided for war and resolved to bring it about by every expedient which shall not too directly violate the public opinion—a third not absolutely desirous of war but solicitous at all events to excite and keep alive irritation and ill humor between the U. States and Great Britain, not unwilling in the pursuit of this object to expose the peace of the country to imminent hazards.

The views of the first party in respect to the questions between G. Britain and us favor the following course of conduct—To take effectual measures of military preparation, creating in earnest force and revenue—to vest the president with important powers respecting navigation and commerce for ulterior contingencies—to endeavor by another effort of negotiation, confided to hands able to manage it and friendly to the object, to obtain reparation for the wrongs we suffer and a demarcation of a line of conduct to govern in future—to avoid 'till the issue of that experiment all measures of a nature to occasion a conflict between the motives which might dispose the British government to do us the justice to which we are entitled and the sense of its own dignity—If that experiment fails then and not till then to resort to reprisals and war.

The views of the second party in respect to the same questions favor the following courses of conduct—to say and to do everything which can have a tendency to stir up the passions of the people and beget a disposition favorable to war—to make use of the inflammation which is excited in the community for the purposes of carrying through measures calculated to disgust Great Britain and to render an accommodation impracticable, without humiliation to her, which they do not believe will be submitted to—in fine, to provoke and bring on war by indirect means without declaring it or even avowing the intention, because they know the public mind is not yet prepared for such an extremity and they fear to encounter the direct responsibility of being the authors of a war.

The views of the third party lead them to favor the measures of the second—but without a perfect coincidence in the result. They weakly hope that they may hector and vapor with success—that the pride of Great Britain will yield to her interest—and that they may accomplish the object of perpetuating animosity between the two countries without involving war.

There are some characters, not numerous, who do not belong to either of these classes—but who fluctuate between them as in the conflict between reason & passion, the one or the other prevails.

It may seem difficult to admit in the situation of this country that there are parties of the description of the two last men who can either systematically meditate war or can be willing to risk it otherwise than by the use of means which they deem necessary to insure reparation for the injuries we experience.

But a due attention to the course of the human passions as recorded in history and exemplified by daily occurrences is sufficient to obviate all difficulty on this head.

Wars oftener proceed from angry and perverse passions than from cool calculations of interest. This position is admitted without difficulty when we are judging of the hostile appearances in the measures of Great Britain towards this country. What reason can there be why it should not be as good a test of similar appearances on our part? As men, it is equally applicable to us—and the symptoms are strong of our being readily enough worked up into a degree of rage and frenzy, which goes very far towards silencing the voice of reason and interest.

Those who compose the parties whose measures have a war-aspect are under the influence of some of the strongest passions that can actuate human conduct. They unite from habitual feeling in an implacable hatred to Great Britain and in a warm attachment to France. Their animosity against the former is inflamed by the most violent resentment for recent and unprovoked injuries—in many instances by personal loss and suffering or the loss and suffering of intimate friends and connections. Their sympathy with the latter is increased by the idea of her being engaged in defending the cause of liberty against a combination of despots who meditate nothing less than the destruction of it throughout the world. In hostility with Britain they seek the gratification of revenge upon a detested enemy with that of serving a favorite friend and in this the cause of liberty. They anticipate also, what is in their estimation a great political good, a more complete and permanent alienation from Great Britain and a more close approximation to France. Those even of them who do not wish the extremity of war consider it as a less evil than a thorough and sincere accommodation with Great Britain and are willing to risk the former rather than lose an opportunity so favorable as the present to extend and rivet the springs of ill will against that nation.

However necessary it is to veil this policy in public—in private there are not much pains taken to disguise it. Some gentlemen do not scruple to say that pacification is and ought to be out of the question.

What has been heretofore said relates only to persons in public character. If we extend our view from these to the community at large, we shall there also find a considerable diversity of opinion—partisans of patience, negotiation, and peace, if possible, and partisans of war. There is no doubt much of irritation now afloat—many advocates for measures tending to produce war. But it would be a great mistake to infer from these appearances that the prevailing sentiment of the country is for war—or that there would be either a willing acquiescence or a zealous cooperation in it if the proceedings of the government should not be such as to render it manifestly beyond question that war was inevitable but by an absolute sacrifice of the rights and interests of the nation—that the race of prudence was completely run and that nothing was done to invite hostility or left undone to avoid it.

It is to my mind unequivocal that the great mass of opinion in the eastern states and in the State of New York is against war if it can be avoided without absolute dishonor or the ultimate sacrifice of essential rights and interests—and I verily believe that the same sentiment is the radical one throughout the U. States, *some* of the towns perhaps excepted, where even it is much to be doubted whether there would not be a minority for the affirmative of the naked question of war or of measures which should be acknowledged to have a tendency to promote or produce it.

The natural inference from such a state of the public mind is—that if measures are adopted with the disapprobation and dissent of a large and enlightened minority of Congress, which in the event should appear to have been obstacles to a peaceable adjustment of our differences with Great Britain—there would be under the pressure of the evils produced by them a deep and extensive dissatisfaction with the conduct of the government—a loss of confidence in it—and an impatience under the measures which war would render unavoidable.

Prosperous as is truly the situation of this country, great as would be the evils of war to it, it would hardly seem to admit of a doubt that no chance for preserving peace ought to be lost or diminished in compliance either with resentment or the speculative ideas which are the arguments for a hostile course of conduct.

At no moment were the indications of a plan on the part of Great Britain to go to war with us sufficiently decisive to preclude the hope of averting it by a negotiation conducted with prudent energy and seconded by such military preparations as should be demonstrative of a resolution eventually to vindicate our rights. The revocation of the instructions of the 6th of November, even with the relaxation of some pretensions which Great Britain has in former wars maintained against neutral powers, is full evidence that if the system was before for war, it was then changed. The events which have taken place in Europe are of a nature to render it probable that such a system will not be revived and that by prudent management we may still escape a calamity which we have the strongest motives internal as well as external to shun.

I express myself thus because it is certainly not an idle apprehension that the example of France (whose excesses are with too many an object of apology if not of justification) may be found to have unhinged the orderly principles of the people of this country and that war, by putting in motion all the turbulent passions and promoting a further assimilation of our principles with those of France, may prove to be the threshold of disorganization and anarchy.

The late successes of France have produced in this country conclusions much too sanguine with regard to the event of the contest. They no doubt afford a high probability of her being able eventually to defend herself, especially under a form of administration of such unexampled vigor as that by which she has of late managed her affairs. But there will be nothing wonderful in a total reverse of fortune during the ensuing campaign. Human nature must be an absolutely different thing in France from what it has hitherto shown itself to be throughout the globe and in all ages if there do not exist in a large proportion of the French nation germs of the profoundest discontent ready to burst into vegetation the moment there should appear an efficacious prospect of protection and shade from the progress of the invading armies. And if having possessed themselves of some of the keys of France, the principle of the commencing campaign should be different from that of the past—active field operations succeeding to the wasteful and dilatory process of sieges—who can say that victory may not so far crown the enterprises of the coalesced powers as to open the way to an internal explosion which may prove fatal to the Republic? 'Tis now evident that another vigorous campaign will be essayed by the allies. The result is and must be incalculable.

To you, Sir, it is unnecessary to urge the extreme precariousness of the events of war. The inference to be drawn is too manifest to escape your penetration. This country ought not to set itself afloat upon an ocean so fluctuating, so dangerous, and so uncertain but in a case of absolute necessity.

That necessity is certainly not yet apparent. The circumstances which have been noticed with regard to the recent change of conduct on the part of G. Britain authorize a strong hope that a negotiation conducted with ability and moderation, and supported at home by demonstrations of vigor and seriousness, would obviate those causes of collision which are the most urgent—might even terminate others which have so long fostered dissatisfaction and enmity. There is room to suppose that the moment is peculiarly favorable to such an attempt. On this point there are symptoms of a common sentiment between the advocates and the opposers of an unembarrassed attempt to negotiate—the former desiring it from the confidence they have in its probable success—the latter from the same cause endeavoring either to prevent its going on under right auspices or to clog it with impediments which will frustrate its effect.

All ostensibly agree that one more experiment of negotiation ought to precede actual war, but there is this serious difference in the practice. The sincere friends of peace and accommodation are for leaving things in a state which will enable Great Britain without abandoning self-respect to do us the justice we seek. The others are for placing things upon a footing which would involve the disgrace or disrepute of having receded through intimidation.

This last scheme indubitably ends in war. The folly is too great to be seriously entertained by the discerning part of those who affect to believe the position—that Great Britain, fortified by the alliances of the greatest part of Europe, will submit to our demands, urged with the face of coercion and preceded by acts of reprisal. She cannot do it without renouncing her pride and her dignity, without losing her consequence and weight in the scale of nations—and consequently it is morally certain that she will not do it. A proper estimate of the operation of the human passions must satisfy us that she would be less disposed to receive the law from us than from any other nation—a people recently become a nation, not long since one of her dependencies, and as yet, if a Hercules—a Hercules in the cradle.

When one nation inflicts injuries upon another, which are causes of war, if this other means to negotiate before it goes to war, the usual and received course is to prepare for war and proceed to negotiation—avoiding reprisals till the issue of the negotiation. This course is recommended by all enlightened writers on the laws of nations as the course of moderation, propriety, and wisdom; and it is that commonly pursued except where there is a disposition to go to war or a commanding superiority of power.

Preparation for war in such cases contains in it nothing offensive. It is a mere precaution for self-defense under circumstances which endanger the breaking out of war. It gives rise to no point of honor which can be a bar to equitable and amicable negotiation. But acts of reprisal speak a contrary effect—they change negotiation into peremptory demand, and they brandish a rod over the party on whom the demand is made. He must be humble indeed if he comply with the demand to avoid the stripe.

Such are the propositions which have lately appeared in the House of Representatives for the sequestration or arrestation of British debts—for the cutting off of all intercourse with Great Britain till she shall do certain specific things. If such propositions pass they can only be regarded as provocatives to a declaration of war by Great Britain.

The sequestration of debts is treated by all writers as one of the highest species of reprisal. It is moreover contrary to the most approved practice of the present century, to what may be safely pronounced to be the modern rule of the law of nations—to what is so plainly dictated by original principles of justice and good faith that nothing but the barbarism of times in which war was the principal business of man could ever have tolerated an opposite practice—to the manifest interest of a people situated like that of the U. States, which, having a vast fund of materials for improvement in various ways, ought to invite into the channels of their industry the capital of Europe by giving to it inviolable security—which, giving little facility to extensive revenue from taxation, ought for its own safety in war to cherish its credit by a religious observance of the maxims of credit in all their branches.

The proposition for cutting off all intercourse with G. Britain has not yet sufficiently developed itself to enable us to pronounce what it truly is. It may be so extensive in its provisions as even to include in fact, though not in form, sequestration by rendering remittances penal or impracticable. Indeed it can scarcely avoid so far interfering with the payment of debts already contracted as in a great degree to amount to a virtual sequestration. But however this may be—being adopted for the express purpose of retaliating or punishing injuries, to continue until those injuries are redressed, it is in the spirit of a reprisal—its principle is avowedly coercion—a principle directly opposite to that of negotiation, which supposes an appeal to the reason and justice of the party. Caustic and stimulant in the highest degree, it cannot fail to have a correspondent effect upon the minds of those against whom it is directed. It cannot fail to be viewed as originating in motives of the most hostile and overbearing kind—to stir up all the feelings of pride and resentment in the nation as well as in the cabinet—and consequently to render negotiation abortive.

It will be wonderful if the immediate effect of either of these measures be not either war or the seizure of our vessels wherever they are found, on the ground of keeping them as hostages for the debts due to the British merchants, and on the additional ground of the measures themselves being either acts of hostility or evidence of a disposition to hostility.

The interpretation will naturally be that our views, originally pacific, have changed with the change in the affairs of France, and are now bent towards war.

The measures in question, besides the objection to them resulting from their tendency to produce war, are condemned by a comprehensive and enlightened view of their operation in other respects.

They cannot but have a malignant influence upon our public and mercantile credit. They will be regarded abroad as violent and precipitate. It will be said there is no reliance to be placed on the steadiness or solidity of concerns with this people. Every gust that arises in the political sky is the signal for measures tending to destroy their ability to pay or to obstruct the course of payment. Instead of a people pacific, forbearing, moderate, and of rigid probity we see in them a people turbulent, hasty, intemperate, and loose—sporting with their individual obligations and disturbing the general course of their affairs with levity and inconsiderateness.

Such will indubitably be the comments upon our conduct. The favorable impressions now entertained of the character of our government and nation will infallibly be reversed.

The cutting off of intercourse with Great Britain to distress her seriously must extend to the prohibition of all her commodities indirectly as well as directly. Else it will have no other operation than to transfer the trade between the two countries to the hands of foreigners to our disadvantage more than to that of Great Britain.

If it extends to the total prohibition of her commodities, however brought, it deprives us of a supply for which no substitute can be found elsewhere, a supply necessary to us in peace and more necessary to us if we are to go to war. It gives a sudden and violent blow to our revenue which cannot easily if at all be repaired from other resources. It will give so great an interruption to commerce as may very possibly interfere with the payment of the duties which have heretofore accrued and bring the treasury to an absolute stoppage of payment—an event which would cut up credit by the roots.

The consequences of so great and so sudden a disturbance of our trade, which must affect our exports as well as our imports, are not to be calculated. An excessive rise in the price of foreign commodities—a proportional decrease of price and demand for our own commodities—the derangement of our revenue and credit—these circumstances united may occasion the most dangerous dissatisfactions & disorders in the community and may drive the government to a disgraceful retreat—independent of foreign causes.

To adopt the measure in *terrorem* and postpone its operation will be scarcely a mitigation of the evil. The expectation of it will as to our imports have the effect of the reality, since we must obtain what we want chiefly upon credit. Our supply and our revenue therefore will suffer nearly as much as if there was an immediate interruption.

The effect with regard to our peace will be the same. The principle, being menace and coercion, will equally recommend resistance to the policy as well as the pride of the other party. 'Tis only to consult our own hearts to be convinced that nations, like individuals, revolt at the idea of being guided by external compulsion. They will at least only yield to that idea after resistance has been fruitlessly tried in all its forms.

'Tis as great an error for a nation to overrate as to underrate itself. Presumption is as great a fault as timidity. 'Tis our error to overrate ourselves and to underrate Great Britain. We forget how little we can annoy, how much we may be annoyed.

'Tis enough for us, situated as we are, to be resolved to vindicate our honor and our rights in the last extremity. To precipitate a great conflict of any sort is utterly unsuited to our condition, to our strength, or to our resources. This is a truth to be well weighed by every wise and dispassionate man as the rule of public action.

There are two ideas of immense consequence to us in the event of war. The disunion of our enemies—the perfect union of our own citizens. Justice and moderation united with firmness are the means to secure both these advantages. Injustice or intemperance will lose both.

Unanimity among ourselves, which is the most important of the two ideas, can only be secured by its being manifest, if war ensues, that it was inevitable by another course of conduct. This cannot and will not be the case if measures so intemperate as those which are meditated take place. The inference will be that the war was brought on by the design of some and the rashness of others. This inference will be universal in the northern states, and to you, Sir, I need not urge the importance of those states in war.

Want of unanimity will naturally tend to render the operations of war feeble and heavy—to destroy both effort and perseverance. War undertaken under such auspices can scarcely end in anything better than an inglorious and disadvantageous peace. What worse it may produce is beyond the reach of human foresight.

The foregoing observations are designed to convey to the mind of the president information of the true state of things at the present juncture and to present to his consideration the general reasons which have occurred to me against the course of proceeding which appears to be favored by a majority of the House of Representatives.

My solicitude for the public interest, according to the view I have of it, and my real respect and regard for him to whom I address myself lead me to subjoin some reflections of a more delicate nature.

The crisis is such a one as involves the highest responsibility on the part of everyone who may have to act a part in it. It is one in which every man will be understood to be bound to act according to his judgment without concession to the ideas of others. The president, who has by the Constitution a right to object to laws which he deems contrary to the public interest, will be considered as under an indispensable obligation to exercise that right against any measure, relating to so vast a point as that of the peace of the country, which shall not accord with his opinion. The consideration of its having been adopted by both Houses of Congress and of respect for their opinion will have no weight in such a case as a reason for forbearing to exercise the right of objection. The consequence is that the not objecting will be deemed conclusive evidence of approbation and will implicate the president in all the consequences of the measure.

In such a position of things it is therefore of the utmost importance to him as well as to the community that he should trace out in his own mind such a plan as he thinks it would be eligible to pursue and should endeavor by proper and constitutional means to give the deliberations of Congress a direction towards that plan.

Else he runs the risk of being reduced to the dilemma either of assenting to measures which he may not approve, with a full responsibility for consequences—or of objecting to measures which have already received the sanction of the two houses of Congress, with the responsibility of having resisted and probably prevented what they meditated. Neither of these alternatives is a desirable one.

It seems advisable, then, that the president should come to a conclusion whether the plan ought to be preparation for war and negotiation unencumbered by measures which forbid the expectation of success—or immediate measures of a coercive tendency to be accompanied with the ceremony of a demand of redress. For I believe there is no middle plan between those two courses.

If the former appears to him to be the true policy of the country, I submit it as my conviction that it is *urgent* for him to demonstrate that opinion as a preventive of wrong measures and future embarrassment.

The mode of doing it which occurs is this—to nominate a person, who will have the confidence of those who think peace still within our reach, and who may be thought qualified for the mission as envoy extraordinary to Great Britain—to announce this to the one as well as the other House of Congress with an observation that it is done with an intention to make a solemn appeal to the justice and good sense of the British government to avoid if possible an ulterior rupture and adjust the causes of misunderstanding between the two countries—and with an earnest recommendation that vigorous and effectual measures may be adopted to be prepared for war should it become inevitable—abstaining for the present from measures which may be contrary to the spirit of an attempt to adjust existing differences by negotiation.

Knowing as I do, Sir, that I am among the persons who have been in your contemplation to be employed in the capacity I have mentioned, I should not have taken the present step had I not been resolved at the same time to advise you with decision to drop me from the consideration and to fix upon another character. I am not unapprised of what has been the bias of your opinion on the subject. I am well aware of all the collateral obstacles which exist and I assure you in the utmost sincerity that I shall be completely and entirely satisfied with the election of another.

I beg leave to add that of the persons whom you would deem free from any constitutional objections—Mr. Jay is the only man in whose qualifications for success there would be thorough confidence, and him whom alone it would be advisable to send. I think the business would have the best chance possible in his hands. And I flatter myself that his mission would issue in a manner that would produce the most important good to the nation.

Let me add, Sir, that those whom I call the sober-minded men of the country look up to you with solicitude upon the present occasion. If happily you should be the instrument of still rescuing the country from the dangers and calamities of war, there is no part of your life, Sir, which will produce to you more real satisfaction or true glory than that which shall be distinguished by this very important service.

In any event I cannot doubt, Sir, that you will do justice to the motives which impel me and that you will see in this proceeding another proof of my sincere wishes for your honor & happiness, and anxiety for the public weal.

With the truest respect and attachment   I have the
Honor to be   Sir   Your most obedient & humble servant
Alexander Hamilton

Letter to Isaac Holmes, June 17, 1794

Sir,

I have received your letter of the 19th of May with its enclosures. The transaction which it communicates is in a high degree exceptionable and afflicting.

When the citizens of any country institute a government, as long as that government subsists, they can only act through the constitutional and legal organs. The exercise therefore of an actual control over the measures of the constituted authorities, even by the body of the people, as it can never take place without involving a state of revolution and subversion of the established government, is inadmissible, except in those great cases which justify a nation in resuming its delegated powers and changing its civil constitution. For a small part of the citizens to undertake to exercise such a control is a culpable usurpation not only of the rights of government but of the original authority of the nation, which cannot be tolerated but upon principles destructive of social order and amounting in practice to anarchy.

The sober, enlightened, & virtuous part of the citizens of Charlestown cannot but be deeply penetrated with these truths, and will no doubt on cool reflection condemn the very irregular and improper interference which took place in the case you announce.

By the Constitution, our national treaties are expressly declared to be the *supreme law of the land*. The authority of the ordinary legislature to abrogate any of their stipulations is very questionable, and certainly an intention to abrogate any of them ought never to be inferred from general expressions applied to a general measure, without a manifest and particular eye to the stipulation intended to be abrogated. These positions are incontestable. Hence the executive, on mature reflection, was of opinion that the general terms of the embargo laws did not control the effect of that article of our treaty with Sweden which exempts its vessels and merchandize from embargo in the ports of the U. States. And it is even understood that, when this matter arose in discussion in Congress, it was an admitted point that if our treaty truly granted that exemption to Sweden, it would not be taken away by the embargo resolutions. The determination of this point necessarily devolved on the executive, as charged with the execution of those resolutions.

What shall we say then of the attempt of a part of the citizens of Charlestown to overrule this determination? How can they reconcile it to their duty towards the government or towards the nation of which they are a part? Is it a light matter to interrupt the course of national treaties? What answer could they make to the people of the U. States should they involve them in a contest with a foreign power by impeding the operation of a treaty with such power?

But the expostulation, to be commensurate with all the dangerous tendencies of the proceeding, would be endless. No presence of moderation in the manner can at all palliate it.

I trust you will have possessed the attorney of the district of all the facts which peculiarly fell within your knowledge and observation, in order that if the circumstances were in his judgment of a nature to authorize legal animadversion, he might submit them to the proper tribunal. It cannot be doubted that the public tribunals & all temperate good citizens would concur in discountenancing so pernicious a precedent. The sincere respect & esteem which I have been long accustomed to entertain for the citizens of Charlestown oblige me to believe that but a small part of them could have concurred in so inconsiderate a measure.

With great consideration   I am sir   Your obedt ser

Letter to George Washington, August 2, 1794

Sir,

In compliance with your requisition, I have the honor to submit my opinion as to the course which it will be advisable for the president to pursue in regard to the armed opposition recently given in the four western counties of Pennsylvania to the execution of the laws of the U. States laying duties upon spirits distilled within the United States and upon stills.

The case upon which an opinion is required is summarily as follows. The four most western counties of Pennsylvania, since the commencement of those laws a period of more than three years, have been in steady and violent opposition to them. By formal public meetings of influential individuals, whose resolutions and proceedings had for undisguised objects to render the laws odious, to discountenance a compliance with them, and to intimidate individuals from accepting and executing offices under them—by a general spirit of opposition (thus fomented) among the inhabitants—by repeated instances of armed parties going in disguise to the houses of the officers of the revenue and inflicting upon them personal violence and outrage—by general combinations to forbear a compliance with the requisitions of the laws by examples of injury to the property and insult to the persons of individuals who have shown by their conduct a disposition to comply, and by an almost universal noncompliance with the laws—their execution within the counties in question has been completely frustrated.

Various alterations have been made in the laws by the legislature to obviate as far as possible the objections of the inhabitants of those counties.

The executive on its part has been far from deficient in forbearance, lenity, or a spirit of accommodation.

But neither the legislative nor the executive accommodations have had any effect in producing compliance with the laws.

The opposition has continued and matured, till it has at length broken out in acts which are presumed to amount to treason.

Armed collections of men, with the avowed design of opposing the execution of the laws, have attacked the house of the inspector of the revenue, burnt and destroyed his property, and shed the blood of persons engaged in its defense—have made prisoner of the marshal of the district and did not release him till for the safety of his life he stipulated to execute no more processes within the disaffected counties—have compelled both him and the inspector of the revenue to fly the country by a circuitous route to avoid personal injury, perhaps assassination—have proposed the assembling of a convention of delegates from these counties and the neighboring ones of Virginia, probably with a view to systematize measures of more effectual opposition—have forcibly seized, opened, & spoliated a mail of the United States.

What in this state of things is proper to be done?

The president has, with the advice of the heads of the departments and the attorney general, caused to be submitted all the evidence of the foregoing facts to the consideration of an associate judge under the act entitled, "An Act to provide for calling forth the Militia to execute the laws of the Union, Suppress Insurrection, and repel Invasion."

If the judge shall pronounce that the case described in the second section of that act exists—it will follow that a competent force of militia should be called forth and employed to suppress the insurrection and support the civil authority in effectuating obedience to the laws and the punishment of offenders.

It appears to me that the very existence of government demands this course and that a duty of the highest nature urges the chief magistrate to pursue it. The Constitution and laws of the United States contemplate and provide for it.

What force of militia shall be called out, and from what state or states?

The force ought, if attainable, to be an imposing one, such, if practicable, as will deter from opposition, save the effusion of the blood of citizens, and secure the object to be accomplished.

The quantum must of course be regulated by the resistance to be expected. 'Tis computed that the four opposing counties contain upwards of sixteen thousand males of 16 years and more, that of these about seven thousand may be expected to be armed. 'Tis possible that the union of the neighboring counties of Virginia may augment this force. 'Tis not impossible that it may receive an accession from some adjacent counties of this state on this side of the Allegheny Mountain.

To be prepared for the worst, I am of opinion, that twelve thousand militia ought to be ordered to assemble, 9000 foot and 3000 horse. I should not propose so many horse but for the probability that this description of militia will be more easily procured for the service.

From what state or states shall these come?

The law contemplates that the militia of a state in which an insurrection happens, if willing & sufficient, shall first be employed, but gives power to employ the militia of other states in the case either of refusal or insufficiency.

The governor of Pennsylvania, in an official conference this day, gave it explicitly as his opinion to the president that the militia of Pennsylvania alone would be found incompetent to the suppression of the insurrection.

This opinion of the chief magistrate of the state is presumed to be a sufficient foundation for calling in, in the first instance, the aid of the militia of the neighboring states.

I would submit, then, that Pennsylvania be required to furnish 6000 men of whom 1000 to be horse, New Jersey 2000 of whom 800 to be horse, Maryland 2000 of whom 600 to be horse, Virginia 2000 of whom 600 to be horse.

Or perhaps it may be as eligible to call upon each state for such a number of troops, leaving to itself the proportion of horse and foot according to convenience. The militia called for to rendezvous at Carlisle in Pennsylvania & Cumberland Fort in Virginia on the 10th of September next.

The law requires that previous to the using of force a proclamation shall issue, commanding the insurgents to disperse and return peaceably to their respective abodes within a limited time. This step must of course be taken.

The application of the force to be called out and other ulterior measures must depend on circumstances as they shall arise.

With the most perfect respect   I have the Honor to be
Sir Your Most Obedient Servant

Tully No. I, August 23, 1794

For the American Daily Advertiser

To *the* PEOPLE *of the* UNITED STATES.

Letter I

It has from the first establishment of your present Constitution been predicted that every occasion of serious embarrassment which should occur in the affairs of the government—every misfortune which it should experience, whether produced from its own faults or mistakes or from other causes, would be the signal of an attempt to overthrow it, or to lay the foundation of its overthrow, by defeating the exercise of constitutional and necessary authorities. The disturbances which have recently broken out in the western counties of Pennsylvania furnish an occasion of this sort. It remains to see whether the prediction which has been quoted proceeded from an unfounded jealousy excited by partial differences of opinion, or was a just inference from causes inherent in the structure of our political institutions. Every virtuous man, every good citizen, and especially every true republican must fervently pray that the issue may confound and not confirm so ill-omened a prediction.

Your firm attachment to the government you have established cannot be doubted.

If a proof of this were wanting to animate the confidence of your public agents, it would be sufficient to remark that as often as any attempt to counteract its measures appear, it is carefully prepared by strong professions of friendship to the government, and disavowals of any intention to injure it. This can only result from a conviction that the government carries with it your affections, and that an attack upon it to be successful must veil the stroke under appearances of good will.

It is therefore very important that you should clearly discern in the present instance the shape in which a design of turning the existing insurrection to the prejudice of the government would naturally assume. Thus guarded, you will more readily discover and more easily shun the artful snare which may be laid to entangle your feelings and your judgment, and will be the less apt to be misled from the path by which alone you can give security and permanency to the blessings you enjoy, and can avoid the incalculable mischiefs incident to a subversion of the just and necessary authority of the laws.

The design alluded to, if it shall be entertained, would not appear in an open justification of the principles or conduct of the insurgents, or in a direct dissuasion from the support of the government. These methods would produce general indignation and defeat the object. It is too absurd and shocking a position to be directly maintained, that forcible resistance by a sixtieth part of the community to the representative will of the whole, and its constitutional laws expressed by that will, and acquiesced in by the people at large, is justifiable or even excusable. It is a position too untenable and disgustful to be directly advocated—that the government ought not be supported in exertions to establish the authority of the laws against a resistance so incapable of justification or excuse.

The adversaries of good order in every country have too great a share of cunning, too exact a knowledge of the human heart, to pursue so unpromising a cause. Those among us would take upon the present occasion one far more artful, and consequently far more dangerous.

They would unite with good citizens, and perhaps be among the loudest in condemning the disorderly conduct of the insurgents. They would agree that it is utterly unjustifiable, contrary to the vital principle of republican government, and of the most dangerous tendency—But they would, at the same time, slyly add, that excise laws are pernicious things, very hostile to liberty (or perhaps they might more smoothly lament that the government had been imprudent enough to pass laws so contrary to the genius of a free people), and they would still more cautiously hint that it is enough for those who disapprove of such laws to submit to them—too much to expect their aid in enforcing them upon others. They would be apt to intimate further that there is reason to believe that the executive has been to blame, sometimes by too much forbearance, encouraging the hope that laws would not be enforced, at other times in provoking violence by severe and irritating measures; and they would generally remark, with an affectation of moderation and prudence, that the case is to be lamented, but difficult to be remedied; that a trial of force would be delicate and dangerous; that there is no foreseeing how or where it would end; that it is perhaps better to temporize, and by mild means to allay the ferment and afterwards to remove the cause by repealing the exceptionable laws. They would probably also propose, by anticipation of and in concert with the views of the insurgents, plans of procrastination. They would say, if force must finally be resorted to let it not be till after Congress have been consulted, who, if they think fit to persist in continuing the laws, can make additional provisions for enforcing their execution. This too, they would argue, will afford an opportunity for the public sense to be better known, which (if ascertained to be in favor of the laws) will give the government a greater assurance of success in measures of coercion.

By these means, artfully calculated to divert your attention from the true question to be decided, to combat by prejudices against a particular system, a just sense of the criminality and danger of violent resistance to the laws; to oppose the suggestion of misconduct on the part of government to the fact of misconduct on the part of the insurgents; to foster the spirit of indolence and procrastination natural to the human mind, as an obstacle to the vigor and exertion which so alarming an attack upon the fundamental principles of public and private security demands; to distract YOUR opinion on the course proper to be pursued, and consequently on the propriety of the measures which may be pursued. They would expect (I say) by these and similar means, equally insidious and pernicious, to abate YOUR just indignation at the daring affront which has been offered to your authority and YOUR zeal for the maintenance and support of the laws, to prevent a competent force, if force is finally called forth, from complying with the call—and thus to leave the government of the Union in the prostrate condition of seeing the laws trampled under foot by an unprincipled combination of a small portion of the community, habitually disobedient to laws, and itself destitute of the necessary aid for vindicating their authority.

Virtuous and enlightened citizens of a now happy country! ye could not be the dupes of artifices so detestable, of a scheme so fatal; ye cannot be insensible to the destructive consequences with which it would be pregnant; ye cannot but remember that the government is YOUR OWN work—that those who administer it are but your temporary agents; that YOU are called upon not to support their power, BUT YOUR OWN POWER. And you will not fail to do what your rights, your best interests, your character as a people, your security as members of society conspire to demand of you.

Tully

Tully No. II, August 26, 1794

For the American Daily Advertiser

To the **PEOPLE** *of the* **UNITED STATES.**

Letter II

It has been observed that the means most likely to be employed to turn the insurrection in the western country to the detriment of the government would be artfully calculated among other things "to divert your attention from the true question to be decided."

Let us see then what is this question. It is plainly this—shall the majority govern or be governed? Shall the nation rule or be ruled? Shall the general will prevail or the will of a faction? Shall there be government or no government?

It is impossible to deny that this is the true and the whole question. No art, no sophistry can involve it in the least obscurity.

The Constitution *you* have ordained for yourselves and your posterity contains this express clause, "The Congress *shall have power* to lay and collect taxes, duties, imposts, and *Excises*, to pay the debts, and provide for the common defense and general welfare of the United States." You have then, by a solemn and deliberate act, the most important and sacred that a nation can perform, pronounced and decreed that your representatives in Congress shall have power to lay excises. You have done nothing since to reverse or impair that decree.

Your representatives in Congress, pursuant to the commission derived from you, and with a full knowledge of the public exigencies, have laid an excise. At three succeeding sessions they have revised that act, and have as often, with a degree of unanimity not common, and after the best opportunities of knowing your sense, renewed their sanction to it, you have acquiesced in it, it has gone into general operation, and *you* have actually paid more than a million dollars on account of it.

But the four western counties of Pennsylvania undertake to rejudge and reverse your decrees. You have said, "The Congress *shall have power* to lay *Excises*." They say, "The Congress *shall not have* this power." Or what is equivalent—they shall not exercise it:—for a *power* that may not be exercised is a nullity. Your representatives have said, and four times repeated it, "an excise on distilled spirits *shall* be collected." They say it *shall not* be collected. We will punish, expel, and banish the officers who shall attempt the collection. We will do the same by every other person who shall dare to comply with your decree expressed in the constitutional character, and with that of your representative expressed in the laws. The sovereignty shall not reside with you but with us. If you presume to dispute the point by force—we are ready to measure swords with you; and if unequal ourselves to the contest we will call in the aid of a foreign nation. We will league ourselves with a foreign power.*

If there is a man among us who shall affirm that the question is not what it has been stated to be—who shall endeavor to perplex it by ill-timed dec-lamations against excise laws—who shall strive to paralyze the efforts of the community by invectives or insinuations against the government—who shall inculcate directly or indirectly that force ought not to be employed to compel the insurgents to a submission to the laws, if the pending experiment to bring them to reason (an experiment which will immortalize the moderation of the government) shall fail; such a man is not a good citizen; such a man, however he may prate and babble republicanism, is not a republican; he attempts to set up the *will* of a part against the *will* of the whole, the *will* of a *faction* against the *will* of *nation*, the pleasure of a *few* against *your* pleasure; the violence of a lawless combination against the sacred authority of laws pronounced under your indisputable commission.

Mark such a man, if such there be. The occasion may enable you to dis-criminate the *true* from *pretended republicans, your* friends from the friends of *faction*. 'Tis in vain that the latter shall attempt to conceal their pernicious principles under a crowd of odious invectives against the laws. *Your* answer is this: "*We* have already in the constitutional act decided the point against you, and against those for whom you apologize. *We* have pronounced that *excises* may be laid and consequently that they are not, as you say, inconsistent with liberty. Let our will be first obeyed and then we shall be ready to consider the reason which can be afforded to prove our judgment has been erroneous: and if they convince us to cause them to be observed. We have not neglected the means of amending in a regular course the constitutional act. And we shall know how to make our sense be respected whenever we shall discover that any part of it needs correction. But as an earnest of this, it is our intention to begin by securing obedience to our authority from those who have been bold enough to set it at defiance. In a full respect for the laws we discern the reality of our power and the means of providing for our welfare as occasion may require; in the contempt of the laws we see the annihilation of our power; the possibility, and the danger of its being usurped by others & of the despotism of individuals succeeding to the regular authority of the nation."

That a fate like this may never await *you*, let it be deeply imprinted in your minds and handed down to your latest posterity that there is no road to *des-potism* more sure or more to be dreaded than that which begins at *anarchy*.

Tully

---

* *Note*—Threats of joining the British are actually thrown out—how far the idea may go is not known.

Tully No. III, August 28, 1794

For the American Daily Advertiser

To the **PEOPLE** *of the* **UNITED STATES**

Letter III

If it were to be asked, what is the most sacred duty and the greatest source of security in a republic? the answer would be, an inviolable respect for the Constitution and laws—the first growing out of the last. It is by this, in a great degree, that the rich and powerful are to be restrained from enterprises against the common liberty—operated upon by the influence of a general sentiment, by their interest in the principle, and by the obstacles which the habit it produces erects against innovation and encroachment. It is by this, in a still greater degree, that caballers, intriguers, and demagogues are prevented from climbing on the shoulders of faction to the tempting seats of usurpation and tyranny.

Were it not that it might require too lengthy a discussion, it would not be difficult to demonstrate that a large and well organized republic can scarcely lose its liberty from any other cause than that of anarchy, to which a contempt of the laws is the high road.

But, without entering into so wide a field, it is sufficient to present to your view a more simple and a more obvious truth, which is this—that a sacred respect for the constitutional law is the vital principle, the sustaining energy of a free government.

Government is frequently and aptly classed under two descriptions, a government of force and a government of laws; the first is the definition of despotism—the last, of liberty. But how can a government of laws exist where the laws are disrespected and disobeyed? Government supposes control. It is the power by which individuals in society are kept from doing injury to each other and are brought to cooperate to a common end. The instruments by which it must act are either the authority of the laws or force. If the first be destroyed, the last must be substituted; and where this becomes the ordinary instrument of government there is an end to liberty.

Those, therefore, who preach doctrines, or set examples, which undermine or subvert the authority of the laws, lead us from freedom to slavery; they incapacitate us for a government of laws and consequently prepare the way for one of force, for mankind must have government of one sort or another.

There are indeed great and urgent cases where the bounds of the constitution are manifestly transgressed, or its constitutional authorities so exercised as to produce unequivocal oppression on the community, and to render resistance justifiable. But such cases can give no color to the resistance, by a comparatively inconsiderable part of a community, of constitutional laws distinguished by no extraordinary features of rigor or oppression, and acquiesced in by the body of the community.

Such a resistance is treason against society, against liberty, against everything that ought to be dear to a free, enlightened, and prudent people. To tolerate were to abandon your most precious interests. Not to subdue it were to tolerate it. Those who openly or covertly dissuade you from exertions adequate to the occasion are your worst enemies. They treat you either as fools or cowards, too weak to perceive your interest and your duty, or too dastardly to pursue them. They therefore merit and will no doubt meet your contempt.

To the plausible but hollow harangues of such conspirators, ye cannot fail to reply, how long, ye Catilines, will you abuse our patience.

Tully

Tully No. IV, September 2, 1794

The prediction mentioned in my first letter begins to be fulfilled. Fresh symptoms every moment appear of a dark conspiracy hostile to your government, to your peace abroad, to your tranquility at home. One of its orators dares to prostitute the name of FRANKLIN by annexing it to a publication as insidious as it is incendiary. Aware of the folly and the danger of a direct advocation of the cause of the insurgents, he makes the impudent attempt to enlist your passions in their favor—by false and virulent railings against those who have heretofore represented you in Congress. The foreground of the piece presented you with a bitter invective against that wise, moderate, and pacific policy, which in all probability will rescue you from the calamities of a foreign war, with an increase of true dignity and with additional luster to the American name and character. Your representatives are delineated as corrupt, pusillanimous, and unworthy of your confidence, because they did not plunge headlong into measures which might have rendered war inevitable, because they contented themselves with preparing for it, instead of making it, leaving the path open to the executive for one last and solemn effort of negotiation—because they did not display either the promptness of gladiators or the blustering of bullies—but assumed that firm yet temperate attitude which alone is suited to the representatives of a brave but rational people—who deprecated war though they did not fear it—and who have a great and solid interest in peace which ought only to be abandoned when it is unequivocally ascertained that the sacrifice is absolutely due to the vindication of their honor and the preservation of their essential rights—because in fine, your representatives wished to give an example to the world that the boasted moderation of republican governments was not (like the patriotism of our political barkers) an empty declamation but a precious reality.

The sallies of a momentary sensibility, roused and stung by injury, were excusable. It was not wonderful that the events of war were under the first impressions heard from good and even prudent men. But to revive them at this late hour, when fact and reflection unite to condemn them, to arraign a conduct which has elevated the national character to the highest point of true glory—to hope to embark you in the condemnation of that conduct, and to make your indignation against it useful to the cause of insurrection and treason, are indications of a wrong-headedness, perverseness, or profligacy for which it is not easy to find terms of adequate reprobation.

Happily the plotters of mischief know ye not. They derive what they mistake for your image from an original in their own heated and crooked imaginations, and they hope to mold a wise, reflecting, and dispassionate people to purposes which presuppose an ignorant unthinking and turbulent herd.

But the declamations against your representatives for their love of peace is but the preface to the main design. That design is to alienate you from the support of the laws by the specter of an "odious excise system, baneful to liberty, engendered by corruption, and nurtured by the INSTRUMENTALITY (favored word, fruitful source of mountebank wit) of the enemies of freedom." To urge the execution of that system would manifest, it is said, an intemperate spirit; and to excite your disapprobation of that course you are threatened with the danger of a civil war, which is called the consummation of human evil.

To crown the outrage upon your understandings, the insurgents are represented as men who understand the principles of freedom & know the horrors and distresses of anarchy, and who therefore must have been tempted to hostility against the laws by a RADICAL DEFECT EITHER in the government or in those entrusted with its administration. How thin the partition which divides the insinuation from the assertion that the government is in fault and the insurgents in the right.

Fellow citizens, a name, a sound has too often had influence on the affairs of nations; an excise has too long been the successful watchword of party. It has even sometimes led astray well meaning men. The experiment is now to be tried whether there be any spell in it of sufficient force to unnerve the arm which it may be found necessary to raise in defense of law and order.

The jinglers who endeavor to cheat us with the sound have never dared to venture into the fair field of argument. They are conscious that it is easier to declaim than to reason on the subject. They know it to be better to play a game with the passions and prejudices than to engage seriously with the understanding of the auditory.

You have already seen that the merits of excise laws are immaterial to the question to be decided—that you have prejudged the point by a solemn constitutional act, and that until you shall have revoked or modified that act resistance to its operation is a criminal infraction of the social compact, an inversion of the fundamental principles of republican government, and a daring attack upon YOUR sovereignty which you are bound by every motive of duty and self-preservation to withstand and defeat. The matter might safely be suffered to rest here, but I shall take a future opportunity to examine the reasonableness of the prejudice which is inculcated against excise laws—and which has become the pretext for excesses tending to dissolve the bands of society.

Fellow citizens—You are told that it will be intemperate to urge the execution of the laws which are resisted—What? Will it be indeed intemperate in your chief magistrate, sworn to maintain the Constitution, charged faithfully to execute the laws, and authorized to employ for that purpose force when the ordinary means fail—will it be intemperate in him to exert that force, when the Constitution and the laws are opposed by force? Can he answer it to his conscience, to you, not to exert it?

Yes, it is said, because the execution of it will produce civil war, the consummation of human evil.

Fellow citizens—Civil war is undoubtedly a great evil. It is one that every good man would wish to avoid, and will deplore if inevitable. But it is incomparably a less evil than the destruction of government. The first brings with it serious but temporary and partial ills—the last undermines the foundations of our security and happiness—where should we be if it were once to grow into a maxim that force is not to be used against the seditious combinations of parts of the community to resist the laws? This would be to give a CARTE BLANCHE to ambition—to licentiousness, to foreign intrigue, to make you the prey of the gold of other nations—the sport of the passions and vices of individuals among yourselves. The hydra anarchy would rear its head in every quarter. The goodly fabric you have established would be rent asunder and precipitated into the dust. You knew how to encounter civil war rather than surrender your liberty to foreign domination—you will not hesitate now to brave it rather than surrender your sovereignty to the tyranny of a faction—you will be as deaf to the apostles of anarchy now as you were to the emissaries of despotism then. Your love of liberty will guide you now as it did then—you know that the POWER of the majority and LIBERTY are inseparable—destroy that, and this perishes. But in truth that which can properly be called a civil war is not to be apprehended—unless, from the act of those who endeavor to fan the flame by rendering the government odious. A civil war is a contest between two GREAT parts of the same empire. The exertion of the strength of the nation to suppress resistance to its laws by a sixtieth part of itself is not of that description.

After endeavoring to alarm you with the horrors of civil war—an attempt is made to excite your sympathy in favor of the armed faction by telling you that those who compose it are men who understand the principles of freedom and know the horrors and distresses of anarchy, and must therefore have been prompted to hostility against the laws by a radical defect either in the government or in its administration.

Fellow citizens! For an answer to this you have only to consult your senses. The natural consequence of radical defect in a government or in its administration is national distress and suffering—look around you—Where is it? Do you feel it? Do you see it?

Go in quest of it beyond the Allegheny, and instead of it you will find that there also a scene of unparalleled prosperity upbraids the ingratitude and madness of those who are endeavoring to cloud the bright face of our political horizon and to mar the happiest lot that beneficent Heaven ever indulged to undeserving mortals.

When you have turned your eyes towards that scene—examine the men whose knowledge of the principles of freedom is so emphatically vaunted—where did they get their better knowledge of those principles than that which you possess? How is it that you have been so blind or tame as to remain quiet, while they have been goaded into hostility against the laws by a RADICAL DEFECT in the government or its administration?

Are you willing to yield them the palm of discernment, of patriotism, or of courage?

Tully

Letter to Edmund Randolph, September 11, 1794

Dr. Sir,

I cannot entertain a doubt that Mr. Jaudenes's request for a guard ought to be complied with. The protection due to a foreign minister is absolute, and the courtesy of nations dictates that *military* means shall be used in cases where there may be doubt of the adequateness of the civil—as here where the menace of assassination may require an armed guard. Nor have I the least doubt that the standing forces can legally be applied to this purpose, whatever may be said of the militia. We have here an officer and twelve dragoon who may be used. But I take it for granted an escort of volunteers from New York or New Jersey may without difficulty be had. I really think the United States would be disagreeably compromitted by a refusal.

Yours with esteem
A Hamilton

Letter to George Washington, September 19, 1794

Sir,

Upon full reflection I entertain an opinion that it is advisable for me, on public ground, considering the connection between the immediate ostensible cause of the insurrection in the western country and my department, to go out upon the expedition against the insurgents. In a government like ours it cannot but have a good effect for the person who is understood to be the adviser or proposer of a measure, which involves danger to his fellow citizens, to partake in that danger: While, not to do it, might have a bad effect. I therefore request your permission for the purpose.

My intention would be not to leave this till about the close of the month so as to reach one of the columns at its ultimate point of rendezvous. In the meantime, I take it for granted General Knox will arrive, and the arrangements which will be made will leave the treasury department in a situation to suffer no embarrassment by my absence; which if it be thought necessary may terminate about or shortly after the meeting of Congress.

With perfect respect, & the truest   attachment,

I have the honor to be,   Sir, Yor: obt. Servt.

Letter to George Washington, December 2, 1794

The secretary of the treasury has the honor respectfully to make the following representation to the president of the United States, in order that he may determine on the expediency of laying the subject of it before Congress. The procuring of military supplies generally is with great propriety vested by law in the Department of the Treasury. That department from situation may be expected to feel a more habitual solicitude for economy than any other, and to possess more means of information respecting the best modes of obtaining supplies. It is, however, important that the particular arrangement should be such as to enable the department to execute the trust in the best manner. This branch of the public business forms a very considerable one of the public expenditure. Including supplies for the navy, it is so extensive as, to be well executed, would occupy the whole time & attention of one person, possessing the requisite qualifications. This, with the growth of the country, must be every year more & more the case. It cannot therefore be conducted in detail by the head of the department, or by any existing officer of it now charged with other duties, without being less well executed than it ought to be, or interfering with other essential duties, or without a portion of both these inconveniences, to the material detriment of the public service. Experience has already verified the position.

It must then of necessity either be confided to a special agent employed by the head of the department, or to a new officer of the department to be constituted by law & to act under the direction & superintendence of that head. The last mode is preferable to the first for obvious reasons.

Wherever an object of public business is likely to be permanent, it is more fit that it should be transacted by an officer of the government regularly constituted than by the agent of a department specially intrusted. The officer can be placed by law under more effectual checks. In the present case that idea is particularly important. The person entrusted ought to be prohibited under penalties from all dealing on his own account in the objects of supply. The duration & emoluments of a mere agency being precarious, a well-qualified man disposed to make the necessary sacrifices of other pursuits & to devote himself exclusively to the business could with much greater difficulty, if at all, be found.

The compensation to such an officer ought it is conceived to weigh nothing as an objection. Independent of the equivalent expense arising from the necessity of employing & compensating an agent, it is morally certain that the close, constant, & undivided attention of a person charged exclusively with this object, & in condition, for that reason, to make the minute as well as extensive enquiries & investigations which are often requisite, would produce savings to the United States with which the salary of the officer could bear no comparison. It is equally evident that it would contribute greatly to punctuality, dispatch, & efficiency in procuring the supplies.

Respectfully submitted.
Alexander Hamilton
Secy of the Treasy

The Cause of France, 1794

The cause of France! We are every day told that this is a cause which ought to engage our warmest affections, our best wishes, and there are not a few who think that we ought to hazard upon it our dearest interests. If we ask what is the cause of France, the ready answer is that it is *the cause of liberty*. It is the cause of a nation nobly struggling for the rights of man against a combination of despots and tyrants laboring to destroy them—of a nation on whose fate our own is suspended.

Let us dare to look this question in the face. The world has been scourged with many fanatical sects in religion—who inflamed by a sincere but mistaken zeal have perpetuated under the idea of serving God the most atrocious crimes. If we were to call the cause of such men the cause of religion, would not everyone agree that it was an abuse of terms?

The best apology to be made for the terrible scenes (of which every new arrival shocks us with the dreadful detail) is the supposition that the ruling party in France is actuated by a zeal similar in its nature (though different in its object) to that which influences religious fanatics. Can this political frenzy be dignified with the honorable appellation of the cause of liberty with any greater propriety than the other kind of frenzy would be denominated the cause of religion?

But even this comparison is too favorable to the ruling party in France. Judging from their acts, we are authorized to pronounce the cause in which they are engaged not the cause of liberty, but the cause of vice, atheism, and anarchy.

The French Revolution, 1794

In the early periods of the French Revolution, a warm zeal for its success was in this country *a sentiment truly universal*. The love of liberty is here the ruling passion *of the citizens of the U. States*, pervading every class, animating every bosom. As long therefore as the revolution of France bore the marks of being the cause of liberty, it united all hearts, concentered all opinions. But this unanimity of approbation has been for a considerable time decreasing. The excesses which have constantly multiplied, with greater and greater aggravations, have successively though slowly detached reflecting men from their partiality for an object which has appeared less and less to merit their regard. Their reluctance to abandon it has, however, been proportioned to the ardor and fondness with which they embraced it. They were willing to overlook many faults—to apologize for some enormities—to hope that better justifications existed than were seen—to look forward to more calm and greater moderation, after the first shocks of the political earthquake had subsided. But instead of this they have been witnesses to one volcano succeeding another, the last still more dreadful than the former, spreading ruin and devastation far and wide—subverting the foundations of right, security, and property, of order, morality, and religion—sparing neither sex nor age, confounding innocence with guilt, involving the old and the young, the sage and the madman, the long-tried friend of virtue and his country and the upstart pretender to purity and patriotism—the bold projector of new treasons with the obscure in indiscriminate and profuse destruction. They have found themselves driven to the painful alternative of renouncing an object dear to their wishes or of becoming by the continuance of their affection for it accomplices with vice, anarchy, depotism, and impiety.

But though an afflicting experience has materially lessened the number of the admirers of the French Revolution among us, and has served to chill the ardor of many more, who profess still to retain their attachment to it from what they suppose to be its ultimate tendency; yet the effect of experience has been thus far much less than could reasonably have been expected. The predilection for it still continues extensive and ardent. And, what is extraordinary, it continues to comprehend men who are able to form a just estimate of the information which destroys its title to their favor.

It is not among the least perplexing phenomena of the present times that a people like that of the U. States—exemplary for humanity and moderation, surpassed by no other in the love of order and a knowledge of the true principles of liberty, distinguished for purity of morals and a just reverence for religion, should so long persevere in partiality for a state of things the most cruel, sanguinary, and violent that ever stained the annals of mankind, a state of things which annihilates the foundations of social order and true liberty, confounds all moral distinctions and *substitutes to* the mild & beneficent religion of the Gospel a gloomy, persecuting, and desolating atheism. To the eye of a wise man, this partiality is the most inauspicious circumstance that has appeared in the affairs of this country. It leads involuntarily and irresistibly to apprehensions concerning the soundness of our principles and the stability of our welfare. It is natural to fear that the transition may not be difficult from the approbation of bad things to the imitation of them, a fear which can only be mitigated by a careful estimate of the extraneous causes that have served to mislead the public judgment.

But though we may find in these causes a solution of the fact calculated to abate our solicitude for the consequences, yet we cannot consider the public happiness as out of the reach of danger so long as our principles continue to be exposed to the debauching influence of admiration for an example which, it will not be too strong to say, presents the caricature of human depravity. And the pride of national character at least can find no alleviation for the wound which must be inflicted by so ill-judged, so unfortunate a partiality.

If there be any thing solid in virtue—the time must come when it will have been a disgrace to have advocated the Revolution of France in its late stages.

This is a language to which the ears of the people of this country have not been accustomed. Everything has hitherto conspired to confirm the pernicious fascination by which they are enchained. There has been a positive and a negative conspiracy against the truth which has served to shut out its enlightening ray. Those who always float with the popular gale, perceiving the prepossession of the people, have administered to it by all the acts in their power—endeavoring to recommend themselves by an exaggerated zeal for a favorite object. Others through timidity, caution, or an ill-judged policy, unwilling to expose themselves to the odium of resisting the general current of feeling, have betrayed by silence that truth which they were unable not to perceive. Others, whose sentiments have weight in the community, have been themselves the sincere dupes of _____. Hence the voice of reason has been stifled, and the nation has been left unadmonished to travel on in one of the most degrading delusions that ever disparaged the understandings of an enlightened people.

To recall them from this dangerous error—to engage them to dismiss their prejudices & consult dispassionately their own good sense—to lead them to an appeal from their own enthusiasm to their reason and humanity, would be the most important service that could be rendered to the U. States at the present juncture. The error entertained is not on a mere speculative question. The French Revolution is a political convulsion that in a great or less degree shakes the whole civilized world, and it is of real consequence to the principles and of course to the happiness of a nation to estimate it rightly.

Report on the Petition of William Gardner, January 31, 1795

To the Speaker of the House of Representatives

The secretary of the treasury, to whom was referred the petition of William Gardner, commissioner of loans for New Hampshire, respectfully reports thereupon as follows:

There is no branch of the public service which more than this requires such an arrangement as will secure a selection of fit characters willing to accept the office and to continue in it. The system of the transfers of stock at fourteen different offices, and from one office to another, and of paying interest at each, is necessarily extremely complicated, requiring great accuracy and punctuality everywhere to prevent its running into disorder and producing very serious hazards and inconveniences to the public and to individuals—A system which is without example in any other country, but which local circumstances and the public engagements have rendered, and continue to render, indispensable. The responsibility, importance, and delicacy of the trust which it implies are witnessed by the simple statement of the fact. It is only to consider what is the nature of the power, as it regards the implication of the public in pecuniary responsibility which is confided to so many individuals, to be convinced that it is essential to make effectual provision for obtaining and keeping competent and unexceptionable agents. It is a subject which even ought to excite particular solicitude in this respect.

It cannot be doubted that an essential mean to this end will be adequate compensations. It cannot be expected in a country where talents for business, united with integrity and character, are in high demand, and in which the expense of living at the places where public business must be carried on is and is likely to continue high, that the government will be so well served without liberal compensations for the service. There is no truth more clear to the eye of reason, nor better established by experience, than that undue parsimony, in this particular, is in time the very worst economy. It tends to throw the business of the nation into hands unqualified or unworthy of trust—whence, of course, it will be ill done—disorders and even frauds will ensue; and the pecuniary loss sustained in one year, perhaps in one day, by the infidelity or inability of unfit agents may exceed the difference of compensation which would have procured fit ones for a long series of years. True economy, as applied to a nation, does not consist in the penurious apportionment of the compensations of its officers, but in the steady adherence to an enlightened and comprehensive system, which, among other effects, placing the management of its affairs in able and faithful hands, causes all its great pecuniary operations to be conducted both with skill and integrity. The experience of the United States, at various periods, sufficiently attests this fact.

These observations do not aim at countenancing prodigality even in this branch of public expenditure; they are only designed to imply that parsimony, in this particular, is not, as it seems by some to be thought, the great hinge of national economy—that carried too far, it turns against its own object and produces the worst effects of prodigality. There is, no doubt, measure in this, as in every other thing; though the compensations should be adequate, they ought not to be excessive. But in adjusting the measure, it is essential to weigh well the nature of the trust—the talents necessary for it—the uses to which they can be turned in private life for the benefit of the possessor, and the indemnification which he will consequently expect to be induced to serve the public—the degree of character which is requisite, and the probable extent of emolument which will command the due degree of character—the expense of living where the service is to be performed.

In the case of the commissioners of loans, the extent of the occupation which they will respectively have, though a criterion of allowance, is not the only one. Similar qualifications are necessary with regard to all of them, whether having more or less business to attend to. And the power of all being equal, the trust with respect to all is equally delicate. There should be nowhere a man who is not an intelligent man of business, of established integrity, and of respectability of character. It merits reflection also that it will sometimes happen that the official duties of the officer may not be sufficient to occupy him wholly, yet sufficient to interfere and perhaps incompatible with the effectual pursuit of other business for which he may be qualified.

In the particular case referred to him, the secretary, combining and weighing to the best of his judgment all the considerations which belong to it, is of opinion that it is just and expedient to allow a yearly salary of one thousand dollars for compensation and all expenses, except stationery.
Which is respectfully submitted,

Alexander Hamilton,
Secretary of the Treasury

Letter to George Washington, January 31, 1795

Sir,

Agreeably to the intimation heretofore given, I have the honor now to tender you my resignation of the office of secretary of the treasury and to be

With sincere respect and affectionate attachment
Sir   Your most Obedient & humble servant

Explanatory Notes

1   This piece was evidently written for publication, but it is incomplete and breaks off here. See *PAH*, 14: 450 notes 1 and 3.
2   Hamilton was here drawing on the title of John Dryden's 1678 tragedy, *All for Love: or, The World Well Lost.*
3   John Dunlap, publisher of *Dunlap's American Daily Advertiser*. See *PAH*, 15: 193 n. 1.
4   The manuscript is incomplete and breaks off at this point.
5   This promise was made in the sixth *Pacificus* paper.

PART 3

Federalist Party Leader: 1795–1800

Letter to Rufus King,
February 21, 1795

My Dear King,

The unnecessary, capricious, & abominable assassination of the national honor by the rejection of the propositions respecting the unsubscribed debt in the House of Representatives haunts me every step I take, and afflicts me more than I can express. To see the character of the government and the country so sported with, exposed to so indelible a blot, puts my heart to the torture. Am I then more of an American than those who drew their first breath on American ground? Or what is it that thus torments me at a circumstance so calmly viewed by almost everybody else? Am I a fool—a romantic quixot—Or is there a constitutional defect in the American mind? Were it not for yourself and a few others, I could adopt the reveries of De Paux as substantial truths, and would say with him that there is something in our climate which belittles every animal, human or brute.

I conjure you, my friend, make a vigorous stand for the honor of your country. Rouse all the energies of your mind, and measure swords in the Senate with the great slayer of public faith—the hackneyed *veteran* in the violation of public engagements. Prevent him if possible from triumphing a second time over the prostrate credit* and injured interests of his country. Unmask his false and horrid hypothesis. Display the immense difference between an able statesman and the *man of subtleties*. Root out the distempered and noisome *weed* which is attempted to be planted in our political garden—to choke and wither in its infancy the fair plant of public credit.

I disclose to you without reserve the state of my mind. It is discontented and gloomy in the extreme. I consider the cause of good government as having been put to an issue & the verdict against it.

Introduce I pray you into the Senate, when the bill comes up, the clause which has been rejected, freed from embarrassment by the bills of credit bearing interest on the nominal value. Press its adoption in this the most unexceptionable shape, & let the *yeas & nays* witness the result.

Among other reasons for this is my wish that the true friends of public credit may be distinguished from its enemies. The question is too great a one

---

* Witness the 40 for 1 scheme, a most unskillful measure, to say the best of it.

not to undergo a thorough examination before the community. It would pain me not to be able to distinguish. Adieu.

God bless you
A. Hamilton

P.S. Do me the favor to revise carefully the course of the bill respecting the unsubscribed debt & let me know the particulars. I wish to be able to judge more particularly of the underplot I suspect.

The Defense No. I, July 22, 1795

It was to have been foreseen that the treaty which Mr. Jay was charged to negotiate with Great Britain, whenever it should appear, would have to contend with many perverse dispositions and some honest prejudices. That there was no measure in which the government could engage so little likely to be viewed according to its intrinsic merits—so very likely to encounter misconception, jealousy, and unreasonable dislike. For this many reasons may be assigned.

It is only to know the vanity and vindictiveness of human nature to be convinced that while this generation lasts there will always exist among us men irreconcilable to our present national Constitution—embittered in their animosity in proportion to the success of its operation and the disappointment of their inauspicious predictions. It is a material inference from this that such men will watch with Lynx's eyes for opportunities of discrediting the proceedings of the government, and will display a hostile and malignant zeal upon every occasion where they think there are any prepossessions of the community to favor their enterprises. A treaty with Great Britain was too fruitful an occasion not to call forth all their activity.

It is only to consult the history of nations to perceive that every country, at all times, is cursed by the existence of men who, actuated by an irregular ambition, scruple nothing which they imagine will contribute to their own advancement and importance. In monarchies, supple courtiers; in republics, fawning or turbulent demagogues, worshipping still the idol power wherever placed, whether in the hands of a prince, or of the people, and trafficking in the weaknesses, vices, frailties, or prejudices of the one or the other. It was to have been expected that such men, counting more on the passions than on the reason of their fellow citizens, and anticipating that the treaty would have to struggle with prejudices, would be disposed to make an alliance with popular discontent, to nourish it, and to press it into the service of their particular views.

It was not to have been doubted that there would be one or more foreign powers indisposed to a measure which accommodated our differences with Great Britain and laid the foundation of future good understanding, merely because it had that effect.

Nations are never content to confine their rivalships and enmities to themselves. It is their usual policy to disseminate them as widely as they can, regardless how far it may interfere with the tranquility or happiness of the nations which they are able to influence. Whatever pretentions may be made, the world is yet remote from the spectacle of that just and generous policy, whether in the cabinets of republics or of kings, which would dispose one nation, in its intercourses with another, satisfied with a due proportion of privileges and benefits, to see that other pursue freely its true interest with regard to a third, though at the expense of no engagement, nor in violation of any rule of friendly or fair procedure. It was natural that the contrary spirit should produce efforts of foreign counteraction to the treaty, and it was certain that the partisans of the counteracting power would second its efforts by all the means which they thought calculated to answer the end.

It was known that the resentment produced by our revolution war with Great Britain had never been entirely extinguished, and that recent injuries had rekindled the flame with additional violence. It was a natural consequence of this that many should be disinclined to any amicable arrangement with Great Britain, and that many others should be prepared to acquiesce only in a treaty which should present advantages of so striking and preponderant a kind as it was not reasonable to expect could be obtained, unless the United States were in a condition to give the law to Great Britain, and as, if obtained under the coercion of such a situation, could only have been the short-lived prelude of a speedy rupture to get rid of them.

Unfortunately, too, the supposition of that situation has served to foster exaggerated expectations, and the absurd delusion to this moment prevails, notwithstanding the plain evidence to the contrary, which is deducible from the high and haughty ground still maintained by Great Britain against victorious France.

It was not to be mistaken that an enthusiasm for France and her revolution throughout all its wonderful vicissitudes has continued to possess the minds of the great body of the people of this country, and it was to be inferred that this sentiment would predispose to a jealousy of any agreement or treaty with her most persevering competitor—a jealousy so excessive as would give the fullest hope to insidious arts to perplex and mislead the public opinion. It was well understood that a numerous party among us, though disavowing the design, because the avowal would defeat it, have been steadily endeavoring to make the United States a party in the present European war, by advocating all those measures which would widen the breach between us and Great Britain, and by resisting all those which could tend to close it; and it was morally certain that this party would eagerly improve every circumstance which could serve to render the treaty odious, and to frustrate it, as the most effectual road to their favorite goal.

It was also known beforehand that personal and party rivalships of the most active kind would assail whatever treaty might be made, to disgrace, if possible, its organ.

There are three persons prominent in the public eye as the successor of the actual president of the United States in the event of his retreat from the station: Mr. Adams, Mr. Jay, Mr. Jefferson.

No one has forgotten the systematic pains which have been taken to impair the well earned popularity of the first gentleman. Mr. Jay, too, has been repeatedly the object of attacks with the same view. His friends as well as his enemies anticipated that he could make no treaty which would not furnish weapons against him—and it were to have been ignorant of the indefatigable malice of his adversaries to have doubted that they would be seized with eagerness and wielded with dexterity.

The peculiar circumstances which have attended the two last elections for governor of this state have been of a nature to give the utmost keenness to party animosity. It was impossible that Mr. Jay should be forgiven for his double, and in the last instance triumphant, success, or that any promising opportunity of detaching from him the public confidence should pass unimproved.

Trivial facts frequently throw light upon important designs. It is remarkable that in the toasts given on the 4th of July, wherever there appears a direct or indirect censure on the treaty, it is pretty uniformly coupled with compliments to Mr. Jefferson and to our late governor Mr. Clinton, with an evident design to place those gentlemen in contrast with Mr. Jay, and decrying him to elevate them. No one can be blind to the finger of party spirit visible in these and similar transactions. It indicates to us clearly one powerful source of opposition to the treaty.

No man is without his personal enemies. Preeminence even in talents and virtue is a cause of envy and hatred of its possessor. Bad men are the natural enemies of virtuous men. Good men sometimes mistake and dislike each other.

Upon such an occasion as the treaty, how could it happen otherwise than that *personal enmity* would be unusually busy, enterprising, and malignant?

From the combined operation of these different causes, it would have been a vain expectation that the treaty would be generally contemplated with candor and moderation, or that reason would regulate the first impressions concerning it. It was certain, on the contrary, that however unexceptionable its true character might be, it would have to fight its way through a mass of unreasonable opposition; and that time, examination, and reflection would be requisite to fix the public opinion on a true basis. It was certain that it would become the instrument of a systematic effort against the national government and its administration, a decided engine of party to advance its own views at the hazard of the public peace and prosperity.

The events which have already taken place are a full comment of these positions. If the good sense of the people does not speedily discountenance the projects which are on foot, more melancholy proofs may succeed.

Before the treaty was known, attempts were made to prepossess the public mind against it. It was absurdly asserted that it was not expected by the people that Mr. Jay was to make any treaty, as if he had been sent, not to accommodate differences by negotiation and agreement, but to dictate to Great Britain the terms of an unconditional submission.

Before it was published at large, a sketch, calculated to produce false impressions, was handed out to the public through a medium noted for hostility to the administration of the government. Emissaries flew through the country, spreading alarm and discontent: the leaders of clubs were everywhere active to seize the passions of the citizens and preoccupy their judgments against the treaty.

At Boston it was published one day, and the next a town meeting was convened to condemn it, without ever being read; without any serious discussion, sentence was pronounced against it.

Will any man seriously believe that in so short a time an instrument of this nature could have been tolerably understood by the greater part of those who were thus induced to a condemnation of it? Can the result be considered as anything more than a sudden ebullition of popular passion, excited by the artifices of a party which had adroitly seized a favorable moment to surprise the public opinion? This spirit of precipitation and the intemperance which accompanied it prevented the body of merchants and the greatest part of the most considerate citizens from attending the meeting, and left those who met wholly under the guidance of a set of men who, with two or three exceptions, have been the uniform opposers of the government.

The intelligence of this event had no sooner reached New York than the leaders of the clubs were seen haranguing in every corner of the city to stir up our citizens into an imitation of the example of the meeting at Boston. An invitation to meet at the City Hall quickly followed, not to consider or discuss the merits of the treaty, but to unite with the meeting at Boston to address the president against its ratification.

This was immediately succeeded by a handbill full of invectives against the treaty as absurd as they were inflammatory, and manifestly designed to induce the citizens to surrender their reason to the empire of their passions.

In vain did a respectable meeting of the merchants endeavor by their advice to moderate the violence of these views and to promote a spirit favorable to a fair discussion of the treaty; in vain did a respectable body of citizens of every description attend for that purpose. The leaders of the clubs resisted all discussion, and their followers, by their clamors and vociferations, rendered it impracticable, notwithstanding the wish of a manifest majority of the citizens convened upon the occasion.

Can we believe that the leaders were really sincere in the objections they made to a decision, or that the great and mixed mass of citizens then assembled had so thoroughly mastered the merits of the treaty as that they might not have been enlightened by such a discussion?

It cannot be doubted that the real motive to the opposition was the fear of a discussion, the desire of excluding light, the adherence to a plan of surprise and deception. Nor need we desire any fuller proof of that spirit of party which has stimulated the opposition to the treaty than is to be found in the circumstances of that opposition.

To every man who is not an enemy to the national government, who is not a prejudiced partisan, who is capable of comprehending the argument and passionate enough to attend to it with impartiality, I flatter myself I shall be able to demonstrate satisfactorily in the course of some succeeding papers—

1. That the treaty adjusts in a reasonable manner the points in controversy between the United States and Great Britain, as well those depending on the inexecution of the treaty of peace as those growing out of the present European war.
2. That it makes no improper concessions to Great Britain, no sacrifices on the part of the United States.
3. That it secures to the United States equivalents for what they grant.
4. That it lays upon them no restrictions which are incompatible with their honor or their interest.
5. That in the articles which respect war it conforms to the laws of nations.
6. That it violates no treaty with nor duty toward any foreign power.
7. That compared with our other commercial treaties it is, upon the whole, entitled to a preference.
8. That it contains concessions of advantages by Great Britain to the United States which no other nation has obtained from the same power.
9. That it gives to her no superiority of advantages over other nations with whom we have treaties.
10. That interests of primary importance to our general welfare are promoted by it.
11. That the too probable result of a refusal to ratify is war, or what would be still worse, a disgraceful passiveness under violations of our rights, unredressed and unadjusted; and consequently, that it is the true interest of the United States that the treaty should go into effect.

It will be understood that I speak of the treaty as advised to be ratified by the Senate—for this is the true question before the public.

Camillus

The Defense No. XXXVI, January 2, 1796

It is now time to fulfill my promise of an examination of the constitutionality of the treaty. Of all the objections which have been contrived against this instrument, those relating to this point are the most futile. If there be a political problem capable of complete demonstration, the constitutionality of the treaty in all its parts is of this sort. It is even difficult to believe that any man in either house of Congress who values his reputation for discernment or sincerity will publicly hazard it by a serious attempt to controvert the position.

It is nevertheless too much a fashion with some politicians, when hard-pressed on the expediency of a measure, to entrench themselves behind objections to its constitutionality. Aware that there is naturally in the public mind a jealous sensibility to objections of that nature, which may predispose against a thing otherwise acceptable if even a doubt in this respect can be raised, they have been too forward to take advantage of this propensity without weighing the real mischief of the example. For, however it may serve a temporary purpose, its ultimate tendency is, by accustoming the people to observe that alarms of this kind are repeated with levity and without cause, to prepare them for distrusting the cry of danger when it may be real. Yet the imprudence has been such that there has scarcely been an important public question which has not involved more or less of this species of controversy.

In the present case the motives of those who may incline to defeat the treaty are unusually strong for creating if possible a doubt concerning its constitutionality. The treaty having been ratified on both sides, the dilemma plainly is between a violation of the Constitution by the treaty and a violation of the Constitution by obstructing the execution of the treaty.

The VI Article of the Constitution of the U. States declares that "that Constitution and the laws of the U. States made in pursuance thereof, and *all Treaties made or which shall be made under the authority of the U. States*, shall be the *Supreme law of the land*, any thing in the constitution or laws of any State to the contrary notwithstanding." A law of the land till revoked or annulled by the competent authority is binding not less on each branch or department of the government than on each individual of the society. Each house of Congress collectively as well as the members of it separately are under a constitutional obligation to observe the injunctions of a preexisting law and to give it effect. If they act otherwise they infringe the Constitution, the theory of which knows in such case no discretion on their part. To resort to first principles for their justification in assuming such a discretion is to go out of the Constitution for an authority which they cannot find in it—it is to usurp the original character of the people themselves—it is in principle to prostrate the government.

The cases must be very extraordinary that can excuse so violent an assumption of discretion. They must be of a kind to authorize a revolution in government, for every resort to original principles in derogation from the established constitution partakes of this character.

Recalling to view that all but the first ten articles of the treaty are liable to expire at the termination of two years after the present war, if the objection to it in point of constitutionality cannot be supported, let me ask who is the man hardy enough to maintain that the instrument is of such a nature as to justify a revolution in government?

If this can be answered in the affirmative, adieu to all the securities which nations expect to derive from constitutions of government. They become mere bubbles subject to be blown away by every breath of party. The precedent would be a fatal one. Our government from being fixed and limited would become revolutionary and arbitrary. All the provisions which our Constitution with so much solemnity ordains "for forming a more perfect union, establishing justice, insuring domestic tranquility, providing for the common defense, promoting the general welfare and securing the blessings of liberty to ourselves and our Posterity," evaporate and disappear.

Equally will this be the case if the rage of party spirit can meditate, if the momentary ascendancy of party in a particular branch of the govt. can effect, and if the people can be so deceived as to tolerate, that the pretense of a violation of the Constitution shall be made the instrument of its actual violation.

This, however, cannot be. There are already convincing indications, on the very subject before us, that the good sense of the people will triumph over prejudice and the arts of party, that they will finally decide according to their true interest, and that any transient or partial superiority which may exist, if abused for the purpose of infracting the Constitution, will consign the perpetrators of the infraction to ruin and disgrace. But, alas, what consolation would there be in the ruin of a party for the ruin of the Constitution!

It is time to enter upon the momentous discussion. The question shall be examined under the four following views: 1. In relation to the theory of the Constitution. 2. In relation to the manner in which it was understood by the convention who framed it & by the people who adopted it. 3. In relation to the practice upon a similar power in the Confederation. 4. In relation to the practice under our present Constitution prior to the treaty with G.B. In all these relations the constitutionality of that treaty can be vindicated beyond the possibility of a serious doubt.

I. As to the theory of the Constitution. The Constitution of the U. States distributes its powers into three departments—legislative, executive, judiciary. The 1. Article defines the structure and specifies various powers of the legislative department. The second article establishes the organization and powers of the executive department. The third article does the same with regard to the judiciary department. The 4 & 5 & the 6 article, which is the last, are a miscellany of particular provisions.

The 1st article declares that "all *legislative powers* granted by the Constitution shall be vested in a Congress of the U. States which shall consist of a Senate & House of Representatives."

The 2nd article, which organizes and regulates the executive department, declares that "the Executive Power shall be vested in a President of the U. States of America" and, proceeding to detail particular authorities of the executive, it declares that "The President shall have power, by and with the advice and consent of the Senate, To Make Treaties, provided two thirds of the Senators present concur." There is in no part of the Constitution an explanation of this power to make treaties, any definition of its objects or delineation of its bounds. The only other provision in the Constitution respecting it is in the 6th article, which provides, as already noticed, that all treaties made or which shall be made under the authority of the U. States shall be the supreme law of the land; and this, notwithstanding anything in the constitution or laws of any state to the contrary.

It was impossible for words more comprehensive to be used than those which grant the power to make treaties. They are such as would naturally be employed to confer a *plenipotentiary* authority. A power "to make Treaties," granted in these indefinite terms, extends to all kinds of treaties and with all the latitude which such a power under any form of government can possess. The power "*to make*" implies a power to act *authoritatively* and *conclusively*, independent of the after clause which expressly places treaties among the supreme laws of the land. The thing to be made is a treaty; with regard to the objects of the treaty, there being no specification, there is of course a *carte blanche*. The general proposition must therefore be that whatever is a proper subject of compact between nation & nation may be embraced by a treaty between the president of the U. States, with the advice and consent of the Senate, and the correspondent organ of a foreign state.

The authority being general, it comprises of course whatever cannot be shown to be necessarily an exception to it.

The only constitutional exception to the power of making treaties is that it shall not change the Constitution, which results from this fundamental maxim, that a delegated authority cannot rightfully transcend the constituting act unless so expressly authorized by the constituting power. A treaty for example cannot transfer the legislative power to the executive department, nor the power of this last department to the judiciary; in other words, it cannot stipulate that the president and not Congress shall make laws for the U. States; that the judges and not the president shall command the national forces &c.

Again there is also a *natural* exception to the power of making treaties, as there is to every other delegated power, which respects abuses of authority in palpable and extreme cases. On natural principles, a treaty which should manifestly betray or sacrifice primary interests of the state would be null. But this presents a question foreign from that of the modification or distribution of constitutional powers. It applies to the case of the pernicious exercise of a power where there is legal competency. Thus the power of treaty, though extending to the right of making alliances offensive and defensive, may yet be exercised in making an alliance so obviously repugnant to the safety of the state as to justify the non-observance of the contract.

Beyond these exceptions to the power, none occurs that can be supported.

Those which have been insisted upon towards invalidating the treaty with Great Britain are not even plausible. They amount to this, that a treaty can establish nothing between the U. States and a foreign nation which it is the province of the legislative authority to regulate in reference to the U. States alone. It cannot for instance establish a particular rule of commercial intercourse between the U. States & G. Britain because it is provided in the Constitution that Congress shall "have power *to regulate commerce with foreign nations.*" This is equivalent to affirming that all the objects upon which the legislative power may act in relation to our own country are excepted out of the power to make treaties.

Two obvious considerations refute this doctrine. One, that the power to make treaties and the power to make laws are different things, operating by different means, upon different subjects; the other, that the construction resulting from such a doctrine would defeat the power to make treaties, while its opposite reconciles this power with the power of making laws.

The power to make laws is "the power of pronouncing authoritatively the will of the nation as to all persons and things over which it has jurisdiction"; or it may be defined to be "the power of prescribing rules binding upon all persons and things over which the nation has jurisdiction." It acts compulsively upon all persons, whether foreigners or citizens, and upon all things, within its territory; and it acts in like manner upon its own citizens and their property without its territory in certain cases and under certain limitations. But it can have no obligatory action whatsoever upon a foreign nation or any person or thing within the jurisdiction of such foreign nation.

The power of treaty, on the other hand, is the power by *agreement,* convention, or *compact* to establish rules binding upon *two* or *more* nations, their respective citizens, and property. The rule established derives its reciprocal obligation from promise, from the faith which the contracting parties pledge to each other, not from the power of either to prescribe a rule for the other. 'Tis not here the will of a superior that commands, tis the consent of two independent parties that contract.

The means which the power of legislation employs are *laws* which it enacts, or rules which it enjoins; the subject upon which it acts is *the nation of whom it is*, the persons and property within the jurisdiction of that nation. The means which the power of treaty employs are *contracts* with other nations, who may or may not enter into them; the subject upon which it acts is the *nations contracting* and those persons and things *of each* to which the contract relates. Though a treaty may effect what a law can, yet a law cannot effect what a treaty may. These discriminations are obvious and decisive; and however the operation of a treaty may in some things resemble that of a law, no two ideas are more distinct than that of *legislating* and that of *contracting*.

It follows that there is no ground for the inference pretended to be drawn, that the legislative powers of Congress are excepted out of the power of making treaties. It is the province of the latter to do what the former cannot do. Congress (to pursue still the case of regulating trade) may regulate by law our own trade and that which foreigners *come* to carry on with us, but they cannot regulate the trade which we may *go* to carry on in foreign countries; they can give to us no rights, no privileges there. This must depend on the will and regulation of those countries; and consequently it is the province of the power of treaty to establish the rule of commercial intercourse *between* foreign nations and the U. States. The legislature may regulate our own trade, but treaty only can regulate the mutual trade between our own and another country.

The Constitution accordingly considers the power of treaty as different from that of legislation. This is proved in two ways. 1. That while the Constitution declares that all the *legislative* powers which it grants shall be vested *in Congress*, it vests the power of making treaties in *the president* with consent of the Senate. 2. That the same article by which it is declared that the executive power shall be vested in a president and in which sundry executive powers are detailed, gives the power to make treaties to the president, with the auxiliary agency of the Senate. Thus the power of making treaties is placed in the class of executive authorities, while the force of law is annexed to its results. This agrees with the distribution commonly made by theoretical writers—though perhaps the power of treaty from its peculiar nature ought to form a class by itself.

When it is said that Congress shall have power to regulate commerce with foreign nations, this has reference to the distribution of the general legislative power of regulating trade between the national and the particular governments, and serves merely to distinguish the right of regulating our external trade as far as it can be done by law, which is vested in Congress, from that of regulating the trade of a state within itself, which is left to each state.

This will the better appear from the entire clause—"The Congress shall have power to regulate Commerce with foreign Nations and among the several States and with the Indian Tribes," which is the same as if it had been said, "The whole power of regulating trade *by law* shall reside in Congress, except as to the Trade within a State, the power to regulate which shall remain with such state." But it is clearly foreign to that mutual regulation of trade between the U. States and other nations which from the necessity of mutual consent can only be performed by treaty. 'Tis indeed an absurdity to say that the power of regulating trade by law is incompatible with the power of regulating it by treaty, since the former can by no means do what the latter can alone accomplish. Consequently 'tis an absurdity to say that the *legislative* power of regulating trade is an exception to the power of making treaties.

Laws are the acts of legislation of a particular nation for itself. Treaties are the acts of the legislation of several nations for themselves jointly & reciprocally. The legislative power of one state cannot reach the cases which depend on the joint legislation of two or more states. For this, resort must be had to the *pactitious* power or the power of treaty. This is another attitude of the subject displaying the fallacy of the proposition that the legislative powers of Congress are exceptions to or limitations of the power of the president, with the aid of the Senate, to make treaties.

Camillus

The Defense No. XXXVII, January 6, 1796

It shall now be shown that the objections to the treaty founded on its pretended interference with the powers of Congress tend to render the power of making treaties in a very great degree if not altogether nominal. This will be best seen by an enumeration of the cases of pretended interference.

I. The power of Congress to lay taxes is said to be impaired by those stipulations which prevent the laying of duties on particular articles, which also prevent the laying of higher or other duties on British commodities than on the commodities of other countries and which restrict the power of increasing the difference of duties on British tonnage and on goods imported in British bottoms.

II. The power of Congress to regulate trade is said to be impaired by the same restrictions respecting duties, inasmuch as they are intended & operate as regulations of trade—by the stipulations against prohibitions in certain cases and in general by all the rights, privileges, immunities, and restrictions in trade which are contained in the treaty, all which are so many regulations of commerce, which are said to encroach upon the legislative authority.

III. The power of Congress to establish a uniform rule of naturalization is said to be interfered with by those provisions of the treaty which secure to the settlers within the precincts of the British posts the right of becoming citizens of the U. States, and those which in certain cases remove the disability of alienism as to property.

IV. The power of Congress "to define and punish piracies and felonies committed on the high seas and offenses against the law of Nations" is said to be contravened by those parts of the treaty which declare that certain acts shall be deemed piracy, which constitute certain other things offenses, & stipulate the reciprocal punishment of them by each.

V. It is also said that the Constitution is violated in relation to that provision which declares that "no money shall be drawn from the Treasury but in consequence of appropriations made by law"—by those parts of the treaty which stipulate compensations to certain commissioners and indemnifications to G. Britain in certain cases to be adjusted and pronounced by the commissioners, and generally by all those parts which may involve an expenditure of money.

VI. The Constitution is said to be violated in that part which requires the establishment of *officers* of the U. States by law—by those stipulations of the treaty which without the intervention of law provide for the appointment of commissioners.

VII. The Constitution is said to be violated in that part which empowers Congress to dispose of and make all needful rules and regulations respecting the *territory* or other property of the U. States, by those provisions of the treaty which respect the adjustment boundary in the cases of the rivers St. Croix & Mississippi.Lastly, the Constitution is said to be violated in its provisions concerning the judiciary department by those parts of the treaty which contemplate the confiding to the determination of commissioners certain questions between the two nations.

A careful inspection of the treaty with these objections in view will discover that of the 28 articles which compose it at least seventeen are involved in the charge of unconstitutionality and these seventeen comprise all the provisions which adjust past controversies or establish rules of commercial intercourse between the parties. The other eleven, which are the 1st, 10th, 17th, 18th, 19th, 20th, 22nd, 23rd and 24th, except the first, are made up of provisions which have reference to war, the first merely declaring that there shall be peace between the parties. And it is a question even with respect to all of these, except the 1st & 10th, whether they also are not implicated in the charge, inasmuch as some of their dispositions have commercial relations. Is not this alone sufficient to bring under strong suspicion the validity of the principles which impeach the constitutionality of the instrument?

It must have been observed, that the argument in the last number is applicable to all the legislative powers of Congress, as well as to that of regulating trade which was selected by way of illustration, the ground of it being common to all. Indeed the instance of the regulation of trade is that which is most favorable to the opposite doctrine—since foreign nations are named in the clause, the true intent of which, however, has been explained.

The same reasoning too would extend the power of treaties to those objects which are consigned to the legislation of individual states; but here the Constitution has announced its meaning in express terms, by declaring that the treaties which have been and shall be made under the authority of the U. States shall be the supreme law of the land, *any thing in the Constitution or laws of any state to the contrary notwithstanding*. This manifestly recognizes the supremacy of the power of treaties over the laws of particular states and goes even a step farther.

The obvious reason for this special provision in regard to the laws of individual states is that there might otherwise have been room for question whether a treaty of the Union could embrace objects the internal regulation of which belonged to the separate authorities of the states. But with regard to the U. States there was no room for a similar question. The power of treaty could not but be supposed commensurate with all those objects to which the legislative power of the Union extended.

It is a question among some theoretical writers—whether a treaty can repeal *preexisting* laws? This question must always be answered by the particular form of government of each nation. In our Constitution, which gives *ipso facto* the force of law to treaties, making them equally with the acts of Congress the supreme law of the land, a treaty must necessarily repeal an antecedent law contrary to it, according to the legal maxim that *"leges posteriores priores contrarias abrogant."**

But even in those forms of government in which there may be room for such a question, it is not understood that a treaty containing stipulations which require the repeal of antecedent laws is on that account unconstitutional and null. The true meaning is that the antecedent laws are not *ipso facto* abrogated by the treaty. But the legislature is nevertheless bound in good faith under the general limitation stated in another place to lend its authority to remove obstacles which previous laws might oppose to the fair execution of a treaty.

One instance of the inconsistency prevailing in the arguments against the treaty negotiated by Mr. Jay is observable on this point. To get rid of the infractions of our treaty of peace with G. Britain by certain laws of particular states, it is strenuously maintained that treaties control the laws of states. To impeach the constitutionality of the treaty under consideration, it is objected that in some points it interferes with the objects of state legislation. The express provision of the Constitution in this particular quoted above has not been sufficient to check the rage for objection.

The absurdity of the alleged interferences will fully appear by showing how they would operate upon the several kinds of treaties usual among nations. These may be classed under three principal heads: 1. Treaties of commerce. 2. Treaties of alliance. 3 Treaties of peace.

Treaties of commerce are of course excluded, for every treaty of commerce is a system of rules devised to regulate and govern the trade between contracting nations, invading directly the *exclusive* power of regulating trade which is attributed to Congress.

Treaties of alliance, whether defensive or offensive, are equally excluded, and this on two grounds—1. because it is their immediate object to define a case or cases in which one nation shall take part with another in war, contrary, in the sense of the objection to that clause of the Constitution which gives to Congress the power of declaring war, and 2. because the succors stipulated, in whatever shape they may be, must involve an expenditure of money—not to say that it is common to stipulate succors in money either in the first instance or by way of alternative. It will be pertinent to observe incidentally in this place that even the humane and laudable provision in the XXII article, which all have approved, is within the spirit of the objection, for the effect of this is to restrain the power and discretion of Congress to grant reprisals till there has been an unsuccessful demand of justice.

3. Treaties of peace are also excluded, or at the least are so narrowed as to be in the greatest number of cases impracticable. The most common conditions of

* Posterior laws abrogate those which are prior to them if contradictory.

these treaties are restitutions or cessions of territory on one side or on the other, frequently on both sides, regulations of boundary, restitutions, & confirmations of property—pecuniary indemnifications for injuries or expenses. It will probably not be easy to find a precedent of a treaty of peace which does not contain one or more of these provisions as the basis of the cessation of hostilities, and they are all of them naturally to be looked for in an agreement which is to put an end to the state of war between conflicting nations. Yet they are all precluded by the objections which have been enumerated—pecuniary indemnifications by that which respects the appropriation of money; restitutions, or cessions of territory or property, regulations of boundary, by that which respects the right of Congress to dispose of and make all needful rules and regulations concerning the territory and property of the U. States. It is to be observed likewise that cessions of territory are almost always accompanied with stipulations in favor of those who inhabit the ceded territory securing personal privileges and private rights of property; neither of which could be acceded to on the principle of that objection, which relates to the power of naturalization; for this power has reference to two species of rights, those of privilege and those of property. An act allowing a foreigner to hold real estate is so far an act of naturalization, since it is one of the consequences of alienism not to be able to hold real estate.

It follows that if the objections which are taken to the treaty on the point of constitutionality are valid, the president, with the advice and consent of the Senate, can make neither a treaty of commerce nor alliance, and rarely, if at all, a treaty of peace. It is probable that on a minute analysis there is scarcely any species of treaty which would not clash, in some particular, with the principle of those objections; and thus, as was before observed, the power to make treaties granted in such comprehensive and indefinite terms and guarded with so much precaution would become essentially nugatory.

This is so obviously against the principles of sound construction, it at the same time exposes the government to so much impotence in one great branch of political power, in opposition to a main intent of the Constitution—and it tends so directly to frustrate one principal object of the institution of a general government—the convenient management of our external concerns—that it cannot but be rejected by every discerning man who will examine and pronounce with sincerity.

It is against the principles of sound construction, because these teach us that every instrument is so to be interpreted that all the parts may if possible consist with each other and have effect. But the construction which is combated would cause the legislative power to destroy the power of making treaties. Moreover, if the power of the executive department be inadequate to the making of the several kinds of treaties which have been mentioned, there is then no power in the government to make them, for there is not a syllable in the Constitution which authorizes either the legislative or judiciary department to make a treaty with a foreign nation. And our Constitution would then exhibit the ridiculous spectacle of a government without a power to make treaties with foreign nations: a result as inadmissible as it is absurd, since in fact our Constitution grants the power of making treaties in the most explicit and ample terms to the president with the advice and consent of the Senate.

On the contrary, all difficulty is avoided by distinguishing the provinces of the two powers according to ideas which have been always familiar to us and which were never exposed to any question till the treaty with G. Britain gave exercise to the subtleties of party spirit.

By confining the power to make laws within its proper sphere & restricting its action to the establishment of rules for our own nation and those foreigners who come within our jurisdiction, and by assigning to the power of treaty the office of concerting those rules of mutual intercourse and connection between us and foreign nations which require their consent as well as our own; allowing to it the latitude necessary for this purpose, a harmonious agreement is preserved between the different powers of the government—that to make laws and that to make treaties between the authority of the legislative & the authority of the executive department.

Hence, though Congress by the Constitution have power to lay taxes, yet a treaty may restrain the exercise of it in particular cases: for a nation like an individual may abridge its moral power by agreement and the organ charged with the legislative power of a nation may be restrained in its operation by the agreements of the organ of its *federative* power or power to contract. Let it be remembered that the nation is the CONSTITUENT, & that the executive within its sphere is no less the organ of its will than the legislature.

Though Congress are empowered to make regulations of trade, yet they are not exclusively so empowered but regulations of trade may also be made by treaty, and where other nations are to be bound by them must be made by treaty.

Though Congress are authorized to establish a uniform rule of naturalization, yet this contemplates only the ordinary cases of internal administration. In particular & extraordinary cases, those in which the pretensions of a foreign government are to be managed—a treaty may also confer the rights and privileges of citizens. Thus the absolute cession and plenary dominion of a province or district possessed by our arms in war may be accepted by the treaty of peace on the condition that its inhabitants shall in their persons and property enjoy the privileges of citizens.

The same reasoning applies to all the other instances of supposed infraction of the legislative authority with regard to piracies and offences against the laws of nations, with regard to expenditures of money, with regard to the appointment of officers, with regard to the judiciary tribunals, with regard to the disposal and regulation of national territory & property. In all these cases the power to make laws and the power to make treaties are concurrent and coordinate. The latter and not the former must act where the cooperation of other nations is requisite.

As to what respects the commissioners agreed to be appointed, they are not in a strict sense OFFICERS. They are *arbitrators* between the two countries. Though in the constitutions, both of the U. States and of most of the individual states, a particular mode of appointing officers is designated, yet in practice it has not been deemed a violation of the provision to appoint commissioners or special agents for special purposes in a different mode.

As to the provision which restricts the issuing of money from the treasury to cases of appropriation by law, and which from its intrinsic nature may be considered as applicable to the exercise of every power of the government, it is in no sort touched by the treaty. The constant practice of the government, the cause of an expenditure or the contract which incurs it, is a distinct thing from the appropriation for satisfying it. Thus the salary of a public officer is fixed by one law, the appropriation for its payment by another. So, the treaty only stipulates what may be a cause of expenditure. An appropriation by law will still be requisite for actual payment.

As to the disposal & regulation of the territory and property of the U. States, this will be naturally understood of dispositions and regulations purely domestic and where the title is not disputed by a foreign power. Where there are interfering claims of foreign powers, as neither will acknowledge the right of the other to decide, TREATY must directly or indirectly adjust the dispute.

So far then is it from being true that the power of treaty can extend to nothing upon which, in relation to ourselves, the legislative power may act—that it may rather be laid down as a general rule that a treaty may do between different nations whatever the legislative power of each may do with regard to itself. The exceptions to this rule are to be deduced from the unfitness & inconvenience of its application to particular cases and are of the nature of abuses of a general principle.

In considering the power of legislation in its relations to the power of treaty, instead of saying that the objects of the former are excepted out of the latter, it will be more correct, indeed it will be entirely correct, to invert the rule and to say that the power of treaty is the power of making exceptions in particular cases to the power of legislation. The stipulations of treaty are in good faith restraints upon the exercise of the last mentioned power. Where there is no treaty it is completely free to act. Where there is a treaty, it is still free to act in all the cases not specially excepted by the treaty. Thus Congress is free to regulate trade with a foreign nation with whom we have no treaty of commerce in such manner as they judge for the interest of the U. States, and they are also free so to regulate it with a foreign nation with whom we have a treaty, in all the points which that treaty does not specifically except. There is always therefore great latitude for the exercise of the legislative power of regulating trade with foreign nations, notwithstanding any treaties of commerce which may be formed.

The effect of a treaty to impose restraints upon the legislative power may in some degree be exemplified by the case of the compacts which the legislative power itself makes, as with regard to the public debt. Its own compacts are in good faith exceptions to its power of action. Treaties with foreign powers for obvious reasons are much stronger exceptions.

Camillus

The Defense No. XXXVIII, January 9, 1796

The manner in which the power of treaty as it exists in the Constitution was understood by the Convention in framing it, and by the people in adopting it, is the point next to be considered.

As to the sense of the Convention, the secrecy with which their deliberations were conducted does not permit any formal proof of the opinions and views which prevailed in digesting the power of treaty. But from the *best opportunity of knowing the fact*, I aver that it was understood *by all* to be the intent of the provision to give to that power the most ample latitude to render it competent to all the stipulations which the exigencies of national affairs might require—competent to the making of treaties of alliance, treaties of commerce, treaties of peace and every other species of convention usual among nations and competent in the course of its exercise to control & bind the legislative power of Congress. And it was emphatically for this reason that it was so carefully guarded, the cooperation of two thirds of the Senate with the president being required to make a treaty. I appeal for this with confidence to every member of the Convention—particularly to those in the two houses of Congress. Two of these are in the House of Representatives, Mr. Madison & Mr. Baldwin. It is expected by the adversaries of the treaty that these gentlemen will in their places obstruct its execution. However this may be, I feel a confidence that neither of them will deny the assertion I have made. To suppose them capable of such a denial were to suppose them utterly regardless of truth.

But though direct proof of the views of the Convention on the point cannot be produced—yet we are not wholly without proof on this head. Three members of the Convention dissented from the Constitution, Mr. Mason, Mr. Gerry, & Mr. Randolph. Among the reasons for his dissent published by Mr. Mason we find this clause: "By declaring all treaties supreme laws of the land, the executive and the Senate have, *in many cases*, an *exclusive* power of *legislation*, which might have been avoided by proper distinctions with respect to treaties, and *requiring the assent of the House of Representatives* where it could be done with safety." This shows the great extent of the power in the conception of Mr. Mason—that in many cases it amounted to an *exclusive power of legislation;* nor did he object to the extent, but only desired that it should have been further guarded, by certain distinctions and by requiring in certain cases the assent of the House of Representatives.

Among the objections to the Constitution addressed by Mr. Gerry to the legislature of Massachusetts we find one to have been "that treaties of the *highest importance* might be formed by the president with the advice of two thirds of a *quorum* of the Senate." This shows his idea of the magnitude of the power; and impliedly admitting as well as Mr. Mason the propriety of this, he seems only to have desired that the concurrence of the Senate should have embraced two thirds of the *whole body* instead of two thirds of a *quorum*. But how small and how insignificant would the power of treaty be, according to the doctrine lately advanced with regard to its constitutional limit?

As to the sense of the community in the adoption of the Constitution this can only be ascertained from two sources, the writings for and against the Constitution and the debates in the several state conventions.

I possess not at this moment materials for an investigation which would enable me to present the evidence they afford. But I refer to them with confidence for proof of the fact that the organization of the power of treaty in the Constitution was attacked and defended, with an admission on both sides of its being of the character which I have assigned to it. Its great extent & importance—its effect to control by its stipulations the legislative authority were mutually taken for granted—and, upon this basis, it was insisted by way of objection—that there were not adequate guards for the safe exercise of so vast a power—that there ought to have been reservations of certain rights, a better disposition of the power to impeach, and a participation, general or special, of the House of Representatives. The reply to these objections, acknowledging the delicacy and magnitude of the power, was directed to show that its organization was a proper one and that it was sufficiently guarded.*

* *Federalist* Vol II, No. XLII has these passages: "the power to make treaties and to receive and send ambassadors speak their own propriety. Both of them are comprised in the Articles of Confederation *with the difference only* that the former is *disembarrassed* by the plan of the Convention of an exception by which treaties might be substantially frustrated by regulations of the states." This plainly alludes to the *proviso* which has been cited and commented upon. "It is true that when treaties of commerce stipulate for the appointment of articles the admission of foreign consuls may fall within the power of making commercial treaties" and in No. LXIV are these passages "the power of making treaties is an important one, especially *as it relates to war, peace, and commerce;* and it should not be delegated but in such a mode and with such precautions as will afford the *highest security* that it will be exercised by men the best qualified for the purpose and in the manner most conducive to the public good." "There are few who will not admit that the affair of *trade* and *navigation* should be regulated by a system cautiously formed and steadily pursued and that both our treaties and our laws should correspond with and be made to promote it." "Some are displeased with it (that is the power of treaty) not on account of any errors or defects in it, but because as the treaties when made are to have the force of laws they should be made only by men invested with legislative authority"—"others though content that treaties should be made in the mode proposed are averse to their being the *supreme laws* of the land." It is generally understood that two persons were concerned in the writings of these papers who from having been members of the convention had a good opportunity of knowing its views—and were under no temptation at that time, in this particular, to misrepresent them. In the address and reasons of dissent of the minority of the convention of Pennsylvania to their constituents they state that they had suggested the following proposition among others for an *amendment* to the constitution: "That no treaty which shall be directly opposed to the existing laws of the United States in Congress assembled shall be valid *until* such laws shall be repealed or made conformable to such treaty." This shows that it was understood that the power of treaty in the Constitution extended to abrogating even *preexisting* laws of the United States which was

The manner of exercising a similar power under the CONFEDERATION shall now be examined.

To judge of the similarity of the provision it will be useful to quote the terms in which it is made. They are these: "The U. States in Congress assembled shall have the sole and exclusive right & power of *entering into treaties and alliances, provided that no treaty of commerce* shall be made whereby the legislative power of the respective states shall be restrained from imposing such imposts and duties on foreigners as their own people are subjected to or from prohibiting the importation or exportation of any species of commodities whatsoever." (Article IX)

It will not be disputed that the words "treaties and alliances" are of equivalent import and of no greater force than the single word TREATIES. An alliance is only a species of treaty, a *particular* of a *general*. And the power of *"entering into treaties,"* which terms confer the authority under which the former government acted, will not be pretended to be stronger than the power *"to make treaties,"* which are the terms constituting the authority under which the present government acts. It follows that the power respecting treaties under the former and that under the present government are similar.

But though similar, that under the present government is more comprehensive; for it is divested of the restriction in the proviso cited above—and is fortified by the express declaration that its acts shall be valid notwithstanding the constitution or laws of any state. This is evidence (as was the fact) of a disposition in the Convention to disembarrass and reinforce the power of making treaties.

It ought not to pass unnoticed that an important argument results from the *proviso* which accompanies the power granted by the Confederation as to the natural extent of this power. The declaration that no treaty of commerce shall be made restraining the legislative power of a state from &c, imposing such duties and imposts on foreigners as their own people are subject to, or from prohibiting the importation or exportation of any species of commodities whatsoever, is an admission 1. that the general power of entering into treaties includes that of making treaties of commerce, and 2. that without the limitation in the proviso, a treaty of commerce might have been made which would restrain the legislative authority of the state in the points interdicted by that proviso.

Let it not be said that the proviso by implication granted the power to make treaties of commerce; for besides that this is inconsistent with the more obvious meaning of the clause—the first article of the Confederation leaves to the states

thought exceptionable; while no objection was made to the idea of its controlling future exercises of the legislative power. The same address states in another place that the president and Senate "may form treaties with foreign nations that may control and abrogate the constitution and laws of the several states." In the 2nd volume of the debates of the convention of Virginia, which is the only part I possess—there are many passages that show the great extent of the power of treaty in the opinion of the speakers on both sides. As quotation would be tedious, I will content myself with referring to the papers where they will be found (viz) 91, 99, 131, 137, 143, 147, 150, 186. It will in particular appear that while the opposers of the Constitution denied the power of the House of Representatives to break in upon or control the power of treaties, the friends of the Constitution did not affirm the contrary but merely contended that the House of Representatives might check by its *influence* the president and Senate on the subject of treaties.

individually every power not *expressly* delegated to the U. States in Congress assembled. The power of Congress therefore to make a treaty of commerce and every other treaty they did make—must be vindicated on the ground that the express grant of power to enter into treaties & alliances is a *general*, which necessarily includes as *particulars* the various treaties they have made & the various stipulations of those treaties.

Under this power thus granted & defined, the alliance with France was contracted; guaranteeing in the case of a defensive war her West India possessions, and when the *casus federis* occurs obliging the U. States to make war for the defense of those possessions, and consequently to incur the expenses of war.

Under the same power, treaties of commerce were made with France, the U. Netherlands, Sweden, and Prussia. Besides that every treaty of commerce is necessarily a *regulation* of commerce between the parties—it has been shown in the antecedent comparison of those treaties with the one lately negotiated that they produce the specific effects of restraining the legislative power from imposing higher or other duties on the articles of those nations than on the like articles of other nations and from extending prohibitions to them which shall not equally extend to other nations the most favored; and thus abridge the exercise of the legislative power to tax, and the exercise of the legislative power to regulate trade. These treaties likewise define & establish the same case of piracy which is defined in the treaty with G. Britain. Moreover the treaty with France, as has been elsewhere shown with regard to rights of property, *naturalizes* the whole French nation.

The Consular Convention with France, negotiated likewise under the same power, grants to the consuls of that country various authorities and jurisdictions, some of the *judicial* nature, which are actual transfers to them of portions of the internal jurisdiction and ordinary judiciary power of the country, the exercise of which our government is bound to aid with its whole strength. It also grants exemptions to French consuls from certain kinds of taxes & to them and French citizens from all personal services, all which are very delicate interferences with our internal police and ordinary jurisdiction.

Under the same power the treaty with *Morocco* was formed, which besides various other regulations relative to war and several relative to trade, contains the rule that neither party shall make war without a previous demand of reparation, in restraint of the general discretionary power of Congress to declare war.

Under the same power, the treaty of peace with Great Britain was made. This treaty contains the establishment of a boundary line between the parties which, in part, is arbitrary and could not have been predicated upon precise antecedent right. It prohibits the future confiscation of the property of adherents to G. Britain, declares that no person shall on account of the part he took in the war suffer any future loss or damage in his person, liberty, or property, and provides for the release of such persons from confinement & the discontinuance of prosecutions against them. It is difficult to conceive a higher act of control both of the legislative & judiciary authority than by this article. These provisions are analogous in principle to those stipulations which in the second and ninth articles of the treaty under examination have given occasion to a constitutional objection.

Under the same power, various treaties with Indians inhabiting the territory of the U. States have been made establishing arbitrary lines of boundary with them, which determine the right of soil on the one side and on the other. Some of these treaties proceed on the principle of the U. States having conquered the Indian country and profess to make gratuitous concessions to them of the lands which are left to their occupation. There is, also, a feature of importance common to these treaties, which is the withdrawing of the protection of the U. States from those of their citizens who intrude on Indian lands, leaving them to be punished at the pleasure of the Indians.

Hence it appears that, except as to the stipulation for appointing commissioners, the treaties made under the Confederation contain all the features identically or by analogy which are topics of constitutional objection to the treaty before us. They restrain in certain instances the legislative power to lay taxes. They make numerous and equivalent regulations of trade—they confer the benefits of naturalization as to property. They define cases of piracy—they create causes of expenditure. They direct and modify the power of war. They erect *within the country* tribunals unknown to our constitutions & laws in cases to which they are competent, whereas the treaty with G.B. only provides for the appointment of arbitrators in cases to which our tribunals & laws are incompetent. And they make dispositions concerning the territory & property of the U. States.

It is true that some of the treaties made under the former government, though subsequent to the proposing of the Articles of Confederation to the states, were prior to the final adoption of these Articles; but still it is presumable that the treaties were negotiated with an eye to the powers of the *pending* national compact. Those with Great Britain, Sweden, Prussia, & Morocco, & the convention with France, were posterior to the completion of that compact.

It may perhaps be argued that a more extensive construction of the power of treaty in the Confederation than in our present Constitution was countenanced by the Union in the same body of legislative powers with the power of treaty. But this argument can have no force when it is considered that the principal legislative powers with regard to the objects embraced by the treaties of Congress were not vested in that body but remained with the individual states. Such are the power of *specific* taxation, the power of regulating trade, the power of naturalization, &c.

If in theory the objects of legislative power are excepted out of the power of treaty, this must have been equally, at least, the case with the legislative powers of the state governments as with those of the U. States. Indeed, the argument was much stronger for the exception where distinct governments were the depositories of the legislative power than where the same government was the depository of that power and of the power of treaty. Nothing but the intrinsic force of the power of treaty could have enabled it to penetrate the separate spheres of the state governments. The practice under the confederation, for so many years acquiesced in by all the states, is therefore a conclusive illustration of the power of treaty and an irresistible refutation of the novel and preposterous doctrine which impeaches the constitutionality of that lately negotiated. If the natural import of the terms used in the Constitution were less clear and decisive than they are, that practice is a commentary upon them and fixes their sense. For the sense in which certain terms were practiced upon a prior constitution of government must be presumed to have been intended in using the like terms in a subsequent constitution of government for the same nation.

Accordingly, the practice under the present govt. before the late treaty has corresponded with that sense.

Our treaties with several Indian nations regulate and change the boundaries between them & the U. States—and in addition to compensations in gross they stipulate the payment of certain specific & perpetual annuities. Thus a treaty in August 1790 with the *Creeks* (Article 4th) promises them the yearly sum of one thousand five hundred dollars. And similar features are found in subsequent treaties with the Six Nations, the Cherokees, and the North Western Indians. This last has *just* been ratified by the *unanimous voice* of the Senate. It stipulates an annuity of 9500 dollars and relinquishes to the Indians a large tract of land which they had by preceding treaties ceded to the U. States.

Hence we find that our former treaties under the present government, as well as one subsequent to that under consideration, contradict the doctrine set up against its constitutionality—in the important particulars of making dispositions concerning the territory and property of the U. States—and binding them to raise and pay money. These treaties have not only been made by the president and ratified by the Senate, without any impeachment of their constitutionality, but the House of Representatives has heretofore concurred and without objection in carrying them into effect by the requisite appropriation of money.

The consular *convention* with France stands in a peculiar predicament. It was negotiated under the former government and ratified under the present; and so may be regarded as a treaty of both governments, illustrative of the extent of the power of treaty in both. The delicate and even the extraordinary nature of the provisions it contains have been adverted to. Though all reflecting men have thought ill of the propriety of some of them, as inconveniently breaking in upon our interior administration, legislative, executive, and judiciary; only acquiescing in them from the difficulty of getting rid of stipulations entered into by our public agents under competent powers, yet no question has been heard about their constitutionality. And Congress have by law assisted their execution by making our judicial tribunals and the public force of the country auxiliary to the decrees of the foreign tribunals which they authorize within our territory.

If it should be said that our Constitution, by making all former treaties and engagements as obligatory upon the United States under that Constitution as they were under the Confederation, rendered the ratification of the convention a matter of necessity—the answer is that either the engagements which it contracted were already conclusive or they were not—if the former, there was no need of a ratification, if the latter, there was no absolute obligation to it. And in every supposition, a ratification by the president with the consent of the Senate could have been predicated only upon the power given in the present

Constitution in relation to treaties, and to have any validity must have been within the limit of that power.

But it has been heretofore seen that the inference from this instrument is no less strong if referred to the power under the Confederation than if referred to the power under the present Constitution.

How happens it that all these invasions of the Constitution, if they were such, were never discovered, and that the departments of the government & all parties in the public councils should have cooperated in giving them a sanction? Does it not prove that ALL were convinced that the power of treaty applied in our exterior relations to objects which in the ordinary course of internal administration & in reference to ourselves were of the cognizance of the legislative power? and particularly that the former was competent to bind the latter in the delicate points of raising and appropriating money? If competent to this, what legislative power can be more sacred, more out its reach?

Let me now ask (and a very solemn question it is, especially for those who are bound by oath to support the Constitution)—Has it not been demonstrated that the provisions in the treaty are justified by the true & manifest interpretation of the Constitution, sanctioned by the practice upon a similar power under the Confederation, and by the practice in other instances under the present government?

If this has been demonstrated, what shall we think of the candor & sincerity of the objections which have been erected on the basis of a contrary supposition? Do they not unequivocally prove that the adversaries of the treaty have been resolved to discredit it by every artifice they could invent? That they have not had truth for their guide & consequently are very unfit guides for the public opinion, very unsafe guardians of the public weal?

It is really painful & disgusting to observe sophisms so miserable as those which question the constitutionality of the treaty retailed to an enlightened people and insisted upon with so much seeming fervency & earnestness. It is impossible not to bestow on sensible men who act this part—the imputation of hypocrisy. The absurdity of the doctrine is too glaring to permit even charity itself to suppose it sincere. If it were possible to imagine that a majority in any branch of our government could betray the Constitution and trifle with the nation so far as to adopt and act upon such a doctrine—it would be time to despair of the republic.

There would be no security at home, no respectability abroad. Our constitutional charter would become a dead letter & the organ of our government for foreign affairs would be treated with derision whenever he should hereafter talk of negotiation or treaty. May the great Ruler of Nations avert from our country so grievous a calamity!*

Camillus

* It is very probable that a treaty with Algiers is now on its way to the U. States which may be expected to contain similar stipulations with that with Morocco. This treaty, which will have cost the U. States no trifling sum & will be of very great value to our trade, must fall equally on the doctrine which I oppose.

Opinion on the Georgia Repeal Act, March 25, 1796[1]

Case

The legislature of the state of Georgia, by an act of the 7th January, 1795, directed a sale to be made of a certain tract of land, therein described to James Gunn and others, by the name of the Georgia company, upon certain conditions therein specified. The sale was made pursuant to the act: the conditions of the sale were performed by the purchasers, and a regular grant made to them, accordingly, of the said tract of land. Subsequent thereto, the said legislature has passed an act, whereby, on the suggestion of unconstitutionality, for various reasons (prout the act), and also of fraud and corruption, in application to the legislative body, the first act, and the grants thereupon, are declared null and void.

On the foregoing case, the opinion of counsel is desired, whether the title of the grantees and their assigns, the latter being *bona fide* purchasers of them, for valuable considerations, be valid? Or, whether the last mentioned act be of force to annul the grant?

Answer

Never having examined the title of the state of Georgia to the lands in question, I have no knowledge whether that state was, itself, entitled to them, and in capacity to make a valid grant. I can, therefore, have no opinion on this point. But, assuming it, in the argument, as a fact, that the state of Georgia had, at the time of the grant, a good title to the land, I hold that the revocation of it is void, and that the grant is still in force.

Without pretending to judge of the original merits or demerits of the purchasers, it may be safely said to be a contravention of the first principles of natural justice and social policy, without any judicial decision of facts, by a positive act of the legislature, to revoke a grant of property regularly made for valuable consideration, under legislative authority, to the prejudice even of third persons on every supposition innocent of the alleged fraud or corruption; and it may be added that the precedent is new of revoking a grant on the suggestion of corruption of a legislative body. Nor do I perceive sufficient ground for the suggestion of unconstitutionality in the first act.

In addition to these general considerations, placing the revocation in a very unfavorable light, the Constitution of the United States, article first, section tenth, declares that no state shall pass a law impairing the obligations of contract. This must be equivalent to saying no state shall pass a law revoking, invalidating, or altering a contract. Every grant from one to another, whether the grantor be a state or an individual, is virtually a contract that the grantee shall hold and enjoy the thing granted against the grantor, and his representatives. It therefore appears to me that taking the terms of the Constitution in their large sense, and giving them effect according to the general spirit and policy of the provisions, the revocation of the grant by the act of the legislature of Georgia, may justly be considered as contrary to the Constitution of the United States and therefore null. And that the courts of the United States, in cases within their jurisdiction, will be likely to pronounce it so.

Alex. Hamilton

Design for a Seal for the United States, May 1796

A globe with Europe and part of Africa on one side—America on the other—the Atlantic Ocean between. The portion occupied by America to be larger than that occupied by Europe. A COLOSSUS to be placed on this globe, with one foot on Europe, the other extending partly over the Atlantic towards America, having on his head a *quintuple* crown, in his right hand an *iron* scepter projected but broken in the middle—in his left hand a *Pileus* reversed, the staff entwined by a snake with its head downward having the staff in its mouth and folding in its tail (as if in the act of strangling) a label with these words "Rights of Man."

Upon a base, supported by fifteen columns, erected on the continent of America, to be placed the *Genius* of America, represented by *Pallas*—a female figure with a firm composed countenance, in an attitude of defiance, clothed in armor with a golden breast plate, a spear in her right hand and an *Ægis* or shield in her left, decorated with the scales of justice instead of the Medusa's head—her helmet encircled with wreaths of olive—her spear striking upon the scepter of the Colussus and breaking it obliquely over her head a radiated crown or *glory*.

Explanation

The globe is an ancient symbol of universal dominion. This, with the Colossus alluding to the Directory will denote the project of acquiring it—the position of one leg of the Colossus will signify the *attempt* to extend it to America. The columns will represent the American states. Pallas as the genius of America will denote that though loving peace (of which the olive wreath is the emblem) yet guided by *wisdom,* or an enlightened sense of her own rights and interests, she is determined to exert and does successfully exert her *valor* in breaking the scepter of the tyrant. The *glory* is the usual type of Providential interposition.

It would improve it if it did not render it too complicated to represent the ocean in tempest & Neptune striking with his trident the projected leg of the Colossus.

But perhaps instead of all this it may suffice to have the figure of Pallas on horse back, the harp placed on the columns, these on a small mount—her spear breaking a scepter projected by a *herculean arm*.

The War in Europe,
September–December 1796

Every step of the progress of the present war in Europe has been marked with horrors. If the perpetration of them was confined to those who are the acknowledged instruments of despotic power, it would excite less surprise—but when they are acted by those who profess themselves to be the champions of the rights of man, they naturally occasion both wonder and regret. Passing by the extreme severities which the French have exercised in Italy, what shall we think of the following declaration of *Jourdan* to the inhabitants of Germany.

Good God! is it then a *crime* for men to defend their own government and country? Is it a punishable offence in the Germans that they will not accept from the French what they offer as liberty, at the point of the bayonet? This is to confound all ideas of morality and humanity; it is to trample upon all the rights of man and nations. It is to restore the ages of barbarism. According to the laws and practice of modern war, the peasantry of a country, if they remain peaceably at home, are protected from other harm than a contribution to the necessities of the invading army. Those who join the armies of their country and fight with them are considered and treated as *other soldiers*. But the present French doctrine is that they are to be treated as *rebels* and *criminals*. German *patriotism* is a heinous offence in the eyes of French PATRIOTS. How are we to solve this otherwise than by observing that the French are influenced by the same spirit of domination which governed the ancient Romans! These considered themselves as having a right to be the masters of the world and to treat the rest of mankind as their vassals.

How clearly is it proved by all ____ that the praise of a ____ world is justly due to Christianity.[2] War, by the influence of the humane principles of that religion, had been stripped of half its terrors. The *French* renounce Christianity & they relapse into barbarism. War resumes the same hideous and savage form which it wore in the ages of *Roman* and Gothic violence.

Letter from Alexander Hamilton to _____, November 8, 1796

Our excellent president, as you have seen, has declined a reelection. 'Tis all-important to our country that his successor shall be a safe man. But it is far less important who of many men that may be named shall be the person than that it shall not be Jefferson. We have every thing to fear if this man comes in, and from what I believe to be an accurate view of our political map I conclude that he has too good a chance of success, and that good calculation, prudence, and exertion were never more necessary to the Federal cause than at this very critical juncture. All personal and partial considerations must be discarded, and every thing must give way to the great object of excluding Jefferson. It appears to be a common opinion (and I think it a judicious one) that Mr. Adams and Mr. Pinckney (late minister to England) are to be supported on our side for president and vice president. New York will be unanimous for both. I hope New England will be so too. Yet I have some apprehensions on this point, lest the fear that he may outrun Mr. Adams should withhold votes from Pinckney. Should this happen, it will be, in my opinion, a most unfortunate policy. It will be to take one only instead of two chances against Mr. Jefferson, and, well weighed, there can be no doubt that the exclusion of Mr. Jefferson is far more important than any difference between Mr. Adams and Mr. Pinckney. At foot is my calculation of chances between Adams and Jefferson. 'Tis too precarious. Pinckney has the chance of some votes southward and westward, which Adams has not. This will render our prospect in the main point, the exclusion of Jefferson, far better.

Relying on the strength of your mind, I have not scrupled to let you see the state of mine. I never was more firm in an opinion than in the one I now express, yet in acting upon it there must be much caution and reserve.

Excerpt from The Answer, December 8, 1796

For The Minerva

The French Republic have, at various times during the present war, complained of certain principles and decisions of the American government as being violations of its neutrality or infractions of the treaty made with France in the year 1778. These complaints were principally made in the year 1793, and explanations, which till now were deemed satisfactory, were made by Mr. Jefferson's correspondence in August of that year. They are now not only renewed with great exaggeration, but the French government have directed that it should be done *in the tone of reproach, instead of the language of friendship*. The apparent intention of this menacing tone, at this particular time, is to influence timid minds to vote agreeable to their wishes in the election of president and vice president, and probably with this view the memorial was published in the newspapers. This is certainly a practice that must not be permitted. If one foreign minister is permitted to publish what he pleases to the people in the name of his government, every other foreign minister must be indulged with the same right. What then will be our situation on the election of a president and vice president, when the government is insulted, the persons who administer it traduced, and the electors menaced by public addresses from these intriguing agents? Poland, that was once a respectable and powerful nation, but is now a nation no longer, is a melancholy example of the danger of foreign influence in the election of a chief magistrate. Eleven millions of people have lost their independence from that cause alone. What would have been the conduct of the French Directory if the American minister had published an elaborate and inflammatory address to the people of France against the government, reprobating the conduct of those in power, and extolling that of the party opposed to them? They would have done as the Parliament of England did in 1727, when the emperor's resident presented an insolent memorial to the king and published it next day in the newspapers. "All parties concurred in expressing the highest indignation and resentment at the affront offered to the government by the memorial delivered by Monsieur Palm, and more particularly at this audacious manner of appealing from the government to the people under the pretext of applying for reparation and redress of supposed injuries." In consequence of an address from both houses, Monsieur Palm was ordered to quit England immediately. And is it not necessary that we should adopt some remedy adequate to this evil, to avoid these serious consequences which may otherwise be apprehended from it?

The Warning No. I, January 27, 1797

There are appearances too strong not to excite apprehension that the affairs of this country are drawing fast to an eventful crisis. Various circumstances daily unfolding themselves authorize a conclusion that France has adopted a system of conduct towards the neutral maritime nations generally which amount to little less than actual hostility. I mean the total *interruption* of their trade with the ports of her enemies: A pretension so violent, and at the same time so oppressive, humiliating, and ruinous to them, that they cannot submit to it without not only the complete sacrifice of their commerce but their absolute degradation from the rank of sovereign and independent states.

It seems to have become latterly a primary object in the policy of France to make the principal attack upon Great Britain through her commerce in order, by extinguishing the sources of her revenue and credit, to disable her from continuing the war and compel her to accept any conditions of peace which her antagonist may think fit to prescribe. It is to this plan we are to attribute the unjustifiable treatment of Tuscany in the seizure of Leghorn, and shutting her ports against the English, contrary to the will of her own government. The same plan has dictated the attempts which appear to have been made to oblige Naples to exclude Great Britain from her ports during the present war. And there have been indications of a design to effect a similar restraint on all the Italian states and expel the British trade wholly from the Mediterranean. The same object of wounding Great Britain through her commerce has been promoted by the war into which Spain has been drawn, and may be considered as the principal advantage expected from it: While it is likewise understood to be the intention to force Portugal to suspend her commercial relations with Great Britain. The late decree forbidding the importation of British manufactures into France is a further proof of the eagerness with which the policy of destroying the British commerce is pursued, since it is presumable from the derangement of French manufactures by the war that there must have been a convenience in the supply which that importation has afforded.

'Tis obviously to the same origin that we are to trace the decree lately communicated by the French minister to our government with respect to the intended treatment of the trade of neutrals and the spoliations which ours has for some time past suffered. While neutral nations were permitted to enjoy securely their rights, besides the direct commerce between them and the British dominions, the commerce of Great Britain would be carried on in neutral bottoms, even with the countries where it was denied access in British bottoms. It follows that the abridgement of neutral rights is essential to the scheme of destroying the British commerce: And here we find the true solution of those unfriendly proceedings, on the part of France towards this country, which are hypocritically charged to the account of the treaty with Great Britain and other acts of pretended infidelity in our government.

Did we need a confirmation of this truth, we should find it in the intelligence lately received from Cadiz. We are informed through a respectable channel* that *Danish* and *Swedish* as well as *American* vessels carried into that port by French cruisers have with their cargoes been condemned and confiscated by the French Consular Tribunal there, on the declared principle of intercepting the trade of neutrals with the ports of the enemies of France. This indiscriminate spoliation of the commerce of neutral powers is a clear proof that France is actuated not by particular causes of discontent given by our government but by a general plan of policy.

The practice upon the decree is a comment much broader than the text. The decree purports that France would observe towards neutrals the same conduct which they permitted her enemies to observe towards them. But the practice goes a great deal further. None of the enemies of France, even at the height of their power and presumption, ever pretended totally to cut off the trade of neutrals with her ports. This is a pretension reserved for her to increase the catalogue of extraordinary examples, of which her revolution has been so fruitful.

The allegations of discontent with this country are evidently a mere coloring to the intended violation of its rights by treaty as well as by the laws of nations. Some pretext was necessary, and this has been seized. It will probably appear hereafter that *Denmark* and *Sweden* have been mocked with a similar tale of grievances. It is indeed already understood that Sweden, outraged in the person of her representative, has been obliged to go the length of withdrawing her minister from Paris.

The complaints of France may be regarded principally as weapons furnished to her adherents to defend her cause notwithstanding the blows she inflicts. Her aim has been in every instance to seduce the people from their government, and by dividing to conquer and oppress. Hitherto happily the potent spells of this political sorcery have in most countries been counteracted and dissipated by the sacred flame of patriotism. One melancholy exception serves as a warning to the rest of mankind to shun the fatal snare. It is nevertheless humiliating that there are men among us depraved enough to make use of the arms she has furnished in her service—and to vindicate her aggressions as the effects of a just resentment provoked by the ill conduct of our government. But the artifice will not succeed. The eyes of the people of this country are everyday more and more opened to the true character of the politics of France. And the period is fast approaching when it will be universally seen in all its intrinsic deformity.

* *Note*: Mr. Iznardi, our Consul at Cadiz, lately arrived who mentioned the fact as here stated, adding without reserve that the principle abovementioned is avowed in the correspondence of the French Consul at Cadiz.

The desire of a power at war to destroy the commerce of its enemy is a natural effect of the state of war, and while exercised within bounds consistent with the rights of nations who are not engaged in the contest is entirely justifiable. But when it manifestly overleaps these bounds and indulges in palpable violations of neutral rights, without even the color of justification in the usages of war, it becomes an intolerable tyranny—wounds the sovereignty of nations and calls them to resistance by every motive of self-preservation and self-respect.

The conduct of France from the commencement of her successes has by gradual developments betrayed a spirit of universal domination; an opinion that she has a right to be the legislatrix of nations; that they are all bound to submit to her mandates, to take from her their moral, political, and religious creeds; that her plastic and regenerating hand is to mold them into whatever shape she thinks fit, & that her interest is to be the sole measure of the rights of the rest of the world. The specious pretense of enlightening mankind and reforming their civil institutions is the varnish to the real design of subjugating them. The vast projects of a Louis the XIV dwindle into insignificance compared with the more gigantic schemes of his republican successors.

Men well informed and unprejudiced early discovered the symptoms of this spirit. Reasoning from human nature they foresaw its growth with success; that from the love of dominion inherent in the heart of man the rulers of the most powerful nation in the world, whether a monarch, a Committee of Safety, or a Directory, will for ever aim at an undue empire over other nations—and that this disposition, inflamed as it was by enthusiasm, if encouraged by a continuation of success, would be apt to exhibit itself during the course of the French Revolution in excesses of which there has been no example since the days of Roman greatness.

Every day confirms the justice of that anticipation. It is now indispensable that the disagreeable and menacing truth should be exposed in full day to the people of America—that they should contemplate it seriously and prepare their minds for extremities which nothing short of abject submission may be able to avert. This will serve them as an armor against the machinations of traitorous men, who may wish to make them instruments of the ambition of a foreign power, to persuade them to concur in forging chains for mankind, and to accept as their reward the despicable privilege of wearing them a day later than others.

Already in certain circles is heard the debasing doctrine that France is determined to reduce us to the alternative of war with her enemies or war with herself and that it is our interest and safety to elect the former.

There was a time when it was believed that a similar alternative would be imposed by Great Britain. At this crisis there was but one sentiment. The firmest friends of moderation and peace no less than the noisiest partisans of violence and war resolved to elect war with that power which should drive us to the election. This resolution was the dictate of morality & honor, of a just regard to national dignity and independence. If any consideration, in any situation, should degrade us into a different resolution, we that instant espouse crime and infamy; we descend from the high ground of an independent people and stoop to the ignominious level of vassals. I trust there are few Americans who would not cheerfully encounter the worst evils of a contest with any nation on earth rather than subscribe to so shameful an abdication of their rank as men and citizens.

Americus

The Warning No. II, February 7, 1797

Independent of the commands of honor, the coolest calculations of interest forbid our becoming the instruments of the ambition of France by associating with her in the war. The question is no longer the establishment of liberty on the basis of republican government. This point the enemies of France have ceased to dispute. The question now is whether she shall be aggrandized by new acquisitions and her enemies reduced by dismemberments to a degree which may render her the mistress of Europe, and consequently in a great measure of America. This is truly the remaining subject of contention.

They who understood the real strength and resources of France before the present war knew that she was intrinsically the most powerful nation of Europe. The incidents of the war have displayed this fact in a manner which is the astonishment of the world. If France can finally realize her present plan of aggrandizement, she will attain to a degree of greatness and power which, if not counteracted by internal disorder, will tend to make her the terror and the scourge of nations. The spirit of moderation in a state of overbearing power is a phenomenon which has not yet appeared and which no wise man will expect ever to see. It is certain that a very different spirit has hitherto marked the career of the new republic; and it is due to truth to add that the ardent, impetuous, and military genius of the French affords perhaps less prospect of such a spirit in them than in any other people.

'Twere therefore contrary to our true interest to assist in building up this colossus to the enormous size at which she aims. 'Twere a policy as shortsighted as mean to seek safety in a subserviency to her views, as the price of her clemency. This at best would be but a temporary respite from the rod; if indeed that can be called a respite, which is of itself the sacrifice of a real to a nominal independence.

These reflections are not designed to rouse a spirit of hostility against France, or to inculcate the idea that we ought of choice to participate in the war against her. They are intended merely to fortify the motives of honor, which forbid our stooping to be *compelled* either to submit, without resistance, to a virtual war on her part—or to avert her blows by engaging in the war on her side.

When it was the opinion that France was defending the cause of liberty, it was a decisive argument against embarking with her in the contest that it would expose us to hazards and evils infinitely disproportioned to the assistance we could render. Now that the question plainly is whether France shall give the law to mankind, the addition of our opposition to her plan could have too little influence upon the event to justify our willingly encountering the certain dangers and mischiefs of the enterprise. 'Tis our true policy to remain at peace, if we can, to negotiate our subjects of complaint as long as they shall be at all negotiable, to bear all that a free and independent people is at liberty to bear, to defer a resort to arms 'till a last effort of negotiation shall have demonstrated that there is no alternative but the surrender of our sovereignty or the defense of it—that the only option is between infamy or war. But if unhappily this period shall ever arrive, it will impose a sacred and indispensable duty to meet the contest with firmness, and relying on a just providence confidently to commit the issue to the God of battles!

While it is a consolation to know that our government on this as on other trying occasions will act with perfect prudence, and will do every thing that honor permits to preserve peace: Yet it is not to be forgotten that there is a point at which forbearance must stop—beyond which moderation were baseness— where we must halt and make a stand for our rights or cease to pretend to any.

When the indiscriminate seizure of our vessels by British cruisers under the order of the sixth of November, 1793,[3] had brought our affairs with Great Britain to a crisis which led to the measure of sending a special envoy to that country to obtain relief and reparation, it was well understood that the issue of that mission was to determine the question of peace or war between the two nations. In like manner it is to be expected that our executive will make a solemn and final appeal to the justice and interest of France, will insist in mild but explicit terms on the renunciation of the pretension to intercept the lawful commerce of neutrals with the enemies of France, and the institution of some equitable mode of ascertaining and retributing the losses which the exercise of it has inflicted upon our merchants. If the experiment shall fail, there will be nothing left but to repel aggression and defend our commerce and independence. The resolution to do this will then be imposed on the government by a painful but irresistible necessity, and it were an outrage to the American name and character to doubt that the people of the United States will approve the resolution, and will support it with a constancy worthy of the justice of their cause and of the glory they have heretofore deserved and acquired.

No: let this never be doubted! The servile minions of France—those who have no sensibility to injury but when it comes from Great Britain, who are unconscious of any rights to be protected against France, who at a moment when the public safety more than ever demands a strict union between the people and their government traitorously labor to detach them from it, and to turn against the government for pretended faults the resentment which the real oppressions of France ought to inspire—these wretched men will discover in the end that they are as insignificant as they are unprincipled. They will find that they have vainly flattered themselves with the cooperation of the great body of those men with whom the spirit of party has hitherto associated them. In such an extremity the adventitious discriminations of party will be lost in the patriotism and pride of the American character. Good citizens of every political denomination will remember that they are Americans—that when their country is in danger the merit or demerit of particular measures is no longer a question—that it is the duty of all to unite their efforts to guard the national rights, to avert national humiliation, and to withstand the imposition of a foreign yoke. The true and genuine spirit of 1776, not the vile counterfeits of it which so often disgust our eyes and our ears, will warn every truly American heart and light up in it a noble emulation to maintain inviolate the rights and unsullied the honor of the nation. It will be proved to the confusion of all false patriots that we did not break the fetters of one foreign tyranny to put on those of another. It will be again proved to the world that we understand our rights and have the courage to defend them.

But there is still ground to hope that we shall not be driven to this disagreeable extremity. The more deliberate calculations of France will probably rescue us from the present embarrassment. If she perseveres in her plan she must inevitably add all the neutral powers to the number of her enemies. How will this fulfill the purpose of destroying the commerce of Great Britain? The commerce of those powers with France will then entirely cease and be turned more extensively into the channels of Great Britain, protected by her navy with the cooperation of the maritime force of those powers. The result will be the reverse of what is projected by the measure. The commerce and revenue of Britain will in all likelihood be augmented rather than diminished, and her arms will receive an important reinforcement.

Violent and unjust measures commonly defeat their own purpose. The plan of starving France was of this description and operated against the views of its projectors. The plan now adopted by France of cutting off the trade of neutrals with her enemies, alike violent and unjust, will no doubt end in similar disappointment. Let us hope that it will be abandoned and that ultimate rupture will be avoided—but let us also contemplate the possibility of the contrary and prepare our minds seriously for the unwelcome event.

Americus

The Warning No. III,
February 21, 1797

The Paris accounts inform us that France has lately exercised towards Genoa an act of atrocious oppression, which is an additional and a striking indication of the domineering and predatory spirit by which she is governed. This little republic, whose territory scarcely extends beyond the walls of her metropolis, has been compelled, it seems, to ransom herself from the talons of France by a contribution of nearly a million of dollars, a large sum for her contracted resources. For this boon, "the French government engages on its part to *renounce all claims upon Genoa*, to *forget* what has passed during the present war, to forbear any future demands." It would appear from this that France to color the odious exaction, besides the pretense of misconduct towards her in the present war, has not disdained to resort to the stale and pitiful device of reviving some antiquated and derelict claim upon the country itself. In vain did the signal hazards encountered by Genoa to preserve her neutrality in defiance of the host of enemies originally leagued against France, in vain did the character and title of republic plead for a more generous treatment: the attractions of plunder predominated. The spirit of rapine, callous to the touch of justice, blind to the testimony of truth, deaf to the voice of entreaty, had marked out and devoted the victim. There was no alternative but to compound or perish.

If it be even supposed, though this has never appeared, that at some period of the war Genoa may be chargeable with acts of questionable propriety in relation to France, it is manifest that it ought to be attributed to the necessity of a situation which must have obliged her to temporize. A very small and feeble state in the midst of so many great conflicting powers, parts of her territories occupied by armies which she was unable to oppose—it were a miracle indeed if her conduct in every particular will bear the test of a rigorous scrutiny. But if at any time the pressure of circumstances may have occasioned some slight deviation, there is nevertheless full evidence of a constant solicitude on the part of Genoa to maintain to the utmost of her ability a sincere neutrality. It is impossible to forget the glorious stand which she at one time made against the imperious efforts of Great Britain to force her from her neutral position. The magnanimous and exemplary fortitude which she displayed on that occasion excited in this country universal admiration and must have made a deep impression. 'Tis only to recollect that instance to be satisfied that the treatment which she has just experienced from France merits the indignant execration of mankind. Unfortunate Genoa! how little didst thou imagine that thou wert destined so soon to be compelled to purchase thy safety from the crushing weight of that hand which ought to have been the first to rise in thy defense.

How fruitful, at the same time, of instruction to us is this painful example! The most infatuated partisans of France cannot but see in it an unequivocal proof of the rapacious and vindictive policy which dictates her measures. All men must see in it that the flagrant injuries, which we are now suffering from her, proceed from a general plan of domination and plunder, from a disposition to prostrate nations at her feet, to trample upon their necks, to ravish from them whatever her avidity or convenience may think fit to dedicate to her own use.

The last intelligence from France seems to dispel the doubt whether the depredations in the West Indies may not have resulted from misapprehension or abuse of the orders of the French government. It is now understood to be a fact that the cruisers of France everywhere are authorized to capture and bring in all vessels bound to the ports of her enemies.

This plan is pregnant with the worst evils which are to be dreaded from the declared and unqualified hostility of any foreign power. If France, after being properly called upon to renounce it, shall persevere in the measure, there cannot be a question but that open war will be preferable to such a state. By whatever name treachery or pusillanimity may attempt to disguise it, 'tis in fact war, war of the worst kind, WAR ON ONE SIDE. If we can be induced to submit to it longer than is necessary to ascertain that it cannot be averted by negotiation, we are undone as a people. Whether our determination shall be to lock up our trade by embargoes, or to permit our commerce to continue to float an unprotected prey to French cruisers, our degradation and ruin will be equally complete. The destruction of our navigation & trade, the annihilation of our mercantile capital, the dispersion & loss of our seamen obliged to emigrate for subsistence, the extinction of our revenue, the fall of public credit, the stagnation of every species of industry, the general impoverishment of our citizens, these will be minor evils in the dreadful catalogue. Some years of security and exertion would repair them. But the humiliation of the American mind would be a lasting and a mortal disease in our social habit. Mental debasement is the greatest misfortune that can befall a people. The most pernicious of conquests which a state can experience is a conquest over that elevated sense of its own rights which inspires a due sensibility to insult and injury, over that virtuous pride of character which prefers any peril or sacrifice to a final submission to oppression, and which regards national ignominy as the greatest of national calamities.

The records of history contain numerous proofs of this truth. But an appeal to them is unnecessary. Holland and Italy present to our immediate observation examples as decisive as deplorable. The former within the last years has undergone two revolutions by the intervention of foreign powers without even a serious struggle. Mutilated of precious portions of its territory at home by pretended benefactors but real despoilers, its dominions abroad slide into the possession of its enemies rather as derelicts than as the acquisitions of victory. Its fleets surrender without a blow. Important only by the spoils which it offers, no less to its friends than to its enemies—every symptom about is portentous of national annihilation.

With regard to Italy, 'tis sufficient to say that she is debased enough not even to dare to take part in a contest on which at this moment her destiny is suspended.

Moderation in every nation is a virtue. In weak or young nations it is often wise to take every chance by patience and address to divert hostility and in this view to *hold parley* with insult and injury—but to *capitulate* with oppression, rather to surrender at discretion to it, is in any nation that has any power of resistance as foolish as it contemptible. The honor of a nation is its life. Deliberately to abandon it is to commit an act of political suicide. There is treason in the sentiment avowed in the language of some, and betrayal by the conduct of others, that we ought to bear anything from France rather than go to war with her. The nation which can prefer disgrace to danger is prepared for a master and deserves one.

The Warning No. IV, February 27, 1797

The emissaries of France, when driven from every other expedient for extenuating her depredations, have a last refuge in the example of Great Britain. The treatment which we receive from France (say they) is not worse than that which was received from Great Britain. If this apology were founded in fact it would still be a miserable subterfuge. For what excuse is it to France, or what consolation to us, that she, our boasted friend and benefactress, treats us only not worse than a power which is stigmatized as an envious rival and an implacable foe?

The conduct of Great Britain appealed to in justification of France was admitted by all to be inexcusable. The Gallic faction thought it so extreme as to call for immediate reprisals. The real patriots differed from them only in thinking that an armed negotiation to end in reprisals if unattended with success was preferable to immediate hostility. How dare the men who at that period were the clamorous champions of our national dignity, how dare they (I ask) now to stand forth the preachers, not of moderation (for in the propriety of this all unite), but of tame submission, but of a servility abject enough to love and cherish the hand which despoils us, to kiss the rod which stings us with unprovoked lashes? What logic, what magic can render innocent or venial in France that which was so critical and odious in Great Britain?

The pretext (we know) of France is that we have permitted Great Britain to treat us in the same manner and that she acts on the principle of a just retaliation, and her deluded or debauched adherents are mean or prostitute enough to reecho the excuse.

Let us grant for argument sake all that can be pretended on this subject, namely, that through want of energy in our administration or from the opinion which it entertained of the situation of the country, there has been too much patience under the oppressions of Great Britain—is this really a justification to France? Is a defect of vigor in the government of one country, or an under estimate of ill means for repelling injury, a sufficient cause for another government lavish in professions of friendship to imitate towards it the aggressions which it has suffered from another? What in private life would be said of the man who, calling himself the friend of another, because the last had too passively allowed a third, the enemy of both, to wrest from him a portion of his property, should deduce from this a pretext to strip him of the remainder? Has language epithets too severe for such a character? Is not the guilt of unjust violence in a case like this aggravated by that of hypocrisy and perfidy?

But this is not our only reply. The truth is (and a truth we may boldly proclaim) that we never did tolerate the aggressions of Great Britain, that we have steadily resisted them and resisted with success. In the respectable attitude of an armed negotiation, seconded by the self-denying and very influential measure of an embargo—we sent to demand a revocation of the orders under which we suffered and retribution for the losses we had sustained. The orders were revoked and the retribution has been stipulated and the stipulation is in a course of honorable and liberal execution. The redress of ancient grievances on the ground of a reciprocity demanded by every principle of rectitude has been superadded to that of more recent ones. Our flag at this moment proudly waves on the ramparts which had been so long detained from us, and Indian butcheries along the whole extent of our vast frontier have been terminated. More than this: the redress obtained from Great Britain was a principal cause of the happy accommodation of our dispute with Spain of the recognition of our right to navigate the Mississippi and of the establishment of a southern boundary equal to our most sanguine wishes.* These are the fruits (and immense fruits they are) of a vigorous though temperate resistance to the aggressions of Great Britain.

'Tis therefore in every sense false that our government has *permitted* Great Britain to *do* as France is now *doing*. Except here and there, the accidental irregularity of the command of a particular ship—there is not one clear right which the laws of nations entitle us to claim that is not now respected by Great Britain, and to a degree unusual in the history of the treatment of neutral nations by great belligerent powers.

It follows that the suggestion on which France bottoms her ill treatment of us is a frivolous and colorless pretext. 'Tis to confound all just ideas to consider a temporary forbearance as a permission or acquiescence—to pretend to retaliate upon an injured party the injury which it has endured from another, to pretend above all to retaliate that injury after it is passed, has ceased, and has been redressed. We are bound to conclude that our real crime in the eye of France is that we had the temerity to think and to act for ourselves, & did not plunge headlong into war with G.B., that the principal streams of our commerce from the national relations of demand and supply flow through the channels of her commerce, and that the booty which it offers to rapacity exceeds the organized means of protection.

But a country containing five millions of people, the second in the number of its seamen, that sinew of maritime power, with an export of sixty millions, understanding its rights, not deficient in spirit to vindicate them, if compelled against its will to exert its strength and resources, will under the guidance of patriotic and faithful councils be at no loss to convince its despoilers that there is as much folly as wickedness in such a calculation. This reflection ought at once

* *Note*: This consequence was foreseen & foretold. And the prediction is confirmed by that part of the declaration of war of Spain against B which makes it a charge against the latter that in the treaty with the U.S., she had "no respect or consideration for the known rights of Spain" and in the sudden disappearance after that treaty of the obstacles which had so long impeded our negotiations with Spain.

to console and animate us, though the remembrance of former friendship & a spirit of virtuous moderation will induce us still to wish that there may be some error in appearances, that the views of France are not as violent & as hostile as they seem to be—that an amicable explanation may still dispel the impending clouds and brighten the political horizon with a happy reconciliation.

The Warning No. V,
March 13, 1797

I have asserted that the conduct of Great Britain towards us and other neutral powers has been at no period so exceptionable as that of France at the present juncture. A more distinct view of this truth may be useful, which will be assisted by a retrospect of the principal acts of violation on both sides.

Though the circumstance was contemporarily disclosed in all of our newspapers, yet so blind and deaf were we rendered by our partiality for France that few among us till very lately have been aware that the first of those acts is fairly chargeable upon her. Such notwithstanding is the fact. The first in order of time is a decree of the National Convention of the 9th of May, 1793, which, reciting that neutral flags are not respected by the enemies of France, and enumerating some instances of alleged violation, proceeds to authorize the vessels of war and cruisers of France to arrest and conduct into her ports *all neutral vessels* which are found *laden in whole* or in *part* with *provisions belonging to neutrals*, or *merchandises* belonging to *the enemies* of France, the latter to be confiscated as prize for the benefit of the captors, the former to be detained but paid for according to their value at the places for which they were destined.

The instances enumerated as the pretext for so direct and formal an attack upon the rights of neutral powers, except two, turn upon the pretension to capture the goods of an enemy in the ships of a friend. Of the remaining two, one is the case of an American vessel going from *Falmouth* to *St. Maloes* with a cargo of wheat, which the decree states was taken by an English frigate and carried into Guernsey, where the agents of the English government detained the cargo, upon a promise to pay the value, as not being for French account; the other is the case of some French passengers going in a *Genoese* vessel from *Cadiz* to *Bayonne*, who were plundered on the passage by the crew of an English privateer.

There is no question but that Great Britain, from the beginning of the war, has claimed and exercised the right of capturing the property of her enemies found in neutral bottoms; and it has been unanswerably demonstrated that for this she has the sanction of the general law of nations. But France, from the exercise of that right by Great Britain when not forbidden by any treaty, can certainly derive no justification for the imitation of the practice, in opposition to the precise and peremptory stipulations of her treaties. Every treaty which established the rule of *"free ships free goods"* must have contemplated the unequal operation of that rule to the contracting parties, when one was at peace, the other at war; looking for indemnification to the correspondent right of taking friends' property in enemies ships, and to the reciprocal effect of the rule when the state of peace and war should be reserved. To make its unequal operation in an existing war an excuse for disregarding the rule is therefore a subterfuge for a breach of faith, which hardly seeks to save appearances. France, as she was once, would have blushed to use it. It is one among many instances of the attempts of revolutionary France to dogmatize mankind out of its reason, as if she expected to work a change in the faculties as well as in the habits and opinions of men.

The case of the American vessel carried to Guernsey is that of a clear infraction of neutral right. But standing singly it was insufficient[4] evidence of a plan of the British government to pursue the principle. It countenanced *suspicion* of a secret order for the purpose, but it did not amount to *proof* of such an order. There might have been misapprehension or misrepresentation; or if neither was the case the circumstance was resolvable into the mere irregularity of particular agents—it is unjustifiable to ascribe to a government as the result of a premeditated plan and to use as the ground of reprisals a single case of irregularity happening in a detached portion of the dominions of that government. France was bound to have waited for more full evidence. There was no warrant in a solitary precedent for general retaliation, even if we could admit the detestable doctrine that the injustice of one belligerent power towards neutral nations is a warrant for similar injustice in another.

The violation of the courtesy of war in the instance of the French passengers, however brutal in itself, was truly a frivolous pretext for the decree. The frequency of irregular conduct in the commanders and crews of privateers, even in contempt of the regulations of their own governments, naturally explains such a transaction into the cupidity of individuals, and forbids the imputation of it to their government. There never was a war in which similar outrages did not occur in spite of the most sincere endeavors to prevent them.

The natural and plain conclusion is that the decree in question was a wanton proceeding in the French government, uncountenanced by the previous conduct either of its enemies or of the neutral nations who were destined to punishment for their faults.

For the first order of the British government authorizing the seizure of provisions is dated the 6th of June 1793, nearly a month posterior to the French decrees. And there is not the least vestige of any prior order; the presumption is that none ever existed. If any had existed, the course of things has been such as to afford a moral certainty that it would have appeared. The subsequent date of the British order is a strong confirmation of the argument that the affair of the vessel carried to Guernsey was nothing more than a particular irregularity.

The publicity of all the proceedings of the French government, and the celerity of communication between Paris and London, leave no doubt that the decree of May the 9th was known in London before the order of June the 6th. It follows that France herself furnished to Great Britain the example and the pretext for the most odious of the measures with which she is chargeable, and that, so far as precedent can justify crime, Great Britain may find in the conduct of France the vindication of her own.

An obvious reflection presents itself. How great were the infatuations of France thus to set the example of an interruption of neutral commerce in provisions, in the freedom of which she was so much more interested than her adversaries! If the detention of the cargo at Guernsey was a bait, we cannot but be astonished at the stupid levity with which it was swallowed.

We are no less struck with the eager precipitancy with which France seized the pretext for a formal and systematic invasion of the rights of neutral powers, equally regardless of the obligations of treaty and of the injunctions of the laws of nations. The presumption of the connivance of a neutral power in infractions of its rights is the only colorable ground for the French idea of retaliation on the sufferers. Here the yet early stage of the war and the recency of the facts alleged as motives to the decree preclude the supposition of connivance. The unjust violence of France, consequently, in resorting to retaliation stands without the slightest veil. From this prominent trait we may distinguish, without possibility of mistake, the real character of her system.

Americus

Notes on Conduct with Great Britain, April 10, 1797

It must be acknowledged by all who can comprehend the subject that the present situation of the U. States is in an extreme degree critical, demanding in our public councils a union of the greatest prudence with the greatest firmness. To appreciate rightly the course which ought to be pursued it is an essential preliminary to take an accurate view of the situation.

That the preservation of peace is a leading article in the policy of this country has been peculiarly the tenet of the friends of the government. It is a tenet supported by conclusive reasons. In addition to the general motives to peace which are common to other nations—it is of the utmost consequence to us that our progress to that degree of maturity which puts humanly speaking our fortunes absolutely in our hands shall not be retarded by a premature war.

But the state of affairs externally and internally suggests the strongest imaginable auxiliary motives to avoid, if possible, at this time a rupture with France. Externally we behold France most formidably successful—extending too her connections and influence, while the affairs of her remaining enemies decline. The late events in Italy have for the present put that country entirely in the power of France with all its resources. It was evident that the emperor had made a violent exertion for the relief of Mantua. The issue has been to him a terrible one. He will probably be able to bring forward new and powerful forces, but it is likely to be attended with great difficulty and embarrassment—and there is too much reason to suspect that these new forces will be under the disadvantage of *raw troops* contending with veterans led by a general who seems to have chained victory to his chair. It would seem too that France has awed or seduced Naples into her alliance. And who can say what she may not do as to Venice? Does not everything seem to promise her the entire command of Italy and its cooperation against the emperor?

What is the situation of Great Britain? Triumphant at sea but deeply, if not mortally, wounded in her vital part, in that which is the vital energy of the opposition to France—I mean in her pecuniary system. The late measures with regard to the bank, however veiled, amount to nothing less than a stoppage of payment and an act of bankruptcy in that institution. The magic which surrounded it and gave it its principal force exists no longer. Opinion must be injured and with it credit. The consequences are incalculable. An incapacity to afford further subsidies or loans to the emperor may be inferred with almost moral certainty. Though the great national resources of England and the universal interest in public credit may arrest and abridge the extent of the evil, yet it is scarcely possible that it shall not very much enervate the future efforts against France, & it may be expected to fortify extremely the desire of peace in the nation.

The conduct of the present emperor of Russia is at best equivocal. Having departed from the engagements of his predecessor towards the emperor, it is in the course of calculation that he may be thrown into the opposite scale. What is the king of Prussia about? Nothing friendly to the emperor of Germany, if we may reason from his conduct for sometime past—though if we were to reason from his solid interest we ought to conclude that he would not be willing to have France for a contiguous neighbor commanding Holland, and the emperor of Germany so weakened as to be a counterpoise neither to *France* nor *Russia*. Yet a crooked policy pursuing some immediate interest seems most likely to be his governing motive.

According to appearances, then, there is great danger that the emperor and England may be compelled to subscribe to the conditions of France, or to continue the contest on unequal and ruinous terms. It is true in the shifting scenes of Europe the political hemisphere may quickly wear a totally different aspect, but such as it is it exhibits every evil omen to the enemies of France.

To be involved in a contest with France at this time and under such circumstances would be in the highest degree inauspicious. If the war continues between her and her present enemies, the contest can still promise nothing but evil to us without a possibility of gain. If a sudden peace in Europe takes place and we are left to contend alone, the prospect is a most uncomfortable one. France will have large bodies of troops that she will be glad to get rid of and it cannot be doubted that she will be governed by a spirit of *domination* and *revenge*.

Internally, though our situation in this respect mends, it is certain that there is a very large party infatuated by a blind devotion to France. Who will guarantee that in a contest so dangerous these men on considerations of ambition, fear, interest, and predilection would not absolutely join France? There is at least enough of danger of this to furnish a strong reason for avoiding, if possible, rupture.

In the South we have a vast body of blacks. We know how successful the French have been in inoculating this description of men, and we ought to consider them as the probable auxiliaries of France. Let us add that we may have to contend on the South & West with Spain & all the savage tribes they can influence.

The aggregate of these considerations is little less than awful.

In such a state of things large and dispassionate views are indispensable. Neither the suggestion of pride nor timidity ought to guide. There ought to be much cool calculation united with much *calm* fortitude. The government ought to be all intellect, while the people ought to be all feeling.

The result is in my mind that there ought to be 1. a further attempt to negotiate & 2. vigorous preparation for war with an intermediate embargo.

As to a further attempt to negotiate—let a commission extraordinary consisting of three persons be sent to France, and let *Jefferson* or *Madison* be at the head of this commission, perhaps as the ostensible minister, but obliged to cooperate with his colleagues & to conform to the major opinion. Let General *Pinckney* be one of the commission, and let Mr. King or Mr. Cabot or some other able man of the northern region be the third. If thought expedient the com. may go to Amsterdam & announce their mission by a courier asking for passports &c.

Let two leading principles of action be prescribed to these commissioners. They must not directly or indirectly acknowledge any fault or culpability in the U. States—they must not stipulate any succor to France of any kind or in any shape in the present war—they must stipulate nothing inconsistent with any existing treaty with another power.

What may they do? They may now modify our treaties with France so as to assimilate the commercial one with that with Great Britain and so as mutually to *do away*, or liquidate with an eye to future *defensive* wars, the guarantee contained in the treaty of alliance, substituting specific succors in defined cases to the *general guarantee.*

This measure will keep open the door of accommodation and give us the chance of favorable events. It will furnish a bridge to the pride of France to retreat. It will give her the motive of endeavoring to strengthen her party by appearing to yield peace to a leader of that party. It will convince the people completely that the government is at least as solicitous to avoid war with France as it was to avoid it with Great Britain. It will take from the partisans of France the argument that as much has not been done in her case as in that of Great Britain & thus it will contribute, if the measure fails, to the all important end of uniting opinion at home.

Let us see the objections to this measure and the answers they admit.

Objection 1. The conduct of France has been so violent & insulting towards us that we cannot without disgrace make a further overture for negotiation.

Answer. This was the opinion of many with regard to Great Britain when Mr. Jay was sent, & in all appearance her conduct was very outrageous. Yet our moderation on that occasion not only averted war but raised the character of the country abroad. It is true France has gone much further than Great Britain ever did. But on the other hand the state of things and of opinion requires greater circumspection in the case of France than was necessary in that of Great Britain. If we couple this measure with others which will evince that we are in earnest about defending ourselves and repelling aggression, our honor will be saved and our moderation only will be displayed. When also it shall be known that our ministers were prohibited from unworthy concessions, it will be demonstrated that we did nothing more than wave *punctilio* in favor of peace. It is often, too, wise by some early *condescension* to avoid the danger of future *humiliation.* Our country is not a military one. Our people are divided. France may present herself to their imaginations as the terrible and invincible conqueror of Europe. Who will answer for their fortitude and exertion under such circumstances? Will it not be prudent to avoid, if we can, the experiment by a little condescension now?

But this is not all. The measure will tend to *unite* and *fortify*, & this may ensure that very fortitude which in a different state of things might be wanting. It may beget the noble resolution to die in the last ditch.

2 Object: The sending of a man unfriendly to the course of our government & devoted to France may give an opportunity to play into the hands of France & leave greater odium upon the government for not acceding to inadmissible terms of accommodation. He may be a medium of cabal between France and the party rather than the negotiator of accommodation.

Answer. There is perhaps more weight in this than in any other objection which can be made. But it seems to admit of a satisfactory answer. First. It goes further in ascribing *turpitude* to the character in question than perhaps is warrantable. It is far from certain that he would be disposed to make an absolute sacrifice of his country, and it is to be remembered that in accepting the appointment with known restrictions he agrees to their reasonableness & engages his reputation upon the issue of success. Considerable securities result from these considerations. But admit the disposition to do what is feared, if he is coupled with men of address, a counter game may be played & such a complexion may be given to the thing as may put both him and France entirely in the wrong. All will depend on the characters combined. Pinckney, it may be depended on, is a man of honor & loves his country. Unite with him a man of *skill* and an effectual counteraction is provided. Such a man can certainly be found in a case where the government may command any of its citizens.

3 Objection. If the measure succeeds under such a man it will strengthen his hands and through him increase the influence of France, from which it is of the utmost importance to emancipate the country.

Answer. There will be some evil of this sort. But this must be weighed against the good obtained. That will be the preservation of peace in the most dangerous crisis that can well be imagined. Besides, the credit of the measure will at least be divided between the authors & the agent. The president and the government will have a large share. And the poison will carry with it its antidote. Moreover, it is morally certain that the course of things in France will furnish every day some new cure to a moral and orderly people like the people of this country. But this objection such as it is lies against the *person*, not the *measure*.

4th Objection. The conduct of France has been such as to free us from the shackles of treaties which present only nominal advantages to us or such as in future will be real to her (alluding chiefly to the mutual guarantee).

Answer. This may be true, but the consequence can only take place in a final rupture. And this would be to stake perhaps our political existence against a partial encumbrance. Surely it could not be wise to attempt to disengage ourselves from our connection with France by a war with her at such a juncture. It might happen that in the end we might be obliged to consent to be fettered in a much greater degree, and increase rather than diminish the evil for which the rupture was hazarded. Expediency is so clearly against it that it is unnecessary to examine the morality of such a policy.

Objection 5. The conduct of France leaves no hope that such a measure will be useful or even that the mission will be heard. There will then be pure disgrace without any advantage.

Answer. The course of things in France does not authorize us to expect any very steady plan there. Events within and without will govern—and there may exist when the minister arrives a good disposition to receive and hear him. The refusal to receive a minister plenipotentiary may mean only *an ordinary one to reside* & may not extend to an extraordinary one *pro hac vice*. But suppose the worst, it will tend to the most precious of all things, *union* at home. The repetition of effort to avoid war and of insult from France will have the most happy influence upon the temper of our country.

Object 6. The policy of remodifying our treaty of alliance is very questionable. It converts a vague into a specific contract, and substitutes precise obligations to such as each party may interpret according to its convenience.

Answer. This is not an essential part of the plan & may be rejected if thought inexpedient.

But considering the treaty of alliance as the *price* no less than the instrument of the assistance from France, morality, which is most consistent with good policy, requires it should be paid. The genuine meaning of that alliance as to the obligation of the U. States seems to be that when France is *really* & *truly* engaged in a *defensive* war & her West India possessions are attacked, the U. States ought to assist in their defense with their whole force. In future the U. States will not have the excuse of *inability*. They are becoming daily a powerful nation. They must then either evade their obligation or as often as France is engaged in a defensive war with a maritime power take part with her with their whole force. Hence they may be exposed to frequent wars. The denial of their duty besides the guilt & disgrace of broken faith may not avoid that consequence, for as it would be a just, so it might be the actual, cause of war with the ally.

The vagueness of the obligation as a source of reciprocal controversy is in itself an evil which it would be important to get rid of.

Specific succors by either party to the other would not necessarily have the effect of involving the giver in war. It is settled that such succors in consequence of a treaty antecedent to the war are not a cause of war.

It would therefore seem to be a great point to the U. States to convert its obligation into that of a specific succor to be defined & thus lessen the danger of a quarrel either with France or its enemies and likewise the evils of a general war.

It is bad to be under obligations which it will be a violation of good faith not to perform & which it will certainly compromit the peace of the country to perform.

In addition to the reasons already given for pacificatory measures are these cogent ones. The plan of the government and of the Federal party has been to avoid becoming a party in the present war. If any measure it has taken is either the cause or pretext of a war with France, the end will be lost. The credit of preserving peace will not exist. The wisdom of the plan pursued will be questioned. The confidence in the government will be shaken. The adverse party will acquire the reputation & the influence of superior foresight. The evil avoided will be forgotten. The evil incurred will be felt. The doubt entertained by many of the justifiableness of the treaty with G.B. in respect to France may increase with suffering and danger—& the management of affairs may be thrown into the hands of the opposite party by the voice of the people & the government & the country sacrificed to France.

Hence it is all important to avoid war if we can—if we cannot, to strengthen as much as possible the opinion that it proceeds from the *unreasonableness* of France.

As to preparation for war they ought in my opinion to consist of these particulars.

I.   Revenue, which ought to go as far as not to be really oppressive. A large sum may be raised within this limit. The objects may be hereafter designated.

II. A loan of five millions of dollars on the basis of that revenue. This may be put on a footing which will ensure its gradual yet timely success.

III. The completion of the three frigates with all possible speed & the purchase of *twenty* ships the most fit to be armed and equipped as cutters & sloops of war. These will serve to guard our trade against the Pickeroons of France in the West Indies which are chiefly dangerous. They are to be used in the first instance merely as convoys with instructions purely defensive—prohibited from cruising for prizes or from attacking, or from *capturing except when attacked.*

IV. Instructions to our minister in Great Britain, if the negotiation fails, to endeavor to purchase from Great Britain or obtain on a loan two ships of the line & three frigates. It will be her interest to do this as she has more ships than she can well man & our men employed in them will increase the force to be employed against the common enemy. This may be the most expeditious mode to augment our navy.

V.   To grant commissions to such of our merchantmen as choose to take them authorizing them to arm and defend themselves but not to cruise and not to capture unless attacked.

VI. To lay a general embargo with authority to the president to grant licenses to sail, if the vessels go themselves armed or with convoys either of our own or of any foreign nation. This will serve our vessels and our seamen without arresting our trade. In a short time it will go on as usual under protection.

VII. To raise upon the *establishment* some additional artillery and two thousand additional cavalry. These will be useful guards against the insurrection of the southern negroes—and they will be a most precious arm in case of invasion. Cavalry will be of infinite importance as auxiliary to *new* against *veteran* troops.

VIII. The establishment of a provisional army of twenty thousand infantry. They may be engaged to serve if a war breaks out with any foreign power, and may receive *certain* emoluments in the meantime—clothes, full wages when they assemble to exercise, a dollar per month at other times. This corps must be regularly organized & officered by the United States. The officers to take rank with those of the establishment. Its advantage will be to have a body of men at a small expense ready for emergencies. The chance of not being employed will facilitate the obtaining of the men on moderate terms.

There may be a disposition to rely wholly on the militia on three grounds—the supposed improbability of an invasion—the belief that militia are sufficient—the expense in the first instance.

Those who may think an invasion improbable ought to remember that it is not long since there was a general opinion the U. States was in no danger of war. They see how difficult it has been and is to avoid one. They ought to suspect that the present opinion that there is no danger of invasion may be as chimerical as that other which experience proves to be false.

If France can transport her troops here, what is to hinder an invasion? Will she not be very likely to imagine that numerous partisans will join her standard so as to enable her to effect a revolution & place us more completely under her influence? What if the corps destined to this service be lost? Will it not be to get rid of an encumbrance rather than to sustain a loss? While the war with Great Britain continues it will be difficult though not impossible to throw any considerable corps into our country. But if the war with G. Britain should end there is no longer anything to hinder. It is then an event so much in the compass of possibility that it ought to enter seriously into our calculations by anticipation. The situation of Europe is so extraordinary that the most improbable enterprises in ordinary times become now probable.

Should an invasion take place, though the militia & after-raised troops may finally rescue us, yet there will be no comparison in the expense and evils with or without such a corps prepared beforehand as the *trunk* of our military force.

IX. Fortification of our principal ports. This ought seriously to be attended to, but it is a source of expense not requited beyond the utility to embrace more than the principal port in each state.

In addition to these measures it may be proper by some religious solemnity to impress seriously the minds of the people. A philosopher may regard the present course of things in Europe as some great providential dispensation. A Christian can hardly view it in any other light. Both these descriptions of persons must approve a national appeal to Heaven for protection. The politician will consider this as an important mean of influencing opinion, and will think it a valuable resource in a contest with France to set the religious ideas of his countrymen in active competition with the atheistical tenets of their enemies. This is an advantage which we shall be very unskillful if we do not improve to the utmost. And the impulse cannot be too early given. I am persuaded a day of humiliation and prayer, besides being very proper, would be extremely useful.

Perhaps attempts to engage the *good offices*, not the *mediation*, of some other foreign powers may be useful. In this light Spain, Holland, & Prussia present themselves. This, however, is a very delicate point.

But we have a further object in the mission—to obtain compensation and redress for the spoliations on our trade. This is an object which our government ought not to lose sight of. Here, however, it may be expedient to facilitate the matter by allowing as an offset to France some of her gratuities during the late war. It is useful to get rid of obligations as fast and as fully as we can, for we see the compensation hitherto claimed is nothing less than the sacrifice of our independence.

Excerpt from an Answer to Questions Proposed by the President of the U. States, April 29, 1797

To The first. It is difficult to fix the precise point at which indignity or affront from one state to another ceases to be negotiable without absolute humiliation and disgrace. It is for the most part a relative question—relative to the comparative strength of the parties—the motives for peace or war—the antecedent relations—the circumstances of the moment as well with regard to other nations as to those between whom the question arises. The conduct of France exclusive of the refusal of Mr. Pinckney is no doubt very violent, insulting, and injurious. The treatment of Mr. Pinckney, if it does not pass, certainly touches upon the utmost limit of what is tolerable. Yet it is conceived that under all the singular and very extraordinary circumstances of the case, further negotiation may be admitted without the absolute humiliation and disgrace, which ought perhaps never to be incurred—to avoid which it is probably always wise to put even the political existence of a nation upon the hazard of the die.

The triumphs of France have been such as to confound and astonish mankind. Several of the principal powers of Europe, even England herself, have found it necessary or expedient in greater or less degrees to submit to some humiliation from France. At the present juncture the course of her affairs & the situation of her enemies more than ever admonishes those who are in danger of becoming so, and who are not able to oppose barriers to her progress, to temporize. The mind of mankind, tired with the suffering or spectacle of a war fatal beyond example, is prepared to see more than usual forbearance in powers not yet parties to it who may be in danger of being involved. It is prepared to view as only prudent what in other circumstances would be deemed dishonorable submission.

The U. States have the strongest motives to avoid war. They may lose a great deal; they can gain nothing. They may be annoyed much and can annoy comparatively little. 'Tis even a possible event *that they may be left alone to contend with the conquerors of Europe.* When interests so great invite and dangers so great menace, delicacy is called upon to yield a great deal to prudence. And a considerable degree of humiliation may, without *ignominy*, be encountered to avoid the possibility of much greater and a train of incalculable evils.

The former relations of the U. States to France—the agency of that power in promoting our revolution—are reasons in the nature of things for not lightly running into a quarrel with—even for bearing and forbearing to a considerable extent. There is perhaps in such a case peculiar dignity in moderation.

France in declining to receive Mr. Pinckney has not gone to the *ne plus ultra*. She has declined to receive a minister till grievances of which she complains are redressed. She has not absolutely ordered away a minister as the preliminary to war. She has mingled some qualifications. It is not even clear that she means to say she will not receive an *extraordinary* minister. This leaves some vacant ground between her act and *rupture*. The U. States may occupy it by a further attempt at negotiation. This further attempt seems to be that which must carry us to the point beyond which we cannot go.

Besides the object of *explanation* to satisfy *France*, we have the most serious grievances *to complain of* and of which to *seek redress*. This last will be a principal object of an extraordinary mission. It will not be to make *submissions* but to *explain* and to demand *reparation*. This double object contains a great *salvo* for the national honor.

We have just seen in the case of Sweden the negotiation in some way or other of a similar insult. Though the refusal of our minister as being more pretextless is more offensive, yet the forbearance of Sweden is a precedent of some force for us.

As to our own country—There is a general and strong desire of peace—and with a considerable party still a particular repugnance to war with France. The state of public opinion is not likely to consider a farther attempt at negotiation as too humiliating. It may be safely taken for granted that it will approve such an attempt as prudent—& that at home it will have no other effect than to lay the foundation for great *union* and *constancy* in case of failure.

But to preserve character abroad—and esteem for the government at home, it is essential that the idea of further negotiation be accompanied by measures that shall demonstrate a spirit of resistance in case of failure—that shall yield present protection—and promise future security.

With this *adjunct*, it is believed that the government in pursuing the plan for further negotiation will raise rather than depress the character of the nation abroad & will preserve the dignity of the American mind & the esteem of the American people.

The enunciation of one measure by the executive ought therefore to be accompanied with a decisive recommendation of the other course. In doing this, however, it will be wise to avoid all expressions that may look like menacing France with what we intend to do. The attempt to negotiate must be put upon the foot of an *appeal* to her *justice* and *friendship*. The recommendation of preparatory & defensive precautions must be put on the foot of *present necessity* in reference to the actual & ruinous depredations on our trade and the possibility of *future dangers* which it may not be *in our power to avert*.

Excerpt from a Letter to William Hamilton, May 2, 1797

Some days since I received with great pleasure your letter of the 10th. of March. The mark it affords of your kind attention, and the particular account it gives me of so many relations in Scotland, are extremely gratifying to me. You no doubt have understood that my father's affairs at a very early day went to wreck, so as to have rendered his situation during the greatest part of his life far from eligible. This state of things occasioned a separation between him and me, when I was very young, and threw me upon the bounty of my mother's relations, some of whom were then wealthy, though by vicissitudes to which human affairs are so liable they have been since much reduced and broken up. Myself at about sixteen came to this country. Having always had a strong propensity to literary pursuits, by a course of steady and laborious exertion I was able by the age of nineteen to qualify myself for the degree of Bachelor of Arts in the College of New York and to lay a foundation, by preparatory study, for the future profession of the law.

The American Revolution supervened. My principles led me to take part in it. At nineteen I entered into the American army as captain of artillery. Shortly after, I became by his invitation aide de camp to General Washington, in which station I served till the commencement of that campaign which ended with the siege of York, in Virginia, and the capture of Cornwallis's army. This campaign I made at the head of a corps of light infantry, with which I was present at the siege of York and engaged in some interesting operations.

At the period of the peace with Great Britain, I found myself a member of Congress by appointment of the legislature of this state.

After the peace, I settled in the City of New York in the practice of the law; and was in a very lucrative course of practice when the derangement of our public affairs by the feebleness of the general confederation drew me again reluctantly into public life. I became a member of the Convention which framed the present Constitution of the U. States; and having taken part in this measure, I conceived myself to be under an obligation to lend my aid towards putting the machine in some regular motion. Hence I did not hesitate to accept the offer of President Washington to undertake the office of secretary of the treasury.

In that office I met with many intrinsic difficulties, and many artificial ones proceeding from passions not very worthy, common to human nature, and which act with peculiar force in republics. The object, however, was effected of establishing public credit and introducing order into the finances.

Public office in this country has few attractions. The pecuniary emolument is so inconsiderable as to amount to a sacrifice to any man who can employ his time with advantage in any liberal profession. The opportunity of doing good, from the jealousy of power and the spirit of faction, is too small in any station to warrant a long continuance of private sacrifices. The enterprises of party had so far succeeded as materially to weaken the necessary influence and energy of the executive authority, and so far diminish the power of doing good in that department as greatly to take the motives which a virtuous man might have for making sacrifices. The prospect was even bad for gratifying in future the love of fame, if that passion was to be the spring of action.

The union of these motives, with the reflections of prudence in relation to a growing family, determined me, as soon as my plan had attained a certain maturity, to withdraw from office. This I did by a resignation about two years since, when I resumed the profession of the law in the City of New York under every advantage I could desire.

It is a pleasing reflection to me that since the commencement of my connection with General Washington to the present time I have possessed a flattering share of his confidence and friendship.

Having given you a brief sketch of my political career, I proceed to some further family details.

Excerpts from The Reynolds Pamphlet, 1797

The spirit of Jacobinism, if not entirely a new spirit, has at least been clothed with a more gigantic body and armed with more powerful weapons than it ever before possessed. It is perhaps not too much to say that it threatens more extensive and complicated mischiefs to the world than have hitherto flowed from the three great scourges of mankind, WAR, PESTILENCE, and FAMINE. To what point it will ultimately lead society it is impossible for human foresight to pronounce, but there is just ground to apprehend that its progress may be marked with calamities of which the dreadful incidents of the French revolution afford a very faint image. Incessantly busied in undermining all the props of public security and private happiness, it seems to threaten the political and moral world with a complete overthrow.

A principal engine by which this spirit endeavors to accomplish its purposes is that of calumny. It is essential to its success that the influence of men of upright principles, disposed and able to resist its enterprises, shall be at all events destroyed. Not content with traducing their best efforts for the public good, with misrepresenting their purest motives, with inferring criminality from actions innocent or laudable, the most direct falsehoods are invented and propagated with undaunted effrontery and unrelenting perseverance. Lies often detected and refuted are still revived and repeated, in the hope that the refutation may have been forgotten or that the frequency and boldness of accusation may supply the place of truth and proof. The most profligate men are encouraged, probably bribed, certainly with patronage if not with money, to become informers and accusers. And when tales, which their characters alone ought to discredit, are refuted by evidence and facts which oblige the patrons of them to abandon their support, they still continue in corroding whispers to wear away the reputations which they could not directly subvert. If, luckily for the conspirators against honest fame, any little foible or folly can be traced out in one whom they desire to persecute, it becomes at once in their hands a two-edged sword by which to wound the public character and stab the private felicity of the person. With such men nothing is sacred. Even the peace of an unoffending and amiable wife is a welcome repast to their insatiate fury against the husband.

In the gratification of this baleful spirit, we not only hear the Jacobin newspapers continually ring with odious insinuations and charges against many of our most virtuous citizens; but, not satisfied with this, a measure new in this country has been lately adopted to give greater efficacy to the system of defamation—periodical pamphlets issue from the same presses, full freighted with misrepresentation and falsehood, artfully calculated to hold up the opponents of the faction to the jealousy and distrust of the present generation and, if possible, to transmit their names with dishonor to posterity. Even the great and multiplied services, the tried and rarely equaled virtues of a Washington, can secure no exemption.

How then can I, with pretensions every way inferior, expect to escape? And if truly this be, as every appearance indicates, a conspiracy of vice against virtue, ought I not rather to be flattered that I have been so long and so peculiarly an object of persecution? Ought I to regret if there be anything about me so formidable to the faction as to have made me worthy to be distinguished by the plentitude of its rancor and venom?

It is certain that I have had a pretty copious experience of its malignity. For the honor of human nature it is to be hoped that the examples are not numerous of men so greatly calumniated and persecuted, as I have been, with so little cause.

I dare appeal to my immediate fellow citizens of whatever political party for the truth of the assertion that no man ever carried into public life a more unblemished pecuniary reputation than that with which I undertook the office of secretary of the treasury, a character marked by an indifference to the acquisition of property rather than an avidity for it.

With such a character, however natural it was to expect criticism and opposition as to the political principles which I might manifest or be supposed to entertain, as to the wisdom or expediency of the plans which I might propose, or as to the skill, care, or diligence with which the business of my department might be executed, it was not natural to expect, nor did I expect, that my fidelity or integrity in a pecuniary sense would ever be called in question.

But on this head a mortifying disappointment has been experienced. Without the slightest foundation, I have been repeatedly held up to the suspicions of the world as a man directed in his administration by the most sordid views, who did not scruple to sacrifice the public to his private interest, his duty and honor to the sinister accumulation of wealth.

Merely because I *retained* an opinion once common to me and the most influential of those who opposed me, *that the public debt ought to be provided for on the basis of the contract upon which it was created*, I have been wickedly accused with wantonly increasing the public burden many millions in order to promote a stockjobbing interest of myself and friends.

Merely because a member of the House of Representatives entertained a different idea from me as to the legal effect of appropriation laws, and did not understand accounts, I was exposed to the imputation of having committed a deliberate and criminal violation of the laws and to the suspicion of being a defaulter for millions, so as to have been driven to the painful necessity of calling for a formal and solemn inquiry.

The inquiry took place. It was conducted by a committee of fifteen members of the House of Representatives—a majority of them either my decided political enemies or inclined against me, some of them the most active and intelligent of my opponents, without a single man, who being known to be friendly to me, possessed also such knowledge and experience of public affairs as would enable him to counteract injurious intrigues. Mr. Giles of Virginia, who had commenced the attack, was of the committee.

The officers and books of the treasury were examined. The transactions between the several banks and the treasury were scrutinized. Even my *private accounts* with those institutions were laid open to the committee, and every possible facility given to the inquiry. The result was a complete demonstration that the suspicions which had been entertained were groundless.

Those which had taken the fastest hold were that the public monies had been made subservient to loans, discounts, and accommodations to myself and friends. The committee in reference to this point reported thus: "It appears from the affidavits of the cashier and several officers of the bank of the United States and several of the directors, the cashier, and other officers of the bank of New York, that the secretary of the treasury never has either *directly* or *indirectly*, for himself or any other person, procured any discount or credit from either of the said banks upon the basis of any public monies which at any time have been deposited therein under his direction: And the committee are *satisfied* that *no monies* of the United States, whether *before* or *after* they have passed to the credit of the treasurer have ever been *directly* or *indirectly* used for or applied to *any purposes* but those of the government, except so far as all monies deposited in a bank are concerned in the *general operations* thereof."

The report, which I have always understood was unanimous, contains in other respects, with considerable detail, the materials of a complete exculpation. My enemies, finding no handle for their malice, abandoned the pursuit.

Yet, unwilling to leave any ambiguity upon the point, when I determined to resign my office, I gave early previous notice of it to the House of Representatives, for the declared purpose of affording an opportunity for legislative crimination, if any ground for it had been discovered. Not the least step towards it was taken. From which I have a right to infer the universal conviction of the House that no cause existed, and to consider the result as a complete vindication.

On another occasion, a worthless man of the name of Fraunces found encouragement to bring forward to the House of Representatives a formal charge against me of unfaithful conduct in office. A committee of the House was appointed to inquire, consisting in this case also partly of some of my most intelligent and active enemies. The issue was an unanimous exculpation of me as will appear by the following extract from the journals of the House of Representatives of the 19th of February 1794.

The House resumed the consideration of the report of the Committee, to whom was referred the memorial of Andrew G. Fraunces: whereupon,

"*Resolved*, That the reasons assigned by the secretary of the treasury for refusing payment of the warrants referred to in the memorial are fully sufficient to justify his conduct; and that in the whole course of this transaction the secretary and other officers of the treasury have acted a meritorious part towards the public."

"*Resolved*, That the charge exhibited in the memorial, against the secretary of the treasury, relative to the purchase of the pension of Baron de Glaubeck, is wholly illiberal and groundless."*

Was it not to have been expected that these repeated demonstrations of the injustice of the accusations hazarded against me would have abashed the enterprise of my calumniators? However natural such an expectation may seem, it would betray an ignorance of the true character of the Jacobin system. It is a maxim deeply engrafted in that dark system that no character, however upright, is a match for constantly reiterated attacks, however false. It is well understood by its disciples that every calumny makes some proselytes and even retains some, since justification seldom circulates as rapidly and as widely as slander. The number of those who from doubt proceed to suspicion and thence to belief of imputed guilt is continually augmenting; and the public mind, fatigued at length with resistance to the calumnies which eternally assail it, is apt in the end to sit down with the opinion that a person so often accused cannot be entirely innocent.

Relying upon this weakness of human nature, the Jacobin scandal club, though often defeated, constantly return to the charge. Old calumnies are served up afresh, and every pretext is seized to add to the catalogue. The person whom they seek to blacken, by dint of repeated strokes of their brush, becomes a demon in their own eyes, though he might be pure and bright as an angel but for the daubing of those wizard painters.

Of all the vile attempts which have been made to injure my character, that which has been lately revived in No. V and VI of the *History of the United States* for 1796 is the most vile.[5] This it will be impossible for any *intelligent*, I will not say *candid*, man to doubt, when he shall have accompanied me through the examination.

I owe perhaps to my friends an apology for condescending to give a public explanation. A just pride with reluctance stoops to a formal vindication against so despicable a contrivance and is inclined rather to oppose to it the uniform evidence of an upright character. This would be my conduct on the present occasion, did not the tale seem to derive a sanction from the names of three men of some weight and consequence in the society: a circumstance which I trust will excuse me for paying attention to a slander that without this prop would defeat itself by intrinsic circumstances of absurdity and malice.

The charge against me is a connection with one James Reynolds for purposes of improper pecuniary speculation. My real crime is an amorous connection with his wife, for a considerable time with his privity and connivance, if not originally brought on by a combination between the husband and wife with the design to extort money from me.

---

* Would it be believed after all this that Mr. Jefferson, vice president of the United States, would write to this Fraunces friendly letters? Yet such is the fact as will be seen in the Appendix, Nos. XLIV & XLV.

This confession is not made without a blush. I cannot be the apologist of any vice because the ardor of passion may have made it mine. I can never cease to condemn myself for the pang which it may inflict in a bosom eminently entitled to all my gratitude, fidelity, and love. But that bosom will approve that even at so great an expense I should effectually wipe away a more serious stain from a name which it cherishes with no less elevation than tenderness. The public too will I trust excuse the confession. The necessity of it to my defense against a more heinous charge could alone have extorted from me so painful an indecorum...

Thus has my desire to destroy this slander completely led me to a more copious and particular examination of it than I am sure was necessary. The bare perusal of the letters from Reynolds and his wife is sufficient to convince my greatest enemy that there is nothing worse in the affair than an irregular and indelicate amour. For this, I bow to the just censure which it merits. I have paid pretty severely for the folly and can never recollect it without disgust and self-condemnation. It might seem affectation to say more.

To unfold more clearly the malicious intent by which the present revival of the affair must have been influenced—I shall annex an affidavit of Mr. Webster, tending to confirm my declaration of the utter falsehood of the assertion that a menace of publishing the papers which have been published had arrested the progress of an attempt to hold me up as a candidate for the office of president. Does this editor imagine that he will escape the just odium which awaits him by the miserable subterfuge of saying that he had the information from a respectable citizen of New York? Till he names the author the inevitable inference must be that he has fabricated the tale.

Alexander Hamilton

The Stand No. I,
March 30, 1798

The enlightened friend of America never saw greater occasion of disquietude than at the present juncture. Our nation, through its official organs, has been treated with studied contempt and systematic insult; essential rights of the country are perseveringly violated, and its independence and liberty eventually threatened, by the most flagitious, despotic, and vindictive government that ever disgraced the annals of mankind; by a government marching with hasty and colossal strides to universal empire, and, in the execution of this hideous project, wielding with absolute authority the whole physical force of the most enthralled but most powerful nation on earth. In a situation like this, how great is the cause to lament, how afflicting to every heart alive to the honor and interest of its country, to observe that distracted and inefficient councils, that a palsied and unconscious state of the public mind, afford too little assurance of measures adequate either to the urgency of the evils which are felt, or to the magnitude of the dangers which are in prospect.

When Great Britain attempted to wrest from us those rights without which we must have descended from the rank of freedom, a keen and strong sense of injury and danger ran with electric swiftness through the breasts of our citizens. The mass and weight of talents, property, and character hastened to confederate in the public cause. The great body of our community everywhere burnt with a holy zeal to defend it, and were eager to make sacrifices on the altar of their country.

If the nation with which we were called to contend was then the preponderating power of Europe; if by her great wealth and the success of her arms she was in a condition to bias or to awe the cabinets of princes; if her fleets covered and domineered over the ocean, facilitating depredation and invasion; if the penalties of rebellion hung over an unsuccessful contest; if America was yet in the cradle of her political existence; if her population little exceeded two millions; if she was without government, without fleets or armies, arsenals or magazines, without military knowledge—still her citizens had a just and elevated sense of her rights, were thoroughly awake to the violence and injustice of the attack upon them, saw the conduct of her adversary without apology or extenuation; and, under the impulse of these impressions and views, determined with little short of unanimity to brave every hazard in her defense. This magnanimous spirit was the sure pledge that all the energies of the country would be exerted to bring all its resources into action, that whatever was possible would be done towards effectual opposition; and this, combined with the immense advantage of distance, warranted the expectation of ultimate success. The event justified the expectation and rewarded the glorious spirit from which it was derived.

Far different is the picture of our present situation! The FIVE TYRANTS of France, after binding in chains their own countrymen, after prostrating surrounding nations, and vanquishing all external resistance to their revolutionary despotism at home, without the shadow of necessity, with no discernible motive other than to confirm their usurpation and extend the sphere of their domination abroad—These implacable TYRANTS obstinately and remorselessly persist in prolonging the calamities of mankind, and seem resolved as far as they can to multiply and perpetuate them. Acting upon the pretension to universal empire, they have at length, in fact though not in name, decreed war against all nations not in league with themselves; and towards this country, in particular, they add to a long train of unprovoked aggressions and affronts the insupportable outrage of refusing to receive the extraordinary ambassadors whom we sent to endeavor to appease and conciliate. Thus have they, in regard to us, filled up the measure of national insult and humiliation. 'Tis not in their power, unless we are accomplices in the design, to sink us lower. 'Tis only in our own power to do this by an abject submission to their will.

But though a knowledge of the true character of the citizens of this country will not permit it to be suspected that a majority either in our public councils or in the community can be so degraded or infatuated, yet to the firm and independent lover of his country there are appearances at once mortifying and alarming.

Among those who divide our legislative councils, we perceive hitherto, on the one side, unremitting efforts to justify or excuse the despots of France, to vilify and discredit our own government, of course to destroy its necessary vigor, and to distract the opinions and to damp the zeal of our citizens, what is worse, to divert their affections from their own to a foreign country: on the other side, we have as yet seen neither expanded views of our situation, nor measures at all proportioned to the seriousness and extent of the danger. While our independence is menaced, little more is heard than of guarding our trade, and this too in very feeble and tremulous accents.

In the community, though in a sounder state than its representatives, we discover the vestiges of the same divisions which enervate our councils. A few, happily a contemptible few, prostituted to a foreign enemy, seem willing that their country should become a province to France. Some of these dare even to insinuate the treasonable and parricidal sentiment that in case of invasion they would join the standard of France. Another and a more considerable part are weak enough to appear disposed to sacrifice our commerce, to endure every indignity and even to become tributary, rather than to encounter war or increase the chances of it; as if a nation could preserve any rights, could even retain its freedom, which should conduct itself on the principle of passive obedience to injury and outrages; as if the debasement of the public mind did not include the debasement of the individual mind and the dereliction of whatever adorns or exalts human nature; as if there could be any security in compounding with tyranny and injustice by degrading compliances; as if submission to the existing violations of our sovereignty would not invite still greater, and whet the appetite to devour us by the allurement of an unresisting prey; as if war was ever to be averted by betraying unequivocally a pusillanimous dread of it as the greatest of all evils.

This country has doubtless powerful motives to cultivate peace. It was its policy, for the sake of this object, to go a great way in yielding secondary interests, and to meet injury with patience as long as it could be done without the manifest abandonment of essential rights, without absolute dishonor. But to do more than this is suicide in any people who have the least chance of contending with effect. The conduct of our government has corresponded with the cogent inducements to a pacific system. Towards Great Britain it displayed forbearance—towards France it has shown humility. In the case of Great Britain, its moderation was attended with success. But the inexorable arrogance and rapacity of the oppressors of unhappy France bar all the avenues to reconciliation as well as to redress, accumulating upon us injury and insult till there is no choice left between resistance and infamy.

My countrymen! can ye hesitate which to prefer? can ye consent to taste the brutalizing cup of disgrace, to wear the livery of foreign masters, to put on the hateful fetters of foreign bondage? Will it make any difference to you that the badge of your servitude is a *cap* rather than an *epaulet?* Will tyranny be less odious because FIVE instead of ONE inflict the rod? What is there to deter from the manful vindication of your rights and your honor?

With an immense ocean rolling between the United States and France—with ample materials for shipbuilding, and a body of hardy seamen more numerous and more expert than France can boast, with a population exceeding five millions, spread over a wide extent of country, offering no one point the seizure of which, as of the great capitals of Europe, might decide the issue, with a soil liberal of all the productions that give strength and resource, with the rudiments of the most essential manufactures capable of being developed in proportion to our want, with a numerous and in many quarters well appointed militia, with respectable revenues and a flourishing credit, with many of the principle sources of taxation yet untouched, with considerable arsenals and the means of extending them, with experienced officers ready to form an army under the command of the same illustrious chief who before led them to victory and glory, and who, if the occasion should require it, could not hesitate again to obey the summons of his country—what a striking and encouraging contrast does this situation in many respects form to that in which we defied the thunder of Britain? What is there in it to excuse or palliate the cowardice and baseness of a tame surrender of our rights to France?

The question is unnecessary. The people of America are neither idiots nor dastards. They did not break one yoke to put on another. Though a portion of them have been hitherto misled; yet not even these, still less the great body of the nation, can be long unaware of the true situation, or blind to the treacherous arts by which they are attempted to be hoodwinked. The unfaithful and guilty leaders of a foreign faction, unmasked in all their intrinsic deformity, must quickly shrink from the scene, appalled and confounded. The virtuous whom they have led astray will renounce their exotic standard. Honest men of all parties will unite to maintain and defend the honor and the sovereignty of their country.

The crisis demands it. 'Tis folly to dissemble. The despots of France are waging war against us. Intoxicated with success and the inordinate love of power, they actually threaten our independence. All amicable means have in vain been tried towards accommodation. The problem now to be solved is whether we will maintain or surrender our sovereignty. To maintain it with firmness is the most sacred of duties, the most glorious of tasks. The happiness of our country, the honor of the American name demands it. The genius of independence exhorts to it. The secret mourning voice of oppressed millions in the very country whose despots menace us admonish to it by their suffering example. The offended dignity of man commands us not to be accessary to its further degradation. Reverence to the SUPREME GOVERNOR of the universe enjoins us not to bow the knee to the modern TITANS who erect their impious crests against him and vainly imagine they can subvert his eternal throne.

But 'tis not enough to resist. 'Tis requisite to resist with energy. That will be a narrow view of our situation which does not contemplate that we may be called, at our very doors, to defend our independence and liberty, and which does not provide against it by bringing into activity and completely organizing all the resources of our country. A respectable naval force ought to protect our commerce, and a respectable army ought both to diminish the temptation to invasion by lessening the apparent chance of success, and to guarantee us, not only against the final success of such an attempt, but against the serious though partial calamities which in that case would certainly await us if we have to rely on militia alone against the enterprises of veteran troops, drenched in blood and slaughter and led by a skillful and daring chief!

Titus Manlius

The Stand No. II,
April 4, 1798

The description of VICE by a celebrated poet may aptly be applied to the REVOLUTIONARY GOVERNMENT of France. It is,

> "A MONSTER of such horrid mien,
> As to be *hated*, needs but to be *seen*."[6]

Unfortunately, however, for mankind a species of moral pestilence has so far disordered the mental eye of a considerable portion of it as to prevent a distinct view of the deformities of this prodigy of human wickedness and folly. It is the misfortune of this country in particular that too many among its citizens have seen the monster in all its dreadful transformations with complacency or toleration. Nor is it among the least of the contradictions of the human mind that a religious, moral, and sober people should have regarded with indulgence so frightful a volcano of atheism, depravity, and absurdity; that a gentle and humane people should have viewed without detestation so hateful an instrument of cruelty and bloodshed; that a people having an enlightened and ardent attachment to genuine liberty should have contemplated without horror so tremendous an engine of despotism and slavery. The film indeed begins to be removed, but the vision of many of those who have been under its influence is not yet restored to the necessary energy or clearness.

It is of the last importance to our national safety and welfare that the remaining obscurity should be speedily dispelled. Till this shall be the case, we shall stand on the brink of a precipice.

To exhibit the hydra in all its horrible preeminence of guilt and mischief would require volumes. Slight sketches chiefly to portray its character in reference to other nations are all that will comport with the plan of these papers.

In retracing the progress of a war which has immersed Europe in blood and calamity, it is an error as common as it is strange to acquit France of responsibility and to throw the whole blame upon her adversaries. This is a principal source of the indulgence which is shown to the extravagances and enormities of her revolution. And yet the plainest facts demonstrate that the reverse of this supposition is far more agreeable to truth. It required all the bold imposing pretenses of the demagogues of France, all the docile partiality of a warm admiration for her revolution, to have secured a moment's success to so glaring a deception.

The origin of the war is usually charged to the treaty of *Pilnitz* and to the counter-revolutionary projects of the parties to it.

To this day we are without authentic and accurate evidence of the nature of that treaty. Taking its existence for granted, there is not the least proof that it comprehended any other powers than *Austria, Prussia,* and *Sardinia.** Beyond these, therefore, unless suspicion be substituted for fact, it could not afford even a pretext for hostility. It is likewise certain[†] that after the date assigned to the treaty of *Pilnitz* the emperor, who was the reputed head of the confederacy, gave strong proof of the renunciation of its object, if hostile to the revolution, by signifying, through his ministers, to all the foreign courts his determination to acquiesce in the constitution of 1792, accepted by Louis the XVI.

The diplomatic correspondence between *France* and *Austria*, which preceded the rupture, evinces that the treaty of *Pilnitz* was not the cause of the war, for it is not even mentioned. The immediate ostensible cause, as it there appears, was the refusal of Austria to disarm in compliance with the peremptory demand of France; a demand to which this apparently very reasonable reply was given, that France had previously armed to a greater extent; and that Austria could not safely reduce her force while France remained in so disturbed and inflamed a state as to leave her neighbors every moment exposed to the enterprises of her revolutionary fervor. There is no absolute criterion by which it can be pronounced whether this reply was merely a pretext or the dictate of a serious apprehension. But it is certain that the correspondence discovers great appearance of candor and moderation on the part of the imperial cabinet, and it is not to be denied that the state of effervescence of the French nation at this juncture furnished real cause of alarm to the neighboring governments.

It is then, at best, problematical, whether France in declaring war, as she did at the same time against *Austria* and *Prussia*, was actuated by the conviction that it was necessary to anticipate and disconcert the unfriendly views of those powers; or whether the war, as has been suggested with great probability, was fought by the republican party as a mean of embarrassing the executive government and paving the way for the overthrow of the royalty. Two things, well established, are instructive on this point. The one, that the king was driven against his wish, by a ministry forced upon him by the popular party, to propose the declaration of war, which he considered as the tomb of his family—the other, that BRISSOT, the head of the then prevailing faction, some time afterwards exultingly boasted, that *"but for this war the revolution of the tenth of August would never have taken place; that but for this war, France would never have been a republic."*

Admitting, nevertheless, that the true source of the war with Austria and Prussia is enveloped in some obscurity, there is none as to the wars in which France became subsequently engaged. It is clear as to them that she was the original aggressor.

It appeared from contemporary testimony that one of the first acts of that assembly which dethroned the king was, in a paroxysm of revolutionary frenzy,

---

* I am not certain that ever Sardinia was a party. Writing from memory some minute circumstances may be misstated.
† See State paper by Debret.

to declare itself "A COMMITTEE OF INSURRECTION of the whole human race, for the purpose of overturning all existing governments." This extravagant declaration surpasses anything to be found in the ample records of human madness. It amounted to an act of hostility against mankind. The republic of America, no less than the despotism of Turkey, was included in the anathema. It breathed that wild and excessive spirit of fanaticism, which would scruple no means of establishing its favorite tenets; and which, in its avowed object, threatening the disorganization of all governments, warranted a universal combination to destroy the monstrous system of which it was the soul.

The decrees of the 19th of November and 15th of December 1792 were modifications of the same spirit. The first offered fraternity and assistance to every people who should wish to recover their liberty, and charged the executive power to send orders to their generals to give that assistance and to defend *those citizens* who had been or might be vexed for the cause of liberty. The last declared that the French nation would *treat as* enemies *any people* who, refusing or *renouncing liberty* and *equality*, were desirous of *preserving*, recalling, or entering into accommodation with their *prince* and *privileged casts*.

The first was a general signal to insurrection and revolt. It was an invitation to the seditious of every country, in pursuit of chimerical schemes of more perfect liberty, to conspire under the patronage of France against the established government, however free. To assist a people in a reasonable and virtuous struggle for liberty, already begun, is both justifiable and laudable; but to incite to revolution everywhere, by indiscriminate offers of assistance before hand, is to invade and endanger the foundations of social tranquility. There is no term of reproach or execration too strong for so flagitious an attempt.

The last of the two decrees is not merely in spirit—it is in terms equivalent to a manifesto of war against every nation having a prince or nobility. It declares explicitly and formally that the French nation will *treat as enemies every people* who may desire to preserve or restore a government of that character.

It is impossible not to feel the utmost indignation against so presumptuous and so odious a measure. It was not only to scatter the embers of a general conflagration in Europe—it was to interfere coercively in the interior arrangements of other nations—it was to dictate to them, under the penalty of the vengeance of France, what form of government they should live under—it was to forbid them to pursue their political happiness in their own way—it was to set up the worst of all despotisms, a despotism over opinion, not against one nation, but against almost all nations. With what propriety is the interference of the powers, *ultimately* coalesced against France, in her interior arrangements, imputed to them as an unpardonable crime, when her leaders had given so terrible an example, and had provoked retaliation as a mean of self-preservation?*

---

* If it be true, as pretended, that Austria and Prussia first interfered in this way with France, it was no plea for her to retaliate on all the rest of Europe. Great Britain in particular, as far as appears, had observed a fair neutrality. Yet the principle of the French decree was emphatically pointed against her, by the open reception of deputations of malcontents and public declarations to them on behalf of the French government, avowing the desire of seeing all thrones overturned, of a National Convention and a Republican revolution in England.

These decrees preceded the transactions which immediately led to rupture between France and the other powers, Austria and Prussia excepted.

It is idle to pretend that they did not furnish to those powers just cause of war. There is no rule of public law better established or on better grounds than that whenever one nation unequivocally avows maxims of conduct dangerous to the security and tranquility of others, they have a right to attack her, and to endeavor to disable her from carrying her schemes into effect. They are not bound to wait till inimical designs are matured for action, when it may be too late to defeat them.

How far it may have been wise in a particular government to have taken up the gauntlet, or if in its option to have left France to the fermentations of the pernicious principles by which its leaders were actuated, is a question of mere expediency, distinct from the right. It is also a complicated and difficult question—one which able and upright men might decide different ways. But the right is still indisputable. The moment the Convention vomited forth those venomous decrees, all the governments threatened were justifiable in making war upon France.

Neither were they bound to be satisfied with after-explanations or qualifications of the principles which had been declared. They had a right to judge conscientiously whether reliance could be placed on any pretended change of system, and to act accordingly. And while the power of France remained in the same men who had discovered such hostile views, and while the effervescence of the public mind continued at its height, there could not have been, in the nature of things, any security in assurances of greater moderation. Fanaticism is a spirit equally fraudulent and intractable. Fanatics may dissemble the better to effect their aims, but they seldom suddenly reform. No faith is due to the reformation which they may affect, unless it has been the work of time and experience.

But whether a wrong or a right election in point of expediency may have been made by all or any of the powers, which after the passing of those decrees became engaged in hostility with France, it is not the less true that her government was the first aggressor and is primarily chargeable with the evils which have followed. This conclusion is greatly aided by the striking fact that it was France which declared war, not only against Austria and Prussia, but against England, Spain, Sardinia, and Holland.

Two very important inferences result from the facts which have been presented—one, that in blowing up the dreadful flame which has overwhelmed Europe in misfortune, France is the party principally culpable—the other, that the prominent original feature of her revolution is the spirit of proselytism, or the desire of new modeling the political institution of the rest of the world according to her standard. The course of the revolutions also demonstrates that whatever change of system may have been at anytime pretended, or however the system may in particular instances have yielded to a temporary policy, it has continued in the main to govern the conduct of the parties who have successively triumphed and tyrannized.

Titus Manlius

The Stand No. III, April 7, 1798

In reviewing the disgusting spectacle of the French revolution, it is difficult to avert the eye entirely from those features of it which betray a plan to disorganize the human mind itself, as well as to undermine the venerable pillars that support the edifice of civilized society. The attempt by the rulers of a nation to destroy all religious opinion, and to pervert a whole people to atheism, is a phenomenon of profligacy reserved to consummate the infamy of the unprincipled reformers of France. The proofs of this terrible design are numerous and convincing.

The animosity to the Christian system is demonstrated by the single fact of the ridiculous and impolitic establishment of the decades, with the evident object of supplanting the Christian Sabbath. The inscription by public authority on the tombs of the deceased, affirming death to be an eternal sleep witness the desire to discredit the belief of the immortality of the soul. The open profession of atheism in the Convention,* received with acclamations; the honorable mention on its journals of a book professing to prove the *nothingness* of all religion;† the institution of a festival to offer public worship to a courtesan decorated with the pompous title of "GODDESS OF REASON"; the congratulatory reception of impious children appearing in the hall of the Convention to lisp blasphemy against the King of Kings; are among the dreadful proofs of a conspiracy to establish atheism on the ruins of Christianity—to deprive mankind of its best consolations and most animating hopes—and to make a gloomy desert of the universe.

Latterly the indications of this plan are not so frequent as they were, but from time to time something still escapes which discovers that it is not renounced. The late address of *Bonaparte* to the Directory is an example. That unequalled conqueror, from whom it is painful to detract; in whom one would wish to find virtues worthy of his shining talents, profanely unites RELIGION (not superstition) with royalty and the feudal system as the scourges of Europe for centuries past. The decades likewise remain the CATAPULTA which is to batter down Christianity.

Equal pains have been taken to deprave the morals as to extinguish the religion of the country, if indeed morality in a community can be separated from religion. It is among the singular and fantastic vagaries of the French revolution

---

* By Dupont, Danton &c.
† Written and presented by Anacharsis Clootz, calling himself orator of the human race.

that while the Duke of Brunswick was marching to Paris a new law of divorce was passed, which makes it as easy for a husband to get rid of his wife, and a wife of her husband, as to discard a worn out habit.* To complete the dissolution of those ties which are the chief links of domestic and ultimately of social attachment, the journals of the Convention record with guilty applause accusations preferred by children against the lives of their parents.

It is not necessary to heighten the picture by sketching the horrid group of proscriptions and murders which have made of France a den of pillage and slaughter, blackening with eternal opprobrium the very name of man.

The pious and the moral weep over these scenes as a sepulcher destined to entomb all they revere and esteem. The politician who loves liberty sees them with regret as a gulf that may swallow up the liberty to which he is devoted. He knows that morality overthrown (and morality *must* fall with religion), the terrors of despotism can alone curb the impetuous passions of man and confine him within the bounds of social duty.

But let us return to the conduct of revolutionary France towards other nations, as more immediately within our purpose.

It has been seen that she commenced her career as the champion of universal liberty; and, proclaiming destruction to the governments which she was pleased to denominate despotic, made a tender of fraternity and assistance to the nation whom they oppressed. She, at the same time, disclaimed conquest and aggrandizement.

But it has since clearly appeared that at the very moment she was making these professions, and while her diplomatic agents were hypocritically amusing foreign courts† with conciliatory explanations and promises of moderation, she was exerting every faculty, by force and fraud, to accomplish the very conquest and aggrandizement which she insidiously disavowed.

The people of Belgium, ensnared by fair pretenses, believed that in abandoning the defense of their country and the cause of their ancient sovereign they acquired a title to enjoy liberty under a government of their own choice, protected by France. Contrary to the hopes which were inspired—contrary to the known will of a large majority of that people, contrary to all their religious and national prejudices—they have been compelled to become departments of France. And their violated temples have afforded a rich plunder to aliment further conquest and oppression.

The Dutch, seduced by the same arts to facilitate rather than obstruct the entrance of a French army into their country, thought they were only getting rid of their stadtholder and nobles, and were to retain their territory, and their wealth secured by such a civil establishment as they should freely choose. Their reward is the dismemberment of their country and the loss of their wealth by exhausting contributions; and they are obliged to take a government dictated by

---

* This law it is understood has been lately modified, in consequence of its manifestly pernicious tendency; but upon a plan which, according to the opinion of the best men in the two Councils, lately banished, would leave the evil in full force.

† England among the rest.

a faction openly countenanced and supported by France. Completely a province of France in imitation of their frantic masters, they are advancing with rapid strides to a lawless tyranny at home.*

France, professing eternal hatred to kings, was to be the tutelary genius of republics—HOLLAND, GENOA, VENICE, the SWISS CANTONS, and the UNITED STATES are agonizing witnesses of her sincerity.

Of undone *Holland*, no more need be said; nothing remains for us but to exercise tender sympathy in the unfortunate fate of a country which generosity lent its aid to establish our independence, and to deduce from her melancholy example an instructive lesson to repel with determined vigor the mortal embrace of her seducer and destroyer.

Genoa, a speck on the globe, for having at every hazard resisted the efforts of the enemies of France to force her from a neutral station, is recompensed with the subversion of her government and the pillage of her wealth by compulsory and burdensome contributions.

VENICE is no more! In vain had she preserved a faithful neutrality, when perhaps her interposition might have inclined the scale of victory in Italy against France. A few of her citizens kill† some French soldiers. Instant retaliation takes place. Every atonement is offered. Nothing will suffice but the overthrow of her government. 'Tis effected. Her own citizens attracted by the lure of democracy become accessory to it, and receive a popular government at the hand of France. What is the sequel—what the faith kept with them? It suits France to bribe the emperor to a surrender of the Netherlands and to peace, that she may pursue her projects elsewhere with less obstacle. It suits France to extend her power and commerce by the acquisition of portions of the *Venetian* territories. The bribe is offered and accepted. VENICE is divided. She disappears from the mass of nations. The tragedy of Poland is reacted with circumstances of aggravated atrocity. France is perfidious enough to sacrifice a people who at her desire had consented to abrogate their *privileged casts* to the chief of those despots against whom she had vowed eternal hatred.

The Swiss cantons—the boast of republicans—the model to which they have been glad to appeal in proof that a republican government may consist with the order and happiness of society—the old and faithful allies of France, who are not even pretended to have deviated from a sincere neutrality—what are they at this moment? Perhaps like Venice, *a story told!* The despots of France had found pretenses to quarrel with them—commotions were excited—the legions of France were in march to second the insurgents. Little other hope remains than that the *death* of this respectable people will be as glorious as their *life*, that they will sell their independence as dearly as they bought it. But why despair of a brave and virtuous people who appear determined to meet the impending danger with a countenance emulous of their ancient renown?

---

* By the last accounts some of their most independent citizens have been seized and imprisoned merely for the constitutional exercise of their opinion.

† Were they not French agents employed to create the pretext?

The United States—what is their situation? Their sovereignty trampled in the dust and their commerce bleeding at every pore, speak in loud accents the spirit of oppression and rapine, which characterizes the usurpers of France. But of this a distinct view is requisite and will be taken.

In these transactions we discover ambition and fanaticism marching hand in hand—bearing the ensigns of hypocrisy, treachery, and rapine. The dogmas of a false and fatal creed second the weapons of ambition. Like the prophet of Mecca, the tyrants of France press forward with the alcoran of their faith in one hand and the sword in the other—They proselyte, subjugate, and debase— no distinction is made between republic and monarchy—all must alike yield to the aggrandizement of the "GREAT NATION": the distinctive, the arrogant appellation lately assumed by France to assert in the face of nations her superiority and ascendency. Nor is it a mere title with which vanity decorates itself. It is the substantial claim of dominion. France, swelled to a gigantic size and aping ancient Rome, except in her virtues, plainly meditates the control of mankind, and is actually giving the law to nations. Unless they quickly rouse and compel her to abdicate her insolent claim, they will verify the truth of that philosophy which makes man in his natural state a quadruped, and it will only remain for the miserable animal, converting his hands into paws in the attitude of prone submission, to offer his patient and servile back to whatever burdens the LORDLY TYRANTS of France may think fit to impose.

Titus Manlius

The Stand No. IV,
April 12, 1798

In the pursuit of her plan of universal empire, the two objects which now seem chiefly to occupy the attention of France are a new organization of Germany favorable to her influence and the demolition of Great Britain. The subversion and plunder, first of Portugal, next of Spain, will be merely collateral incidents in the great drama of iniquity.

In the new distribution of the territories, population, and political power of the Germanic body, which has been announced as in contemplation of the Directory, three characters are conspicuous—a disposition to build up rivals to the imperial chief, strong enough to feel the sentiment of competition but too weak to hazard it alone, who will therefore stand in need of the patronage of France, and as a consequence will facilitate her influence in the affairs of the empire—a generosity in making compensation, at the expense of others, for the spoils with which she has aggrandized herself—a facility in transferring communities, like herds of cattle, from one master to another, without the privilege of an option. In a project like this, it is impossible to overlook the plain indications of a restless, overbearing ambition, combined with a total disregard of the rights and wishes of nations. The people are counted for nothing, their masters for everything.

The conduct of France towards Great Britain is the copy of that of Rome towards Carthage. Its manifest aim is to destroy the principal obstacle to a domination over Europe. History proves that Great Britain has repeatedly upheld the balance of power there, in opposition to the grasping ambition of France. She has no doubt occasionally employed the pretense of danger as the instrument of her own ambition, but it is not the less true that she has been more than once an essential and an effectual shield against real danger. This was remarkably the case in the reign of Louis the XIVth, when the security of Europe was seriously threatened by the successful enterprises of that very ambitious monarch.

The course of the last negotiation between France and Britain leaves no doubt that the former was resolved against peace on any practicable terms. This of itself indicates that the destruction of the latter is the direct object in view. But this object is not left to inference. It has been fastidiously proclaimed to the world—and the necessity of crushing the TYRANT of the SEA has been trumpeted as a motive to other powers to acquiesce in the execution of a plan by which France endeavors to become the tyrant both of sea and land. The understanding of mankind has, at the same time, been mocked with the proposition that the peace of Europe would be secured by the aggrandizement of France on the ruins of her rivals; because then, it is said, having nothing to fear, she would have no motive to attack; as if moderation was to be expected from a government or people having the power to impose its own will without control. The peace of Europe would in such case be the peace of vassalage.

Towards the execution of the plan of destroying Great Britain, the rights of other nations are openly and daringly invaded. The confiscation is decreed of all vessels with their cargoes, if composed in any part of articles of British fabric; and all nations are to be compelled to shut their ports against the meditated victim. Hamburgh is stated to have already reluctantly yielded to this humiliating compulsion.

While the demolition of Great Britain is eagerly pursued as a primary object, that of Portugal seems designed to form an episode in the tragedy. Her fears had induced her to buy a peace. The money which she had paid was the immediate instrument of the revolution of September last—Yet no sooner had the news of pacification with the emperor reached Paris than pretenses were sought to elude the ratification of the purchased treaty. A larger tribute was demanded, more, probably, than it was expected Portugal would be able to pay, to serve as an excuse for marching an army to revolutionize and plunder.* The blow may perhaps be suspended by further sacrifices, but it is not likely to be finally averted.

Spain, too, was in a fair way of enjoying the fruits of her weakness in putting on the yoke of France and of furnishing another proof of the general scheme of aggrandizement and oppression. The demand of the cession of *Louisiana*, long pressed upon her, had at length become categoric. The alternative was to comply or offend. The probability is that before this time, the cession has been made and *Spain* has learnt, to her cost, that the chief privilege of an ally of France is to be plundered at discretion. With the acquisition of Louisiana, the foundation will be laid for stripping her of South America and her mines, and perhaps for dismembering the United States. The magnitude of this mighty mischief is not easy to be calculated.

Such vast projects and pretensions pursued by such unexampled means are full evidence of a plan to acquire an absolute ascendant among nations. The difficulties in the final execution of a plan of this kind are, with many, decisive reasons against its existence. But in the case of ancient Rome did it not in fact exist, and was it not substantially realized? Does the experience of the present day warrant the opinion that men are not as capable of mad and wicked projects as they were at any former period? Does not the conduct of the French government display a vastness and sublimation of views, and enormity of ambition, and a destitution of principle, which render the supposition of such a design probable? Has not a more rapid progress been made towards its execution than was ever made by Rome in an equal period? In their intercourse with foreign nations, do not the Directory affect an ostentatious imitation of Roman pride and superiority? Is it not natural to conclude that the same spirit points to the same ends?

* Such is the account of this transaction received through authentic channels.

The project is possible. The evidence of its existence is strong, and it will be the wisdom of every other state to act upon the supposition of its reality.

Let it be understood that the supposition does not imply the intention to reduce all other nations formally to the condition of provinces. This was not done by Rome in the zenith of her greatness. She had her provinces and she had her allies. But her allies were in fact her vassals. They obeyed her nod. Their princes were deposed and created at her pleasure.

Such is the proud preeminence to which the ambition of France aspires! After securing as much territory as she thinks it expedient immediately to govern, after wresting from Great Britain and attaching to herself the command of the sea, after despoiling Spain of the riches of Mexico and Peru, after attaining by all these means to a degree of strength sufficient to defy and awe competition, she may be content, under the modest denomination of allies, to rule the rest of the world by her frown or her smile.

The character of the actual Directory of France justifies the imputation to them of any project the most extravagant and criminal. Viewed internally, as well as externally, their conduct is alike detestable. They have overturned the constitution which they were appointed to administer with circumstances of barefaced guilt that disgrace a revolution, before so tarnished as seemed scarcely to admit of greater degradation; and have erected in its stead a military despotism, clothed but not disguised with the mere garb of the constitution which they have abolished. In the accomplishment of this usurpation, they have assassinated one of their colleagues* and seized and banished another, together with all those members of the two councils who were disposed and able to combat their pernicious aims. They have done more; not content with rendering themselves masters of the two councils, and converting them into the mere pageants of national representation, they have thought it proper to secure their own power by exiling or imprisoning such private citizens as they feared might promote the future election of men hostile to their views, on the futile pretense of a counterrevolutionary plot to be effected by *royalizing* the elections. Thus have they not only monopolized all the power for the present, but they have made provisions for its perpetuation, so long at least as the PRAETORIAN BANDS will permit.

No impartial man can doubt that the plot charged upon the exiled members is a forgery. The characters of several of the accused bely it. *Barthelemy* and *Pichegru* are virtuous men. The former has long merited and possessed this character. The latter has given numerous proofs of a good title to it—his only fault seems to have been that of enthusiasm in the worst of causes. Neither of them, like Dumourier, had been from his entrance on public life marked out as the votary of an irregular ambition. The alleged object of the plot, as to such men, from the circumstances of the conjuncture, was wholly improbable;

---

* Carnot—as was reported at the time, and as is confirmed by nothing having been since heard of him. He had been too deeply in the horrid secrets of the violent party. It was necessary to silence him.

nothing like satisfactory proof has come to light. But the decisive argument of their innocence is that the usurpers did not dare to confront them with a fair legal accusation and trial. It was so clearly their interest and policy to have justified themselves by establishing the guilt of the accused, if in their power, that the omission to attempt it is the demonstration of its impossibility. Having all authority in their own hands, and the army at their devotion, they had nothing to fear from the pursuit; and they must have foreseen that the banishment, without trial, would finally marshal public opinion against them. There can be little doubt that the people of France at this moment regard, with compassion and regret, the banished directors and deputies, and with horror and detestation the authors of their disgrace. But the people of France internally are annihilated. To their liberty and happiness this last usurpation gave a more fatal blow than any or all of the former. It has more of system in it, and being less sanguinary is less likely to provoke resistance from despair.

The inference from the transaction is evident. The real crime of the banished was the desire of arresting the mad career of the Directory and of restoring peace to France, in the hope that peace might tend to settle the government on the foundations of order, security, and tranquility. The majority of the Directory foresaw that peace would not prove an element congenial with the duration of their power; or perhaps under the guidance of Sieyes, the conjuror of the scene, they judged it expedient to continue in motion the revolutionary wheel till matters were better prepared for creating a new DYNASTY and a new ARISTOCRACY,* to regenerate the exploded monarchy of France with due regard to their own interest.

Thus we perceive that the interior conduct of the Directory has the same characters with their exterior—the same irregular ambition, the same contempt of principle, the same boldness of design, the same temerity of execution. From such men, what is not to be expected? The development of their recent conduct towards the United States will no doubt confirm all the inferences to be drawn from other parts of the portrait, and will contribute to prove that there is nothing too abandoned or too monstrous for them to meditate or attempt.

Who that loves his country or respects the dignity of his nature would not rather perish than subscribe to the prostration of both before such men and such a system? What sacrifice, what danger is too great to be incurred in opposition to both? What security in any compromise with such unprincipled tyranny? What safety but in union, in vigor, in preparation for every extremity, in a decisive and courageous stand for the rights and honor of our injured and insulted country?

Titus Manlius

---

* There is good evidence that this is at bottom the real plan of the Abbe Sieyes; and some of the most influential in the Executive Department are his creatures.

The Stand No. V,
April 16, 1798

To estimate properly the conduct of revolutionary France towards the United States the circumstances which have reciprocally taken place must be viewed together. It is a WHOLE, not a PART, which is to be contemplated. A rapid summary, nevertheless, of the most material is all that can be presented.

Not only the unanimous good wishes of the citizens of this country spontaneously attached themselves to the revolution of France in its first stages, but no sooner was the change from monarchy to a republic officially announced than our government, consulting the principles of our own revolution and the wishes of our citizens, hastened to acknowledge the new order of things. This was done to the last minister sent by Louis the XVI before the arrival of the first envoy from the republic. Genet afterwards came—his reception by the government was cordial, by the people enthusiastic.

The government did not merely receive the minister of the Republic, in fact, and defer the obligation of treaties till the contest concerning its establishment had been terminated by success: But giving the utmost latitude to the maxim that real treaties bind nations notwithstanding revolutions of government, ours did not hesitate to admit the immediate operations of the antecedent treaties between the two countries; though the revolution could not be regarded as yet fully accomplished; though a warrant for a contrary policy might have been found in the example of France herself; and though the treaties contained several stipulations which gave to her important preferences relative to war & which were likely to give umbrage to the powers coalesced against her.

In acknowledging the Republic, the U. States preceded every other nation. It was not till a long time after that any of the neutral powers followed the example. Had prudence been exclusively consulted, our government might not have done all that it did at this juncture, when the case was very nearly Europe in arms against France.

But good faith and a regard to consistency of principle prevailed over the sense of danger. It was resolved to encounter it, qualifying the step by the manifestation of a disposition to observe a sincere neutrality as far as should consist with the stipulations of treaty. Hence the proclamation of neutrality.

It ought to have no small merit in the eyes of France that at so critical a period of her affairs, we were willing to run risks so imminent. The fact is that it had nearly implicated us in the war on her side at a juncture when all calculations were against her, and when it was certain she could have afforded us no protection or assistance.

What was the return? *Genet* came with neutrality on his lips but war in his heart. The instructions published by himself and his practice upon them demonstrate that it was the premeditated plan to involve us in the contest not by a candid appeal to the judgment, friendship, or interest of our country but by alluring the avarice of bad citizens into acts of predatory hostility by instituting within our territory military expeditions against nations with whom we were at peace. And when it was found that our executive would not connive at this insidious plan, bold attempts were made to create a schism between the people and the government and consequently to sow the seeds of civil discord, insurrection, and revolution. Thus began the Republic.

It is true that the *Girondist* faction, having been subverted by that of Robespierre, our complaint of the agent of the former was attended with success. The spirit of vengeance came in aid of the justice of our demand. The offending minister was recalled with disgrace. But Robespierre did not fail in a public speech to give a gentle hint of delinquency in the United States, sufficiently indicating that the *authors* and the *manner* were more in fault in his opinion than the thing. It was not then expedient to quarrel with us. There was still a hope that a course of things, or more dextrous management, might embark us in the war as an auxiliary to France.

The treaties were made by us the criterion of our duty; but as they did not require us to go to war, as France did never even pretend this to be the case, listening to the suggestions not only of interest but of safety, we resolved to endeavor to preserve peace. But we were equally resolved to fulfill our real obligations in every respect. We saw without murmur our property seized in belligerent vessels; we allowed to French ships of war and privateers all the peculiar exclusive privileges in our ports to which they were entitled by our treaties upon fair construction, *upon a construction fully concurred in by the political leader* of the adherents to France*—we went further and gratuitously suffered her to sell her prizes in our country, in contravention perhaps of the true principles of neutrality—we paid to her new government the debt contracted by us with the old not only as fast as it became due, but by an anticipation which did not give pleasure to her enemies. While our government was faithful, our citizens were zealous. Not content with good wishes, they adventured their property and credit in the furnishing of supplies to an extent that showed in many cases the cooperation of zeal with interest. Our country, our merchants, and our ships in the gloomy periods of her revolution have been the organs of succors to France to a degree which give us an undoubted title to the character of very useful friends.

Reverse the medal. France from the beginning has violated essential points in the treaties between the two countries. The first formal *unequivocal* act by either of the belligerent parties interfering with the rule that "free ships make

* Mr. Jefferson.

free goods" was a decree of the French Convention. This violation has been persisted in and successive violations added till they amount to a general war on our commerce.

First the plea of necessity repelled our feeble and modest complaints of infractions. Next the plea of delinquencies on our part was called in aid of the depredations which it was found convenient to practice upon our trade. Our refusal to record privileges not granted by our treaties but claimed by misconstructions destitute even of plausibility, privileges which would have put us at once in a state of war with the enemies of France, the reciprocal application to them of principles originally established against their remonstrances in favor of France,* occasioned embarrassments to her privateers, arising from the established forms of our courts and the necessity of vigilance to frustrate her efforts to entangle us against our will in the war—delays in giving relief in a few instances rendered unavoidable by the nature of our government and the great extent of our territory—these were so many topics of bitter accusation against our government and of insult as rude as was unmerited. Our citizens, in judging whether the accusation was captious or well founded, ought to bear in mind that most of the transactions on which it was predicated happened under the administrations of *Jefferson* and *Randolph*, and, as is well ascertained, with their full assent & cooperation. They will not readily suppose that these *very cunning* men were the dupes of colleagues actuated by ill will towards France; but they will discover in this union of opinion among men of very opposite principles a strong probability that our government acted with propriety and that the dissatisfaction of France, if more than a color, was unreasonable.

Hitherto the progress no less than the origin of our controversy with France exhibits plain marks of a disposition on her part to disregard those provisions in the treaties which it was our interest should be observed by her, to exact from us a scrupulous performance of our engagements and even the extension of them beyond their true import—to embroil us with her enemies contrary to our inclination and interest and without even the allegation of a claim upon our faith—to make unreasonable demands upon us the grounds of complaints against us and excuses to violate our property and rights, to divide our nation and to disturb our government.

Many of the most determined advocates of France among us appear latterly to admit that previous to the treaty with Great Britain the complaints of France against the U. States were frivolous, those of the United States against France real and serious. But the treaty with G. Britain, it is affirmed, has changed the ground. This, it is said, has given just cause of discontent to France—this has brought us to the verge of war with our first ally and best friend—to this fatal instrument are we indebted for the evils we feel and the still greater which impend over our heads.

* This was the case as to the horses procured by the British in Virginia. France had before freely procured military supplies in our country. The British minister had remonstrated. The reply, adhered to, was that belligerent powers had a right to procure supplies in a neutral country.

These suggestions are without the shadow of foundation; they prove the infatuated devotion to a foreign power of those who invented them and the easy credulity of those with whom they have obtained currency. The evidence of a previous disposition in France to complain without cause and to injure without provocation is a sufficient comment upon the resentment she professes against the treaty. The partiality or indulgence with which the ill treatment received from her prior to that event was viewed by her decided partisans is a proof of the facility with which they credit her pretenses and palliate her aggressions.

The most significant of the charges against the treaty, as it respects France, is that it abandoned the rule of free ships making free goods—that it extended unduly the list of contraband articles and gave color to the claim of a right to subject provisions to seizure—that a treaty of amity with the enemy of France in the midst of a war was a mark of preference to that enemy and of ill will to her. The replies which have been given to these charges are conclusive.

As to the first point—The stipulation of two powers to observe between themselves a particular rule in their respective wars, a rule too innovating upon the general law of nations, can on no known or reasonable principle of interpretation be construed to intend that they will insist upon that rule with all other nations, and will make no treaty with any, however beneficial in other respects, which does not comprehend it. To tie up the will of a nation and its power of providing for its own interests to so immense an extent required a stipulation in positive terms. In vain shall we seek in the treaty for such a stipulation or its equivalent. There is not even a single expression to imply it. The idea is consequently no less ridiculous than it is novel. The contemporary proceedings, legislative and judiciary, of our government show that it was not so understood in this country. Congress even declined to become a formal party to the armed neutrality of which it was the basis, unwilling to be pledged for the coercive maintenance of a principle which they were only disposed to promote by particular pacts. It is equally futile to seek to derive the obligation of the U. States to adhere to this rule from the supposition of a change in the law of nations by the force of that league. Neither theory nor practice warrants the attributing so important an effect to a military association springing up in the war and ending with it, not having had the universal consent of nations nor a course of long practice to give it a sanction.

Were it necessary to resort to an auxiliary argument, it might be said with conclusive force that France, having before our treaty with Great Britain violated in practice the rule in question, absolved us from all obligation to observe it, if any did previously exist.

As to the second point—it has been repeatedly demonstrated that the enumeration of contraband in the treaty with Great Britain is agreeable to the *general* law of nations. But this is a matter from its nature liable to vary according to relative situation, and to be variously modified not only between different nations but between one nation and different nations. Thus in our treaty with Great Britain some articles are enumerated which are omitted in that with France; in that with France some articles are inserted which are omitted in that with Britain. But it is perhaps the first time that a diversity of this sort has been deemed a ground of umbrage to a third party.

With regard to provisions, the treaty only decides that where *by the law of nations* they are subject to seizure, they are to be paid for. It does not define or admit any new case. As to its giving color to abuse in this respect, this if true would amount to nothing. For till some abuse has actually happened and been tolerated to the prejudice of France there was no cause of complaint. The possibility of abuse from a doubtful construction of a treaty between two powers is no subject of offence to a third. It is the fact which must govern. According to this indisputable criterion, France has had no cause to complain on this account; for since the ratification of the treaty no instance of the seizure of provisions has occurred, & it is known that our government protested against such a construction.

Further, the treaty has made no change whatever in the actual antecedent state of things to the disadvantage of France.

Great Britain had before the treaty with the sanction of our government acted upon the principles as to free ships making free goods and generally as to the affair of contraband which the treaty recognizes. Nor was that sanction merely tacit but explicit and direct. It was even diplomatically communicated to the agents of France. If there was anything wrong therefore in this matter, it was chargeable, not upon the treaty, but upon the prior measures of the government, which had left these points mere points of form in the treaty.

The remaining charge against that instrument involves a species of political metaphysics. Neither the theory of writers nor the history of nations will bear out the position that a treaty of amity, between a neutral state and one belligerent party, not granting either succors or new privileges relative to war, not derogating from any obligation of the neutral state to the other belligerent party, is a cause of umbrage to the latter. There can be no reason why a neutral power should not settle differences or adjust a plan of intercourse beneficial to itself with another power because this last happens to be at war with a third. All this must be a mere question of courtesy, and might be uncourteous or otherwise according to circumstances, but never a ground of quarrel. If there even might have been want of courtesy in the U. States to have entered into a treaty of this sort with the enemy of France, had they volunteered it without cogent motives—there could be none in the particular situation. They were led to the treaty by preexisting differences which had nearly ripened to a rupture and the amicable settlement of which affected very important interests. No favorable conjunction for this settlement was to be lost. The settlement, by the usual formulas in such cases, would amount to a treaty of amity.

Thus is it evident that the treaty, like all the rest, has been a mere pretense for ill treatment. But admitting that this was not the case, that it really afforded some cause of displeasure, was this of a nature to admit of no atonement, or of none short of the humiliation of our country?

If the contrary must be conceded, it is certain that our government has done all that was possible towards reconciliation, and enough to have satisfied any reasonable or just government.

France after the treaty proceeded to inflict still deeper wounds upon our commerce. She has endeavored to intercept and destroy it with all the ports of her enemies. Nor was this the worst. The spoliation has frequently extended to our trade with her own dominions, attended with unparalleled circumstances of rapacity and violence.

The diplomatic representative of the French government to the U. States was ordered to deliver to our government a most insulting manifesto and then to withdraw.

Yet our government, notwithstanding this accumulation of wrongs, after knowing that it had been repeatedly outraged in the person of one minister, condescended to send another specially charged to endeavor to conciliate. This minister was known to unite fidelity to his country with principles friendly to France and her revolution. It was hoped that the latter would make him acceptable and that he would be able by amicable explanations and overtures to obviate misunderstanding and restore harmony. He was not received.

Though it was very problematical whether the honor of the U. States after this permitted a further advance, yet the government, anxious if possible to preserve peace, concluded to make another and more solemn experiment. A new mission, confided to three extraordinary ministers, took place. They were all three in different degrees men well affected to France and her revolution. They were all men of high respectability and among the purest characters of our country. Their powers and instructions were so ample as to have extorted from the most determined opposers of the government, in the two houses of Congress, a reluctant approbation in this instance of the president's conduct.

In contempt of established usage and of the respect due to us as an independent people, with the deliberate design of humbling and mortifying our government, these special and extraordinary ministers have been refused to be received. Admitting all the charges brought against us by France to be well founded, still ministers of that description ought on every principle to have been accredited and conferred with, 'till it was ascertained that they were not ready to do as much as was expected. Not to pursue this course was to deny us the rank of an independent nation; it was to treat us as Great Britain did while we were yet contending with her for this character.

Instead of this, informal agents, probably panders and mistresses, are appointed to intrigue with our envoys. These, attending only to the earnest wish of their constituents for peace, stoop to the conference. What is the misshapen result?

MONEY, MONEY is the burden of the discordant song of these foul birds of prey. Great indignation is at first professed against expressions in the president's speech of May last. The reparation of a disavowal is absolutely due to the honor of the Directory and of the republic; but it turns out that there is a practicable substitute more valuable. The honor of both being a marketable commodity—is ready to be committed for gold.

A douceur of 50,000 pounds sterling for the special benefit of the Directory was to pave the way. Instead of reparation for the spoliations of our commerce exceeding twenty millions of dollars, a loan equal to the amount of them is to be made by us to the French government. Then perhaps a mode might be settled for the liquidation of the claims of our merchants to be compensated at some future period. The depredations nevertheless were to continue till the treaty should be concluded, which from the distance between the two countries must at all events take a great length of time, and might be procrastinated indefinitely at the pleasure of the Directory.

In addition to all this we must purchase of the Directory at par Dutch inscriptions to the amount of thirty-two millions of florins and look to the ability of the Batavian Republic to redeem them. Already are these assignats depreciated to half their nominal value and in all probability will come to nothing, serving merely as a flimsy veil to the extortion of a further & immense contribution.

"Money, a great deal of money"* is the cry from the first to last; and our commissioners are assured that without this they may stay in Paris six months without advancing a step. To enforce the argument they are reminded of the fate of Venice.

At so hideous a compound of corruption and extortion, at demands so exorbitant and degrading, there is not a spark of virtuous indignation in an American breast which will not kindle into a flame. And yet there are men—could it have been believed? There are men to whom this country gave birth—vile and degenerate enough to run about the streets to contradict, to palliate, to justify, to preach the expediency of compliance. Such men merit all the detestation of all their fellow citizens; and there is no doubt that with time and opportunity they will merit much more from the offended justice of the laws.

T.M.

* "Il faut de l'argent—il faut beaucoup d'argent."

The Stand No. VI,
April 19, 1798

The inevitable conclusion from the facts which have been presented is that revolutionary France has been and continues to be governed by a spirit of proselytism, conquest, domination, and rapine. The detail well justifies the position that we may have to contend at our very doors for our independence and liberty.

When the wonders achieved by the arms of France are duly considered, the possibility of the overthrow of Great Britain seems not to be chimerical. If by any of those extraordinary coincidences of circumstances, which occasionally decide the fate of empires, the meditated expedition against England shall succeed, or if by the immense expense to which that country is driven and the derangement of her commerce by the powerful means employed to that end, her affairs shall be thrown into such disorder as may enable France to dictate to her the terms of peace; in either of these unfortunate events the probability is that the U. States will have to choose between the surrender of their sovereignty, the new modeling of their government according to the fancy of the Directory, the emptying of their wealth by contributions into the coffers of the greedy and insatiable monster—and resistance to invasion in order to compel submission to those ruinous conditions.

In opposition to this, it is suggested that the interest of France concurring with the difficulty of execution is a safeguard against the enterprise. It is asked what incentives sufficiently potent can stimulate to so unpromising an attempt?

The answer is—the strongest passions of bad hearts—inordinate ambition, the love of domination, that prime characteristic of the despots of France—the spirit of vengeance for the presumption of having thought and acted for ourselves, a spirit which has marked every step of the revolutionary leaders—the fanatical egotism of obliging the rest of the world to adapt their political system to the French standard of perfection—the desire of securing the future control of our affairs by humbling and ruining the independent supporters of their country and of elevating the partisans and tools of France—the desire of entangling our commerce with preferences and restrictions which would give to her the monopoly—these passions the most imperious, these motives the most enticing to a crooked policy, are sufficient persuasives to undertake the subjugation of this country.

Added to these primary inducements, the desire of finding an outlet for a part of the vast armies which on the termination of the European war are likely to perplex and endanger the men in power would be an auxiliary motive of great force. The total loss of the troops sent would be no loss to France. Their cupidity would be readily excited to the undertaking by the prospect of dividing among themselves the fertile lands of this country. Great Britain once silenced, there would be no insuperable obstacle to the transportation. The divisions among us, which have been urged to our commissioners as one motive to a compliance with the unreasonable demands of the Directory, would be equally an encouragement to invasion. It would be believed that a sufficient number would flock to the standard of France to render it easy to quell the resistance of the rest. Drunk with success, nothing would be thought too arduous to be accomplished.

It is too much a part of our temper to indulge an overweening security. At the close of our revolution war the phantom of perpetual peace danced before the eyes of everybody. We see at this early period with how much difficulty war has been parried and that with all our efforts to preserve peace we are now in a state of partial hostility. Untaught by this experience, we now seem inclined to regard the idea of invasion as incredible and to regulate our conduct by the belief of its improbability. Who would have thought eighteen months ago that Great Britain would have been at this time in serious danger of invasion from France? Is it not now more probable that such a danger may overtake us than it was then that it would so soon assail G.B.?

There are currents in human affairs when events at other times no[7] less than miraculous are to be considered as natural and simple. Such were the eras of Macedonian, of Roman, of Gothic, of Saracen inundation. Such is the present era of French fanaticism. Wise men, when they discover the symptoms of a similar era, look for prodigies and prepare for them with foresight and energy.

Admit that in our case invasion is upon the whole improbable; yet if there are any circumstances which pronounce that the apprehension of it is not absolutely chimerical, it is the part of wisdom to act as if it was likely to happen. What are the inconveniences of preparation compared with the infinite magnitude of the evil if it shall surprise us unprepared? They are lighter than air weighed against the smallest probability of so disastrous a result.

But what is to be done? Is it not wiser to compound on any terms than to provoke the consequences of resistance?

To do this is dishonor—it is ruin—it is death. Waiving other considerations there can be no reliance on its efficacy. The example of Portugal teaches us that it is to purchase disgrace, not safety. The cravings of despotic rapacity may be appeased but they are not to be satisfied. They will quickly renew their fires and call for new sacrifices in proportion to the facility with which the first were made. The situation of France is likely to make plunder for a considerable time to come an indispensable expedient of government. Excluding the great considerations of public right and public policy, and bringing the matter to the simple test of pecuniary calculation, resistance is to be preferred to submission. The surrender of our whole wealth would only procure respite, not safety. The disbursements for war will chiefly be at home. They will not necessarily carry away our riches, and they will preserve our honor and give us security.

But in the event supposed, can we oppose with success? There is no event in which we may not look with confidence to a successful resistance. Though G. Britain should be impolitic or wicked enough (which is hoped to be impossible) to compromise her differences with France by an agreement to divide the U. States, according to the insulting threat of the agents of France, still it is in our power to maintain our independence and baffle every enemy. The people of the U. States from their number, situation, and resources are invincible if they are provident and faithful to themselves.

The question returns—what is to be done? Shall we declare war? No—there are still chances for avoiding a general rupture which ought to be taken. Want of future success may bring the present despots to reason. Every day may produce a revolution which may substitute better men in their place and lead to honorable accommodation.

Our true policy is, in the attitude of calm defiance, to meet the aggressions upon us by proportionate resistance, and to prepare vigorously for further resistance. To this end, the chief measures requisite are to invigorate our treasury by calling into activity the principal untouched resources of revenue—to fortify in earnest our chief seaports—to establish foundries and increase our arsenals—to create a respectable naval force and to raise with the utmost diligence a considerable army. Our merchant vessels ought to be permitted not only to arm themselves but to sink or capture their assailants. Our vessels of war ought to cruise on our coast and serve as convoys to our trade. In doing this, they also ought to be authorized not only to sink or capture assailants, but likewise to capture & bring in privateers found hovering within twenty leagues of our coast. For this last measure, precedent if requisite is to be found in the conduct of neutral powers on other occasions.

This course, it will be objected, implies a state of war. Let it be so. But it will be a limited and mitigated state of war, to grow into general war or not at the election of France. What may be that election will probably depend on future and incalculable events. The continuation of success on the part of France would insure war. The want of it might facilitate accommodation. There are examples in which states have been for a long time in a state of partial hostility without proceeding to general rupture. The duration of this course of conduct on our part may be restricted to the continuance of the two last decrees of France, that by which the trade of neutrals with the ports of her enemies has been intercepted, and that by which vessels and their cargoes, if composed in whole or in part of British fabrics, are liable to seizure and condemnation.

The declared suspension of our treaties with France is a measure of evident justice and necessity. It is the natural consequence of a total violation on one side. It would be preposterous to be fettered by treaties which are wholly disregarded by the other party. It is essentially our interest to get rid of the guarantee in the treaty of alliance, which on the part of France is likely to be henceforth nugatory; on the part of the U. States it is a substantial and dangerous stipulation; obliging them in good faith to take part with France in any future defensive war in which her West India colonies may be attacked. The consular convention is likewise a mischievous instrument devised by France in the spirit of extending her influence into other countries and producing to a certain extent *imperium in imperio*.

It may be happy for the U. States that an occasion has been furnished by France in which with good faith they may break through these trammels, readjusting when reconciliation shall take place a basis of connection or intercourse more convenient and more eligible.

The resolution to raise an army, it is to be feared, is that one of the measures suggested which will meet with greatest obstacle; and yet it is the one which ought most to unite opinion. Being merely a precaution for internal security, it can in no sense tend to provoke war, and looking to eventual security in a case which if it should happen would threaten our very existence as a nation, it is the most important.

The history of our revolution war is a serious admonition to it. The American cause had nearly been lost for want of creating in the first instance a solid force commensurate in duration with the war. Immense additional expense and waste and a variety of other evils were incurred which might have been avoided.

Suppose an invasion, & that we are left to depend on militia alone. Can it be doubted that a rapid and formidable progress would in the first instance be made by the invader? Who can answer what dismay this might inspire—how far it might go to create general panic—to rally under the banners of the enemy the false and the timid? The imagination cannot without alarm anticipate the consequences. Prudence commands that they shall be guarded against. To have a good army on foot will be best of all precautions to prevent as well as to repel invasion.

The propriety of the measure is so palpable that it will argue treachery or incapacity in our councils if it be not adopted. The friends of the government owe it to their own characters to press it; its opposers can give no better proof that they are not abandoned to a foreign power than to concur in it. The public safety will be more indebted to its advocates than to the advocates of any other measure, in proportion as our independence & liberty are of more consequence than our trade.

It is the fervent wish of patriotism that our councils and nation may be united and resolute. The dearest interests call for it. A great public danger commands it. Every good man will rejoice to embrace the adversary of his former opinions if he will now by candor and energy evince his attachment to his country. Whoever does not do this consigns himself to irrevocable dishonor. But 'tis not the triumph over a political rival which the true lover of his country desires—'tis the safety, 'tis the welfare of that country—and he will gladly share with his bitterest opponent the glory of defending and preserving her. Americans! rouse! Be unanimous, be virtuous, be firm, exert your courage, trust in heaven, and nobly defy the enemies both of god and man!

T.M.

The Stand No. VII,
April 21, 1798

The dispatches from our envoys have at length made their appearance. They present a picture of the French government exceeding in turpitude whatever was anticipated from the previous intimations of their contents. It was natural to expect that the perusal of them would have inspired a universal sentiment of indignation and disgust, and that no man calling himself an American would have had the hardihood to defend, or even to palliate, a conduct so atrocious. But it is already apparent that an expectation of this kind would not have been well founded.

There are strong symptoms that the men in power in France understand better than ourselves the true character of their faction in this country, at least of its leaders; and that as to these, the agents who conferred with our envoys were not mistaken in predicting that the unreasonableness of the demands upon us would not serve to detach the party from France, or to reunite them to their own country. The high-priest of this sect, with a tender regard for the honor of the immaculate Directory, has already imagined several ingenious distinctions to rescue them from the odium and corruption unfolded by the dispatches.[8] Among these is the suggestion that there is no proof of the privity of the Directory—all may have been the mere contrivance of the minister for foreign relations.

The presumption from so miserable a subterfuge is that had the propositions proceeded immediately from the Directory, the cry from the same quarter would have been—there is no evidence that the councils or nation approved of them; they at least are not implicated; the friendship of the two republics ought not to be disturbed on account of the villainy of the transitory and fugitive organs of one of them. The inventor of the subterfuge, however, well knew that the executive organ of a nation never comes forward in person to negotiate with foreign ministers; and that unless it be presumed to direct and adopt what is done by its agents, it may always be sheltered from responsibility or blame. The recourse to so pitiful an evasion betrays in its author a systematic design to excuse France at all events—to soften a spirit of submission to every violence she may commit—and to prepare the way for implicit subjection to her will. To be the proconsul of a despotic Directory over the United States, degraded to the condition of a province, can alone be the criminal, the ignoble aim of so seditious, so prostitute a character.

The subaltern mercenaries go still farther. Publications have appeared endeavoring to justify or extenuate the demands upon our envoys and to inculcate the slavish doctrine of compliance. The United States, it is said, are the aggressors and ought to make atonement; France assisted them in their revolution with loans, and they ought to reciprocate the benefit; peace is a boon worth the price required for it, and it ought to be paid. In this motley form, our country is urged to sink voluntarily, and without a struggle, to a state of tributary vassalage. Americans are found audacious and mean enough to join in the chorus of a foreign nation, which calls upon us to barter our independence for a respite from the lash.

The charge of aggression upon the United States is false; and if true, the reparation, from the nature of the case, ought not to be pecuniary. This species of indemnification between nations is only proper where there has been pecuniary injury.

The loans received by us from France were asked as a favor, on the condition of reimbursement by the United States, and were freely granted for a purpose of mutual advantage. The advances to be made by us were exacted as the price of peace. Though in name loans, they would be in fact contributions by the coercion of a power which has already wrested from our citizens an immense property, for which it owes to them compensation.

To pay such a price for peace is to prefer peace to independence. The nation which becomes tributary takes a master.* Peace is doubtless precious, but it is a bauble compared with national independence, which includes national liberty. The evils of war to resist such a precedent are insignificant compared with the evil of the precedent. Besides that there could be no possible security for the enjoyment of the object for which the disgraceful sacrifice was made.

To disguise the poison, misrepresentation is combined with sophistry. It is alleged that finally no more was asked than that the United States should purchase sixteen millions of Dutch inscriptions, and that by doing this they would have secured compensation to their citizens for depredations on their trade to four times the amount, with an intermission of the depredations; that no hazard of ultimate loss could have attended the operation, because the United States owed the Dutch a much larger sum which would be a pledge for payment or discount.

This is a palpable attempt to deceive. The first propositions were such as to have been represented in a former paper; but it appears in the sequel that the French agents, seeing the inflexible opposition of our envoys to their plan, and hoping to extort finally a considerable sum, though less than at first contemplated, relaxed so far in their demands as to narrow them down to the payment of a douceur of twelve hundred thousand livres with a positive engagement to advance to the French government a sum equal to the amount of the spoliations

---

* The argument of what has been done in the cases of *Algerines* and *Indians* has nothing pertinent but in the comparison of relative ferocity. In this view, the claim of the Directory is indisputable—but in every other it is preposterous. It is the general practice of civilized nations to pay barbarians—there is no point of honor to the contrary. But as between civilized nations, the payment of tribute by one to another is by the common opinion of mankind a badge of servitude.

of our trade, and a further engagement to send to our government for power to purchase of France thirty two millions of the inscriptions (12,800,000 dollars) in return for all which our envoys were to be permitted to remain six months in Paris, depredations on our trade during that time were to be suspended, and a commission of five persons was to be appointed to liquidate the claims for past depredations, which were to be satisfied "in a *time* and *manner* to be agreed upon." The substance of these demands is to pay immediately twelve hundred thousand livres and to bind ourselves to pay absolutely twenty millions of dollars more (the estimated amount of the spoliations) for what?—barely for the acknowledgement of a debt to our citizens, which without it is not the less due, and for a suspension of *hostilities** for six months.

Afterwards, in a conversation between the French minister himself and one of our envoys, the propositions assumed still another form. The United States were required to purchase of France at par sixteen millions of inscriptions, and to promise *further aid when in their power*. This *arrangement being first made* and not before, France was to take measures for reimbursing the equitable demands of our citizens on account of captures.

The purchase of the inscriptions was to be preliminary. The arrangement for reimbursing our merchants was to follow. The nature of it was not explained, but it is to be inferred from all that preceded that the expedient of the advance of an equal sum by the United States would have been pressed as the basis of the promised arrangement.

This last proposal was in its principle as bad as either of the former, its tendency worse. The promise of future assistance would have carried with it the privilege to repeat at pleasure the demand of money, and to dispute with us about our ability to supply; and it would have immediately embarked us as an *associate* with France in the war. It was to promise her the most effectual aid in our power, and that of which she stood most in need.

The scheme of concealment was a trick. The interest of France to engage us in the war against Great Britain, as a mean of wounding her commerce, is too strong to have permitted the secret to be kept by her. By the ratification of the treaty, in which the Senate must have concurred, too many would have obtained possession of the secret to allow it to remain one. While it did, the apprehension of discovery would have enabled France to use it as an engine of unlimited extortion. But a still greater objection is that it would have been infamous in the United States thus covertly to relinquish their neutrality, and with equal cowardice and hypocrisy to wear the mask of it, when they had renounced the reality.

The idea of securing our advances by means of the debt which we owe to the Dutch is without foundation. The creditors of the United States are the *private citizens* of the Batavian republic. Their demands could not be opposed by a claim of our government upon their government. The only shape in which it

---

* It is observable that the French give themselves the denomination of *hostilities* to their depredations upon us. Our Jacobins would have us consider them as gentle caresses.

could be attempted must be in that of reprisals for the delinquency of the government. But this would not only be a gross violation of principle—it would be contrary to *express* stipulations in the contracts for the loans.*

In the same spirit of deception, it has also been alleged that our envoys, by giving the douceur of twelve hundred thousand livres and agreeing to send for powers to make a loan, might have obtained a suspension of depredations for six months. There is not a syllable in the dispatches to countenance this assertion. A large advance in addition, either on the basis of the spoliations or by way of purchase of the inscriptions, is uniformly made the condition of suspending hostilities.

Glosses so false and insidious as these, in a crisis of such imminent public danger, to mislead the opinion of our nation concerning the conduct and views of a foreign enemy, are shoots from a very pernicious trunk. Opportunity alone is wanting to unveil the treason which lurks at the core.

What signifies the quantum of the contribution, had it been really as unimportant as is represented? 'Tis the principle which is to be resisted at every hazard. 'Tis the pretension to make us tributary, in opposition to which every American ought to resign the last drop of his blood.

The pratings of the Gallic faction at this time remind us of those of the British faction at the commencement of our revolution. The insignificance of a duty of three pence per pound on tea was echoed and re-echoed as the bait to an admission of the right to bind us in all cases whatsoever.

The tools of France incessantly clamor against the treaty with Britain as the just cause of the resentment of France. It is curious to remark that in the conferences with our envoys this treaty was never once mentioned by the French agents. Particular passages in the speech of the president are alone specified as a ground of dissatisfaction. This is at once a specimen of the fruitful versatility with which causes of complaint are contrived, and of the very slight foundations on which they are adopted. A temperate expression of sensibility at an outrageous indignity, offered to our government by a member of the Directory, is converted into a mortal offence. The tyrants will not endure a murmur at the blows they inflict.

But the dispatches of our envoys, while they do not sanction the charge preferred by the Gallic faction against the treaty, confirm a very serious charge which the friends of the government bring against that faction. They prove, by the unreserved confession of her agents, that France places absolute dependence on this party in every event, and counts upon their devotion to her as an encouragement to the hard conditions which they attempt to impose. The people of this country must be infatuated indeed, if after this plain confession they are at a loss for the true source of the evils they have suffered or may hereafter suffer from the despots of France. 'Tis the unnatural league of a portion of our citizens with the oppressors of their country.

Titus Manlius

---

* They all provide against seizure or sequestration by way of reprisals, &c.

Letter to George Washington, May 19, 1798

My Dear Sir,

At the present dangerous crisis of public affairs, I make no apology for troubling you with a political letter. Your impressions of our situation, I am persuaded, are not different from mine. There is certainly great probability that we may have to enter into a very serious struggle with France, and it is more and more evident that the powerful faction which has for years opposed the government is determined to go every length with France. I am sincere in declaring my full conviction, as the result of a long course of observation, that they are ready to *new model* our constitution under the *influence* or *coercion* of France—to form with her a perpetual alliance *offensive* and *defensive*—and to give her a monopoly of our trade by *peculiar* and *exclusive* privileges. This would be in substance, whatever it might be in name, to make this country a province of France. Neither do I doubt that her standard displayed in this country would be directly or indirectly seconded by them in pursuance of the project I have mentioned.

It is painful and alarming to remark that the opposition faction assumes so much a geographical complexion. As yet from the south of Maryland nothing has been heard but accents of disapprobation of our government and approbation of or apology for France. This is a most portentous symptom & demands every human effort to change it.

In such a state of public affairs it is impossible not to look up to you, and to wish that your influence could in some proper mode be brought into direct action. Among the ideas which have passed through my mind for this purpose—I have asked myself whether it might not be expedient for you to make a circuit through Virginia and North Carolina under some pretense of health &c. This would call forth addresses, public dinners, &c., which would give you an opportunity of expressing sentiments in answers, toasts &c., which would throw the weight of your character into the scale of the government and revive an enthusiasm for your person that may be turned into the right channel.

I am aware that the step is delicate & ought to be well considered before it is taken. I have even not settled my own opinion as to its propriety—but I have concluded to bring the general idea under your view, confident that your judgment will make a right choice and that you will take no step which is not well calculated. The conjuncture, however, is extraordinary & now or very soon will demand extraordinary measures.

You ought also to be aware, My Dear Sir, that in the event of an open rupture with France, the public voice will again call you to command the armies of your country; and though all who are attached to you will from attachment, as well as public considerations, deplore an occasion which should once more tear you from that repose to which you have so good a right—yet it is the opinion of all those with whom I converse that you will be compelled to make the sacrifice. All your past labor may demand to give it efficacy this further, this very great sacrifice.

Adieu My Dear Sir   Respectfully & Affecly Yr very obed servt
A. Hamilton

Letter to George Washington, June 2, 1798

My Dear Sir,

I have before me your favor of the 27th of May.

The suggestion in my last was an indigested thought begotten by my anxiety. I have no doubt that your view of it is accurate & well founded.

It is a great satisfaction to me to ascertain what I had anticipated in hope, that you are not determined in an *adequate emergency* against affording once more your military services. There is no one but yourself that could unite the public confidence in such an emergency, independent of other considerations—and it is of the last importance that this confidence should be *full* and *complete*. As to the wish of the country it is certain that it will be *ardent* and *universal*. You intimate a desire to be informed what would be my part in such an event as to entering into military service. I have no scruple about opening myself to you on this point. If I am invited *to a station in which the service I may render may be proportioned to the sacrifice I am to make*—I shall be willing to go into the army. If you command, the place in which I should hope to be most useful is that of Inspector General with a command in the line. This I would accept. The public must judge for itself as to whom it will employ; but every individual must judge for himself as to the terms on which he will serve and consequently must estimate himself his own pretensions. I have no knowledge of any arrangement contemplated, but I take it for granted the services of all the former officers worth having may be commanded & that your choice would regulate the executive. With decision & care in selection, an excellent army may be formed.

The view you give of the prospects in the south is very consoling. The public temper seems everywhere to be travelling fast to a right point. This promises security to the country in every event.

> I have the honor to remain very truly My Dr. Sir
> Yr. faithful & Affectionate servant
> A. Hamilton

Letter to Oliver Wolcott, Jr., June 29, 1798

Dear Sir,

I have this moment seen a bill brought into the Senate entitled a Bill to define more particularly the crime of Treason &c. There are provisions in this bill which according to a cursory view appear to me highly exceptionable & such as more than anything else may endanger civil war. I have not time to point out my objections by this post but I will do it tomorrow. I hope sincerely the thing may not be hurried through. Let us not establish a tyranny. Energy is a very different thing from violence. If we make no false step we shall be essentially united, but if we push things to an extreme we shall then give to faction *body* & solidarity.

Yrs. truly
A Hamilton

Excerpt from a Letter to Stephen Van Rensselaer, January 27, 1799

As to an insolvent law, these are my ideas. There is a serious doubt whether any such law, passed by a legislature subsequent to the adoption of the Constitution of the U. States, will not be an infringement of that article which forbids a state to pass "any law impairing the obligation of contracts." I think it the better opinion that it will. What way so effectual to impair the obligation of a contract as to defeat the means which the established laws allow for its enforcement? In the eye of a human forum, the essence of the obligation of a contract consists in the sanctions by which it is carried into execution; by which, as between debtor & creditor, the former can obtain a satisfaction, whether by exertion of the person or property of the debtor.

This difficulty out of the way I should feel no great objection to a law like the following—

Providing that after a debtor shall have been imprisoned by his creditor upon execution for a term of five years, it shall be in the discretion of commissioners to examine into the circumstances of the case, and to liberate the debtor from imprisonment, upon the condition, however, of a surrender of all the property he has & leaving all he may acquire afterwards to be subject to the demands of his creditors—in order to which the debtor to account every five years on oath before the commissioners for whatever surplus he may have acquired, they to direct what dividend shall be made among the creditors and to permit him to retain from time to time so much as they may think expedient for carrying on whatever business he may be engaged in, having regard to the interest of his creditors. His liberty also, so long as he shall be called to account to be exempt from execution, the same as before his insolvency.

The commissioners to be selected and designated by the Council of Appointment with competent allowances. These may arise from fees.

Letter to Theodore Sedgwick, February 2, 1799

What, My Dear Sir, are you going to do with Virginia? This is a very serious business, which will call for all the wisdom and firmness of the government. The following are the ideas which occur to me on the occasion.

The first thing in all great operations of such a government as ours is to secure the opinion of the people. To this end, the proceedings of Virginia and Kentucky with the two laws complained of should be referred to a special committee. That committee should make a report exhibiting with great luminousness and particularity the reasons which support the constitutionality and expediency of those laws—the tendency of the doctrines advanced by Virginia and Kentucky to destroy the Constitution of the U. States—and, with calm dignity united with pathos, the full evidence which they afford of a regular conspiracy to overturn the government. And the report should likewise dwell upon the inevitable effect, and probably the intention, of these proceedings to encourage a hostile foreign power to decline accommodation and proceed in hostility. The government must not merely defend itself but must attack and arraign its enemies. But in all this, there should be great care to distinguish the people of Virginia from the legislature, and even the greater part of those who may have concurred in the legislature from the chiefs; manifesting indeed a strong confidence in the good sense and patriotism of the people, that they will not be the dupes of an insidious plan to disunite the people of America, to break down their Constitution & expose them to the enterprises of a foreign power.

This report should conclude with a declaration that there is no cause for a repeal of the laws. If, however, on examination any modifications consistent with the general design of the laws, but instituting better guards, can be devised, it may be well to propose them as a bridge for those who may incline to retreat over. Concessions of this kind adroitly made have a good rather than a bad effect. On a recent though hasty revision of the Alien law, it seems to me deficient in precautions against abuse and for the security of citizens. This should not be.

No pains or expense should be spared to disseminate this report. A little pamphlet containing it should find its way into every house in Virginia.

This should be left to work and nothing to court a shock should be adopted.

In the meantime the measures for raising the military force should proceed with activity. 'Tis much to be lamented that so much delay has attended the execution of this measure. In times like the present, not a moment ought to have been lost to secure the government so powerful an auxiliary. Whenever the experiment shall be made to subdue a refractory & powerful state by militia, the event will shame the advocates of their sufficiency. In the expedition against the western insurgents, I trembled every moment lest a great part of the militia should take it into their heads to return home rather than go forward.

When a clever force has been collected, let them be drawn towards Virginia, for which there is an obvious pretext—& then let measures be taken to act upon the laws & put Virginia to the test of resistance.

This plan will give time for the fervor of the moment to subside, for reason to resume the reins, and by dividing its enemies will enable the government to triumph with ease.

As an auxiliary measure, it is very desirable that the Provisional Army Bill should pass & that the executive should proceed to the appointment of the officers. The tendency of this needs no comment.

Yrs. affecy
A. Hamilton

Letter to Timothy Pickering, February 21, 1799

My Dear Sir,

The multiplicity of my avocations, joined to imperfect health, has delayed the communication you desired respecting St. Domingo. And what is worse, it has prevented my bestowing sufficient thought to offer at present anything worth having.

No regular system of liberty will, at present, suit St. Domingo. The government, if independent, must be military—partaking of the feudal system.

A hereditary chief would be best, but this I fear is impracticable.

Let there be then—

A single executive to hold his place for life.

The person to succeed on a vacancy to be either the officer *next in command in the island at the time of the death* of the predecessor, or the person who by plurality of voices of the commandants of regiments shall be designated within a certain time. In the meantime, the principal military officers to administer.

All the males within certain ages to be arranged in military corps and to be compellable to military service. This may be connected with the tenure of lands.

Let the supreme judiciary authority be vested in twelve judges to be chosen for life by the *generals* or chief military officers.

Trial by jury in all criminal causes not military to be established. The mode of appointing them must be regulated with reference to the general spirit of the establishment.

Every law inflicting capital or other corporal punishment, or levying a tax or contribution in any shape, to be proposed by the executive to an Assembly composed of the generals & commandants of regiments for their sanction or rejection.

All other laws to be enacted by the sole authority of the executive.

The powers of war & treaty to be in the executive.

The executive to be obliged to have three ministers—of finance, war, & foreign affairs—whom he shall nominate to the generals for their approbation or rejection.

The colonels & generals, when once appointed, to hold their offices during good behavior, removeable only by conviction of an infamous crime in due course of law or the sentence of a court martial cashiering them.

Court martials for trial of officers & capital offence to be not less than 12, & well guarded as to mode of appointment.

Duties of import & export, taxes on lands & buildings, to constitute the chief branches of revenue.

These thoughts are very crude, but perhaps they may afford some hints.

How is the sending an agent to Toussaint to encourage the independence of St. Domingo & a minister to France to negotiate an accommodation reconciliable to consistency or good faith?

Yrs. Truly
A.H.

Letter to James McHenry, March 18, 1799

Beware, my Dear Sir, of magnifying a riot into an insurrection by employing in the first instance an inadequate force. 'Tis better far to err on the other side. Whenever the government appears in arms it ought to appear like a Hercules, and inspire respect by the display of strength. The consideration of expense is of no moment compared with the advantages of energy. 'Tis true this is always a relative question—but 'tis always important to make no mistake. I only offer a principle and a caution.

A large corps of auxiliary cavalry may be had in Jersey, New York, Delaware, Maryland without interfering with farming pursuits.

Will it be inexpedient to put under marching orders a large force provisionally, as in eventual support of the corps to be employed—to awe the disaffected?

Let all be well considered.

Yrs. truly
A. Hamilton

Excerpt from a Letter to James McHenry, April 20, 1799

As I do not conceive the United States to be now at war in the legal import of that term (which I construe to be a state not of *partial* but of *general* hostility), I consider it as beyond my power to approve or execute such sentences as by the Articles of War are referred to the president in time of peace. But while I think it my duty on this ground to transmit the sentence without acting upon it, I feel myself called upon by a profound conviction of the necessity of some severe examples to check a spirit of desertion which, for want of them in time past has become too prevalent, respectfully to declare my opinion that the confirmation and execution of the sentence are of material consequence to the prosperous course of the military service. The crime of desertion is in this instance aggravated by the condition of the offender, who is a sergeant, and by the breach of trust, in purloining the money which was in his hands for the pay of his company.

Letter to James McHenry, May 3, 1799

Sir,

After mature reflection on the subject of your letter of the 26th of last month, I am clearly of opinion that the president has no power to make alone the appointment of Officers to the Battalion, which is to be added to the second Regiment of Artillerists and Engineers.

In my opinion *vacancy* is a relative term and presupposes that the office has been once filled. If so, the power to fill the vacancy is not the power to make an original appointment. The phrase "Which may have happened" serves to confirm this construction. It implies casualty—and denotes such offices as having been once filled have become vacant by accidental circumstances. This at least is the most familiar and obvious sense, and in a matter of this kind it could not be advisable to exercise a doubtful authority.

It is clear that independent of the authority of a special law, the president cannot fill a vacancy which happens during a session of the Senate.

With great respect   I am Sir Yr.   Obedt. servt.

A. Hamilton

Letter to James McHenry, May 18, 1799

Sir,

It is urgent that arms for the troops to be raised be at the respective regimental rendezvouses as speedily as possible. Military pride is to be excited and kept up by military parade. No time ought to be lost in teaching the recruits the use of arms. Guards are necessary as soon as there are soldiers, and these require arms.

When I came to see the hats furnished for the Twelfth Regiment, I was disappointed and distressed. The Commander in Chief recommended cocked-hats. This always means hats cocked on three sides. I was assured that cocked hats were provided. I repeated the assurance to the officers. But the hats received are only capable of being cocked on one side, and the brim is otherwise so narrow as to consult neither good appearance nor utility. They are also without cockades and loops.

Nothing is more necessary than to stimulate the vanity of soldiers. To this end a smart dress is essential. When not attended to, the soldier is exposed to ridicule and humiliation. If the articles promised to him are defective in quality or appearance, he becomes dissatisfied; and the necessity of excusing the public delinquency towards them is a serious bar to the enforcement of discipline. The government of the country is not now in the indigent situation in which it was during our revolution war. It possesses amply the means of placing its military on a respectable footing; and its dignity and its interest equally require that it shall act in conformity with this situation. This course is indeed indispensable if a faithful, zealous, and well regulated army is thought necessary to the security or defense of the country.

With great respect   I have the honor to be
Sir   Yr. Obed serv

Letter to James McHenry, May 27, 1799

Sir,

The returns from every quarter show that desertion prevails to a ruinous extent. For this the remedies are: 1. greater attention to discipline. 2. additional care in furnishing the supplies due to the soldiery of such quality and with such exactness as will leave no real cause of dissatisfaction. 3. the forbearance to enlist foreigners, and, lastly, energy in the punishment of offenders.

To promote the first will be my peculiar care. The second, I doubt not, will have from you all the attention due to a matter of primary importance. The third I hope soon to receive your instructions to put in execution. As to the fourth, I must entreat that you will make such a representation to the president as will convince him of the absolute necessity, where his agency must intervene, of giving effect to the sentences of the courts. His determination upon one some time since reported to you has not yet been received.[9] I expect it with great solicitude; there cannot occur a more fit case for exemplary punishment. If this culprit escapes, the example of his impunity will have a most malignant aspect towards the service. I repeat it, Sir, this is a point of such essential consequence that you cannot bestow too much pains to satisfy the president that severity is indispensable. It is painful to urge a position of this kind, especially where life is concerned, but a military institution must be worse than useless—it must be pernicious if a just severity does not uphold and enforce discipline.

With great respect   I have the honor to be
Sir   Your Obt sert.

General Orders, June 6, 1799

Pursuant to the instructions from the secretary of war, the following additions to the "Rules and Regulations respecting the Recruiting Service" are to be observed.

"None but *Citizens* of the United States shall be enlisted. Persons not born within the said states, who were within the same on the fourth day of July, 1776, shall be deemed citizens for the purpose of enlistment. Every person not born within the United States, who may have migrated hither since that day, must produce a certificate of naturalization from some competent magistrate or court before he can be enlisted; and every person whosoever, not born within the United States, before he can be enlisted, must produce proof by ye. affidavits of two reputable inhabitants of the county, within which he shall offer himself to be enlisted, taken and certified by some magistrate authorized to administer oaths, that he has resided within such county for at least one year immediately preceding the time when he shall so offer himself to be enlisted: The said certificates & affidavits, when respectively necessary, shall be produced to the officer who shall first muster any recruit, to whom they are applicable after he shall have joined his regiment, towards the justification of the officer by whom he shall have been enlisted.

"Apprentices shall on no pretext be enlisted. If any apprentice shall be enlisted through ignorance of the officer enlisting him, he shall be discharged, first refunding and returning any money or other articles which he may have received."

Major General Hamilton enjoins the strict observance of these regulations as points of material consequence to the service. He equally enjoins a particular attention to those parts of the original rules and regulations which forbid the enlistment of persons in a state of intoxication, and limit the ages within which recruits must be enlisted. It is learned with regret that in several instances they have not been sufficiently attended to. A faithful army is to be preferred to a numerous one; and a regard to justice and propriety in the conduct of every part of the military service cannot fail ultimately to promote the honor and interest of those concerned in it, as well as the public good.

It is expected that the commanders of regiments will carefully attend to all willful or negligent breaches of these rules, and if any occur will exert the means which the Articles of War provide for repressing disorders & neglects to the prejudice of good order and military discipline.

Letter to James McHenry, July 29, 1799

Sir,

I have the honor to acknowledge the receipt of your letter of the 25 instant enclosing a warrant for the execution of Sergeant Hunt.[10]

I have reflected carefully on the point submitted to our joint consideration, and upon the whole I incline to the side of forbearance.

The temper of our country is not a little opposed to the frequency of capital punishment. Public opinion, in this respect, though it must not have too much influence, is not wholly to be disregarded. There must be some caution not to render our military system odious by giving it the appearance of being sanguinary.

Considering too the extreme lenity in time past, there may be danger of shocking even the opinion of the army by too violent a change. The idea of cruelty inspires disgust, and ultimately is not much more favorable to authority than the excess of lenity.

Neither is it clear that one example so quickly following upon the heels of another, in the same corps, will materially increase the impression intended to be made or answer any valuable purpose.

If for any or all of these reasons the utility of the measure be doubtful in favor of life, it ought to be foresworn. It is the true policy of the government to maintain an attitude which shall express a reluctance to strike united with a firm determination to do it whenever it shall be essential.

It is but too certain that it will not be long before other instances will occur in which the same punishment will be decried for the same offence. To disseminate the examples of executions, so far as they shall be indispensable, will serve to render them more efficacious.

Under these impressions if I hear nothing to the contrary from you by the return of the post I shall issue an order to the following effect: "That though the president has fully approved the sentence of Sergeant Hunt and from the heinous nature of his conduct considers him as a very fit subject for punishment—yet being unwilling to multiply examples of severity, however just, beyond what experience may show to be indispensable and hoping that the good faith and patriotism of the soldiery will spare him the painful necessity of frequently resorting to them, he has thought fit to authorize a remission of the punishment; directing nevertheless that Sergeant Hunt be degraded from his station."

I request to be speedily instructed.

With great respect &c

Letter to James McHenry, August 5, 1799

If there be anything in my general order lately sent you which imputes to the secretary of war ignorance or inattention, I agree with you, my dear friend, that it ought not to have been there. I add that if done with design it would be a *very culpable* indecorum. But if it does bear this construction, I have very clumsily executed my own intention. And I give you my honor that so far from being sensible of it, my aim was quite the reverse.

I have already told you my opinion that the letter from you to Capt. Frye was in the view of military etiquette irregular. It ought to have been addressed to Major Hoops. If my memory serves me right it refers to the muster by Capt. Frye & thus gives him the pretext of your sanction. It was necessary to do away this inference and at the same time to obviate in the mind of the army the idea of irregularity on your part. My object was to reconcile these two things.

The means I employed were these two suggestions—1. That the intermediate circumstances were unknown to you. In this you see nothing amiss. 2. That from a disposition to give *facility* to the service you *overlooked* the inconsistency of what was done with your *instructions*. Does this imply ignorance or inattention? I think not. Every superior sometimes *overlooks*, that is, *forbears to take notice of*, the incompatibility of the conduct of an inferior with his instructions, though he clearly perceives (and consequently acts neither from ignorance nor inattention) that incompatibility—but willing to give facility to the service in the particular instance, he thinks it best to wave any objection to what has been done & even to give effect to it. In civil & military life this has happened to myself, and yet to hear it stated would not in my opinion charge me with ignorance or inattention. There may often be good reasons for *overlooking* a fault which we *perceive*. To *overlook* is very different from *not to see* or not to attend to. It is in one sense to excuse, to forbear to punish or animadvert upon. And it seems to me that it is plainly in this sense that it is used in the general order. Most certainly it was intended so to be.

Now let me rebuke you in turn. How could you imagine that I entertain an opinion that you have *wantonly* or ignorantly given orders to inferior officers within the command of their superior? It is to injure my friendship for you to suppose that I could think you had *wantonly* done so. That you may have done so through want of a *strict habit* on the subject or perhaps from some incorrectness of ideas with regard to military etiquette, I have indeed believed, but nothing worse. And I cannot think that this belief ought to give you pain. It only implies that you have not been long enough called by situation to contemplate or practice upon that etiquette to have formed exact notions of it and a habit of conforming to it. I do not myself pretend to be an adept in this species of knowledge, though I have endeavored to systematize my ideas on the subject. They are these in brief that the Department of War may regularly correspond with the *civil staff* or officers charged with the business of *expenditure & supply in its various branches* without passing through the medium of the chief military officer. But that in all other matters the correspondence ought to be with him exclusively—saving the cases of sudden emergency in which the object would suffer by using him as the medium.

Yrs. Affecy
A.H.

Letter to Thomas Lloyd Moore, October 6, 1799

Sir,

It is afflicting to learn that such a dispute as you state in your letter of the third instant should have occurred between two officers of the American army. Particular attachment to *any foreign nation* is an exotic sentiment which, where it exists, must derogate from the exclusive affection due to our own country. Partiality to France at this late date is a bad symptom. The profession of it by Captain Johnson, in my opinion, does him no honor. How far it ought to impair confidence must depend in a degree on personal character. But as often as a similar bias is manifested, the conduct of the person ought to engage the vigilant attention of his commanding officer. I hesitate as to what my duty requires on the occasion and must think further of the matter. You will be pleased to ascertain and inform me whether Lt. Irving be an American citizen or not.

You will receive another letter of this date on the subject of winter quarters.

With Considr & esteem   I am, Sir   yr obt St

Letter to Jonathan Dayton, October–November, 1799

An accurate view of the internal situation of the U. States presents many discouraging reflections to the enlightened friends of our government and country. Notwithstanding the unexampled success of our public measures at home and abroad—notwithstanding the instructive comments afforded by the disastrous & disgusting scenes of the French Revolution, public opinion has not been ameliorated—sentiments dangerous to social happiness have not been diminished—on the contrary there are symptoms which warrant the apprehension that among the most numerous class of citizens errors of a very pernicious tendency have not only preserved but have extended their empire. Though something may have been gained on the side of men of information and property, more has probably been lost on that of persons of different description. An extraordinary exertion of the friends of government, aided by circumstances of momentary impression, gave in the last election for members of Congress a more favorable countenance to some states than they had before worn. Yet it is the belief of well informed men that no real or desirable change has been wrought in those states. On the other hand it is admitted by close observers that some of the parts of the Union which in time past have been the soundest have of late exhibited signs of a gangrene begun and progressive.

It is likewise apparent that opposition to the government has acquired more system than formerly—is bolder in the avowal of its designs—less solicitous than it was to discriminate between the Constitution and the administration—more open and more enterprising in its projects.

The late attempt of Virginia & Kentucky to unite the state legislatures in a direct resistance to certain laws of the Union can be considered in no other light than as an attempt to change the government.

It is stated, in addition, that the opposition party in Virginia, the headquarters of the faction, have followed up the hostile declarations which are to be found in the resolutions of their General Assembly by an actual preparation of the means of supporting them by force—That they have taken measures to put their militia on a more efficient footing—are preparing considerable arsenals and magazines and (which is an unequivocal proof how much they are in earnest) have gone so far as to lay new taxes on their citizens.

Amidst such serious indications of hostility, the safety and the duty of the supporters of the government call upon them to adopt vigorous measures of counteraction. It will be wise in them to act upon the hypothesis that the opposers of the government are resolved, if it shall be practicable, to make its existence a question of force. Possessing as they now do all the constitutional powers, it will be an unpardonable mistake on their part if they do not exert them to surround the Constitution with new ramparts and to disconcert the schemes of its enemies.

The measures proper to be adopted may be classed under ___ heads:

1. Establishments which will extend the influence and promote the popularity of the government.

Under this head three important expedients occur—1. The extension of the judiciary system. 2. The improvement of the great communications as well interiorly as coastwise by turnpike roads. 3. The institution of a society with funds to be employed in premiums for new inventions, discoveries, and improvements in agriculture and in the arts.

The extension of the judiciary system ought to embrace two objects—one the subdivision of each state into small districts (suppose Connecticut into four and so in proportion) assigning to each a judge with a moderate salary— the other the appointment in each country of conservators or justices of the peace with only ministerial functions and with no other compensations than fees for the services they shall perform.

This measure is necessary to give efficacy to the laws, the execution of which is obstructed by the want of similar organs and by the indisposition of the local magistrates in some states. The Constitution requires that *judges* shall have fixed salaries—but this does not apply to mere justices of the peace without judicial powers. Both those descriptions of persons are essential as well to the energetic execution of the laws as to the purpose of salutary patronage.

The thing would no doubt be a subject of clamor, but it would carry with it its own antidote, and when once established would bring a very powerful support to the government.

The improvement of the roads would be a measure universally popular. None can be more so. For this purpose a regular plan should be adopted coextensive with the Union to be successively executed—and a fund should be appropriated sufficient for the basis of a loan of a million of dollars. The revenue of the Post Office naturally offers itself. The future revenue from tolls would more than reimburse the expense; and public utility would be promoted in every direction.

The institution of a society with the aid of proper funds to encourage agriculture and the arts, besides being productive of general advantage, will speak powerfully to the feelings and interests of those classes of men to whom the benefits derived from the government have been heretofore the least manifest.

2. Provisions for augmenting the means and consolidating the strength of the government.

A million of dollars may without difficulty be added to the revenue by increasing the rates of some existing indirect taxes and by the addition of some new items of a similar character. The direct taxes ought neither to be increased nor diminished.

Our naval force ought to be completed to six ships of the line, twelve frigates, and twenty four sloops of war. More at this juncture would be disproportioned to our resources. Less would be inadequate to the end to be accomplished.

Our military force should for the present be kept upon its actual footing, making provision for a reenlistment of the men for five years in the event of a settlement of differences with France—with this condition that in case of peace between Great Britain France and Spain, the U. States being then also at peace, all the privates of twelve additional regiments of infantry and of the regiment of dragoons exceeding twenty to a company shall be disbanded. The corps of artillerists may be left to retain the numbers which it shall happen to have; but without being recruited until the number of privates shall fall below the standard of the infantry & dragoons. A power ought to be given to the president to augment the four old regiments to their war establishment.

The laws respecting volunteer companies & the *Eventual Army* should be rendered permanent, and the executive should proceed without delay to organize the latter. Some modifications of the discretion of the president will, however, be proper in a permanent law. And it will be a great improvement of the plan if it shall be thought expedient to allow the enlistment, for the purpose of instruction, of a corps of sergeants equal to the number requisite for the Eventual Army.

The institution of a military academy will be an auxiliary of great importance.

Manufactories of every article, the woolen parts of clothing included, which are essential to the supply of the army, ought to be established.

3. Arrangements for confirming and enlarging the legal powers of the government.

There are several temporary laws which in this view ought to be rendered permanent, particularly that which authorizes the calling out of the militia to suppress unlawful combinations and insurrections.

An article ought to be proposed to be added to the Constitution for empowering Congress to open canals in all cases in which it may be necessary to conduct them through the territory of two or more states or through the territory of a state and that of the U. States. The power is very desirable for the purpose of improving the prodigious facilities for inland navigation with which nature has favored this country. It will also assist commerce and agriculture by rendering the transportation of commodities more cheap and expeditious. It will tend to secure the connection by facilitating the communication between distant portions of the Union. And it will be a useful source of influence to the government.

Happy would it be if a clause would be added to the Constitution enabling Congress, on the application of any considerable portion of a state containing not less than a hundred thousand persons, to erect it into a separate state on the condition of fixing the quota of contributions which it shall make towards antecedent debts, if any there shall be, reserving to Congress the authority to levy within such state the taxes necessary to the payment of such quota, in case of neglect on the part of the state. The subdivision of the great states is indispensable to the security of the general government and with it of the Union. Great states will always feel a rivalship with the common head, will often be disposed to machinate against it, and in certain situations will be able to do it with decisive effect. The subdivision of such states ought to be a cardinal point in the Federal policy: and small states are doubtless best adapted to the purposes of local regulation and to the preservation of the republican spirit. This suggestion, however, is merely thrown out for consideration. It is feared that it would be inexpedient & even dangerous to propose at this time an amendment of the kind.

4. Laws for restraining and punishing incendiary and seditious practices.

It will be useful to declare that all such writings &c which at common law are libels if leveled against any officer whatsoever of the U. States shall be cognizable in the courts of U. States.

To preserve confidence in the officers of the general government by preserving their reputations from malicious and unfounded slanders is essential to enable them to fulfill the ends of their appointment. It is therefore both constitutional and politic to place their reputations under the guardianship of the courts of the United States. They ought not to be left to the cold and reluctant protection of state courts, always temporizing, sometimes disaffected.

But what avail laws which are not executed? Renegade aliens conduct more than one of the most incendiary presses in the U. States—and yet in open contempt and defiance of the laws they are permitted to continue their destructive labors. Why are they not sent away? Are laws of this kind passed merely to excite odium and remain a dead letter? Vigor in the executive is at least as necessary as in the legislative branch. If the president requires to be stimulated, those who can approach him ought to do it.

Letter to Josiah Ogden Hoffman, November 6, 1799

Sir,

"GREENLEAFS NEW DAYLY ADVERTISER" of this morning contains a publication entitled "Extract of a letter from Philadelphia dated September 20th," which charges me with being at the "bottom" of an "effort recently made to suppress the AURORA" (a newspaper of that city) by pecuniary means.

It is well known that I have long been the object of the most malignant calumnies of the faction opposed to our government, through the medium of the papers devoted to their views. Hitherto I have forborne to resort to the laws for the punishment of the authors or abettors; and were I to consult personal considerations alone I should continue in this course, repaying hatred with contempt. But public motives now compel me to a different conduct. The design of that faction to overturn our government, and with it the great pillars of social security and happiness in this country, becomes every day more manifest, and has of late acquired a degree of system which renders them formidable. One principal engine for effecting the scheme is by audacious falsehoods to destroy the confidence of the people in all those who are in any degree conspicuous among the supporters of the government: an engine which has been employed in time past with too much success, and which unless counteracted in future is likely to be attended with very fatal consequences. To counteract it is therefore a duty to the community.

Among the specimens of this contrivance, that which is the subject of the present letter demands peculiar attention. A bolder calumny, one more absolutely destitute of foundation, was never propagated. And its dangerous tendency needs no comment, being calculated to inspire the belief that the independence and liberty of the press are endangered by the intrigues of ambitious citizens and by foreign gold.

In so flagrant a case, the force of the laws must be tried. I therefore request that you will take immediate measures towards the prosecution[11] of the persons who conduct the enclosed paper.

With great consideration   I am Sir   yr Obed ser

Excerpt from a Letter to James McHenry, November 23, 1799

Sir,

The near approach of a session of Congress will naturally lead you to the consideration of such measures for the improvement of our military system as may require legislative sanction.

Under this impression, I am induced now to present to you some objects which appear to me very interesting, and shall take the liberty to add, hereafter, such others as shall have occurred.

One which I have always thought of primary importance is a military academy. This object has repeatedly engaged the favorable attention of the administration, and some steps towards it have been taken. But these, as yet, are very inadequate—a more perfect plan is in a high degree desirable.

No sentiment is more just than this, that in proportion as the circumstances & policy of a country forbid a large military establishment, it is important that as much perfection as possible should be given to that which may at any time exist.

Since it is agreed that we are not to keep on foot numerous forces instructed and disciplined, military science in its various branches ought to be cultivated, with peculiar care, in proper nurseries; so that there may always exist a sufficient body of it ready to be imparted and diffused, and a competent number of persons qualified to act as instructors to the additional troops which events may successively require to be raised. This will be to substitute the elements of an army to the thing itself, and it will greatly tend to enable the government to dispense with a large body of standing forces, from the facility which it will give of forming officers and soldiers promptly upon emergencies.

No sound mind can doubt the essentiality of military science in time of war, any more than the moral certainty that the most pacific policy on the part of a government will not preserve it from being engaged in war more or less frequently. To avoid great evils, it must either have a respectable force prepared for service, or the means of preparing such a force with expedition. The latter, most agreeable to the genius of our government and nation, is the object of a military academy.

I propose that this academy shall consist of five schools—One to be called "The Fundamental School"—another "The School of Engineers & Artillerists"—another "The School of Cavalry"—another "The School of Infantry"—and a fifth "The School of the Navy"—and of the following officers and persons—

Letter to Charles Cotesworth Pinckney, December 22, 1799

Sir,

The death of our beloved commander in chief was known to you before it was to me. I can be at no loss to anticipate what have been your feelings. I need not tell you what are mine. Perhaps no friend of his has more cause to lament, on personal account, than myself. The public misfortune is one which all the friends of our government will view in the same light. I will not dwell on the subject. My imagination is gloomy, my heart sad.

Enclosed is an order relative to the occasion which speaks its own object.

With the sincerest esteem and most affectionate regard   I remain Sir   Yr very Obed ser

Letter to Tobias Lear, January 2, 1800

Dr. Sir,

Yr. letter of the 15 of Decr. last was delayed in getting to hand by the circumstance of its having gone to N. York while I was at Phila. and of its having arrived at Phila. after I had set out on my return to N. York.

The very painful event which it announces had, previously to the receipt of it, filled my heart with bitterness. Perhaps no man in this community has equal cause with myself to deplore the loss. I have been much indebted to the kindness of the general, and he was an aegis very essential to me. But regrets are unavailing. For great misfortunes it is the business of reason to seek consolation. The friends of General Washington have very noble ones. If virtue can secure happiness in another world, he is happy. In this the seal is now put upon his glory. It is no longer in jeopardy from the fickleness of fortune.

Adieu &c

Excerpt from a Letter to Rufus King, January 5, 1800

At home, everything is in the main well, except as to the perverseness and capriciousness of one and the spirit of faction of many.

Our measures, from the first cause, are too much the effect of momentary impulse. Vanity and jealousy exclude all counsel. Passion wrests the helm from reason.

The irreparable loss of an inestimable man removes a control which was felt and was very salutary.

The leading friends of the government are in a sad dilemma. Shall they risk a serious schism by an attempt to change? Or shall they annihilate themselves and hazard their cause by continuing to uphold those who suspect or hate them, & who are likely to propose a course for no better reason than because it is contrary to that which they approve?

The spirit of faction is abated nowhere. In Virginia it is more violent than ever. It seems demonstrated that the leaders there, who possess completely all the powers of the local government, are resolved to possess those of the national, by the most dangerous combinations, & if they cannot effect this, to resort to the employment of physical force. The want of disposition in the people to second them will be the only preventive. It is believed that it will be an effectual one.

In the two houses of Congress we have a decided majority. But the dread of unpopularity is likely to paralyze it and to prevent the erection of additional buttresses to the Constitution: a fabric which can hardly be stationary and which will retrograde if it cannot be made to advance.

In the mass of the people the dispositions are not bad. An attachment to the system of peace continues. No project contrary to it could easily conciliate favor. Good will towards the government in my opinion predominates—though a numerous party is still actuated by an opposite sentiment and some vague discontents have a more diffused influence. Sympathy with the French Revolution acts in a much narrower circle than formerly; but the jealousy of monarchy, which is as active as ever, still furnishes a hand by which the factious mislead well meaning persons.

Letter to Martha Washington, January 12, 1800

I did not think it proper, madam, to intrude amidst the first effusions of your grief. But I can no longer restrain my sensibility from conveying to you an imperfect expression of my affectionate sympathy in the sorrows you experience. No one better than myself knows the greatness of your loss, or how much your excellent heart is formed to feel it in all its extent. Satisfied that you cannot receive consolation, I will attempt to offer none. Resignation to the will of Heaven, which the practice of your life ensures, can alone alleviate the sufferings of so heart-rending an affliction.

There can be few who equally with me participate in the loss you deplore. In expressing this sentiment, I may without impropriety allude to the numerous and distinguished marks of confidence and friendship, of which you have yourself been a witness; but I cannot say in how many ways the continuance of that confidence and friendship was necessary to me in future relations.

Vain, however, are regrets. From a calamity which is common to a mourning nation who can expect to be exempt? Perhaps it is even a privilege to have a claim to a larger portion of it than others.

I will only add, madam, that I shall deem it a real and a great happiness if any future occurrence shall enable me to give you proof of that respectful and cordial attachment with which I have the honor to be

Your obliged & very obedient servant

Letter to Theodore Sedgwick, February 27, 1800

Dear Sir,

When will Congress probably adjourn? Will any thing be settled as to a certain *Election?* Will my presence be requisite as to this or any other purpose and when? I observe more and more that by the jealousy and envy of some, the miserliness of others, and the concurring influence of *all foreign powers*, America, if she attains to greatness, must *creep* to it. Well be it so. Slow and sure is no bad maxim. Snails are a wise generation.

Yrs. truly
A.H.

P.S. Unless for indispensable reasons, I had rather not come.

Letter to Henry Lee, March 7, 1800

My dear Sir,

The letters to which you allude in yours of the 5th instant have never been seen by me. The truth is that I pay very little attention to such newspaper ebullitions, unless some friend points out a particular case which may demand attention.

But be assured once for all that it is not easy for these miscreants to impair the confidence in and friendship for you which are long habits of my mind. So that you may join me in looking with indifference upon their malicious efforts.

You have mistaken a little an observation in my last. Believe me that I feel no despondency of any sort. As to the country it is too young and vigorous to be quacked out of its political health—and as to myself I feel that I stand on ground which, sooner or later, will ensure me a triumph over all my enemies.

But, in the mean time I am not wholly insensible of the injustice which I from time to time experience, and of which, in my opinion, I am at this moment the victim.[12] Perhaps my sensibility is the effect of an exaggerated estimate of my services to the U. States—but on such a subject every man will judge for himself. And if he is misled by his vanity he must be content with the mortifications to which it exposes him. In no event, however, will any displeasure I may feel be at war with the public interest. This in my eyes is sacred.

Adieu

Letter to Oliver Wolcott, Jr., March 12, 1800

Sir,

I have written to you heretofore respecting Mr. Benjamin Wells, who acted as an excise officer in the western part of Pennsylvania at the time of the disturbances there. But this gentleman has just arrived here, and requests me to mention his case again to you. I comply with his request.

It appeared from what I saw and heard at the time that Mr. Wells distinguished himself by persevering exertions to carry the laws into effect. He was, of course, marked out as an object of vengeance. The losses which he sustained were very considerable, and proceeded from the zeal he had displayed in support of the government. To repair his losses, and reward his zeal, is, therefore, a duty imposed on the government by the principles both of justice and policy. It is imposed by justice, for the injuries were committed by persons in disguise, or under circumstances which render it impossible to discover the offenders. It is vain therefore to refer Mr. Wells to the individuals by whose acts he suffered. This is to tell him that his losses will never be repaired. Policy speaks in this case the same language with justice.

Mr. Wells suffered in consequence of his efforts to support the government and of his attention to duty. Will the government then refuse to make him compensation? To do so will be to violate the plainest maxims of policy, as it will effectually damp the zeal of public officers in every future case of difficulty. It is not to be expected that individuals will expose their persons to violence and their property to destruction in support of a government that has not generosity sufficient to reward those who suffer in its cause. There appears to me to be no doubt of the meritorious exertions of Mr. Wells. Even if there were some doubt, yet the excellent effect which the measure is calculated to produce on public officers will prove a full compensation for the money that may be advanced. I recollect to have mentioned to Mr. Wells and other persons in the same capacity that I considered the govt. as bound to indemnify them. So far, therefore, as my opinion could pledge the government, it was pledged. In giving this opinion, I thought I was promoting the best interests of the nation. And it appears to me that the government will very widely mistake its policy in refusing to allow these men all reasonable claims.

Letter to Timothy Pickering, March 15, 1800

Dear Sir,

The bearer of this, Mr. DuPont, formerly consul at Charles Town, is personally known to you. He comes with the rest of his family to establish themselves in the United States. They are desirous of being favorably viewed by our government and my intervention for this purpose has been requested.

Enclosed is a letter from General Pinckney which speaks for itself. All that has come to my knowledge of this particular gentleman is recommendatory of him, as far as situation has permitted. I have always understood that his sentiments toward this country have been amicable & that he has not been very deeply tinctured with the revolutionary spirit of his own, though circumstances have placed him in office under the new government. And I believe if ever diseased, he is now perfectly cured. He is afraid that some expressions respecting the influence of the British government in this country may have given an ill impression. He explains by saying 1st that they are qualified. 2nd that they were a necessary concession to the prejudices of the persons to whom his observations were addressed, calculated to procure attention to the conciliatory plan which he recommended by screening him from the suspicion of being a corrupted partisan of this country. This solution seems to me an admissible one. In addressing enthusiasts it is commonly requisite to adopt a little of their nonsense.

He has delivered me a paper which he sent to the *Aurora* to be published but which he says was suppressed and something of an insidious complexion substituted. He delivers the true communication that it may be seen what he really did.

I am much mistaken if his father be not really a benevolent, well disposed man. Indeed the family generally impress us here agreeably, & we are inclined to augur well of them.

Very truly yrs
A. Hamilton

Letter to James McHenry, March 21, 1800

Dear Sir,

Though from repeated reflection and action upon the subject my opinion was well made up when I received your letter of the 19th, yet I thought it proper once more to review the matter before I complied with your request.

The principle of the doctrine advanced by the accountant will go much farther than the position which he now avows: namely, "that no authority short of Congress can make allowances to an officer beyond the emoluments fixed to his office by law." It will go the length of denying to the executive in all its branches any discretion, not confirmed by some special law, to *call forth* and *compensate* any services, not merely of officers, but of any other persons, which are not indicated and provided for by particular statutes. It will interdict the employment and compensation of a citizen, as a *writer* or even as an *express*, no less than that of an officer for either purpose. The foundation of the doctrine must be that there is no power in the executive to subject the public to expense in any case not specially provided for by law. What substantial difference can there be between employing a private citizen for some contingent service and paying him for it, and employing an officer for something *not within the sphere of his official duty* and compensating him for it? I discover none in theory; for as to such extra service he is a private citizen, and I know of no law that declares a distinction.

It is certain that in the course of the discharge of its trusts there will occur numerous instances in which the public service must stagnate or the executive must employ and compensate agents not contemplated by special laws. It follows in my opinion that he must have an inherent right to do it—under these restrictions that it ought to be relative to some object confided to his agency by the Constitution or by the laws, and that no money ought actually to be paid for which there is not an appropriation by statute either with particular reference to the purpose or under the general denomination of contingencies. This is in my opinion a right necessarily implied—nor do I see why the executive may not claim the exercise of implied powers as well as the legislative. In a word, there is no public function which does not include the exercise of implied as well as express authority.

This reasoning as far as I know is consonant with the practice of every government, and with that of ours as well under the Confederation as under the present Constitution.

If my memory deceives me not, there was an act of Congress prohibiting the union of two offices in the same person with distinct compensations. Yet this did not hinder the allowance of special compensations to officers for special and extra service. Still less did it hinder the indemnifications for extra expenses of an officer in peculiar situations. Such compensations and indemnifications were, I believe, made by the executive boards under the former government. Indeed, I am unusually mistaken if the uniform practice of the Treasury and War Departments under this government does not recognize the rule for which I contend and regret that which is advanced by the accountant.

This practice too has been right. A different one will be found in experience—a fatal clog in the wheels of public business. The administration at large is interested in discountenancing it and that spirit of cavil in the accountant on which it is founded, and which my observations in my present station have convinced me is ruinous to the military department of the government.

There was not an appropriation law passed while I was at the head of the Treasury which did not sanction my principle. There was always, I believe, a sum for the contingencies of the War Department. The power to incur charges which involve expense not falling under any specific head presupposes the right to employ agents and engage services not particularly contemplated by law. I always viewed such appropriations as a virtual sanction of the right, including in them a warranty if necessary, to exercise the power. Such too was the practical construction.

Nobody knows better the truth in this respect than Mr. Wolcott. Nobody ought more decidedly to frown upon the dangerous metaphysics of Mr. Simmons. The recognition of his doctrine will be a fatal precedent in the administration. It will be a palsy destructive of all energy in the govt. Considering the disposition which prevails among certain men in a certain body there ought to be more than a common anxiety not to establish such a fetter upon executive operations.

Yrs

Letter to John Jay,
May 7, 1800

Dear Sir,

You have been informed of the loss of our election in this city. It is also known that we have been unfortunate throughout Long Island & in West Chester. According to the returns hitherto, it is too probable that we lose our senators for this district.

The moral certainty therefore is that there will be an Anti-federal majority in the ensuing legislature, and this very high probability is that this will bring *Jefferson* into the chief magistracy, unless it be prevented by the measure which I shall now submit to your consideration, namely the immediate calling together of the existing legislature.

I am aware that there are weighty objections to the measure, but the reasons for it appear to me to outweigh the objections. And in times like these in which we live it will not do to be over-scrupulous. It is easy to sacrifice the substantial interests of society by a strict adherence to ordinary rules.

In observing this, I shall not be supposed to mean that any thing ought to be done which integrity will forbid—but merely that the scruples of delicacy and propriety, as relative to a common course of things, ought to yield to the extraordinary nature of the crisis. They ought not to hinder the taking of a *legal* and *constitutional* step to prevent an *atheist* in religion and a *fanatic* in politics from getting possession of the helm of the state.

You, Sir, know in a great degree the Antifederal party; but I fear that you do not know them as well as I do. Tis a composition indeed of very incongruous materials, but all tending to mischief—some of them to the overthrow of the government by stripping it of its due energies, others of them to a revolution after the manner of Bonaparte. I speak from indubitable facts, not from conjectures & inferences.

In proportion as the true character of this party is understood is the force of the considerations which urge to every effort to disappoint it. And it seems to me that there is a very solemn obligation to employ the means in our power.

The calling of the legislature will have for object the choosing of electors by the people in districts. This (as Pennsylvania will do nothing) will insure a majority of votes in the U. States for Federal candidates.

The measure will not fail to be approved by all the Federal party, while it will no doubt be condemned by the opposite. As to its intrinsic nature, it is justified by unequivocal reasons for *public safety*.

The reasonable part of the world will I believe approve it. They will see it as a proceeding out of the common course but warranted by the particular nature of the crisis and the great cause of social order.

If done the motive ought to be frankly avowed. In your communication to the legislature, they ought to be told that temporary circumstances had rendered it probable that without their interposition the executive authority of the general government would be transferred to hands hostile to the system heretofore pursued with so much success and dangerous to the peace happiness and order of the country—that under this impression from facts convincing to your own mind you had thought it your duty to give the existing legislature an opportunity of deliberating whether it would not be proper to interpose and endeavor to prevent so great an evil by referring the choice of electors to the people distributed into districts.

In weighing this suggestion you will doubtless bear in mind that popular governments must certainly be overturned & while they endure, prove engines of mischief—if one party will call to its aid all the resources which *vice* can give and if the other, however pressing the emergency, confines itself within all the ordinary forms of delicacy and decorum.

The legislature can be brought together in three weeks. So that there will be full time for the objects; but none ought to be lost.

Think well, my Dear Sir, of this proposition. Appreciate the extreme danger of the crisis; and I am unusually mistaken in my view of the matter if you do not see it right and expedient to adopt the measure.[13]

Respectfully & Affecty   Yrs.

A. Hamilton

Letter to Theodore Sedgwick, May 10, 1800

Dear Sir,

I am very sorry for the information contained in your letter of the 7th. But I am not intimate enough with Dexter to put myself upon paper to him. If on his return I can catch him at New York I shall have a particular conversation with him.

He is, I am persuaded, much mistaken as to the opinion entertained of Mr. Adams by the Federal party. Were I to determine from my own observation I should say *most* of the *most influential men* of that party consider him as a very *unfit* and *incapable* character.

For my individual part my mind is made up. I will never more be responsible for him by my direct support—even though the consequence should be the election of *Jefferson*. If we must have an *enemy* at the head of the government, let it be one whom we can oppose & for whom we are not responsible, who will not involve our party in the disgrace of his foolish and bad measures. Under *Adams* as under *Jefferson* the government will sink. The party in the hands of whose chief it shall sink will sink with it, and the advantage will all be on the side of his adversaries.

Tis a notable expedient for keeping the Federal party together to have at the head of it a man who hates and is despised by those men of it who in time past have been its most efficient supporters.

If the cause is to be sacrificed to a weak and perverse man, I withdraw from the party & act upon my own ground—never certainly against my principles, but in pursuance of them in my own way. I am mistaken if others will not do the same.

The only way to prevent a fatal schism in the Federal party is to support G. Pinckney in good earnest.

If I can be perfectly satisfied that Adams & Pinckney will be upheld in the east with entire good faith, on the ground of conformity I will, wherever my influence may extend, pursue the same plan. If not, I will pursue Mr. Pinckney as my single object.

Adieu Yrs. truly
A.H.

Letter to James McHenry, May 15, 1800

If, My Dear McHenry, your retreat is from any circumstances painful to yourself, I regret it with all the sincerity of a real friend; otherwise I congratulate you.[14] It is impossible that our public affairs can proceed under the present chief or his Antifederal rival without loss of reputation to all the agents. Happy those who are released from the fetter.

But, my friend, we are not to be discouraged. Zeal and fortitude are more than ever necessary. A new and more dangerous *era* has commenced. Revolution and a new order of things are aroused in this quarter. Property, liberty, and even life are at stake. The friends of good principles must be more closely linked, more watchful, and more decided than they have been. Of this enough for the present—more hereafter. Can we not see each other, without my coming to Philadelphia, before you go to Maryland?

Yrs. Affecty.
A. Hamilton

Letter to John Adams, August 1, 1800

Sir,

It has been repeatedly mentioned to me that you have, on different occasions, asserted the existence of a *British faction* in this country, embracing a number of leading or influential characters of the *Federal Party* (as usually denominated), and that you have sometimes named me, at other times plainly alluded to me, as one of this description of persons: And I have likewise been assured that of late some of your warm adherents, for electioneering purposes, have employed a corresponding language.

I must, Sir, take it for granted that you cannot have made such assertions or insinuations without being willing to avow them and to assign the reasons to a party who may conceive himself injured by them. I therefore trust that you will not deem it improper that I apply directly to yourself, to ascertain from you, in reference to your own declarations, whether the information I have received has been correct or not, and if correct what are the grounds upon which you have founded the suggestion.

With respect   I have the honor to be   Sir   Your obedient servt.
Alexander Hamilton

Letter to Oliver Wolcott, Jr., August 3, 1800

Dear Sir,

I have two days since written to Mr. Adams a *respectful* letter on the subject I heretofore mentioned to you. Occupations at court prevented its being sooner done.

But I wait with impatience for the statement of facts which you promised me. It is plain that unless we give our reasons in some form or other— Mr. Adams's personal friends seconded by the Jacobins will completely *run us down in the public opinion*. Your name in company with mine that of T. Pickering &c. is in full circulation as one of the *British Faction* of which Mr. Adams has talked so much.

I have serious thoughts of giving to the public my opinion respecting Mr. Adams with my reasons in a letter to a friend with my signature. This seems to me the most authentic way of conveying the information & best suited to the plain dealing of my character. There are, however, reasons against it, and a very strong one is that some of the principal causes of my disapprobation proceed from yourself & other members of the administration who would be understood to be the sources of my information whatever cover I might give the thing.

What say you to this measure? I could predicate it on the fact that I am abused by the friends of Mr. Adams who ascribe my opposition to pique & disappointment & would give it the shape of a *defense of myself*.

You have doubtless seen *The Aurora* publications of Treasury documents & the manner in which my name is connected with it. These publications do harm with the ignorant, who are the greatest number. I have thoughts of instituting an action of slander to be tried by a struck jury against the editor. If I do it I should claim you & the supervisors, collectors, & loan officers of all the states from Maryland to N. York inclusively as witnesses to demonstrate completely the malice & falsity of the accusation. What think you of this? You see I am in a very belligerent humor.

But I remember that at the outset before the sums payable for interest pensions &c. were ascertained, I placed the money in the hands of the paying officers upon estimate & that to avoid disappointment I made the estimates large. Pray look into this & see how far it may give any color to the calumny.

Let me hear from you soon.

Yrs. very truly
A. Hamilton

Letter to James A. Bayard, August 6, 1800

Dear Sir,

The President of Columbia College in this city has resigned, & we are looking out for a successor. Dr. Wharton has occurred to me as a character worthy of inquiry, & the great confidence I feel in your judgment & candor induces me to have recourse to you. We are extremely anxious to have a well-qualified man, as this is the only thing wanting to render our institution very flourishing. We have two *very good* professors, one of the languages, the other of mathematics & natural philosophy—and we have a professor of chemistry (this branch having been lately made a part of the academic course), together with better funds, as I believe, than any similar institution in the U. States. I mention these particulars to impress you with the importance of our college to the cause of literature, & with the duty which thence results of peculiar circumspection & care in the choice of a president. It is essential that he be a gentleman in his manners, as well as a sound & polite scholar—that his moral character be irreproachable, that he possess energy of body & mind, & be of a disposition to maintain discipline without *undue austerity*, & in the last place that his politics be of the right sort. I beg you to inform me particularly how far Dr. Wharton meets this description, in what if anything he fails. You will of course see the propriety of mentioning nothing about this inquiry. In the present eventful crisis of our affairs, a mutual communication of information & opinions among influential men of the Federal party may be attended with some advantage to their cause. Under this impression I shall give you a summary of the state of things north of the Delaware; south of it your information is likely to be as good as mine, & accordingly I shall request your view of what is to be expected in that quarter. In New Hampshire there is no doubt of Federal electors, but there is a decided partiality for Mr. Adams. I took pains to possess Governor Gilman, whose influence is very preponderating, of the errors and defects of Mr. Adams, and of the danger that no candidate can prevail, by mere Federal strength, consequently of the expediency & necessity of unanimously voting for General Pinckney (who in the South may get some Anti-Federal votes) as the best chance of excluding Mr. Jefferson. The governor appeared convinced of the soundness of these views, & cautiously gave me to expect his cooperation. Yet I do not count upon New Hampshire for more than two things, one, an unanimous vote for Mr. Adams; the other, no vote for any Anti-Federalist. In Massachusetts almost all the leaders of the first class are dissatisfied with Mr. Adams & enter heartily into the policy of supporting General Pinckney. But most of the leaders of the 2nd class are attached to Mr. Adams & fearful of jeopardizing his election by promoting that of Gen. Pinckney. And the mass of the people are well affected to him & to his administration. Yet I have strong hopes that by the exertions of the principal Federalists, Masstts. will unanimously vote for *Adams & Pinckney*. Rhode Island is in a state somewhat uncertain. Schisms have grown up from personal rivalships, which have been improved by the Anti-federalists to strengthen their interests. Governor Fenner expresses a hope that there will be 2 Anti-Federal electors, but our friends reject this idea as wholly improbable. But I am not quite convinced that they know the ground. In every event, however, I expect Mr. A. will have there an unanimous vote. I think nothing can be relied upon as to General Pinckney. Connecticut will I doubt not unanimously vote for General P: but being very much displeased with Mr. A. it will require the explicit advice of certain gentlemen to induce them to vote for him. No Anti-Federalist has any chance there. About Vermont I am not as yet accurately informed; but I believe *Adams & Pinckney* will both have all the votes. In New York all the votes will certainly be for Jefferson & Burr. New Jersey does not stand as well as she used to do; the Antis hope for the votes of this state. But I think they will be disappointed. If the electors are Federal, Pinckney will certainly be voted for; & Adams will be or not as leading friends shall advise. Adding to this view of the northern what I have understood of the southern quarter, our prospects are not brilliant. There seems to be too much probability that Jefferson or Burr will be President. The latter is intriguing with all his might in New Jersey, Rhode Island, & Vermont. And there is a possibility of some success to his intrigues. He counts positively on the universal support of the Antis & that by some adventitious aid from other quarters he will overtop his friend Jefferson. Admitting the first point the conclusion may be realized. And if it is, Burr will certainly attempt to reform the government *a la Bonaparte*. He is as unprincipled & dangerous a man as any country can boast, as true a *Catiline* as ever met in midnight conclave.

With sincere esteem & regard I am

A.H.

Excerpt from a Letter to Charles Carroll of Carrollton, August 7, 1800

As between Pinckney & Adams, I give a decided preference to the first. If you have not heard enough to induce you to agree in this opinion I will upon your request enter into my reasons. Mr. Adams has governed & must govern from *impulse* and *caprice*, under the influence of the two most mischievous of passions for a politician, to an extreme that to be portrayed would present a caricature—*vanity* and *jealousy*. He has already disorganized & in a great measure prostrated the Federal party. Under his auspices the government can scarcely fail to decline, & with him the Federal party will be disgraced. This is my anticipation on mature reflection. Will not Maryland vote by her legislature? I am aware of strong objections to the measure; but if it be true, as I suppose, that our opponents aim at revolution & employ all means to secure success, the contest must be very unequal if we *not only* refrain from *unconstitutional* and *criminal* measures but even from such as may offend against the *routine of strict decorum*.

Letter to William Jackson, August 26, 1800

My dear Jackson,

Never was there a more ungenerous persecution of any man than of myself. Not only the worst constructions are put upon my conduct as a public man, but it seems my birth is the subject of the most humiliating criticism.

On this point, as on most others which concern me, there is much mistake—though I am pained by the consciousness that it is not free from blemish.

I think it proper to confide to your bosom the real history of it, that among my friends you may if you please wipe off some part of the stain which is so industriously impressed.

The truth is that on the question who my parents were, I have better pretensions than most of those who in this country plume themselves on ancestry.

My grandfather by the mother's side of the name of Faucette was a French Huguenot who emigrated to the West Indies in consequence of the revocation of the Edict of Nantes and settled in the Island of Nevis, and there acquired a pretty fortune. I have been assured by persons who knew him that he was a man of letters and much of a gentleman. He practiced as a physician; whether that was his original profession or one assumed for livelihood after his emigration is not to me ascertained.

My father, now dead, was certainly of a respectable Scotch family. His father was, and the son of his eldest brother now is, Laird of Grange. His mother was the sister of an ancient baronet, *Sir Robert Pollock*.

Himself being a younger son of a numerous family was bred to trade. In capacity of merchant he went to St. Kitts, where from too generous and too easy a temper he failed in business, and at length fell into indigent circumstances. For some time he was supported by his friends in Scotland, and for several years before his death by me. It was his fault to have had too much pride and too large a portion of indolence—but his character was otherwise without reproach and his manners those of a gentleman.

So far I may well challenge comparison, but the blemish remains to be unveiled.

A Dane, a fortune-hunter of the name of *Lavine*, came to Nevis bedizened with gold, and paid his addresses to my mother, then a handsome young woman having a *snug* fortune. In compliance with the wishes of her mother, who was captivated by the glitter of the ___, but against her own inclination, she married Lavine. The marriage was unhappy and ended in a separation by divorce. My mother afterwards went to St. Kitts, became acquainted with my father, and a marriage between them ensued, followed by many years cohabitation and several children.

But unluckily it turned out that the divorce was not absolute but qualified, and thence the second marriage was not lawful. Hence when my mother died, the small property which she left went to my half brother, Mr. Lavine, who lived in South Carolina and was for a time partner with Mr. Kane. He is now dead.

As to my father's family, Mr. McCormick of this city, merchant, can give testimony and will corroborate what I have stated.

Yours truly and affectionately.
Alexander Hamilton

Letter to James McHenry, August 27, 1800

Indeed, my dear Mac, I have not enough the gift of second sight to foresee what N. England will do. The mass of the people there are attached to Adams, and the leaders of the second class pretty generally. The leaders of the first class pretty generally promote the joint support of *Adams & Pinckney*, either because they dislike Adams or hate & fear Jefferson. Upon the whole I believe, though not with perfect assurance, that Pinckney will have almost all the votes of N.E.—Adams will have all.

The state of New Jersey is more uncertain than I could wish. Parties will be too nicely balanced there. But our friends continue confident of a favorable result. If the electors in the state are Federal they will certainly vote for Pinckney, and I rather think will do with respect to Mr. Adams what may be thought right.

In New York there is no chance for *any Federal candidate*.

I think at all events Maryland had better choose by the legislature. If we have a majority of Federal votes throughout we can certainly exclude Jefferson & if we please, bring the question between Adams & Pinckney to the House of Representatives.

We fight *Adams* on very unequal grounds—because we do not disclose the motives of our dislike. The exposition of these is very important, but how? I would make it & put my name to it but I cannot do it without its being conclusively inferred that as to very material facts I must have derived my information from members of the administration. Yet without this we have the air of mere *caballers* & shall be completely run down in the public opinion.

I have written a letter of which I shall send a copy to you, another to Wolcott. If I am not forbidden, Col. Ogden, to whom it will be addressed, will commit it to the newspapers.

Yrs. truly & Affecty

A.H.

Letter to Oliver Wolcott, Jr., September 26, 1800

Dear Sir,

As I hinted to you some time since, I have drafted a letter which it is my wish to send to influential individuals in the New England states. I hope from it two advantages, the promoting of Mr. Pinckney's election and the vindication of ourselves.

You may depend upon it a very serious impression has been made on the public mind by the partisans of Mr. Adams to our disadvantage; that the facts hitherto known have very partially impaired the confidence of the body of the Federalists in Mr. Adams, who for want of information are disposed to regard his opponents as factious men. If this cannot be counteracted, our characters are the sacrifice. To do it facts must be stated with some authentic stamp. Decorum may not permit going into the newspapers, but the letter may be addressed to so many respectable men of influence as may give its contents general circulation.

What say you to the measure? Anonymous publications can now effect nothing.

Some of the most delicate of the facts stated I hold from the three ministers, yourself particularly—and I do not think myself at liberty to take the step without your consent. I never mean to bring proof—but to stand upon the credit of my own veracity.

Say quickly what is to be done, for there is no time to spare. Give me your opinion not only of the measure but of the *fashion* & *spirit* of the letter in regard to utility & propriety. If there are exceptionable ideas or phrases note them.

As it is a first draft there is much I should myself mend. But I have not now leisure for it previous to your inspection.

Yrs. truly
A.H.

Letter to John Adams, October 1, 1800

Sir,

The time which has elapsed since my letter of the first of August was delivered to you precludes the further expectation of an answer.

From this silence, I will draw no inference; nor will I presume to judge of the fitness of silence on such an occasion on the part of the chief magistrate of a republic, towards a citizen who without a stain has discharged so many important public trusts.

But this much I will affirm, that by whomsoever a charge of the kind mentioned in my former letter may, at any time, have been made or insinuated against me, it is a base, wicked, and cruel calumny, destitute even of a plausible pretext to excuse the folly or mask the depravity which must have dictated it.

With due respect   I have the honor to be
Sir   Your obed Servt
A. Hamilton

Letter from Alexander Hamilton, Concerning the Public Conduct and Character of John Adams, Esq., President of the United States, October 24, 1800

Sir,

Some of the warm personal friends of Mr. Adams are taking unwearied pains to disparage the motives of those Federalists who advocate the equal support of Gen. Pinckney at the approaching election of president and vice president. They are exhibited under a variety of aspects equally derogatory. Sometimes they are versatile, factious spirits, who cannot be long satisfied with any chief, however meritorious—Sometimes they are ambitious spirits, who can be contented with no man that will not submit to be governed by them—Sometimes they are intriguing partisans of Great Britain, who, devoted to the advancement of her views, are incensed against Mr. Adams for the independent impartiality of his conduct.

In addition to a full share of the obloquy vented against this description of persons collectively, peculiar accusations have been devised to swell the catalogue of my demerits. Among these, the resentment of disappointed ambition forms a prominent feature. It is pretended that had the president, upon the demise of General Washington, appointed me commander in chief, he would have been, in my estimation, all that is wise and good and great.

It is necessary, for the public cause, to repel these slanders by stating the real views of the persons who are calumniated and the reasons of their conduct.

In executing this task, with particular reference to myself, I ought to premise that the ground upon which I stand is different from that of most of those who are confounded with me as in pursuit of the same plan. While our object is common, our motives are variously dissimilar. A part, well affected to Mr. Adams, have no other wish than to take a double chance against Mr. Jefferson. Another part, feeling a diminution of confidence in him, still hope that the general tenor of his conduct will be essentially right. Few go as far in their objections as I do. Not denying to Mr. Adams patriotism and integrity, and even talents of a certain kind, I should be deficient in candor were I to conceal the conviction that he does not possess the talents adapted to the *administration* of government, and that there are great and intrinsic defects in his character which unfit him for the office of chief magistrate.

To give a correct idea of the circumstances which have gradually produced this conviction, it may be useful to retrospect to an early period.

I was one of that numerous class who had conceived a high veneration for Mr. Adams on account of the part he acted in the first stages of our revolution. My imagination had exalted him to a high eminence as a man of patriotic, bold, profound, and comprehensive mind. But in the progress of the war, opinions were ascribed to him which brought into question, with me, the solidity of his understanding. He was represented to be of the number of those who favored the enlistment of our troops annually, or for short periods, rather than for the term of the war; a blind and infatuated policy, directly contrary to the urgent recommendation of General Washington, and which had nearly proved the ruin of our cause. He was also said to have advocated the project of appointing yearly a new commander of the army, a project which, in any service, is likely to be attended with more evils than benefits; but which, in ours, at the period in question, was chimerical, from the want of persons qualified to succeed, and pernicious, from the peculiar fitness of the officer first appointed, to strengthen, by personal influence, the too feeble cords which bound to the service, an ill-paid, ill-clothed, and undisciplined soldiery.

It is impossible for me to assert at this distant day that these suggestions were brought home to Mr. Adams in such a manner as to ascertain their genuineness; but I distinctly remember their existence, and my conclusion from them, which was, that, if true, they proved this gentleman to be infected with some visionary notions, and that he was far less able in the practice than in the theory of politics. I remember also that they had the effect of inducing me to qualify the admiration which I had once entertained for him, and to reserve for opportunities of future scrutiny a definitive opinion of the true standard of his character.

In this disposition I was when, just before the close of the war, I became a member of Congress.

The situation in which I found myself there was far from being inauspicious to a favorable estimate of Mr. Adams.

Upon my first going into Congress I discovered symptoms of a party already formed, too well disposed to subject the interests of the United States to the management of France. Though I felt, in common with those who had participated in our Revolution, a lively sentiment of good will towards a power whose cooperation, however it was and ought to have been dictated by its own interest, had been extremely useful to us, and had been afforded in a liberal and handsome manner; yet, tenacious of the real independence of our country, and dreading the preponderance of foreign influence as the natural disease of popular government, I was struck with disgust at the appearance, in the very cradle of our republic, of a party actuated by an undue complaisance to foreign power; and I resolved at once to resist this bias in our affairs: a resolution which has been the chief cause of the persecution I have endured in the subsequent stages of my political life.

Among the fruits of the bias I have mentioned were the celebrated instructions to our commissioners for treating of peace with Great Britain, which, not only as to final measures, but also as to preliminary and intermediate negotiations, placed them in a state of dependence on the French ministry humiliating to themselves and unsafe for the interests of the country. This was the more exceptionable as there was cause to suspect that in regard to the two cardinal points of the fisheries and the navigation of the Mississippi, the policy of the cabinet of Versailles did not accord with the wishes of the United States.

The commissioners, of whom Mr. Adams was one, had the fortitude to break through the fetters which were laid upon them by those instructions; and there is reason to believe that by doing it they both accelerated the peace with Great Britain and improved the terms, while they preserved our faith with France.

Yet a serious attempt was made to obtain from Congress a formal censure of their conduct. The attempt failed, and instead of censure, the praise was bestowed which was justly due to the accomplishment of a treaty advantageous to this country, beyond the most sanguine expectation. In this result, my efforts were heartily united.

The principal merit of the negotiation with Great Britain in some quarters has been bestowed upon Mr. Adams; but it is certainly the right of Mr. Jay, who took a lead in the several steps of the transaction no less honorable to his talents than to his firmness. The merit, nevertheless, of a full and decisive cooperation, is justly due to Mr. Adams.

It will readily be seen that such a course of things was calculated to impress me with a disposition friendly to Mr. Adams. I certainly felt it, and gave him much of my consideration and esteem.

But this did not hinder me from making careful observations upon his several communications and endeavoring to derive from them an accurate idea of his talents and character. This scrutiny enhanced my esteem in the main for his moral qualifications, but lessened my respect for his intellectual endowments. I then adopted an opinion, which all my subsequent experience has confirmed, that he is a man of an imagination sublimated and eccentric, propitious neither to the regular display of sound judgment nor to steady perseverance in a systematic plan of conduct; and I began to perceive what has been since too manifest, that to this defect are added the unfortunate foibles of a vanity without bounds and a jealousy capable of discoloring every object.

Strong evidence of some traits of this character is to be found in a journal of Mr. Adams, which was sent by the then secretary of foreign affairs to Congress. The reading of this journal extremely embarrassed his friends, especially the delegates of Massachusetts, who more than once interrupted it and at last succeeded in putting a stop to it, on the suggestion that it bore the marks of a private and confidential paper, which, by some mistake, had gotten into its present situation, and never could have been designed as a public document for the inspection of Congress. The good humor of that body yielded to the suggestion.

The particulars of this journal cannot be expected to have remained in my memory—but I recollect one which may serve as a sample. Being among the guests invited to dine with the Count de Vergennes, minister for foreign affairs, Mr. Adams thought fit to give a specimen of American politeness by conducting Madame de Vergennes to dinner; in the way, she was pleased to make retribution in the current coin of French politeness—by saying to him, "*Monsieur Adams, vous etes le* Washington *de negociation*."* Stating the incident, he makes this comment upon it: "These people have a very pretty knack of paying compliments." He might have added, they have also a very dexterous knack of disguising a sarcasm.

This opinion, however, which I have avowed, did not prevent my entering cordially into the plan of supporting Mr. Adams for the office of vice president under the new Constitution. I still thought that he had high claims upon the public gratitude and possessed a substantial worth of character, which might atone for some great defects. In addition to this, it was well known that he was a favorite of New England, and it was obvious that his union with General Washington would tend to give the government, in its outset, all the strength which it could derive from the character of the two principal magistrates.

But it was deemed an essential point of caution to take care that accident or an intrigue of the opposers of the government should not raise Mr. Adams, instead of General Washington, to the first place. This, every friend of the government would have considered as a disastrous event; as well because it would have displayed a capricious operation of the system in elevating to the first station a man intended for the second; as because it was conceived that the incomparably superior weight and transcendent popularity of Gen. Washington rendered his presence at the head of the government, in its first organization, a matter of primary and indispensable importance. It was therefore agreed that a few votes should be diverted from Mr. Adams to other persons, so as to insure to General Washington a plurality.

Great was my astonishment, and equally great my regret, when afterwards I learned from persons of unquestionable veracity that Mr. Adams had complained of unfair treatment in not having been permitted to take an equal chance with General Washington by leaving the votes to an uninfluenced current.

The extreme egotism of the temper which could blind a man to considerations so obvious as those that had recommended the course pursued cannot be enforced by my comment. It exceeded all that I had imagined, and showed, in too strong a light, that the vanity which I have ascribed to him existed to a degree that rendered it more than a harmless foible.

* Mr. Adams, you are the Washington of negotiation.

Mr. Adams was elected vice president. His public conduct in that station was satisfactory to the friends of the government, though they were now and then alarmed by appearances of some eccentric tendencies.

It is, in particular, a tribute due from me to acknowledge that Mr. Adams, being in quality of vice president *ex officio* one of the trustees of the Sinking Fund, I experienced from him the most complete support, which was the more gratifying to me as I had to struggle against the systematic opposition of Mr. Jefferson, seconded occasionally by Mr. Randolph. Though it would be an ill compliment to Mr. Adams not to presume that the support which he gave me was the dictate of his sense of the public interest, yet so cordial and useful a cooperation, at a moment when I was assailed with all the weapons of party rancor, won from me an unfeigned return of the most amicable sentiments.

I lost no opportunity of combating the prejudices industriously propagated against him by his political enemies, and, for a considerable time, went quite as far as candor would permit to extenuate the failings which more and more alarmed and dissatisfied his friends.

The epoch at length arrived when the retreat of General Washington made it necessary to fix upon a successor. By this time men of principal influence in the Federal Party, whose situation had led them to an intimate acquaintance with Mr. Adams's character, began to entertain serious doubts about his fitness for the station; yet his pretensions in several respects were so strong that after mature reflection, they thought it better to indulge their hopes than to listen to their fears. To this conclusion the desire of preserving harmony in the Federal Party was a weighty inducement. Accordingly it was determined to support Mr. Adams for the chief magistracy.

It was evidently of much consequence to endeavor to have an eminent Federalist vice president. Mr. Thomas Pinckney of South Carolina was selected for this purpose. This gentleman, too little known in the North, had been all his life time distinguished in the south for the mildness and amiableness of his manners, the rectitude and purity of his morals, and the soundness and correctness of his understanding, accompanied by a habitual discretion and self-command, which has often occasioned a parallel to be drawn between him and the venerated Washington. In addition to these recommendations, he had been, during a critical period, our minister at the Court of London, and recently envoy extraordinary to the Court of Spain; and in both these trusts he had acquitted himself to the satisfaction of all parties. With the Court of Spain he had effected a treaty which removed all the thorny subjects of contention that had so long threatened the peace of the two countries, and stipulated for the United States, on their southern frontier and on the Mississippi, advantages of real magnitude and importance.

Well informed men knew that the event of the election was extremely problematical; and, while the friends of Mr. Jefferson predicted his success with sanguine confidence, his opposers feared that he might have at least an equal chance with any Federal candidate.

To exclude him was deemed by the Federalists a primary object. Those of them who possessed the best means of judging were of opinion that it was far less important whether Mr. Adams or Mr. Pinckney was the successful candidate than that Mr. Jefferson should not be the person; and on this principle it was understood among them that the two first mentioned gentlemen should be equally supported, leaving to casual accessions of votes in favor of the one or the other to turn the scale between them.

In this plan I united with good faith in the resolution, to which I scrupulously adhered, of giving to each candidate an equal support. This was done wherever my influence extended, as was more particularly manifested in the state of New York, where all the electors were my warm personal or political friends, and all gave a concurrent vote for the two Federal candidates.

It is true that a faithful execution of this plan would have given Mr. Pinckney a somewhat better chance than Mr. Adams, nor shall it be concealed that an issue favorable to the former would not have been disagreeable to me, as indeed I declared at the time in the circles of my confidential friends.* My position was that if chance should decide in favor of Mr. Pinckney, it probably would not be a misfortune, since he, to every essential qualification for the office, added a temper far more discreet and conciliatory than that of Mr. Adams.

This disposition on my part at that juncture proves, at least, that my disapprobation of Mr. Adams has not originated in the disappointment to which it has been uncandidly attributed. No private motive could then have entered into it. Not the least collision or misunderstanding had ever happened between that gentleman and myself—on the contrary, as I have already stated, I had reason individually to be pleased with him.

No: The considerations which had reconciled me to the success of Mr. Pinckney were of a nature exclusively public. They resulted from the disgusting egotism, the distempered jealousy, and the ungovernable indiscretion of Mr. Adams's temper, joined to some doubts of the correctness of his maxims of administration. Though in matters of finance he had acted with the Federal Party, yet he had more than once broached theories at variance with his practice. And in conversation he repeatedly made excursions in the field of foreign politics which alarmed the friends of the prevailing system.

The plan of giving equal support to the two Federalist candidates was not pursued. Personal attachment for Mr. Adams, especially in the New England states, caused a number of the votes to be withheld from Mr. Pinckney and thrown away. The result was that Mr. Adams was elected president by a majority of two votes and Mr. Jefferson vice president.

This issue demonstrated the wisdom of the plan which had been abandoned and how greatly, in departing from it, the cause had been sacrificed to the man. But for a sort of miracle, the departure would have made Mr. Jefferson president. In each of the states of Pennsylvania, Virginia, and

* I appeal particularly to Lt. Governor Van Rensselaer and R. Troup, Esq.

North Carolina, Mr. Adams had one vote. In the two latter states, the one vote was as much against the stream of popular prejudice as it was against the opinions of the other electors. The firmness of the individuals who separated from their colleagues was so extraordinary as to have been contrary to all probable calculation. Had only one of them thrown his vote into the other scale, there would have been an equality and no election. Had two done it, the choice would have fallen upon Mr. Jefferson.

No one, sincere in the opinion that this gentleman was an ineligible and dangerous candidate, can hesitate in pronouncing that in dropping Mr. Pinckney too much was put at hazard, and that those who promoted the other course acted with prudence and propriety.

It is a fact which ought not to be forgotten that Mr. Adams, who had evinced discontent because he had not been permitted to take an equal chance with General Washington, was enraged with all those who had thought that Mr. Pinckney ought to have had an equal chance with him. But in this there is perfect consistency. The same turn of temper is the solution of the displeasure in both cases.

It is to this circumstance of the equal support of Mr. Pinckney that we are in a great measure to refer the serious schism which has since grown up in the Federal Party.

Mr. Adams never could forgive the men who had been engaged in the plan, though it embraced some of his most partial admirers. He has discovered bitter animosity against several of them. Against me, his rage has been so vehement as to have caused him more than once to forget the decorum which, in his situation, ought to have been an inviolable law. It will not appear an exaggeration to those who have studied his character to suppose that he is capable of being alienated from a system to which he has been attached because it is upheld by men whom he hates. How large a share this may have had in some recent aberrations cannot easily be determined.

Occurrences which have either happened or come to light since the election of Mr. Adams to the presidency confirming my unfavorable forebodings of his character have given new and decisive energy, in my mind, to the sentiment of his unfitness for the station.

The letter which has just appeared in the public prints, written by him while vice president to Tench Coxe, is of itself conclusive evidence of the justness of this sentiment. It is impossible to speak of this transaction in terms suited to its nature without losing sight that Mr. Adams is the president of the United States.

This letter avows the *suspicion* that the appointment of Mr. Pinckney to the Court of London had been procured or promoted by British influence. And considering the parade with which the story of the Duke of Leeds is told, it is fair to consider that circumstance as the principal, if not the sole, ground of the odious and degrading suspicion.

Let any man of candor or knowledge of the world pronounce on this species of evidence.

It happened unfortunately for the Pinckneys, that, while boys, and long before our revolution, they went to school with a British Duke, who was afterwards minister of the British government for the foreign department. This indiscreet Duke, perhaps for no better reason than the desire of saying something to a parting American minister and the want of something better to say, divulges to him the dangerous secret that the two Pinckneys had been his classmates, and goes the alarming length of making enquiry about their health. From this it is sagaciously inferred that these gentlemen have "*many powerful old friends in England*"; and from this again that the Duke of Leeds (of course of the number of these old friends) had procured by intrigue the appointment of one of his classmates to the Court of London; or, in the language of the letter, that much British influence had been exerted in the appointment.

In the school of jealousy, stimulated by ill will, logic like this may pass for substantial; but what is it in the school of reason and justice?

Though this contaminating connection of the Pinckneys with the Duke of Leeds in their juvenile years did not hinder them from fighting for the independence of their native country throughout our revolution, yet the supposition is that the instant the war was terminated it transformed them from the soldiers of liberty into the tools of the British monarchy.

But the hostility of the Pinckneys to Mr. Adams, evidenced by their "long intrigue" against him, of which he speaks in the letter, is perhaps intended as a still stronger proof of their devotion to Great Britain—the argument may be thus understood: Mr. Adams is the bulwark of his country against foreign influence. The batteries of every foreign power, desirous of acquiring an ascendant in our affairs, are of consequence always open against him—and, the presumption therefore must be, that every citizen who is his enemy is the confederate of one or another of those foreign powers.

Let us, without contesting this argument of self-love, examine into the facts upon which its applicability must depend.

The evidence of "the long intrigue" seems to be that the family of the Pinckneys contributed to limit the duration of Mr. Adams's commission to the Court of London to the term of three years, in order to make way for some of themselves to succeed him. This, it must be confessed, was a long-sighted calculation in a government like ours.

A summary of the transaction will be the best comment on the inference which has been drawn.

The resolution of Congress by which Mr. Adams's commission was limited was a general one, applying to the commissions of all ministers to foreign Courts. When it was proposed and adopted, it is certain that neither of the two Pinckneys was a member of Congress; and it is believed that they were both at Charleston, in South Carolina, their usual place of abode, more than eight hundred miles distant from the seat of government.

But they had, it seems, a *cousin*, Mr. Charles Pinckney, who was in Congress; and this cousin it was who moved the restrictive resolution. Let us enquire who seconded and who voted for it.

It was seconded by Mr. Howell, a member from Rhode Island, *the very person who nominated Mr. Adams as Minister to Great Britain*, and was voted for by the four eastern states, with New York, New Jersey, Maryland, and South Carolina. Mr. Gerry, always a zealous partisan of Mr. Adams, was among the supporters of the resolution. To make out this to be a machination of the two Pinckneys, many things must be affirmed: First, that their cousin Charles is always subservient to their views (which would equally prove that they have long been, and still are, opposers of the Federal administration)—Second, that this cunning wight had been able to draw the *four eastern states* into his plot, as well as New York, New Jersey, Maryland, and South Carolina—Third, that the Pinckneys could foresee, at the distance of three years, the existence of a state of things which would enable them to reap the fruit of their contrivance.

Would not the circumstances better warrant the suspicion that the resolution was a contrivance of the friends of Mr. Adams, to facilitate in some way his election, and that Mr. Pinckney was their coadjutor rather than their prompter?

But the truth most probably is that the measure was a mere precaution to bring under frequent review the propriety of continuing a minister at a particular court, and to facilitate the removal of a disagreeable one without the harshness of formally displacing him. In a policy of this sort, the cautious maxims of New England would very naturally have taken a lead.

Thus in the very grounds of the suspicion, as far as they appear, we find its refutation. The complete futility of it will now be illustrated by additional circumstances.

It is a fact that the rigor with which the war was prosecuted by the British armies in our southern quarter had produced among the friends of our revolution there more animosity against the British Government than in the other parts of the United States: and it is a matter of notoriety in the same quarter that this disposition was conspicuous among the Pinckneys and their connections. It may be added that they were likewise known to have been attached to the French Revolution, and to have continued so till long after the appointment of Mr. Thomas Pinckney to the Court of London.

These propensities of the gentlemen were certainly not such as to make them favorites of Great Britain, or the appointment of one of them to that court an object of particular solicitude.

As far as appeared at the time, the idea of nominating Mr. Thomas Pinckney originated with the then president himself: but whatever may have been its source, it is certain that it met the approbation of the whole administration, Mr. Jefferson included. This fact alone will go far to refute the surmise of a British agency in the appointment.

Supposing that, contrary to all probability, Great Britain had really taken some unaccountable fancy for Mr. Pinckney, upon whom was her influence exerted?

Had the virtuous, circumspect *Washington* been ensnared in her insidious toils? Had she found means for once to soften the stern, inflexible hostility of Jefferson? Had Randolph been won by her meretricious caresses? Had Knox, the uniform friend of Mr. Adams, been corrupted by her seducing wiles? Or was it all the dark work of the *alien* secretary of the treasury? Was it this arch juggler, who debauched the principles or transformed the prejudices of Mr. Pinckney; who persuaded the British government to adopt him as a pliant instrument; who artfully induced the president to propose him as of his own selection; who lulled the zealous vigilance of Jefferson and Randolph, and surprised the unsuspecting friends of Knox?

But when the thing had been accomplished, no matter by what means, it was surely to have been expected that the man of its choice would have been treated at the Court of London with distinguished regard, and that his conduct towards that court would have been marked, if not by some improper compliances, at least by some displays of extraordinary complaisance.

Yet, strange as it may appear upon Mr. Adams's hypothesis, it might be proved, if requisite, that neither the one nor the other took place. It might be proved that, far from Mr. Pinckney's having experienced any flattering distinctions, incidents not pleasant to his feelings had occurred, and that in the discharge of his official functions he had advanced pretensions in favor of the United States from which, with the approbation of the then secretary of state, Mr. Jefferson, he was instructed to desist.

What will Mr. Adams or his friends reply to all these facts? How will he be excused for indulging and declaring, on grounds so frivolous, a suspicion so derogatory of a man so meritorious—of a man who has acted in a manner so unexceptionable?

But a more serious question remains: How will Mr. Adams answer to the government and to his country for having thus wantonly given the sanction of his opinion to the worst of the aspersions which the enemies of the administration have impudently thrown upon it? Can we be surprised that such a torrent of slander was poured out against it, when a man, the second in official rank, the second in the favor of the friends of the government, stooped to become himself one of its calumniators? It is peculiarly unlucky for Mr. Adams in this affair that he is known to have desired, at the time, the appointment which was given to Mr. Pinckney. The president declined the measure, thinking that it was compatible neither with the spirit of the Constitution nor with the dignity of the government, to designate the vice president to such a station.

This letter, better than volumes, develops the true, the unfortunate character of Mr. Adams.

The remaining causes of dissatisfaction with him respect his conduct in the office of president, which, in my opinion, has been a heterogeneous compound of right and wrong, of wisdom and error.

The outset was distinguished by a speech which his friends lamented as temporizing. It had the air of a lure for the favor of his opponents at the expense of his sincerity; but being of an equivocal complexion, to which no precise design can be annexed, it is barely mentioned as a circumstance which, in conjunction with others of a more positive tint, may serve to explain character.

It is in regard to our foreign relations that the public measures of Mr. Adams first attract criticism.

It will be recollected that General Pinckney, the brother of Thomas, and the gentleman now supported together with Mr. Adams, had been deputed by President Washington as successor to Mr. Monroe, and had been refused to be received by the French government in his quality of minister plenipotentiary.

This, among those of the well-informed who felt a just sensibility for the honor of their country, excited much disgust and resentment. But the opposition party, ever too ready to justify the French government at the expense of their own, vindicated or apologized for the ill treatment: and the mass of the community, though displeased with it, did not appear to feel the full force of the indignity.

As a final effort for accommodation, and as a mean, in case of failure, of enlightening and combining public opinion, it was resolved to make another, and a more solemn, experiment, in the form of a commission of three.

This measure (with some objections to the detail) was approved by all parties; by the Antifederalists, because they thought no evil so great as the rupture with France; by the Federalists, because it was their system to avoid war with every power, if it could be done without the sacrifice of essential interests or absolute humiliation.

Even such of them who conceived that the insults of the French government and the manifestation of its ill will had already gone far enough to call for measures of vigor, perceiving that the nation was not generally penetrated with the same conviction, and would not support with zeal measures of that nature unless their necessity was rendered still more apparent, acquiesced in the expediency of another mission. They hoped that it would serve either to compose the differences which existed, or to make the necessity of resistance to the violence of France palpable to every good citizen.

The expediency of the step was suggested to Mr. Adams, through a Federal channel, a considerable time before he determined to take it. He hesitated whether it could be done after the rejection of General Pinckney without national debasement. The doubt was an honorable one; it was afterwards very properly surrendered to the cogent reasons which pleaded for a further experiment.

The event of this experiment is fresh in our recollection. Our envoys, like our minister, were rejected. Tribute was demanded as a preliminary to negotiation. To their immortal honor, though France at the time was proudly triumphant, they repelled the disgraceful pretension. Americans will never forget that General Pinckney was a member, and an efficient member, of this commission.

This conduct of the French government, in which it is difficult to say whether despotic insolence or unblushing corruption was most prominent, electrified the American people with a becoming indignation. In vain the partisans of France attempted to extenuate. The public voice was distinct and audible. The nation, disdaining so foul an overture, was ready to encounter the worst consequences of resistance.

Without imitating the flatterers of Mr. Adams, who, in derogation from the intrinsic force of circumstances, and from the magnanimity of the nation, ascribe to him the whole merits of producing the spirit which appeared in the community, it shall with cheerfulness be acknowledged that he took upon the occasion a manly and courageous lead—that he did all in his power to rouse the pride of the nation—to inspire it with a just sense of the injuries and outrages which it had experienced, and to dispose it to a firm and magnanimous resistance; and that his efforts contributed materially to the end.

The friends of the government were not agreed as to ulterior measures. Some were for immediate and unqualified war, others for a more mitigated course: the dissolution of treaties, preparation of force by land and sea, partial hostilities of a defensive tendency, leaving to France the option of seeking accommodation or proceeding to open war. The latter course prevailed.

Though not as bold and energetic as the other, yet, considering the prosperous state of French affairs when it was adopted, and how many nations had been appalled and prostrated by the French power—the conduct pursued bore sufficiently the marks of courage and elevation to raise the national character to an exalted height throughout Europe.

Much is it to be deplored that we should have been precipitated from this proud eminence without necessity, without temptation.

The latter conduct of the president forms a painful contrast to his commencement. Its effects have been directly the reverse. It has sunk the tone of the public mind—it has impaired the confidence of the friends of the government in the executive chief—it has distracted public opinion—it has unnerved the public councils—it has sown the seeds of discord at home and lowered the reputation of the government abroad. The circumstances which preceded aggravate the disagreeableness of the results. They prove that the injudicious things which have been acted were not the effects of any regular plan but the fortuitous emanations of momentary impulses.

The session which ensued the promulgation of the dispatches of our commissioners was about to commence. Mr. Adams arrived at Philadelphia from his seat at Quincy. The tone of his mind seemed to have been raised rather than depressed.

It was suggested to him that it might be expedient to insert in his speech of Congress a sentiment of this import: That after the repeatedly rejected advances of this country, its dignity required that it should be left with France in future to make the first overture; that if, desirous of reconciliation, she should evince the disposition by sending a minister to this government, he would be received with the respect due to his character, and treated with in the frankness of a sincere desire of accommodation.

The suggestion was received in a manner both indignant and intemperate.

Mr. Adams declared as a sentiment which he had adopted on mature reflection: *That if France should send a minister tomorrow, he would order him back the day after.*

So imprudent an idea was easily refuted. Little argument was requisite to show that by a similar system of retaliation, when one government in a particular instance had refused the envoy of another, nations might entail upon each other perpetual hostility, mutually barring the avenues of explanation.

In less than forty-eight hours from this extraordinary sally, the mind of Mr. Adams underwent a total revolution—he resolved not only to insert in his speech the sentiment which had been proposed to him, but to go farther, and to declare that if France would give explicit assurances of receiving a minister from this country with due respect, he would send one.

In vain was this extension of the sentiment opposed by all his ministers as being equally incompatible with good policy and with the dignity of the nation—he obstinately persisted, and the pernicious declaration was introduced.

I call it pernicious, because it was the groundwork of the false steps which have succeeded.

The declaration recommended to the president was a prudent one.

The measures of Congress, by their mitigated form, showed that an eye had been still kept upon pacification. A numerous party were averse from war with France at any rate. In the rest of the community a strong preference of honorable accommodation to final rupture was discernible, even amidst the effusions of resentment.

The charges which we had exhibited in the face of the world against the French government were of a high and disgraceful complexion; they had been urged with much point and emphasis.

To give an opening to France, to make conciliatory propositions, some salve for her pride was necessary. It was also necessary she should be assured that she would not expose herself to an affront by a refusal to receive the agent whom she might employ for that purpose. The declaration proposed fulfilled both objects.

It was likely to have another important advantage. It would be a new proof to the American people of the moderate and pacific temper of their government, which would tend to preserve their confidence, and to dispose them more and more to meet inevitable extremities with fortitude and without murmurs.

But the supplement to the declaration was a blamable excess. It was more than sufficient for the ends to be answered. It waived the point of honor, which, after two rejections of our ministers, required that the next mission between the two countries should proceed from France. After the mortifying humiliations we had endured, the national dignity demanded that this point should not be departed from without necessity. No such necessity could be pretended to exist: moreover, another mission by us would naturally be regarded as evidence of a disposition on our part to purchase the friendship of revolutionary France, even at the expense of honor, an impression which could hardly fail to injure our interests with other countries: and the measure would involve the further inconvenience of transferring the negotiation from this country, where our government could regulate it according to its own view of exigencies, to France, where that advantage would be enjoyed by her government, and where the power of judging for us must be delegated to commissioners, who, acting under immense individual responsibility, at a distance too great for consultation, would be apt to act with hesitancy and irresolution, whether the policy of the case required concession or firmness. This was to place it too much in the power of France to manage the progress of the negotiation according to events.

It has been said that Paris was wisely preferred as the place of negotiation, because it served to avoid the caballings of a French minister in this country. But there is not enough in this argument to counterbalance the weighty considerations on the other side. The intrigues of Genet and his successors were perplexing to the government chiefly because they were too well seconded by the prepossessions of the people. The great alteration in public opinion had put it completely in the power of our executive to control the machinations of any future public agent of France. It ought also to be remembered that if France has not known agents, she never will be without secret ones, and that her partisans among our citizens can much better promote her cause than any agents she can send. In fact, her agents, by their blunders, were in the event rather useful than pernicious to our affairs.

But is it likely that France would have sent a minister to this country? When we find that from calculations of policy she could brook the ignominy which the publication of the dispatches of our commissioners was calculated to bring upon her; and, stifling her resentment, could invite the renewal of negotiation; what room can there be to doubt that the same calculations would have induced her to send a minister to this country when an opening was given for it?

The French minister for foreign relations, through the French diplomatic agent at the Hague, had opened a communication with Mr. Murray, our resident there, for the purpose of reviving negotiation between the two countries. In this manner, assurances were given that France was disposed to treat, and that a minister from us would be received and accredited. But they were accompanied with intimations of the characters proper to be employed, and who would be likely to succeed; which was exceptionable, both as it savored of the pretension (justly censured by the president himself) of prescribing to other governments how they were to manage their own affairs; and as it might, according to circumstances, be construed into a tacit condition of the promise to receive a minister. Overtures so circuitous and informal, through a person who was not the regular organ of the French government for making them, to a person who was not the regular organ of the American government for receiving them, might be a very fit mode of preparing the way for the like overtures in a more authentic and obligatory shape: But they were a very inadequate basis for the institution of a new mission.

When the President pledged himself in his speech to send a minister, if satisfactory assurances of a proper reception were given, he must have been understood to mean such as were direct and official, not such as were both informal and destitute of a competent sanction.

Yet upon this loose and vague foundation, Mr. Adams precipitately nominated Mr. Murray as envoy to the French Republic, without previous consultation with any of his ministers. The nomination itself was to each of them, even to the secretary of state, his constitutional counselor in similar affairs, the first notice of the project.

Thus was the measure wrong, both as to mode and substance.

A president is not bound to conform to the advice of his ministers. He is even under no positive injunction to ask or require it. But the Constitution presumes that he will consult them, and the genius of our government and the public good recommend the practice.

As the president nominates his ministers, and may displace them when he pleases, it must be his own fault if he be not surrounded by men who for ability and integrity deserve his confidence. And if his ministers are of this character, the consulting of them will always be likely to be useful to himself and to the state. Let it even be supposed that he is a man of talents superior to the collected talents of all his ministers (which can seldom happen, as the world has seen but few Fredericks), he may, nevertheless, often assist his judgment by a comparison and collision of ideas. The greatest genius, hurried away by the rapidity of its own conceptions, will occasionally overlook obstacles which ordinary and more phlegmatic men will discover, and which, when presented to his consideration, will be thought by himself decisive objections to his plans.

When, unhappily, an ordinary man dreams himself to be a Frederick, and through vanity refrains from counseling with his constitutional advisers, he is very apt to fall into the hands of miserable intriguers, with whom his self-love is more at ease, and who without difficulty slide into his confidence, and by flattery govern him.

The ablest men may profit by advice. Inferior men cannot dispense with it; and if they do not get it through legitimate channels, it will find its way to them through such as are clandestine and impure.

Very different from the practice of Mr. Adams was that of the modest and sage Washington. He consulted much, pondered much, resolved slowly, resolved surely.

And as surely Mr. Adams might have benefited by the advice of his ministers.

The stately system of not consulting ministers is likely to have a further disadvantage. It will tend to exclude from places of primary trust the men most fit to occupy them.

Few and feeble are the interested inducements to accept a place in our administration. Far from being lucrative, there is not one which will not involve pecuniary sacrifice to every *honest* man of preeminent talents. And has not experience shown that he must be fortunate indeed if even the successful execution of his task can secure to him consideration and fame? Of a large harvest of obloquy he is sure.

If excluded from the counsels of the executive chief, his office must become truly insignificant. What able and virtuous man will long consent to be so miserable a pageant?

Everything that tends to banish from the administration able men tends to diminish the chances of able counsels. The probable operation of a system of this kind must be to consign places of the highest trust to incapable honest men, whose inducement will be a livelihood, or to capable dishonest men, who will seek indirect indemnifications for the deficiency of direct and fair inducements.

The precipitate nomination of Mr. Murray brought Mr. Adams into an awkward predicament.

He found it necessary to change his plan in its progress, and instead of one to nominate three envoys, and to super-add a promise, that, though appointed, they should not leave the United States till further and more perfect assurances were given by the French government.

This remodification of the measure was a virtual acknowledgement that it had been premature. How unseemly was this fluctuation in the executive chief. It argued either instability of views or want of sufficient consideration beforehand. The one or the other, in an affair of so great moment, is a serious reproach.

Additional and more competent assurances were received; but before the envoys departed intelligence arrived of a new revolution in the French government which, in violation of the constitution, had expelled two of the Directory.

Another revolution: Another constitution overthrown: Surely here was reason for a pause, at least till it was ascertained that the new Directory would adhere to the engagement of its predecessors and would not send back our envoys with disgrace.

In the then posture of French affairs, which externally as well as internally were unprosperous, a pause was every way prudent. The recent revolution was a valid motive for it.

Definitive compacts between nations, called real treaties, are binding, notwithstanding revolutions of governments. But to apply the maxim to ministerial acts, preparatory only to negotiation, is to extend it too far; to apply it to such acts of an unstable revolutionary government (like that of France at that time) is to abuse it.

Had any policy of the moment demanded it, it would have been not at all surprising to have seen the new Directory disavowing the assurance which had been given and imputing it as a crime to the ex-Directors, on the pretense that they had prostrated the dignity of the Republic by courting the renewal of negotiation with a government which had so grossly insulted it.

Yet our envoys were dispatched without a ratification of the assurance by the new Directory, at the hazard of the interests and the honor of the country.

Again, the dangerous and degrading system of not consulting ministers was acted upon.

When the news of the revolution in the Directory arrived, Mr. Adams was at his seat in Massachusetts. His ministers addressed to him a joint letter communicating the intelligence and submitting to his consideration whether that event ought not to suspend the projected mission. In a letter which he afterwards wrote from the same place, he directed the preparation of a draft of instructions for the envoys and intimated that their departure would be suspended *for some time*.

Shortly after, he came to Trenton, where he adjusted with his ministers the tenor of the instructions to be given; but he observed a profound silence on the question whether it was expedient that the mission should proceed. The morning after the instructions were settled, he signified to the secretary of state that the envoys were immediately to depart.

He is reported to have assigned as the reason of his silence that he knew the opinions of his ministers from their letter, that he had irrevocably adopted an opposite one, and that he deemed it most delicate not to embarrass them by a useless discussion.

But would it not have been more prudent to have kept his judgment in some degree in suspense till after an interview and discussion with his ministers? Ought he to have taken it for granted that the grounds of his opinion were so infallible that there was no possibility of arguments being used which were sufficient to shake them? Ought he not to have recollected the sudden revolution which his judgment had undergone in the beginning of the business, and to have inferred from this that it might have yielded in another instance to better lights? Was it necessary for him, if he had had a conference with his ministers, to have alarmed their delicacy by prefacing the discussion with a declaration that he had fixed an unalterable opinion? Did not the intimation respecting a suspension of the departure of the envoys imply that this would continue till there was a change of circumstances? Was it not a circumstance to strengthen expectation in the ministers when consulted about the instructions that they would be heard as to the principal point, previous to a definitive resolution?

Giving Mr. Adams credit for sincerity, the desultoriness of his mind is evinced by the very different grounds upon which, at different times, he has defended the propriety of the mission.

Sometimes he has treated with ridicule the idea of its being a measure which would terminate in peace; asserting that France would not accommodate, on terms admissible by the United States, and that the effect to be expected from the mission was the demonstration of this truth and the union of public opinion on the necessity of war.

Sometimes, and most frequently, he has vindicated the measure as one conformable with the general and strong wish of the country for peace, and as likely to promote that desirable object.

It is now earnestly to be hoped that the final issue of the mission, in an honorable accommodation, may compensate for the sacrifice of consistency, dignity, harmony, and reputation at which it has been undertaken.

But even in relation to the adjustment of differences with the French Republic, the measure was injudicious. It was probable that it would delay, rather than accelerate, such an adjustment.

The situation of French affairs, at the time of the overtures for renewing the negotiation, coincides with the solicitude which was manifested for that object, to render it likely that, at this juncture, France really desired accommodation. If this was so, it is presumable (as observed in another place) that, had not the declaration about sending a minister to her intervened, she would have sent one to us with adequate powers and instructions. Towards a minister here, our government might have acted such a part as would have hastened a conclusion; and the minister, conforming to the impressions of his government when he was sent, it is not improbable that a desirable arrangement might sometime since have been effected.

Instead of this, the mode pursued naturally tended to delay. A lapse of time, by changing the circumstances, is very apt to change the views of governments. The French agents, charged with the negotiation at Paris, could find little difficulty in protracting it till events (such as the fate of a campaign) should be ascertained as a guide to rise or fall in their pretensions. And in this way obstacles might supervene which would not have existed in the beginning, and which might render accommodation impracticable—or practicable only on terms injurious to our interests.

Thus, on every just calculation, whatever may be the issue, the measure, in reference either to our internal or foreign affairs, even to our concerns with France herself, was alike impolitic.

It is sometimes defended by the argument that when our commissioners departed there were circumstances in the position of Europe which made a general peace during the succeeding winter probable, and that it would have been dangerous for this country, remote as it is from Europe, to have been without agents on the spot authorized to settle its controversy with France at the same epoch. The country, it is said, might otherwise have been left in the perilous situation of having a subsisting quarrel with France after she had disembarrassed herself of all her European enemies.

The idea that a general peace was likely to happen during that winter was, I know, entertained by Mr. Adams himself; for, in a casual conversation at Trenton he expressed it to me, and I supported a different opinion. But waiving now a discussion of the point, and admitting that the expectation was entertained on substantial grounds, though it has not been verified by experience, still the argument derived from it is not valid.

The expediency of the measure must be tested by the state of things when it had its inception. At the time the foundation was laid for it by the speech, when even the nomination of Mr. Murray took place, the affairs of France and of her enemies portended a result very inauspicious to her, and very different from that of a general peace, on conditions which would leave her the inclination or the power to prosecute hostilities against this country.

But even on the supposition of other prospects, Mr. Adams had the option of a substitute far preferable to the expedient which he chose.

He might secretly and confidentially have nominated one or more of our ministers actually abroad for the purpose of treating with France, with *eventual* instructions predicated upon appearances of an approaching peace.

An expedient of this sort, merely provisionary, could have had none of the bad effects of the other. If the secret was kept, it could have had no inconvenient consequences; if divulged, it would have been deemed here and elsewhere a prudent precaution only, recommended by the distant situation of the country, to meet future casualties with which we might otherwise not have been able to keep pace. To the enemies of France it could have given no ill impression of us; to France no motive to forbear other conciliatory means, for one and the same reason, namely, because the operation was to be eventual.

There are some collateral incidents connected with this business of the mission which it may not be useless to mention, as they will serve still farther to illustrate the extreme propensity of Mr. Adams's temper to jealousy.

It happened that I arrived at Trenton a short time before the president— Chief Justice Ellsworth a short time after him. This was considered as evidence of a combination between the heads of departments, the chief justice, and myself to endeavor to influence or counteract him in the affair of the mission.

The truth, nevertheless, most certainly is that I went to Trenton with General Wilkinson, pursuant to a preconcert with him of some weeks standing, to accelerate, by personal conferences with the secretary of war, the adoption and execution of arrangements which had been planned between that general and myself for the future disposition of the Western Army; that when I left New York upon this journey I had no expectation whatever that the president would come to Trenton, and that I did not stay at this place a day longer than was indispensable to the object I have stated. General Wilkinson, if necessary, might be appealed to, not only as knowing that this was a real and sincere purpose of my journey, but as possessing satisfactory evidence that in all probability I had no anticipation of the movement of the president.

As to Chief Justice Ellsworth, the design of his journey was understood to be to meet his colleague, Governor Davy, at the seat of the government, where they would be at the fountain head of information and would obtain any lights or explanations which they might suppose useful. This was manifestly a very natural and innocent solution of the chief justice's visit, and I believe the true one.

Yet these simple occurrences were to the jealous mind of Mr. Adams "confirmations strong" of some mischievous plot against his independence.

The circumstance which next presents itself to examination is the dismission of the two secretaries, Pickering and McHenry. This circumstance, it is known, occasioned much surprise and a strong sensation to the disadvantage of Mr. Adams.

It happened at a peculiar juncture, immediately after the unfavorable turn of the election in New York, and had much the air of an explosion of combustible materials which had been long prepared, but which had been kept down by prudential calculations respecting the effect of an explosion upon the friends of those ministers in the state of New York. Perhaps, when it was supposed that nothing could be lost in this quarter, and that something might be gained elsewhere by an atoning sacrifice of those ministers, especially Mr. Pickering, who had been for some time particularly odious to the opposition party, it was determined to proceed to extremities. This, as a mere conjecture, is offered for as much as it may be worth.

One fact, however, is understood to be admitted, namely, that neither of the dismissed ministers had given any new or recent cause for their dismission.

A primary cause of the state of things which led to this event is to be traced to the ungovernable temper of Mr. Adams. It is a fact that he is often liable to paroxysms of anger which deprive him of self-command and produce very outrageous behavior to those who approach him. Most if not all his ministers, and several distinguished members of the two Houses of Congress, have been humiliated by the effects of these gusts of passion.

This violence, and the little consideration for them which was implied in declining to consult them, had occasioned great dryness between the president and his ministers, except, I believe, the secretary of the navy.

The neglect was of course most poignant to Mr. Pickering, because it had repeatedly operated in matters appertaining to his office. Nor was it in the disposition of this respectable man, justly tenacious of his own dignity and independence, to practice condescensions towards an imperious chief. Hence the breach constantly grew wider and wider, till a separation took place.

The manner of the dismission was abrupt and uncourteous, ill-suited to a man who, in different stations, had merited so much from his country.

Admitting that when the president and his minister had gotten into a situation thus unpleasant, a separation was unavoidable, still, as there was no surmise of misconduct, the case required a frank politeness, not an uncouth austerity.

But the remark most interesting in this particular to the character of the president is that it was by his own fault that he was brought into a situation which might oblige him to displace a minister whose moral worth has his own suffrage, and whose abilities and services have that of the public.

The dismission of this minister was preceded by a very curious circumstance. It was, without doubt, announced as a thing shortly to happen in an opposition circle, before any friend of the government had the slightest suspicion of it. This circumstance, taken in connection with the period at which it happened, naturally provokes the conjecture that there may have been some collateral inducements to the step.

The dismission of the secretary at war took place about the same time. It was declared in the sequel of a long conversation between the president and him, of a nature to excite alternately pain and laughter; pain, for the weak and excessive indiscretions of a chief magistrate of the United States; laughter at the ludicrous topics which constituted charges against this officer.

A prominent charge was that the secretary, in a report to the House of Representatives, had *eulogized General Washington* and had attempted to eulogize General *Hamilton*, which was adduced as one proof of a combination, in which the secretary was engaged, to depreciate and injure him, the president.

Wonderful! passing Wonderful! that an eulogy of the dead patriot and hero, of the admired and beloved Washington, consecrated in the affections and reverence of his country, should, in any shape, be irksome to the ears of his successor!

Singular, also, that an encomium on the officer, first in rank in the armies of the United States, appointed and continued by Mr. Adams, should in his eyes have been a crime in the head of the War Department, and that it should be necessary, in order to avert his displeasure, to obliterate a compliment to that officer from an official report.

Another principal topic of accusation was that the secretary had, with the other ministers, signed the joint letter which had been addressed to the president respecting a suspension of the mission to France. It was ostentatiously asked how he or they should pretend to know anything of *diplomatic affairs*, and it was plainly intimated that it was presumption in them to have intermeddled in such affairs.

A variety of things equally frivolous and *outré* passed. By way of episode, it fell to my lot to be distinguished by a torrent of gross personal abuse; and I was accused of having contributed to the loss of the election in New York out of ill will to Mr. Adams: a notable expedient truly for giving vent to my ill will. Who is so blind as not to see that if actuated by such a motive I should have preferred by the success of the election to have secured the choice of electors for the State of New York, who would have been likely to cooperate in the views by which I was governed?

To those who have not had opportunities of closely inspecting the weaknesses of Mr. Adams's character, the details of this extraordinary interview would appear incredible; but to those who have had these opportunities, they would not even furnish an occasion of surprise. But they would be, to all who knew their truth, irrefragable proofs of his unfitness for the station of chief magistrate.

Ill treatment of Mr. McHenry cannot fail to awaken the sympathy of every person well acquainted with him. Sensible, judicious, well-informed, of an integrity never questioned, of a temper which, though firm in the support of principles, has too much moderation and amenity to offend by the manner of doing it—I dare pronounce that he never gave Mr. Adams cause to treat him, as he did, with unkindness. If Mr. Adams thought that his execution of his office indicated a want of the peculiar qualifications required for it, he might have said so with gentleness, and he would have only exercised a prerogative entrusted to him by the Constitution to which no blame could have attached; but it was unjustifiable to aggravate the deprivation of office by humiliating censures and bitter reproaches.

The last material occurrence in the administration of Mr. Adams of which I shall take notice is the pardon of *Fries* and other principals in the late insurrection in Pennsylvania.

It is a fact that a very refractory spirit has long existed in the western counties of that state. Repeatedly have its own laws been opposed with violence and as often, according to my information, with impunity.

It is also a fact which everybody knows that the laws of the Union in the vital article of revenue have been twice resisted in the same state by combinations so extensive, and under circumstances so violent, as to have called for the employment of military force, once under the former president, and once under the actual president, which together cost the United States nearly a million and a half of dollars.

In the first instance it happened that by the early submission of most of the leaders, upon an invitation of the government, few offenders of any consequence remained subject to prosecution. Of these, either from the humanity of the juries or some deficiency in the evidence, not one was capitally convicted. Two poor wretches only were sentenced to die, one of them little short of an idiot, the other a miserable follower in the hindmost train of rebellion, both beings so insignificant in all respects that, after the lenity shown to the chiefs, justice would have worn the mien of ferocity if she had raised her arm against them. The sentiment that their punishment ought to be remitted was universal; and the president, yielding to the special considerations, granted them pardons.

In the last instance, some of the most important of the offenders were capitally convicted—one of them by the verdicts of two successive juries. The general opinion of the friends of the government demanded an example as indispensable to its security.

The opinion was well founded. Two insurrections in the same state, the one upon the heels of the other, demonstrated a spirit of insubordination or disaffection which required a strong corrective. It is a disagreeable fact, forming a weighty argument in the question, that a large part of the population of Pennsylvania is of a composition which peculiarly fits it for the intrigues of factious men, who may desire to disturb or overthrow the government. And it is an equally disagreeable fact that disaffection to the national government is in no other state more general, more deeply rooted, or more envenomed.

The late Governor Mifflin himself informed me that in the first case insurrection had been organized down to the very liberties of Philadelphia, and that had not the government anticipated it, a general explosion would speedily have ensued.

It ought to be added that the impunity so often experienced had made it an article in the creed of those who were actuated by the insurgent spirit that neither the general nor the state government dared to inflict capital punishment.

To destroy this persuasion, to repress this dangerous spirit, it was essential that a salutary rigor should have been exerted, and that those who were under the influence of the one and the other should be taught that they were the dupes of a fatal illusion.

Of this, Mr. Adams appeared so sensible that while the trials were pending he more than once imprudently threw out that the accused must found their hopes of escape either in their innocence or in the lenity of the juries, since from him, in case of conviction, they would have nothing to expect. And a very short time before he pardoned them, he declared with no small ostentation that the mistaken clemency of Washington on the former occasion had been the cause of the second insurrection, and that he would take care there should not be a third by giving the laws their full course against the convicted offenders.

Yet he thought proper, as if distrusting the courts and officers of the United States, to resort through the attorney general to the counsel of the culprits for a statement of their cases; in which was found, besides some objections of form, the novel doctrine, disavowed by every page of our law books, that treason does not consist of resistance by force to a public law, unless it be an act relative to the militia or other military force.

And upon this, or upon some other ground not easy to be comprehended, he of a sudden departed from all his former declarations, and against the unanimous advice of his ministers, with the attorney general, came to the resolution, which he executed, of pardoning all those who had received sentence of death.

No wonder that the public was thunderstruck at such a result—that the friends of the government regarded it as a virtual dereliction—it was impossible to commit a greater error. The particular situation of Pennsylvania, the singular posture of human affairs, in which there is so strong a tendency to the disorganization of government—the turbulent and malignant humors which exist, and are so industriously nourished throughout the United States; every thing loudly demanded that the executive should have acted with exemplary vigor, and should have given a striking demonstration that condign punishment would be the lot of the violent opposers of the laws.

The contrary course which was pursued is the most inexplicable part of Mr. Adams's conduct. It shows him so much at variance with himself, as well as with sound policy, that we are driven to seek a solution for it in some system of concession to his political enemies, a system the most fatal for himself and for the cause of public order of any that he could possibly devise. It is by temporizings like these that men at the head of affairs lose the respect both of friends and foes—it is by temporizings like these that in times of fermentation and commotion governments are prostrated, which might easily have been upheld by an erect and imposing attitude.

I have now gone through the principal circumstances in Mr. Adams's conduct which have served to produce my disapprobation of him as chief magistrate. I pledge my veracity and honor that I have stated none which are not either derived from my own knowledge or from sources of information in the highest degree worthy of credit.

I freely submit it, Sir, to your judgment whether the grounds of the opinion I have expressed are not weighty; and whether they are not sufficient to exculpate those Federalists who favor the equal support of Mr. Pinckney from all blame, and myself in particular from the unworthy imputation of being influenced by private resentment.

At the same time, I will admit, though it should detract from the force of my representations, that I have causes of personal dissatisfaction with Mr. Adams. It is not my practice to trouble others with my individual concerns, nor should I do it at present but for the suggestions which have been made. Even with this incentive, I shall do it as little as possible.

The circumstances of my late military situation have much less to do with my personal discontent than some others. In respect to them, I shall only say that I owed my appointment to the station and rank I held to the *express stipulation* of General Washington when he accepted the command of the army, afterwards *peremptorily insisted upon* by him in *opposition* to the *strong wishes* of the president; and that, though second in rank, I was not promoted to the first place when it became vacant by the death of the commander in chief. As to the former, I should have had no cause to complain if there had not been an apparent inconsistency in the measures of the president; if he had not nominated me *first* on the list of major generals and attempted afterwards to place me *third* in rank. As to the latter, the chief command not being a matter of routine, the not promoting me to it cannot be deemed a wrong or injury; yet certainly I could not see in the omission any proof of good will or confidence—or of a disposition to console me for the persecutions which I had incessantly endured. But I dismiss the subject, leaving to others to judge of my pretensions to the promotion, and of the weight, if any, which they ought to have had with the president.

On other topics my sensations are far less neutral. If, as I have been assured from respectable authorities, Mr. Adams has repeatedly indulged himself in virulent and indecent abuse of me; if he has denominated me a man destitute of every moral principle; if he has stigmatized me as the leader of a British faction; then certainly I have right to think that I have been most cruelly and wickedly traduced; then have I right to appeal to all those who have been spectators of my public actions; to all who are acquainted with my private character, in its various relations, whether such treatment of me by Mr. Adams is of a nature to weaken or to strengthen his claim to the approbation of wise and good men; then will I so far yield to the consciousness of what I am as to declare that in the cardinal points of public and private rectitude, above all in pure and disinterested zeal for the interests and service of this country—I shrink not from a comparison with any arrogant pretender to superior and exclusive merit.

Having been repeatedly informed that Mr. Adams had delineated me as the leader of a British faction, and having understood that his partisans, to counteract the influence of my opinion, were pressing the same charge against me, I wrote him a letter on the subject, dated the first of August last. No reply having been given by him to this letter, I, on the first of the present month, wrote him another, of both which letters I send you copies.

Of the purity of my public conduct in this, as in other particulars, I may defy the severest investigation.

Not only is it impossible for any man to give color to this absurd charge by a particle of proof or by any reasonable presumption, but I am able to show that my conduct has uniformly given the lie to it.

I never advised any connection* with Great Britain other than a commercial one; and in this I never advocated the giving to her any privilege or advantage which was not to be imparted to other nations. With regard to her pretensions as a belligerent power in relation to neutrals, my opinions while in the administration, to the best of my recollection, coincided with those of Mr. Jefferson. When in the year 1793 her depredations on our commerce discovered a hostile spirit, I recommended one definitive effort to terminate differences by negotiation, to be followed, if unsuccessful, by a declaration of war. I urged in the most earnest manner the friends of the administration in both houses of Congress to prepare by sea and land for the alternative, to the utmost extent of our resources; and to an extent far exceeding what any member of either party was found willing to go. For this alternative I became so firmly pledged to the friends and enemies of the administration, and especially to the president of the United States, in writing as well as verbally, that I could not afterwards have retracted without a glaring and disgraceful inconsistency. And being thus pledged, I explicitly gave it as my opinion to Mr. Jay, envoy to Great Britain, that *"unless an adjustment of the differences with her could be effected on solid terms, it would be better to do nothing."* When the treaty arrived, it was not without full deliberation and some hesitation that I resolved to support it. The articles relative to the settlement of differences were upon the whole satisfactory, but there were a few of the others which appeared to me of a different character. The article respecting contraband, though conformable with the general law of nations, was not in all its features such as could have been

---

* I mean a lasting connection. From what I recollect of the train of my ideas, it is possible I may at some time have suggested a *temporary* connection for the purpose of cooperating against France in the event of a definitive rupture; but of this I am not certain, as I well remember that the expediency of the measure was always problematical in my mind, and that I have occasionally discouraged it.

wished. The XXVth article, which gave asylum in our ports, under certain exceptions, to privateers with their prizes, was in itself an ineligible one, being of a nature to excite the discontent of nations against whom it should operate, and deriving its justification from the example before set of an equivalent stipulation in our treaty with France. The XIIth article was in my view inadmissible. The enlightened negotiator, not unconscious that some parts of the treaty were less well arranged than was to be desired, had himself hesitated to sign: but he had resigned his scruples to the conviction that nothing better could be effected, and that aggregately considered the instrument would be advantageous to the United States. On my part, the result of mature reflection was that as the subjects of controversy which had threatened the peace of the two nations, and which implicated great interests of this country, were in the essential points well adjusted, and as the other articles would expire in twelve years after the ratification of the treaty, it would be wise and right to confirm the compact, with the exception of the XIIth article. Nevertheless, when an account was received that the British cruisers had seized provisions going to ports of the French dominions, not in fact blockaded or besieged, I advised the president to ratify the treaty conditionally only, that is, with express instructions not to exchange ratifications, unless the British government would disavow a construction of the instrument authorizing the practice and would discontinue it.

After the rejection of Mr. Pinckney by the government of France, immediately after the installment of Mr. Adams as president, and long before the measure was taken, I urged a member of Congress, then high in the confidence of the president, to propose to him the immediate appointment of three commissioners, of whom Mr. *Jefferson*, or Mr. *Madison* to be one, to make another attempt to negotiate. And when afterwards commissioners were appointed, I expressly gave it as my opinion that indemnification for spoliations should not be a *sine qua non* of accommodation. In fine, I have been disposed to go greater lengths to avoid rupture with France than with Great Britain, to make greater sacrifices for reconciliation with the former than with the latter.

In making this avowal I owe it to my own character to say that the disposition I have confessed did not proceed from predilection for France (revolutionary France, after her early beginnings, has been always to me an object of horror), nor from the supposition that more was to be feared from France, as an enemy, than from Great Britain (I thought that the maritime power of the latter could do us most mischief), but from the persuasion that the sentiments and prejudices of our country would render war with France a more unmanageable business than war with Great Britain.

Let any fair man pronounce whether the circumstances which have been disclosed bespeak the partisan of Great Britain or the man exclusively devoted to the interests of this country. Let any delicate man decide whether it must not be shocking to an ingenuous mind to have to combat a slander so vile, after having sacrificed the interests of his family, and devoted the best part of his life to the service of that country, in counsel and in the field.

It is time to conclude—The statement which has been made shows that Mr. Adams has committed some positive and serious errors of administration; that in addition to these he has certain fixed points of character which tend naturally to the detriment of any cause of which he is the chief, of any administration of which he is the head; that by his ill humors and jealousies he has already divided and distracted the supporters of the government; that he has furnished deadly weapons to its enemies by unfounded accusations, and has weakened the force of its friends by decrying some of the most influential of them to the utmost of his power; and let it be added, as the necessary effect of such conduct, that he has made great progress in undermining the ground which was gained for the government by his predecessor, and that there is real cause to apprehend it might totter, if not fall, under his future auspices. A new government, constructed on free principles, is always weak, and must stand in need of the props of a firm and good administration, till time shall have rendered its authority venerable and fortified it by habits of obedience.

Yet with this opinion of Mr. Adams I have finally resolved not to advise the withholding from him a single vote. The body of Federalists, for want of sufficient knowledge of facts, are not convinced of the expediency of relinquishing him. It is even apparent that a large proportion still retain the attachment which was once a common sentiment. Those of them, therefore, who are dissatisfied, as far as my information goes, are, generally speaking, willing to forbear opposition and to acquiesce in the equal support of Mr. Adams with Mr. Pinckney, whom they prefer. Have they not a claim to equal deference from those who continue attached to the former? Ought not these, in candor, to admit the possibility that the friends who differ from them act not only from pure motives but from cogent reasons? Ought they not, by a cooperation in General Pinckney, to give a chance for what will be a *safe* issue, supposing that they are right in their preference, and the best issue, should they happen to be mistaken? Especially since by doing this they will increase the probability of excluding a third candidate, of whose unfitness all sincere Federalists are convinced. If they do not pursue this course, they will certainly incur an immense responsibility to their friends and to the government.

To promote this cooperation, to defend my own character, to vindicate those friends who with myself have been unkindly aspersed, are the inducements for writing this letter. Accordingly, it will be my endeavor to regulate the communication of it in such a manner as will not be likely to deprive Mr. Adams of a single vote. Indeed, it is much my wish that its circulation could forever be confined within narrow limits. I am sensible of the inconveniences of giving publicity to a similar development of the character of the chief magistrate of our country, and I lament the necessity of taking a step which will involve that result. Yet to suppress truths, the disclosure of which is so interesting to the public welfare as well as to the vindication of my friends and myself, did not appear to me justifiable.

The restraints to which I submit are a proof of my disposition to sacrifice to the prepossessions of those with whom I have heretofore thought and acted, and from whom in the present question I am compelled to differ. To refrain from a decided opposition to Mr. Adams's re-election has been reluctantly sanctioned by my judgment, which has been not a little perplexed between the unqualified conviction of his unfitness for the station contemplated and a sense of the great importance of cultivating harmony among the supporters of the government, on whose firm union hereafter will probably depend the preservation of order, tranquility, liberty, property, the security of every social and domestic blessing.

Letter to Oliver Wolcott, Jr., December 16, 1800

It is now, my Dear Sir, ascertained that Jefferson or Burr will be president, and it seems probable that they will come with equal votes to the House of Representatives. It is also circulated here that in this event the Federalists in Congress, or some of them, talk of preferring Burr. I trust New England at least will not so far lose its head as to fall into this snare. There is no doubt but that upon every virtuous and prudent calculation Jefferson is to be preferred. He is by far not so dangerous a man and he has pretensions to character.

As to *Burr*, there is nothing in his favor. His private character is not defended by his most partial friends. He is bankrupt beyond redemption, except by the plunder of his country. His public principles have no other spring or aim than his own aggrandizement per *fas* et *nefas*. If he can, he will certainly disturb our institutions to secure to himself *permanent power* and with it *wealth*. He is truly the *Catiline* of America—& if I may credit Major Wilcocks, he has held very vindictive language respecting his opponents.

But early measures must be taken to fix on this point the opinions of the Federalists. Among them, from different motives—Burr will find partisans. If the thing be neglected he may possibly go far.

Yet it may be well enough to throw out a lure for him, in order to tempt him to start for the plate & thus lay the foundation of dissension between the two chiefs.

You may communicate this letter to *Marshall & Sedgwick*.

Let me hear speedily from you in reply.

Yrs. Affectly
A. Hamilton

Excerpt from a Letter to Theodore Sedgwick, December 22, 1800

I entirely agree with you, My Dear Sir, that in the event of Jefferson and Burr coming to the House of Representatives, the former is to be preferred. The appointment of Burr as president would disgrace our country abroad. No agreement with him could be relied upon. His private circumstances render disorder a necessary resource. His public principles offer no obstacle. His ambition aims at nothing short of permanent power and wealth in his own person. For heaven's sake, let not the Federal party be responsible for the elevation of this man.

Letter to Harrison Gray Otis, December 23, 1800

Burr loves nothing but himself, thinks of nothing but his own aggrandizement, and will be content with nothing short of permanent power in his own hands. No compact that he should make with any passion in his breast, except ambition, could be relied upon by himself. How then should we be able to rely upon any agreement with him? Jefferson, I suspect, will not dare much. Burr will dare everything, in the sanguine hope of effecting everything.

Excerpt from a Letter to Gouverneur Morris, December 24, 1800

Another subject—*Jefferson* or *Burr?*—the former without all doubt. The latter in my judgment has no principle, public or private—could be bound by no agreement—will listen to no monitor but his ambition; & for this purpose will use the *worst* part of the community as a ladder to climb to permanent power & an instrument to crush the better part. He is bankrupt beyond redemption, except by the resources that grow out of war and disorder, or by a sale to a foreign power, or by great peculation. War with Great Britain would be the immediate instrument. He is sanguine enough to hope everything—daring enough to attempt everything—wicked enough to scruple nothing. From the elevation of such a man, heaven preserve the country!

Let our situation be improved to obtain from Jefferson assurances on certain points—the maintenance of the present system, especially on the cardinal articles of public credit, a *navy, neutrality*.

Make any discreet use you think fit of this letter.

Yrs. truly
A. Hamilton

Letter to Gouverneur Morris, December 26, 1800

Dear Sir,

The post of yesterday gave me the pleasure of a letter from you. I thank you for the communication. I trust that a letter which I wrote you the day before the receipt of yours will have duly reached you as it contains some very free & confidential observations ending in two results—1. That The Convention with France ought to be ratified as the least of two evils. 2. That *on the same ground Jefferson* ought to be preferred to *Burr*.

I trust the Federalists will not finally be so mad as to vote for the *latter*. I speak with an intimate & accurate knowledge of character. His elevation can only promote the purposes of the desperate and profligate. If there be a man in the world I ought to hate, it is Jefferson. With *Burr* I have always been personally well. But the public good must be paramount to every private consideration. My opinion may be freely used with such reserves as you shall think discreet.

Yrs.   very truly
A.H.

Letter to James A. Bayard, December 27, 1800

Dear Sir,

Several letters to myself & others from the city of Washington excite in my mind extreme alarm on the subject of the future president. It seems nearly ascertained that *Jefferson & Burr* will come into the house of Rs. with equal votes, and those letters express the probability that the Federal party may prefer the latter. In my opinion a circumstance more ruinous to them, or more disastrous to the country, could not happen. This opinion is dictated by a long & close attention to the character, with the best opportunities of knowing it, an advantage for judging which few of our friends possess, & which ought to give some weight to my opinion. Be assured, my dear Sir, that this man has no principle, public or private. As a politician his sole spring of action is an inordinate ambition; as an individual he is believed by friends as well as foes to be without *probity*, and a voluptuary by system, with habits of expense that can be satisfied by no fair expedients. As to his talents, great management & cunning are the predominant features—he is yet to give proofs of those solid abilities which characterize the statesman. Daring & energy must be allowed him, but these qualities under the direction of the worst passions are certainly strong objections, not recommendations. He is of a temper to undertake the most hazardous enterprises because he is sanguine enough to think nothing impracticable, and of an ambition which will be content with nothing less than *permanent* power in his own hands. The maintenance of the existing institutions will not suit him, because under them his power will be too narrow & too precarious; yet the innovations he may attempt will not offer the substitute of a system *durable & safe*, calculated to give lasting prosperity & to unite liberty with strength. It will be the system of the day, sufficient to serve his own turn, & not looking beyond himself. To execute this plan, as the good men of the country cannot be relied upon, the worst will be used. Let it not be imagined that the difficulties of execution will deter or a calculation of interest restrain. The truth is that under forms of government like ours, too much is practicable to men who will without scruple avail themselves of the bad passions of human nature. To a man of this description possessing the requisite talents, the acquisition of permanent power is not a chimera. I *know* that Mr. Burr does not view it as such, & I am sure there are no means too atrocious to be employed by him. In debt vastly beyond his means of payment, with all the habits of excessive expense, he cannot be satisfied with the regular emoluments of any office of our government. Corrupt expedients will be to him a *necessary* resource. Will any prudent man offer such a president to the temptations of foreign gold? No engagement that can be made with him can be depended upon. While making it he will laugh in his sleeve at the credulity of those with whom he makes it—and the first moment it suits his views to break it, he will do so.* Let me add that I could scarcely name a discreet man of either party in our state who does not think Mr. Burr the most unfit man in the U. S. for the office of president. Disgrace abroad, ruin at home are the probable fruits of his elevation. To contribute to the disappointment and mortification of Mr. J. would be on my part only to retaliate for unequivocal proofs of enmity; but in a case like this it would be base to listen to personal considerations. In alluding to the situation I mean only to illustrate how strong must be the motives which induce me to promote *his* elevation in exclusion of another. For Heaven's sake, my dear Sir, exert yourself to the utmost to save our country from so great a calamity. Let us not be responsible for the evils which in all probability will follow the preference. All calculations that may lead to it must prove fallacious.

Accept the assurances of my esteem,
A. Hamilton

---

* A recent incident will give you an idea of his views as to foreign politics. I dined with him lately. His toasts were: "The French Republic." "The commissioners who negotiated the convention." "Bonaparte." "The Marquis La Fayette." His doctrines that it would be the interest of this country to permit the indiscriminate sale of prizes by the belligerent *powers* & the building & equipment of vessels, a project amounting to nothing more nor less (with the semblance of equality) than to turn all our naval resources into the channel of France, and compel G. Britain to war. Indeed, Mr. Burr must have war as the instrument of his ambition & cupidity. The peculiarity of the occasion will excuse my mentioning *in confidence* the occurrences of a private table.

Excerpt from a Letter to James Ross, December 29, 1800

Dear Sir,

Letters which myself and others have received from Washington give me much alarm at the prospect that Mr. Burr may be supported by the Federalists in preference to Mr. Jefferson. Be assured, my Dear Sir, that this would be a fatal mistake. From a thorough knowledge of the character I can pronounce with confidence that Mr. Burr is the last man in the U. States to be supported by the Federalists.

1. It is an opinion firmly entertained by his enemies and not disputed by his friends that as a man he is deficient in *honesty*. Some very sad stories are related of him. That he is bankrupt for a large *deficit* is certain.
2. As a politician, discerning men of both parties admit that he has but one principle—to *get* *power* by *any* means and to *keep* it by *all* means.
3. Of an ambition too irregular and inordinate to be content with institutions that leave his power precarious, he is of too bold and sanguine a temper to think any thing too hazardous to be attempted or two difficult to be accomplished.
4. As to talents, they are great for management and intrigue—but he is yet to give the first proofs that they are equal to the art of governing well.
5. As to his theory, no mortal can tell what it is. Institutions that would serve his own purpose (such as the government of France of the present day), not such as would promise lasting prosperity and glory to the country, would be his preference because he cares only for himself and nothing for his country or glory.
6. Certain that his irregular ambition cannot be supported by *good* men, he will *court* and *employ* the worst men of all parties as the most eligible instruments. Jacobinism in its most pernicious form will scourge the country.
7. As to foreign policies, war will be a necessary mean of power and wealth. The animosity to the British will be the handle by which he will attempt to wield the nation to that point: Within a fortnight he has advocated positions which if acted upon would in six months place us in a state of war with that power—

From the elevation of such a man, may heaven preserve the country. Should it be by the means of the Federalists, I should at once despair. I should see no longer anything upon which to rest the hope of public or private prosperity.

No: let the Federalists vote for Jefferson. But as they have much in their power, let them improve the situation to obtain some assurances from him.

1. The preservation of the actual system of finance & public credit.
2. The support and gradual increase of the navy.
3. A bona fide neutrality toward the belligerent powers.
4. The preservation in office of our friends, except in the great departments in respect to which & to future appointments he ought to be at liberty to promote his friends.

Letter to Oliver Wolcott, Jr., December, 1800

Your last letter, My Dear Sir, has given me great pain, not only because it informed me that the opinion in favor of Mr. Burr was increasing among the Federalists, but because it also told me that Mr. Sedgwick was one of its partisans. I have a letter from this gentleman in which he expresses decidedly his preference of Mr. Jefferson. I hope you have been mistaken and that it is not possible for him to have been guilty of so great duplicity.

There is no circumstance which has occurred in the course of our political affairs that has given me so much pain as the idea that Mr. Burr might be elevated to the presidency by the means of the Federalists. I am of opinion that this party has hitherto solid claims of merit with the public, and so long as it does nothing to forfeit its title to confidence I shall continue to hope that our misfortunes are temporary and that the party will ere long emerge from its depression. But if it shall act a foolish or unworthy part in any capital instance, I shall then despair.

Such without doubt will be the part it will act, if it shall seriously attempt to support Mr. Burr in opposition to Mr. Jefferson. If it fails, as after all is not improbable, it will have riveted the animosity of that person, will have destroyed or weakened the motives to moderation which he must at present feel, and it will expose them to the disgrace of a defeat in an attempt to elevate to the first place in the government one of the worst men in the community. If it succeeds, it will have done nothing more nor less than place in that station a man who will possess the boldness and daring necessary to give success to the Jacobin system instead of one who for want of that quality will be less fitted to promote it.

Let it not be imagined that Mr. Burr can be won to the Federal views. It is a vain hope. Stronger ties, and stronger inducements than they can offer, will impel him in a different direction. His ambition will not be content with those objects which virtuous men of either party will allot to it, and his situation and his habits will oblige him to have recourse to corrupt expedients, from which he will be restrained by no moral scruples. To accomplish his ends he must lean upon unprincipled men and will continue to adhere to the myrmidons who have hitherto seconded him. To these he will no doubt add able rogues of the Federal party, but he will employ the rogues of all parties to overrule the good men of all parties and to prosecute projects which wise men of every description will disapprove.

These things are to be inferred with moral certainty from the character of the man. Every step in his career proves that he has formed himself upon the model of *Catiline*, and he is too coldblooded and too determined a conspirator ever to change his plan.

What would you think of these toasts and this conversation at his table within the last three or four weeks? 1. The French Republic. 2. The commissioners on both sides who negotiated the Convention. 3. Bonaparte. 4. La Fayette. What would you think of his having seconded the positions that it was the interest of this country to allow the belligerent powers to bring in and sell their prizes and build and equip ships in our ports? Do you not see in this the scheme of war with Great Britain as the instrument of power and wealth? Can it be doubted that a man who has all his life speculated upon the popular prejudices will consult them in the object of a war when he thinks it expedient to make one? Can a man who, despising democracy, has chimed in with all its absurdities be diverted from the plan of ambition which must have directed this course? They who suppose it must understand little of human nature.

If Jefferson is president, the whole responsibility of bad measures will rest with the Anti-federalists. If Burr is made so by the Federalists, the whole responsibility will rest with them. The other party will say to the people: We intended him only for Vice President. Here he might have done very well or been at least harmless. But the Federalists, to disappoint us and a majority of you, took advantage of a momentary superiority to put him in the first place. He is therefore their president and they must answer for all the evils of his bad conduct. And the people will believe them.

Will any reasonable calculation on the part of the Federalists uphold the policy of assuming so great a responsibility in the support of so unpromising a character?

The negative is so manifest that had I not been assured of the contrary I should have thought it impossible that assent to it would have been attended with a moment's hesitation.

Alas! when will men consult their reason rather than their passions? Whatever they may imagine, the desire of mortifying the adverse party must be the chief spring of the disposition to prefer Mr. Burr. This disposition reminds me of the conduct of the Dutch monied men who, from hatred of the old aristocracy, favored the admission of the French into Holland to overturn everything.

Adieu to the Federal Troy if they once introduce this Grecian horse into their citadel.

Trust me, my dear friend. You cannot render a greater service to your country than to resist this project. Far better will it be to endeavor to obtain from Jefferson assurances on some cardinal points—1. The preservation of the actual fiscal system. 2. Adherence to the neutral plan. 3. The preservation & gradual increase of the navy. 4. The continuance of our friends in the offices they fill, except in the great departments in which he ought to be left free.

Adieu My Dr. Sir   Yrs. ever

A. Hamilton

Explanatory Notes

1 This is the act that the Supreme Court later ruled unconstitutional in *Fletcher v. Peck* 10 U.S. (6 Cranch) 87 (1810).

2 The missing passages reflect Hamilton's original manuscript.

3 Hamilton actually left the date blank, but it was supplied by his editors. See *PAH*, 20: 511 n.3.

4 Hamilton's original reads "sufficient," but we think "insufficient" is clearly indicated by the context.

5 Hamilton refers here to a pamphlet by James Thomson Callender. See *PAH*, 21: 243 n. 15.

6 Here Hamilton is quoting—slightly incorrectly—Epistle II of Alexander Pope's *Essay on Man*. Pope uses "frightful," not Hamilton's "horrid."

7 Hamilton's original sentence does not included the word "no," but we believe the context clearly indicated that he intended it.

8 Hamilton here appears to refer to Thomas Jefferson. See *PAH*, 21: 442 n. 4 and 409 n. 2.

9 The case to which Hamilton refers was one of desertion, for which the offender had been sentenced to death. See *PAH*, 23: 152 n. 1 and 56 n. 2.

10 This is the same case as that mentioned in the letter of May 27, 1799.

11 Hoffman, the recipient of this letter, was the attorney general of the State of New York. See *PAH*, 24: 6 n. 1.

12 Hamilton apparently refers to the fact that President Adams did not appoint him to succeed Washington as lieutenant general and commanding officer of the United States Army. See *PAH*, 24: 299 n. 2.

13 Here Hamilton was indeed mistaken in his view of how Jay would regard such a proposal. Jay wrote on the letter: "Proposing a measure for party purposes wh. I think it wd. not become me to adopt." See *PAH*, 24: 467 n. 4.

14 McHenry, along with Timothy Pickering, had just resigned from his post in the Adams administration.

PART 4

Elder Statesman: 1801–1804

Excerpts from An Address to the Electors of the State of New York, March 21, 1801

Fellow Citizens!

We lately addressed you on the subject of the ensuing election for governor and lieutenant governor—recommending to your support Stephen Van Rensselaer and James Watson. Since that we have seen the address of our opponents, urging your preference of George Clinton and Jeremiah Van Rensselaer.

The whole tenor of our address carries with it the evidence of a disposition to be temperate and liberal, to avoid giving occasion to mutual recrimination. It would have been agreeable to us to have seen a like disposition in our adversaries, but we think it cannot be denied that their address manifests a different one. It arraigns the principles of the Federalists with extreme acrimony, and, by the allusion to Great Britain in the preposterous figure of the mantle, attributes to them a principle of action which every signer of the address knows to have no existence, and which for its falsehood and malice merits indignation and disdain.

So violent an attack upon our principles justifies and calls for an exhibition of those of our opponents. To your good sense, to your love of country, to your regard for the welfare of yourselves and families, the comment is submitted.

The pernicious spirit which has actuated many of the leaders of the party denominated Antifederal, from the moment when our national Constitution was first proposed down to the present period, has not ceased to display itself in a variety of disgusting forms. In proportion to the prospect of success it has increased in temerity. Emboldened by a momentary triumph in the choice of our national chief magistrate, it seems now to have laid aside all reserve and begins to avow projects of disorganization with the sanction of the most respectable names of the party, which before were merely the anonymous ravings of incendiary newspapers.

This precipitation in throwing aside the mask will, we trust, be productive of happy effects. It will serve to show that the mischievous designs ascribed to the party have not been the effusions of malevolence, the inventions of political rivalship, or the visionary forebodings of an over-anxious zeal; but that they have been just and correct inferences from an accurate estimate of characters and principles. It will serve to show that moderate men, who have seen in our political struggles nothing more than a competition for power and place, have been deceived; that in reality the foundations of society, the essential interests of our nation, the dearest concerns of individuals are staked upon the eventful contest. And, by promoting this important discovery, it may be expected to rally the virtuous and the prudent of every description round a common standard, to endeavor by joint efforts to oppose mounds to that destructive torrent which in its distant murmuring seemed harmless, but in the portentous roaring of its nearer approach menaces our country with all the horrors of revolutionary frenzy.

To what end, fellow citizens, has your attention been carried across the Atlantic to the revolution of France and to that fatal war of which it has been the source? To what end are you told that this is the most interesting conflict man ever witnessed, that it is a war of principles—a war between equal and unequal rights, between republicanism and monarchy, between liberty and tyranny?

What is there in that terrific picture which you are to admire or imitate? Is it the subversion of the throne of the *Bourbons* to make way for the throne of the *Bonapartes?* Is it the undistinguishing massacre in prisons and dungeons of men, women and children? Is it the sanguinary justice of a revolutionary tribunal, or the awful terrors of a guillotine? Is it the rapid succession of revolution upon revolution, erecting the transient power of one set of men upon the tombs of another? Is it the assassinations which have been perpetrated, or the new ones which are projected? Is it the open profession of impiety in the public assemblies, or the ridiculous worship of a Goddess of Reason, or the still continued substitution of decades to the Christian Sabbath? Is it the destruction of commerce, the ruin of manufactures, the oppression of agriculture? Or is it the pomp of war, the dazzling glare of splendid victories, the bloodstained fields of Europe, the smoking cinders of desolated cities, the afflicting spectacle of millions precipitated from plenty and comfort to beggary and misery? If it be none of these things, what is it?

Perhaps it is the existing government of France of which your admiration is solicited?

Here, fellow citizens, let us on our part invite you to a solemn pause. Mark, we beseech you, carefully mark, in this result the fruit of those extravagant and noxious principles which it is desired to transplant into our happy soil.

Behold a consul for ten years elected, *not by the people*, but by a Conservatory Senate, *self-created* and self-*continued for life*; a magistrate who to the plentitude of executive authority adds the peculiar and vast prerogative of an exclusive right to originate every law of the republic.

Behold a legislature elected, *not by the people*, but by the same Conservatory Senate, one branch for fourteen, the other for ten years—one branch with a right to debate the law proposed by the consul but not to propose—another branch with a right neither to debate nor propose; but merely to assent or dissent; leaving to the people nothing more than the phantom of representation, or the useless privilege of designating one *tenth* of their whole mass as *candidates* indiscriminately for the offices of the state, according to the *option* of the Conservatory Senate.

Behold in this magic lantern of republicanism the odious form of real despotism garnished and defended by the bayonets of more than five hundred thousand men in disciplined array.

Do you desire an illustration of the practical effect of this despotic system, read it in the last advices from France. Read it in the exercise of a power by the chief consul, recognized to belong to him by the Conservatory Senate, to banish indefinitely the citizens of France without trial, without the formality of a legislative act. Then say where can you find a more hideous despotism?—Or, what ought ye to think of those men who dare to recommend to you as the bible of your political creed the principles of a revolution which in its commencement, in its progress, in its termination (if termination it can have, before it has overthrown the civilized world) is only fitted to serve as a beacon to warn you to shun the gulfs, the quicksands, and the rocks of those enormous principles?

Surely ye will applaud neither the wisdom nor the patriotism of men who can wish you to exchange the fair fabric of republicanism which you now enjoy, modeled and decorated by the hand of federalism, for that tremendous form of despotism which has sprung up amidst the volcanic eruptions of *principles at war* with all past and present experience, at war with the nature of man.

Or was the allusion to France and her revolution, to the war of principles of which you have heard, and intended to familiarize your ears to a war of arms, as one of the blessings of the new order of things? Facts, which cannot be mistaken, demonstrate that in the early period of the French revolution it was the plan of our opponents to engage us in the war as associates of France. But at this late hour, when even the pretense of supporting the cause of liberty has vanished, when acquisition and aggrandizement have manifestly become the only, the exclusive objects of this war, it was surely to have been expected that we should have been left to retain the advantage of a pacific policy.

If there are men who hope to gratify their ambition, their avarice, or their vengeance by adding this country to the league of Northern Powers, in the fantastic purpose of an extension of neutral rights, the great body of the people will hardly, we imagine, see in this project benefits sufficiently solid and durable to counterbalance the certain sacrifices of present advantages and the certain sufferings of positive evils inseparable from a state of war.

Let us now attend to some other parts of this extraordinary address.

You are told that there are many in the bosom of our country who have long aimed at unequal privileges and who have too well succeeded, by arrogating to themselves the right to be considered as the only friends of the Constitution, the guardians of order and religion, by the lavish abuse of their opponents, and by representing opposition to particular plans of administration as hostility to the government itself.

What is meant by this aiming at unequal privileges?

If we are to judge of the end by the means stated to have been used, the charge amounts to this, that the Federalists have sought to retain in their own hands, by the suffrages of the people, the exercise of the powers of the government.

Admitting the charge to be true, have not the Antifederalists pursued exactly the same course? Have they not labored incessantly to monopolize the power of our national and state governments? Whenever they have had it, have they not strained every nerve to keep it? Why is it a greater crime in the Federalists than in their rivals to aim at an ascendant in the councils of our country?

It is true, as alleged, that the Federalists insisted upon their superior claim to be considered as the friends of our Constitution and have imputed to their adversaries improper and dangerous designs; but it is equally true that these have asserted a similar claim, have advanced the pretension of being the only republicans and patriots, have charged their opponents with being in league with Great Britain to establish monarchy, have imputed to men of unblemished characters for probity, in high public offices, corruption and peculation, and have persisted in the foul charge after its falsity had been ascertained by solemn public inquiry; and in their wanton and distempered rage for calumny have not scrupled to brand even a Washington as a *tyrant*, a *conspirator*, a *peculator*.

It is true that the Federalists have represented the leaders of the other party as hostile to our national Constitution, but it is not true that it was because they have been unfriendly to *particular plans* of its administration.

It is because as a party and with few exceptions they were violent opposers of the adoption of the Constitution itself, predicted from it every possible evil, and painted it in the blackest colors as a monster of political deformity.

It is because the amendments subsequently made, meeting scarcely any of the important objections which were urged, leaving the structure of the government and the mass and distribution of its powers where they were, are too insignificant to be with any sensible man a reason for being reconciled to the system if he thought it originally bad.

It is because they have opposed not *particular* plans of the administration but the general course of it, and almost all the measures of material consequence; and this too, not under one man or set of men but under all the successions of men.

It is because as there have been no alterations of the Constitution sufficient to change the opinion of its merits, and as the practice under it has met with the severest reprobation of the party, there is no circumstance from which to infer that they can really have been reconciled to it.

It is because the newspapers under their direction have from time to time continued to decry the Constitution itself.

It is because they have openly avowed their attachment to the excessive principles of the French revolution and to leading features in the crude forms of government which have appeared only to disappear, utterly inconsistent with the sober maxims upon which our federal edifice was reared, and with essential parts in its structure. As specimens of this, it is sufficient to observe that they have approved the unity of the legislative power in one branch and have been loud in their praises of an Executive Directory, that five-headed monster of faction and anarchy.

It is because they have repeatedly shown, and in their present address again show, that they contemplate innovations in our public affairs which without doubt would disgrace and prostrate the government.

On these various and strong grounds have the Federalists imputed to their opponents disaffection to the national Constitution. As yet they have no reason to retract the charge. To future proofs of repentance and reconciliation must an exculpation be referred. The Antifederalists have acquired the administration of the national government. Let them show by a wise and virtuous management that they are its friends, and they shall then have all the credit of so happy a reformation; but till then their assertions cannot be received as proofs.

And if the views which the signers of the address now boldly avow should unfortunately be those which should regulate the future administration of the government, the tokens of their amity would be as pernicious as could possibly be the tokens of their most deadly hatred.

They enumerate, as the crimes of the Federalists, the funding system, the national debt, the taxes which constitute the public revenue, the British treaty, the federal city, the mint, a mausoleum, the sedition law, and a standing army; and they tell us in plain terms that these are "abuses no longer to be suffered."

Let it be observed in the first place, that these crying sins of our government are not to be placed exclusively to the account of the Federalists, that for some of them the other party are chiefly responsible, and that in others they have participated.

As to the *federal city*—It is not to be denied that this was a favorite of the illustrious Washington. But it is no less certain that it was warmly patronized by Mr. Jefferson, Mr. Madison, and the great majority of the members who at the time composed the opposition in Congress and who are now influential in the Antifederal party. It is also certain that the measure has never been a favorite of a majority of the Federal party.

As to the *mint*, it was not at all a measure of party: With slight diversities of opinion about some of the details it was approved by both parties.

As to the MAUSOLEUM, it has not taken place at all. The bill for erecting it was lost in the Senate, where the Federalists have a decided majority; and instead of it an appropriation of fifty thousand dollars was made for erecting an equestrian statue, *agreeably to a resolution of Congress passed under the old confederation*. Is there an American who would refuse this memorial of gratitude to the man who is the boast of his country, the honor of his age?

As to the FUNDING SYSTEM, it was thus far a measure of both parties that both agreed there should be a FUNDING SYSTEM. In the formation of it the chief points of difference were: 1. A discrimination between original holders and transferees of the public debt. 2. A provision for the general debt of the union, leaving to each state to make separate provision for its particular debt.

Happily for our country, by the rejection of the first, which would have been an express violation of contracts, the faith of the government was preserved, its credit maintained and established.

Happily for our country, by not pursuing the last, unity, simplicity, and energy were secured to our fiscal system. The entanglements of fourteen conflicting systems of finance were avoided: The same mass of debt was included in one general provision, instead of being referred to fourteen separate provisions—more comprehensive justice was done, the states which had made extraordinary exertions for the support of the common cause were relieved from the unequal pressure of burdens which must have crushed them, and the people were saved from the immense difference of expense between a collection of the necessary revenues by one set of officers or by fourteen different sets.

The truth then, fellow citizens, is this—both parties agreed that there should be a *funding* system. And the particular plan which prevailed was most agreeable to the contract of the government—most conducive to general and equal justice among the states and individuals—to order and efficiency in the finances—to economy in the collection.

Ought not these ideas to have governed? What is meant by holding up the funding system as an abuse no longer to be tolerated?

What is the funding system? It is nothing more nor less than the *pledging of adequate funds or revenues for paying the interest and for the gradual redemption of the principal* of that very debt which was the sacred price of independence. The country being unable to pay off the principal, what better could have been done?

Is it recollected that long before our revolution most of the states had their funding systems? They emitted their paper money, which is only another phrase for certificates of debt, and they pledged funds for its redemption, which is but another phrase for *funding* it. What then is there so terrible in the idea of a funding system?

Those who may have been accustomed under some of the state governments to gamble in the floating paper, and, when they had monopolized a good quantity of it among themselves at low prices, to make partial legislative provisions for the payment of the particular kinds, would very naturally be displeased with a fixed and permanent system, which would give to the evidences of debt a stable value and lop off the opportunities for gambling speculations; but men who are sensible of the pernicious tendency of such a state of things will rejoice in a plan which was designed to produce and *has produced* a contrary result.

What have been the effects of this system?—An extension of commerce and manufactures, the rapid growth of our cities and towns, the consequent prosperity of agriculture and the advancement of the farming interest. All this was effected by giving life and activity to a capital in the public obligations, which was before dead, and by converting it into a powerful instrument of mercantile and other industrious enterprise.

We make these assertions boldly because the fact is exemplified by experience and is obvious to all discerning men. Our opponents in their hearts know it to be so.

As to the public debt—The great mass of it was not *created* by the Federalists peculiarly. It was contracted by all who were engaged in our councils during our revolutionary war. The Federalists have only had a principal agency in providing for it. No man can impute that to them as a crime who is not ready to avow the fraudulent and base doctrine that it is wiser and better to *cheat* than to *pay* the creditors of a nation.

It is a fact certain and notorious that under the administration of the first secretary of the treasury ample provision was made, not only for paying the interest of this debt but for extinguishing the principal in a moderate term of years.

But it is alleged that this debt has been increased and is increasing.

On this point we know that malcontent individuals make the assertion and exhibit statements intended to prove it. But this we also know, that a committee of the House of Representatives particularly charged with the inquiry have stated and reported the contrary; and we think that more credit is due to their representation than to that of individuals—especially as nothing is easier than in a matter of this sort to make plausible statements which, though utterly false, cannot be detected except by those who possess all the materials of a complex calculation, who are qualified and who will take the pains to make it.

We know likewise that extraordinary events have compelled our government to extraordinary expenditures—An Indian war, for some time disastrous, but terminated on principles likely to give durable tranquility to our frontier. Two insurrections, fomented by the opposition to the government. The hostilities of a foreign power encouraged by the undissembled sympathies of the same opposition, which obliged the government to arm for defense and security: These things have retarded the success of the efficacious measures which have been adopted for the discharge of our debt; measures which with a peaceable and orderly course of things, accelerated by the rapid growth of our country, are sufficient in a few years without any new expedient to exonerate it from the whole of its present debt.

These, fellow citizens, are serious truths well known to most of our opponents, but what they shamefully endeavor to disfigure and disguise.

As to *taxes*, they are evidently inseparable from government. It is impossible without them to pay the debts of the nation, to protect it from foreign danger, or to secure individuals from lawless violence and rapine.

It is always easy to assert that they are heavier than they ought to be, always difficult to refute the assertion—which cannot ever be attempted without a critical review of the whole course of public measures. This gives an immense advantage to those who make a trade of complaint and censure.

But, fellow citizens, it is in our power to state to you in relation to this subject and upon good information one material fact.

There is perhaps no item in the catalogue of our taxes which has been more unpopular than that which is called the DIRECT TAX.

This tax may emphatically be placed to the account of the opposite party; it was always insisted upon by them as preferable to taxes of the indirect kind. And it is a truth capable of full proof that Mr. *Madison*, second in the confidence of the Antifederal party, the confidential friend of Mr. Jefferson, and now secretary of state by his nomination, was the proposer of this tax. This was done in a committee of the last House of Representatives of which he was a member—was approved by that committee and referred to the late secretary of the treasury, Mr. Wolcott, with *instructions* to prepare a plan as to the *mode*.

Let it be added that it was a principle of the Federal party never to resort to this species of tax but in time of war or hostility with a foreign power, that it was in such a time when they did resort to it—and that the occasion ceasing by the prospect of an accommodation, it has been resolved by them not to renew the tax.

As to the *British treaty*, it is sufficient to remind you of the extravagant predictions of evil prior[1] to its ratification and to ask you, in what have they been realized? You have seen our peace preserved, you have seen our western posts surrendered, our commerce proceed with success in its wonted channels, and our agriculture flourish to the extent of every reasonable wish. And you have been witnesses to none of the mischiefs which were foretold. You will then conclude with us that the clamors against this treaty are the mere ebullitions of ignorance, of prejudice, and of faction.

As to the *sedition law*, we refer you to the debates in Congress for the motives and nature of it—More would prolong too much this reply, already more lengthy than we could wish. We will barely say that the most essential object of this act is to declare the courts of the United States competent to the cognizance of those slanders against the principal officers and departments of the federal government which at common law are punishable as libels, with the liberal and important mitigation of allowing the truth of an accusation to be given in evidence in exoneration of the accuser. What do you see in this to merit the execrations which have been bestowed on the measure?

As to a *standing army*—there is none except four small regiments of infantry insufficient for the service of guards in the numerous posts of our immense frontiers, stretching from Niagara to the borders of Florida, and two regiments of artillery which occupy in the same capacity the numerous fortifications along our widely extended sea-coast. What is there in this to affright or disgust?

If these corps are to be abolished, substitutes must be found in the militia. If the experiment shall be made, it is easy to foretell that it will prove not a measure of economy but a heavy bill of additional cost, and like all other visionary schemes will be productive only of repentance and a return to a plan injudiciously renounced.

This exposition of the measures which have been represented to you as abuses *no longer to be suffered* (mark the strength of the phrase) will, we trust, serve to satisfy you of the violence and absurdity of those crude notions which govern our opposers, if we believe them to be sincere.

Happily for our country, however, there has just beamed a ray of hope that these violent and absurd notions will not form the rule of conduct of the person whom the party have recently elevated to the head of our national affairs.

In the speech of the new president upon assuming the exercise of his office, we find among the articles of his creed, "the honest payment of our DEBT, and sacred preservation of the PUBLIC FAITH." The funding system, the national debt, the British treaty are not therefore in his conception abuses, which if no longer to be tolerated would be of course to be abolished.

But we think ourselves warranted to derive from the same source a condemnation still more extensive of the opinions of our adversaries. The speech characterizes our present government "as a Republican Government, in the *full tide* of successful *experiment*." Success in the *experiment* of a government is success in the *practice* of it, and this is but another phrase for an administration, in the main, wise and good. That administration has been hitherto in the hands of the Federalists.

Here then, fellow citizens, is an open and solemn protest against the principles and opinions of our opponents, from a quarter which as yet they dare not arraign.

In referring to this speech, we think it proper to make a public declaration of our approbation of its contents: We view it as virtually a candid retraction of past misapprehensions and a pledge to the community that the new president will not lend himself to dangerous innovations but in essential points will tread in the steps of his predecessors.

In doing this he prudently anticipates the loss of a great portion of that favor which has elevated him to his present station. Doubtless it is a just foresight. Adhering to the professions he has made, it will not be long before the body of the Antifederalists will raise their croaking and ill-omened voices against him: But in the talents, the patriotism, and the firmness of the Federalists he will find more than an equivalent for all that he shall lose.

All those of whatever party who may desire to support the moderate views exhibited in the presidential speech will unite against the violent projects of the men who have addressed you in favor of Mr. Clinton, and against a candidate who in all past experience has evinced that he is likely to be a fit instrument of these projects.

Fellow citizens, we beseech you to consult your *experience* and not listen to tales of evil, which exist only in the language, not even in the imaginations of those who deal them out. This experience will tell you that our opposers have been uniformly mistaken in their views of our Constitution, of its administration, in all the judgments which they have pronounced of our public affairs; and consequently that they are unfaithful or incapable advisers. It will teach you that you have eminently prospered under the system of public measures pursued and supported by the Federalists.

In vain are you told that you owe your prosperity to your own industry and to the blessings of Providence. To the latter doubtless you are primarily indebted. You owe to it among other benefits the Constitution you enjoy and the wise administration of it by virtuous men as its instruments. You are likewise indebted to your own industry. But has not your industry found aliment and incitement in the salutary operation of your government—in the preservation of order at home—in the cultivation of peace abroad—in the invigoration of confidence in pecuniary dealings—in the increased energies of credit and commerce—in the extension of enterprise ever incident to a good government well administered? Remember what your situation was immediately before the establishment of the present Constitution. Were you then deficient in industry more than now? If not, why were you not equally prosperous? Plainly because your industry had not at that time the vivifying influences of an efficient and well conducted government....

We shall not discuss how far it is probable that the radical antipathy of Mr. Clinton to the vital parts of our national Constitution has given way to the little formal amendments which have since been adopted. We are glad to be assured that it has. It gives us pleasure to see proselytes to the truth; nor shall we be over curious to enquire how men get right if we can but discover that they are right. If happily the possession of the power of our once detested government shall be a talisman to work the conversion of all its enemies, we shall be ready to rejoice that good has come out of evil.

But we dare not too far indulge this pleasing hope. We know that the adverse party has its *Dantons*, its *Robespierres*, as well as its *Brissots*, and its *Rolands*; and we look forward to the time when the sects of the former will endeavor to confound the latter and their adherents, together with the Federalists, in promiscuous ruin.

In regard to these sects, which compose the pith and essence of the Antifederal party, we believe it to be true that the contest between us is indeed a war of principles—a war between tyranny and liberty, but not between monarchy and republicanism. It is a contest between the tyranny of Jacobinism, which confounds and levels everything, and the mild reign of rational liberty, which rests on the basis of an efficient and well balanced government, and through the medium of stable laws shelters and protects the life, the reputation, the prosperity, the civil and religious rights of every member of the community.

'Tis against these sects that all good men should form an indissoluble league. To resist and frustrate their machinations is alike essential to every prudent and faithful administration of our government, whoever may be the depositaries of the power.

The Examination Number I, December 17, 1801

Instead of delivering a *speech* to the House of Congress at the opening of the present session the president has thought fit to transmit a *Message*. Whether this has proceeded from pride or from humility, from a temperate love of reform or from a wild spirit of innovation, is submitted to the conjectures of the curious. A single observation shall be indulged—since all agree that he is unlike his predecessors in essential points, it is a mark of consistency to differ from them in matters of form.

Whoever considers the temper of the day must be satisfied that this Message is likely to add much to the popularity of our chief magistrate. It conforms, as far as would be tolerated at this early stage of our progress in political perfection, to the bewitching tenets of that illuminated doctrine which promises man, ere long, an emancipation from the burdens and restraints of government, giving a foretaste of that pure felicity which the apostles of this doctrine have predicted. After having, with infinite pains and assiduity, formed the public taste for this species of fare, it is certainly right for those whom the people have chosen for their caterers to be attentive to the gratification of that taste. And should the viands which they may offer prove baneful poisons instead of wholesome aliments, the justification is both plain and easy—*good patriots must, at all events, please the people*. But those whose patriotism is of the OLD SCHOOL, who differ so widely from the disciples of the new creed that they would rather risk incurring the displeasure of the people by speaking unpalatable truths than betray their interest by fostering their prejudices, will never be deterred by an impure tide of popular opinion from honestly pointing out the mistakes or the faults of weak or wicked men who may have been selected as guardians of the public weal.

The Message of the president, by whatever motives it may have been dictated, is a performance which ought to alarm all who are anxious for the safety of our government, for the respectability and welfare of our nation. It makes, or aims at making, a most prodigal sacrifice of constitutional energy, of sound principle, and of public interest to the popularity of one man.

The first thing in it which excites our surprise is the very extraordinary position that though *Tripoli had declared war in form* against the United States, and had enforced it by actual hostility, yet that there was not power, for want of *the sanction of Congress*, to capture and detain her cruisers with their crews.

When the newspapers informed us that one of these cruisers, after being subdued in a bloody conflict, had been liberated and permitted quietly to return home, the imagination was perplexed to divine the reason. The conjecture naturally was that, pursuing a policy too refined perhaps for barbarians, it was intended by that measure to give the enemy a strong impression of our magnanimity and humanity. No one dreamt of a scruple as to the *right* to seize and detain the armed vessel of an open and avowed foe, vanquished in battle. The enigma is now solved, and we are presented with one of the most singular paradoxes ever advanced by a man claiming the character of a statesman. When analyzed, it amounts to nothing less than this, that *between* two nations there may exist a state of complete war on the one side—of peace on the other.

War, of itself, gives to the parties a mutual right to kill in battle and to capture the persons and property of each other. This is a rule of natural law, a necessary and inevitable consequence of the state of war. This state between two nations is completely produced by the act of one—it requires no concurrent act of the other. It is impossible to conceive the idea that one nation can be in full war with another, and this other not in the same state with respect to its adversary. The moment therefore that two nations are, in an absolute sense, at war, the public force of each may exercise every act of hostility which the general laws of war authorize against the persons and property of the other. As it respects this conclusion, the distinction between offensive and defensive war makes no difference. That distinction is only material to discriminate the aggressing nation from that which defends itself against attack. The war is offensive on the part of the state which makes it; on the opposite side it is defensive: but the rights of both, as to the measure of hostility, are equal.

It will be readily allowed that the constitution of a particular country may limit the organ charged with the direction of the public force in the use or application of that force, even in time of actual war: but nothing short of the strongest negative words, of the most express prohibitions, can be admitted to restrain that organ from so employing it as to derive the fruits of actual victory by making prisoners of the persons and detaining the property of a vanquished enemy. Our Constitution happily is not chargeable with so great an absurdity. The framers of it would have blushed at a provision so repugnant to good sense, so inconsistent with national safety and convenience.[2] That instrument has only provided affirmatively that "The Congress shall have power to declare War," the plain meaning of which is that it is the peculiar and exclusive province of Congress, *when the nation is at peace*, to change that state into a state of war, whether from calculations of policy or from provocations or injuries received: in other words, it belongs to Congress only *to go to war*. But when a foreign nation declares or openly and avowedly makes war upon the United States, they are then by the very fact already *at war*, and any declaration on the part of Congress is nugatory: it is at least unnecessary. This inference is clear in principle and has the sanction of established practice. It is clear in principle, because it is self-evident that a declaration by one nation against another produces at once a complete state of war between both, and that no declaration on the other side can at all vary their relative situation: and in practice it is well known that nothing is more common than when war is declared by one party to prosecute mutual hostilities without a declaration by the other.

The doctrine of the Message includes the strange absurdity that without a declaration of war by Congress, our public force may destroy the life but may not restrain the liberty or seize the property of an enemy. This was exemplified in the very instance of the Tripolitan corsair. A number of her crew were slaughtered in the combat, and after she was subdued she was set free with the remainder. But it may perhaps be said that she was the assailant and that resistance was an act of mere defense and self-preservation. Let us then pursue the matter a step further. Our ships had blockaded the Tripolitan Admiral in the bay of Gibraltar; suppose he had attempted to make his way out, without first firing upon them: if permitted to do it, the blockade was a farce; if hindered by force, this would have amounted to more than a mere act of defense; and if a combat had ensued, we should then have seen an unequivocal illustration of the unintelligible right to take the life but not to abridge the liberty or capture the property of an enemy.

Let us suppose an invasion of our territory, previous to a declaration of war by Congress. The principle avowed in the Message would authorize our troops to kill those of the invader if they should come within the reach of their bayonets, perhaps to drive them into the sea and drown them; but not to disable them from doing harm by the milder process of making them prisoners and sending them into confinement. Perhaps it may be replied that the same end would be answered by disarming and leaving them to starve. The merit of such an argument would be complete by adding that should they not be famished before the arrival of their ships with a fresh supply of arms, we might then, if able, disarm them a second time and send them on board their fleet to return safely home.

The inconvenience of the doctrine in practice is not less palpable than its folly in theory. In every case it presents a most unequal warfare. In the instance which has occurred the vanquished barbarian got off with the loss of his guns. Had he been victorious, the Americans, whose lives might have been spared, would have been doomed to wear out a miserable existence in slavery and chains. Substantial benefits would have rewarded his success; while on our side, life, liberty and property were put in jeopardy for an empty triumph. This, however, was a partial inconvenience—cases may arise in which evils of a more serious and comprehensive nature would be the fruits of this visionary and fantastical principle. Suppose that, in the recess of Congress, a foreign maritime power should unexpectedly declare war against the United States and send a fleet and army to seize Rhode Island, in order from thence to annoy our trade and our seaport towns. Till the Congress should assemble and declare war, which would require time, our ships might, according to the hypothesis of the Message, be sent by the president to fight those of the enemy as often as they should be attacked, but not to capture and detain them: If beaten, both vessels and crews would be lost to the United States: if successful, they could only disarm those they had overcome and must suffer them to return to the place of common rendezvous, there to equip anew for the purpose of resuming their depredations on our towns and our trade.

Who could restrain the laugh of derision at positions so preposterous, were it not for the reflection that in the first magistrate of our country they cast a blemish on our national character? What will the world think of the fold when such is the shepherd?

Lucius Crassus

Excerpts from The Examination Number III, December 21, 1801

Had our laws been less provident than they have been, yet must it give us a very humble idea of the talents of our president as a statesman to find him embarrassed between an absolute abandonment of revenue and an inconvenient accumulation of treasure. Pursuing the doctrine professed by his *sect* that our public debt is a national *curse* which cannot too promptly be removed, and adhering to the* assurance which he has virtually given that a sponge, the *favorite instrument*, shall not be employed for the purpose, how has it happened that he should have overlooked the simple and obvious expedient of using the supposed excess of income as a remedy for so great a mischief?... .

In addition to objects of national security, there are many purposes of great public utility to which the revenues in question might be applied. The improvement of the communications between the different parts of our country is an object well worthy of the national purse, and one which would abundantly repay to *labor* the portion of its *earnings* which may have been borrowed for that purpose. To provide roads and bridges is within the direct purview of the Constitution. In many parts of the country, especially in the western territory, a matter in which the Atlantic states are equally interested, aqueducts and canals would also be fit subjects of pecuniary aid from the general government. In France, England, and other parts of Europe, institutions exist supported by public contributions, which eminently promote agriculture and the arts: such institutions merit imitation by our government: they are of the number of those which directly and sensibly recompense *labor* for what it lends to their agency.

To suggestions of the last kind the adepts of the new school have a ready answer: *Industry will succeed and prosper in proportion as it is left to the exertions of individual enterprise.* This favorite dogma, when taken as a general rule, is true; but as an exclusive one, it is false and leads to error in the administration of public affairs. In matters of industry, human enterprise ought, doubtless, to be left free in the main, not fettered by too much regulation; but practical politicians know that it may be beneficially stimulated by prudent aids and encouragements on the part of the government. This is proved by numerous examples too tedious to be cited, examples which will be neglected only by indolent and temporizing rulers, who love to loll in the lap of epicurean ease, and seem to

* One of the essential principles of government is "*the honest payment of our debts and sacred preservation of the public faith.*"—Inaugural Speech.

imagine that to govern well is to amuse the wondering multitude with sagacious aphorisms and oracular sayings.

What has been observed is sufficient to render it manifest that, independent of the extinguishment of the debt, the revenues proposed to be yielded up would find ample and very useful employment for a variety of public purposes. Already in possession of so valuable a resource; having surmounted the difficulties, which, from the opinions and habits of our citizens, obstruct, in this, more than in any other country, every new provision for adding to our public income; certainly without a colorable presence of there being a grievous or undue pressure on the community—how foolish will it be to resign the boon, perhaps in a short time to be compelled again to resort to it; and for that purpose to hazard a repetition of the obstacles which have been before encountered and overcome; which, however, gave birth to one insurrection and may give birth to another? Infatuated must be the councils from which so injurious a project has proceeded!

But admitting the position that there is an excess of income which ought to be relinquished, still the proposal to surrender the *internal revenue* is impolitic. It ought to be carefully preserved as not being exposed to the casualties incident to our intercourse with foreign nations and therefore the most certain. It ought to be preserved as reaching to descriptions of persons who are not proportionably affected by the impost, and as tending for this reason to distribute the public burden more equitably. It ought to be preserved because if revenue can really be spared, it is best to do it in such a manner as will conduce to the relief or advancement of our navigation and commerce. Rather let the tonnage duty on American vessels be abolished, and let the duties be lessened on some particular articles on which they may press with inconvenient weight. Let not the merchant be provoked to attempt to evade the duties by the sentiment that his ease or interest is disregarded and that his capital alone is to be clogged and encumbered by the demands of the treasury.

But who and what are the merchants when compared with the patriotic votaries of whiskey in Pennsylvania and Virginia?

Lucius Crassus

The Examination Number V, December 29, 1801

In the rage for change, or under the stimulus of a deep-rooted animosity against the former administrations, or for the sake of gaining popular favor by a profuse display of extraordinary zeal for economy, even our judiciary system has not passed unassailed. The attack here is not so open as that on the revenue; but when we are told that the states individually have "*principal* care of our persons, our property, and our reputation; constituting the great field of human concerns; and that therefore *we may well doubt whether our organization is not too complicated, too expensive;* whether offices and officers have not been multiplied unnecessarily and sometimes injuriously to the service they were meant to promote"; when afterwards it is observed that "the Judiciary System will *of course* present itself to the contemplation of Congress"; and when it appears that pains had been taken to form and communicate a numerical list of all the causes decided since the first establishment of the courts, in order that Congress may be able to judge of the proportion which the institution bears to the business; with all these indications it is not to be misunderstood that the intention was unequivocally to recommend *material* alterations in the system.

No bad thermometer of the capacity of our chief magistrate for government is furnished by the rule which he offers for judging of the utility of the federal courts; namely, the exact *number* of causes which have been by them decided. There is hardly any stronger symptom of a pigmy mind than a propensity to allow greater weight to *secondary* than to *primary* considerations.

It ought at least to have been adverted to that if this circumstance were a perfect criterion, it is yet too early to apply it, especially to the courts recently erected: And it might have merited reflection that it would have been prudent to wait for a more advanced period of the presidential term to ascertain what influence the great change which has lately happened in our *public functionaries* may have on the confidence, which in many parts of the Union has heretofore been reposed in the state courts, so as to prevent a preference of those of the United States.

But to enable us duly to appreciate the wisdom of the projected innovation, it is necessary to review the objects which were designed to be accomplished by the arrangement of the judiciary power as it is seen in the Constitution, and to examine the organization which has been adopted to give effect to those objects.

It is well known to all who were acquainted with the situation of our public affairs when the Constitution was framed, and it is to be inferred from the provisions of the instrument itself, that the objects contemplated, were: 1st. To provide a faithful and efficient organ for carrying into execution the laws of the United States, which otherwise would be a *dead letter*. 2d. To secure the fair interpretation and execution of our treaties with foreign nations. 3d. To maintain harmony between the individual states, not only by an independent and impartial mode of determining controversies between them, but by frustrating the effects of partial laws in any one injurious to the rights of the citizens of another. 4th. To guard generally against the invasions of property and right by fraudulent and oppressive laws of particular states enforced by their own tribunals. 5th. To guard the rights and conciliate the confidence of foreigners by giving them the option of tribunals created by and responsible to the general government, which, having the immediate charge of our external relations, including the care of our national peace, might be expected to be more tenacious of such an administration of justice as would leave to the citizens of other countries no real cause of complaint. 6th. To protect reciprocally the rights and inspire mutually the confidence of the citizens of different states in their intercourse with each other, by enabling them to resort to tribunals so constituted as to be essentially free from local bias or partiality. 7th. To give the citizens of each state a fair chance of impartial justice through the medium of those tribunals in cases in which the titles to property might depend on the conflicting grants of different states. These were the immensely important objects to be attained by the institution of an adequate judiciary power in the government of the United States. Nor did its institution depend upon mere speculative opinion, though indeed even that would have been sufficient to indicate the expediency of the measure: but experience had actually in a variety of ways demonstrated its necessity.

The treaties of the United States had been infracted by state laws, put in execution by state judicatories. The rights of property had been invaded by the same means in numerous instances, as well with respect to foreigners as to citizens, as well between citizens of different states as between citizens of the same state. There were many cases in which lands were held or claimed under adverse grants of different states having rival pretensions, and in respect to which the local tribunals, even if not fettered by the local laws, could hardly be expected to be impartial. In several of the states the courts were so constituted as not to afford sufficient assurance of a pure, enlightened, and independent administration of justice, an evil which in some of them still continues. From these different sources serious mischiefs had been felt. The interests of the United States in their foreign concerns had suffered; their reputation had been tarnished; their peace endangered; their mutual harmony had been disturbed or menaced; creditors had been ruined or in a very extensive degree much injured; confidence in pecuniary transactions had been destroyed and the springs of industry had been proportionably relaxed. To these circumstances, as much, perhaps, as to any other that accompanied a defective social organization, are we to attribute that miserable and prostrate situation of our affairs which immediately before the establishment of our present national Constitution filled every intelligent lover of his country with affliction and mortification. To the institution of a competent judiciary, little less than to any one provision in that Constitution, is to be ascribed the rapid and salutary renovation of our affairs which succeeded.

The enumeration* of the component parts of the judicial power in the Constitution has an evident eye to the several objects which have been stated: And considering their vast magnitude, no sound politician will doubt that the principal question with the administration ought to be how to give the greatest efficacy to this essential part of the system, in comparison with which the more or less of expense must be a matter of trivial moment. The difference of expense between an enlarged and a contracted plan may be deemed an atom in the great scale of national expenditure. The fulfillment of the important ends of this part of our constitutional plan, though with but a small degree of additional energy, facility, or convenience, must infinitely overbalance the consideration of such difference of expense.

The number of causes which have been tried in these courts, as already intimated, can furnish but a very imperfect test by which to decide upon their utility or necessity. Their existence alone has a powerful and salutary effect. The liberty to use them, even where it is not often exercised, inspires confidence in the intercourse of business. They are viewed as beneficent guardians whose protection may be claimed when necessary. They induce caution in the state courts, and promote in them a more attentive, if not a more able administration of justice. Though in some districts of the Union the federal courts are seldom resorted to, in others they are used in an extensive degree, particularly as between foreigners and citizens, and between citizens of different states.

That their organization throughout the U. States ought to be uniform will not be denied; and it is evident that it ought to be regulated by the situation of those parts in which a greater degree of employment denotes the courts to be most necessary: Of consequence, if the quantity of business were at all a guide, the scenes in which there is the greatest employment for the federal courts ought to furnish the rule of computation; it ought not to be sought for in the aggregate of business throughout the Union. In reference to this point, it is likewise material to observe that, from the manner in which the federal courts were constituted previous to the last arrangement, *the organization* of the state courts was so much better adapted to expedition as to afford a strong motive for giving them

---

* "Sec. II. The judicial power shall extend to all cases in law and equity, arising under this constitution, the laws of the United States and treaties made, or which shall be made, under their authority; to all cases affecting ambassadors, other public ministers and consuls; to all cases of admiralty and maritime jurisdiction; to controversies to which the United States shall be a party; to controversies between two or more states, between a state and citizens of another state, between citizens of different states, between citizens of the same state claiming lands under grants of different states, and between a state, or the citizens thereof, and foreign states, citizens or subjects."

a preference. The establishment of circuit courts, as now modified, will vary that circumstance and therefore attract more business; but it is evident that it must require a course of years fully to exemplify its operations, which cannot be seen in a few months or in a single year. To attempt, therefore, to draw important inferences from the short experience hitherto had is worse than puerile.

Lucius Crassus

The Examination Number VI, January 2, 1802

In answer to the observations in the last number it may perhaps be said that the Message meant nothing more than to condemn the recent *multiplication* of federal courts and to bring them back to their original organization: considering it as adequate to all the purposes of the Constitution, to all the ends of justice and policy.

Towards forming a right judgment on this subject, it may be useful to those who are not familiar with the subject to state briefly what was the former and what is the present establishment.

The former consisted of one Supreme Court with six judges, who, twice a year made the tour of the United States, distributed into three circuits, for the trial of causes arising in the respective districts of each circuit; and of fifteen district courts, each having a single judge. The present consists of one Supreme Court with the like number of judges, to be reduced on the first vacancy happening to five; of six circuit courts, having three distinct judges each, excepting one circuit which has only a single circuit judge; and of twenty-two district courts with a judge for each as before: In both plans the Supreme Court is to hold two terms at the seat³ of government, and the circuit courts to be holden twice a year in each district. The material difference in the two plans, as it respects the organs by which they are executed, is reducible to the creation of twenty-three additional judges: sixteen for the six circuits courts, seven for the superadded district courts, and the addition of the necessary clerks, marshals, and subordinate officers of seven courts. This shows at a single view that the difference of expense as applied to the United States is of trifling consideration.

But here an enquiry naturally presents itself: why was the latter plan substituted to the former and more economical one? The solution is easy and satisfactory. The first was inadequate to its object and incapable of being carried into execution. The extent of the United States is manifestly too large for the due attendance of the six judges in the circuit courts. The immense journeys they were obliged to perform kept them from their families for several successive months in every year; this rendered the office a grievous burden and had a strong tendency to banish or exclude men of the best talents and characters from these important stations. It is known to have been no light inducement with one chief justice, whose health was delicate, to quit that office for another attended with less bodily fatigue; and it is well understood that other important members of the Supreme Court were prepared to resign their situations if there had not been some alteration of the kind which has taken place. It was also no uncommon circumstance for temporary interruptions in the health of particular judges, of whom only one was attached to a circuit, to occasion a failure in the sessions of the courts, to the no small disappointment, vexation, and loss of the suitor. At any rate the necessity of visiting, within a given time, the numerous parts of an extensive circuit unavoidably rendered the sessions of each court so short that where suits were in any degree multiplied or intricate there was not time to get through the business with due deliberation. Besides all this, the incessant fatigues of the judges of the Supreme Court, and their long and frequent absences from home, prevented that continued attention to their studies, which even the most learned will confess to be necessary for those entrusted in the last resort with questions frequently novel, always of magnitude, affecting not only the property of individuals but the rights of foreign nations and the Constitution of the country.

For these reasons it became necessary either to renounce the circuit courts or to constitute them differently: the latter was preferred. The United States were divided into six circuits, with a proper number of judges to preside over each. No man of discernment will pretend that the number of circuits is too great. Surely three states forming an area of territory equal to that possessed by some of the first powers of Europe must afford a quantity of business fully sufficient to employ three judges on a circuit, twice a year, and certainly not less than this will suffice for the dispatch of business, whether the number of causes be small or great. The inconsiderable addition made to the number of the district courts will hardly excite criticism, and does not, therefore, claim a particular discussion, nor will their necessity be generally questioned. They are almost continually occupied with revenue and admiralty causes, besides the great employment collaterally given to the judges in the execution of the Bankrupt Act, which probably must increase instead of being diminished.

Perhaps it may be contended that the circuit courts ought to be abolished altogether, and the business for which they are designed left to the state courts, with a right of appeal to the Supreme Court of the United States. Indeed, it is probable that this was the true design of the intimation in the Message. *A disposition to magnify the importance of the particular states, in derogation from that of the United States*, is a feature in that communication not to be mistaken. But to such a scheme there are insuperable objections. The right of appeal is by no means equal to the right of applying, in the first instance, to a tribunal agreeable to the suitor. The *desideratum* is to have impartial justice, at a moderate expense, administered "promptly and without delay"; not to be obliged to seek it through the long and tedious and expensive process of an appeal. It is true that in causes of sufficient magnitude an appeal ought to be open, which includes the possibility of going through that process: but when the courts of original jurisdiction are so constituted as not only to deserve but to inspire confidence, appeals, from the inevitable inconvenience attached to them, are exceptions to the general rule of redress; where the contrary is the situation they become the general rule itself. Appeals then multiplied to a pernicious extent, while the difficulties to which they are liable operate in numerous instances as a preventative of justice, because they fall with most weight on the least wealthy suitor. It is to be remembered that the cases in which the federal courts would be preferred are those where there would exist some distrust of the state courts; and this distrust would be a fruitful source of appeals. To say that there could be no good cause for this distrust, and that the danger of it is imaginary, is to be wiser than experience and wiser than the Constitution. The first officer of the government, when speaking in his official capacity, has no right to attempt to be thus wise. His duty exacts of him that he should respectfully acquiesce in the spirit and ideas of that instrument under which he is appointed.

The detail would be invidious, perhaps injurious; else it would be easy to show that however great the confidence to which the tribunals in some of the states are entitled, there is just cause for suspicion as to those of others; and that in respect to a still greater number it would be inexpedient to delegate to them the care of interests which are specially and properly confided to the government of the United States.

The plan of using the state courts as substitutes for the circuit courts of the Union is objectionable in another view. The citizens of the United States have a right to expect from those who administer our government the efficacious enjoyment of those privileges as suitors for which the Constitution has provided. To *turn them round*, therefore, from the enjoyment of those privileges in originating their causes to the eventual and dilatory resource of an appeal is in a great degree to defeat the object contemplated. This is a consideration of much real weight, especially to the merchants in our commercial states.

In the investigation of our subject, it is not to be forgotten that the right to employ the agency of the state courts for executing the laws of the Union is liable to question and has, in fact, been seriously questioned. This circumstance renders it the more indispensable that the permanent organization of the federal judiciary should be adapted to the prompt and vigorous execution of those laws.

The right of Congress to discontinue judges, once appointed, by the abrogation of the courts for which they were appointed, especially as it relates to their emoluments, offers matter for a very nice discussion, but which shall now be but superficially touched.

On the one head it is not easy to maintain that Congress cannot abolish courts which having been once instituted are found in practice to be inconvenient and unnecessary: On the other, if it may be done so as to include the annihilation of existing judges, it is evident that the measure may be used to defeat that clause of the Constitution which renders the duration and emoluments of the judicial office coextensive with the good behavior of the officer; an object essential to the independence of the judges, the security of the citizen, and the preservation of the government.

As a medium which may reconcile opposite ideas and obviate opposite inconveniences, it would perhaps be the best and safest practical construction to say that though Congress may abolish the courts, yet shall the actual judges retain their character and their emoluments, with the authorities of office, so far as they can be exercised elsewhere than in the courts. For this construction a precedent exists in the last arrangement of the judiciary. Though the number of judges of the Supreme Court is reduced from six to five, yet the actual reduction is wisely deferred to the *happening of a vacancy*. The expense of continuing the salaries of the existing incumbent cannot prudently be put in competition with the advantage of guarding from invasion one of the most precious provisions in the Constitution. Nor ought it to be without its weight that this modification will best comport with good faith on the part of government towards those who had been invited to accept offices not to be held by an uncertain tenure but during *good behavior*.

Weighing maturely all the very important and very delicate considerations which appertain to the subject, would a wise or prudent statesman hazard the consequences of immediately unmaking at one session courts and judges which had only been called in into being at the one preceding? Delectable indeed must be the work of disorganization to a mind which can thus rashly advance in its prosecution! Infatuated must that people be who do not open their eyes to projects so intemperate—so mischievous! Who does not see what is the ultimate object? "*Delenda est Carthago*"—ill-fated Constitution, which Americans had fondly hoped would continue for ages, the guardian of public liberty, the source of national prosperity!

Lucius Crassus

The Examination Number VII, January 7, 1802

The next exceptionable feature in the Message is the proposal to abolish all restriction on naturalization arising from a previous residence. In this the president is not more at variance with the concurrent maxims of all commentators on popular governments than he is with himself. The Notes on Virginia are in direct contradiction to the Message and furnish us with strong reasons against the policy now recommended. The passage alluded to is here presented: Speaking of the *population* of America, Mr. Jefferson there says, "Here I will beg leave to propose a doubt. The present desire of America is to produce rapid population by as great *importations of foreigners* as possible. *But is this founded in good policy?*" "Are there no inconveniences to be thrown into the scale against the advantage expected from a multiplication of numbers by the *importation of foreigners?* It is for the happiness of those united in society to harmonize as much as possible in matters which they must of necessity transact together. Civil government being the sole object of forming societies, its administration must be conducted by common consent. Every species of government has its specific principles: Ours, perhaps, are more peculiar than those of any other in the universe. *It is a composition of the freest principles of the English constitution* with others, derived from natural right and reason. To these nothing can be more opposed than the maxims of absolute monarchies. Yet from such we are to expect the *greatest number of emigrants. They will bring with them the principles of the governments they leave, imbibed in their early youth; or if able to throw them off, it will be in exchange for an unbounded licentiousness, passing as is usual from one extreme to another. It would be a miracle were they to stop precisely at the point of temperate liberty. Their principles with their language they will transmit to their children.* In proportion to their numbers, *they will share with us in the legislation.* They will infuse *into it their spirit, warp and bias its direction, and render it a heterogeneous, incoherent, distracted mass.* I may appeal to experience, during the present contest, for a verification of these conjectures: but if they be not certain in event, are they not possible, are they not probable? *Is it not safer to wait with patience for the attainment of any degree of population desired or expected?* May not our government be more homogeneous, *more peaceable, more durable?* Suppose 20 millions of republican Americans, thrown all of a sudden into France, what would be the condition of that kingdom? If it would be more turbulent, less happy, less strong, we may believe that the addition of half a million of foreigners to our present numbers would produce a similar effect here." Thus wrote Mr. Jefferson in 1781—Behold the reverse of the medal. The Message of the president contains the following sentiments: "A denial of citizenship under a residence of 14 years is a denial to a great proportion of those who ask it, & controls a policy pursued from their first settlement by many of these states and *still believed of consequence to their prosperity*. And shall we refuse to the unhappy fugitives from distress *that hospitality* which the savages of the wilderness extended to our fathers arriving in this land? Shall oppressed humanity find no asylum on this globe? Might not the general character and capabilities of a citizen be safely communicated to *everyone* manifesting a bona fide purpose of embarking his life and fortune permanently with us?"

But if gratitude can be allowed to form an excuse for inconsistency in a public character, in *The Man of the People*; a strong plea of this sort may be urged in behalf of our president. It is certain that had the late election been decided entirely by native citizens, had foreign auxiliaries been rejected on both sides, the man who ostentatiously vaunts that the *doors of public honor and confidence have been burst open to him* would not now have been at the head of the American nation. Such a proof then of virtuous discernment in the *oppressed fugitives* had an imperious claim on him to a grateful return, and without supposing any very uncommon share of *self-love* would naturally be a strong reason for a revolution in his opinions.

The pathetic and plaintive exclamations by which the sentiment is enforced might be liable to much criticism, if we are to consider it in any other light than as a flourish of rhetoric. It might be asked in return, does the right to *asylum* or *hospitality* carry with it the right to suffrage and sovereignty? And what indeed was the courteous reception which was given to our forefathers by the savages of the wilderness? When did these humane and philanthropic savages exercise the policy of incorporating strangers among themselves on their first arrival in the country? When did they admit them into their huts, to make part of their families, and when did they distinguish them by making them their sachems? Our histories and traditions have been more than apocryphal if anything like this kind and gentle treatment was really lavished by the much-belied savages upon our thankless forefathers. But the remark occurs, had it all been true, prudence inclines to trace the history farther and ask what has become of the nations of savages who exercised this policy? And who now occupies the territory which they then inhabited? Perhaps a useful lesson might be drawn from this very reflection.

But we may venture to ask what does the president really mean by insinuating that we treat aliens coming to this country with inhospitality? Do we not permit them quietly to land on our shores? Do we not protect them equally with our own citizens in their persons and reputation, in the acquisition and enjoyment of property? Are not our courts of justice open for them to seek redress of injuries? And are they not permitted peaceably to return to their own country whenever they please, and to carry with them all their effects? What then means this worse than idle declamation?

The impolicy of admitting foreigners to an immediate and unreserved participation in the right of suffrage, or in the sovereignty of a republic, is as much a received axiom as anything in the science of politics and is verified by the experience of all ages. Among other instances, it is known that hardly anything contributed more to the downfall of Rome than her precipitate communication of the privileges of citizenship to the inhabitants of Italy at large. And how terribly was Syracuse scourged by perpetual seditions when, after the overthrow of the tyrants, a great number of foreigners were suddenly admitted to the rights of citizenship? Not only does ancient but modern, and even domestic, history furnish evidence of what may be expected from the dispositions of foreigners when they get too early footing in a country. Who wields the scepter of France and has erected a despotism on the ruins of a republic? A foreigner. Who rules the councils of our own ill-fated, unhappy country? And who stimulates persecution on the heads of its citizens for daring to maintain an opinion and for exercising the rights of suffrage? *A foreigner!*[4] Where is the virtuous pride that once distinguished Americans? Where the indignant spirit which in defense of principle hazarded a revolution to attain that independence now *insidiously* attacked?

Lucius Crassus

The Examination Number VIII, January 12, 1802

Resuming the subject of our last paper, we proceed to trace still farther the consequences that must result from a too unqualified admission of foreigners to an equal participation in our civil and political rights.

The safety of a republic depends essentially on the energy of a common national sentiment; on a uniformity of principles and habits; on the exemption of the citizens from foreign bias and prejudice; and on that love of country which will almost invariably be found to be closely connected with birth, education, and family.

The opinion advanced in the Notes on Virginia is undoubtedly correct that foreigners will generally be apt to bring with them attachments to the persons they have left behind, to the country of their nativity, and to its particular customs and manners. They will also entertain opinions on government congenial with those under which they have lived, or, if they should be led hither from a preference to ours, how extremely unlikely is it that they will bring with them that *temperate love of liberty* so essential to real republicanism? There may as to particular individuals, and at particular times, be occasional exceptions to these remarks, yet such is the general rule. The influx of foreigners must, therefore, tend to produce a heterogeneous compound; to change and corrupt the national spirit; to complicate and confound public opinion; to introduce foreign propensities. In the composition of society, the harmony of the ingredients is all important, and whatever tends to a discordant intermixture must have an injurious tendency.

The United States have already felt the evils of incorporating a large number of foreigners into their national mass; it has served very much to divide the community and to distract our councils by promoting in different classes different predilections in favor of particular foreign nations and antipathies against others. It has been often likely to compromit the interests of our own country in favor of another. In times of great public danger there is always a numerous body of men of whom there may be just grounds of distrust; the suspicion alone weakens the strength of the nation, but their force may be actually employed in assisting an invader.

In the infancy of the country, with a boundless waste to people, it was politic to give a facility to naturalization; but our situation is now changed. It appears from the last census that we have increased about one third in ten years; after allowing for what we have gained from abroad, it will be quite apparent that the natural progress of our own population is sufficiently rapid for strength, security, and settlement. By what has been said it is not meant to contend for a total prohibition of the right of citizenship to strangers, nor even for the very long residence which is now a prerequisite to naturalization, and which of itself goes far towards a denial of that privilege. The present law was merely a temporary measure adopted under peculiar circumstances and perhaps demands revision. But there is a wide difference between closing the door altogether and throwing it entirely open, between a postponement of fourteen years and an immediate admission to all the rights of citizenship. Some reasonable term ought to be allowed to enable aliens to get rid of foreign and acquire American attachments; to learn the principles and imbibe the spirit of our government; and to admit of at least a probability of their feeling a real interest in our affairs. A residence of at least five years ought to be required.

If the rights of naturalization may be communicated by parts, and it is not perceived why they may not, those peculiar to the conducting of business and the acquisition of property might with propriety be at once conferred upon receiving proof, by certain prescribed solemnities, of their intention to become citizens, postponing all political privileges to the ultimate term. To admit foreigners indiscriminately to the rights of citizens the moment they put foot in our country, as recommended in the Message, would be nothing less than to admit the Grecian Horse into the citadel of our liberty and sovereignty.

Lucius Crassus

The Examination Number IX, January 18, 1802

The leading points of the Message have been sufficiently canvassed, and it is believed to have been fully demonstrated that this communication is chargeable with all the faults which were imputed to it on the outset of the Examination. We have shown that it has made or attempted to make prodigal sacrifices of constitutional energy, of sound principle, and of public interest. In the doctrine respecting war there is a senseless abandonment of the just and necessary authority of the executive department in a point material to our national safety. In the proposals to relinquish the internal revenue there is an attempt to establish a precedent ruinous to our public credit; calculated to prolong the burden of the debt, and generally to enfeeble and sink the government by depriving it of resources of great importance to its respectability, to the accomplishment of its most salutary plans, to its power of being useful. In the attack upon the judiciary establishment there is a plain effort to impair that organ of the government, one on which its efficiency and success absolutely depend. In the recommendation to admit indiscriminately foreign emigrants of every description to the privileges of American citizens on their first entrance into our country there is an attempt to break down every pale which has been erected for the preservation of a national spirit and a national character, and to let in the most powerful means of perverting and corrupting both the one and the other.

This is more than the moderate opponents of Mr. Jefferson's elevation ever feared from his administration; much more than the most wrongheaded of his own sect dared to hope; it is infinitely more than any one who had read the fair professions in his Inaugural Speech could have suspected. Reflecting men must be dismayed at the prospect before us. If such rapid strides have been hazarded in the very gristle of his administration, what may be expected when it shall arrive to manhood? In vain was the collected wisdom of America convened at Philadelphia. In vain were the anxious labors of a Washington bestowed. Their works are regarded as nothing better than empty bubbles destined to be blown away by the mere breath of a disciple of Turgot, a pupil of *Condorcet*.

Though the most prominent features of the Message have been portrayed and their deformity exhibited in true colors, there remain many less important traits not yet touched, which, however, will materially assist us in determining its true character. To particularize them with minuteness would employ more time and labor than the object deserves, yet to pass them by wholly without remark would be to forego valuable materials for illustrating the true nature of the performance under examination.

There remains to be cursorily noticed a disposition in our chief magistrate far more partial to the state governments than to our national government, to pull down rather than to build up our federal edifice—to vilify the past administration of the latter—to court for himself popular favor by artifices not to be approved of, either for their dignity, their candor, or their patriotism.

Why are we emphatically and fastidiously told that "the states individually have the *principal* care of our *persons*, our *property*, and our *reputation, constituting the great field of human concerns*"? Was it to render the state governments more dear to us, more the objects of affectionate solicitude? Nothing surely was necessary on this head; they are already the favorites of the people, and if they do not forfeit the advantage by a most gross abuse of trust must, by the very nature of the objects confided to them, continue always to be so. Was it then to prevent too large a portion of affection from being bestowed on the general government? No pains on this head were requisite, not only for the reason just assigned, but for the further reason that the more peculiar objects of this government, though no less essential to our prosperity than those of the state governments, oblige it often to act upon the community in a manner more likely to produce aversion than fondness. Accordingly every day furnishes proof that it is not the *spoiled child of the many*. On this point the high example of the president himself is pregnant with instruction. Was it to indicate the supreme importance of the state governments over that of the United States? This was as little useful as it was correct. Considering the vast variety of humors, prepossessions, and localities, which in the much diversified composition of these states militate against the weight and authority of the general government, if union under that government is necessary it can answer no valuable purpose to depreciate its importance in the eyes of the people. It is not correct, because to the care of the federal government are confided directly those great general interests on which all particular interests materially depend: our safety in respect to foreign nations; our tranquility in respect to each other; the foreign and mutual commerce of the states; the establishment and regulation of the money of the country; the management of our national finances; indirectly, the security of liberty by the guarantee of a republican form of government to each state; the security of property by the interdiction of laws violating the obligation of contracts & issuing the emissions of paper money under state authority (from both of which causes the right of property had experienced serious injury); the prosperity of agriculture and manufactures as intimately connected with that of commerce, and as depending in a variety of ways upon the agency of the general government: In a word, it is the province of the general government to manage the greatest number of those concerns in which its provident *activity* and *exertion* are of most importance to the people; and we have only to compare the state of our country antecedent to its establishment with what it has been since to be convinced that the most operative causes of public prosperity depend upon that general government. It is not meant by what has been said to insinuate that the state governments are not extremely useful in their proper spheres; but the object is to guard against the mischiefs of exaggerating their importance in derogation from that of the general government. Every attempt to do this is, remotely, a stab at the Union of these states; a blow to our collective existence as one people—and to all the blessings which are interwoven with that sacred fraternity.

If it be true as insinuated that "our organization is too complicated—too expensive"—let it be simplified; let this, however, be done in such a manner as not to mutilate, weaken, and eventually destroy our present system, but in a manner to increase the energy and insure the duration of our national government, the rock of our political salvation.

In this insinuation, and in the suggestion that "offices and officers have been unnecessarily multiplied"; in the intimation that appropriations have not been sufficiently specific, and that the system of accountability to a single department has been disturbed; in this and in other things, too minute to be particularized, we discover new proofs of the disposition of the present executive unjustly and indecorously to arraign his predecessors.

As far as the Message undertakes to specify any instance of the improper complexity of our organization, namely, in the instance of the judiciary establishment, the late administration has been already vindicated.

As to the "*undue* multiplication of offices and officers," it is substantially a misrepresentation. It would be nothing less than a miracle if in a small number of instances it had not happened that particular offices and officers might have been dispensed with. For in the early essays of a new government, in making the various establishments relative to the affairs of a nation, some mistakes in this respect will arise, notwithstanding the greatest caution. It must happen to every government that in the hurry of a new plan, some agents will occasionally be employed who may not be absolutely necessary; and this where there is every inclination to economy. Similar things may have happened under our past administration. But any competent judge who will take the trouble to examine into it will be convinced that there is no just cause for blame in this particular.

The president has not pointed out the causes to which he applies the charge; but he has communicated information of some retrenchments which he has made, and probably intends that the truth shall be inferred from this.

Three instances are particularly presented; these shall be briefly examined; it will be seen that they do not justify the imputation. They respect certain ministers at foreign courts, some navy agents at particular ports, and some inspectors of the revenue in particular states.

As to the first, it is believed to be a pretty just idea that we ought not greatly to multiply diplomatic agencies. Three permanent ones may perhaps be found sufficient in the future progress of our affairs: for *France, Spain*, and *England*. The expediency of having these is recognized by the conduct of our present chief magistrate. But others must be employed, and during particular seasons it may be wise to do it for a considerable length of time. Indeed there is strong ground for an opinion entertained by very sensible men that there ought to be a permanent minister at every court with which we have extensive commercial relations.

Two other ministers were employed by both the former administrations, one with Portugal, the other with Holland; and it is asserted without fear of denial that this was done by the first president with the approbation of Mr. Jefferson. One other minister was employed by the late president at the Court of Berlin.

A commercial treaty with Portugal is admitted on all hands and for obvious reasons to be particularly desirable, as very interesting branches of our commerce are carried on in the Portuguese dominions. We are still without any such treaty. To send to that court a diplomatic agent to endeavor to effect one was a measure of evident propriety; to recall them before a treaty has been effected must be of questionable expediency. The views and circumstances of nations change; and an opportunity may occur, at some particular conjuncture, for effecting what was not before possible, which may be lost by the want of a fit agent on the spot to embrace it. But admitting that the experiment has now been sufficiently tried to justify its abandonment, still it does not follow that it was unwise to have continued it as long as was; and as this must at least rest in opinion, the continuance, if upon an erroneous calculation in this particular, is no proof of a "disposition to multiply offices" or officers. And those who consider the nature and extent of our commercial relations with Portugal will not cease to think it problematical whether the expense of a diplomatic agent, especially in a situation in which nothing has been defined by treaty, ought to stand in competition with the benefits which may result from the presence of a minister at the court of that kingdom. This consideration alone is sufficient to repel the charge.

Lucius Crassus

Draft of a Resolution for the Legislature of New York for the Amendment of the Constitution of the United States, January 29, 1802

Resolved, as the sense of the Legislature, that the following amendments ought to be incorporated into the Constitution of the United States as a necessary safeguard in the choice of a president and vice president against pernicious dissensions as the most eligible mode of obtaining a full and fair expression of the public will in such election.

1st. That Congress shall from time to time divide each state into districts equal to the whole number of senators and representatives from such state in the Congress of the United States, and shall direct the mode of choosing an elector of president and vice president in each of the said districts, who shall be chosen by citizens who have the qualifications requisite for electors of the most numerous branch of the state legislature, and that the districts shall be formed, as nearly as may be, with an equal proportion of population in each, and of counties and, if necessary, parts of counties contiguous to each other, except when there may be any detached portion of territory not sufficient of itself to form a district which then shall be annexed to some other part nearest thereto.

2nd. That in all future elections of president and vice president the persons voted for shall be particularly designated by declaring which is voted for as president and which as vice president.

Resolved, that the president of the Senate and Speaker of the Assembly transmit a copy of the preceding resolutions to the senators and representatives in Congress from this state with an earnest request that they would use their best exertions for obtaining the adoption of the above amendments or other amendments in substance equivalent so as that the president and vice president may be separately designated in voting for them and that the electors for both may be chosen in distinct districts.

Remarks on the Repeal of the Judiciary Act, February 11, 1802[5]

To these remarks General Hamilton rose again to reply—he remarked in substance that he had fostered the hope that on this occasion, by cautiously avoiding to say anything on the point of the constitutionality of the proposed repeal, and stating only the opinion of the New York bar on that of its *inexpediency*, there would have been but one sentiment—He regretted, deeply regretted, that on this point there was a diversity of sentiment; he foresaw the unhappy effects that would hence result; he deplored them, not from any private or contracted view, but turning his eye inward on his heart, and looking to heaven as the witness of his motives, he declared he knew of none that influenced him but the sincerest attachment to the public good. So far as respected the unconstitutionality of the proposed repeal, he had no hesitation in avowing his own opinion. He considered it a most direct and fatal violation of the most essential, the most *vital* principle of the Constitution. The independence of the judges once destroyed, the Constitution is gone, it is a dead letter; it is a vapor which the breath of faction in a moment may dissipate, and this boasted Union, the labor of true patriots, the hope of our country, which in the last 12 years has raised us to the most enviable height of prosperity, dissolves and dies.

He had cherished the idea, he said, that this part of the Constitution was the last that party violence would attack. That although certain extensions of executive authority, certain changes in the finances, or in diplomatic arrangements abroad might take place, yet that the essential rights of the judiciary in which foreigners and citizens, but more especially the mercantile interests of the U. States are so deeply concerned, would have been preserved inviolate. He had looked forward to many evils that he thought likely to flow from the known principles of the leading characters now in authority, but indeed he had not calculated on such a rapid progression of evil. He had little hope that anything that could now be *said* or done would assist in averting the impending blow. He knew full well that the plan now going into effect had long been meditated and resolved on, and hence his zeal was much abated, yet could anything he could do have any effect in saving the Constitution from the fatal blow that now menaced it, he would labor day and night; he would not give "sleep to his eyes, nor slumber to his eye-lids," while he had hope to support his exertions; nay, "I would give a drop of my heart's blood," said he, to save this *vital* principle of the Constitution. There is no motive which induced me to put my life at hazard through our revolutionary war that would not now as powerfully operate on me to put it again in jeopardy in defense of the independence of the judiciary; for remember what is said this night; if this fatal measure is not by *some means* arrested, if the *laws* are not suffered to control the passions of individuals, through the organs of an extended, firm, and independent judiciary, the bayonet must. There is no alternative; we must be ruled by municipal law or by—a military force: and I beg gentlemen to recollect what I now say, without aspiring to the character of a prophet, that if this rash, unadvised repeal takes place, mutual confidence will be destroyed—the union will gradually crumble to pieces and in a few, very few years, the present confederation will either be parceled out into separate territories with clashing interests, and you will see the hand of brother, raised to shed a brother's blood, or you will see this country become the prey of a usurper, and sink into the calm of a military despotism. On those gentlemen, then, who truly value our republican government, I call to banish for an instant the influence of party spirit and to lend their aid in extinguishing a rising conflagration, which threatens to involve this devoted country in miseries incalculable. On the point of *expediency*, he observed that he could, in no one point of view, consider the proposed repeal as defensible. Every gentleman present who had been concerned in business depending in the circuit court of the United States knew, without his going into details, the vices of the *old system*. Many of its defects were indeed removed by the present, which, however, was not to be considered as perfect. On this, certain improvements could be advantageously engrafted—which would render it a very eligible and convenient system. But he was surprised, greatly surprised indeed, to hear any gentleman who had any respect to his own character risk an opinion that the district courts, with the Supreme Court of the United States, were fully competent to all the business of the United States. The business of the former, he said, from revenue and admiralty causes, and from what arose under the late bankrupt law, furnished full employ for the most industrious judge. Besides, if all suits were originally to be commenced in the district courts, no suitor would rest satisfied with the decision of a single man, but would remove the cause for a final hearing to the Supreme Court of the United States, in which case parties would be constantly obliged to travel with papers and vouchers from the extremities of the Union to the seat of government, there to retain new counsel, be at heavy expenses, and far from their families, which would produce inconveniences that would not long be submitted to.

The Examination Number XII, February 23, 1802

From the manner in which the subject was treated in the fifth and sixth numbers of *The Examination*, it has been doubted whether the writer did or did not entertain a decided opinion as to the power of Congress to abolish the offices and compensations of judges, once instituted and appointed pursuant to a law of the United States. In a matter of such high constitutional moment it is a sacred duty to be explicit. The progress of a bill lately brought into the Senate for repealing the law of the last session, entitled "An act to provide for the more convenient organization of the courts of the U. States," with the avowed design of superseding the judges who were appointed under it, has rendered the question far more serious than it was while it rested merely on the obscure suggestion of the Presidential Message. 'Till the experiment had proved the fact, it was hardly to have been imagined that a majority of either house of Congress, whether from design or error, would have lent its sanction to a glaring violation of our national compact, in that article which of all others is the most essential to the efficiency and stability of the government; to the security of property; to the safety and liberty of person. This portentous and frightful phenomenon has nevertheless appeared. It frowns with malignant and deadly aspect upon our Constitution. Probably before these remarks shall be read that Constitution will be no more! It will be numbered among the numerous victims of democratic frenzy, and will have given another and an awful lesson to mankind—the prelude perhaps of calamities to this country, at the contemplation of which imagination shudders!

With such a prospect before us, nothing ought to be left unessayed, to open the eyes of thinking men to the destructive projects of those mountebank politicians who have been too successful in perverting public opinion and in cheating the people out of their confidence; who are advancing with rapid strides in the work of disorganization—the sure forerunner of tyranny; and who, if they are not arrested in their mad career, will, ere long, precipitate our nation into all the horrors of anarchy.

It would be vanity to expect to throw much additional light upon a subject which has already exhausted the logic and eloquence of some of the ablest men of our country; yet it often happens that the same arguments placed in a new attitude, and accompanied with illustrations which may have escaped the ardor of a first research, serve both to fortify and to extend conviction. In the hope that this may be the case, the discussion shall be pursued with as much perspicuity and brevity as can be attained.

The words of the Constitution are: "The Judges *both* of the Supreme and Inferior Courts *shall hold their offices during good behavior*, and shall at stated times receive for their services a compensation which *shall not be diminished during their continuance in office.*"

Taking the literal import of the terms as the criterion of their true meaning, it is clear that the *tenure* or *duration* of the office is limited by no other condition than the *good behavior* of the incumbent. The words are imperative, simple, and unqualified: "The Judges *shall hold their offices during good behavior.*" Independent therefore of any artificial reasoning to vary the nature and obvious sense of the words, the provision must be understood to vest in the judge a right to the office, indefeasible but by his own misconduct.

It is consequently the duty of those who deny this right to show either that there are certain presumptions of intention deducible from other parts of the constitutional instrument, or certain general principles of constitutional law or policy, which ought to control the literal and substitute a different meaning.

As to presumptions of intention different from the import of the terms, there is not a syllable in the instrument from which they can be inferred; on the contrary, the latter member of the clause cited affords very strong presumption the other way.

From the injunction that the compensation of the judges shall not be diminished, it is manifest that the Constitution intends to guard the independence of those officers against the legislative department: because, to this department *alone* would have belonged the power of diminishing their compensations.

When the Constitution is thus careful to tie up the legislature from taking away part of the compensation, is it possible to suppose that it can mean to leave that body at full liberty to take away the whole? The affirmative imputes to the Constitution the manifest absurdity of holding to the Legislature this language: "You shall not *weaken* the independence of the judicial character by exercising the power of *lessening* his emolument, but you may *destroy* it altogether by exercising the greater power of *annihilating* the recompense with the office." No mortal can be so blind as not to see that by such a construction the restraint intended to be laid upon the legislature by the injunction not to lessen the compensations becomes absolutely nugatory.

In vain is a justification of it sought in that part of the same article which provides that "The Judicial power of the United States shall be vested in one Supreme Court and in such Inferior Courts as the Congress *may* from time to time ordain and establish." The position that a discretionary power to institute inferior courts includes virtually a power to abolish them, if true, is nothing to the purpose. The abolition of a court does not necessarily imply that of its judges. In contemplation of law, the court and the judge are distinct things. The court may have a legal existence, though there may be no judge to exercise its powers. This may be the case either at the original creation of a court, previous to the appointment of a judge, or subsequently by his death, resignation, or removal: In the last case, it could not be pretended that the court had become extinct by the event. In like manner, the office of the judge may subsist, though the court in which he is to officiate may be suspended or destroyed. The duties of a judge, as the office is defined in our jurisprudence, are two fold—judicial and ministerial. The latter may be performed out of court, and often without reference to it. As conservator of the peace, which every judge is *ex officio*, many things are done not connected with a judicial controversy, or to speak technically, with a *lis pendens*. This serves to illustrate the idea that the office is something different from the court, which is the place or situation for its principal action, yet not altogether essential to its activity. Besides, a judge is not the less a judge when out of court than when in court. The law does not suppose him to be always in court, yet it does suppose him to be always in office, in vacation as well as in term. He has also a property or interest in his office which entitles him to civil actions and to recompense in damages for injuries that affect him in relation to his office; but he cannot be said to have a property or interest in the court of which he is a member. All these considerations confirm the hypothesis that the court and the judge are distinct legal entities, and therefore may exist the one independently of the other.

If it be replied, that the office is an incident to the court, and that the abolition of the principal includes that of the incidents—the answer to this is that the argument may be well founded as to all subsequent appointments, but not as to those previously made. Though there be no office to be filled in future, it will not follow that one already vested in an individual by a regular appointment and commission is thereby vacated and divested. Whether this shall or shall not happen must depend on what the Constitution or the law has declared with regard to the *tenure* of the office. Having pronounced that this shall be during good behavior, it will preserve the office, to give effect to that tenure for the benefit of the possessor. To be consistent with itself, it will require and prescribe such a modification and construction of its own acts as will reconcile its power over the future with the rights which have been conferred as to the past.

Let it not be said that an office is a mere trust for public benefit and excludes the idea of a property or a vested interest in the individual. The first part of the proposition is true—the last false. Every office combines the two ingredients of an interest in the possessor and a trust for the public. Hence it is that the law allows the officer redress by a civil action for an injury in relation to his office, which presupposes property or interest. This interest may be defeasible at the pleasure of the government, or it may have a fixed duration, according to the constitution of the office. The idea of a vested interest holden even by a permanent tenure, so far from being incompatible with the principle that the primary and essential end of every office is the public good, may be conducive to that very end by promoting a diligent, faithful, energetic, and independent execution of the office.

But admitting, as seems to have been admitted by the speakers on both sides the question, that the judge must fall with the court, then the only consequence will be that Congress cannot abolish a court once established. There is no rule of interpretation better settled than that different provisions in the same instrument, on the same subject, ought to be so construed, as, if possible, to comport with each other, and give a reasonable effect to all.

The provision that "The Judiciary Power shall be vested in one Superior Court and in such inferior courts as the Congress *may* from time to time ordain and establish" is immediately followed by this other provision: "The judges *both* of the Supreme and Inferior Courts shall hold their offices during good behavior."

The proposition that a power to do includes virtually a power to undo, as applied to a legislative body, is generally but not universally true. All *vested rights* form an exception to the rule. In strict theory, there is no lawful or moral power to divest by a subsequent statute a right vested in an individual by a prior: And accordingly it is familiar to persons conversant with legal studies that the repeal of a law does not always work the revocation or divestiture of such rights.

If it be replied that though a legislature might act immorally and wickedly in abrogating a vested right, yet the legal *validity* of its act for such a purpose could not be disputed; it may be answered that this odious position, in any application of it, is liable to question in every limited constitution (that is, in every constitution which, in its theory, does not suppose the whole power of the nation to be lodged in the legislative body*)—and that it is certainly false in its application to a legislature the authorities of which are defined by a positive written constitution, as to everything which is contrary to the actual provisions of that constitution. To deny this is to affirm that the *delegated* is paramount to the *constituent* power. It is in fact to affirm there are *no constitutional limits to the legislative authority*.

The enquiry then must be whether the power to abolish inferior courts, if implied in that of creating them, is not abridged by the clause which regulates the tenure of judicial office.

The first thing which occurs in this investigation is that the power to abolish is at most an implied or incidental power, and as such will the more readily yield to any express provision with which it may be inconsistent.

The circumstance of giving to Congress a discretionary power to establish inferior courts instead of establishing them specifically in the Constitution has, with great reason, been ascribed to the impracticability of ascertaining beforehand the number and variety of courts which the development of our national affairs might indicate to be proper, especially in relation to the progress of new settlements and the creation of new states. This rendered a discretionary power to *institute* courts indispensable, but it did not alike render indispensable a power to abolish those which were once instituted. It was conceived that with intelligence, caution, and care, a plan might be pursued in the institution of courts which would render abolitions unnecessary. Indeed it is not presumable with regard to establishments of such solemnity and importance, making part of the *organization* of a principal department of the government, that a

* As in the Parliament of Great Britain.

fluctuation of plans was anticipated. It is therefore not essential to suppose that the power to destroy was intended to be included in the power to create: Thus the words "to ordain and establish" may be satisfied by attributing to them only the latter effect.

Consequently, when the grant of the power to institute courts is immediately succeeded by the declaration that the judges of those courts shall *hold* their offices during good behavior; if the exercise of the power to abolish the courts cannot be reconciled with the actual holding or enjoyment of the office, according to the prescribed tenure, it will follow that the power to abolish is interdicted. The implied or hypothetical power to destroy the office must give way to the express and positive right of holding it during good behavior. This is agreeable to the soundest rules of construction; the contrary is in subversion of them.

Equally in vain is a justification of the construction adopted by the advocates of the repeal attempted to be derived from a distinction between the supreme and inferior courts. The argument that as the former is established by the Constitution it cannot be annulled by a legislative act, though the latter which must owe their existence to such an act may by the same authority be extinguished, can afford no greater stability to the office of a judge of the Supreme Court than to that of a judge of an inferior court. The Constitution does indeed establish the Supreme Court, but it is altogether silent as to the number of the judges. This is as fully left to legislative discretion as the institution of inferior courts, and the rule that a power to undo is implied in the power to do is therefore no less applicable to the reduction of the number of the judges of the Supreme Court than to the abolition of the inferior courts. If the former are not protected by the clause which fixes the tenure of office, they are no less at the mercy of the legislature than the latter: And if that clause does protect them, its protection must be equally effectual for the judges of the inferior courts. Its efficacy in either case must be founded on the principle that it operates as a restraint upon the legislative discretion; and if so, there is the like restraint in both cases, because the very same words in the very same sentence define conjunctly the tenure of the offices of the two classes of judges. No sophistry can elude this conclusion.

It is therefore plain to a demonstration that the doctrine which affirms the right of Congress to abolish the judges of the inferior courts is absolutely fatal to the independence of the judiciary department. The observation that so gross an abuse of power as would be implied in the abolition of the judges of the Supreme Court ought not to be supposed can afford no consolation against the extreme danger of the doctrine. The terrible examples before us forbid our placing the least confidence in that delusive observation. Experience, sad experience warns us to dread every extremity—to be prepared for the worst catastrophe that can happen.

Lucius Crassus

To the New York Evening Post, February 24, 1802

We might well be excused from taking any notice of such a writer as the author of the leading article in the *Citizen* of this morning; but as in one instance he has pretended to state facts in reply to what was said in the *Evening Post* respecting the opinions held in the Convention by Mr. Hamilton and by Mr. Madison, some answer may be expected. Mr. Hamilton had been charged with holding an opinion in favor of monarchy, and it had been said he proposed a monarchy to the Convention. This was denied. It is now replied that he proposed a "system composed of three branches, an Assembly, a Senate, and a Governor; that the Assembly should be *elected by the people* for three years, and that the Senate and Governor should likewise be *elected by the people* during good behavior." Thus the charge is at length reduced to specific terms. Before it can be decided, however, whether this would be a *monarchy* or a *republic*, it seems necessary to settle the meaning of those terms.

No exact definitions have settled what is or is not a *republican government* as contradistinguished from a *monarchical*. Every man who speaks or writes on the subject has an arbitrary standard in his own mind. The mad democrat will have nothing republican which does not accord with his own mad theory—He rejects even representation. Such is the opinion held by a man now one of Mr. Jefferson's ministers. Some authors denominate every government a monarchy in which the executive authority is placed in a single hand, whether for life or for years, and whether conferred by election or by descent. According to this definition the actual government of the United States, and of most states, is a *monarchy*.

In practice, the terms republic and republican have been applied with as little precision. Even the government of England, with a powerful hereditary king, has been repeatedly spoken of by authors as a commonwealth or republic. The late government of Holland, with a hereditary Stadtholder, was constantly so denominated. That of Poland, previous to the dissolution of the state, with an executive for life, was never called by any other name.

The truth seems to be that all governments have been deemed republics in which a large portion of the sovereignty has been vested in the whole or in a considerable body of the people, and that none have been deemed monarchies, as contrasted with the republican standard, in which there has not been an *hereditary* chief magistrate.

Were we to attempt a correct definition of a republican government, we should say, "That is a republican government in which both the executive and legislative organs are appointed by a popular election and hold their offices upon a responsible and defeasible tenure." If this be not so, then the tenure of good behavior for the judicial department is antirepublican, and the government of this state is not a republic: If the contrary, then a government would not cease to be republican because a branch of the legislature, or even the executive, held their offices during good behavior. In this case the two essential criteria would still concur—The creation of the officer by a popular election, and the possibility of his removal in the course of law by accusation before and conviction by a competent tribunal.

How far it may be expedient to go, even within the bounds of the theory, in framing a Constitution, is a different question, upon which we pretend not to give our opinion. It is enough for the purpose of our assertion if it be *in principle* correct. For even then, upon the statement of the *Citizen* himself, General Hamilton did never propose *a monarchy*.

Thus much too we will add, that whether General Hamilton at any stage of the deliberations of the Convention did or did not make the proposition ascribed to him, it is certain that his more deliberate and final opinion, adopted a moderate term of years for the duration of the office of president, as also appears by a plan of a constitution *in writing now in this city*, drawn up by that gentleman in detail.

Whether the first system presented by Mr. Hamilton was the one to which he gave a decided preference it would be difficult to say, since we find him adopting and proposing a different one in the course of the sitting of the convention. It may have been his opinion was nearly balanced between the two; nay it is possible he may have really preferred the one last proposed and that the former, like many others, was brought forward to make it the subject of discussion and see what would be the opinions of different gentlemen on so momentous a subject. And it is now repeated with confidence that the *Virginia* delegation did vote for the most energetic form of government and that Mr. Madison was of the number. But we desire to be distinctly understood that it was never intended by mentioning this circumstance to impeach the purity of Mr. Madison's motives. To arraign the morals of any man because he entertains a speculative opinion on government different from ourselves is worse than arrogance. He who does so must entertain notions in ethics extremely crude, and certainly unfavorable to virtue.

The Examination Number XIII, February 27, 1802

The advocates of the power of Congress to abolish the judges endeavor to deduce a presumption of intention favorable to their doctrine from this argument—The provision concerning the tenure of office (say they) ought to be viewed as a restraint upon the executive department, *because* to this department belongs the power of removal; in like manner as the provision concerning the diminution of compensations ought to be regarded as a restraint upon the legislative department, *because* to this department belongs the power of regulating compensations: The different members of the clause ought to be taken distributively in conformity with the distribution of power to the respective departments.

This is certainly the most specious of the arguments which have been used on that side. It has received several pertinent and forcible answers. But it is believed to be susceptible of one still more direct and satisfactory, which is not recollected to have been yet given.

If, in the theory of the Constitution, there was but one way of *defeating the tenure* of office, and that exclusively appertaining to the executive authority, it would be a natural and correct inference that this authority was solely contemplated in a constitutional provision upon the subject. But the fact is clearly otherwise. There are two modes known to the Constitution in which the tenure of office may be affected—one the abolition of the office, the other the removal of the officer. The first is a legislative act and operates by removing the office from the person—the last is an executive act and operates by removing the person from the office. Both equally cause the tenure, enjoyment, or *holding* of the office to cease.

This being the case, the inference which has been drawn fails. There is no ground for the presumption that the Constitution, in establishing the tenure of an office, had an exclusive eye to one only of the two modes in which it might be affected. The more rational supposition is that it intended to reach and exclude both, because this alone can fulfill the purpose which it appears to have in view: And it ought neither to be understood to aim at less than its language imports, nor to employ inadequate means for accomplishing the end which it professes. Or, the better to elucidate the idea by placing it in another form, it may be said that since in the nature of things the legislative, equally with the executive organ, may by different modes of action affect the tenure of office, when the Constitution undertakes to prescribe what that tenure shall be, it ought to be presumed to intend to guard that which shall have been prescribed against the interference of either department.

In an instrument abounding with examples of restrictions on the legislative discretion, there is no difficulty in supposing that one was intended in every case in which it may be fairly inferred, either from the words used or from the object to be effected.

While the reason which has been stated refers the provision respecting the tenure of judicial office as well to the executive as to the legislative department, were it necessary to examine to which, if to either of them, it ought to be deemed most appropriate, there could be no difficulty in selecting the latter rather than the former. The *tenure* of an office is one of its essential *qualities*. A provision, therefore, which is destined to prescribe or define this quality may be supposed to have a more peculiar reference to that department which is empowered to constitute the office, either as directory to it in the exercise of its power or as fixing what otherwise would be left to its discretion.

It is constantly to be recollected that the terms of the provision do not look particularly to either department. They are general: "The Judges shall hold their offices during good behavior." 'Tis not from the terms, therefore, that an exclusive applicability to the executive organ can be inferred. On the contrary, they must be narrowed to give them only this effect.

It is different as to the provision concerning compensations. Though equally general in the terms, this can have no relation but to the legislative department, *because*, as before observed, that department alone would have had power to diminish the compensations. But this reason for confining that provision to one department, namely, the power of affecting the compensations, so far from dictating a similar appropriation of the other provision, looks a different way and requires by analogy that the latter should be applied to both the departments, each having a power of affecting the tenure of office in a way peculiar to itself. Nor can it be too often repeated, because it is a consideration of great force, that the design so conspicuous in the former of those two provisions, to secure the independence of the judges against legislative influence, is a powerful reason for understanding the latter in a sense calculated to advance the same important end rather than in one which must entirely frustrate it.

A rule of constitutional law opposed to our construction is attempted to be derived from the maxim that the power of legislation is always equal and that a preceding can never bind or control a succeeding legislature by its acts, which therefore must always be liable to repeal at the discretion of the successor.

The misapplication or too extensive application of general maxims or propositions, true in their genuine sense, is one of the most common and fruitful sources of false reasoning. This is strongly exemplified in the present instance. The maxim relied upon can mean nothing more than that as to all those matters which a preceding legislature was free to establish and revoke, a succeeding legislature will be equally free. The latter may do what the former could have done, or it may undo what the former could have undone. But unless it can be maintained that the power of ordinary legislation is in itself illimitable, incontrollable, incapable of being bound either by its own acts or by the injunctions or prohibitions of a constitution, it will follow that the body invested with that power may bind itself and may bind its successor, so that neither itself nor its successor can of right revoke acts which may have been once done. To say that a legislature may bind itself but not its successor is to affirm that the latter has not merely an equal but a greater power than the former, else it could not do what the former was unable to do. Equality of power only will not suffice for the argument. On the other hand, to affirm that a legislature cannot bind itself is to assert that there can be no valid pledge of the public faith, that no right can be vested in an individual or collection of individuals, whether of property or of any other description, which may not be resumed at pleasure.

Without doubt a legislature binds itself by all those acts which engage the public faith; which confer on individuals permanent rights, either gratuitously or for valuable consideration; and in all these instances, a succeeding one is not less bound. As to a right which may have been conferred by an express provision of the Constitution defining the condition of the enjoyment; or as to an institution or matter in its nature permanent, which the Constitution may have confided to an act of the legislature; its authority terminates with the act that vests the right or makes the establishment. A case of the first sort is exemplified in the office of a judge; of the last, in the creation of a new state, which has been very pertinently mentioned as a decisive instance of power in a legislature to do a thing which being done is irrevocable.

But whatever may be the latitude we assign to the power of a legislature over the acts of a predecessor, it is nothing to the purpose so long as it shall be admitted that the Constitution may bind and control the legislature. With this admission, the simple inquiry must always be—has or has not the Constitution in the particular instance bound the legislature? And the solution must be sought in the language, nature, and end of the provision. If these warrant the conclusion that the legislature was intended to be bound, it is perfect nonsense to reply that this cannot be so because a legislature cannot bind itself by its own acts, or because the power of one legislature is equal to that of another. What signifies this proposition, if the Constitution has power to bind the legislature and has in fact bound it in a given case? Can a general rule disprove the fact of an exception which it is admitted may exist? If so, the argument is always ready and equally valid to disprove any limitation of the legislative discretion.

Compelled, as they must be, to desist from the use of the argument in the extensive sense in which it has been employed, if its inventors should content themselves with saying that at least the principle adduced by them ought to have so much of force as to make the exception to it depend on an express provision—it may be answered that in the case under consideration there is an express provision. No language can be more precise or peremptory than this: "The Judges, *both* of the Supreme and Inferior Courts, shall hold their offices during good behavior." If this be not an express provision, it is impossible to devise one. But the position that an express provision is necessary to form an exception is itself unfounded. Wherever it is clear, whether by a circumstance expressed or by one so implied as to leave no reasonable doubt, that a limitation of the authority of the legislature was designed by the Constitution, the intention ought to prevail.

A very strong confirmation of the true intent of the provision respecting the tenure of judicial office results from an argument by analogy. In each of the articles which establishes any branch of the government, the duration of office is a prominent feature. Two years for the House of Representatives, six for the Senate, four for the president and vice president, are the respective terms of duration; and for the judges the term of good behavior is allotted. It is presumable that each was established in the same spirit, as a point material in the organization of the government and of a nature to be properly fundamental. It will not be pretended that the duration of office prescribed as to any other department is within the reach of legislative discretion. And why shall that of judicial officers form an exception? Why shall the Constitution be supposed less tenacious of securing to this organ of the sovereign power a fixed duration than to any other? If there be anything which ought to be supposed to be peculiarly excepted out of the power of the ordinary legislature, it is emphatically the organization of the several constituent departments of the government, which in our system are the *legislative*, *executive*, and *judiciary*. Reasons of the most cogent nature recommend that the stability and independence of the last of these three branches should be guarded with particular circumspection and care.

Lucius Crassus

Letter to Gouverneur Morris, February 29, 1802

My Dr. Sir,

Your letter of the 22nd is the third favor for which I am indebted to you since you left N. York.

Your frankness in giving me your opinion as to the expediency of an application of our bar to Congress obliges me. But you know we are not readily persuaded to think we have been wrong. Were the matter to be done over I should pursue the same course. I did not believe the measure would be useful as a preventative, and for the people an expression of an opinion by letter would be as good as in a memorial. It appeared to me best because it saved our delicacy and because in the abstract I am not over fond of the precedent of the bar addressing Congress. But I did what I thought likely to do more good—*I induced* the Chamber of Commerce to send a memorial.

As to the rest, I should be a very unhappy man if I left my tranquility at the mercy of the misinterpretations which friends as well as foes are fond of giving to my conduct.

Mine is an odd destiny. Perhaps no man in the U. States has sacrificed or done more for the present Constitution than myself—and contrary to all my anticipations of its fate, as you know from the very beginning I am still laboring to prop the frail and worthless fabric. Yet I have the murmurs of its friends no less than the curses of its foes for my rewards. What can I do better than withdraw from the scene? Every day proves to me more and more that this American world was not made for me.

The suggestions with which you close your letter suppose a much sounder state of the public mind than at present exists. Attempts to make a show of a general *popular* dislike of the pending measures of the government would only serve to manifest the direct reverse. Impressions are indeed making but as yet within a very narrow sphere. The time may ere long arrive when the minds of men will be prepared to make an offer to *recover* the Constitution, but the many cannot now be brought to make a stand for its preservation. We must wait awhile.

I have read your speeches with great pleasure. They are truly worthy of you. Your real friends had many sources of satisfaction on account of them. The conspiracy of Dulness was at work. It chose to misinterpret your moderation in certain transactions of a personal reference. A public energetic display of your talents and principles was requisite to silence the cavillers. It is now done. You, friend Morris, are by *birth* a native of this country but by *genius* an exotic. You mistake if you fancy that you are more a favorite than myself or that you are in any sort upon a theater suited to you.

Adieu   Yrs. ever
A.H.

The Examination Number XIV, March 2, 1802

In the course of the debate in the Senate, much verbal criticism has been indulged; many important inferences have been attempted to be drawn from distinctions between the words *shall* and *may*. This species of discussion will not be imitated, because it is seldom very instructive or satisfactory. These terms, in particular cases, are frequently synonymous, and are imperative or permissive, directing or enabling, according to the relations in which they stand to other words. It is, however, certain that the arguments even from this source greatly preponderate against the right of Congress to abolish the judges.

But there has been one argument, rather of a verbal nature, upon which some stress has been laid which shall be analyzed, principally to furnish a specimen of the wretched expedients to which the supporters of the repeal are driven. It is this: "The tenure of an office is not synonymous with its existence. Though Congress may not annul the tenure of a judicial office while the office itself continues, yet it does not follow that they may not destroy its existence."

The constituent parts of an office are its authorities, duties, and duration. These may be denominated the elements of which it is composed. Together they form its *essence* or *existence*.* It is impossible to separate even in idea the duration from the existence: The office must cease to exist when it ceases to have duration. Let it be observed that the word *tenure* is not used in the Constitution, and that in the debate it has been the substitute for duration. The words "The Judges shall hold their offices during good behavior" are equivalent to these other words, The offices of the judges shall endure or last so long as they behave well.

The conclusions from these principles are that existence is a *whole* which includes tenure or duration as a part, that it is impossible to annul the existence of an office without destroying its tenure, and consequently that a prohibition to destroy the tenure is virtually and substantially a prohibition to abolish the office. How contemptible then the sophism that Congress may not destroy the tenure but may annihilate the office!

It has now been seen that this power of annihilation is not reconcilable with the language of the constitutional instrument, and that no rule of constitutional law which has been relied upon will afford it support. Can it be better defended by any principle of constitutional policy?

* The remuneration or recompense is not added, because it is most properly an accessory.

To establish the affirmative of this question, it has been argued that if the judges hold their offices by a title absolutely independent of the legislative will, the judicial department becomes a colossal and overbearing power, capable of degenerating into a permanent tyranny, at liberty, if audacious and corrupt enough, to render the authority of the legislature nugatory by expounding away the laws, and to assume a despotic control over the rights of person and property.

To this argument (which supposes the case of a palpable abuse of power) a plain and conclusive answer is that the Constitution has provided a complete safeguard in the authority of the *House of Representatives* to impeach, of the *Senate* to condemn. The judges are in this way amenable to the public justice for misconduct, and, upon conviction, removable from office. In the hands of the legislature itself is placed the weapon by which they may be put down and the other branches of the government protected. The pretended danger, therefore, is evidently imaginary—the security perfect!

Reverse the medal. Concede to the legislature a legal discretion to abolish the judges; where is the defense? where the security for the judicial department? There is absolutely none. This most valuable member of the government, when rightly constituted the surest guardian of person and property, of which stability is a prime characteristic; losing at once its most essential attributes, and doomed to fluctuate with the variable tide of faction, degenerates into a disgusting mirror of all the various, malignant, and turbulent humors of party spirit.

Let us not be deceived. The real danger is on the side of that foul and fatal doctrine, which emboldens its votaries with daring front and unhallowed step, to enter the holy temple of justice and pluck from their seats the venerable personages who, under the solemn sanction of the Constitution, are commissioned to officiate there; to guard that sacred compact with jealous vigilance; to dispense the laws with a steady and impartial hand; unmoved by the storms of faction, unawed by its powers, unseduced by its favors; shielding right and innocence from every attack; resisting and repressing violence from every quarter. 'Tis from the triumph of that execrable doctrine that we may have to date the downfall of our government and with it, of the whole fabric of republican liberty. Who will have the folly to deny that the definition of despotism is the concentration of all the powers of government in one person or in one body? Who is so blind as not to see that the right of the legislature to abolish the judges at pleasure destroys the independence of the judicial department and swallows it up in the impetuous vortex of legislative influence? Who is so weak as to hope that the executive, deprived of so powerful an auxiliary, will long survive? What dispassionate man can withstand the conviction that the boundaries between the departments will be thenceforth nominal, and that there will be no longer more than one active and efficient department?

It is a fundamental maxim of free government that the three great departments of power, *legislative*, *executive*, and *judiciary*, shall be essentially distinct and independent the one of the other. This principle, very influential in most of our state constitutions, has been particularly attended to in the Constitution of the United States, which, in order to give effect to it, has adopted a precaution peculiar to itself in the provisions that forbid the legislature to vary in any way the compensation of the *president*, to diminish that of a *judge*.

It is a principle equally sound that though in a government like that of Great Britain, having an hereditary chief with vast prerogatives, the danger to liberty by the predominance of one department over the other is on the side of the executive, yet in popular forms of government this danger is chiefly to be apprehended from the legislative branch.

The power of legislation is in its own nature the most comprehensive and potent of the three great subdivisions of sovereignty. It is the will of the government; it prescribes universally the rule of action, and the sanctions which are to enforce it. It creates and regulates the public force, and it commands the public purse. If deposited in an elective representative of the people, it has, in most cases, the body of the nation for its auxiliary, and generally acts with all the momentum of popular favor. In every such government it is consequently an organ of immense strength. But when there is an hereditary chief magistrate, clothed with dazzling prerogatives and a great patronage, there is a powerful counterpoise which, in most cases, is sufficient to preserve the equilibrium of the government; in some cases to incline the scale too much to its own side.

In governments wholly popular or representative there is no adequate counterpoise. Confidence in the most numerous, or legislative department, and jealousy of the executive chief, form the genius of every such government. That jealousy, operating in the constitution of the executive, causes this organ to be intrinsically feeble; and withholding in the course of administration accessory means of force and influence, is for the most part vigilant to continue it in a state of impotence. The result is that the legislative body in this species of government possesses additional resources of power and weight, while the executive is rendered much too weak for competition, almost too weak for self-defense.

A third principle, not less well founded than the other two, is that the judiciary department is naturally the weakest of the three. The sources of strength to the legislative branches have been briefly delineated. The executive by means of its several active powers, of the dispensations of honors and emoluments and of the direction of the public force, is evidently the second in strength. The judiciary, on the other hand, can ordain nothing. It commands neither the purse[6] nor the sword. It has scarcely any patronage. Its functions are not active but deliberative. Its main province is to declare the meaning of the laws, and in extraordinary cases it must even look up to the executive aid for the execution of its decisions. Its chief strength is in the veneration which it is able to inspire by the wisdom and rectitude of its judgments.

This character of the judiciary clearly indicates that it is not only the weakest of the three departments of power but, also as it regards the security and preservation of civil liberty, by far the safest. In a conflict with the other departments it will be happy if it can defend itself—to annoy them is beyond its power. In vain would it singly attempt enterprises against the rights of the citizen. The other departments could quickly arrest its arm and punish its temerity. It can only then become an effectual instrument of oppression when it is combined with one of the more active and powerful organs, and against a combination of this sort the true and best guard is a complete independence on each and both of them. Its dependence on either will imply and involve a subserviency to the views of the department on which it shall depend. Its independence of both will render it a powerful check upon the others and a precious shield to the rights of persons and property. Safety, liberty, are therefore inseparably connected with the real and substantial independence of the courts and judges.

It is plainly to be inferred from the instrument itself that these were governing principles in the formation of our Constitution: that they were in fact so will hereafter be proved by the contemporary exposition of persons who must be supposed to have understood the views with which it was framed, having been themselves members of the body that framed it. Those principles suggest the highest motives of constitutional policy against that construction which places the existence of the judges at the mercy of the legislature. They instruct us that to prevent a concentration of powers, the *essence of despotism*, it is essential that the departments among which they shall be distributed should be effectually independent of each other; and that it being impossible to reconcile this independence with a right in any one or two of them to annihilate at discretion the organs of the other, it is contrary to all just reasoning to imply or infer such a right. So far from its being correct that an express interdiction is requisite to deprive the legislature of the power to abolish the judges that the very reverse is the true position. It would require a most express provision, susceptible of no other interpretation, to confer on that branch of the government an authority so dangerous to the others, in opposition to the strong presumptions which, in conformity with the fundamental maxims of free government, arise from the care taken in the Constitution to establish and preserve the reciprocal and complete independence of the respective branches, first by a separate organization of the departments, next by a precise definition of the powers of each, lastly by precautions to secure to each a permanent support.

Lucius Crassus

The Examination Number XV, March 3, 1802

It is generally understood that the essays under the title of the *Federalist*, which were published at New York while the plan of our present federal Constitution was under the consideration of the people, were principally written by two persons* who had been members of the Convention which devised that plan and whose names are subscribed to the instrument containing it. In these essays† the principles advanced in the last number of this Examination are particularly stated and strongly relied upon in defense of the proposed Constitution, from which it is a natural inference that they had influenced the views with which the plan was digested. The full force of this observation will be best perceived by a recurrence to the work itself, but it will appear clearly enough from the following detached passages.

"One of the principal objections inculcated by the more respectable *adversaries* to the Constitution is its supposed violation of the political maxim that the *legislative, executive* and *judiciary* departments ought to be *separate* and *distinct.*" "No *political truth* is certainly of *greater intrinsic value*, or is stamped with the authority of more enlightened patrons of liberty, than that on which the objection is founded. The *accumulation* of all power, legislative, executive, and judiciary, in the same hands, whether of one, a few, or many; whether hereditary, self-appointed or elective, may justly be pronounced the *very definition* of tyranny."‡ "Neither of the three departments ought to possess *directly* or *indirectly* an *overruling influence* over the others in the administration of their respective powers." "But the most difficult task is to provide some *practical security* for each *against the invasion* of the others."

"Experience assures us that the efficacy of *parchment barriers* has been greatly overrated, and that some *more adequate defense is indispensably necessary* for the more feeble against the more powerful members of the government. The legislative department is everywhere extending the sphere of its activity and drawing all power into its impetuous vortex." "In a representative republic, where the executive magistracy is carefully limited both in the extent and the duration of its power; and where the legislative power is exercised by an assembly, which is inspired by a supposed influence over the people with an intrepid confidence in its own strength; which is sufficiently numerous to feel all the passions

---

* James Madison, now Secretary of State, Alexander Hamilton, formerly Secretary of the Treasury.
† Particularly Nos. XLVII to LI inclusive, and Nos. LXXVIII to LXXXII inclusive.
‡ No. XLVII.

which actuate a multitude; yet not so numerous as to be incapable of pursuing the objects of its passions, by means which reason prescribes; *it is against the enterprising ambition of this department, that the people ought to indulge all their jealousy and exhaust all their precautions.*" Again, "The *tendency* of republican governments is to an *aggrandizement of the legislature at the expense of the other departments.*"

These passages recognize as a fundamental maxim of free government that the three departments of power ought to be separate and distinct, consequently that neither of them ought to be able to exercise, either directly or indirectly, an *overruling influence* over any other. They also recognize as a truth, indicated by the nature of the system and verified by experience, that in a representative republic, the legislative department is the "Aaron's Rod" most likely to swallow up the rest, and therefore to be guarded against with particular care and caution: And they inculcate that parchment barriers (or the formal provisions of a constitution designating the respective boundaries of authority), having been found ineffectual for protecting the more feeble against the most powerful members of the government, some more adequate defense, some practical security is necessary. What this was intended to be will appear from subsequent passages.

"To what expedient shall we finally resort for maintaining in practice the necessary partition of power among the several departments as laid down in the Constitution?" "As all exterior provisions are found to be inadequate, the defect must be supplied by so contriving the interior structure of the government as that its several constituent departments may, by their mutual relations, be the means of keeping each other in their proper places."*

These passages intimate the "*practical security*" which ought to be adopted for the preservation of the weaker against the stronger members of the government. It is so to contrive its interior structure that the constituent organs may be able to *keep each other* in their *proper places*, an idea essentially incompatible with that of making the *existence* of one dependent on the *will* of another. It will be seen afterwards how this structure is to be so contrived.

"In order to lay a *foundation* for that separate and distinct exercise of the different powers of government, which to a certain extent is admitted on all hands to be essential to the preservation of liberty, it is evident that each department should have a will of its own, and consequently should be so constituted that the members of each should have *as little agency* as possible in the appointment of the members of the others. This principle rigorously adhered to would require that all the appointments for the several departments should be drawn from the same fountain of authority, the people." But "In the constitution of the judiciary department it might be inexpedient to insist rigorously on the principle; first, because peculiar qualifications being essential in the members, the primary consideration ought to be to select that mode of choice which best secures these qualifications; secondly, because *the permanent tenure* by which

* No. LI.

the appointments are held in that department must soon destroy all sense of dependence on the authority conferring them."

"It is equally evident that the members of each department should be as little dependent as possible on those of the others for the emoluments annexed to their offices. Were the executive magistrate or the *judges* not independent of the legislature in this particular, *their independence in every other* would be merely nominal." "The great security against a concentration of the several powers in the same department consists in giving to those who administer each department the *necessary constitutional means and personal motives* to resist encroachments of the others." "But it is not possible to give to each department an equal power of self-defense. In republican governments the legislative authority necessarily predominates."

The means held out as proper to be employed, for enabling the several departments to keep each other in their proper places, are:

1. To give to each such an *organization* as will render them essentially independent of one another. 2. To secure to each a *support* which shall not be at the discretionary disposal of any other. 3. To establish between them such *mutual relations of authority* as will make one a check upon another and enable them reciprocally to resist encroachments and confine one another within their proper spheres.

To accomplish the first end, it is deemed material that they should have as little agency as possible in the appointment of one another and should all emanate directly from the same fountain of authority—the people: And that it being expedient to relax the principle in respect to the judiciary department, with a view to a more select choice of its organs, this defect in the creation ought to be remedied by a *permanent tenure* of office, which certainly becomes nominal and nugatory if the existence of the office rests on the pleasure of the legislature. The principle that the several organs should have as little agency as possible in the appointment of each other is directly opposed to the claim in favor of one of a discretionary agency to destroy another. The second of the proposed ends is designed to be effected by the provisions for fixing the compensations of the executive and judicial departments—The third by the qualified negative of the executive, or the acts of the two houses of Congress; by the right of one of these houses to accuse; of the other to try and punish the executive and judicial officers; and lastly, by the right of the judges, as interpreters of the laws, to pronounce unconstitutional acts void.

These are the means contemplated by the Constitution for maintaining the limits assigned to itself and for enabling the respective organs of the government to keep each other in their proper places, so that they may not have it in their power to domineer the one over the other and thereby in effect, though not in form, to concentrate the powers in one department, overturn the government, and establish a tyranny. Unfortunate if these powerful precautions shall prove insufficient to accomplish the end and to stem the torrent of the imposter—INNOVATION disguised in the specious garb of *Patriotism!*

The views which prevailed in the formation of the Constitution are further illustrated by these additional comments from the same source.*

"As liberty can have nothing to fear from the judiciary alone, but would have everything to fear from its union with either of the other departments; that as all the effects of such an union must ensue from a dependence of the former on the latter, notwithstanding a nominal and apparent separation; that as from the natural feebleness of the judiciary, it is in continual jeopardy of being overpowered, awed, or influenced by its coordinate branches; and that as nothing can contribute so much to its firmness and independence as *permanency in office*, this quality may therefore be justly regarded as an indispensable ingredient in its constitution, and in a great measure as the citadel of the public justice and the public security."

"The complete independence of the courts of justice is peculiarly essential in a limited constitution. Limitations can be preserved in practice no other way than through the medium of the courts of justice to declare all acts contrary to the manifest tenor of the Constitution void."

Then follows a particular discussion of the position that it is the right and the duty of the courts to exercise such an authority, to repeat which would swell this number to an improper size.

The essence of the argument is that every act of a delegated authority contrary to the tenor of the commission under which it is exercised is void, consequently that no legislative act inconsistent with the Constitution can be valid. That it is not a natural presumption that the Constitution intended to make the legislative body the final and exclusive judges of their own powers; but more rational to suppose that the courts were designed to be an intermediate body between the people and the legislature, in order, among other things, to keep the latter within the bounds assigned to its authority. That the interpretation of the laws being the peculiar province of the courts, and a Constitution being in fact a fundamental law superior in obligation to a statute, if the Constitution and the statute are at variance the former ought to prevail against the latter; the will of the people against the will of the agents; and the judges ought in their quality of interpreters of the laws to pronounce and adjudge the truth, namely, that the unauthorized statute is a nullity.

"Nor (continues the commentator) does this conclusion by any means suppose a superiority of the judicial to the legislative power. It only supposes that the power of the people is superior to both; and that where the will of the legislature declared in its statute stands in opposition to that of the people declared in the Constitution, the judges ought to be governed by the latter rather than the former. They ought to regulate their decisions by the fundamental laws rather than by those which are not fundamental."

"If then the courts of justice are to be considered as the bulwarks of a limited constitution against legislative encroachments, this consideration will afford a strong argument for the permanent tenure of judicial offices."

* No. LXXVIII.

But no proposition can be more manifest than that this permancy of tenure must be nominal if made defeasible at the pleasure of the legislature, and that it is ridiculous to consider it as an obstacle to encroachments of the legislative department if this department has a discretion to vacate or abolish it directly or indirectly.

In recurring to the comments which have been cited, it is not meant to consider them as evidence of anything but of the views with which the Constitution was framed. After all, the instrument must speak for itself. Yet to candid minds, the contemporary explanation of it by men who had had a perfect opportunity of knowing the views of its framers must operate as a weighty collateral reason for believing the construction agreeing with this explanation to be right, rather than the opposite one. It is too cardinal a point to admit readily the supposition that there was misapprehension; and whatever motives may have subsequently occurred to bias the impressions of the one or the other of the purposes alluded to, the situation in which they wrote exempts both from the suspicion of an intention to misrepresent in this particular. Indeed, a course of argument more accommodating to the objections of the adversaries of the Constitution would probably have been preferred as most politic, if the truth, as conceived at the time, would have permitted a modification. Much trouble would have been avoided by saying, "The legislature will have a complete control over the judges by the discretionary power of reducing the number of those of the Supreme Court and of abolishing the existing judges of the inferior courts by the abolition of the courts themselves." But this pretension is a novelty reserved for the crooked ingenuity of after-discoveries.

Lucius Crassus

Letter to Gouverneur Morris, March 4, 1802

My Dear Sir,

You have seen certain resolutions unanimously pass our legislature for amending the Constitution 1. by designating separately the candidates for president and vice president 2. by having the electors chosen by the people in districts under the direction of the national legislature.

After mature reflection I was thoroughly confirmed in my first impression that it is true Federal policy to promote the adoption of these amendments.

Of the first, not only because it is in itself right that the people should know whom they are choosing, & because the present mode gives all possible scope to intrigue and is dangerous, as we have seen, to the public tranquility—but because in everything which gives opportunity for juggling arts, our adversaries will nine times out of ten excel us.

Of the second, because it removes thus far the intervention of the state governments and strengthens the connection between the federal head and the people, and because it diminishes the means of party combination, in which also the burning zeal of our opponents will be generally an overmatch for our temperate flame.

I shall be very happy that our friends may think with me & that no temporary motive may induce them to let slip the precious occasion, in which personal motives induce the other party to forget their true policy.

We are told here that at the close of your birth day feast a strange *apparition* which was taken for the *V. P.* appeared among you and toasted "the union of all honest men." I often hear at the corner of the streets important Federal secrets of which I am ignorant. This may be one.

If the story be true, 'tis a good thing if we use it well. As an *instrument* the person will be an auxiliary of *some* value; as a chief he will disgrace and destroy the party. I suspect, however, the folly of the mass will make him the latter, and from the moment it shall appear that this is the plan it may be depended upon much more will be lost than gained. I know of no important character who has a less *founded* interest than the man in question. His talents may do well enough for a particular plot but they are ill-suited to a great and wise *drama*. But what has wisdom to do with weak man? Adieu

Yrs. truly
A.H.

Letter to Charles Cotesworth Pinckney, March 15, 1802

You will probably have learned before this reaches you that the act of last session for the better organization of the judiciary department has been repealed, and I take it for granted that you will with me view this measure as a vital blow to the Constitution. In my opinion, it demands a systematic and persevering effort *by all constitutional means* to produce a revocation of the precedent and to restore the Constitution.

For this purpose I deem it essential that there should be without delay a meeting and conference of a small number of leading Federalists from different states.

Unless there shall be a plan of conduct proceeding from such a source, our measures will be disjointed, discordant, and of course ineffectual. There is also a further danger which may attend the want of a plan capable of fixing opinions and determining objects.

There are among us *incorrect men with very incorrect* views, which may lead to *combinations* and *projects* injurious to us as a party, and very detrimental to the country.

These considerations have determined me to make an attempt to bring about such a meeting. And it has occurred that the first Monday of May next at the City of Washington may be a convenient time and place.

A general meeting of the Society of the Cincinnati is to be then and there held. I have likewise taken the liberty to request the attendance of Governor Davie of North Carolina. In the event of your concurring in sentiment with me, it will be expedient for you to second my invitation to him.

With the truest esteem and most affectionate regard

The Examination Number XVI, March 19, 1802

The president, as a politician, is in one sense particularly unfortunate. He furnishes frequent opportunities of arraying him against himself—of combating his opinions at one period by his opinions at another. Without doubt, a wise and good man may on proper grounds relinquish an opinion which he has once entertained, and the change may even serve as a proof of candor and integrity. But with such a man, especially in matters of high public importance, changes of this sort must be rare. The contrary is always a mark either of a weak and versatile mind, or of an artificial and designing character, which, accommodating its creed to circumstances, takes up or lays down an article of faith just as may suit a present convenience.

The question in agitation, respecting the judiciary department, calls up another instance of opposition between the former ideas of Mr. Jefferson and his recent conduct. The leading positions which have been advanced as explanatory of the policy of the Constitution in the structure of the different departments, and as proper to direct the interpretation of the provisions which were contrived to secure the independence and firmness of the judges, are to be seen in a very emphatical and distinct form in the Notes on Virginia. The passage in which they appear deserves to be cited at length, as well for its intrinsic merit as by way of comment upon the true character of its author; presenting an interesting contrast between the maxims which experience had taught him while governor of Virginia and those which now guide him as the official head of a great party in the United States.

It is in these words—

"All the powers of government, legislative, executive and judiciary, result to the legislative body. The concentrating these in the same hands is precisely the definition of despotic government. It will be no alleviation that these powers will be exercised by a plurality of hands and not by a single one. One hundred and seventy-three despots would surely be as oppressive as one. Let those who doubt it turn their eyes on the Republic of Venice. As little will it avail us that they are chosen by ourselves. An *elective despotism* was not the government we fought for; but one which should not only be founded on free principles, but in which the powers of government should be so divided and balanced among several bodies of magistracy as that no one could transcend their legal limits without being effectually *checked* and *restrained* by the others. For this reason that Convention which passed the ordinance of government laid its foundation on this basis, that the legislative, executive and judiciary departments should be separate and distinct, so that no person should exercise the powers of more than one of them at the same time. *But no barrier was provided between these several powers.* The judiciary and executive members were left dependent on the legislative for their subsistence in office, and some of them for their continuance in it. If therefore the legislature assumes executive and judiciary powers, no opposition is likely to be made; nor if made can be effectual; because in that case they may put their proceedings into the form of an act of assembly, which will render them obligatory on the other branches. They have accordingly *in many instances decided rights* which should have been left to *judiciary controversy*, and *the direction of the executive, during the whole time of their session, is becoming habitual and familiar.*"

This passage fully recognizes these several important truths: that the tendency of our governments is towards a CONCENTRATION of the POWERS of the different departments in the LEGISLATIVE BODY, that such a CONCENTRATION is precisely the DEFINITION OF DESPOTISM, and that an effectual *barrier* between the respective departments ought to exist. It also, by a strong implication, admits that offices during *good behavior* are independent of the legislature for their continuance in office. This implication seems to be contained in the following sentence: "The judiciary and executive members were left dependent on the legislature for their subsistence in office, and *some* of them *for their continuance in it.*" The word "*some*" implies that *others* were not left thus dependent; and to what description of officers can the exception be better applied than to the judges, the tenure of whose offices was *during good behavior?*

The sentiments of the president, delivered at a *period* when he can be supposed to have been under no improper bias, must be regarded by all those who respect his judgment as no light evidence of the truth of the doctrine for which we contend. Let us, however, resume and pursue the subject on its merits, without relying upon the aid of so variable and fallible an authority.

At an early part of the discussion in this Examination, a construction of the Constitution was suggested to which it may not be amiss to return: It amounts to this, that Congress have power to new-model or even to abrogate an inferior court, but not to abolish the office or emoluments of a judge of such court previously appointed. In the Congressional debates, some of the speakers against the repealing law appear to have taken it for granted that the *abrogation of the court* must draw with it the *abolition of the Judges*, and therefore have denied in totality the power of abrogation. In the course of these papers, too, it has been admitted that if the preservation of the judges cannot be reconciled with the power to annul the court, then the existence of this power is rightly denied. But in an affair of such vast magnitude, it is all-important to survey with the utmost caution the ground to be taken, and then to take and maintain it with inflexible fortitude and perseverance. Truth will be most likely to prevail when the arguments which support it stop at a temperate mean, consistent with practical convenience. Excess is always error. There is hardly any theoretic hypothesis which, carried to a certain extreme, does not become practically false. In construing a Constitution, it is wise, as far as possible to pursue a course which will reconcile essential principles with convenient modifications. If guided by this spirit in the great question which seems destined to decide the fate of our government, it is believed that the result will accord with the construction that *Congress have a right to change or abolish inferior courts, but not to abolish the actual judges.*

Towards the support of this construction it has been shown in another place that the courts and the judges are distinct legal *entities*, which, in contemplation of law, may exist independently the one of the other—mutually related, but not inseparable. The act proposed to be repealed exemplifies this idea in practice. It abolishes the district courts of Tennessee and Kentucky and transfers their judges to one of the circuit courts. Though the authorities and jurisdiction of those courts are vested in the circuit court to which the judges are transferred, yet the *identity of the courts* ceases. It cannot be maintained that courts so different in their organization and jurisdiction are the same; nor could a legislative transfer of the judges have been constitutional but upon the hypothesis that the office of a judge may survive the court of which he is a member: a *new appointment* by the executive of two additional judges for the circuit court would otherwise have been necessary.

This precedent in all its points is correct and exhibits a rational operation of the construction which regards the office of the judge, as distinct from the court, as one of the elements or constituent parts of which it is composed: not as a mere incident that must perish with its principal.

It will not be disputed that the Constitution might have provided *in terms*, and with effect, that an inferior court which had been *established by law* might by law be abolished; nevertheless, that the judges of such courts should retain the offices of judges of the United States, with the emoluments before attached to their offices. The operation of such a provision would be that when the court was abolished, all the functions to be executed in that court would be suspended, and the judge could only continue to exert the authorities and perform the duties which might before have been performed without reference to causes pending in court; but he would have the capacity to be annexed to another court, without the intervention of a new appointment, and by that annexation simply to *renew* the exercise of the authorities and duties which had been suspended.

If this might have been the effect of positive and explicit provision, why may it not likewise be the result of provisions which, presenting opposite considerations, point to the same conclusion as a compromise calculated to reconcile those considerations with each other and to unite different objects of public utility? Surely the affirmative infringes no principle of legal construction, transgresses no rule of good sense.

Let us then inquire whether there are not in this case opposite and conflicting considerations demanding a compromise of this nature? On the one hand, it is evident that if an inferior court once instituted, though found inconvenient, cannot be abolished, this is to entail upon the community the mischief, be it more or less, of a first error in the administration of the government. On the other hand, it is no less evident that if the judges hold their offices at the discretion of the legislature, they cease to be a coordinate and become a dependent branch of the government, from which dependence mischiefs infinitely greater are to be expected.

All these mischiefs, the lesser as well as the greater, are avoided by saying, "*Congress may abolish the courts, but the judges shall retain their offices with the appurtenant emoluments.*" The only remaining inconvenience then will be one too insignificant to weigh in a national scale, that is, the expense of the compensations of the incumbents during their lives. The future and permanent expense will be done away.

But will this construction secure the benefits proposed by the Constitution from the independent tenure of judicial office? Substantially it will. The main object is to preserve the judges from being influenced by an apprehension of the loss of the advantages of office. As this loss could not be incurred, that influence would not exist. Their firmness could not be assailed by the danger of being superseded and perhaps *consigned to want*. Let it be added that when it was understood not to be in the power of the legislature to deprive the judges of their offices and emoluments, it would be a great restraint upon the factious motives which might induce the abolition of a court. This would be much less likely to happen unless for genuine reasons of public utility, and of course there would be a much better prospect of the stability of judiciary establishments.

Lucius Crassus

The Examination Number XVII, March 20, 1802

It was intended to have concluded the argument respecting the judiciary department with the last number. But a speech lately delivered* in the House of Representatives having since appeared, which brings forward one new position, and reiterates some others in a form well calculated to excite prejudice, it may not be useless to devote some further attention to the subject.

The new position is that the clause of the Constitution enabling the judges to hold their offices during good behavior ought to be understood to have reference to the executive only, BECAUSE ALL OFFICES ARE HOLDEN OF THE PRESIDENT!!

This is a second example of a doctrine contrary to every republican idea, broached in the course of this debate by the advocates of the repealing law.† Had a Federalist uttered the sentiment, the cry of monarchy would have resounded from one extremity of the United States to the other. It would have been loudly proclaimed that the mask was thrown aside by a glaring attempt to transform the servants of the people into the supple tools of presidential ambition. But now, to justify a plain violation[7] of the Constitution, and serve a party purpose, this bold and dangerous position is avowed without hesitation or scruple from a quarter remarkable for the noisy promulgation of popular tenets.

The position is not correct, & it is of a nature to demand the indignant reprobation of every real republican. In the theory of all the American constitutions, offices are holden of the government, in other words of the PEOPLE *through the* GOVERNMENT. The appointment is indeed confined to a particular organ, and in instances in which it is not otherwise provided by the Constitution or the laws the removal of the officer is left to the pleasure or discretion of that organ. But both these acts suppose merely an instrumentality of the organ from the necessity or expediency of the people's acting in such cases by an agent. They do not suppose the substitution of the agent to the people as the object of the fealty or allegiance of the officer.

It is said that the word *holden* is a technical form denoting tenure and implying that there is one who holds, another of whom the thing is holden. This assertion is indeed agreeable to the common use of the word in our law books. But it

---

* By Mr. Giles.
† The other is the denial of the right of the courts to keep the legislature within its constitutional bounds by pronouncing laws which transgress them inoperative.

is hardly to be presumed that it was employed in the Constitution in so artificial a sense. It is more likely that it was designed to be the equivalent of the words *possess, enjoy*. Yet let the assertion be supposed correct. In this case, it must also be remembered that the term in this *technical* sense includes two things, the quantity of interest in the subject holden, and the meritorious consideration upon which the grant is made; which, in many cases includes service or rent, in all *fealty*; this last forming emphatically the link or tie between the lord and the tenant, the sovereign and the officer. Will any one dare to say that fealty or allegiance, as applied to the government of the United States, is due from the officer to the president? Certainly it is not. It is due to the people in their political capacity. If so, it will follow that the office is holden not of the president but of the *nation*, government, or state.

It is remarkable that the Constitution has everywhere used the language "Officers of the United States," as if to denote the relation between the officer and the sovereignty; as if to exclude the dangerous pretension that he is the mere creature of the executive; accordingly, he is to take an oath "to support the Constitution," that is, an oath of fidelity to the government, but no oath of any kind to the *president*.

In the theory of the British government it is entirely different; there the majesty of the nation is understood to reside in the prince. He is deemed the real sovereign. He is emphatically the fountain of honor. Allegiance is due to him, and consequently public offices are in the true notion of *tenure* holden of him. But in our Constitution the president is not the sovereign; the sovereignty is vested in the government, collectively; and it is of the sovereignty, strictly and technically speaking, that a public officer holds his office.

If this view of the matter be just, the basis of the argument, in point of fact, fails; and the principle of it suggests an opposite conclusion, namely, that the condition of *good behavior* is obligatory on the whole government and ought to operate as a barrier against any authority by which the displacement of the judges from their office may be directly or indirectly effected.

In the same speech, much stress has been laid on the words "during their continuance in office," as implying that the compensation of the judge was liable to cease by a legislative discontinuance of the office. If the words had been during *the continuance of the office*, the argument would have been pertinent; but as they stand, a different inference, if any, is to be drawn from them. They seem rather to relate to the continuance of the *officer* than to that of the *office*. But in truth, an inference either way it is a pitiful subtlety. The clause is neutral; its plain and simple meaning being that the compensation shall not be diminished while the judge retains the office. It throws no light whatever on the question *how he may lawfully cease to possess it*.

Another point is pressed with great earnestness and with greater plausibility. It is this, that the Constitution must have intended to attach recompense to service, and cannot be supposed to have meant to bestow compensation where, in the opinion of the legislature, no service was necessary. Without doubt, the Constitution does contemplate service as the ground of compensation; but it likewise takes it for granted that the legislature will be circumspect in the institution of offices, and especially that it will be careful to establish none of a permanent nature which will not be permanently useful. And with this general presumption the Constitution anticipates no material inconvenience from the permanency of judicial offices connected with permanent emoluments. And though it should have foreseen that cases might happen in which the service was not needed, yet there is no difficulty whatever in the supposition that it was willing to encounter the trivial contingent evil of having to maintain a few superfluous officers in order to obtain the immense good of establishing and securing the independence of the courts of justice. A readiness of the officer to render service to the will of the government is the consideration as to him for continuing the compensation. But the essential inducement is the public utility incident to the independency of the judicial character. As to the supposition of an enormous abuse of power by creating a long list of sinecures and a numerous host of pensioners, whenever such a thing shall happen it will constitute one of those extreme cases which, on the principle of necessity, may authorize extra-constitutional remedies. But these are cases which can never be appealed to for the interpretation of any constitution which, in meting out the power of the government, must be supposed to adjust them on the presumption of a fair execution.

A further topic of argument is that our doctrine would equally restrain the legislature from abolishing offices held during pleasure. But this is not true. The two things stand on different ground. First, the executive has such an agency in the enacting of laws that as a general rule the displacement of the officer cannot happen against his pleasure. Second, the pleasure of the president, in all cases not particularly excepted, is understood to be subject to the direction of the law. Third, an officer during pleasure, having merely a revocable interest, the abolition of his office is no infringement of his right. In substance he is a tenant *at the will of the government,* liable to be discontinued by the executive organ in the form of a removal, by the legislative in the form of an abolition of the office. These different considerations reconcile the legislative authority to abolish with the prerogative of the chief magistrate to remove, and with the temporary right of individuals to hold. And therefore there is no reason against the exercise of such an authority, nothing to form an exception to the *general competency of the legislative power to provide for the public welfare.* Very different is the case as to the judges. The most persuasive motives of public policy, the safety of liberty itself, require that the judges shall be independent of the legislative body, in order to maintain effectually the separation between the several departments: The provision that their compensation shall not be diminished is a clear constitutional indication that their independence was intended to be guarded against the legislature. The express declaration that they shall hold their offices during good behavior, that is, upon a condition *dependent on themselves*, is repugnant to the hypothesis that they shall hold at the *mere pleasure of others*. Provisions which profess to confer rights on individuals are always entitled to a liberal interpretation in support of the rights and ought not, without necessity, to receive an interpretation subversive of them. Provisions which respect the organization of a co-ordinate branch of the government ought to be construed in such a manner as to procure for it stability and efficiency rather than in such a manner as render it weak, precarious, and dependent. These various and weighty reasons serve to establish strong lines of discrimination between judicial and other officers, and to prove that no inference can be drawn from the power of the legislature as to the latter which will be applicable to the former.

One more defense of this FORMIDABLE CLAIM is attempted to be drawn from the example of the judiciary establishment of G. Britain. It is observed that this establishment, the theme of copious eulogy on account of the independence of the judges, places those officers upon a footing far less firm than will be that of the judges of the U. States, even admitting the right of Congress to abolish their offices by abolishing the courts of which they are members: And as one proof of the assertion it is mentioned that the English judges are removable by the king on the address of the two houses of Parliament.

All this might be very true, and yet prove nothing as to what is or ought to be the construction of our Constitution on this point. It is plain from the provision respecting compensation that the framers of that Constitution intended to prop the independence of our judges beyond the precautions which have been adopted in England in respect to the judges of that country, and the intention apparent in this particular is an argument that the same spirit may have governed other provisions. Cogent reasons have been assigned, applicable to our system and not applicable to the British system, for securing the independence of our judges against the legislative as well as against the executive power.

It is alleged that the statute of Great Britain of the 13 of William III was the model from which the framers of our Constitution copied the provisions for the independence of our judiciary. It is certainly true that the idea of the tenure of office during good behavior, found in several of our constitutions, is borrowed from that source. But it is evident that the framers of our federal system did not mean to confine themselves to that model. Hence the restraint of the legislative discretion as to compensation; hence the omission of the provision for the removal of the judges by the executive on the application of the two branches of the legislature, a provision which has been imitated in some of the state governments.

This very omission affords no light inference that it was the intention to depart from the principle of making the judges removable from office by the cooperation or interposition of the legislative body. Why else was this qualification of the permanent tenure of the office, which forms a conspicuous feature in the British statute and in some of the state constitutions, dropped in the plan of the federal government?

The insertion of it in the British statute may also be supposed to have been dictated by the opinion that without a special reservation the words *during good behavior* would have imported an irrevocable tenure. If so, the precaution will serve to fortify our construction.

But however it may seem in theory, in fact the difference in the genius of the two governments would tend to render the independence of the judges more secure under the provision of the British statute than it would be in this country upon the construction which allows to Congress the right to abolish them. The reason is this—From the constitution of the British monarchy the thing chiefly to be apprehended is an overbearing influence of the Crown upon the judges. The jealousy of executive influence resting upon more powerful motives in that country than in this, it may be expected to operate as a stronger obstacle there than here, to an improper combination between the executive and legislative departments to invade the judiciary. Moreover, the British executive has greater means of resisting parliamentary control than an American executive has of resisting the control of an American legislature; consequently the former would be in less danger than the latter of being driven to a concurrence in measures hostile to the independence of the judges: And in both these ways there would be greater security for the British than for the American judges.

Thus is it manifest that in every attitude in which the subject has been placed the argument is victorious against the power of Congress to abolish the judges. But what, alas! avails the demonstration of this important truth? The fatal blow has been struck! It is no longer possible to arrest the rash and daring arm of power! Can the proof that it has acted without right, without warrant—can this heal the wound? Can it renovate the perishing Constitution?—Yes, let us hope that this will be the case. Let us trust that the monitory voice of true patriotism will at length reach the ears of a considerate people and will rouse them to a united and vigorous exertion for the restoration of their VIOLATED CHARTER, not by means either disorderly or guilty, but by means which the Constitution will sanction and reason approve. Surely this will be so—A people, who descrying tyranny at a distance and guided only by the light of just principles, before they had yet felt the scourge of oppression, could nobly hazard all in the defense of their rights—A people, who sacrificing their prejudices on the altar of experience, and spurning the artifices of insidious demagogues, could, as a deliberate act of national reason, adopt and establish for themselves a Constitution which bid fair to immortalize their glory and their happiness, such a people, though misled for a period, will not be the final victims of a delusion, alike inauspicious to their reputation and to their welfare. They will not long forget the fame they have so justly merited, nor give the world occasion to ascribe to accident what has hitherto been imputed to wisdom. They will disdain to herd with the too long list of degraded nations who have bowed their necks to unworthy idols of their own creating—who, immolating their best friends at the shrine of falsehood, have sunk under the yoke of sycophants and betrayers. They will open their eyes and see the precipice on which they stand! They will look around and select from among the throng the men who have heretofore established a claim to their confidence, the solid basis of able and faithful service; and they will with indignation and scorn banish from their favor the wretched impostors who, with honeyed lips and guileful hearts, are luring them to destruction! Admonished by the past, and listening again to the counsels of *real* friends, they will make a timely retreat from the danger which threatens—they will once more arrange themselves under the banners of the Constitution, with anxious care will repair the breaches that have been made, and will raise new mounds against the future assaults of open or secret enemies!

Lucius Crassus

Letter to John Dickinson, March 29, 1802

I was not, My Dear Sir, insensible to the kind attention shown me by your letter of the 30th of November last. But till very lately the subject has been so extremely painful to me that I have been under a necessity of flying from it as much as possible. Time and effort and occupation have at length restored the tranquility of my mind sufficiently to permit me to acknowledge the kindness of those friends who were good enough to manifest their sympathy in my misfortune.

Be assured, Sir, that consolation from you on such an occasion was particularly welcome to me, and that I shall always remember it with a grateful sense. The friendship of the wise and good rises in value in proportion as we learn to form a just estimate of human character and opinion.

That estimate too has a tendency to reconcile us to the departure of those who are dear to us from a world which holds out to virtue many snares, few, very few, supports or recompenses. I do assure you, Sir, that as soon as the calm of reason returned, this consideration had no small influence in disposing me to resign, with diminished regret, the eldest and *brightest* hope of my family. Happy those who deduce from it motives to seek in earnest a higher, and far more substantial, bliss than can ever be found in this chequered, this ever varying scene!

> Accept the assurances of most sincere and
> cordial respect esteem and regard
> A. Hamilton

Letter to Benjamin Rush, March 29, 1802

Dear Sir,

I felt all the weight of the obligation which I owed to you and to your amiable family for the tender concern they manifested in an event, beyond comparison, the most afflicting of my life. But I was obliged to wait for a moment of greater calm to express my sense of the kindness.

My loss is indeed great. The highest as well as the eldest hope of my family has been taken from me. You estimated him rightly—He was truly a fine youth. But why should I repine? It was the will of heaven; and he is now out of the reach of the seductions and calamities of a world, full of folly, full of vice, full of danger—of least value in proportion as it is best known. I firmly trust also that he has safely reached the haven of eternal repose and felicity.

You will easily imagine that every memorial of the goodness of his heart must be precious to me. You allude to one recorded in a letter to your son. If no special reasons forbid it, I should be very glad to have a copy of that letter.

Mrs. Hamilton, who has drunk deeply of the cup of sorrow, joins me in affectionate thanks to Mrs. Rush and yourself. Our wishes for your happiness will be unceasing.

Very sincerely & cordially   Yrs.

A. Hamilton

Letter to James A. Bayard, April 6, 1802

Amidst the humiliating circumstances which attend our country, all the sound part of the community must find cause of triumph in the brilliant display of talents which have been employed, though without success, in resisting the follies of an infatuated administration. And your personal friends will not have much reason for mortification on account of the part you have performed in the interesting scene. But, my dear Sir, we must not content ourselves with a temporary effort to oppose the approach of the evil. We must derive instruction from the experience before us; and, learning to form a just estimate of the things to which we have been attached, there must be a systematic & persevering endeavor to establish the fortune of a great empire on foundations much firmer than have yet been devised. What will signify a vibration of power, if it cannot be used with confidence or energy, & must be again quickly restored to hands which will prostrate much faster than we shall be able to rear under so frail a system? Nothing will be done till the structure of our national edifice shall be such as naturally to control eccentric passions & views, and to keep in check demagogues & knaves in the disguise of patriots. Yet I fear a different reasoning will prevail, and an eagerness to recover lost power will betray us into expedients which will be injurious to the country, & disgraceful & ruinous to ourselves. What meant the *apparition* & the *toast* which made part of the *afterpiece* of the *birth day festival?* Is it possible that some new intrigue is about to link the Federalists with a man who can never be anything else than the bane of a good cause? I dread more from this than from all the contrivances of the bloated & senseless junta of Virginia. The Feds. & Antifeds. of this state united in certain amendments to the Constitution now before your house, having for objects, 1st to discriminate the candidates for the presidency & vice presidency, 2nd to have the electors of these officers chosen by the people in districts under the direction of Congress. Both these appear to me points of importance in true Federal calculation. Surely the scene of last session ought to teach us the intrinsic demerits of the existing plan. It proved to us how possible it is for a man in whom no party has confidence, & who deserves the confidence of none, by mere intrigue & accident, to acquire the first place in the government of our nation; and it also proved to us how serious a danger of convulsion & disorder is incident to the plan. On this point things have come to my knowledge, improper for a letter, which would astonish you. Surely we ought by this time to have learnt that whatever multiplied the opportunities & means of cabal is more favorable to our adversaries than to us. They have certainly the advantage in the game, by greater zeal, activity, and subtlety, & especially by an abandonment of principle. On all these accounts it is our true policy to abridge the facilities to cabal as much as possible in all our public institutions & measures. As to the second of the amendments, it has ever appeared to me as sound principle to let the federal government rest as much as possible on the shoulders of the people and as little as possible on those of the state legislatures. The proposition accords with this principle, & in my view it is further recommended by its tendency to exclude *combination*, which I am persuaded in the general & permanent course of things will operate more against than for us. Col. Burr without doubt will resist these amendments. And he may induce some of our friends to play into his hands. But this will be a very bad calculation, even admitting the inadmissible idea that he ought to be adopted as a chief of the Federal party. We never can have him fairly in our power till we render his situation absolutely hopeless with his old friends. While the indiscriminate voting prevails he will find it his interest to play fast & loose and to keep himself in a state to be at the head of the Antifederal party. If these hopes are cut off, he will immediately set about forming a third party of which he will be the head, and then if we think it worth the while we can purchase him with his flying squadron. These observations are of course hypothetical. For to my mind the elevation of Mr. Burr by Federal means to the chief magistracy of the U. States will be the worst kind of political suicide.

Adieu my dear Sir   Yours very sincerely

A. Hamilton

The Examination Number XVIII, April 8, 1802

In order to cajole the people the Message abounds with all the commonplace of popular harangue and prefers claims of merit for circumstances of equivocal or of trivial value. With pompous absurdity are we told of the "*multiplication of men, susceptible of happiness*" (as if this susceptibility were a privilege peculiar to our climate), "*habituated to self-government, and valuing its blessings above all price.*" Fortunate will it be if the present favorites of the people do not, before their reign is at an end, transform those blessings into curses, so serious and heavy as to make even despotism a desirable refuge from the elysium of democracy.

In a country the propensities of which are opposed even to necessary burdens, an alarm is attempted to be excited about the general tendency of government "to leave to labor the *smallest* portion of its earnings on which it can subsist, and to *consume the residue* of what it was instituted to guard." It might have been well to have explained whether it is the *whole* of the earnings of labor which government is instituted to guard, or only the *residue* after deducting what is *necessary to enable it* to fulfill the duty of protection. Representatives who share with their constituents in an excessive jealousy of executive abuses are cantingly admonished to "circumscribe discretionary powers over money," though they are known to be already so limited, as that the executive, even on the prospect of a rupture with a foreign power, would not possess the means of obtaining intelligence the most necessary for the proper direction of its measures. That the new administration has not boldly invaded the laws and withheld the funds applicable to the payment of principal and interest of the public debt is fastidiously proclaimed as *evidence* that "the public faith has been *exactly* maintained." The praise of a spirit of economy is attempted to be gained by the suppression of a trifling number of officers (a majority of whom had become unnecessary by the mere change of circumstances), and by declaiming with affectation against "*the multiplication of officers and the increase of expense.*" The proposition to reduce our insignificant *military establishment* (the actual number of troops probably not exceeding that which is intended to be retained) cannot be suggested without tickling our ears with the trite but favorite maxim that "*a standing army ought not to be kept up in time of peace.*" To make a display of concern for their prosperity—agriculture, manufactures, commerce, and navigation are introduced among the pageants of the piece; but, except as "to protection from *casual* embarrassments," we are sagaciously informed that these "great pillars *of our prosperity* ought to be left *to take care of themselves.*" The carrying trade, however, seems to engage more solicitude, no doubt that we may be terrified by the expectation of future evils from a much traduced instrument,* which *in time past* has done nothing but good, in spite of the gloomy predictions of patriotic seers.

Such are the minor features of this curious performance. Had these been its only blemishes, a regard to national reputation would have forbidden a comment; but connected as they are with schemes of innovation replete with great present mischief and still greater future danger; designed as they are to varnish over projects which threaten to precipitate our nation from an enviable height of prosperity to that low and abject state from which it was raised by the establishment and wise administration of our present government—they become entitled to notice as additional indications of character and disposition.

The merits of the Message have now been pretty fully discussed; but before it is dismissed it may be useful to take a view of it in another and a different light as one link in a chain of testimony which the force of circumstances, at every step of the new administration, extorts from them in favor of their predecessors.

The president, on the threshold of office, at the first opportunity of speaking to his constituents, in his very inaugural speech, full of a truth which the most rancorous prejudice cannot obscure, and not sufficiently reflecting on the inferences which would be drawn, proclaims aloud to the world that a government, which he had disapproved in its institution and virulently opposed in its progress, was in THE FULL TIDE OF SUCCESSFUL EXPERIMENT. In the last address he again unconsciously becomes the panegyrist of those whom he seeks to depreciate. The situation in which (humanly speaking) we have been preserved by the prudent and firm councils of the preceding administrations, amidst the revolutionary and convulsive throes, amidst the desolating conflicts of Europe, is there a theme of emphatic gratulation. It shall not be forgotten, as the solitary merit of the address, that we are reminded of the *gratitude due to heaven* for the blessings of this situation. Amidst the spurious symptoms of a spirit of reform, it is consoling to observe one which, in charity, ought to be supposed genuine. But it would not have diminished our conviction of its sincerity if the instruments of Providence in the accomplishment of the happy work had not been entirely overlooked, since this would have been evidence of a willingness to acknowledge and retract error—to make reparation for injury. But though they have been overlooked by the Message, the American people ought never for a moment to forget them. Their efforts and their struggles, their moderation and their energy, their care and their foresight; the mad and malignant opposition of their political adversaries; the charges of pusillanimity and perfidy lavished on the declaration of neutrality; the resistance to measures for avoiding a rupture with Great Britain; the attempt to rush at once into reprisals; the cry for war with the enemies of France as the enemies of republican liberty; all these things should be forever imprinted on the memory of a just

* The Treaty with Great Britain.

and vigilant nation. And in recollecting them, they should equally recollect that the opposers of the salutary plans to which they are so much indebted were and are the zealous partisans of the present head of our government; who have at all times submitted to his influence and implicitly obeyed his nod; who never would have pursued with so much vehemence the course they did had they known it to be contrary to the views of their chief: nor should it be forgotten that this chief in the negotiation with the British minister, conducted by him as secretary of state, acted precisely as if it had been his design to widen, not to heal, the breach between the two countries; that he at first *objected* to the declaration of neutrality; was afterwards reluctantly dragged into the measures connected with it; was believed by his friends not to approve the system of conduct of which he was the official organ; was publicly and openly accused by the then agent of the French Republic with duplicity and deception, with having been the first to inflame his mind with ill impressions of the principles and views of leading characters in our government, not excepting the revered WASHINGTON; that this chief, at a very critical period of our affairs in reference to the war of Europe, withdrew from the direction of that department peculiarly charged with the management of our foreign relations, evidently to avoid being more deeply implicated in the consequences of the position which had been assumed by the administration; but on the hollow presence of a dislike to public life and a love of philosophic retirement. Citizens of America—mark the sequel and learn from it instruction! You have been since agitated to the center, to raise to the first station in your government the very man who, at a conjuncture when your safety and your welfare demanded his stay, early relinquished a subordinate but exalted and very influential post, on a presence as frivolous as it has proved to be insincere! Was *he*, like the virtuous WASHINGTON, forced from a beloved retreat by the unanimous and urgent call of his country? No: he stalked forth the champion of faction, having never ceased in the shade of his retreat by all the arts of intrigue to prepare the way to that elevation for which a restless ambition impatiently panted.

The undesigned eulogy of the men *who have been slandered out of the confidence of their fellow citizens* has not been confined to the situation of the country, as connected with the war of Europe. In the view given of the very flourishing state of our finances, the worst of the calumnies against those men is refuted, and it is admitted that in this article of vital importance to the public welfare their measures have been provident and effectual beyond example. To the charge of a design to saddle the nation with a perpetual debt, a plain contradiction is given by the concession that the provisions which have been made for it are so ample as even to justify the relinquishment of a part no less considerable than the *whole of the internal revenue*. The same proposal testifies the brilliant success of our fiscal system generally and that it is more than equal to all that has been undertaken, to all that has been promised to the nation.

The report of the secretary of the treasury, as published, confirms this high commendation of the conduct of the *former administrations*. After relieving each state from the burden of its particular debt by assuming the payment of it on account of the United States, in addition to the general debt of the nation; after settling the accounts between the states relatively to their exertions for the common defense in our revolutionary war, and providing for the balances found due to such of them as were creditors; after maintaining with complete success an obstinate and expensive war with the Indian tribes; after making large disbursements for the suppression of two insurrections against the government; after liberal contributions to the Barbary powers to induce them to open to our merchants the trade of the Mediterranean; after incurring a responsibility for indemnities to a large amount due to British merchants, in consequence of infractions of the treaty of peace by some of the states; after heavy expenditures for creating and supporting a navy and for other preparations to guard our independence and territory against the hostilities of a foreign nation; after the accomplishment of all these very important objects, it is now declared to the United States by the present head of the treasury, by the confidential minister of the present chief magistrate, the most subtle and implacable of the enemies of the former administrations, "That the actual revenues of the Union are sufficient *to defray all the expenses civil and military* of government *to the extent authorized by existing laws,* to meet ALL THE ENGAGEMENTS OF THE UNITED STATES, *and to discharge in fifteen years and a half* THE WHOLE OF OUR PUBLIC DEBT"—foreign as well as domestic, *new* as well as *old.* Let it be understood that the revenues spoken of were *all provided under the two first administrations,* and that the "existing laws" alluded to were all passed under the same administrations; consequently, that *the revenues had not been increased nor the expenses diminished by the men who now hold the reins:* and then let it be asked whether so splendid a result does not reflect the highest credit on those who in times past have managed the affairs of the nation? Does not the picture furnish matter not only for consolation but even for exultation to every true friend of his country? And amidst the joy which he must feel in the contemplation, can he be so unjust as to refuse the tribute of commendation to those by whose labors his country has been placed on so fair an eminence? Will he endure to see any part of the fruits of those labors blasted or hazarded by a voluntary surrender of any portion of the means which are to insure the advantages of so bright a prospect?

In vain will envy or malevolence reply, "The happy situation in which we are placed is to be attributed not to the labors of those who have heretofore conducted our affairs, but to an unforeseen and unexpected progress of our country." Candor and truth will answer—Praise is always due to public men who take their measures in such a manner as to derive to the nation the benefit of favorable circumstances which are possible, as well as of those which are foreseen. If proportionate provision had not been made concurrently with the progress of our national resources, the effect of them would not have been felt as to the past and would not have been matured as to the future.

But why should it be pretended that this progress was not anticipated? In past experience there were many data for calculation. The ratio of the increase of our population had been observed and stated; the extent and riches of our soil were known; the materials for commercial enterprise were no secret; the probable effect of the measures of the government to foster and encourage navigation, trade, and industry was well understood; and especially the influence of the means which were adapted to augment our active capital, and to supply a fit and adequate medium of circulation towards the increase of national wealth, was declared and insisted upon in official reports. Though adventitious circumstances may have aided the result, it is certain that a penetrating and comprehensive mind could be at no loss to foresee a progress of our affairs, similar to what has been experienced. Upon this anticipation the assumption of the state debts and other apparently bold measures of the government were avowedly predicated, in opposition to the feeble & contracted views of the little politicians who now triumph in the success of their arts and enjoy the benefits of a policy which they had neither the wisdom to plan nor the spirit to adopt—idly imagining that the cunning of a demagogue and the talents of a statesman are synonymous. Consummate in the paltry science of courting and winning popular favor, they falsely infer that they have the capacity to govern, and they will be the last to discover their error. But let them be assured that the people will not long continue the dupes of their pernicious sorceries. Already the cause of truth has derived this advantage from the crude essays of their chief, that the film has been removed from many an eye. The credit of great abilities was allowed him by a considerable portion of those who disapproved his principles; but the short space of nine months has been amply sufficient to dispel that illusion, and even some of his most partial votaries begin to suspect that they have been mistaken in the OBJECT OF THEIR IDOLATRY.

Lucius Crassus

Letter to James Bayard, April 1802

Dear Sir,

Your letter of the 12th inst. has relieved me from some apprehension. Yet it is well that it should be perfectly understood by the truly sound part of the Federalists that there do in fact exist intrigues in good earnest between several individuals not unimportant of the Federal party and the person in question, which are bottomed upon motives & views by no means auspicious to the real welfare of the country. I am glad to find that it is in contemplation to adopt a plan of conduct. It is very necessary; & to be useful it must be efficient & comprehensive in the means which it embraces, at the same time that it must meditate none which are not really constitutional & patriotic. I will comply with your invitation by submitting some ideas which from time to time have passed through my mind. Nothing is more fallacious than to expect to produce any valuable or permanent results, in political projects, by relying merely on the reason of men. Men are rather reasoning than reasonable animals, for the most part governed by the impulse of passion. This is a truth well understood by our adversaries, who have practiced upon it with no small benefit to their cause. For at the very moment they are eulogizing the reason of men & professing to appeal only to that faculty, they are courting the strongest & most active passion of the human heart—*VANITY!*

It is no less true that the Federalists seem not to have attended to the fact sufficiently, and that they erred in relying so much on the rectitude & utility of their measures as to have neglected the cultivation of popular favor by fair & justifiable expedients. The observation has been repeatedly made by me to individuals with whom I particularly conversed & expedients suggested for gaining good will which were never adopted. Unluckily, however, for us in the competition for the passions of the people our opponents have great advantages over us, for the plain reason that the vicious are far more active than the good passions, and that to win the latter to our side we must renounce our principles & our objects, & unite in corrupting public opinion till it becomes fit for nothing but mischief. Yet unless we can contrive to take hold of & carry along with us some strong feelings of the mind we shall in vain calculate upon any substantial or durable results. Whatever plan we may adopt to be successful must be founded on the truth of this proposition. And perhaps it is not very easy for us to give it full effect, especially not without some deviations from what on other occasions we have maintained to be right. But in determining upon the propriety of the deviations, we must consider whether it be possible for us to succeed without in some degree employing the weapons which have been employed against us, & whether the actual state & future prospect of things be not such as to justify the reciprocal use of them. I need not tell you that I do not mean to countenance the imitation of things intrinsically unworthy, but only of such as may be denominated irregular, such as in a sound & stable order of things ought not to exist. Neither are you to infer that any revolutionary result is contemplated. In my opinion the present Constitution is the standard to which we are to cling. Under its banners, *bona fide* must we combat our political foes—rejecting all changes but through the channel itself provides for amendments. By these general views of the subject have my reflections been guided. I now offer you the outline of the plan which they have suggested. Let an association be formed to be denominated "The Christian Constitutional Society." Its objects to be

1st. The support of the Christian religion.

2nd. The Support of the Constitution of the United States.

Its Organization

1st. A directing council consisting of a president & 12 members, of whom 4 and the president to be a quorum.

2nd. A sub-directing council in each state consisting of a vice president and 12 members, of whom 4 with the vice president to be a quorum, and

3rd. As many societies in each state as local circumstances may permit to be formed by the sub-directing council.

The Meeting at Washington to nominate the *president* & *vice president*, together with *4 Members of each* of the councils, who *are to complete* their own numbers respectively.

Its Means

1st. The diffusion of information. For this purpose not only the newspapers but pamphlets must be largely employed, and to do this a fund must be created. 5 dollars annually for 8 years to be contributed by each member who can really afford it (taking care not to burden the less able brethren) may afford a competent fund for a competent time. It is essential to be able to disseminate *gratis* useful publications. Whenever it can be done, & there is a press, clubs should be formed to meet once a week, read the newspapers, and prepare essays, paragraphs, &ct.

2nd. The use of all lawful means in concert to promote the election of *fit men*. A lively correspondence must be kept up between the different societies.

3rd. The promoting of institutions of a charitable & useful nature in the management of Federalists. The populous cities ought particularly to be attended to. Perhaps it will be well to institute in such places 1st

Societies for the relief of emigrants—2nd Academies each with one professor for instructing the different classes of mechanics in the principles of mechanics.

& Elements of Chemistry.[8] The cities have been employed by the Jacobins to give an impulse to the country. And it is believed to be an alarming fact that while the question of presidential election was pending in the House of Rs, parties were organized in several of the cities, in the event of there being no election, to cut off the leading Federalists and seize the government.

An act of association to be drawn up in concise general terms. It need only designate the "name," "objects," & contain an engagement to promote the objects by all lawful means, and particularly by the diffusion of information. This act to be signed by every member.

The foregoing to be the principal engine. In addition, let measures be adopted to bring as soon as possible the repeal of the judiciary law before the Supreme Court. Afterwards, if not before, let as many legislatures as can be prevailed upon instruct their senators to endeavor to procure a repeal of the repealing law. The body of New England speaking the same language will give a powerful impulse. In Congress our friends to *propose* little, to agree candidly to all good measures, & to resist & expose all bad. This is a general sketch of what has occurred to me. It is at the service of my friends for so much as it may be worth. With true esteem & regard

Dr Sir   Yours
A.H.

Letter to Rufus King, June 3, 1802

My Dear Sir,

I have been long very delinquent towards you as a correspondent and am to thank you that you have not cast me off altogether as an irretrievable reprobate. But you knew how to appreciate the causes and you have made a construction equally just and indulgent.

In your last you ask my opinion about a matter delicate and important, both in a public and in a personal view. I shall give it with the frankness to which you have a right, and I may add that the impressions of your other friends, so far as they have fallen under my observation, do not differ from my own. While you were in the midst of a negotiation interesting to your country, it was your duty to keep your post. You have now accomplished the object and have the good fortune not very common of having the universal plaudit. This done, it seems to me most advisable that you return home. There is little probability that your continuance in your present station will be productive of much positive good. Nor are circumstances such as to give reason to apprehend that the substitute for you, whoever he may be, can do much harm. Your stay or return, therefore, as it regards our transatlantic concerns, is probably not material: While your presence at home may be useful in ways which it is not necessary to particularize. Besides, it is questionable whether you can continue longer in the service of the present administration consistently with what is due as well to your own character as to the common cause. I am far from thinking that a man is bound to quit a public office merely because the administration of the government may have changed hands. But when those who have come into power are undisguised persecutors of the party to which he has been attached and study with ostentation to heap upon it every indignity and injury—he ought not in my opinion to permit himself to be made an exception or to lend his talents to the support of such characters. If in addition to this it be true that the principles and plans of the men at the head of affairs tend to the degradation of the government and to their own disgrace, it will hardly be possible to be in any way connected with them without sharing in the disrepute which they may be destined to experience.

I wish I had time to give you a comprehensive & particular map of our political situation. But more than a rude outline is beyond my leisure, devoted as I am more than ever to my professional pursuits.

You have seen the course of the administration hitherto, especially during the last session of Congress; and I am persuaded you will agree in opinion with me that it could hardly have been more diligent in mischief. What, you will ask, has been and is likely to be the effect on the public mind?

Our friends are sanguine that a great change for the better has been wrought and is progressive. I suppose good has been done—that the Federalists have been reconciled and cemented—have been awakened and alarmed. Perhaps too there may be some sensible and moderate men of the adverse party who are beginning to doubt. But I as yet discover no satisfactory symptoms of a revolution of opinion in the *mass* "informe in gens cui lumen ademptum."[9] Nor do I look with much expectation to any serious alteration until inconveniences are extensively felt or until time has produced a disposition to coquet it with new lovers. Vibrations of power, you are aware, are of the genius of our government.

There is, however, a circumstance which may accelerate the fall of the present party. There is certainly a most serious schism between the chief and his heir apparent, a schism absolutely incurable, because founded in the breasts of both in the rivalship of an insatiable and unprincipled ambition. The effects are already apparent and are ripening into a more bitter animosity between the partisans of the two men than ever existed between the Federalists and Antifederalists.

Unluckily we are not as neutral to this quarrel as we ought to be. You saw how far our friends in Congress went in polluting themselves with the support of the second personage for the presidency. The cabal did not terminate there. Several men, of no inconsiderable importance among us, like the enterprising and adventurous character of this man and hope to soar with him to power. Many more through hatred to the chief and through an impatience to recover the reins are linking themselves with the vice chief, almost without perceiving it and professing to have no other object than to make use of him, while he knows that he is making use of them. What this may end in, it is difficult to foresee.

Of one thing only I am sure, that in no event will I be directly or indirectly implicated in a responsibility for the elevation or support of either of two men, who in different senses are in my eyes equally unworthy of the confidence of intelligent or honest men.

Truly, My dear Sir, the prospects of our country are not brilliant. The mass is far from sound. At headquarters a most visionary theory presides. Depend upon it, this is the fact to a great extreme. No army, no navy, no *active* commerce—national defense not by arms but by embargoes, prohibition of trade &c.—as little government as possible within—these are the pernicious dreams which as far and as fast as possible will be attempted to be realized. Mr. Jefferson is distressed at the codfish having latterly emigrated to the southern coast lest the people there should be tempted to catch them, and commerce of which we have already too much receive an accession. Be assured this is no pleasantry but a very sober anecdote.

Among Federalists old errors are not cured. They also continue to dream, though not quite so preposterously as their opponents. "All will be very well (say they) when the power once more gets back into Federal hands. The people convinced by experience of their error will repose a *permanent* confidence in good men." Rescum teneatis—Adieu.

Yrs. ever
A.H.

Letter to Charles Cotesworth Pinckney, December 29, 1802

My Dear Sir,

A garden, you know, is a very usual refuge of a disappointed politician. Accordingly, I have purchased a few acres about 9 miles from town, have built a house, and am cultivating a garden. The melons in your country are very fine. Will you have the goodness to send me some seed both of the water & muss melons?

My daughter adds another request, which is for three or four of your peroquets. She is very fond of birds. If there be any thing in this quarter the sending of which can give you pleasure, you have only to name them. As farmers a new source of sympathy has risen between us, and I am pleased with everything in which our likings and tastes can be approximated.

Amidst the triumphant reign of Democracy,[10] do you retain sufficient interest in public affairs to feel any curiosity about what is going on? In my opinion the follies and vices of the administration have as yet made no material impression to their disadvantage. On the contrary, I think the malady is rather progressive than upon the decline in our northern quarter. The last *lullaby* message, instead of inspiring contempt, attracts praise. Mankind are forever destined to be the dupes of bold & cunning imposture.

But a difficult *knot* has been twisted by the incident of the cession of Louisiana and the interruption of the deposit at New Orleans. You have seen the soft turn given to this in the message. Yet we are told the president in conversation is very stout. The great embarrassment must be how to carry on war without taxes. The pretty scheme of substituting economy to taxation will not do here, and a war would be a terrible comment upon the abandonment of the internal revenue. Yet how is popularity to be preserved with the western partisans if their interests are tamely sacrificed? Will the artifice be for the chief to hold a bold language and the subalterns to act a public part? Time must explain.

You know my general theory as to our western affairs. I have always held that the unity of our empire and the best interests of our nation require that we should annex to the U. States all the territory east of the Mississippi, New Orleans included. Of course I infer that in an emergency like the present, energy is wisdom.

Adieu My Dear Sir   Ever Yrs
A.H.

For the Evening Post,
February 8, 1803

Since the question of independence, none has occurred more deeply interesting to the United States than the cession of Louisiana to France. This event threatens the early dismemberment of a large portion of our country: more immediately the safety of all the southern states; and remotely the independence of the whole union. This is the portentous aspect which the affair presents to all men of sound and reflecting minds of whatever party, and it is not to be concealed that the only question which now offers itself is, how is the evil to be averted?

The strict right to resort at once to WAR, if it should be deemed expedient, cannot be doubted. *A manifest and great danger* to the nation: the nature of the cession to France, extending to ancient limits without respect to our rights by treaty; the direct infraction of an important article of the treaty itself in withholding the deposit of New Orleans; either of these affords justifiable cause of war, and that they would authorize immediate hostilities is not to be questioned by the most scrupulous mind.

The whole is then a question of expediency. Two courses only present. First, to negotiate and endeavor to purchase, and if this fails, to go to war. Secondly, to seize at once on the Floridas and New Orleans and then negotiate.

A strong objection offers itself to the first. There is not the most remote probability that the ambitious and aggrandizing views of Bonaparte will commute the territory for money. Its acquisition is of immense importance to France and has long been an object of her extreme solicitude. The attempt therefore to purchase, in the first instance, will certainly fail, and in the end war must be resorted to, under all the accumulation of difficulties caused by a previous and strongly fortified possession of the country by our adversary.

The second plan is, therefore, evidently the best. First, because effectual: the acquisition easy; the preservation afterwards easy: The evils of a war with France at this time are certainly not very formidable: Her fleet crippled and powerless, her treasury empty, her resources almost dried up, in short, gasping for breath after a tremendous conflict which, though it left her victorious, left her nearly exhausted under her extraordinary exertions. On the other hand, we might count with certainty on the aid of Great Britain with her powerful navy.

Secondly, this plan is preferable because it affords us the only chance of avoiding a long-continued war. When we have once taken possession, the business will present itself to France in a new aspect. She will then have to weigh the immense difficulties, if not the utter impracticability of wresting it from us.

In this posture of affairs she will naturally conclude it is her interest to bargain. Now it may become expedient to terminate hostilities by a purchase, and a cheaper one may reasonably be expected.

To secure the better prospect of final success, the following auxiliary measures ought to be adopted.

The army should be increased to ten thousand men, for the purpose of ensuring the preservation of the conquest. Preparations for increasing our naval force should be made. The militia should be classed, and effectual provision made for raising on an emergency 40,000 men. Negotiations should be pushed with Great Britain, to induce her to hold herself in readiness to cooperate fully with us, at a moment's warning.

This plan should be adopted and proclaimed before the departure of our envoy.

Such measures would astonish and disconcert Bonaparte himself; our envoy would be enabled to speak and treat with effect; and all Europe would be taught to respect us.

These ideas have been long entertained by the writer, but he has never given himself the trouble to commit them to the public, because he despaired of their being adopted. They are now thrown out with very little hope of their producing any change in the conduct of administration, yet, with the encouragement that there is a strong current of public feeling in favor of decisive measures.

If the president would adopt this course, he might yet retrieve his character, induce the best part of the community to look favorably on his political career, exalt himself in the eyes of Europe, save the country, and secure a permanent fame. But for this, alas! Jefferson is not destined!

Pericles

Purchase of Louisiana,
July 5, 1803

Purchase of Louisiana. At length the business of New Orleans has terminated favorably to this country. Instead of being obliged to rely any longer on the force of treaties for a place of deposit, the jurisdiction of the territory is now transferred to our hands and in future the navigation of the Mississippi will be ours unmolested. This, it will be allowed, is an important acquisition, not, indeed, as territory, but as being essential to the peace and prosperity of our western country, and as opening a free and valuable market to our commercial states. This purchase has been made during the period of Mr. Jefferson's presidency and, will, doubtless, give eclat to his administration. Every man, however, possessed of the least candor and reflection will readily acknowledge that the acquisition has been solely owing to a fortuitous concurrence of unforeseen and unexpected circumstances, and not to any wise or vigorous measures on the part of the American government.

As soon as we experienced from Spain a direct infraction of an important article of our treaty, in withholding the deposit of New Orleans, it afforded us justifiable cause of war and authorized immediate hostilities. Sound policy unquestionably demanded of us to begin with a prompt, bold, and vigorous resistance against the injustice: to seize the object at once; and having this *vantage ground*, should we have thought it advisable to terminate hostilities by a purchase, we might then have done it on almost our own terms. This course, however, was not adopted, and we were about to experience the fruits of our folly when another nation has found it her interest to place the French government in a situation substantially as favorable to our views and interests as those recommended by the Federal party here, excepting indeed that we should probably have obtained the same object on better terms.

On the part of France the short interval of peace had been wasted in repeated and fruitless efforts to subjugate St. Domingo; and those means which were originally destined to the colonization of Louisiana had been gradually exhausted by the unexpected difficulties of this ill-starred enterprise.

To the deadly climate of St. Domingo, and to the courage and obstinate resistance made by its black inhabitants, are we indebted for the obstacles which delayed the colonization of Louisiana till the auspicious moment when a rupture between England and France gave a new turn to the projects of the latter and destroyed at once all her schemes as to this favorite object of her ambition.

It was made known to Bonaparte that among the first objects of England would be the seizure of New Orleans and that preparations were even then in a state of forwardness for that purpose. The First Consul could not doubt that if an English fleet was sent thither, the place must fall without resistance; it was obvious, therefore, that it would be in every shape preferable that it should be placed in the possession of a neutral power; and when, besides, some millions of money, of which he was extremely in want, were offered him, to part with what he could no longer hold, it affords a moral certainty that it was to an accidental state of circumstances, and not to wise plans, that this cession at this time has been owing. We shall venture to add that neither of the ministers through whose instrumentality it was effected will ever deny this or even pretend that previous to the time when a rupture was believed to be inevitable there was the smallest chance of inducing the First Consul, with his ambitious and aggrandizing views, to commute the territory for any sum of money in their power to offer. The real truth is, Bonaparte found himself absolutely compelled by situation to relinquish his darling plan of colonizing the banks of the Mississippi: and thus have the government of the United States, by the unforeseen operation of events, gained what the feebleness and pusillanimity of its miserable system of measures could never have acquired. Let us then, with all due humility, acknowledge this as another of those signal instances of the kind interpositions of an overruling Providence, which we more especially experienced during our revolutionary war, & by which we have more than once been saved from the consequences of our errors and perverseness.

We are certainly not disposed to lessen the importance of this acquisition to the country, but it is proper that the public should be correctly informed of its real value and extent as well as of the terms on which it has been acquired. We perceive by the newspapers that various & very vague opinions are entertained; and we shall therefore venture to state our ideas with some precision as to the territory; but until the instrument of cession itself is published, we do not think it prudent to say much as to the conditions on which it has been obtained.

Prior to the Treaty of Paris 1763, France claimed the country on both sides of the river under the name of Louisiana, and it was her encroachments on the rear of the British colonies which gave rise to the war of 1755. By the conclusion of the treaty of 1763, the limits of the colonies of Great Britain and France were clearly and permanently fixed; and it is from that and subsequent treaties that we are to ascertain what territory is really comprehended under the name of Louisiana. France ceded to Great Britain all the country east and southeast of a line drawn along the middle of the Mississippi from its source to the Iberville, and from thence along that river and the Lakes Maurepas and Pontchartrain to the sea; France retaining the country lying west of the river, besides the town and Island of New Orleans on the east side. This she soon after ceded to Spain, who acquiring also the Floridas by the treaty of 1783, France was entirely shut out from the continent of North America. Spain, at the instance of Bonaparte, ceded to him Louisiana, including the town and island (as it is commonly called) of New Orleans. Bonaparte has now ceded the same tract of country, and this only, to the United States. The whole of East and West-Florida, lying south of Georgia and of the Mississippi Territory, and extending to the Gulf of Mexico, still remains to Spain, who will continue, therefore, to occupy, as formerly, the country along the southern frontier of the United States, and the east bank of the river, from the Iberville to the American line.

Those disposed to magnify its value will say that this western region is important as keeping off a troublesome neighbor and leaving us in the quiet possession of the Mississippi. Undoubtedly this has some force, but on the other hand it may be said that the acquisition of New Orleans is perfectly adequate to every purpose; for whoever is in possession of that has the uncontrolled command of the river. Again, it may be said, and this probably is the most favorable point of view in which it can be placed, that although not valuable to the United States for settlement, it is so to Spain, and will become more so, and therefore at some distant period will form an object which we may barter with her for the Floridas, obviously of far greater value to us than all the immense, undefined region west of the river.

It has been usual for the American writers on this subject to include the Floridas in their ideas of Louisiana, as the French formerly did, and the acquisition has derived no inconsiderable portion of its value and importance with the public from this view of it. It may, however, be relied on, that no part of the Floridas, not a foot of land on the east of the Mississippi, excepting New Orleans, falls within the present cession. As to the unbounded region west of the Mississippi, it is, with the exception of a very few settlements of Spaniards and Frenchmen bordering on the banks of the river, a wilderness through which wander numerous tribes of Indians. And when we consider the present extent of the United States, and that not one sixteenth part of its territory is yet under occupation, the advantage of the acquisition, as it relates to actual settlement, appears too distant and remote to strike the mind of a sober politician with much force. This, therefore, can only rest in speculation for many years, if not centuries to come, and consequently will not perhaps be allowed very great weight in the account by the majority of readers. But it may be added that should our own citizens, more enterprising than wise, become desirous of settling this country and emigrate thither, it must not only be attended with all the injuries of a too widely dispersed population, but by adding to the great weight of the western part of our territory must hasten the dismemberment of a large portion of our country, or a dissolution of the government. On the whole, we think it may with candor be said that whether the possession at this time of any territory west of the river Mississippi will be advantageous is at best extremely problematical. For ourselves, we are very much inclined to the opinion that, after all, it is the Island of N. Orleans, by which the command of a free navigation of the Mississippi is secured, that gives to this interesting cession its greatest value, and will render it in every view of immense benefit to our country. By this cession we hereafter shall hold within our own grasp what we have heretofore enjoyed only by the uncertain tenure of a treaty, which might be broken at the pleasure of another and (governed as we now are) with perfect impunity. Provided therefore we have not purchased it too dear, there is all the reason for exultation which the friends of the administration display and which all Americans may be allowed to feel.

As to the pecuniary value of the bargain, we know not enough of the particulars to pronounce upon it. It is understood generally that we are to assume *debts* of France to our own citizens not exceeding four millions of dollars; and that for the remainder, being a very large sum, 6 per cent stock to be created, and payment made in that. But should it contain no conditions or stipulations on our part, no "tangling alliances," of all things to be dreaded, we shall be very much inclined to regard it in a favorable point of view, though it should turn out to be what may be called a costly purchase. By the way, a question here presents itself of some little moment: Mr. Jefferson in that part of his famous electioneering message, where he took so much pains to present a flattering state of the treasury in so few words that every man could carry it in his noddle and repeat it at the poll, tells us that "experience too so far authorizes us to believe, *if no extraordinary event supervenes, and the expenses which will be actually incurred shall not be greater than was contemplated* by Congress at their last session, that we shall not be disappointed in the expectations formed" that the debt would soon be paid, &c. &c. But the first and only measure of the administration that has really been of any material service to the country (for they have hitherto gone on the strength of the provisions made by their predecessors) is really "*an extraordinary event*," and calls for more money than they have got. According to Mr. Gallatin's report, they had about 40,000 to spare for contingencies, and now the first "*extraordinary event*" that "*supervenes*" calls upon them for several millions. What a poor starveling system of administering a government! *But how is the money to be had? Not by taxing luxury and wealth and whiskey, but by increasing the taxes on the necessaries of life.* Let this be remembered.

But we are exceeding our allowable limits. It may be satisfactory to our readers that we should finish with a concise account of New Orleans itself.

The Island of New Orleans is in length about 150 miles; its breadth varies from 10 to 30 miles. Most of it is a marshy swamp, periodically inundated by the river. The town of New Orleans, situated about 105 miles from the mouth of the river, contains near 1300 houses and about 8000 inhabitants, chiefly Spanish and French. It is defended from the overflowings of the river by an embankment, or *leveé*, which extends near 50 miles.

The rights of the present proprietors of real estate in New Orleans and Louisiana, whether acquired by descent or by purchase, will, of course, remain undisturbed. How they are to be governed is another question; whether as a colony, or to be formed into an integral part of the United States, is a subject which will claim consideration hereafter. The probable consequences of this cession, and the ultimate effect it is likely to produce on the political state of our country, will furnish abundant matter of speculation to the American statesman.

If reliance can be placed on the history given of the negotiation of *Louisiana* in private letters from persons of respectability residing at Paris, and who speak with confidence, the merit of it, after making due allowance for the great events which have borne it along with them, is due to our ambassador, Chancellor Livingston, and not to the Envoy Extraordinary. "The cession was voted in the Council of State on the 8th of April, and Mr. Monroe did not even arrive till the 12th." Judging from Mr. Monroe's former communications to the French government on this subject, we really cannot but regard it as fortunate that the thing was concluded before he reached St. Cloud.

Letter to Timothy Pickering, September 16, 1803

My Dear Sir,

I will make no apology for my delay in answering your inquiry some time since made, because I could offer none which would satisfy myself. I pray you only to believe that it proceeded from anything rather than want of respect or regard. I shall now comply with your request.

The highest toned propositions which I made in the Convention were for a president, Senate, and judges during good behavior—a House of Representatives for three years. Though I would have enlarged the legislative power of the general government, yet I never contemplated the abolition of the state governments; but on the contrary they were, in some particulars, constituent parts of my plan.

This plan was in my conception conformable with the strict theory of a government purely republican, the essential criteria of which are that the principal organs of the executive and legislative departments be elected by the people and hold their offices by a *responsible* and temporary or *defeasible* tenure.

A vote was taken on the proposition respecting the executive. Five states were in favor of it, among those Virginia; and though from the manner of voting, by delegations, individuals were not distinguished, it was morally certain, from the known situation of the Virginia members (six in number, two of them, *Mason* and *Randolph*, possessing popular doctrines) that *Madison* must have concurred in the vote of Virginia. Thus, if I sinned against republicanism, Mr. Madison was not less guilty.

I may truly then say that I never proposed either a president or Senate for life, and that I neither recommended nor meditated the annihilation of the state governments.

And I may add that in the course of the discussions in the Convention, neither the propositions thrown out for debate, nor even those voted in the earlier stages of deliberation, were considered as evidences of a definitive opinion in the proposer or voter. It appeared to me to be in some sort understood that with a view to free investigation experimental propositions might be made, which were to be received merely as suggestions for consideration.

Accordingly, it is a fact that my final opinion was against an executive during good behavior, on account of the increased danger to the public tranquility incident to the election of a magistrate of this degree of permanency. In the plan of a constitution, which I drew up while the convention was sitting & which I communicated to Mr. Madison about the close of it, perhaps a day or two after, the office of president has no greater duration than for three years.[11]

This plan was predicated upon these bases—1. That the political principles of the people of this country would endure nothing but republican government. 2. That in the actual situation of the country, it was in itself right and proper that the republican theory should have a fair and full trial—3. That to such a trial it was essential that the government should be so constructed as to give it all the energy and stability reconcilable with the principles of that theory. These were the genuine sentiments of my heart, and upon them I acted.

I sincerely hope that it may not hereafter be discovered that, through want of sufficient attention to the last idea, the experiment of republican government, even in this country, has not been as complete, as satisfactory, and as decisive as could be wished.

Very truly   Dear Sir Yr friend & servt
A. Hamilton

Speech at a Meeting of Federalists in Albany, New York, February 10, 1804

Reasons why it is desirable that Mr. Lansing rather than Col. Burr should succeed.[12]

1. Col Burr has steadily pursued the track of Democratic policies. This he has done either from *principle* or from *calculation*. If the former, he is not likely now to change his plan, when the Federalists are prostrate and their enemies predominant. If the latter, he will certainly not at this time relinquish the ladder of his ambition and espouse the cause or views of the weaker party.

2. Though detested by some of the leading Clintonians, he is certainly not personally disagreeable to the great body of them; and it will be no difficult task for a man of talents, intrigue, and address possessing this chair of government to rally the great body of them under his standard and thereby to consolidate for personal purposes the mass of Clintonians, his own adherents among the Democrats, and such Federalists as from personal good will or interested motives may give him support.

3. The effect of his elevation will be to reunite under a more adroit, able, and daring chief the now scattered fragments of the Democratic party and to reinforce it by a strong detachment from the Federalists. For though virtuous Federalists who from miscalculation may support him, would afterwards relinquish his standard, a large number from various motives would continue attached to it.

4. A further effect of his elevation by the aid of Federalists will be to present to the confidence of New England a man already the man of the Democratic leaders of that country, and towards whom the mass of the people have no weak predilection as their countryman, as the grandson of President Edwards, and the son of President Burr. In vain will certain men resist this predilection when it can be said that he was chosen governor of this state, in which he was best known principally or in a great degree by the aid of Federalists.

5. This will give him fair play to disorganize New England if so disposed, a thing not very difficult when the strength of the Democratic party in each of the N. E. states is considered and the natural tendency of our civil institutions is duly weighed.

6. The ill opinion of Jefferson and jealousy of the ambition of Virginia is no inconsiderable prop of good principles in that country. But these causes

are leading to an opinion that a dismemberment of the Union is expedient. It would probably suit Mr. Burr's views to promote this result to be the chief of the northern portion—And placed at the head of the state of New York no man would be more likely to succeed.

7. If he be truly, as the Federalists have believed, a man of irregular and insatiable ambition; if his plan has been to rise to power on the ladder of Jacobinic principles, it is natural to conclude that he will endeavor to fix himself in power by the same instrument, that he will not lean on a fallen and falling party, generally speaking of a character not to favor usurpation and the ascendancy of a despotic chief. Every day shows more and more the much to be regretted tendency of governments entirely popular to dissolution and disorder. Is it rational to expect that a man who had the sagacity to foresee this tendency, and whose temper would permit him to bottom his aggrandizement on popular prejudices and vices, would desert this system at a time when more than ever the state of things invites him to adhere to it?

8. If Lansing is governor his personal character affords some security against pernicious extremes, and at the same time renders it morally certain that the Democratic party, already much divided and weakened, will molder and break asunder more and more. This is certainly a state of things favorable to the future ascendancy of the wise and good. May it not lead to a recasting of parties by which the Federalists will gain a great accession of force from former opponents? At any rate, is it not wiser in them to promote a course of things by which schism among the Democrats will be fostered and increased, than one likely, upon a fair calculation to give them a chief better able than any they have yet had to unite and direct them and in a situation to infuse rottenness in the only part of our country which still remains sound—the Federal states of New England?

Propositions on the Law of Libel, February 15, 1804

I. The liberty of the press consists in the right to publish with impunity truth with good motives for justifiable ends, though reflecting on govt., magistracy, or individuals.

II. That the allowance of this right is essential to the preservation of free governmt. The disallowance of it fatal.

III. That its abuse is to be guarded against by subjecting the exercise of it to the animadversion and control of the tribunals of justice; but that this control cannot safely be entrusted to a permanent body of magistracy and requires the effectual cooperation of court and jury.

IV. That to confine the jury to the mere question of publication and the application of terms, without the right of inquiry into the intent or tendency, reserving to the court the exclusive right of pronouncing upon the construction, tendency, and intent of the alleged libel, is calculated to render nugatory the function of the jury, enabling the court to make a libel of any writing whatsoever the most innocent or commendable.

V. That it is the general rule of criminal law that the intent constitutes the crime, and that it is equally a general rule that the intent, mind, or *quo animo* is an inference of fact to be drawn by the jury.

VI. That if there are exceptions to this rule they are confined to cases on which not only the principal fact but its circumstances can be and are specifically defined by statute or judicial precedents.

VII. That in respect to libel there is no such specific and precise definition of facts and circumstances to be found; that consequently it is difficult if not impossible to pronounce that any writing is per se and exclusive of all circumstances libelous: That its libelous character must depend on intent and tendency the one and the other being matter of fact.

VIII. That the definitions or descriptions of libels to be found in the books predicate them upon some malicious or mischievous intent or tendency, to expose individuals to hatred or contempt, or to occasion a disturbance or breach of the peace.

IX. That in determining the character of a libel, the truth or falsehood is in the nature of things a material ingredient, though the truth may not always be decisive but being abused may still admit of a malicious and mischievous intent which may constitute a libel.

X. That in the Roman law, one source of the doctrine of libel, the truth in cases interesting to the public may be given in evidence. That the ancient statutes probably declaratory of the common make the falsehood an ingredient of the crime; that ancient precedents in the court of justice correspond, and that the precedents to this day charge a malicious intent.

XI. That the doctrine of excluding the truth as immaterial originate in a tyrannical and polluted source, the Court of Star Chamber, and that though it prevailed a considerable length of time, yet there are leading precedents down to the Revolution and ever since in which a contrary practice prevailed.

XII. That this doctrine being against reason and natural justice, and contrary to the original principles of the common law enforced by statutory provisions, precedents which support it deserve to be considered in no better light than as *malus usus* which ought to be abolished.

XIII. That in the general distribution of powers in our system of jurisprudence, the cognizance of law belongs to the court, of fact to the jury; that as often as they are not blended the power of the court is absolute and exclusive. That in civil cases it is always so and may rightfully be so exerted. That in criminal cases the law and fact being always blended, the jury for reasons of a political and peculiar nature, for the security of life and liberty, is entrusted with the power of deciding both law and fact.

XIV. That this distinction results.

1. From the ancient forms of pleading in civil cases, none but special pleas being allowed in matter of law, in criminal none but the general issue.

2. From the liability of the jury to attaint on civil cases and the general power of the court, as its substitute in granting new trials and from the exemption of the jury from attaint in criminal cases and the defect of power to control their verdicts by new trials; the test of every legal power being its capacity to produce a definitive effect liable neither to punishment nor control.

XV. That in criminal cases nevertheless the court are the constitutional advisers of the jury in matter of law; who may compromit their consciences by lightly or rashly disregarding that advice; but may still more compromit their consciences by following it, if exercising their judgments with discretion and honesty they have a clear conviction that the charge of the court is wrong.

Letter to Robert G. Harper, February 19, 1804

Dr Sir,

Since the receipt of your letter on the subject of the impeachment of the judges, this is perhaps the first moment that indifferent health and excessive occupation have permitted a reply.

I view the attempts which are making completely in the light you do, and have very little doubt that they are in prosecution of a deliberate plan to prostrate the independence of the judicial department and substitute to the present judges creatures of the reigning party, who will be the supple instruments of oppression and usurpation, under the forms of the Constitution. This being my apprehension of the matter, I shall not be backward to give the scheme all practicable resistance; and certainly, if an impeachment shall be instituted and other prior and indispensable duties will permit, I shall cheerfully aid in the defense of the accused, as a very high obligation. It is not, however, in my power to promise absolutely attendance, because the possibility of it must depend on the time of trial. There is hardly a sitting of our circuit or supreme court at which there are not causes depending which involve the whole fortunes of individuals who place a material reliance on my efforts. Propriety or good faith would not permit me to be absent during these periods; and though the public cause might call me elsewhere I should be convinced that it would be in hands (exclusive of mine) in which it would have every possible advantage.

But notwithstanding the opinion I have expressed, it will not surprise me if the execution of the plan is suspended. It is certain that in this state leading men of the popular party either disapprove the attempt or are fearful of its influence upon the affairs of the party. Hints will probably go to the prompters at Washington which may induce, if not a relinquishment, a postponement.

The Republican party (soi disant) are greatly distracted in this state. The violence of their measures, added to the disappointments of partisans who have been candidates for office, has produced a mass of discontent which threatens their power. Col. Burr intends to profit by it, if he can, and has no bad chance of being lifted to the chair of government by the united efforts of personal adherents among the Democrats, malcontents of the same party, and Federalists too angry to reason.

One consequence of the distraction of the party is the declining of Governor Clinton to be candidate at the next election. A very respectable man as to private character, Chancellor Lansing, is the substitute. He had secretly many competitors and is far from being a general favorite of the party. From this moment it is destined to be split into fragments, unless hereafter reunited under the more skillful, adroit, and able lead of Col. Burr.

You will conclude from this that I do not look forward to his success with pleasure. The conclusion will be true. It is an axiom with me that he will be the most dangerous chief that *Jacobinism* can have; and, in relation to the present question, a full persuasion that he will reunite under him the popular party and give it new force for personal purposes—that a dismemberment of the Union is likely to be one of the first fruits of his elevation, and the overthrow of good principles in our only sound quarter, the north, a result not very remote.

I had rather see Lansing governor & the party broken to pieces. This will be no bad state of things for those who really love their country & understand its true interest.

Yrs. with sincere regard
A. Hamilton

P.S. Since writing the foregoing Chancellor Lansing has declined and chief Justice Lewis is the substitute. Burr's prospect has extremely brightened.

To an Unknown Correspondent, April 13, 1804

Dear Sir,

The post of today brought me a letter from you, and another from Mr. ____. I have no doubt but the latter would serve you if he could, but he cannot at this time.

On the whole I would advise you to return to New York and accept any respectable employment in your way, 'till an opportunity of something better shall occur. 'Tis by patience and perseverance that we can expect to vanquish difficulties, and better an unpleasant condition.

Arraign not the dispensations of Providence—they must be founded in wisdom and goodness; and when they do not suit us, it must be because there is some fault in ourselves which deserves chastisement, or because there is a kind intent to correct in us some vice or failing of which, perhaps, we may not be conscious; or because the general plan requires that we should suffer partial ill.

In this situation it is our duty to cultivate resignation, and even humility, bearing in mind, in the language of the Poet, that it was "*Pride which lost the blest abodes.*"

> With esteem and regard, &c.
> A. Hamilton.

Statement on an Impending Duel With Aaron Burr, June 28–July 10, 1804

On my expected interview with Col. Burr, I think it proper to make some remarks explanatory of my conduct, motives, and views.

I am certainly desirous of avoiding this interview, for the most cogent reasons.

1. My religious and moral principles are strongly opposed to the practice of dueling, and it would even give me pain to be obliged to shed the blood of a fellow creature in a private combat forbidden by the laws.
2. My wife and children are extremely dear to me, and my life is of the utmost importance to them, in various views.
3. I feel a sense of obligation towards my creditors, who, in case of accident to me, by the forced sale of my property, may be in some degree sufferers. I did not think myself at liberty, as a man of probity, lightly to expose them to this hazard.
4. I am conscious of no *ill-will* to Col. Burr, distinct from political opposition, which, as I trust, has proceeded from pure and upright motives.

Lastly, I shall hazard much, and can possibly gain nothing by the issue of the interview.

But it was, as I conceive, impossible for me to avoid it. There were *intrinsic* difficulties in the thing and *artificial* embarrassments from the manner of proceeding on the part of Col. Burr.

Intrinsic—because it is not to be denied that my animadversions on the political principles, character, and views of Col. Burr have been extremely severe, and on different occasions I, in common with many others, have made very unfavorable criticisms on particular instances of the private conduct of this gentleman.

In proportion as these impressions were entertained with sincerity and uttered with motives and for purposes which might appear to me commendable, would be the difficulty (until they could be removed by evidence of their being erroneous) of explanation or apology. The disavowal required of me by Col. Burr, in a general and indefinite form, was out of my power, if it had really been proper for me to submit to be so questioned; but I was sincerely of opinion that this could not be, and in this opinion I was confirmed by that of a very moderate and judicious friend whom I consulted. Besides that Col. Burr appeared to me to assume, in the first instance, a tone unnecessarily peremptory and menacing, and in the second, positively offensive. Yet I wished, as far as might be practicable, to leave a door open to accommodation. This, I think, will be inferred from the written communications made by me and by my direction, and would be confirmed by the conversations between Mr. van Ness and myself, which arose out of the subject.

I am not sure whether under all the circumstances I did not go further in the attempt to accommodate than a punctilious delicacy will justify. If so, I hope the motives I have stated will excuse me.

It is not my design by what I have said to affix any odium on the conduct of Col. Burr in this case. He doubtless has heard of animadversions of mine which bore very hard upon him, and it is probable that as usual they were accompanied with some falsehoods. He may have supposed himself under a necessity of acting as he has done. I hope the grounds of his proceeding have been such as ought to satisfy his own conscience.

I trust, at the same time, that the world will do me the justice to believe that I have not censured him on light grounds or from unworthy inducements. I certainly have had strong reasons for what I may have said, though it is possible that in some particulars I may have been influenced by misconstruction or misinformation. It is also my ardent wish that I may have been more mistaken than I think I have been, and that he by his future conduct may show himself worthy of all confidence and esteem, and prove an ornament and blessing to his country.

As well because it is possible that I may have injured Col. Burr, however convinced myself that my opinions and declarations have been well founded, as from my general principles and temper in relation to similar affairs—I have resolved, if our interview is conducted in the usual manner, and it pleases God to give me the opportunity, to *reserve* and *throw away* my first fire, and I *have thoughts* even of *reserving* my second fire—and thus giving a double opportunity to Col. Burr to pause and to reflect.

It is not, however, my intention to enter into any explanations on the ground. Apology, from principle I hope, rather than pride, is out of the question.

To those who, with me, abhorring the practice of dueling, may think that I ought on no account to have added to the number of bad examples—I answer that my *relative* situation, as well in public as private aspects, enforcing all the considerations which constitute what men of the world denominate honor, impressed on me (as I thought) a peculiar necessity not to decline the call. The ability to be in future useful, whether in resisting mischief or effecting good, in those crises of our public affairs which seem likely to happen, would probably be inseparable from a conformity with public prejudice in this particular.

A.H.

Letter to Elizabeth Hamilton, July 4, 1804

This letter, my very dear Eliza, will not be delivered to you unless I shall first have terminated my earthly career, to begin, as I humbly hope from redeeming grace and divine mercy, a happy immortality.

If it had been possible for me to have avoided the interview, my love for you and my precious children would have been alone a decisive motive. But it was not possible without sacrifices which would have rendered me unworthy of your esteem. I need not tell you of the pangs I feel from the idea of quitting you and exposing you to the anguish which I know you would feel. Nor could I dwell on the topic lest it should unman me.

The consolations of religion, my beloved, can alone support you; and these you have a right to enjoy. Fly to the bosom of your God and be comforted. With my last idea I shall cherish the sweet hope of meeting you in a better world.

Adieu, best of wives and best of women. Embrace all my darling children for me.

Ever yours,
A.H.

Letter to Elizabeth Hamilton, July 10, 1804

My beloved Eliza,

Mrs. Mitchell is the person in the world to whom as a friend I am under the greatest obligations. I have not hitherto done my duty to her. But resolved to repair my omission as much as possible, I have encouraged her to come to this country and intend, if it shall be in my power, to render the evening of her days comfortable. But if it shall please God to put this out of my power and to enable you hereafter to be of service to her, I entreat you to do it and to treat her with the tenderness of a sister.

This is my second letter.

The scruples of a Christian have determined me to expose my own life to any extent rather than subject myself to the guilt of taking the life of another. This must increase my hazards & redoubles my pangs for you. But you had rather I should die innocent than live guilty. Heaven can preserve me and I humbly hope will; but in the contrary event, I charge you to remember that you are a Christian. God's Will be done. The will of a merciful God must be good.

Once more Adieu my darling, darling wife
A.H.

Letter to Theodore Sedgwick, July 10, 1804

My Dear Sir,

I have received two letters from you since we last saw each other—that of the latest date being the 24 of May. I have had in hand for some time a long letter to you, explaining my view of the course and tendency of our politics and my intentions as to my own future conduct. But my plan embraced so large a range that owing to much avocation, some indifferent health, and a growing distaste for politics, the letter is still considerably short of being finished. I write this now to satisfy you that want of regard for you has not been the cause of my silence.

I will here express but one sentiment, which is that dismemberment of our empire will be a clear sacrifice of great positive advantages without any counterbalancing good, administering no relief to our real disease, which is Democracy, the poison of which by a subdivision will only be the more con-centered in each part, and consequently the more virulent.

King is on his way for Boston, where you may chance to see him and hear from himself his sentiments.

God bless you
A.H.

Explanatory Notes

1 The original says "persons" but Hamilton surely meant "prior."
2 Hamilton had written "inconvenience," but this was probably inadvertent. The context strongly suggests "convenience."
3 The original reads "scat of government." It is hard to avoid the conclusion that this should read "seat," as we have corrected it to read.
4 This is likely a reference to Albert Gallatin, Swiss immigrant and Jefferson's secretary of the treasury. See *PAH*, 25: 494 n. 5.
5 These remarks were made to a meeting of the New York City bar and are here presented as they were published in the New York *Commercial Advertiser*. See *PAH*, 25: 520 n. 1.
6 The original says "press" but Hamilton must have intended "purse" in this context.
7 The original reads "resolution" but we think this emendation a sound one.

8 In the margin Hamilton marked this paragraph "especially confidential." See *PAH*, 25: 608.

9 Hamilton's editors note that this is from Virgil's *Aeneid*, book 3, line 659. It is a description of the Cyclops. The full quotation is: "Monstrum horrendum informe ingens cui lumen ademptum." It is literally translated: "a dreadful monster, shapeless, huge, and blind." See *PAH*, 26: 13 n. 6.

10 Hamilton had written "Decomocracy," intending, we think, "Democracy."

11 Hamilton is mistaken here. Whatever he may have thought about the issue at the end, or after the end, of the Convention, the "Plan of Government" to which he refers retains the executive serving during good behavior that he had proposed earlier in the convention. See Volume I, Part 3 of the present work.

12 The issue here is who should be elected governor of New York.

APPENDIX

Hamilton's Death and Legacy

Letter from Benjamin Moore to William Coleman, July 12, 1804[1]

Mr. Coleman,

The public mind being extremely agitated by the melancholy fate of that great man, ALEXANDER HAMILTON, I have thought it would be grateful to my fellow citizens, would provide against misrepresentation, and perhaps be conducive to the advancement of the cause of religion, were I to give a narrative of some facts which have fallen under my own observation during the time which elapsed between the fatal duel and his departure out of this world.

Yesterday morning, immediately after he was brought from Hoboken to the house of Mr. Bayard at Greenwich, a message was sent informing me of the sad event, accompanied by a request from General Hamilton that I would come to him for the purpose of administering the holy Communion. I went; but being desirous to afford time for serious reflection, and conceiving that under existing circumstances it would be right and proper to avoid every appearance of precipitancy in performing one of the most solemn offices of our religion, I did not then comply with his desire. At one o'clock I was again called on to visit him. Upon my entering the room and approaching his bed, with the utmost calmness and composure he said, "My dear Sir, you perceive my unfortunate situation, and no doubt have been made acquainted with the circumstances which led to it. It is my desire to receive the Communion at your hands. I hope you will not conceive there is any impropriety in my request." He added, "It has for some time past been the wish of my heart, and it was my intention to take an early opportunity of uniting myself to the church, by the reception of that holy ordinance." I observed to him that he must be very sensible of the delicate and trying situation in which I was then placed; that however desirous I might be to afford consolation to a fellow mortal in distress; still, it was my duty as a minister of the Gospel to hold up the law of God as paramount to all other law; and that, therefore, under the influence of such sentiments, I must unequivocally condemn the practice which had brought him to his present unhappy condition. He acknowledged the propriety of these sentiments and declared that he viewed the late transaction with sorrow and contrition. I then asked him, "Should it please God to restore you to health, Sir, will you never be again engaged in a similar transaction, and will you employ all your influence in society to discountenance this barbarous custom?" His answer was, "That, Sir, is my deliberate intention."

I proceeded to converse with him on the subject of his receiving the Communion; and told him that with respect to the qualifications of those who wished to become partakers of that holy ordinance, my inquiries could not be made in language more expressive than that which was used by our Church. "Do you sincerely repent of your sins past? Have you a lively faith in God's mercy through Christ, with a thankful remembrance of the death of Christ? And are you disposed to live in love and charity with all men?" He lifted up his hands and said, "With the utmost sincerity of heart I can answer those questions in the affirmative—I have no ill will against Col. Burr. I met him with a fixed resolution to do him no harm. I forgive all that happened." I then observed to him that the terrors of the divine law were to be announced to the obdurate and impenitent, but that the consolations of the Gospel were to be offered to the humble and contrite heart, that I had no reason to doubt his sincerity and would proceed immediately to gratify his wishes. The Communion was then administered, which he received with great devotion, and his heart afterwards appeared to be perfectly at rest. I saw him again this morning, when, with his last faltering words, he expressed a strong confidence in the mercy of God through the intercession of the Redeemer. I remained with him until 2 o'clock this afternoon, when death closed the awful scene—he expired without a struggle, and almost without a groan.

By reflecting on this melancholy event, let the humble believer be encouraged ever to hold fast that precious faith which is the only source of true consolation in the last extremity of nature. Let the infidel be persuaded to abandon his opposition to that Gospel which the strong, inquisitive, and comprehensive mind of a HAMILTON embraced, in his last moments, as the truth from heaven. Let those who are disposed to justify the practice of dueling be induced by this simple narrative to view with abhorrence that custom which has occasioned in irreparable loss to a worthy and most afflicted family: which has deprived his friends of a beloved companion, his profession of one of its brightest ornaments, and his country of a great statesman and a real patriot.

With great respect,   I remain   your friend and servant,

Benjamin Moore

Letter from David Hosack to William Coleman, August 17, 1804

Dear Sir,

To comply with your request is a painful task; but I will repress my feelings while I endeavor to furnish you with an enumeration of such particulars relative to the melancholy end of our beloved friend Hamilton as dwell most forcibly on my recollection.

When called to him upon his receiving the fatal wound, I found him half sitting on the ground, supported in the arms of Mr. Pendleton. His countenance of death I shall never forget. He had at that instant just strength to say, "This is a mortal wound, Doctor," when he sunk away and became to all appearance lifeless. I immediately stripped up his clothes, and soon, alas! ascertained that the direction of the ball must have been through some vital part. His pulses were not to be felt; his respiration was entirely suspended; and upon laying my hand on his heart, and perceiving no motion there, I considered him as irrecoverably gone. I, however, observed to Mr. Pendleton that the only chance for his reviving was immediately to get him upon the water. We therefore lifted him up and carried him out of the wood to the margin of the bank, where the bargemen aided us in conveying him into the boat, which immediately put off. During all this time I could not discover the least symptom of returning life. I now rubbed his face, lips, and temples, with spirits of hartshorn, applied it to his neck and breast, and to the wrists and palms of his hands, and endeavored to pour some into his mouth. When we had got, as I should judge, about 50 yards from the shore, some imperfect efforts to breathe were for the first time manifest: in a few minutes he sighed and became sensible to the impression of the hartshorn, or the fresh air of the water: He breathed; his eyes, hardly opened, wandered, without fixing upon any objects; to our great joy he at length spoke: "My vision is indistinct," were his first words. His pulse became more perceptible; his respiration more regular; his sight returned. I then examined the wound to know if there was any dangerous discharge of blood; upon slightly pressing his side it gave him pain, on which I desisted. Soon after recovering his sight, he happened to cast his eye upon the case of pistols, and observing the one that he had had in his hand lying on the outside, he said, "Take care of that pistol; it is undischarged, and still cocked; it may go off and do harm—Pendleton knows (attempting to turn his head towards him) that I did not intend to fire at him." "Yes," said Mr. Pendleton, understanding his wish, "I have already made Dr. Hosack acquainted with your determination as to that." He then closed his eyes and remained calm, without any disposition to speak; nor did he say much afterwards, excepting in reply to my questions as to his feelings. He asked me once or twice how I found his pulse; and he informed me that his lower extremities had lost all feeling, manifesting to me that he entertained no hopes that he should long survive. I changed the posture of his limbs, but to no purpose; they had totally lost their sensibility. Perceiving that we approached the shore, he said, "Let Mrs. Hamilton be immediately sent for—let the event be gradually broken to her; but give her hopes." Looking up we saw his friend Mr. Bayard standing on the wharf in great agitation. He had been told by his servant that Gen. Hamilton, Mr. Pendleton, and myself, had crossed the river in a boat together, and too well he conjectured the fatal errand and foreboded the dreadful result. Perceiving, as we came nearer, that Mr. Pendleton and myself only sat up in the stern sheets, he clasped his hands together in the most violent apprehension; but when I called to him to have a cot prepared, and he at the same moment saw his poor friend lying in the bottom of the boat, he threw up his eyes and burst into a flood of tears and lamentation. Hamilton alone appeared tranquil and composed. We then conveyed him as tenderly as possible up to the house. The distresses of this amiable family were such that till the first shock was abated they were scarcely able to summon fortitude enough to yield sufficient assistance to their dying friend.

Upon our reaching the house he became more languid, occasioned probably by the agitation of his removal from the boat. I gave him a little weak wine and water. When he recovered his feelings, he complained of pain in his back; we immediately undressed him, laid him in bed, and darkened the room. I then gave him a large anodyne, which I frequently repeated. During the first day he took upwards of an ounce of laudanum; and tepid anodyne fomentations were also applied to those parts nearest the seat of his pain. Yet were his sufferings, during the whole of the day, almost intolerable. I had not the shadow of a hope of his recovery, and Dr. Post, whom I requested might be sent for immediately on our reaching Mr. Bayard's house, united with me in this opinion. General Rey, the French Consul, also had the goodness to invite the surgeons of the French frigates in our harbor, as they had had much experience in gunshot wounds, to render their assistance. They immediately came; but to prevent his being disturbed I stated to them his situation, described the nature of his wound and the direction of the ball, with all the symptoms that could enable them to form an opinion as to the event. One of the gentlemen then accompanied me to the bed side. The result was a confirmation of the opinion that had already been expressed by Dr. Post and myself.

During the night he had some imperfect sleep; but the succeeding morning his symptoms were aggravated, attended, however, with a diminution of pain. His mind retained all its usual strength and composure. The great source of his anxiety seemed to be in his sympathy with his half distracted wife and children. He spoke to me frequently of them—"My beloved wife and children" were always his expressions. But his fortitude triumphed over his situation, dreadful as it was; once, indeed, at the sight of his children brought to the bedside together, seven in number, his utterance forsook him; he opened his eyes, gave them one look, and closed them again, till they were taken away. As a proof of his extraordinary composure of mind, let me add, that he alone could calm the frantic grief of their mother. "*Remember, my Eliza, you are a Christian,*" were the expressions with which he frequently, with a firm voice, but in pathetic and impressive manner, addressed her. His words, and the tone in which they were uttered, will never be effaced from my memory. At about two o'clock, as the public well knows, he expired.

> Incorrupta fides—nudaque veritas
> Quando ullum invenient parem?
> Multis ille quidem flebilis occidit.[2]

I am, Sir,   Your friend and humble servant,
David Hosack

Gouverneur Morris, Funeral Oration for Alexander Hamilton, July 14, 1804

Fellow Citizens,

If on this sad, this solemn occasion, I should endeavor to move your commiseration, it would be doing injustice to that sensibility which has been so generally and so justly manifested. Far from attempting to excite your emotions, I must try to repress my own, and yet I fear that instead of the language of a public speaker, you will hear only the lamentations of a bewailing friend. But I will struggle with my bursting heart to portray that heroic spirit, which has flown to the mansions of bliss.

Students of Columbia—he was in the ardent pursuit of knowledge in your academic shades, when the first sound of the American war called him to the field. A young and unprotected volunteer, such was his zeal, and so brilliant his service, that we heard his name before we knew his person. It seemed as if God had called him suddenly into existence, that he might assist to save a world!

The penetrating eye of WASHINGTON soon perceived the manly spirit which animated his youthful bosom. By that excellent judge of men he was selected as an aide, and thus he became early acquainted with and was a principal actor in the most important scenes of our Revolution.

At the siege of York, he pertinaciously insisted—and he obtained the command of a Forlorn Hope. He stormed the redoubt, but let it be recorded that not one single man of the enemy perished. His gallant troops, emulating the heroism of their chief, checked the uplifted arm, and spared a foe no longer resisting. Here closed his military career.

Shortly after the war, your favor—no, your discernment called him to public office. You sent him to the convention at Philadelphia: he there assisted in forming that Constitution which is now the bond of our Union, the shield of our defense, and the source of our prosperity. In signing that compact he expressed his apprehension that it did not contain sufficient means of strength for its own preservation, and that in consequence we should share the fate of many other republics and pass through anarchy to despotism. We hoped better things. We confided in the good sense of the American people: and above all we trusted in the protecting Providence of the Almighty. On this important subject he never concealed his opinion. He disdained concealment. Knowing the purity of his heart, he bore it as it were in his hand, exposing to every passenger its inmost recesses. This generous indiscretion subjected him to censure from misrepresentation. His speculative opinions were treated as deliberate designs; and yet you all know how strenuous, how unremitting were his efforts to establish and to preserve the Constitution. If, then, his opinion was wrong, pardon, oh! pardon that single error in a life devoted to your service.

At the time when our government was organized, we were without funds, though not without resources. To call them into action and establish order in the finances, Washington sought for splendid talents, for extensive information, and, above all, he sought for sterling, incorruptible integrity—All these he found in HAMILTON. The system then adopted has been the subject of much animadversion. If it be not without a fault, let it be remembered that nothing human is perfect. Recollect the circumstances of the moment—recollect the conflict of opinion—and above all, remember that *the minister of a republic must bend to the will of the people*. The administration which Washington formed was one of the most efficient, one of the best that any country was ever blessed with. And the result was a rapid advance in power and prosperity, of which there is no example in any other age or nation. The part which Hamilton bore is universally known.

His unsuspecting confidence in professions which he believed to be sincere, led him to trust too much to the undeserving. This exposed him to misrepresentation. He felt himself obliged to resign. The care of a rising family, and the narrowness of his fortune, made it a duty to return to his profession for their support. But though he was compelled to abandon public life, never, no, never for a moment did he abandon the public service. He never lost sight of your interests. I declare to you, before that God in whose presence we are now so especially assembled, that in his most private and confidential conversations the single objects of discussion and consideration were your freedom and happiness.

You well remember the state of things which again called forth Washington from his retreat to lead your armies. You know that he asked for Hamilton to be his second in command. That venerable sage well knew the dangerous incidents of a military profession, and he felt the hand of time pinching life at its source. It was probable that he would soon be removed from the scene, and that his second would succeed to the command. He knew by experience the importance of that place—and he thought the sword of America might safely be confided to the hand which now lies cold in that coffin. Oh! my fellow citizens, remember this solemn testimonial, that he was not ambitious. Yet, he was charged with ambition: and wounded by the imputation, when he laid down his command, he declared in the proud independence of his soul, that he never would accept of any office, unless in a foreign war he should be called on to expose his life in defense of his country. This determination was immovable. It was his fault that his opinions and his resolutions could not be changed. Knowing his own firm purpose, he was indignant at the charge that he sought for place or power. He was ambitious only of glory, but he was deeply solicitous for you. For himself he feared nothing, but he feared that bad men might by false professions acquire your confidence and abuse it to your ruin.

Brethren of the Cincinnati—There lies our chief! Let him still be our model. Like him, after a long and faithful public service, let us cheerfully perform the social duties of private life. Oh! he was mild and gentle. In him there was no offense, no guile. His generous hand and heart were open to all.

Gentlemen of the bar—You have lost your brightest ornament. Cherish and imitate his example. While, like him, with justifiable, with laudable zeal, you pursue the interests of your clients, remember, like him, the eternal principles of justice.

Fellow citizens—You have long witnessed his professional conduct and felt his unrivaled eloquence. You know how well he performed the duties of a citizen—you know that he never courted your favor by adulation or the sacrifice of his own judgment. You have seen him contending against you and saving your dearest interests, as it were, in spite of yourselves. And you now feel and enjoy the benefits resulting from the firm energy of his conduct. Bear this testimony to the memory of my departed friend. I CHARGE YOU TO PROTECT HIS FAME—it is all he has left—all that these poor orphan children will inherit from their father. But, my countrymen, that fame may be a rich treasure to you also. Let it be the test by which to examine those who solicit your favor. Disregarding professions, view their conduct and on a doubtful occasion, ask, *Would Hamilton have done this thing?*

You all know how he perished. On this last scene, I cannot, I must not dwell. It might excite emotions too strong for your better judgment. Suffer not your indignation to lead to any act which might again offend the insulted majesty of the law. On his part, as from his lips, though with my voice—for his voice you will hear no more—let me entreat you to respect yourself.

And now, ye ministers of the everlasting God, perform your holy office and commit these ashes of our departed brother to the bosom of the grave!

Excerpt from a Letter from Charles Cotesworth Pinckney to Col. W.S. Smith, August 18, 1804

Sir,

With deep affliction, I received the account of our irreparable loss by the death of our late President-General. This deplorable event has been sensibly felt and lamented in this part of the Union, even by those who were not personally acquainted with him, and who did not coincide with him in politics. By me, who have witnessed his calm intrepidity and heroic valor on trying occasions, and was acquainted with his transcendent abilities and amiable qualities, and honored with his particular friendship, his loss is most poignantly felt, and his memory will be ever most affectionately revered.

Is there no way of abolishing, throughout the Union, this absurd and barbarous custom, to the observance of which he fell a victim? Dueling is no criterion of bravery; for I have seen cowards fight duels, and I am convinced real courage may often be better shown in the refusal than in the acceptance of a challenge....

Your most obedient servant,
Charles Cotesworth Pinckney,
V. P. G. S. C.

Fisher Ames: A Sketch Of The Character Of Alexander Hamilton, July 1804

"I have a message full of sorrow to deliver to you; would it were not so!—
Achilles is no more."
Hom. Il.

The following sketch, written immediately after the death of the ever to be lamented
HAMILTON, was read to a select company of friends, and at their desire it first
appeared in the Repertory, July, 1804.

There are so many persons, who, from various causes, possess only a superficial
knowledge of the character of eminent men, that it is to be expected, the
extraordinary marks of grief manifested by the public, on the death of General
HAMILTON, will to some appear strange and to others excessive. America,
they may say, has produced many great men—some are dead, and others remain
alive. Why then should we mourn, as if with a sense of desolation and surprise,
for a loss that, by the lot of human nature, has already become familiar; and
why mourn so much, as if all was lost, when we have so many great men left?

But although General HAMILTON has, for some years, withdrawn from
public office to the bar, and has been, in some measure, out of the view and contemplation of his countrymen, there was nevertheless a splendor in his character
that could not be contracted within the ordinary sphere of his employments.

It is with really great men as with great literary works: the excellence of both
is best tested by the extent and durableness of their impression. The public
has not suddenly, but after an experience of five-and-twenty years, taken that
impression of the just celebrity of ALEXANDER HAMILTON, that nothing
but his extraordinary intrinsic merit could have made, and still less could have
made so deep and maintained so long. In this case, it is safe and correct to judge
by effects. We sometimes calculate the height of a mountain by measuring the
length of its shadow.

It is not a party, for party distinctions, to the honor of our citizens be it said,
are confounded by the event; it is a nation that weeps for its bereavement. We
weep, as the Romans did over the ashes of Germanicus. It is a thoughtful, fore-
boding sorrow that takes possession of the heart, and sinks it with no counter-
feited heaviness.

It is here proper and not invidious to remark, that as the emulation excited
by conducting great affairs commonly trains and exhibits great talents, it is seldom the case that the fairest and soundest judgment of a great man's merit is

to be gained, exclusively, from his associates in counsel or in action. Persons of conspicuous merit themselves are, not unfrequently, bad judges and still worse witnesses on this point; often rivals, sometimes enemies, almost always unjust, and still oftener envious or cold; the opinions they give to the public, as well as those they privately form for themselves, are of course discolored with the hue of their prejudices and resentments.

But the body of the people, who cannot feel a spirit of rivalship towards those whom they see elevated by nature and education so far above their heads, are more equitable, and, supposing a competent time and opportunity for information on the subject, more intelligent judges. Even party rancor, eager to maim the living, scorns to strip the slain. The most hostile passions are soothed or baffled by the fall of their antagonist. Then, if not sooner, the very multitude will fairly decide on character, according to their experience of its impression, and as long as virtue, not unfrequently for a time obscured, is ever respectable when distinctly seen, they cannot withhold, and they will not stint, their admiration.

If, then, the popular estimation is ever to be taken for the true one, the uncommonly profound public sorrow, for the death of ALEXANDER HAMILTON, sufficiently explains and vindicates itself. He had not made himself dear to the passions of the multitude by condescending, in defiance of his honor and conscience, to become their instrument. He is not lamented because a skillful flatterer is now mute forever. It was by the practice of no art, by wearing no disguise, it was not by accident, or by the levity or profligacy of party, but in despite of its malignant misrepresentation, it was by bold and inflexible adherence to truth, by loving his country better than himself, preferring its interest to its favor, and serving it when it was unwilling and unthankful, in a manner that no other person could, that he rose, and the *true* popularity, the homage that is paid to virtue, followed him. It was not in the power of party or envy to pull him down, but he rose with the refulgence of a star, till the very prejudice that could not reach was at length almost ready to adore him.

It is indeed no imagined wound that inflicts so keen an anguish. Since the news of his death, the novel and strange events of Europe have succeeded each other unregarded, the nation has been enchained to its subject, and broods over its grief, which is more deep than eloquent, which though dumb, can make itself felt without utterance, and which does not merely pass, but like an electrical shock, at the same instant smites and astonishes, as it passes from Georgia to New Hampshire.

There is a kind of force put upon our thoughts by this disaster that detains and rivets them to a closer contemplation of those resplendent virtues that are now lost, except to memory, and there they will dwell forever.

That writer would deserve the fame of a public benefactor who could exhibit the character of HAMILTON, with the truth and force that all who intimately knew him conceived it; his example would then take the same ascendant as his talents. The portrait alone, however, exquisitely finished, could not inspire genius where it is not; but if the world should again have possession of so rare a gift, it might awaken it where it sleeps, as by a spark from heaven's own altar; for surely if there is anything like divinity in man, it is in his admiration of virtue.

But who alive can exhibit this portrait? If our age, on that supposition more fruitful than any other, had produced two HAMILTONs, one of them might then have depicted the other. To delineate genius one must feel its power; HAMILTON, and he alone, with all its inspirations, could have transfused its whole fervid soul into the picture, and swelled its lineaments into life. The writer's mind, expanding with his own peculiar enthusiasm, and glowing with kindred fires, would then have stretched to the dimensions of his subject.

Such is the infirmity of human nature, it is very difficult for a man who is greatly the superior of his associates, to preserve their friendship without abatement; yet, though he could not possibly conceal his superiority, he was so little inclined to display it, he was so much at ease in its possession, that no jealousy or envy chilled his bosom, when his friends obtained praise. He was indeed so entirely the friend of his friends, so magnanimous, so superior, or more properly so insensible to all exclusive selfishness of spirit, so frank, so ardent, yet so little overbearing, so much trusted, admired, beloved, almost adored, that his power over their affections was entire, and lasted through his life. We do not believe that he left any worthy man his foe who had ever been his friend.

Men of the most elevated minds have not always the readiest discernment of character. Perhaps he was sometimes too sudden and too lavish in bestowing his confidence; his manly spirit, disdaining artifice, suspected none. But while the power of his friends over him seemed to have no limits, and really had none, in respect to those things which were of a nature to be yielded, no man, not the Roman Cato himself, was more inflexible on every point that touched, or only seemed to touch, integrity and honor. With him, it was not enough to be unsuspected; his bosom would have glowed, like a furnace, at its own whispers of reproach. Mere purity would have seemed to him below praise; and such were his habits, and such his nature, that the pecuniary temptations, which many others can only with great exertion and self-denial resist, had no attractions for him. He was very far from obstinate; yet, as his friends assailed his opinions with less profound thought than he had devoted to them, they were seldom shaken by discussion. He defended them, however, with as much mildness as force, and evinced, that if he did not yield, it was not for want of gentleness or modesty.

The tears that flow on this fond recital will never dry up. My heart, penetrated with the remembrance of the man, grows liquid as I write, and I could pour it out like water. I could weep too for my country, which, mournful as it is, does not know the half of its loss. It deeply laments, when it turns its eyes back, and sees what HAMILTON *was*; but my soul stiffens with despair when I think what HAMILTON *would have been*.

His social affections and his private virtues are not, however, so properly the object of public attention, as the conspicuous and commanding qualities that gave him his fame and influence in the world. It is not as Apollo, enchanting the shepherds with his lyre, that we deplore him; it is as Hercules, treacherously slain in the midst of his unfinished labors, leaving the world overrun with monsters.

His early life we pass over; though his heroic spirit in the army has furnished a theme that is dear to patriotism and will be sacred to glory.

In all the different stations in which a life of active usefulness has placed him, we find him not more remarkably distinguished by the extent, than by the variety and versatility of his talents. In every place he made it apparent that no other man could have filled it so well; and in times of critical importance, in which alone he desired employment, his services were justly deemed absolutely indispensable. As secretary of the treasury, his was the powerful spirit that presided over the chaos:

Confusion heard his voice, and wild uproar
Stood ruled... .[3]

Indeed, in organizing the federal government in 1789, every man of either sense or candor will allow, the difficulty seemed greater than the first-rate abilities could surmount. The event has shown that his abilities were greater than those difficulties. He surmounted them—and Washington's administration was the most wise and beneficent, the most prosperous, and ought to be the most popular, that ever was entrusted with the affairs of a nation. Great as was Washington's merit, much of it in plan, much in execution, will of course devolve upon his minister.

As a lawyer, his comprehensive genius reached the principles of his profession; he compassed its extent, he fathomed its profound, perhaps even more familiarly and easily than the ordinary, rules of its practice. With most men law is a trade; with him it was a science.

As a statesman, he was not more distinguished by the great extent of his views, than by the caution with which he provided against impediments, and the watchfulness of his care over right and the liberty of the subject. In none of the many revenue bills which he framed, though committees reported them, is there to be found a single clause that savors of despotic power; not one that the sagest champions of law and liberty would, on that ground, hesitate to approve and adopt.

It is rare that a man who owes so much to nature descends to seek more from industry; but he seemed to depend on industry, as if nature had done nothing for him. His habits of investigation were very remarkable; his mind seemed to cling to his subject till he had exhausted it. Hence the uncommon superiority of his reasoning powers, a superiority that seemed to be augmented from every source, and to be fortified by every auxiliary, learning, taste, wit, imagination, and eloquence. These were embellished and enforced by his temper and manners, by his fame and his virtues. It is difficult, in the midst of such various excellence, to say in what particular the effect of his greatness was most manifest. No man more promptly discerned truth; no man more clearly displayed it; it was not merely made visible, it seemed to come bright with illumination from his lips. But prompt and clear as he was, fervid as Demosthenes, like Cicero full of resource, he was not less remarkable for the copiousness and completeness of his argument, that left little for cavil, and nothing for doubt. Some men take their strongest argument as a weapon, and use no other; but he left nothing to be inquired for more, nothing to be answered. He not only disarmed his adversaries of their pretexts and objections, but he stripped them of all excuse for having urged them; he confounded and subdued as well as convinced. He indemnified them, however, by making his discussion a complete map of his subject, so that his opponents might, indeed, feel ashamed of their mistakes, but they could not repeat them. In fact, it was no common effort that could preserve a really able antagonist from becoming his convert; for the truth, which his researches so distinctly presented to the understanding of others, was rendered almost irresistibly commanding and impressive by the love and reverence which, it was ever apparent, he profoundly cherished for it in his own. While patriotism glowed in his heart, wisdom blended in his speech her authority with her charms.

Such, also, is the character of his writings. Judiciously collected, they will be a public treasure.

No man ever more disdained duplicity or carried frankness further than he. This gave to his political opponents some temporary advantages, and currency to some popular prejudices, which he would have lived down if his death had not prematurely dispelled them. He knew that factions have ever in the end prevailed in free states; and, as he saw no security (and who living can see any adequate?) against the destruction of that liberty which he loved, and for which he was ever ready to devote his life, he spoke at all times according to his anxious forebodings; and his enemies interpreted all that he said according to the supposed interest of their party.

But he ever extorted confidence, even when he most provoked opposition. It was impossible to deny that he was a patriot, and such a patriot as, seeking neither popularity nor office, without artifice, without meanness, the best Romans in their best days would have admitted to citizenship and to the consulate. Virtue so rare, so pure, so bold, by its very purity and excellence inspired suspicion as a prodigy. His enemies judged of him by themselves; so splendid and arduous were his services, they could not find it in their hearts to believe that they were disinterested.

Unparalleled as they were, they were nevertheless no otherwise requited than by the applause of all good men, and by his own enjoyment of the spectacle of that national prosperity and honor which was the effect of them. After facing calumny, and triumphantly surmounting an unrelenting persecution, he retired from office with clean though empty hands, as rich as reputation and an unblemished integrity could make him.

Some have plausibly, though erroneously, inferred, from the great extent of his abilities, that his ambition was inordinate. This is a mistake. Such men as have a painful consciousness that their stations happen to be far more exalted than their talents are generally the most ambitious. HAMILTON, on the contrary, though he had many competitors, had no rivals; for he did not thirst for power, nor would he, as it was well known, descend to office. Of course he suffered no pain from envy when bad men rose, though he felt anxiety for the public. He was perfectly content and at ease in private life. Of what was he ambitious? Not of wealth; no man held it cheaper. Was it of popularity? That weed of the dunghill he knew, when rankest, was nearest to withering. There is no doubt that he desired glory, which to most men is too inaccessible to be an object of desire; but feeling his own force, and that he was tall enough to reach the top of Pindus or of Helicon, he longed to deck his brow with the wreath of immortality. A vulgar ambition could as little comprehend as satisfy his views; he thirsted only for that fame, which virtue would not blush to confer, nor time to convey to the end of his course.

The only ordinary distinction to which, we confess, he did aspire, was military; and for that, in the event of a foreign war, he would have been solicitous. He undoubtedly discovered the predominance of a soldier's feelings; and all that is honor in the character of a soldier was at home in his heart. His early education was in the camp; there the first fervors of his genius were poured forth, and his earliest and most cordial friendships formed; there he became enamored of glory, and was admitted to her embrace.

Those who knew him best, and especially in the army, will believe that if occasions had called him forth, he was qualified, beyond any man of the age, to display the talents of a great general.

It may be very long before our country will want such military talents; it will probably be much longer before it will again possess them.

Alas! the great man who was at all times so much the ornament of our country, and so exclusively fitted in its extremity to be its champion, is withdrawn to a purer and more tranquil region. We are left to endless labors and unavailing regrets.

> Such honors Ilion to her hero paid,
> And peaceful slept the mighty Hector's shade.[4]

Our Troy has lost her Hector.

The most substantial glory of a country is in its virtuous great men; its prosperity will depend on its docility to learn from their example. That nation is fated to ignominy and servitude for which such men have lived in vain. Power may be seized by a nation that is yet barbarous; and wealth may be enjoyed by one that it finds or renders sordid; the one is the gift and the sport of accident, and the other is the sport of power. Both are mutable, and have passed away without leaving behind them any other memorial than ruins that offend taste, and traditions that battle conjecture. But the glory of Greece is imperishable, or will last as long as learning itself, which is its monument; it strikes an everlasting root, and bears perennial blossoms on its grave. The name of HAMILTON would have honored Greece in the age of Aristides. May Heaven, the guardian of our liberty, grant that our country may be fruitful of HAMILTONs, and faithful to their glory!

Excerpt from a Speech of Daniel Webster, March 24, 1831

Gentlemen, you have personal recollections and associations, connected with the establishment and adoption of the Constitution, which are necessarily called up on an occasion like this. It is impossible to forget the prominent agency exercised by eminent citizens of your own, in regard to that great measure. Those great men are now recorded among the illustrious dead; but they have left names never to be forgotten, and never to be remembered without respect and veneration. Least of all can they be forgotten by you, when assembled here for the purpose of signifying your attachment to the Constitution, and your sense of its inestimable importance to the happiness of the people.

I should do violence to my own feelings, Gentlemen, I think I should offend yours, if I omitted respectful mention of distinguished names yet fresh in your recollections. How can I stand here, to speak of the Constitution of the United States, of the wisdom of its provisions, of the difficulties attending its adoption, of the evils from which it rescued the country, and of the prosperity and power to which it has raised it, and yet pay no tribute to those who were highly instrumental in accomplishing the work? While we are here to rejoice that it yet stands firm and strong, while we congratulate one another that we live under its benign influence, and cherish hopes of its long duration, we cannot forget who they were that, in the day of our national infancy, in the times of despondency and despair, mainly assisted to work out our deliverance. I should feel that I was unfaithful to the strong recollections which the occasion presses upon us, that I was not true to gratitude, not true to patriotism, not true to the living or the dead, not true to your feelings or my own, if I should forbear to make mention of ALEXANDER HAMILTON.

Coming from the military service of the country yet a youth, but with knowledge and maturity, even in civil affairs, far beyond his years, he made this city the place of his adoption; and he gave the whole powers of his mind to the contemplation of the weak and distracted condition of the country. Daily increasing in acquaintance and confidence with the people of New York, he saw, what they also saw, the absolute necessity of some closer bond of union for the states. This was the great object of desire. He never appears to have lost sight of it, but was found in the lead whenever anything was to be attempted for its accomplishment. One experiment after another, as is well known, was tried, and all failed. The states were urgently called on to confer such further powers on the old Congress as would enable it to redeem the public faith, or to adopt, themselves, some general and common principle of commercial regulation. But the states had not agreed, and were not likely to agree. In this posture of affairs, so full of public difficulty and public distress, commissioners from five or six of the states met, on the request of Virginia, at Annapolis, in September, 1786. The precise object of their appointment was to take into consideration the trade of the United States; to examine the relative situations and trade of the several states; and to consider how far a uniform system of commercial regulations was necessary to their common interest and permanent harmony. Mr. Hamilton was one of those commissioners; and I have understood, though I cannot assert the fact, that their report was drawn by him. His associate from this state was the venerable Judge Benson,[5] who has lived long, and still lives, to see the happy results of the counsels which originated in this meeting. Of its members, he and Mr. Madison are, I believe, now the only survivors. These commissioners recommended, what took place the next year, a general convention of all the states, to take into serious deliberation the condition of the country, and devise such provisions as should render the constitution of the federal government adequate to the exigencies of the Union. I need not remind you, that of this convention, Mr. Hamilton was an active and efficient member. The Constitution was framed and submitted to the country. And then another great work was to be undertaken. The Constitution would naturally find, and did find, enemies and opposers. Objections to it were numerous, and powerful, and spirited. They were to be answered; and they were effectually answered. The writers of the numbers of the *Federalist*, Mr. Hamilton, Mr. Madison, and Mr. Jay, so greatly distinguished themselves in their discussions of the Constitution that those numbers are generally received as important commentaries on the text, and accurate expositions, in general, of its objects and purposes. Those papers were all written and published in this city. Mr. Hamilton was elected one of the distinguished delegation from the city to the State Convention at Poughkeepsie, called to ratify the new Constitution. Its debates are published. Mr. Hamilton appears to have exerted, on this occasion, to the utmost, every power and faculty of his mind.

The whole question was likely to depend on the decision of New York. He felt the full importance of the crisis; and the reports of his speeches, imperfect as they probably are, are yet lasting monuments to his genius and patriotism. He saw at last his hopes fulfilled; he saw the Constitution adopted, and the government under it established and organized. The discerning eye of Washington immediately called him to that post, which was far the most important in the administration of the new system. He was made secretary of the treasury; and how he fulfilled the duties of such a place, at such a time, the whole country perceived with delight and the whole world saw with admiration. He smote the rock of the national resources, and abundant streams of revenue gushed forth. He touched the dead corpse of the public credit, and it sprung upon its feet. The fabled birth of Minerva, from the brain of Jove, was hardly more sudden or more perfect than the financial system of the United States, as it burst forth from the conceptions of ALEXANDER HAMILTON.

Chancellor James Kent: Memories of Alexander Hamilton, December 10, 1832

To MRS. ELIZABETH HAMILTON:

DEAR MADAM,

You have requested of me "a detailed reply to the several queries subjoined," and you express a hope that you may not in that request "be regarded as asking more than my friendship to your father and husband would readily grant." I beg leave to assure you that it is sufficient that the application comes from the daughter of General Schuyler and the widow of General Hamilton, to make it command all the information within my power to impart; and I have only to regret that neither my memory nor the materials before me are sufficient to meet the extent of my wishes or to equal your expectations. The following are the questions you have proposed: —

1. "Your early acquaintance with my husband—when, and the circumstances of it?"
2. "His appearance and manners then?"
3. "Any facts connected with his history at the bar before he went into the Treasury, or on his return from it?"
4. "Incidents connected with his services in the Convention at Poughkeepsie, and his last speech there?"
5. "Its effects on the decision of the Convention?"
6. "His characteristic manner of speaking; also the manner of Mr. Jay, Chancellor Livingston, and the principal opponents?"
7. "My father's agency in adopting the Constitution, and Judge Benson's?"
8. "Any anecdotes illustrative of his character or strong expressions?"

There are some points mentioned in those queries on which I have not the requisite information, but as you request me not to consider the inquiries as "limiting the answers," and as you suggest that my "information will relate mostly to his political and civil life," I cannot complain that you have not given me "ample room and verge enough."[6] I shall therefore, with your permission, instead of a special and narrow reply to each question, return one general answer embracing the whole range of inquiry, and endeavor to give a brief but faithful detail of the professional and political life of your eminent husband, so far as the same came within my own knowledge or contemporary observation. It will be convenient, and will tend to give method and perspicuity to my recollections, if we divide the historical sketches of your husband's life in the following manner: —

1. From my first personal knowledge of General Hamilton, in 1782, to the call of the Convention in 1787.
2. His services in relation to the origin and adoption of the federal Constitution.
3. His subsequent life.

I

My personal acquaintance with General Hamilton did not commence until some time after the conclusion of the American War, but I was not then ignorant of the character which he had long sustained, nor of the reputation which he had acquired by his talents and services. While I was a clerk in the office of Egbert Benson, the Attorney General, as early as 1782, I heard it said that he was the author of some essays which had recently appeared in one of the public prints under the signature of *The Continentalist*, the purport of which was to show that the powers of Congress under the Confederation were insufficient and ought to be enlarged. Those essays I never saw, but General Hamilton attracted my particular observation as early as July, 1782, when he was appointed a delegate in Congress from this state. The legislature was then sitting at Poughkeepsie, where I resided, and there I saw him for the first time, though I was too young and too obscure to seek or to merit any personal acquaintance. He was in company with Mr. Benson and Colonel Lawrence, and his animated and didactic conversation, far superior to ordinary discourse in sentiment, language, and manner, and his frank and manly deportment interested and engrossed my attention.

In pursuance of that appointment he took his seat in Congress for the first time in the November following, and we there find him promptly and efficiently engaged in the promotion of measures calculated to relieve the embarrassed state of the public finances, and to avert the difficulties and dangers which beset the Union of the States. His efforts to reanimate the powers of the Confederation, and to infuse life, vigor, and credit into that languishing system, were incessant and masterly; and he was sustained in all his views and assisted in all his measures by his friend and illustrious coadjutor, James Madison. Other members of Congress at that period may have been entitled to an equal share of merit, but their services do not appear to have been equally conspicuous and distinguished.

The proceedings of Congress took a new and more decided tone and character while he was a present and active member, between November, 1782, and July, 1783. Within that period a series of active, intrepid, untiring, but fruitless efforts were made to render the national government under the Articles of Confederation adequate to the support of the Union. It is necessary that we should make a slight reference to the prominent proceedings in Congress, during the session I refer to, in order to perceive clearly and appreciate justly the high character of those efforts, which led on, step by step, to the renewal and consolidation of our Union, and to that rapid and glorious elevation of our country which distinguished the administration of Washington. Thus, on the 6th December, 1782, a motion was made by Mr. Hamilton and carried, that the superintendent of finance represent to the legislatures of the several states the indispensable necessity of complying with the requisitions of Congress for raising specified sums of money towards paying a year's interest on the domestic debt of the United States, and defraying the estimated expenses for the year ensuing, and to assure them that Congress was determined to make the fullest justice to the public creditors an invariable object of their counsels and exertion.

On the 11th of the same month he was chairman of a committee which reported the form of an application to the governor of Rhode Island, urging in most persuasive terms the necessity and reasonableness of a concurrence on the part of that state in the grant to Congress of a general import duty of five percent, in order to raise a fund for the discharge of the public debt. The application was to be accompanied with an assurance that such a grant was the most efficacious, the most expedient, and the most unexceptionable plan of finance that Congress could devise for the occasion; and that the increasing discontents of the army, the loud clamors of the public creditors, and the extreme disproportion between the current supplies and the demands of the public service were so many invincible arguments for the fund recommended by Congress; and that calamities of the most menacing nature might be anticipated if that expedient should fail.

So again, on the 16th December, Mr. Hamilton, Mr. Madison, and Mr. Fitzsimmons made a report of a very superior character in relation to the national finances, and in answer to the objections of the Legislature of Rhode Island against the grant of a general impost. The same discussion was afterwards renewed on the 30th January, 1783, by the report of a committee of which Mr. Hamilton was a member, in which it was stated that Congress had long been deeply impressed with the absolute necessity of taking measures to liquidate the public debts, and to secure the payment of interest until the principal could be discharged; and that the inability of Congress to perform its engagements with the public creditors, under the defective compliance of the states, was most apparent. Congress conceived it to be its duty to persevere in its intentions, and to renew and extend its endeavors to procure the establishment of revenues equal to the purpose of funding all the debts of the United States.

On the 20th March, 1783, Mr. Hamilton submitted a plan and recommendation of a duty of five percent *ad valorem* on imported goods, and a land and house tax, to create funds for the discharge of the debts of the Union; for they had been created, as he observed, on the faith of Congress, for the common safety, and it was its duty to make every effort in its power for doing complete justice to the public creditors. He likewise, on the 22nd of March, as chairman of a committee, reported in favor of a grant of five years' full pay to the officers of the army, as a commutation for the half pay for life promised them by Congress.

At last, on the 18th of April, 1783, Congress finally agreed to recommend to the states a grant of power for twenty-five years to levy specified duties on imported goods, to be applied exclusively to the discharge of the principal and interest of the debts contracted on the faith of the United States for supporting the war, and that other funds for the same purposes be supplied by the states. Mr. Madison, Mr. Ellsworth, and Mr. Hamilton were the committee who reported an address to the states, to accompany the resolution of the 18th of April; and it is rare that the records of the United States furnish the example of a document more replete with sound argument, or which equals it in pathetic and eloquent exhortations. But the exertions of Mr. Hamilton did not cease, nor was the patience of Congress exhausted, in suggesting and adopting measures to preserve the public faith and maintain the dignity and authority of the government. The master spirits which animated and swayed the deliberations of Congress had the merit at least of unconquerable perseverance, and of preserving the national honor, while every other valuable attribute of power was lost.

On the 2nd May, 1783, Mr. Hamilton moved a resolution calling upon the states in the most earnest manner to make such payments into the common treasury as might enable Congress to advance to the officers and soldiers of the army a part of their pay before they left the field, that they might return to their respective homes with convenience and satisfaction. He was also one of the committee which reported the resolution that the noncommissioned officers and soldiers enlisted for the period of the war be allowed their firearms and accoutrements, as an extra reward for their long and faithful services. Nor was this the only occasion in which Colonel Hamilton recollected the gratitude that was due for services in the field. On the 30th December, 1782, he was chairman of the committee which reported resolutions highly honorable to Major-General the Baron de Steuben. The sacrifices and services of that *very* meritorious officer, says the report, were deemed justly to entitle him to the distinguished notice of Congress, and to a generous compensation.

On other subjects General Hamilton, while he held a seat in Congress, showed equal solicitude for the preservation of the public faith, and the safety and authority of the Union. He was chairman of the committee which, on the 30th May, 1783, introduced the resolution calling upon the states to remove every legal obstruction under their local jurisdictions, in the way of the active and faithful execution of the fourth and sixth Articles of the Treaty of Peace; and that all future confiscations and prosecutions for acts done during the war should cease; and that the several states be requested to conform to the fifth article of the treaty with that spirit of moderation and liberality which ought to characterize the measures of a free and enlightened nation. His anxiety to preserve the internal peace of the confederacy was manifest by the resolution, which he seconded and supported, that the people of the district called the New Hampshire Grants—then, in point of fact, assuming to be an independent state—be desired to cease to molest the persons or property of those inhabitants who did not acknowledge their jurisdiction; and that, on the other hand, the persons holding commissions under New York also forbear to exercise any authority under the same, to the end that things might remain as they were until a decision could peaceably be made in the controversy. He was likewise chairman of the committee which stated the efforts which had been made on the part of Congress to suppress the mutinous proceedings of part of the troops of the United States, who had insulted Congress, and which eventually compelled them, from the want of sufficient protection from the executive council of Pennsylvania, to remove from Philadelphia to Princeton in New Jersey.

I have alluded to these documentary proofs as affording the most authentic and the most honorable testimony to the spirit and intelligence with which General Hamilton devoted himself, as early as the year 1782 and 1783, and at his own youthful age of twenty-five, to the support of the integrity and welfare of the Union. And it will abundantly appear in the subsequent history of his life that his zeal for the establishment of a national government, competent to preserve us from insult abroad and dissensions at home, and equally well fitted to uphold credit, to preserve liberty, and to cherish our resources, kept increasing; and that his views grew more and more enlarged and comprehensive as we approached the crisis of our destiny. It will hereafter appear, in the course of these narrative recollections, that he did more with his pen and his tongue than any other man, not only in reference to the origin and adoption of the federal Constitution, but also to create and establish public credit, and defend the government and its measures, under the wise and eventful administration of Washington. Though I was not at the time conscious of the distinguished merit of General Hamilton as a member of Congress, yet his high character for genius, wisdom, and eloquence was everywhere known and acknowledged, and when, in the winter of 1784, his pamphlet productions under the signature of *Phocion* appeared, they excited a general sensation. They were addressed "to the considerate citizens of New York," and their object was to protect the rights of all classes of persons inhabiting the southern district of the state; to put a stop to every kind of proscriptive policy and to the creation of legislative disabilities and bills of attainder, as being equally incompatible with the obligations of the Treaty of Peace, the principles of the Constitution, and the dictates of policy. The appeal to the good sense and patriotism of the public was not in vain. It was unanswerable and irresistible. "The force of plain truth carried the work along against the stream of prejudice," and it overcame every obstacle.

A counter pamphlet, under the signature of *Mentor*, written by Doctor Isaac Ledyard, and representing the inhabitants of the southern district who had remained within the enemy's lines as aliens, subject to penalties and disabilities in the discretion of the legislature, was entirely demolished. A bill before the House of Assembly for putting various descriptions of persons out of the protection of government was abandoned. The rising generation, then just entering on the stage of action, readily imbibed those sentiments of temperate civil liberty and of sound constitutional law which he had so clearly taught and so eloquently inculcated. The benign influence of such doctrines was happily felt and retained through the whole course of the generation to whom they were addressed. I speak for myself, as one of that generation, that no hasty productions of the press could have been more auspicious.

In the summer of 1784, Colonel Hamilton attended the circuit court at Poughkeepsie, and I had then an opportunity, for the first time, of seeing him at the bar as a counselor addressing the court and jury. It was an interesting country circuit. Colonel Lawrence of New York, Peter W. Yates of Albany, Egbert Benson (my revered preceptor, and who still lives, a venerable monument of the wisdom, the integrity, the patriotism, and the intrepidity of the sages of the Revolution), and some other gentlemen of the profession, whose names I do not now recollect, attended the court. I was struck with the clear, elegant, and fluent style and commanding manner of Hamilton. At that day everything in law seemed to be new. Our judges were not remarkable for law learning. We had no precedents of our own to guide us. English books of practice, as well as English decisions, were resorted to and studied with the scrupulous reverence due to oracles. Nothing was settled in our courts. Every point of practice had to be investigated, and its application to our courts and institutions questioned and tested. Mr. Hamilton thought it necessary to produce authorities to demonstrate and to guide the power of the court, even in the now familiar case of putting off a cause for the circuit, and to show that the power was to be exercised, as he expressed it, "in sound discretion and for the furtherance of justice." He never made any argument in court in any case without displaying his habits of thinking, and resorting at once to some well-founded principle of law, and drawing his deductions logically from his premises. Law was always treated by him as a science founded on established principles. His manners were gentle, affable, and kind, and he appeared to be frank, liberal, and courteous in all his professional intercourse. This was my impression at the time.

General Hamilton was employed, while at that circuit, by Major Brown, to defend him on the trial of a suit in trover or trespass then pending, for seizing and converting to his own use British goods, under the pretense that they were the result of illicit commerce with the enemy. The country, towards the close of the American War, was exceedingly destitute of clothing and of all the comforts and conveniences which British manufactures had formerly afforded us. The high price of British goods of all kinds and the wants of the country rendered the temptation to illicit trade with the enemy almost irresistible. The Congress of the United States and the legislatures of New York and some other states vainly endeavored, by ordinances and statutes imposing confiscations and penalties, to put a stop to the corrupt and pernicious traffic. The defendant in the case alluded to had been concerned in the seizure of goods alleged to be of that description, though it was understood at that day that there was generally as much of a predatory and lawless spirit in the persons who seized as in those who traded in the noxious goods. The cause became very interesting. Peter

W. Yates, one of the leading counsel for the plaintiff, was subtle, acute, dry, and practical, and he exceeded my highest expectations; Colonel Lawrence was graceful, fluent, and ingenious; but Colonel Hamilton, by means of his fine melodious voice and dignified deportment, his reasoning powers and persuasive address, soared far above all competition. His preeminence was at once and universally conceded. He was pressed by his client to appeal to the feelings of the jury in favor of the poor and meritorious Whigs, against the secret enemies of their country in the character of traders in British goods. I heard him say, at the time, that he would never be found contending against the principles of *Phocion*, and that he told his anxious client that he could not gratify him to the extent of his wishes. He made, notwithstanding, in point of fact, whether he was conscious of it or not, an animated and powerful appeal to the passions and prejudices of the jury. The audience listened with admiration to his impassioned eloquence, and they were almost ready to yield to the truth of the suggestion which he threw into his address, that a British statesman had remarked that the true way to slacken the zeal and break down the stern devotedness of the American Whigs was to open upon them the flood-gates of commerce.

In January, 1785, I attended for the first time the term of the Supreme Court at Albany and was admitted an attorney; and I had the satisfaction to see General Hamilton come forward as an advocate on a much greater occasion, and with distinguished luster. The case I allude to was the following: Chancellor Livingston claimed lands lying on the south bounds of the lower manor of Livingston, and the claim was large in amount of property. In an ejectment suit brought by Chancellor Livingston, as plaintiff, against Hoffman, the cause was tried at the bar of the Supreme Court at Albany, in October term, 1784; and though Mr. Hamilton was one of the counsel for the defendant, *he* was not one of the counsel assigned to sum up the cause before the jury. The cause was tried with great ability by Mr. Ogden of New Jersey and Mr. Benson, the attorney general, on behalf of the defendant. Chancellor Livingston appeared at the bar as an advocate in his own case, and his concluding address to the jury was said to contain a boldness of illustration and a burst of eloquence never before witnessed at our bar. He rebuked severely the opposite counsel for their attacks on the character of one of his ancestors, relative to the early grants of the manor, and for "raking the ashes of the dead in the presence of a great-grandson." He brought his ancestor up from the grave and led him into court to speak for himself, by a daring metaphor which surprised and confounded the audience as well as the jury. He carried his cause, as it were, by a *coup de main* and obtained a verdict, rather by the weight of his character, and the charm and power of his eloquence, than by the force of evidence or the merits of the case.

A new trial was moved for in January term, 1785, on the ground that the verdict was against the evidence. Mr. Benson, Colonel Lawrence, and Colonel Hamilton were in favor of the motion, and Mr. (afterward Chancellor) Lansing and Chancellor Livingston resisted it. I had the pleasure of being

present at the argument, and was a witness of the contest of talent and eloquence between Chancellor Livingston and Colonel Hamilton, the brilliant
and master spirits who controlled on that occasion. All the cases and reasons
contained in the modem English decisions, and especially those which arose
in the time of Lord Mansfield, and which are so well digested and elegantly
illustrated in the third volume of Blackstone's *Commentaries*, were cited and
urged in support of the motion. The Chancellor contended, on the other
hand, that no single authority was to be found in support of the motion,
in the case of a trial and verdict at bar in term time, and that the opposite
counsel, in order to make out their case, were obliged to select parts from
each of several cases, and to make up a piece of diversified mosaic—a motley
compound, destitute equally of symmetry and law. He compared the efforts
of his opponents to the construction of their father's will by Peter Martin
and Jack in *The Tale of the Tub,* and who had found an authority for the
use of shoulder-knots by picking out single letters in different parts of the
instrument. He made a warm and declamatory eulogy upon trial by jury, and
denounced with equal vehemence the judicial authority of Lord Mansfield.
He considered that the trial by jury, with all the other great leading principles
of English liberty, came from their German ancestors, and that a disposition
existed in the then government of England to undermine their Saxon liberties, and especially the inestimable trial by jury. No Englishman, he observed,
was found worthy of the task; a Scotchman must be selected, who had the
talents, subtlety, and love of power calculated to produce the effect; and the
new-fangled doctrines of Lord Mansfield had enlarged and refined upon the
power of awarding new trials, so as at last to resolve the trial by jury into the
discretion of the court. Our Constitution had guarded against the dangerous innovation by declaring that the trial by jury as hereafter used should be
inviolate forever. And yet, no sooner had we established our independence
and organized our courts than the pernicious doctrines alluded to were to
be adopted and called into action. "What would be the exclamation of the
Genius of Liberty, if she were now present in this assembly, and saw the same
gentlemen who had so honorably wielded the sword of war in her defense
now wielding the arbitrary decrees of Lord Mansfield for her destruction?"

The tall and graceful person of Chancellor Livingston, and his polished
wit and classical taste, contributed not a little to deepen the impression
resulting from the ingenuity of his argument, the vivacity of his imagination, and the dignity of his station. Mr. Hamilton had never before met and
encountered at the bar such a distinguished opponent. He appeared to be
agitated with intense reflection. His lips were in constant motion and his
pen rapidly employed during the Chancellor's address to the court. He rose
with dignity and spoke for perhaps two hours in support of his motion. His
reply was fluent and was accompanied with great earnestness of manner and
emphasis of expression. It was marked by a searching and accurate analysis
of the cases and a thorough and familiar acquaintance with all the law and
learning applicable to the subject. He begged leave to suggest, in reference to

the same *Tale of the Tub*, that the Chancellor's interest had blinded his better judgment, and, like Peter's influence over his brother, had turned the brown loaf into mutton. He illustrated the fact that the power of awarding new trials in the discretion of the court had been recognized before the time of Lord Mansfield, and that it was a very reasonable and necessary power, and a vast amelioration and improvement of the trial by jury in property concerns. Without such a salutary control, the rights of property would be unsafe and at the sport of ignorance and prejudice; and trial by jury, instead of being deemed a blessing, would excite the disgust and contempt of mankind. The court had no concern with the political opinions of Lord Mansfield, but it was due to truth to say that his profound learning, clear intellect, and admirable judgment had elevated and adorned the jurisprudence of England; and by his wisdom and purity, while presiding over the English administration of law, he had deservedly gained the reverence of his own age, and his fame would rest in the admiration of posterity.

It was some time before I had another opportunity of hearing Colonel Hamilton speak. I was as yet unknown to him, and as I continued to reside for several years at Poughkeepsie, I did not usually attend the terms of the Supreme Court, either at New York or Albany. Mr. Hamilton was called again into public life, on being elected a member of the Assembly for the City of New York, in April, 1786. The destinies of this country were at that time rapidly approaching a crisis. The Confederation of the states was essentially dissolved, and at the session of the legislature, in the winter of 1787, the active mind and intrepid spirit of Hamilton were displayed in various efforts to surmount difficulties and avert the dangers which surrounded us. The state of Vermont was then in the exercise of independent sovereignty, though not recognized in that capacity. His object was to relieve the state and nation from such a perilous state of things, and he introduced a bill into the House of Assembly, renewing the jurisdiction of this state over the territory in question, and preparing the way for the admission of that state into the Union. The owners of lands in Vermont, under grants from New York, considered their vested interests to be put in jeopardy by the bill, and they were permitted to be heard by counsel at the bar of the House in opposition to it. Richard Harrison addressed the House in a very interesting speech, in which he insisted that the state was bound to employ all the means in its power to recover and protect the rights and property of its citizens, and that, if it was deemed inexpedient to apply force, the state was morally bound and was abundantly able to indemnify its citizens for the loss of their property.

He excited great attention and respect by the perspicuity and strength of his argument, and the suavity of his manner and address. Mr. Hamilton promptly met and answered, in behalf of the House, all the objections to the bill, and he showed, with his usual ability and familiar knowledge of the principles of public law, that the case was one in which the state was dismembered by force without the power to prevent it. Remonstrances had been exhausted. It was in fact a revolution, and it was not the duty of the state, nor was she bound by the fundamental principles of the social compact, to engage in a crusade which must prove disastrous and fruitless, or to undertake to indemnify the claimants in a case of such magnitude.

In this same session Mr. Hamilton made great and manly efforts to prop up and sustain the tottering fabric of the Confederation, and the fallen dignity of Congress. In his comments upon Governor Clinton's speech, he sharply rebuked him for refusing to call the legislature at the special and earnest request of Congress, to take into consideration their recommendation of a grant of an impost to pay the national debt. He regarded the refusal as heaping fresh marks of contempt upon their authority. He pressed upon the House the necessity of complying with the recommendation of Congress. His speech on that subject was taken down in shorthand by Francis Childs and published at large in his daily paper. It was received and perused with very great interest. I well remember how much it was admired, for the comprehensive views which it took of the state of the nation, the warm appeals which it made to the public patriotism, the imminent perils which it pointed out, and the absolute necessity which it showed of some such financial measure to rescue the nation from utter ruin and disgrace.

His argument was left unanswered, without an attempt to reply to it, and the proposition to accede to the grant to Congress of the impost was rejected by a silent vote. But a new era was at hand. The public mind had become prepared for a reorganization and enlargement of the powers of the national government. General Hamilton was destined to display his exalted talents, and his ardent devotedness to his country's glory, on a broader theater and in a more illustrious course of public action. In this same session he was appointed one of the three delegates from this State to the General Convention recommended by Congress to be held at Philadelphia in May, 1787. The sole and express purpose of that Convention was to revise the Articles of Confederation, and report to Congress such alterations as should, when agreed to, render the federal Constitution adequate to the exigencies of government and the preservation of the Union.

II

The second branch of the inquiry brings me to consider the services of General Hamilton in relation to the origin and adoption of the federal Constitution. I never had any means of information respecting the extent and merit of those services, except such as were accessible to the public at large. It was a remark of the Hon. W.S. Johnson, who was a member of the Convention from Connecticut (and which remark was mentioned to me from a very authentic source about that period, though I cannot now recollect the precise time), that if the Constitution should prove to be a failure, Mr. Hamilton would be less responsible than any other member, for he frankly pointed out to the Convention what he apprehended to be its infirmities; and that, on the other hand, if it should operate well the nation would be more indebted to him than to any other individual, for no one labored more faithfully than he did, nor with equal activity, to give the Constitution a fair trial, by guarding against every evil tendency, and by clothing it with all the attributes and stability requisite for its safety and success, and compatible with the principles of the republican theory.

This was the substance, though I cannot give the exact words of the remark, and it is confirmed by all our contemporary information. Mr. Hamilton's avowed object was to make the experiment of a great federative republic, moving in the largest sphere and resting entirely on a popular basis, as complete, satisfactory, and decisive as possible. He considered the best interests and happiness of mankind as deeply, and perhaps finally, involved in the experiment. He knew and said that no other government but a republic would be admitted or endured in this country. Experimental propositions were made in the Convention and received as suggestions for consideration, and he has stated himself that the highest-toned proposition which he ever made was that the president and Senate should be elected by electors chosen by the people, and that they, as well as the judges, should hold their offices during good behavior, and that the House of Representatives should be elected triennially.

But his opinion essentially changed during the progress of the discussions, and he became satisfied that it would be dangerous to the public tranquility to elect, by popular elections, a chief magistrate with so permanent a tenure; and toward the close of the convention his subsequent plan gave to the office of president a duration of only three years.[7] He remained with the Convention to the last, though his colleagues, Robert Yates and John Lansing, Junior, had left it some weeks before; singly representing this state, he heartily assented to and signed the Constitution. It appears to me, therefore, that his friend Gouverneur Morris did him great injustice when he represented him, according to the correspondence contained in Mr. Sparks's *Life of Gouverneur Morris*, as having "had little share in forming the Constitution," and as "hating republican government, because he confounded it with democratical government." All the documentary proof and the current observation at the time lead us to the conclusion that he surpassed all his contemporaries in his exertions to create, recommend, adopt, and defend the Constitution of the United States.

All his actions and all his writings as a public man show that he was the uniform, ardent, and inflexible friend of justice and of national civil liberty. He had fought for our republic during the American War. In his early production as *Phocion* he declared that "the noble struggle we had made in the cause of liberty, had occasioned a kind of revolution in human sentiment; we had the greatest advantages for promoting it that ever a people had; the influence of our example had penetrated the gloomy regions of despotism, and had pointed the way to inquiries which might shake it to its deepest foundations." That immortal work *The Federalist* is the most incontestable evidence of his fervent attachment to the liberties of this country, and of his extreme solicitude for the honor and success of the republican system. His recorded speeches in the state convention, as taken down in short hand at the time by Mr. Childs, and written out by him in the evenings at my house, contain the same sentiments, coming fresh and fervent from his own lips. "I presume I shall not be disbelieved," he said, "when I declare that the establishment of a republican government, on a safe and solid basis, is an object of all others the nearest and most dear to my heart."

General Hamilton confound republican with democratical government! It is contradicted by the whole tenor of his life. While he admitted that the petty republics of Greece and Italy were kept in a state of perpetual vibration between the extremes of tyranny and anarchy, he declared, in the 9th number of *The Federalist*, that "the efficacy of various principles is now well understood, which were either not known at all or imperfectly known to the ancients. The regular distribution of power into distinct departments; the introduction of legislative balances and checks; the institution of courts composed of judges holding their offices during good behavior; the representation of the people in the legislature by deputies of their own election— these are means, and powerful means, by which the excellences of republican government may be retained and its imperfections lessened or avoided." If he doubted of its success from his knowledge of history and his profound reflections upon the infirmities and corrupt passions of mankind, he was none the less anxious to meet those inherent difficulties by a skillful and judicious structure of the republican machinery of government. Nor ought it to be forgotten that one of the last proofs which he gave of his inextinguishable devotion to the popular rights of his countrymen was his gratuitous and glorious forensic effort in favor of trial by jury and the liberty of the press.

At the October term of the Supreme Court at Albany, in 1787, I was, for the first time, personally introduced to Colonel Hamilton. I had the honor of dining at your father's house, in company with him and several other gentlemen, and as the new Constitution had just then appeared, it was of course the engrossing topic of conversation. I was a fixed and diffident listener, without presuming to intrude at all into the discussions of such sages. General Schuyler was full of lively, spirited, and instructive reflections, and he went into details, showing, in his usual calculating manner, the great expense and complicated provisions of our local financial systems, and the order, simplicity, and economy that would attend one national system of revenue.

Mr. Hamilton appeared to be careless and desultory in his remarks, and it occurred to me afterwards how little did I then suppose that he was deeply meditating the plan of the immortal work of *The Federalist*. In the latter part of the same month of October, the essays which compose the volumes of *The Federalist* were commenced in the New York papers. Three or four numbers were published in the course of a week, and they were not concluded until nearly the time of the New York Convention in June, 1788. Those essays, as they successively appeared, were sought after and read, with the greatest avidity and constantly increasing admiration, by all persons favorable to the adoption of the Constitution. Colonel Hamilton was very soon and very generally understood to be the sole, or the principal, author. As the small and humble *Poughkeepsie Journal* was an incompetent vehicle for the re-publication of them, I undertook at first to make an abridgement, or abstract, of them for that paper, and it was the only newspaper then printed in this state, out of the cities of New York and Albany; but this was soon found to be impracticable, and that if it could be done they would lose all their interest and effect. The essays had grown in number sufficient for a small volume early in the spring of 1788, and the first part of them, to the extent of thirty-six numbers, were collected and reprinted, and a large number of the volumes were sent to me at Poughkeepsie for gratuitous distribution. My former master, mentor, and friend, Judge Benson, attended with me a county meeting in Dutchess, called for the nomination of delegates to the Convention, and the volumes were there circulated to the best of our judgments.

The essays composing *The Federalist* made, at the time, a wonderful impression upon reflecting men. The necessity and importance of the union of the states, the utter incompetency of the Articles of Confederation to maintain that union, their fundamental and fatal defects, the infirmities which seemed to be inherent in all ancient and modern confederacies, and the disasters which had usually attended them, and finally, the absolute necessity of a government organized upon the principles, and clothed with the powers and attributes, of that which was then presented to the judgment of the American people—were all of them topics of vast magnitude and affecting most deeply all our foreign and domestic concerns. They were discussed in a masterly manner, and with a talent, strength, information, and eloquence to which we had not been accustomed. The appeal to the good sense and patriotism of the country was not made in vain. It usually met with a warm reception in frank and liberal minds, not blinded by prejudice, nor corrupted by self-interest, nor enslaved by party discipline.

The New York Convention assembled at Poughkeepsie on the 17th June, 1788. It formed the most splendid constellation of the sages and patriots of the Revolution which I had ever witnessed, and the intense interest with which the meeting of the Convention was anticipated and regarded can now scarcely be conceived and much less felt. As I then resided in that village, I laid aside all other business and avocations, and attended the Convention as a spectator, daily and steadily, during the whole six weeks of its session, and was an eye and an ear witness to everything of a public nature that was done or said. The Convention was composed of sixty-five members, and of them nineteen were Federalists, or in favor of the adoption of the Constitution, and forty-six were Anti-Federalists, or against the adoption of it without previous amendments. Not a member of that Convention is now living. The remark will equally apply, as I believe, with but one exception besides myself, to every man who was then a housekeeper either in the village or its environs. That bright and golden age of the Republic may now be numbered "with the years beyond the flood," and I am left almost alone, to recall and enjoy the enchanting vision.

The Convention combined the talents, experience, and weight of character of some of the most distinguished men in the state. Most of them had been disciplined in the discussions, services, and perils of the Revolution. The principal speakers on the Federal side were Mr. Jay (then secretary for foreign affairs), Chancellor Livingston, Mr. Duane (then Mayor of New York), Mr. Harrison, and Colonel Hamilton. On the other side they were the elder Governor Clinton, Mr. (afterwards Chancellor) Lansing, Mr. Jones (afterwards Recorder of New York), John Williams of Washington County, and Gilbert Livingston and Melancthon Smith, delegates from Dutchess. There was no difficulty in deciding at once on which side of the house the superiority in debate existed, yet in the ordinary range of the discussion, it was found that the dignity, candor, and strength of Jay, the polished address and elegant erudition of Chancellor Livingston, the profound sagacity and exhaustive researches of Hamilton, were met with equal pretensions by their opponents, supported by the simplicity and unpretending good sense of Clinton, the popular opinions and plausible deductions of Lansing, the metaphysical mind, prepossessing plainness, and embarrassing subtleties of Smith.

Mr. Hamilton maintained the ascendancy on every question, and being the only person present who had signed the Constitution, he felt and sustained the weight of the responsibility which belonged to his party. He was indisputably preeminent, and all seemed, as by a common consent, to concede to him the burden and the honor of the debate. Melancthon Smith was equally the most prominent and the most responsible speaker on the Anti-Federal side of the Convention. There was no person to be compared to him in his powers of acute and logical discussion. He was Mr. Hamilton's most persevering and formidable antagonist.

But even Smith was routed in every contest. As Hamilton had been a leading member of the national Convention and a leading writer of *The Federalist*, his mind had become familiar with the principles of federal government and with every topic of debate, and it was prompt, ardent, energetic, and overflowing with an exuberance of argument and illustration. The three principal topics of discussion in which Mr. Hamilton was most distinguished and most masterly were: (1) On the importance of the Union, the defects of the Confederation, and the just principles of representation. (2) On the requisite tenure and stability of the Senate. (3) On the power of taxation, and the reserved rights of the states. On each of these subjects he bestowed several speeches, some of which were employed in refutation and reply.

He generally spoke with much animation and energy and with considerable gesture. His language was clear, nervous, and classical. His investigations penetrated to the foundation and reason of every doctrine and principle which he examined, and he brought to the debate a mind filled with all the learning and precedents applicable to the subject. He never omitted to meet, examine, and discover the strength or weakness, the truth or falsehood of every proposition with which he had to contend. His candor was magnanimous and rose to a level with his abilities. His temper was spirited but courteous, amiable and generous, and he frequently made pathetic and powerful appeals to the moral sense and patriotism, the fears and hopes of the assembly, in order to give them a deep sense of the difficulties of the crisis and prepare their minds for the reception of the Constitution.

The style and manner of Smith's speaking was dry, plain, and syllogistic, and it behooved his adversary to examine well the ground on which they started, and not to concede too much at the beginning, or he would find it somewhat embarrassing to extricate himself from a subtle web of sophistry, unless indeed he happened to possess the giant strength of Hamilton, which nothing could withstand. Mr. Smith was a man of remarkable simplicity, and of the most gentle, liberal, and amiable disposition. Though I felt strong political prejudices against Governor Clinton, as the leader of the Anti-Federal party, yet during the course of that Convention I became very favorably struck with the dignity with which he presided, and with his unassuming and modest pretensions as a speaker. It was impossible not to feel respect for such a man, and for a young person not to be somewhat overawed in his presence, when it was apparent in all his actions and deportment that he possessed great decision of character and a stern inflexibility of purpose.

The arguments used by Colonel Hamilton in the debates in the Convention were substantially the same which he had before employed in *The Federalist*. They could not well have been any other, for he had already urged in support of the Constitution all the leading considerations which had led to the plan of it, and which guided the skill of the artists. The wisdom of the commentator was now repeated and enforced by the eloquence of the orator.

In his opening speech Mr. Hamilton preliminarily observed that it was of the utmost importance that the Convention should be thoroughly and deeply impressed with a conviction of the necessity of the Union of the States. If they could but once be entirely satisfied of that great truth, and would duly reflect upon it, their minds would then be prepared to admit the necessity of a government of similar powers and organization with the one before them, to uphold and preserve that Union. It was equally so, he said by way of illustration, with the doctrine of the immortality of the soul, and he believed with Doctor Young that doubts on that subject were one great cause of modern infidelity; for to convince men that they have within them immaterial and immortal spirits is going very far to prepare their minds for the ready reception of Christian truth.

After pointing out the radical defects of the Confederation, and vindicating the popular basis of the new Constitution, he declared his convictions that the latter was a genuine specimen of a representative and republican government; and he hoped and trusted that we had found a cure for our evils, and that the new government would prove, in an eminent degree, a blessing to the nation. He concluded his first great speech with the Patriot's Prayer, "Oh, save my country, Heaven!" in allusion to the brave Cobham, who fell, "his ruling passion strong in death."

His two speeches on the organization, powers, and stability of the Senate were regarded at the time as the best specimens which the debates afforded of the ability and wisdom of a consummate statesman. They were made in opposition to a proposed amendment to the Constitution that no person should be eligible as a Senator for more than six years in any term of twelve years, and that they should at all times, within the period of six years, be subject to recall by the state legislatures, and to the substitution of others. Mr. Hamilton on that occasion took large and philosophical views of the nature of man, his interests, his passions, his pursuits, his duties; and he drew his deductions from the end and design of government, the settled principles of policy, and the history of all other free governments, ancient and modern. He discovered equally an ardent zeal for the success of popular government, and a correct knowledge of those infirmities which had invariably attended it. Instability and a fluctuating policy were the prominent features in most republican systems, and the tendency of such vicious defects was to destroy all sense of pride and national character, and to forfeit the respect and confidence of other nations. He contended, therefore, that in all rational policy we ought to infuse a principle of strength and stability into the structure of our national government, by the creation of a senatorial branch, which should be comparatively small in number, and appointed for considerable periods of time, and inspired with a sense of independence in the exercise of its powers. Upon no other plan would the Senate, either in its legislative or executive character, be able to perform its functions, as the balance-wheel of the machine; or form on the one hand a salutary check to the mischiefs of misguided zeal and a fluctuating policy in the more popular branch, and on the other to the abuses and misrule of the president, in the exercise of the treaty and the appointing powers.

The tendency of federative governments, as all history taught us, was to weakness and dissolution, by gradual and steady encroachments of the members upon the national authority. Our own experience under the Articles of Confederation was a monitory example before our eyes of this fatal tendency. Local governments more readily concentrated popular sympathies and prejudices. The affections naturally grew languid in proportion to the expansion of the circle in which they moved.

Though Mr. Hamilton considered that amendment as tending to destroy the dignity and stability of the national Senate, and give the state legislatures a fatal control in their discretion over the legislative and executive authorities of the Union, it was nevertheless adopted by a vote of all the Anti-Federal members of the Convention, and it was one of the recommendatory amendments annexed to the ratification of the instrument. During the sitting of the Convention, information was received that New Hampshire had adopted the Constitution, and she made the ninth state that had adopted it. That great event wrought at once an important change in the situation of the United States, inasmuch as the Confederation thereby became *ipso facto* dissolved, and the new Constitution had become the lawful government of the states which had ratified it.

But the fact, however momentous, did not seem to disturb the tranquility or shake the purpose of a majority of the Convention. Mr. M. Smith and Mr. Lansing both declared that the event had no influence on their deliberations, and the Convention continued their sharp debate for three weeks subsequent to that information and apparently regardless of it, and until all hopes of an auspicious issue to it seemed to be lost. It was in the midst of that gloomy period, and just before the clouds began to disperse and serene skies to appear, that Mr. Hamilton made one of his most pathetic and impassioned addresses. He urged every motive that he thought ought to govern men, and he touched with exquisite skill every chord of sympathy that could be made to vibrate in the human breast. Our country, our honor, our friends, our posterity were placed in vivid colors before us. He alluded slightly to the distress and degradation which dictated the call for a national Convention, and he portrayed in matchless style the characters of that illustrious assembly, composed undoubtedly of the best and brightest of the American statesmen, who could have had no motive but their country's good. They had lived in "times that tried men's souls." To discriminate might be odious. It could not be so to select Franklin, revered by the wise men of Europe, and Washington, "crowned with laurels, loaded with glory."

Soon thereafter information was received that Virginia had also adopted the Constitution. Colonel Hamilton read a letter to the Convention to that effect from Mr. Madison, and then a visible change took place in the disposition of the house, and led it to think of adopting the Constitution upon certain terms. A resolution to adopt it was before the house when Mr. M. Smith moved an amendment that it be ratified upon condition that certain powers contained in the instrument should not be exercised until a general convention of the states had been called to propose amendments. This proposition was discussed for some days, with increasing agitation and anxiety, and it was at last urged that the adoption of the Constitution would readily be received with that qualification annexed. Mr. Hamilton was strenuous and peremptory in his opinion and advice to the house that such a conditional ratification was void, and would not and could not be accepted by Congress. All expectation from such a source he assured them would prove delusive. The members generally and gradually assumed a more conciliatory tone, and all vehemence in debate seemed to have ceased as by common consent. "We did not come here," said Mr. Jay, "to carry points or gain party triumphs. We ought not to wish it. We were without a national government and on the eve of an untried era. Everything demanded concession and moderation. The laurels of party victory might peradventure be bedewed with the tears or stained with the blood of our fellow citizens."

Colonel Hamilton disclaimed the intention of wounding the feelings of any individual, though he admitted that he had expressed himself, in the course of the debates, in strong language dictated by ardent feelings arising out of the interesting nature of the discussions. On no subject, he observed, had his breast been filled with stronger emotions or agitated with more anxious concern. The spirit of the house was liberal and cheering, and at last Samuel Jones, one of the Anti-Federal members, had the magnanimity to move to substitute the words "in full confidence" in lieu of the words "upon condition." He was supported by Melancthon Smith, who had so eminently distinguished himself throughout the whole course of the session, and by Zephaniah Platt, then first judge of the County of Dutchess, who made a few observations expressing in a plain, frank manner, his sense of duty on that occasion and his determination to follow it. The members who came over from the Anti-Federal side of the House were twelve in number, being four members from Dutchess, four from Queens, three from Suffolk, and one from Washington, and, uniting themselves with the nineteen Federal members from New York, Westchester, Kings, and Richmond, they constituted a majority in the Convention, and the Constitution was ratified on the 26th of July.

I always considered that the gentlemen who made this memorable and unbought sacrifice of prejudice, error, and pride on the altar of patriotism and their country's welfare were entitled to the highest honor. It was quite an heroic effort to quit such a leader as Governor Clinton, and such men as Yates and Lansing, who had been delegates to the General Convention, even though it was to follow their own convictions. It was understood that several other members were inclined to follow the same course, but they could not be brought to desert Governor Clinton, who remained inflexible. Had he consented to vote for the Constitution, the final ratification of it would probably have been unanimous. As it was, the spirit of harmony and conciliation with which the Convention closed was deemed most auspicious by all sincere lovers of their country. Considering the circumstances under which the Convention assembled, the manner in which it terminated afforded a new and instructive example of wisdom and moderation to mankind.

III

The third and last part of the history of General Hamilton to which you have requested my attention relates to his life subsequent to the adoption of the Constitution of the United States. After the Constitution went into operation, in the course of the year 1789, Mr. Hamilton was appointed to the office of secretary of the treasury. While the Constitution was in its progress to maturity, some of his friends had suggested in my hearing that the office of chief justice of the Supreme Court of the United States would be in every way suited to the exercise of his discernment and judgment; and that he was well fitted for it by his accurate acquaintance with the general principles of jurisprudence. Of all this there could have been no doubt. But his versatile talents, adapted equally for the bench or the bar, the field, the Senate house, and the executive cabinet, were fortunately called to act in a more complicated, busy, and responsible station. I found myself by this time upon friendly and familiar terms with Colonel Hamilton. In the winter and spring of 1789, he took a leading and zealous part in the election of governor. He was chairman of the New York Committee of Correspondence, in favor of Judge Yates as a candidate for governor, in opposition to the re-election of Governor Clinton, and he no doubt was the author of some of the circular addresses from that committee. One of them was subscribed by his own hand as chairman, and was circulated in a pamphlet form addressed to the supervisors of each county. All the addresses of the New York committees on each side were collected by me at the time and are now before me; and I cannot but be struck with the spirit of decorum which characterizes their contents, in the midst of the most earnest and the most animated competition. In the printed circulars the committees fairly reasoned before the public the merits of their respective pretensions and candidates.

I was in New York when the House of Representatives was first organized in the beginning of April, 1789, and no spectacle could have been more gratifying. The City Hall had been remodeled and fitted up in elegant style for the reception of Congress, and all ranks and degrees of men seemed to be actuated by one common impulse to fill the galleries as soon as the doors of the House of Representatives were opened for the first time, and to gaze on one of the most interesting fruits of their struggle, a popular assembly summoned from all parts of the United States. Colonel Hamilton remarked to me that, as nothing was to be done the first day, such impatient crowds were evidence of the powerful principle of curiosity. I felt another and better apology in my own breast. I considered it to be a proud and glorious day, the consummation of our wishes; and that I was looking upon an organ of popular will, just beginning to breathe the breath of life, and which might in some future age, much more truly than the Roman Senate, be regarded as the "refuge of nations." At any rate, I dwell upon that recollection with some interest, for it has so happened that I have never since that day been present in the House of Representatives.

Colonel Hamilton filled the office of secretary of the treasury upwards of five years, and his official acts are all before the public, and do not come within the scope of my present inquiry. He resigned the office in January, 1795, after having raised the financial character of the government to an exalted height, and finished those duties which appertained peculiarly to that department on its first institution. Those duties consisted in the establishment of a sound, efficient, and permanent provision for the gradual restoration of public credit, and the faithful discharge of the national debt. No man ever inculcated with more sincerity and zeal a lively sense of the obligations of good faith and the sanctity of contracts. In his view, the true principle to render public credit immortal was always to accompany the creation of debt with the means of extinguishing it. He demonstrated that the creation of a national bank was within the reach of the legitimate powers of the government, and essential to the convenient and prosperous administration of the national finances. He made an able and elaborate report in favor of the encouragement of domestic manufactures, and he seems not to have entertained a doubt of the constitutional right of Congress to exercise its discretion on the subject.

He contended that the encouragement of manufactures tended to create a more extensive, certain, and permanent home market for the surplus produce of land, and that it was necessary, in self-defense, to meet and counteract the restrictive system of the commercial nations of Europe. It was admitted, however, that if the liberal system of Adam Smith had been generally adopted, it would have carried forward nations, with accelerated motion, in the career of prosperity and greatness. The English critics spoke at the time of his report as a strong and able plea on the side of manufactures, and said that the subjects of trade, finance, and internal policy were not often discussed with so much precision of thought and perspicuity of language.

During the time that Colonel Hamilton presided over the Treasury Department, the French Revolution was in action, and a fierce war broke out between Great Britain and the French Republic. He was one of President Washington's cabinet council, and a leading and efficient adviser of the president's proclamation of neutrality in April, 1793, declaring the neutral position of the United States, and his duty and determination, as the chief executive guardian of the laws, to preserve it. That proclamation was the index to the foreign policy of President Washington, and it was temperately and discreetly, but firmly, maintained, under the sage advice and controlling influence of Hamilton, against the arts and intrigues of the French minister to the United States, and against all the force and fury of the tempestuous passions of the times, engendered and influenced by the French democracy. He aided the great American policy of neutrality by his pen, in some fugitive pieces under the signature of *No Jacobin*, and in the more elaborate and elegant essays under the signature of *Pacificus*; and still more so by his opinion and advice in favor of the seasonable mission of Chief Justice Jay to the Court of Great Britain, in the spring of 1794. That envoy was sent on purpose "to vindicate our rights with firmness and to cultivate peace with sincerity," and no one event was attended with more auspicious results, or contributed equally to establish and elevate the pacific policy of Washington, who, having "once saved his country by his valor in war, again saved it by his wisdom in peace."

Mr. Hamilton returned to private life and to the practice of the law in New York in the spring of 1795. He was cordially welcomed and cheered on his return by his fellow citizens, and while he was gradually resuming his profession he felt himself called upon, by a sense of duty, to vindicate by his pen one great act of Washington's administration. Mr. Jay's treaty with Great Britain had been negotiated while he was in office, though it was not ratified by the president and Senate until the summer of 1795. It had honorably adjusted and extinguished the complaints and difficulties between us and Great Britain, and it contributed essentially to continue and strengthen the neutrality of the United States. But it was vehemently opposed and denounced by the party in this country which had originally opposed the Constitution, and which, from being formerly denominated the Anti-Federal, was then called the Democratic party; and it included, of course, all the devoted partisans of France and apologists for the violence and madness of the French rulers.

Mr. Hamilton vindicated the treaty in a series of essays under the signature of *Camillus*. They were written with vast ability, and in clear, strong, and elegant language, and disclosed a familiar acquaintance with all the grievances, claims, doctrines, and principles adjusted, ascertained, and declared by the treaty. Some of the essays are of permanent value, and will be read and cited as long as his name endures, as accurate and lucid commentaries on public law.

My acquaintance with Colonel Hamilton was revived after his return to New York, and it was enlarged and cherished, and eventually terminated in a warm and confidential friendship. Several of the essays of *Camillus* were communicated to me before they were printed, and my attention was attracted by a single fact which fell under my own eye, to the habit of thorough, precise, and authentic research which accompanied all his investigations. He was not content, for instance, with examining Grotius, and taking him as an authority, in any other than the original Latin language in which the work was composed.

Between the years 1795 and 1798 he took his station as the leading counsel at the bar. He was employed in every important and especially in every commercial case. He was a very great favorite with the merchants of New York, and he most justly deserved to be, for he had uniformly shown himself to be one of the most enlightened, intrepid, and persevering friends to the commercial prosperity of this country. Insurance questions, both upon the law and the fact, constituted a large portion of the litigated business in the courts, and much of the intense study and discussion at the bar. The business of insurance was carried on principally by private underwriters, and as the law had not been defined and settled in this country by a course of judicial decisions, and was open to numerous perplexed questions arising out of our neutral trade, and was left, under a complicated mixture of law and fact, very much at large to a jury, the litigation of that kind was immense. Mr. Hamilton had an overwhelming share of it, and though the New York bar could at that time boast of the clear intellect, the candor, the simplicity, and black-letter learning of the elder Jones, the profound and richly varied learning of Harrison, the classical taste and elegant accomplishments of Brockholst Livingston, the solid and accurate, but unpretending common-law learning of Troup, the chivalrous feelings and dignified address of Pendleton, yet the mighty mind of Hamilton would at times bear down all opposition by its comprehensive grasp and the strength of his reasoning powers.

He taught us all how to probe deeply into the hidden recesses of the science, or to follow up principles to their far distant sources. He was not content with the modern reports, abridgments, or translations. He ransacked cases and precedents to their very foundations; and we learned from him to carry our inquiries into the commercial codes of the nations of the European continent, and in a special manner to illustrate the law of insurance by the severe judgment of Emerigon and the luminous commentaries of Valin.

In the spring of 1798, Mr. Hamilton felt himself called upon by a sense of public duty to engage once more in political discussion. It will be recollected, as I once had occasion to observe in a brief review of his public life and writings which was published anonymously soon after his death, that France had long been making piratical depredations upon our commerce; that negotiation and a pacific adjustment had been repeatedly attempted on the part of this country without success; that one minister had been refused an audience; that three ministers extraordinary had been treated with the grossest indignity, and money demanded of the United States on terms the most degrading. The doors of reconciliation being thus barred, we had no honorable alternative left but open and determined resistance. At that portentous period Mr. Hamilton published *The Stand*, or a series under the signature of *Titus Manlius*, with a view to arouse the people of this country to a sense of their impending danger, and to measures of defense which should be at once vigorous and manly.

The plan of this production was communicated to me by Mr. Hamilton before it appeared, and the very signature was a subject of discussion at my office. He wished for some appropriate name from Roman history, applicable to the stand which those ancient Republicans had made against the Gauls, and on examination the name selected was deemed by him the most suitable. In these essays he portrayed in strong and glowing colors the conduct of revolutionary France towards her own people and towards other nations. He showed that she had undermined the main pillars of civilized society; that she had betrayed a plan to disorganize the human mind itself by attempting to destroy all religious opinion and pervert a whole people to atheism; that her ruling passions were ambition and fanaticism; and that she aimed equally to proselyte, subjugate, and debase every government, without distinction, to effect the aggrandizement of the "great nation." All the states, even of the republican form, that fell within her widespread grasp—the United Netherlands, Geneva, the Swiss Cantons, Genoa, and Venice—had already been prostrated by her arms, or her still more formidable caresses.

He then gave a detail of the accumulated insults and injuries which the United States had received from France, and showed that her object was to degrade and humble our government, and prepare the way for revolution and conquest. He concluded, as the result of his work, that we ought to suspend our treaties with France, fortify our harbors, defend our commerce on the ocean, attack their predatory cruisers on our coasts, create a respectable naval force, and raise, or organize and discipline, a considerable army, as an indispensable precaution against attempts at invasion, which might put in jeopardy our very existence as a nation. So undeniable were all these facts, so irresistible were the conclusions which he drew from them, that in the summer of 1798 those measures suggested by Mr. Hamilton were all literally carried into execution by Congress, and received the warm and hearty sanction of the nation. An honorable, proud, and manly sentiment was then enkindled and pervaded the continent; it reflected high honor on our national character, and that character was transmitted to Europe as a means of respect and a pledge of security.

It is well known that General Washington gave his decided approbation to all those measures of national resistance, and that he urged upon government the employment of Colonel Hamilton in the military line. In a letter to President Adams, in September, 1798, he pronounced upon him a noble eulogy. He declared that Colonel Hamilton had been his "principal and most confidential aide; that his acknowledged abilities and integrity had placed him on high ground and made him a conspicuous character in the United States, and even in Europe; that he had the laudable ambition which prompts a man to excel in whatever he takes in hand; that he was enterprising, quick in his perceptions, and that his judgment was intuitively great." Upon the earnest recommendation of Washington, General Hamilton was appointed inspector general of the provisional army that was raised in 1798; but the time which he was necessarily led to bestow on his new military duties did not dissolve his connection with the profession and practice of the law. That military office was but temporary, and he soon resumed his full practice at the bar.

My judicial station in 1798 brought him before me in a new relation, but the familiar friendly intercourse between us was not diminished, and it kept on increasing to the end of his life. At circuits and in term time I was called, in a thousand instances, to attend with intense interest and high admiration to the rapid exercise of his reasoning powers, the sagacity with which he pursued his investigations, his piercing criticisms, his masterly analysis, and the energy and fervor of his appeals to the judgment and conscience of the tribunal which he addressed. If I were to select any two cases in which his varied powers were most strikingly displayed, it would be the case of *Le Guen* v. *Gouverneur and Kemble*, argued before the Court of Errors in the winter of 1800, and the case of *Croswell* advs. *The People,* argued before the Supreme Court in February term, 1804. In the first of those cases the most distinguished counsel of the New York bar were engaged; but what gave peculiar interest to it was the circumstance that Gouverneur Morris, a relative of one of the defendants, gratuitously appeared as their counsel. The action had been originally commenced by Le Guen at law, upon the advice of Mr. Hamilton. The claim was very large in amount, and after expensive trials and the most persevering and irritating litigation, pursued into the court of the last resort. The plaintiff recovered upon technical rules of law strictly and severely applied.

The claim was a commercial one, and was in opposition to the mercantile sense of its justice. The success of it was thought at the time to be due in a very material degree to the overbearing weight and influence of General Hamilton's talents. The case I now allude to, in which Mr. Hamilton and

Mr. Morris were brought into collision, was on an appeal from a decree in Chancery, in which relief on grounds of fraud had been afforded against the judgment at law. The zeal and anxiety which the cause enkindled had been increasing through the whole protracted controversy, and had become very intense at the period of this final review. Everything was calculated to tax to the utmost the powers of those two illustrious statesmen civilians. If the one was superior in logic and law learning, the other was presumed to be his equal in eloquence, imagination, and wit. The appearance of Mr. Morris was very commanding. His noble head, his majestic mien, the dignity of his deportment were all impressive. I have no notes or memorials remaining of the argument in the cause, but my memory serves me to say that it was a most beautiful and captivating display of the genius and varied accomplishments of those orators.

The questions of law involved in the case were indeed dry and technical, nor were the facts of a nature to excite much interest. It was the large amount of property in controversy, the character of the litigation, and, above all, the high reputation of the two leading counsel, that roused such ardent curiosity and anxious expectation. But any cause involving law and fact seems to be sufficient to afford aliment for the brilliant exhibition of minds of such high order and of such intellectual resources. There was, in that case, a mass of facts involving a complicated charge of fraud, and that was enough to command the exertion of the keenest sagacity, a critical severity, shrewd retort, and pathetic appeal. A Jewish house was concerned in the commercial transaction, and that led to affecting allusion to the character and fortunes of that ancient race. Some of the negotiations happened in France, and that produced references to that tremendous Revolution which was then still in its fury, and whose frightful ravages and remorseless pretensions seemed to overawe and confound the nations.

Mr. Morris and Mr. Hamilton equally resorted for illustration to Shakespeare, Milton, and Pope; and when the former complained that his long absence from the bar had caused him to forget the decisions, the latter sportively accounted for it on another principle, and relied on the poetical authority that —

> "Where beams of warm imagination play,
> The memory's soft figures melt away."[8]

The other case I mentioned involved the discussion of legal principles of the greatest consequence. Croswell had been indicted and convicted of a libel upon Thomas Jefferson, then president of the United States. The libel consisted in charging Mr. Jefferson with having paid one Callender, a printer, for grossly slandering George Washington and John Adams, the former presidents; and the defendant offered to prove the truth of the charge. But the testimony was overruled by Chief Justice Lewis, who held the circuit, and he charged the jury that it was not their province to decide on the intent of the defendant, or whether the libel was true or false or malicious, and that those questions belonged exclusively to the court. The motion was for a new trial for misdirection of the judge, and those two great points in the case were elaborately discussed before the Supreme Court, and they were considered by General Hamilton, who appeared gratuitously for the defendant, as affecting very essentially the constitutional right of trial by jury in criminal cases, and the American doctrine of the liberty of the press.

I have always considered General Hamilton's argument in that cause the greatest forensic effort that he ever made. He had bestowed unusual attention to the case, and he came prepared to discuss the points of law with a perfect mastery of the subject. He believed that the rights and liberties of the people were essentially concerned in the vindication and establishment of those rights of the jury and of the press for which he contended. That consideration was sufficient to arouse all the faculties of his mind to their utmost energy. He held it to be an essential ingredient in the trial by jury that, in criminal cases, the law and the fact were necessarily blended by the plea of not guilty, and that the jury had a rightful cognizance of the intent and tendency of the libel, for in the intent consisted the crime. They had a right and they were bound in duty to take into consideration the whole matter of the charge, both as to the law and the fact, for it was all involved in the issue and determined by a general verdict. On the independent exercise of the right of the jury in criminal cases to determine the guilt or innocence of the defendant, according to their judgment and consciences, rested the security of our lives and liberties. Nothing would be more dangerous to the citizens of this country than to place the trial by jury in such cases under the control and dictation of the court. The English history, in its dark and disastrous periods, showed abundantly by its records that the most dangerous, the most sure, the most fatal of tyrannies consisted in selecting and sacrificing single individuals, under the mask and forms of law, by dependent and partial tribunals. We could not too perseveringly cultivate and sustain the rights of the jury in all their common law vigor, as the great guardians of liberty and life, equally against the sport and fury of contending factions, the vindictive persecution of the public prosecutor, and the "machinations of demagogues and tyrants on their imagined thrones."

On the other great question in the case he contended with equal ardor and ability for the admission of the truth in evidence to a qualified extent in justification of the libel. He showed that it depended on the motive and object of the publication whether the truth was or was not a justification.

The liberty of the press was held to consist in the right to publish with impunity the truth, whether it respected government, magistrates, or individuals, provided it was published with good motives and for justifiable ends. The hard doctrines under which his client was convicted came from the Star Chamber, that arbitrary and hated tribunal acting under the government of a permanent body of judges, without the wholesome restraints of a jury. He felt a proud satisfaction in the reflection that the Act of Congress of July, 1798, for preventing certain libels against the government, and which act had been grossly misrepresented, established these two great principles of civil liberty involved in the discussion. It declared that the jury should have the right to determine the law and the fact, under the direction of the court, as in other cases, and that the defendant might give in evidence in his defense the truth of the libel. He was as strenuous for the qualification of the rule allowing the truth of the libel to be shown in the defense as he was for the rule itself.

While he regarded the liberty of the press as essential to the preservation of free government, he considered that a press wholly unchecked, with a right to publish anything at pleasure, regardless of truth or decency, would be, in the hands of unprincipled men, a terrible engine of mischief, and would be liable to be diverted to the most seditious and wicked purposes, and for the gratification of private malice or revenge. Such a free press would destroy public and private confidence, and would overawe and corrupt the impartial administration of justice.

There was an unusual solemnity and earnestness on the part of General Hamilton in this discussion. He was at times highly impassioned and pathetic. His whole soul was enlisted in the cause, and in contending for the rights of the jury and a free press he considered that he was establishing the finest refuge against oppression. The aspect of the times was portentous, and he was persuaded that if he should be able to overthrow the high-toned doctrine contained in the charge of the judge, it would be great gain to the liberties of his country. He entered, by the force of sympathy, into the glorious struggles of English patriots, during oppressive and unconstitutional times, for the rights of juries and for a free press; and the anxiety and tenderness of his feelings and the gravity of his theme rendered his reflections exceedingly impressive. He never before, in my hearing, made any effort in which he commanded higher reverence for his principles, or equal admiration of his eloquence.

Nor were his efforts on that occasion lost to his country. The fruit of them still exists and will remain with posterity, a monument of his glory, though the court was equally divided on the motion he discussed, and therefore decided nothing; yet in the following winter the Legislature of New York passed a declaratory statute, introduced into the House of Assembly by William W. Van Ness, his friend and associate on the trial, admitting the right of the jury in all criminal cases to determine the law and the fact under the direction of the court, and allowing the truth to be given in evidence by the defendant, in every prosecution for a libel; provided that such evidence should not be a justification, unless it should be made satisfactorily to appear that the matter charged as libel was published with good motives and for justifiable ends.

In April, 1804, I held the Circuit Court in the city of New York, and the most interesting interview which I ever had with General Hamilton was at his country seat at Harlem Heights, during the course of that month. He took me out to dine with him and I was detained at his house the next day. We were assailed by a violent easterly storm the night I was there, and the house, standing on high ground, was very much exposed to the fury of the winds as they swept over the island from the "vex'd Atlantic." The solicitude of General Hamilton for my comfort, and his attention and kindness quite affected me. He visited me after I had retired to my chamber, to see that I was sufficiently attended to. In a memorandum which I made a day or two after that visit, and which is now before me, I state in allusion to it that "he never appeared before so friendly and amiable. I was alone, and he treated me with a minute affection that I did not suppose he knew how to bestow. His manners were delicate and chaste, and he appeared, in his domestic state, the plain, modest, and affectionate father and husband."

Gouverneur Morris was to have dined with us, but he sent an apology stating that "the Jacobin winds" had prevented him. We were consequently left to ourselves during the greater part of a day, and the conversation led to a more serious train of reflections on his part than I had ever before known him to indulge. His mind had a cast unusually melancholy.[9] The impending election exceedingly disturbed him, and he viewed the temper, disposition, and passions of the times as portentous of evil, and favorable to the sway of artful and ambitious demagogues. His wise reflections, his sober views, his anxiety, his gentleness, his goodness, his Christian temper, all contributed to render my solitary visit inexpressibly interesting. At that time he revealed to me a plan he had in contemplation, for a full investigation of the history and science of civil government, and the practical results of the various modifications of it upon the freedom and happiness of mankind. He wished to have the subject treated in reference to past experience, and upon the principles of Lord Bacon's inductive philosophy. His object was to see what safe and salutary conclusions might be drawn from an historical examination of the effects of the various institutions heretofore existing, upon the freedom, the morals, the prosperity, the intelligence, the jurisprudence, and the happiness of the people. Six or eight gentlemen were to be united with him in the work, according to his arrangement, and each of them was to take his appropriate part and to produce a volume. If I am not mistaken, Mr. Harrison, Mr. Jay, Mr. Morris, and Mr. King were suggested by him as desirable coadjutors. I recollect that he proposed to assign the subject of ecclesiastical history to the Rev. Dr. Mason, and he was pleased to suggest that he wished me to accept a share of the duty. The conclusions to be drawn from these historical reviews, he intended to reserve for his own task, and this is the imperfect outline of the scheme which then occupied his thoughts. I heard no more of it afterwards, for the business of the court occupied all our attention, and after the May term of that year I saw him no more.

I have very little doubt that if General Hamilton had lived twenty years longer, he would have rivaled Socrates, or Bacon, or any other of the sages of ancient or modern times, in researches after truth and in benevolence to mankind. The active and profound statesman, the learned and eloquent lawyer would probably have disappeared in a great degree before the character of the sage philosopher, instructing mankind by his wisdom and elevating his country by his example. He had not then attained his forty-eighth year, and all his faculties were in their full vigor and maturity, and incessantly busy in schemes to avert distant dangers and to secure the freedom and promote the honor and happiness of his country.

I knew General Hamilton's character well. His life and actions, for the course of twenty-two years, had engaged and fixed my attention. They were often passing under my eye and observation. For the last six years of his life he was arguing causes before me. I have been sensibly struck, in a thousand instances, with his habitual reverence for truth, his candor, his ardent attachment to civil liberty, his indignation at oppression of every kind, his abhorrence of every semblance of fraud, his reverence for justice, and his sound legal principles drawn by a clear and logical deduction from the purest Christian ethics, and from the very foundations of all rational and practical jurisprudence. He was blessed with a very amiable, generous, tender, and charitable disposition, and he had the most artless simplicity of any man I ever knew. It was impossible not to love as well as respect and admire him. He was perfectly disinterested. The selfish principle, that infirmity too often of great as well as of little minds, seemed never to have reached him. It was entirely incompatible with the purity of his taste and the grandeur of his ambition. Everything appeared to be at once extinguished, when it came in competition with his devotion to his country's welfare and glory. He was a most faithful friend to the cause of civil liberty throughout the world, but he was a still greater friend to truth and justice.

He wished the people to enjoy as much political liberty as they were competent to use and not abuse—as much as was consistent with the perfect security of life and social rights, and the acquisition and enjoyment of property. He was satisfied, from profound reflection and from the uniform language of history, that all plans of government founded on any new and extraordinary reform in the morals of mankind were plainly Utopian. The voice of history, the language of Scripture, the study of the nature and character of man, all taught us that mankind were exceedingly prone to error; that they were liable to be duped by flattery, to be seduced by artful, designing men, to be inflamed by jealousies and bad passions; and he was satisfied that the greatest danger to be apprehended in this country was from the natural tendency of the organized and powerful state governments to resist and control the constitutional authority of the federal head. This I know from repeated conversations with him to have been one great ground of uneasiness and apprehension with him as to our future destiny. He knew that factions were the besetting evils of republics. They lead to the tyrannical oppression of minorities, of individuals under the mask and form of law; to the dangerous influence of cunning, intriguing, and corrupt leaders; to civil discord and anarchy, and eventually to an armed master. The fate of all former federative governments and the horrible excesses of the French democracy were before his eyes, and without the aid of his private reflections we can be at no loss, from the reasonings and sentiments in *The Federalist*, to know the quarter from which he apprehended danger and dissension, disunion, and ruin to the nation.

I have thus endeavored, my dear madam, to the best of my ability, and with perfect candor and regard for truth, to satisfy your inquiries. And if what I have written shall afford you consolation, and shall contribute in any small degree to awaken in the present generation an increased attention to the history and character of your illustrious husband, I shall be amply rewarded for my effort.

I am, Madam, with the utmost respect and esteem,
Your friend and ob'd't serv't,
JAMES KENT

Letter from George Washington, February 2, 1795

Dear Sir,

After so long an experience of your public services, I am naturally led, at this moment of your departure from office—which it has always been my wish to prevent—to review them.

In every relation which you have borne to me, I have found that my confidence in your talents, exertions, and integrity has been well placed. I the more freely render this testimony of my approbation, because I speak from opportunities of information which cannot deceive me, and which furnish satisfactory proof of your title to public regard.

My most earnest wishes for your happiness will attend you in your retirement, and you may assure yourself of the sincere esteem, regard, and friendship of

Dear Sir   Your affectionate

Go: Washington

Explanatory Notes

1 Moore was the Episcopal Bishop of New York. He sent this letter to William Coleman for publication in the *New York Evening Post*, of which Coleman was the editor.

2 Hamilton's editors supply the following translation: "When will incorruptible faith and naked truth / Find another his equal? / He has died wept by many." The lines are from Horace's *Odes*, 1.24.7–9. See *PAH*, 26: 347 n. 3.

3 These lines are from Book 3 John Milton's *Paradise Lost*.

4 These are the concluding lines of Alexander Pope's translation of the *Iliad*.

5 Webster is here referring to Egbert Benson, who was the attorney general of New York during the Revolution and later served in the House of Representatives and as a federal judge.

6 This is a line from Thomas Gray's 1757 poem, "The Bard."

7 See our note 11 to Part 4 of this volume.

8 These lines are from Alexander Pope's *Essay on Criticism*.

9 Kent had written "usually" but we think the context indicates that he intended "unusually."

Index

Great Britain (*cont.*)
  October 24, 1800 on Hamilton's
    support of the Jay Treaty with, 456–7
  public debt of US (August 18, 1792) as
    equal to annual expenditure of, 136
  Republic of France's declaration of war
    against, 357
  The Stand series on staying out of war
    between France and, 350–80
  To the New York Evening Post,
    February 24, 1802 on commonwealth
    republic of, 516
  Treaty of 1763 between France and, 564–5
  The Warning series on French attempts
    to cut off maritime trade of neutral
    nations with, 317–32
  See also European war
"Grennleaf's New Dayly Advertising"
  (November 6, 1799), 405
Grotius, Hugo, 166, 167

Hamilton (musical), 1
Hamilton, Alexander
  appreciation of enormous foreign
    policy contributions by, 2
  August 26, 1800 on his parents, 427–8
  December 29, 1802 letter on his purchase
    of land and plans for garden, 560
  as de factor leader of Federalist
    Party, 3
  The Examination series written under
    pseudonym of Lucius Crassus, 3,
    485–507, 511–15, 518–21, 524–7,
    528–44, 549–53
  fatal duel fought with Aaron Burr and
    death of, 3
  his contribution and influence as a
    political thinker, 1–2
  January 31, 1795 letter submitting
    his resignation as secretary of
    treasury, 282
  March 29, 1802 letter on the death of
    his son, 546
  October 24, 1800 on eulogy of
    Washington and attempted eulogy
    of, 452
  October 24, 1800 on injury and abuse
    by Adams upon, 455–9
  as one of the first rank of founders, 1

  Opinion on the Constitutionality of a
    National Bank, February 23, 1791 as
    secretary of treasury, 2, 56–79
  Reynolds Pamphlet (1797) addressing
    slander of his character, 345–9
  The Stand series written under
    pseudonym of Titus Manlius, 358–80
  Statement on an Impending Duel With
    Aaron Burr, June 28-July 10, 1804
    by, 577–8
Hamilton, Elizabeth
  Letter to Elizabeth Hamilton, July 4,
    1804 from Alexander to, 579
  Letter to Elizabeth Hamilton, July 10,
    1804 from Alexander to, 580
  March 29, 1802 letter on death of their
    son, 546
Hamilton, William, 343–4
Harper, Robert G., 574–5
Henfield case verdict, 222
Hoffman, Josiah Ogden, 405
Holland. *See* United Provinces (The
  Netherlands)
Holmes, Isaac, 257–8
Hoops, Adam, 398
House of Representatives *See* US House
  of Representatives
Howell, David, 440
Hunt, Richard, 396–7

impeachment
  The Examination opposition to term
    of judges based on "their good
    behavior," 520–1, 522–3, 524, 539–44
  February 19, 1804 letter on judges
    and, 574–5
  House of Representatives's power
    of, 525
importation of foreigners
  The Examination Number VII, January
    7, 1802 on Jefferson's Message on,
    499–501
  The Examination Number VIII, January
    12, 1802 on Jefferson's Message
    on, 502–3
incorporation. *See* corporations/power of
  incorporation
Indian nations treaties, 309
insurrection

August 5, 1799 letter on Hamilton's
concerns over irregular military
etiquette by McHenry, 398–9
December 2, 1794 letter on how to
better organize procuring supplies
for the, 275–6
*The Examination Number XVIII, April
18, 1802* on proposed reduction
of, 549–50
February 2, 1799 letter on supporting
Provisional Army Bill, 387
February 8, 1803 letter recommending
an increase in, 517
February 21, 1799 on St. Domingo
government and military
hierarchy, 388–9
Federalist and Anti-Federalist positions
on standing army, 482–3
General Orders, June 6, 1799 on
"Rules and Regulation respecting to
Recruiting Service," 395
Hamilton's suggestions for measures to
prepare in case of war, 338–9
June 2, 1798 letter on Hamilton's
willingness to rejoin the, 383
March 18, 1799 letter on making an
insurrection worse by using an
inadequate response by, 390
March 21, 1800 on compensation for
military officers, 415–16
May 3, 1799 letter on filling a battalion
officer vacancy, 393
May 15, 1793 memorandum on
British demands regarding French
privateers, 176–80
May 18, 1799 letter on importance of
providing cocked hats to soldiers, 393
May 19, 1798 letter on possibility
of Washington's return to leading
the, 381–2
May 27, 1799 letter on suggested
remedies to problem of desertion, 394
May 28, 1790 memorandum on arrears
in pay due to soldiers of, 26–30
No Jacobin French ambassador's
actions to recruit US citizens to
French, 224–32
October 6, 1799 letter on dispute
between two officers of the, 400

October 24, 1800 letter on opposition
to annual enlistment of troops
policy, 433
October–November 1799 letter on
period of enlistment in the, 403
September 11, 1794 letter stating that
only when civil means are inadequate
to call upon, 273
Vattel on hostile acts against one nation
without consent on the soil of third
nation, 176–7
See also naval forces
Mitchell, Ann, 580
monarchy
April 18, 1793 comments on US
response to French Revolution
overthrowing the French, 161–74
Louis XVI as the constitutional agent
of French nation, 208–10
moral obligation of allies by treaty to a
nation versus a dethroned, 167–9
nation's dependence on the voluntary
succors derived from a, 165
Sweden passing from republican
government back to an absolute, 229
*To the New York Evening Post,
February 24, 1802* denial by
Hamilton on supposed suggestion
of, 516–17
Vattel on alliances made between
states and not for personal defense
of, 166–7
Vattel on rendering an alliance null
when a nation has disposed of
its, 220–1
See also laws and government
money (paper currency)
as the hinge upon which commerce
turns, 73–4
how banks relate to the collection
of taxes and circulating credit
using, 70–2
January 9, 1790 report on public credit
as necessary for confidence in, 8–25
*Objections and Answers, August
18, 1792* on practice of paper
speculation, 147
payment of the public debt as true final
causes for, 74–5